MW01633785

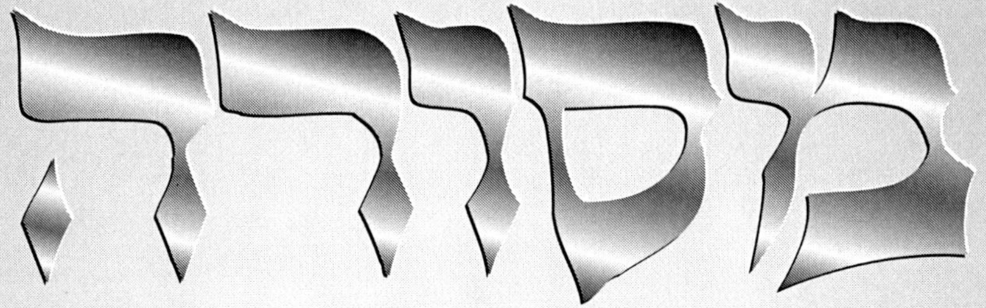

ArtScroll® Series

Rabbi Nosson Scherman / Rabbi Gedaliah Zlotowitz

General Editors

Rabbi Meir Zlotowitz ז"ל, *Founder*

JAFFA FAMILY EDITION

The Priceless Treasure of Bircas

Published by

ARTSCROLL

Mesorah Publications, ltd

ברכת כהנים

Kohanim

HISTORY, HALACHOS, MINHAGIM, AND STORIES

NAFTALI WEINBERGER

INCLUDES OVER 550 TESHUVOS IN HEBREW FROM MARAN RAV CHAIM KANIEVSKY

FIRST EDITION
First Impression ... September 2024

Published and Distributed by
MESORAH PUBLICATIONS, LTD.
313 Regina Avenue / Rahway, N.J. 07065

Distributed in Europe by
LEHMANNS
Unit E, Viking Business Park
Rolling Mill Road
Jarrow, Tyne & Wear NE32 3DP
England

Distributed in Australia & New Zealand by
GOLDS WORLD OF JUDAICA
3-13 William Street
Balaclava, Melbourne 3183
Victoria Australia

Distributed in Israel by
SIFRIATI / A. GITLER — BOOKS
POB 2351
Bnei Brak 51122

Distributed in South Africa by
KOLLEL BOOKSHOP
Northfield Centre, 17 Northfield Avenue
Glenhazel 2192, Johannesburg, South Africa

ARTSCROLL® SERIES
THE PRICELESS TREASURE OF BIRCAS KOHANIM

ITEM CODE: PTBKH
ISBN 10: 1-4226-4173-2
ISBN 13: 978-1-4226-4173-6

Typography by CompuScribe at ArtScroll Studios, Ltd.
Printed in the United States of America.
Bound by Sefercraft, Quality Bookbinders, Ltd., Rahway NJ

We humbly dedicate this work
in memory of

Maran Sar HaTorah
HaGaon HaRav Shmaryahu Yosef Chaim
Kanievsky *zt"l*

מרן הגאון הרב שמריהו יוסף חיים
בן מרן הגאון הרב יעקב ישראל זצ"ל

נבל"ע ט"ו אדר ב' תשפ"ב

whom we were *zocheh* to know
and whose loving advice and counsel
guided us for many years.

Although Rav Chaim treasured every mitzvah,
Bircas Kohanim was one that was special to him.
Indeed, he would frequently advise people
to seek out a minyan that recites Bircas Kohanim
and to focus on the powerful *berachos* it contains.

Rav Chaim took an active interest in the development
and progress of this *sefer* and graced it
with his *haskamah*. It is a privilege for us
to take part in bringing this *sefer* to fruition.
May it be a source of merit to us
and to all of Klal Yisrael.

The Jaffa Family

הסכמות of Maran Rav Chaim Kanievsky זצוק״ל and Rav Moshe Sternbuch שליט״א

בעזה״י

ערב שבועות תש״פ

הנה ידידי הרה״ג ר׳ נפתלי וינברגר שליט״א חיבר ספר חשוב בעניני מצות ברכת כהנים. וטוב עשה שקיבץ וליקט מהרבה מקומות בכדי שיצא חיבור מועיל.

והנני מכירו שנים רבות והוא ת״ח גדול. אמנם אין לסמוך על תשובותי למעשה, כי אני עונה בלי די עיון הנצרך. ויהי רצון שיזכה לנחת מכל יוצ״ח מתוך הרווחה.

חיים קניבסקי

בעזה״י

י״ד אב תשפ״א

אני מצטרף להנ״ל. עיינתי קצת בספר החשוב על המצוה הנשגבה של ברכת כהנים. וכבר איתמחי גברא ואיתמחי קמיעא בספריו הקודמים. ויהי רצון מלפני אבינו שבשמים שנזכה לברכה המשלשת בתורה, ולידבק באלוקינו יתברך שמו, ובעינינו נזכה לראות התגלות כבוד ה׳ בעולמו וביאת משיח צדקינו.

ממני המצפה בכליון ממש לישועת ה׳ ורחמי שמים מרובים.

הסכמות of
Rav Moshe Hillel Hirsch and Rav Dov Landau שליט״א

בס״ד

תאריך ט״ו תמוז תשפ״ג

שמחתי לראות כי ש״ב הרה״ג ר׳ נפתלי וינברגר שליט״א עולה ומתעלה וקנה שם טוב לעצמו בספריו החשובים והמועילים אשר פקיע שמייהו מקדמת דנא.

וכעת עמד לפני תכריך כתביו העתיד לראות אור בספר ׳שי״ח ברכת כהנים׳ וב״ה שזכה כת״ר להקיף בעומק וברוחב סוגיא גדולה זו של נשיאת כפים וברכת כהנים בהלכה ובאגדה. וצירף לזה ברכה מרובה בקונטרס התשובות ממרן שר התורה הגר״ח קניבסקי זצוק״ל אשר נקבצו ובאו בו מאות תשובות בעניני ברכת כהנים מסודרים בסדר נכון ומועיל.

ואברכהו בכל הברכות האמורות בתורה ושיזכה למנוחת הדעת ושלוות הנפש להעמיק ולהגביר חיילים לתורה ולחבר עוד חיבורים טובים ומועילים לזכות בהם את הרבים, ויזכה להרביץ תורה בישראל מתוך ישוב הדעת, בריאות ונחת מכל יוצאי חלציו. ויתברכו עמו כל העוזרים והמסייעים בהכנת ספר חשוב זה.

החותם לכבוד התורה ולומדיה

משה הלל הירש

גם אני מצטרף

דוב לנדו

הסכמה of
Rav Yitzchak Zilberstein שליט״א

Yitzhak Zilberstein
Rabbi of 'Ramat-Elhanan'
Bnei-Brak
Rosh Kollel 'Beit-David' Holon

יצחק זילברשטיין
רב שכונת רמת-אלחנן
בני ברק
ראש כולל ׳בית-דוד׳ – חולון

בס״ד כ״ח תמוז תשפ״ג

זכה הרב המחבר שליט״א במשך שנים רבות ליצוק מים על ידיו של גיסי שר התורה רשכבה״ג מרן רבנו חיים קניבסקי זי״ע אשר לשמו ולזכרו תאות נפשו וזכה לקרבה גדולה עד מאד מצדו. והחכם עיניו בראשו ובעינא פקיחא דיליה זכה וזיכה וקיבל מגיסי זללה״ה על מנת לכלול בספרו אוצר בלום של מאות תשובות שיצאו מלשכת הגזית, מתחת ידו הטהורה של גיסי מרן רבנו חיים קניבסקי זללה״ה, אשר השיב בתורת-חסדו לשואליו בכתב מכל קצווי תבל, מתוך מסירות הגוף והנפש בבחינת ״ותדד שנתי מעיני״. ובתשובות אלו, ימצאו הלומדים הוראות ברורות ועוד ענינים חשובים הקשורים למצות ברכת כהנים.

כמעשהו בראשונה בספריו היקרים, גם בספר הזה לא חסך טורח וממון להעמיד דבר דבור על אופנו בכל מיני מעלות הדפוס והעמיד את תוכם הספר הנפלא כתפוחי זהב במשכיות כסף, ובוודאי גם ספרו זה יהיה לתועלת רבה עבור הכלל ורבים ייאותו לאורו, למען ידעו לברך ולהתברך בברכת הקב״ה. ולכן אמינא לפעלא טבא יישר, וחפץ ה׳ יעלה בידו, שנזכה כולנו להתברך בברכה המשולשת בתורה על ידי נותן התורה.

בברכת התורה

יצחק זילברשטיין

הסכמה of
Rav Elya Ber Wachtfogel שליט״א

ב״ה. שלהי תמוז ה׳תשפ״ג

הובאו לפני גליונות הספר החשוב ״שי״ח ברכת כהנים״ אשר אסף איש טהור הרה״ג רבי נפתלי וינברגר שליט״א וכבר איתמחי גברא ואיתמחי קמיעא בספריו הנפלאים הקודמים שזכו להסכמת גדולי הדור זצ״ל.

ומה גדלה שמחתי לראות תלמודו בידו פרי עמלו ויגיעתו זה כמה שנים, חיבור גדול שלם ומקיף על המצוה הנשגבה של ברכת כהנים אשר על ידי מצוה זו מתברכים כל כלל ישראל בשפע של ברכה מאת הקדוש ברוך הוא ואף הקב״ה בעצמו מתאוה למצוה זו כדאיתא בסוטה (לח, ב): אמר ר׳ יהושע בן לוי מנין שהקב״ה מתאוה לברכת כהנים שנאמר ושמו את שמי על בני ישראל ואני אברכם.

והנה הרב המחבר שליט״א ליקט וערך כל עיקרי ועניני הלכות נשיאת כפים וברכת כהנים מעיקרי הסוגיות ודברי רבותינו הראשונים כמלאכים ועד פסקי האחרונים בספריהם ובתשובותיהם עד הכרעת ההלכה והמנהג למעשה. ועוד זאת הגדיל ועשה יפה בעטו שהביא בספרו תוספת ברכה מרובה, הכרעת דעתם ופסקיהם של גדולי דורנו בהרבה מפרטי השאלות המתעוררות בקיום מצוה זו. וביחוד קונטרס גדול המחזיק תשובות רבות על מצות ברכת כהנים מפי פאר הדור שר התורה מרן הג״ר חיים קניבסקי זצ״ל. אשר כנודע בשער בת רבים תשובות אלו הן בחינת ״תורת חסד״ שהשיב לשואלים בכתב ידו הקדושה במשך למעלה מחמישים שנה, ובמדותיו הנעלות הלהיב רבבות אלפי ישראל בתשובות על מכתביהם, וסלל הדרך על ידי זה בהרבה מקצועות בתורה.

ועברתי על חלק מהספר ונוכחתי לראות שיש בו תועלת מרובה, הן לכהנים שיזכו לקיים מצותם על צד היותר טוב בעז״ה מתוך הלכה ברורה והן לישראל המתברכים, ומברר היטב הדברים ומביא הרבה ידיעות חשובות ונחוצות. והיא זכות גדולה להביא הענינים לפני כהנים, לויים, וישראלים, למען ילמדו לדעת המעשה אשר יעשון אל נכון וגם יכירו וידעו מעלת המצוה הקדושה ונזכה על ידי זה כולנו יחד להיות צינור וכלי לברכת ה׳ ושפע טובה הנאצל ב׳ואני אברכם׳.

ומקרב לב אוהב אברכהו שיזכה להמשיך בעמלו בקנין תורה והרבצתה מתוך מנוחת הנפש והרחבת הדעת ונחת דקדושה, יפוצו מעיינותיו חוצה ורבים יהנו לאורו.

ונזכה במהרה בימינו לבנין בית מקדשנו ותפארתנו, בימיו ובימינו תיוושע ציון בביאת גואל-צדק רוח-אפנו משיח-ה׳ ונזכה לראות כהנים בעבודתם ובדוכנם ולויים בשירם ובזמרם.

מוקירו ומכבדו כערכו הרם

החותם לכבוד התורה הוגי׳ ועמלי׳

אלי׳ בר וכטפוגל

הסכמה of
Rav Yaakov Hillel שליט״א

RABBI YAAKOV HILLEL
ROSH YESHIVAT
HEVRAT AHAVAT SHALOM
45 ARZEY HABIRA ST. JERUSALEM

יעקב משה הלל
ראש ישיבת
חברת אהבת שלום
רח׳ ארזי הבירה 45 ירושלים

בס״ד ב׳ תמוז תשפ״ג פה עיר הקודש ירושלים תובב״א

דברי ברכה והסכמה

שמחתי לראות שהרה״ג רבי נפתלי יחיאל וינברגר שליט״א הולך מחיל אל חיל בלימוד התורה הקדושה, וכבר נודע בשערים עם ספריו הטובים והמועילים שהוציא לאור עולם מקדמת דנא, והנה אתא ואייתי מתניתא בידיה עלים לתרופה מהספר ״שיח ברכת כהנים״ העוסק בהלכות והליכות השייכות למצות ברכת כהנים באהבה, והדברים מלוקטים מספרם של צדיקים בטוב טעם ודעת ומסודרים בסדר נכון לתועלת המברכים והמתברכים החפצים לקיים את המצוה כהלכתה. וקובע ברכה לעצמו קונטרס השאלות והתשובות מאת שר התורה ופאר הדור ה״ה מרן הגר״ח קניבסקי זצ״ל, שיש בו אוצר בלום להרוות צמאון הלומדים ממימיו הנאמנים.

ולכן באתי בשורות אלו בדברי הסכמה וברכה שחפץ ה׳ בידו יצלח ויזכה עוד כהנה וכהנה לשקוד על דלתי התורה, ללמוד וללמד לשמור ולעשות, ולהגדיל תורה ולהאדירה בעוד חיבורים טובים ומתוקנים, ולכוין בהם לאמיתה של תורה, ולא תצא שום תקלה מתחת ידו לעולם, ויתברך בכל ההצלחות ברו״ח ובגש״ם ובכל מילי דמיטב, אכי״ר.

הסכמה of
Rav Shraga Shteinman שליט״א

בס״ד כ׳ תמוז תשפ״ג

מכתב ברכה

כבוד הרב ר׳ נפתלי וינברגר שליט״א

אחדשה״ט

ב״ה שאתם זוכים להמשיך ולהאיר בחלקי התורה, ועתה על מצות ברכת הכהנים, שה׳ אמר על זה ואני אברכם, ומה לנו גדול מזה.

והנה איתא בסוטה (ל״ט ב׳) שאין הכהנים רשאין לעקור רגליהם עד שיגמור ש״צ שים שלום, ואם כן מבואר ששים שלום היא עדיין המשך וחלק מברכת כהנים.

וכן מבואר במגילה (י״ח א׳) ומה ראו לומר שים שלום אחר ברכת כהנים דכתיב ושמו את שמי על בני ישראל ואני אברכם, ברכה דהקב״ה שלום שנאמר ה׳ יברך את עמו בשלום.

ויעזור השם יתברך שתתקיים בנו התפילה שאחר ברכת כהנים אדיר במרום שוכן בגבורה, אתה שלום ושמך שלום, יהי רצון שתשים עלינו ועל כל עמך בית ישראל חיים וברכה למשמרת שלום.

בתפילה וברכה

[signature]

הסכמה of
Rav Gamliel Rabinovitz שליט״א

בס״ד יום ו׳ י״ב מרחשון פעיה״ק ת״ו תשפ״ד

הביא לפני הרב הגאון חו״ב טובא יראתו קודמת לחכמתו הרב נפתלי וינברגר שליט״א אשר ביודעי ומכירי קאמינא ונתתי הסכמה על שאר ספריו בעבר שנתקבלו בתפוצות ישראל. וכעת שב והניף ידו, חבר וליקט וערך ופירש ספר מאד חשוב בשם ״שי״ח ברכת כהנים״ אשר בו בירר וליקט כל הענינים והלכות הקשורות בברכת כהנים בסדר נפלא ובשפה ברורה למצוה גדולה וחשובה זו.

וביותר יש לברכו על אשר אסף איש טהור שו״ת מאת רשכבה״ג רבנו הג״ר חיים קניבסקי זצ״ל וביארם ופירשם כיד ה׳ הטובה עליו. וגם לרבות אשר טוב עשה בעמיו שהביא לפונדק אחד עניני הסגולות ושפע הברכות של ברכת כהנים וגם לרבות עובדות ומנהגים מגדולי ישראל.

ואברכהו בברכת כהן שיפוצו מעינותיו חוצה והמברך את עמו יברכם בברכת שלום ופדות נפשנו בביאת גואל צדק ולהנצל מחבלי משיח אמן

הכו״ח בברכה [illegible]

גמליאל הכהן רבינאוויץ

הסכמה of
Rav Dovid Cohen שליט״א

בס״ד סיון תשפ״ג

יום בשורה הוא לכל עדת בני ישראל בהוצאתו לאור עולם של הספר הנפלא ׳שי״ח ברכת כהנים׳ אשר סידר וערך ברוב כשרון ידידי הדגול הרב הגאון רבי נפתלי וינברגר שליט״א אשר כבר איתמחי גברא ואיתמחי קמיעא בספריו הקודמים שהתקבלו באהבה ובחיבה אצל לומדי התורה, והביאו תועלת מרובה לרבים.

עתה נשא לבו אותו בחכמה להביא את ברכת ה׳ לקהל ה׳ בהוציאו לאור עולם ספר מלא וגדוש ושמו אשר פיו ייקבנו ׳שי״ח ברכת כהנים׳ הכולל כל עניני המצוה הנשגבה של ברכת כהנים בהלכה ובאגדה, בשפה ברורה ונעימה השווה לכל נפש, ולא הניח דבר קטן וגדול שלא בירורו הדק היטב בעומק ובהיקף להגיש מסקנת ותמצית הדברים בדרך קצרה ולשון קל. אשר יש בספר כזה תועלת מרובה להביא ולהשריש את עומק המצוה של ברכת כהנים והוא זכות גדולה מאד לזיכוי הרבים ואשרי חלקו שזכה לזה.

וראה זה חדש שזיכה רבים וזכה לעטר את ספרו בקונטרס שלם ובו תשובות רבות מאד מאת שר התורה מרן רבינו רבי חיים קניבסקי זצ״ל, אשר כ׳אורים ותומים׳ הלך לפני המחנה, וסלל הדרך הישרה בכל חלקי התורה. בקונטרס זה ימצא המעיין תשובות נכוחות וברורות על שאלות רבות מאד הנוגעות לענין מצות ברכת כהנים, אשר יגע וטרח עליהם מרן זללה״ה ביותר, במסירות נפשו לכלל. חסד גדול עשה הרב המחבר עם כלל הציבור להוציא לאור עולם תשובות אלו כפי אשר יצאו מתחת ידי רבינו הגדול זיע״א בכתב ויש מהן שנשנו ונתבררו לכמה וכמה שואלים במשך עשרות שנים ויש בסידורן מלאכה שהיא חכמה.

והנה לפני הרבה שנים הייתי אצל מרן ראש הישיבה הגרא״ל שטינמן זצ״ל ואמר לי שתמוה אצלו מאד לראות אנשים הזקוקים לאיזה ישועה, שמבקשים ומחפשים לקבל ברכות והרבה פעמים נודדים למרחקים בשביל כך, ואף שאין להם שום אסמכתא שיש ענין בברכותיהם של המברכים ואינם שמים אל ליבם שיש להם בסמוך בכל יום ויום ברכה שהקב״ה הבטיח שיש בה כח והיא פועלת שפע של ברכה, היא הברכה שמברכים הכהנים בכל יום. ואינם משתדלים לרדוף ולהשתדל אחר ברכת כהנים. ואז נתעוררתי כי מן הראוי למצוא דרכים לעורר את הלבבות לגודל המשמעות של ברכת כהנים.

זכינו ובס״ד מרובה בא הרב המחבר בספר זה והאריך בהרבה מקורות על גודל מעלתה של ברכה זו אשר כפי הנראה עדיין לא נתברר ענינה כראוי אצל הציבור הרחב. וערך הכל בשפה ברורה דבר דבור על אופנו, שפתים ישק משיב דברים נכוחים.

וזכות גדולה היא בהוצאת ספר זה לעורר את הלבבות, להכיר את ערכה של הברכה ועומק ענינה. ועל ידי זה יתחזק כל אדם בישראל להשתדל בברכת כהנים ובזה יזכה המחבר ונזכה עמו כולנו להתברך ממקור הברכה.

הכו״ח למען קדושת בית אהרן ולמען ברכתם של ישראל

דוד כהן

הסכמה of
Rav Shlomo Kanievsky שליט"א

YESIVA
TIFERET TZION
ישיבת תפארת ציון

הוקמה ונוסדה ע"י הגה"צ
רבי יעקב שניידמן זצ"ל

YESIVA
KIRYAS MELECH
ישיבת קרית.מלך

מיסודו של מרן החזו"א זצללה"ה
בנשיאות יבלח"ט רבן של ישראל
רבנו חיים קניבסקי שליט"א

בראשות
מורנו הגאון הגדול
הרב
שלמה קניבסקי
שליט"א
ראש הישיבה

U.S.A MAILING ADRESS
C/O CHANO ITL. INS. 45 WEST
36 ST 4TH FL. N.Y. N.Y 10018
(212)239-4222 X14

YESHIVA OFFICE
P.O.Box 9
BNEY BRAK, 51100
ISRAEL
TEL 03-6188933
FAX 03-6196002
CELL 050-4111278

ישיבה לצעירים ומשרד:
רח' ירושלים 37-39 בני ברק
ישיבה גבוהה וכולל אברכים:
רח' ר' יהושע 27 בני ברק
רח' ירושלים 42-44 בני ברק
כתובת למשלוח דואר:
ת.ד 9 בני ברק 51100 ישראל
טל. 03-6188933
פקס. 03-6196002
פל. 050-4111278

בס"ד תמוז תשפ"ג

חזיתי איש מהיר במלאכתו לפני מלכים יתייצב, מאן מלכי רבנן. ה"ה ידי"נ הרה"ג ר' נפתלי וינברגר שליט"א אשר ידיו רב לו בהוצאת ספרים חשובים, אשר מביאים תועלת עצומה, וכבר איתמחי גברא בבירור פרטי הדברים בדקדוק עצום.

ובהיותו מקורב מאד לאאמו"ר זצוקללה"ה שנים רבות, ובהיות ששמע פעמים הרבה מאאמו"ר חשיבות של ברכת כהנים ואפי' בחו"ל, דבר המצריך לעתים טרחה לבני אשכנז לילך במיוחד לבית הכנסת של קהילות ספרד ועדות המזרח אשר נהגו בברכת כהנים בכל יום. והרב הנ"ל נאה דורש נאה מקיים, בהיותו בן חו"ל מקפיד זה שנים רבות ללכת לשמוע כמעט בכל יום ברכת כהנים בבית הכנסת של קהילות ספרד. רחש לבו דבר טוב ועלתה בדעתו מחשבה טובה לזכות את הרבים כדרכו בבירור הלכות אלו של ברכת כהנים שאינם מבוררים כ"כ ובפרט בחו"ל שאין נושאין כפיהן רק ביו"ט.

ובירר וקיבץ מתוך אלפי תשובות של אאמו"ר כל התשובות הנוגעים להלכות ברכת כהנים. וכדרכו עשה עבודה עצומה ונפלאה ביחד עם חבר אברכים שהיו מקורבים לאאמו"ר, ועלה בידו חיבור נפלא ובשם "שיח ברכת כהנים" יקרא, ובדין הוא שיטול שכרו.

כמובן שאינני ראוי להיות כשר המסכים ולא לדידי ולדכוותי להעיד על תוכן הדברים, אבל על ידידי הנ"ל שליט"א יכולני להעיד שכל מעשיו שעושה בהוצאת הספרים, הוא עושה בדקדוק ובבירור עצום, בירור אחר בירור ולא ייעף ולא ייגע עד אשר יצא דבר מושלם מתחת ידו, וכמעשיו בראשונים כן מעשיו באחרונים הכל דבר דבור על אופניו.

והנני לברכו שיזכה להגדיל תורה ולהאדירה. ובודאי זכות אאמו"ר זצוקללה"ה שכ"כ הרבה עמל על תורתו תעמוד לו ולזרעו שלא תמוש התורה מפיו ומפי זרעו, ויתקיים בו מקרא שכתוב "ושמו את שמי על בני ישראל ואני אברכם".

הסכמה of
Rav Eliezer Yehuda Finkel שליט״א

Founded in Mir 1817. In Jerusalem 1944 | 580037638 ע״ר | בס״ד נוסדה במיר בשנת תקע״ז. בירושלים בשנת תש״ד

RABBI E.Y. FINKEL

בס״ד   בין המצרים, תשפ״ג

מכתב ברכה

מכתב פתוחי חותם לכבוד מוהר״ר המצויין חו״ב טובא, הג״ר **נפתלי וינברגר** שליט״א, גבור חיל בתורה וביראה אשר יגע בעמלה של תורה וחפץ ה׳ הצליח בידו. וזה כבר כמה חיבורים נפלאים בהרבה מקצועות התורה אשר הרה״ג המחבר הנ״ל הו״ל בעזה״י, בשפה ברורה ובהירה בטוב טעם ודעת, מעשה אומן עשוי לתפארת.

ועתה שוב הניף ידו להעלות עלי גליון, ספר **שו״ח ברכת כהנים** העוסק בהלכות והליכות ברכת הכהנים והמסתעף, ערוך ומוטעם בלשון השוה לכל נפש, ובסופו קובץ תשובות בענינים אלו מרבינו הגדול שר התורה זצוקללה״ה, וכבר איתמחי גברא רבא בספריו הקודמים, בהם הראה כוחו בבהירות נפלאה.

יהי ה׳ עמו להרבות חיילים לתורה לפתוח שערי אורה זו תורה, לשבת באהלה של תורה ללמוד וללמד לשמור ולעשות כשאיפתו הטהורה, וישמחו בו חבריו, ויהא כבוד שמים מתרבה על ידו להגדיל תורה ולהאדירה.

בברכת התורה

הרב אליעזר יהודה פינקל
ראש הישיבה

רח. בית ישראל 3 ת.ד. 5022 ירושלים 9105001 טל. 02-5410999 פקס. 02-5323446 ע״ר 580037638 • 3 Beth Israel St. P.O.B 5022 Jerusalem 9105001 Tel. 02-5410999 Fax. 02-5323446

הסכמה of
Rav Yitzchak Shaul Kanievsky שליט״א

הרב יצחק שאול קניבסקי
שיכון חזון איש, בני ברק

בס״ד

מנחם אב תשפ״ג

הנה ידידי הרב הגאון ר׳ נפתלי וינברגר שליט״א כבר אתמחי גברא וקמיעא בהוצאת ספרו הראשון בהוראת אאמו״ר מרן הגאון זללה״ה, שהיה ר׳ נפתלי אהוב לפניו עד לאחת, ועתה הניף ידו ומוציא לאור ספר נפלא וקדוש על ברכת כהנים שמלא וגדוש מתשובות אאמו״ר מרן הגאון זללה״ה, והמחבר הנ״ל מברר כל תשובה היטב כיד ה׳ הטובה עליו, ואילו זכינו ואאמו״ר ז״ל היה בחיים חיותו בצאת הספר לאור עולם היה שמח שמחה גדולה באשר על ידי הספר יהיה התעוררות על המצוה הגדולה הזאת. ועל ידי זה נזכה כולנו שיתקיים בנו מקרא שכתוב ושמו את שמי על בני ישראל ואני אברכם.

בידידות,

ידידו יצחק שאול בן מרן הגאון הגר״ח קניבסקי
זללה״ה

Table of Contents

Part 4: Facets of the Mitzvah

Part 5: Laws and Customs

Part 6: Collected Responsa of Maran Harav Chaim Kanievsky

Part 7: The Text of Bircas Kohanim and Its Associated Tefillos

Introduction

> We must believe in the power of Bircas Kohanim more than we believe in the power of a *berachah* that we receive from a renowned *tzaddik*. We must enthusiastically pursue the opportunity to hear Bircas Kohanim, and pay attention to the *berachah* with all the reverence and trepidation that it deserves, in the same way that the Jewish people listened to the voices of the Kohanim in the Beis HaMikdash.
>
> — R' Yitzchak Isaac Sher
> (*Leket Sichos Mussar*, vol. 3, p. 152)

Only one vestige remains today of the Kohanim's service in the Beis HaMikdash. Every day in Eretz Yisrael and in Sephardic congregations worldwide, and every Yom Tov in the Diaspora, the Kohanim stand before the *aron kodesh* and turn to the congregation, hands outstretched, as they pronounce Bircas Kohanim, the Torah's benediction, which brings a tremendous blessing to the world and minimizes the Divine punishment ordained for that day. Even today, Bircas Kohanim is a fulfillment of the Torah's mitzvah for the Kohanim to bless the people, which brings Hashem's blessing upon Klal Yisrael.

Sifrei (*Nasso* 42) teaches many different meanings that are contained in the three verses of Bircas Kohanim, and *Netziv* explains (*Emek HaNetziv* ibid.) that all these teachings are based on one principle: Every *berachah* in the universe is included in the fifteen words of Bircas Kohanim.

In his *Siddur,* R' Yaakov Emden (*Hilchos Nesiyas Kapayim*) cites the following teaching of Arizal:

> It is well known that during Bircas Kohanim, the Shechinah (Divine Presence) rests upon the hands of the Kohanim; for the ten fingers of their hands represent the ten *sefiros*. All the blessings that come to the universe must first come to the Jewish nation, and only then do these blessings spread out to the rest of the world. Because Hashem desires to bring merit to the Jewish people, He commanded the Kohanim to strive for the trait of *chesed* (lovingkindness) when they bless their congregation. It is through this mitzvah to lovingly bless the Jewish people that all the goodness that happens in this world and all the miracles and wonders can take place.

In 2011, I went to discuss a personal challenge with R' Chaim Kanievsky. After listening intently he replied, "Concentrate on the words of the blessing of the Kohanim during Bircas Kohanim." I told R' Chaim that I would do my utmost to follow what he said. I then asked him what I should do when I return to my home overseas, as in *chutz laAretz* Bircas Kohanim is performed only on Yom Tov. R' Chaim replied that I should attend Sephardic minyanim, where Bircas Kohanim is performed every day.

As an Ashkenazi who descends from many chassidic Rebbes and grew up in the Borough Park section of Brooklyn, I had little exposure to the Sephardic community and was not aware of their customs. I told R' Chaim that the overseas Sephardim also perform Bircas Kohanim only on Yom Tov, not daily. R' Chaim smiled and patiently replied, "Sephardim worldwide perform Bircas Kohanim every day, as is brought down in *Beis Yosef.*"

I made some quick inquiries afterward and was informed that Sephardim do indeed perform Bircas Kohanim daily! I went back to R' Chaim later that day, thanked him for his advice, and asked him how often I should attend. He replied, *"L'fachot paamayim b'shavua* (at least twice a week)." I later heard that R' Chaim gave this advice to thousands of petitioners.

After hearing from R' Chaim about the tremendous sanctity of Bircas Kohanim and being inspired by its Divine blessings, I delved into the topic some more, but minimally. Later, around 2018, I asked R' Chaim for copies of his handwritten responses to inquiries on the topic of Bircas Kohanim. At the time I was also researching the topic of *shidduchim* in halachah, and asked him for access to the written letters on *shidduchim* as well. He graciously agreed and asked his son R' Yitzchak Shaul to provide me with copies of all his letters on these two subjects.

For many months I worked through the Bircas Kohanim letters with several of R' Chaim's esteemed grandchildren.

As we progressed through R' Chaim's letters, we were fortunate to maintain consistent dialogue with him and obtain indispensable clarifications and expansions on his written answers. A few months later, we asked him if we should publish a book on *Bircas Kohanim* first and then *shidduchim* (as we were working on both), or vice versa. We suggested that perhaps, in light of the positive commandment of *"V'kidashto,"* to show deference to the Kohen (*Vayikra* 21:8), Bircas Kohanim should be given precedence.

Aware as we were of the care R' Chaim took to give priority to Kohanim, we were certain he would concur. As we noted in our biography of R' Chaim, published by ArtScroll/Mesorah, before beginning to reply to the many letters he received daily, R' Chaim would sort the mail and make piles of incoming letters. First, he pulled out any that came from people bearing a surname that might belong to a Kohen, and put them in one pile. He then went through the letters a second time and removed all letters whose writers' names indicated that they might be Leviim, and he left the rest in a "Yisraelim" pile. To fulfill the mitzvah of *"V'kidashto,"* he responded first to the Kohanim, then to the Leviim, and finally to the Yisraelim.

To our surprise, however, R' Chaim smiled and replied: *"Shidduchim kodem"* (we should write about *shidduchim* first). He explained that the urgency of this topic is paramount, and he also noted his distress that so many *bachurim* who reside overseas begin *shidduchim* when they are older; this adversely affects their spiritual purity, and also leaves many girls who reside overseas single, often waiting for many years to marry. All of this, he said, was detrimental to Klal Yisrael.

In January 2022, the book *Rav Chaim Kanievsky on Shidduchim* was published by ArtScroll/Mesorah, followed by a Hebrew edition called *Siach Shidduch* (*Siach* being an acronym for Shmaryahu Yosef Chaim, R' Chaim's full name).

Our team, consisting of several of R' Chaim's grandsons and me, then turned our attention to the topic of Bircas Kohanim.

The treasure trove of the never-before-published responsa of R' Chaim at the end of this book represents a small fraction of the tens of thousands of letters that people sent him on every conceivable Torah topic. When R' Chaim received a letter, he would reply (usually the same day) on a postcard, but he would keep the original letter in his possession, copy his postcard response on the original letter, and store it in his home.

Approximately twenty-five years ago, the renowned Torah supporter Mr. A. Joseph Stern of Edison, New Jersey, undertook the financial responsibility of scanning, preserving, and indexing all R' Chaim's responsa. Mr. Stern's foresight enabled us to readily select the *teshuvos* applicable to Bircas Kohanim, out of thousands of letters, and access more than five thousand letters on Bircas Kohanim with R' Chaim's handwritten responses, spanning over half a century.

It was enlightening to review thousands of letters, primarily from Kohanim from all over the world, with practical questions regarding Bircas Kohanim. I am still awed by the magnitude of R' Chaim's *chesed* for Klal Yisrael in answering them and preserving his responses. Some letters had more than twenty questions, yet he diligently answered every query.

The Gemara states (*Berachos* 31a): "A person should not take leave of his fellow man, except amid discussion of a matter of halachah." It was an indescribable merit to discuss the laws of Bircas Kohanim with R' Chaim and several of his grandchildren during the last few years of his blessed life. Even after his passing, as we worked intensely on this volume, sifting through and curating his rulings, we felt a special connection to him and his boundless *chesed* and mastery of Torah.

In his exceptional humility, R' Chaim says this in the introduction to his *sefer Daas Notah*:

> Although I am not at all qualified to issue rulings, I respond to [inquiries] in order to encourage the writers. However, I regularly warn them not to rely on my response in practice. Rather, they should study the topic on their own if they are qualified or they should ask a qualified halachic authority.

As per R' Chaim's explicit request regarding this book and all other works that quote his rulings and responses, every reader must be guided by his own qualified rav and should not rely solely on these *teshuvos*. Especially when it comes to the topic of Bircas Kohanim, which involves many different customs, one should consult with his own rav to be sure that R' Chaim's response conforms to his own *mesorah*.

Many of his *teshuvos* that have practical applications appear at the end of this volume, in their original Hebrew (as per R' Chaim's direction).

The halachah section of this book is based primarily on the rulings of *Mishnah Berurah*. R' Chaim would frequently say that the *poskim acharonim* (final halachic decisors) are *Mishnah Berurah*, the Chofetz Chaim's magnum opus, and the *Chazon Ish*. We also received R' Chaim's permission to translate relevant portions of his *sefer Shoneh Halachos*, which summarizes the *Mishnah Berurah*.

In 2019, I was present during the weekly learning session R' Chaim had with his brother-in-law R' Yitzchak Zilberstein. Before R' Chaim entered the room, I conversed with R' Yitzchak and he inquired what topic I was writing about. When I answered, "Bircas Kohanim and *shidduchim*," he seemed perplexed. "Are you a Levi?" he asked. "Because I know you are not a Kohen."

"No," I replied, "I am a Yisrael."

"So why are you writing about Bircas Kohanim?"

Hashem put an interesting reply into my mouth. *"Kevod haRav,"* I said, *"ani gam lo tzippor* (I am also not a bird), and I wrote a *sefer* about *shiluach hakan*."

R' Yitzchak was amused by the answer. When R' Chaim came in

to learn with R' Yitzchak, he recounted the exchange to R' Chaim and R' Chaim uncharacteristically laughed heartily.

One of the interesting recollections I have of R' Chaim occurred on Shabbos Parashas Nasso 5772/2012. The biography of his wife, Rebbetzin Batsheva, had been published several days earlier, and we presented the book to him. After quipping that the content was in a language he did not understand, but the pictures appeared to be in Hebrew, he thanked us for publishing the book.

That Shabbos afternoon, when I was in the Lederman shul awaiting *Minchah Gedolah*, R' Chaim came over to me and asked if he could speak to me after Minchah. This had never happened before; R' Chaim never came over *to speak to me*. I was overcome with trepidation, akin to the experience of being called into the principal's office with no inkling of what you did wrong.

After Minchah and *seudah shelishis*, R' Chaim gestured to me to come over. In a soft voice he told me that there was something bothering him a lot about the book. He told me he was worried that the book had caused me a lot of *bittul Torah* (neglecting Torah study), as I had been unable to learn sufficiently while I compiled the book. I countered that he himself had told me in the name of the Chazon Ish that reading biographies of *gedolim* was an effective way to attain *yiras Shamayim*, and he had given me a written approbation for the book! R' Chaim replied that nevertheless I had a lot of *teshuvah* to do for not learning enough Torah while working on the book.

It was the only time R' Chaim reprimanded me. His mild, loving rebuke serves as a constant reminder to dedicate more time for Torah study.

This book is the product of five years of intensive study of the topic of Bircas Kohanim. It is my hope that the many hours of Torah learning involved in researching and compiling this collection of insights into Bircas Kohanim should find favor in the eyes of Hashem, and bring *nachas ruach* to R' Chaim's lofty *neshamah*.

One of the people I was very close to for many years was my wife's grandfather, R' Shmuel HaKohen Roth. As a native of pre-war Munkacz, he merited to perform Bircas Kohanim in the minyan of the Minchas Elazar, the Munkaczer Rebbe. Yet he would say that the most memorable time that he performed Bircas Kohanim was during one of the darkest chapters in our nation's history.

During Shavuos, May 28-29, 5704/1944, he was imprisoned by the Nazis in the city of Mishkoltz (Miskolc), Hungary. The accursed Nazis gave the hundreds of Jews fifteen minutes a day to leave their cells and gather in the prison courtyard. The inmates utilized the time to have a quick minyan for Mussaf. Several Leviim used part of their water ration to wash the hands of the Kohanim. They davened Mussaf together, and R' Shmuel was one of the Kohanim who blessed his fellow prisoners. He told us that this Bircas Kohanim gave him a glimmer of light and hope during his imprisonment and his time in a slave labor camp. After performing Bircas Kohanim on both days of Shavuos, he had a sixth sense that he would survive, even though his parents had been murdered.

When I visited R' Moshe Sternbuch to request his written approbation for this book he told me, "Between the Yidden in Eretz Yisrael and the Sephardic communities throughout the Diaspora, there are more Yidden receiving Bircas Kohanim on a daily basis today than at any time in recent history, and that is a heavenly sign of the coming Redemption."

May all those who read this book gain a deeper appreciation of Bircas Kohanim, and may we merit that the prayers we implore Hashem during the Festivals, וְהָשֵׁב כֹּהֲנִים לַעֲבוֹדָתָם וּלְוִיִּם לְשִׁירָם וּלְזִמְרָם וְהָשֵׁב יִשְׂרָאֵל לִנְוֵיהֶם, *Restore the Kohanim to their service and the Leviim to their song and music; and restore Israel to their dwellings,* be accepted speedily in our days.

Naftali Weinberger

Acknowledgments

My first acknowledgment is to Hashem Yisbarach, to Whom we all owe everything we have in this world. He orchestrated many events that facilitated my relationship with Maran Harav Chaim Kanievsky *zt"l*, ensuring that I would be privileged to be "in the right place at the right time."

My parents, R' Shlomo and Mrs. Gitty Weinberger, and in-laws, R' Heshy and Mrs. Suzi Basch, do so much for my wife and me with boundless devotion and love. We are grateful beyond words to you for being quintessential parents and role models for us and our children.

As we complete the writing of this book, it is difficult to submit it for print without R' Chaim in our midst. When we worked on this book during the last few years of R' Chaim's incredibly productive life, he always made himself available to answer our queries. May we merit to greet him with Mashiach and *techiyas hameisim,* speedily in our days.

A special thank you to my dear son R' Binyomin, who reviewed the manuscript in depth and provided many insightful comments.

Sincere thanks go to R' Chaim's sons, R' Avraham Yeshayah, R' Shlomo, and R' Yitzchak Shaul, and sons-in-law, R' Shraga Shteinman, R' Yitzchak Kolodetsky, R' Yehoshua Tzivyon, R' Zelig Braverman, and R' Dovid Epstein, who all assisted in clarifying various aspects of this incredible mitzvah.

Special thanks to R' Chaim's inimitable and illustrious brother-in-law HaRav Yitzchak Zilberstein for his many insightful halachic clarifications. I have been privileged to listen to his brilliant *shiurim* for about thirty years.

This book could not have been completed without the assistance of R' Chaim's grandsons R' Gedaliah Honigsberg, R' Yaakov Maklev, R' Avraham Yeshayah Shteinman, R' Dovid Kanievsky, and especially R' Aryeh Kolodetsky, all of whom had learning sessions with their grandfather and were able to review and clarify many of his rulings that appear in this book. Special thanks to their wives for allowing their husbands to give up many hours of family time to dedicate themselves to the compilation of the book.

It was a distinct pleasure to work with R' Uri HaKohen Tieger and R' Tzvi Yabrov, who reviewed the Hebrew manuscript and provided many valuable suggestions. Their longstanding relationship with R' Chaim was so close that he asked them to review several of his own *sefarim* prior to publication.

I am grateful to the many rebbeim who taught, guided, and inspired me, specifically (in alphabetical order): R' Asher Arielli, R' Moshe Aharon Friedman, R' Shmuel Kamenetsky, R' Eliezer Yehuda Finkel, R' Chizkiyahu Mishkovsky, R' Tzvi Partzovitz, and R' Moshe Sternbuch.

R' Mechel Cohen and his father R' Mordechai Cohen assisted in researching and clarifying many of the chassidic customs of Bircas Kohanim.

Special thanks to the esteemed Kohanim R' Yosef Fixler and R' Tzodek Katz, who personify blessing Klal Yisrael *b'ahavah*, and who spent many hours assisting in various aspects of the book.

During the years of researching and writing this book, we were assisted by many Kohanim, including R' Ari Brecher, R' Yossi Brecher, R' Yossi Brezel, R' Yaakov Beyda, R' Yoni Czegledi, R' Shmuel Dovid Friedman, R' Dov Kahan, R' Avrohom Cohen, R' Shimon Kaplan, R' Shmuel Dovid Katz, R' Yossi Katz, R' Daniel Asher Kleinman, R' Yehoshua Novoseller, R' Moshe Roth, R' Ezra Maselton, R' Aharon Muller, R' Mutty Muller, R' Yaakov Weisz, and R' Ezra Zafrani.

Among the many other people who assisted us, special gratitude is due to those who contributed immensely: R' Yisroel Besser, R' Yaakov Bistricer, R' Raphael Brus, R' Yehuda Brus, R' Yitzy Dick, R' Natan Feldman, R' Colev Gestetner, R' Amir Jaffa, R' Aharon Kaye, R' Shlomo Lewenstein, R' Rafi Lichtschein, R' Ami Maierovits, R' Eliezer Maierovits, R' Moshe Tzvi Marsh, R' Aryeh Millet, R' Yossi Moskowitz, R' Shimon Yosef Meller, R' Dovid Nachfolger, R' Shmuel Rabinowitz, R' Yussi Rieder, R' Mendy Safrin, R' Elazar Safrin, R' Ido Saka,

R' Moshe Sanders, R' Dov Scheinerman, R' Yitzchak Scheinerman, R' Dov Schon, R' Yaakov Sod, R' Eliyahu Tobal, and R' Elazar Dovid Weinberger.

A special thank you goes to R' Gedaliah Zlotowitz. Under his wise and unwavering leadership, ArtScroll/Mesorah continues its worldwide *harbatzas haTorah* in the tradition of its great and unparalleled founder, my dear friend R' Meir Zlotowitz. Thank you, R' Gedaliah, for your active involvement, creative guidance, and helpful input (from early morning to late at night), which were so vital in shaping and enhancing this book. I would like to especially acknowledge his son R' Ahron Zlotowitz for coordinating and assisting in many aspects of this book.

I am grateful to R' Nosson Scherman, who granted his valuable time to review and refine the work with innumerable editorial suggestions. A special thank you to his esteemed grandson R' Ephraim Scherman, who helped compile and edit the manuscript.

R' Avrohom Biderman assisted in coordinating this book from its early stages and spent much time ensuring that it would be a success.

I am grateful to Mrs. Estie Dicker, who entered corrections and paginated the book with skill, patience, and dedication, ensuring the beauty of every page.

R' Sheah HaKohen Brander, who sets the bar of graphics excellence, made sure that every element of the book has the unique ArtScroll touch and meets the highest standards of design, layout, and typography. I thank his son R' Shloime HaKohen for his help.

My thanks to ArtScroll's graphics master, the incomparable R' Eli Kroen, for his creative and beautiful cover.

My sincere appreciation to R' Yoav Elan, who provided masterful diagrams for the position of the Kohanim's fingers during Bircas Kohanim.

Thank you, R' Mendy Herzberg, for managing the production of this book with your signature pleasantness and professionalism.

R' Moshe Scheinbaum's efficiency and positive energy was of great assistance.

Mrs. Tova Finkelman reviewed the book and offered many important comments. A special thank you to her husband, my dear friend R' Shimon HaKohen Finkelman, for reviewing several chapters.

A special acknowledgment goes to R' Yonah (Jack) Jaffa, who was a close disciple of R' Chaim. Following R' Chaim's advice, R' Yonah diligently attends a Sephardic minyan almost every day to be blessed by the Kohanim. I am honored by his friendship and generous dedication of this book.

R' Yossi Maline translated and edited the material in this book and spent much time enhancing it with his incredible talent and upbeat attitude.

I was fortunate to have this book edited by Mrs. Malky Heimowitz, who rewrote and reorganized the manuscript, masterfully weaving together the chapters of this book, while her husband, R' Yehuda, served as a consultant and sounding board. Their exceptional ability is evident on every page. May Hashem grant them health, strength, and *hatzlachah* to continue disseminating high-quality Torah projects.

Thank you to my dear children, who insist on not being named, for encouraging me to undertake this project and for making it possible for me to spend so much time on it. (They maintain that R' Chaim did not list his children in *his* acknowledgments and the same standard should apply here.) May this book be a special *zechus* for you and your own children and may you all merit good health and success until the coming of Mashiach.

No words could possibly express my gratitude to my *eishes chayil,* Naomi. May Hashem bless us with the best of health and *hatzlachah,* and together may we see continued *nachas* from our dear children, in all areas.

May Hashem's blessings, conveyed to us by His Kohanim, be fulfilled, and may we all merit experiencing Bircas Kohanim in the rebuilt Beis HaMikdash speedily in our days.

Naftali Weinberger
Sivan 5784/June 2024

Part 1:

A Unique Mitzvah

Chapter 1
The Power and Significance of Bircas Kohanim

Hashem Desires Bircas Kohanim

The Gemara (*Sotah* 38b) states: "R' Yehoshua ben Levi said: From where do we know that the Holy One, Blessed is He, desires Bircas Kohanim? For it is written (*Bamidbar* 6:27): וְשָׂמוּ אֶת שְׁמִי עַל בְּנֵי יִשְׂרָאֵל וַאֲנִי אֲבָרְכֵם, *And they shall place My Name upon Bnei Yisrael, and I will bless them."*

How do we see from the above *pasuk* that Hashem desires Bircas Kohanim?

Rashi (*Sotah* ibid.) explains that the *pasuk* gives the Kohanim the authority to "place G-d's Name" upon His people, indicating that the blessing not only benefits the Jewish people, but also, so to speak, fulfills the "need" of Hashem to have His Name pronounced over His people.

Rashi also tells us that R' Yehoshua ben Levi understands the phrase "and I will bless *them*" to mean that when the Kohanim bless the people, Hashem will bless the people as well. But if Hashem intends to bless the people Himself, what is the point of having the Kohanim bless them? We must conclude, says *Maharsha*, that Hashem *desires* that the Kohanim should bestow their blessing upon His people.

Chumash Torah Temimah (*Bamidbar* 6:27, 155) observes that the *pasuk* is not worded as a commandment (וְיָשִׂימוּ, *and they* ***shall*** *place*), and suggests that the word וְשָׂמוּ (*and they* ***will*** *place*) implies a desire — "If only they would place My Name...."

More Than the Infant Desires to Eat

Maharal (*Chiddushei Aggados, Sotah* ibid.) shares a deep understanding of why Hashem "desires" Bircas Kohanim:

Hashem is exalted above all His creations, and one who is positioned above others is inherently a giver to those who are beneath him. *Chazal* say that Hashem "desires" Bircas Kohanim because He longs to bestow blessing upon His people, and that objective is achieved through Bircas Kohanim. We know that "more than the infant desires to eat, his mother desires to feed him," for the power of giving, which is done through an action, is always greater than the power of receiving, which is passive.

The sixty letters of Bircas Kohanim correspond to the שִׁשִּׁים גִּבֹּרִים סָבִיב לָהּ מִגִּבֹּרֵי יִשְׂרָאֵל, *sixty of Israel's mighty encircling [Hashem's resting place]* (*Shir HaShirim* 3:7). Because of its power, Hashem desires Bircas Kohanim, and commanded the Kohanim, *You shall place My Name upon Bnei Yisrael.* As Rashi explains: It is a "need" of the Almighty, so to speak, for the Kohanim to place His Name upon the Jewish people, because He is the ultimate Giver.

Hashem Needs Bircas Kohanim

She'iltos D'R' Achai (125) cites a different version of R' Yehoshua ben Levi's statement: "From where do we know that even the Holy One, Blessed is He, *needs* Bircas Kohanim? For it is written: *And they shall place My Name upon Bnei Yisrael, and I will bless them." Ein Yaakov* (*Sotah* 38b) adds that just as Hashem desired to have a *Mishkan* (Tabernacle) built in this world so that He can rest His Divine spirit among His chosen people (*Shemos Rabbah* 52), He likewise desires Bircas Kohanim so that He can rest His Divine spirit upon the Jewish people.

The King Wants to Hear From You

Sefer Koh Sevarechu[1] says the following (Preface):

A Kohen who goes up to *duchan* should keep this statement of the Gemara at the forefront of his thoughts and realize that Hashem *desires* his Bircas Kohanim! Imagine getting a message from a flesh-and-blood king that he desires to hear from you. Surely, you would be filled with excitement and trepidation. You would carefully prepare and weigh each word that you plan to say, and make certain not to utter a single sentence that could somehow be offensive to the king. At the presentation itself you would enunciate every syllable clearly and try your best to impress the king, knowing that he desires to hear your words.

How much more so when you know that the King of kings, Who rules the entire universe and lives for all eternity, desires to hear your words! When a Kohen reflects upon this, he will be awestruck and will tremble with fear lest he fail to meet Hashem's expectations. If **Hashem desires his blessing**, he must concentrate on each word, with the intent of bringing pleasure to his Creator.

Blessing the Angels; Higher Than the Angels

The Torah introduces the mitzvah of Bircas Kohanim with the words כֹּה תְבָרְכוּ אֶת בְּנֵי יִשְׂרָאֵל אָמוֹר לָהֶם, *So shall you bless Bnei Yisrael, saying to them* (*Bamidbar* 6:23). Rabbeinu Bachaye teaches that the connecting word "*es*" (אֶת) comes to include the ministering angels in the blessing as well. Likewise, *Zohar* states (*Nasso* 169): "R' Yehudah said that the phrase 'saying to *them*' in that *pasuk* **includes all the celestial beings together** with all of humanity down here on earth; all are blessed simultaneously."

Sfas Emes (*Vayechi* 5649) says: "When the Kohanim raise their hands to recite Bircas Kohanim, **the angels of the Upper Worlds descend and the Kohanim of the Lower Worlds rise above them.**"

---

1. Written by R' Yehoshua Elazar HaKohen Chimtzi (1795-1881), who served as a rav in Izmir, Turkey, for many years, later moving to Haifa and serving as a rav there.

Peering Through the Openings

The Midrash relates (*Bamidbar Rabbah* 11:2): When Hashem instructed Aharon and his sons, *So shall you bless Bnei Yisrael,* the Jewish people reacted by saying, "Master of the Universe! Why do you tell the Kohanim to bless us? We only desire and need a blessing from You!"

Hashem responded: "Although I have told the Kohanim to bless you, I shall stand together with them and bless you as well." Thus, the *pasuk* in *Shir HaShirim* states (2:9): הִנֵּה זֶה עוֹמֵד אַחַר כָּתְלֵנוּ מַשְׁגִּיחַ מִן הַחַלֹּנוֹת מֵצִיץ מִן הַחֲרַכִּים, *He was standing behind our wall, observing through the windows, peering through the lattices.* This means that Hashem stands behind the Kohanim, observing through the spaces between their shoulders and peering through the openings created by the spread-out fingers of their raised hands.

Regarding the earlier words of that verse, דּוֹמֶה דוֹדִי לִצְבִי, *My beloved is like a gazelle,* the Midrash (ibid.) says that just as a gazelle leaps through the forest from place to place, so does Hashem leap from one congregation to another, to bestow His blessing on the Jewish people at the time of Bircas Kohanim.

Sefer HaEshkol and others cite these Midrashim as one of the reasons for the prohibition to look at the hands of Kohanim during Bircas Kohanim, even nowadays, since the Shechinah rests on the hands of the Kohanim at this time.

Forbidden to Gaze

Rabbeinu David HaKochavi writes (*Sefer HaBattim, Mitzvas Asei* 25): Because of the exalted nature of Bircas Kohanim, it is forbidden for the Kohanim to gaze at the congregation while reciting the *berachos,* just as it is forbidden for the congregation to gaze at them (see *Chagigah* 16a). This is to avoid becoming distracted and so that they will be able to concentrate on the meaning of the words.

The "Gezeirah" of Bircas Kohanim

After performing Bircas Kohanim, the Kohanim recite a short *tefillah,* which begins with the words *"Ribbono Shel Olam* — Master of the Universe, we have done what You have 'decreed' (*shegazarta*) upon us...."

R' Shlomo HaKohen of Vilna wonders (*Binyan Shlomo* 1:10): Why is Bircas Kohanim referred to as a *gezeirah* (decree)? Wouldn't it be more appropriate to say, "We have done what You have *commanded* us"?

He offers an answer that he heard from his father, based on the first *pasuk* in *Parashas Chukas*. There, the Torah refers to the mitzvah of *parah adumah* (the red heifer) as a *chok* — a mitzvah that cannot be understood with human logic, and the *Targum* translates the word *chok* as *gezeirah* — a decree. This teaches us that a commandment of the Torah that we cannot understand is called a *gezeirah*. Hence the term *"gezeiras hakasuv,"* which is a decree of the Torah that we don't necessarily understand but must comply with nonetheless.

Bircas Kohanim is also a mitzvah that seems counterintuitive. After all, the greatest, most pious Torah sage of the generation, who does not happen to be a Kohen, is compelled to receive a *berachah* through a Kohen — *any* Kohen — even if that Kohen is an ignorant person who is on a far lower spiritual level than he is! Thus, it is indeed apropos to refer to the mitzvah of Bircas Kohanim as a *gezeirah*.

Unconditional Blessing

Raviah (R' Eliezer ben R' Yoel HaLevi, a Rishon) points out (*Teshuvos U'Biurei Sugyos* 1155) that the passage of Bircas Kohanim begins with the commandment כֹּה תְבָרְכוּ אֶת בְּנֵי יִשְׂרָאֵל, *So shall you bless Bnei Yisrael*, and it ends with the promise וַאֲנִי אֲבָרְכֵם, *and I shall bless them*. This is unlike the *berachos* listed in the beginning of *Parashas Bechukosai*, where the Torah stipulates, אִם בְּחֻקֹּתַי תֵּלֵכוּ וְאֶת מִצְוֹתַי תִּשְׁמְרוּ, *If you will follow My decrees and observe My commandments...* then you will receive the blessings. Here, the sixty letters of Bircas Kohanim bring us all the blessings *unconditionally*.

Shaarei Orah (*Shaar* 10), one of the earliest Kabbalistic works, states that it was a great act of kindness toward the Jewish people that Hashem commanded His Kohanim to bless them, because there are times when, in fact, we are not deserving of blessing. We may find ourselves stained with grievous sins that prevent us from receiving any beneficence from Above. What did Hashem do? He gave the Kohanim the keys to the Gates of Mercy, so that whenever they recite Bircas Kohanim the gates are opened, and **an endless flow of mercy and kindness pours down from Heaven — regardless of how undeserving we may be!**

Similarly, the author of *Magen Avraham* writes in his *sefer Zayis Raanan,* on *Yalkut Shimoni* (*Bamidbar* 6:24), that the blessings of Bircas Kohanim are fulfilled even if one did not follow other commandments of Hashem.

Chida (*Devash L'fi,* 30:9, *Levayah*) notes that the blessings found at the beginning of *Parashas Bechukosai* contain all the letters of the *aleph-beis* except the letter *samech* (ס), which has a numerical value of sixty. This is an allusion to the sixty letters of Bircas Kohanim, and the lesson here is that all the *berachos* of the Torah are granted to us only on the condition that we keep the mitzvos — with the exception of Bircas Kohanim! **We receive the blessings of Bircas Kohanim even if we are not deserving!**

Likewise, *Birkei Yosef* (128:19) states that when the community is facing misfortune and they gather together to pray for salvation, it is recommended and appropriate for the Kohanim to first *duchan* during Shacharis and then to pray afterward, for Bircas Kohanim awakens Divine Mercy and allows us to receive gifts from Hashem even when we have not earned them.

The same is recorded in *Kaf HaChaim* (128:270) as well.

Unhindered by Heavenly Justice

When the Kohanim raise their hands and recite Bircas Kohanim, **a great surge of blessing streams down from the Upper Worlds, unimpeded and unhindered by any form of Heavenly Justice that demands that Hashem's kindness be withheld due to our sins.** This is comparable to the incident in which Bilaam attempted to curse the Jewish nation, yet, as the Torah tells us (*Devarim* 23:6), *Hashem, your G-d, refused to listen to Bilaam, and Hashem, your G-d, reversed the curse to a blessing for you, because Hashem, your G-d, loved you* (*Shulchan Aruch HaRav, Likutei Torah,* end of *Parashas Korach*).

In the Merit of the Avos

The *Midrash* (*Bereishis Rabbah* 43:8) teaches that the Jewish nation merited Bircas Kohanim because of the deeds of the Patriarchs.

We know this because the commandment of Bircas Kohanim begins with the word *"koh"* (*"So" shall you bless Bnei Yisrael*), and the same word is found in connection with our forefathers, as follows: R' Yehudah said it is in the merit of Avraham, for Hashem said to Avraham: *Count the stars if you are able to count them. So* (*koh*) *shall your offspring be* (*Bereishis* 15:5). R' Nechemiah said it was in the merit of Yitzchak, as the *pasuk* says, regarding the *Akeidah*: *I and the lad will go yonder* (*ad koh*) (ibid. 22:5). Finally, the Rabbis said it was in the merit of Yaakov, as the Torah says: *So* (*koh*) *shall you say to the House of Yaakov...* (*Shemos* 19:3).

The Power to Bestow Blessing

Midrash Tanchuma (*Vayechi* 7) teaches that the Holy One, Blessed is He, said: In the past, it was necessary for Me to bless people Myself. Thus we find, for example: *G-d blessed Noach and his sons* (*Bereishis* 9:1); *Hashem had blessed Avraham with everything* (ibid. 24:1); *And it was after the death of Avraham that G-d blessed Yitzchak his son* (ibid. 25:11), and so forth. From this point on, however, the Kohanim and the righteous will be the ones who have the power to bestow blessing.

A different Midrash states (*Bamidbar Rabbah* 11:4) that when Avraham Avinu passed away, the Torah tells us: *And it was after the death of Avraham that G-d blessed Yitzchak his son* (*Bereishis* 25:11). Yitzchak, in turn, blessed his son Yaakov, and Yaakov blessed his own twelve sons at the end of his life as well, as the *pasuk* says: *All these are the tribes of Yisrael — twelve — and this is what their father spoke to them and he blessed them* (ibid. 49:28). "From that point on," Hashem decreed, "the *berachos* are in the hands of the Kohanim; it is up to them to bless the Jewish people and to fulfill My promise to Avraham, *you shall be a blessing* (ibid. 12:2)."

Hashem also promised Avraham, *And I will bless those who bless you* (ibid. v. 3). *Midrash Tanchuma* (*Lech Lecha* 4) relates that Hashem told Avraham, "In the future, I will designate one tribe from among your descendants who will be appointed to bless the Jewish people, and that is the tribe of Levi." Avraham asked, "Master of the Universe, who will bless that tribe?" Hashem responded, "When they bless the people, I will bless them, as the Torah states: *Let them place My Name on Bnei Yisrael, and I shall bless them.*"

Speaking to the Jewish people, Hashem said, "In this world, the tribe of Levi blesses you, but in the world of the Future I shall bless you in person, as the *navi*, describing the future Redemption, says: עוֹד יֹאמְרוּ אֶת הַדָּבָר הַזֶּה בְּאֶרֶץ יְהוּדָה ... יְבָרֶכְךָ ה׳ נְוֵה צֶדֶק הַר הַקֹּדֶשׁ, *People will again say this thing in the land of Yehudah... May Hashem bless you, O Abode of Righteousness, O Holy Mountain*" (*Yirmiyah* 31:22).

All the Children of Israel

The Gemara (*Sotah* 38a) teaches: "When the Torah states (*Bamidbar* 6:23), *So shall you bless Bnei Yisrael,* I know only that the Kohanim must bless the sons of Israel (i.e., males born to Jewish parents). From where do we derive that they must also bless converts, women, and emancipated Caananite slaves? To teach this, the Torah states in that very verse, *saying to them,* which implies: Say the blessing to all of them, i.e., all members of the nation."

The Gemara adds that the blessing extends even to the people in the fields, who are unable to come to shul due to circumstances beyond their control.[2]

Similarly, *Sifrei* (*Nasso* 43) states that although the commandment of Bircas Kohanim begins with the words *Let them place My Name on "Bnei Yisrael,"* and the term *"Bnei Yisrael"* usually refers only to males of Jewish descent, the added phrase, *and I shall bless them,* teaches that the blessing of the Kohanim is bestowed upon all Jews, including converts, women, and slaves as well.

Avoiding the Blessing

The halachah is that a Kohen who is called up to *duchan* and fails to do so transgresses three positive commandments.[3] *Beis Yosef* (128:1) cites the opinion of Rabbeinu Manoach that even if the Kohen is not called up, he transgresses the commandment of כֹּה תְבָרְכוּ, *so shall you bless,* by failing to *duchan. Beis Yosef* himself, however, disagrees with this latter ruling of Rabbeinu Manoach.

Regarding a Kohen who avoids the mitzvah of Bircas Kohanim,

2. For an extensive discussion of how the *berachah* spreads, see chapter 17.
3. *Sotah* 38b; *Rambam, Hilchos Tefillah U'Nesias Kapayim* 15:12; *Shulchan Aruch* 128:2.

R' Avraham ben HaRambam writes (*HaMaspik L'Ovdei Hashem,* ch. 28) that although he does not violate any specific transgression, he is still considered a sinner, for he has forfeited the opportunity to fulfill a Torah commandment.

The same holds true for those who avoid *receiving* the *berachah,* as *Kaf HaChaim* writes (128:149) that if one misses Bircas Kohanim and does not have a legitimate excuse for doing so, he demonstrates that the *berachah* has little value to him, and therefore he is certainly not included in the *berachah,* as *Rashi* says (*Sotah* 38b). In fact, he says, even if one is merely passing through a shul, and happens to walk in during Bircas Kohanim, he is not permitted to leave until the Kohanim finish.

Indeed, *Ben Ish Chai* (*Tetzaveh* §19) states that if a person enters a shul just to look for something, or for some other purpose, and at that moment the Kohanim happen to be *duchaning,* he should stop and listen to Bircas Kohanim, and should not leave until it is over. If he himself is a Kohen, and he arrives before the congregation has reached Bircas Kohanim, he may *duchan* for them even if he has already performed the mitzvah earlier that day.

Likewise, the Chofetz Chaim (*Biur Halachah* 128:4) cites from *Chemed Moshe* that it is inappropriate to avoid a positive Torah commandment for no reason. He gives the example of the mitzvah of tzitzis, which one is not obligated to perform unless he is wearing a four-cornered garment — yet one must make the effort to acquire such a garment in order to fulfill the mitzvah. If one chooses to avoid the mitzvah, he is punished *"b'idan rischa"* — at a time when Hashem's anger is manifest in the world, as the Gemara teaches (*Menachos* 41a).

Additionally, *Biur Halachah* (128:24) quotes the Gemara's statement that those who are standing behind the Kohanim are not included in the *berachah,* adding that the same applies to anyone who is in the city but chooses not to go to hear Bircas Kohanim; he, too, is excluded from the *berachah,* even if he faces in the direction of the Kohanim and is not standing "in front of" them. That is because he has demonstrated that in his eyes, the *berachah* is not important enough for him to make the effort of coming to hear it.

Shulchan Aruch HaRav (128:37) reproaches those who do not come to shul for Bircas Kohanim, or who come, but do not stand facing the Kohanim to receive the *berachah*. He writes that anyone who is in the city and is able to come to shul to receive the *berachah* — standing face to face with the Kohanim — and fails to do so demonstrates that the *berachah* is unimportant in his eyes; therefore, he is not included in the blessing.

Even those who are standing in the courtyard of the shul because there is no room for them inside are not included in the *berachah* if they stand on the east side of the shul, which is behind the Kohanim. Rather, they must stand on the west side of the building, opposite the Kohanim. They may also stand on the north or south sides, but facing toward the Kohanim. Likewise, those who sit at the *mizrach* (east) wall in the front of the shul must move from their places during Bircas Kohanim so that they can face the Kohanim.

Understanding the Concepts of Bircas Kohanim

R' Avraham ben HaRambam writes (*HaMaspik L'Ovdei Hashem,* ch. 28): "It is clear that the great blessings of Bircas Kohanim cannot be achieved without the participation of both the Kohanim who pray and the people for whom they are praying. Therefore, it is proper for the congregation to be present to hear the *berachah,* to concentrate on the meaning of the words, and to anticipate the fruits that the *berachah* will surely produce. Thus, it is appropriate for every person to learn and understand the concepts of Bircas Kohanim and to bear them in mind when receiving the *berachah*."

R' Aharon Leib Shteinman writes (*Yemalei Pi Tehilasecha, Iyunim BiTefillah*) that there are many deep secrets hidden in Bircas Kohanim, and the various commentaries say that the Kohanim can simply have in mind that their *berachah* should be understood in accordance with all the intentions of the Torah.

Incredible Power of the Verses

Mishnah Berurah (47:20) explains that the reason we recite the passage of Bircas Kohanim immediately after *Birchos HaTorah* each morning is to begin our Torah study on a positive note and with a *berachah,* so that Hashem will allow us to study and properly understand His Torah with no distractions. He adds that it is permitted to say these verses in the very early morning, before sunrise, even though Bircas Kohanim is not recited at night, because they are being recited for the purpose of Torah study, and are not connected to Bircas Kohanim in any way.

Millions of Mitzvos

Sefer Chareidim (12:8), *Haflaah* (*Kesubos* 24b), and others assert that in addition to the mitzvah for the Kohanim to bless the people, there is a mitzvah for the people to receive the blessing. *Ritva* (*Succah* 31b), however, disagrees.

Aderes[4] (*Cheshbonos Shel Mitzvah*, Mitzvah 378) dismisses the position of the *Chareidim* by quoting *Noda BiYehudah* (*Responsa Yoreh Deah*, vol. 2, 123), who writes that the reason *Shelah* (*Shaar HaOsiyos*, p. 101) counts a particular commandment[5] as a positive mitzvah, in contrast to others who do not, is because of his great love for mitzvos. So it was with *Chareidim* — his greatest desire was to perform as many mitzvos as possible. Since he was not a Kohen and could not perform the mitzvah of Bircas Kohanim, he found a way that he, too, could have a portion in this mitzvah — by receiving the *berachah*. *Chareidim*, with his passion to accumulate mitzvos, distributed millions of mitzvos to other Leviim and Yisraelim worldwide.

Aderes concludes, however, that after further review, he finds support for the position of *Chareidim* in *Rashi*, and therefore feels obligated to retract some of the harsh words he wrote about this being a "new mitzvah" for Leviim and Yisraelim.

Sustaining our Nation

The Shinover Rav, R' Yechezkel Shraga Halberstam, writes in his approbation to the *sefer Avodas Kehunah*: "By publishing this work, you are fulfilling a great mitzvah, which benefits all members of the Jewish people — the Kohanim who recite the *berachos*, the Leviim who wash the hands of the Kohanim, and the Yisraelim who receive the *berachos* — all of them are participating in the mitzvah, as *Rashi* teaches us (*Bamidbar* 6:27). This *sefer* will give everyone

4. R' Eliyahu Dovid Rabinowitz-Teumim (1845-1905).
5. וְסָפְרָה לָּה, *and she must count for herself* (*Vayikra* 15:28).

an appreciation of this beloved mitzvah, which has the power to bring down an outpouring of life and blessing that will sustain our nation until the coming of Mashiach."

Midrash HaGadol (*Nasso* 6:26) states that the merit of Bircas Kohanim stands for the Jewish people in the present time and will stand for us in the future time of Mashiach as well.

Chapter 2
Bircas Kohanim: The Last Vestige of the Beis HaMikdash

Bircas Kohanim is a form of *avodah* (Divine service), akin to the *avodah* that was performed by the Kohanim in the Beis HaMikdash. This is clearly expressed in the Gemara (*Sotah* 38a) that quotes the following Baraisa:

> When the Torah states, כֹּה תְבָרְכוּ אֶת בְּנֵי יִשְׂרָאֵל, *so shall you bless Bnei Yisrael,* it means that the Kohanim must recite the blessing in a standing position. We derive this from a *gezeirah shavah* (Scriptural analogy). R' Nosson says, it is unnecessary to resort to a *gezeirah shavah,* for the Torah states (*Devarim* 10:8), לְשָׁרְתוֹ וּלְבָרֵךְ בִּשְׁמוֹ, *to serve Him and to bless in His Name*. In this *pasuk*, "blessing" is compared to "serving." Just as the Kohen who serves in the Beis HaMikdash does so in a standing position, for it is written (ibid. 18:5), לַעֲמֹד לְשָׁרֵת, *to stand and to serve,* so, too, the Kohen who blesses the nation must do so in a standing position.

This concept is reiterated in *Menachos* (18b), where the Gemara states that a Kohen who does not accept all of the *avodos* that must be performed by Kohanim is not entitled to receive a portion of the *korbanos*. Among the *avodos* listed there is Bircas Kohanim, whether performed inside the Beis HaMikdash or outside; in either venue it is regarded as *avodah*. Elsewhere (*Chullin* 133a), *Rashi* notes that in addition to Bircas Kohanim being performed in the Beis HaMikdash, it is done outside the Beis HaMikdash as well, in every city and shul, inside Eretz Yisrael and abroad.

Likewise, *Rashi* (*Taanis* 26b) explains that the reason a Kohen may not perform Bircas Kohanim while intoxicated is that it is a form of *avodah* (see *Vayikra* 10:9). *Beis Yosef* (128:38) cites Rabbeinu Yerucham (*Nesiv* 3, 6:27:73), who asserts that a Kohen is disqualified only when he reaches the level of Lot's intoxication (see *Bereishis* 19:32), for at that point one is too drunk to pray (*Eruvin* 65a). Apparently, Rabbeinu Yerucham understood that the reason for this halachah is that Bircas Kohanim is considered *tefillah*. *Beis Yosef* disagrees, however, concurring with *Rashi* that Bircas Kohanim is a form of *avodah*, as the Torah states, *to serve Him and to bless in His Name*. That being the case, drinking even one *reviis* (approximately 3-5 ounces) of wine disqualifies a Kohen from performing Bircas Kohanim, just as it disqualifies him from any other *avodah*.

The Same Potency as in the Time of the Beis HaMikdash

Although the Gemara (*Berachos* 32b) states, "Since the day that the Beis HaMikdash was destroyed, a wall of iron has separated between Israel and their Father in Heaven," it is clear from the words of *Tosafos* (*Sotah* 39a, s.v. *Mechitzah*) that this refers only to our prayers, which are not as readily accepted as they were when the Beis HaMikdash stood. With regard to Bircas Kohanim, *Tosafos* explain, there is no separation between us and Hashem, and the blessings of the Kohanim have the same potency today as they did thousands of years ago, in the time of the Beis HaMikdash.

Additionally, *Mishnah Berurah* (128:44) proves, based on *Yerushalmi*, *Bavli*, and Midrashim, that the mitzvah of Bircas Kohanim applies today, even in *chutz laAretz*, just as it did in the Beis HaMikdash.

Washing Hands Before Doing the Avodah

Rambam states[1] that a Kohen must wash his hands until the wrist before Bircas Kohanim "in the same manner that [a Kohen] washes his hands before performing *avodah,*" as the *pasuk* says (*Tehillim* 134:2), שְׂאוּ יְדֵכֶם קֹדֶשׁ וּבָרְכוּ אֶת ה׳, *Lift your hands in the Sanctuary and bless Hashem.*

Radbaz[2] writes:

> The reason Kohanim must wash their hands before Bircas Kohanim is that there is a positive Torah commandment for Kohanim to wash their hands and feet[3] before performing *avodah*, and Bircas Kohanim is an *avodah*, as the *pasuk* says (*I Divrei HaYamim* 23:13), וַיִּבָּדֵל אַהֲרֹן לְהַקְדִּישׁוֹ קֹדֶשׁ קָדָשִׁים הוּא וּבָנָיו עַד עוֹלָם לְהַקְטִיר לִפְנֵי ה׳ לְשָׁרְתוֹ וּלְבָרֵךְ בִּשְׁמוֹ עַד עוֹלָם, *Aharon was set apart, to sanctify him as holy of holies, he and his sons forever, to burn offerings before Hashem, to minister before Him and to bless in His Name forever.*

At the End of the Prayer

R' Avraham ben HaRambam explains (*HaMaspik L'Ovdei Hashem,* ch. 28) why Bircas Kohanim is placed at the end of the chazzan's repetition of *Shemoneh Esrei*:

> The Gemara (*Berachos* 26b) teaches that *tefillah* is a substitute for *korbanos,* and that is why *Chazal* chose to place Bircas Kohanim, when it is performed outside the Beis HaMikdash, at the end of the *tefillah,* just as the mitzvah was performed in the Beis HaMikdash after offering the morning *Korban Tamid.* Indeed, strictly speaking, Bircas Kohanim should be recited only after the Shacharis prayer, which corresponds to the morning *Tamid,* but once it was joined with *tefillah, Chazal* enacted that it should be recited after every *tefillas tzibbur* (that is, after Mussaf and Neilah as well) — with the exception of Minchah, because

1. *Hilchos Tefillah U'Nesias Kapayim* 15:5, cited in *Beis Yosef* 128:6 and *Mishnah Berurah* 128:21.
2. R' Dovid ben Zimra, 1479-1573; *Teshuvos,* vol. 2 #778.
3. *Beis Yosef* 128:8 discusses the custom in some locales for Kohanim to wash their feet as well.

drunkenness (i.e., a Kohen is prohibited from performing the *avodah* after drinking a *reviis* of wine) is prevalent at that time of day.

Avodah Outside the Beis HaMikdash

Rash MiShantz (*Toras Kohanim, Emor* 3:2) writes that since Bircas Kohanim is an *avodah* that may be performed outside the Beis HaMikdash ("*avodah shebachutz*"), even a Kohen who has a blemish (a "*baal mum*") may *duchan*. It is in the same category as other *avodos* that Kohanim do outside the Beis HaMikdash, such as the *sotah* procedure, the *eglah arufah* (decapitation of the calf), and the purification of a *metzora*.

Their Backs Toward the Shechinah

The Kohanim in the Beis HaMikdash would perform Bircas Kohanim on the steps of the Ulam (see *Mishnayos Tamid* 7:2), or on a nearby platform (called a *duchan*, which is the reason the word *duchan* is associated with Bircas Kohanim), with their backs to the Holy of Holies.

Regarding this, the Gemara teaches (*Sotah* 40a), "R' Yitzchak said: Let the awe of a congregation always be upon you, for when the Kohanim recite Bircas Kohanim, their faces are toward the people and their backs are toward the Shechinah (i.e., the *aron kodesh*)."

Rabbeinu Bachaye writes (*Kad HaKemach, Erech Reshus*):

> This is, in fact, a very perplexing matter — how indeed are the Kohanim permitted to turn their backs to the *aron kodesh*? The answer lies in the teaching of *Chazal* that the Shechinah rests upon the raised hands of the Kohanim, as the *Midrash* states (*Bamidbar Rabbah* 11:2): *He was standing behind our wall, observing through the windows...* (*Shir HaShirim* 2:9) — this refers to the Shechinah, which observes through the "windows" — that is, the spaces between the hands of the Kohanim, just as the Shechinah rested between the two *Keruvim* in the Beis HaMikdash. Thus, there is no need for concern if the Kohanim face away from the *aron kodesh*, for at this moment the Shechinah is

not resting in the *aron kodesh*, but upon their hands, which are raised in front of them.

This gives rise to a deeper understanding of the *pasuk* (*Yeshayah* 1:15) וּבְפָרִשְׂכֶם כַּפֵּיכֶם אַעְלִים עֵינַי מִכֶּם, *When you spread your hands [in prayer], I will hide My eyes from you*; so says Hashem when He is angered by the sins of His people. But we may learn from this that at a time of favor, such as when the Kohanim spread their hands to bless the Jewish nation, the opposite is true. At that time, Hashem's Presence is directly in front of the Kohanim, resting upon their hands.

Aruch HaShulchan (128:18) records this halachah as follows: "The chazzan calls out, 'Kohanim!' whereupon the Kohanim turn around to face the congregation, with their backs toward the *aron kodesh*, in fulfillment of the phrase כֹּה תְבָרְכוּ , *so shall you bless*, which means standing face to face with those receiving the blessing, as one person speaks to another (*Sotah* 38a). How beloved are the Jewish people to the Holy One, Blessed is He, that He allows the Kohanim to stand with their backs to the *aron kodesh* in order to bless them!"

Ohr Samei'ach (*Hilchos Tefillah U'Nesias Kapayim* 14:12) explains that this is why the Kohanim say after *duchaning*, "Master of the Universe, we have done what You have 'decreed' upon us. May You do with us that which You have promised us." Bircas Kohanim is referred to as a "decree," for if Hashem had not decreed that we do this, we would never act in such a disrespectful manner on our own.

Even During the Holiest Prayer of the Year

R' Aharon Leib Shteinman would stress that if Hashem is ready to forego His honor for the sake of the congregation, surely a mere mortal must show the greatest deference to the blessing Hashem bestows. R' Aharon Leib added that even during Neilah on Yom Kippur, the holiest *tefillah* of the year, **when the *aron kodesh* remains open, Hashem allows the Kohanim to turn their backs to the *aron kodesh* so that He can bless His children.**

Disqualified From the Avodah of Bircas Kohanim

The Mishnah states (*Menachos* 109a): "The Kohanim who served in the Temple of Chonyo[4] may not serve in the Beis HaMikdash, and, needless to say, the same goes for Kohanim who served in a temple of idolatry." *Tosafos* there quote *Sefer HaZahir*, which says, based on this Mishnah, that a Kohen who abandons his faith is disqualified from Bircas Kohanim — once again indicating that Bircas Kohanim is a form of *avodah*. This ruling in cited in *Beis Yosef* and *Shulchan Aruch* (128:37) and in *Mishnah Berurah* there. (See, however, contemporary rulings cited in chapter 47).

Earning Priestly Gifts Even Today

Raavad (*Toras Kohanim, Shemini*) explains that the mitzvah of Bircas Kohanim applies in all generations, because it is a form of *avodah* that is performed even outside the Beis HaMikdash. He writes: "What type of *avodah* is performed with the Name of Hashem? It is Bircas Kohanim. Thus, through this mitzvah, which is not limited to the Beis HaMikdash, the Kohanim merit to receive the priestly gifts, many of which are given even outside the Beis HaMikdash" (such as the money paid for *pidyon haben* — redemption of a firstborn son).

Inspired by the Avodah

The Gemara (*Bava Basra* 21a) teaches that the Sages enacted that teachers of children should be installed in Yerushalayim, so that any youth could go there and be taught Torah. They based this arrangement on the *pasuk* that says (*Yeshayah* 2:3), כִּי מִצִּיּוֹן תֵּצֵא תוֹרָה וּדְבַר ה׳ מִירוּשָׁלָם, *For Torah shall go forth from Zion and the word of Hashem from Yerushalayim.*

Tosafos explain that the environment of Yerushalayim was

4. Chonyo, the son of the great Kohen Gadol Shimon HaTzaddik, was chosen by his father to succeed him as Kohen Gadol. However, because of an incident related in the Gemara there, Chonyo fled to Alexandria, Egypt, where he erected a temple and offered sacrifices. This became known as the Temple of Chonyo.

particularly conducive to Torah study. When a person beheld the tremendous sanctity of the Beis HaMikdash and saw the Kohanim engaged in the *avodah,* he was inspired to direct his heart to awe of Hashem and the study of Torah.

As noted, the only *avodah* of the Beis HaMikdash that remains in contemporary times is Bircas Kohanim. If we closely heed the words of *Tosafos,* we can utilize the time before Bircas Kohanim to strengthen our fear of Heaven and improve our Torah study. For although *Tosafos* is referring primarily to the many other *avodos* of the Beis HaMikdash, Bircas Kohanim is the only one we merit to have in our times.

Chapter 3
The Incredible Segulah of Bircas Kohanim

In the Merit of Raising the Hands

S*efer HaBahir* (135), the Midrash of the *Tanna* R' Nechuniah ben HaKanah, cites the following statement of R' Yochanan regarding the verse וְהָיָה כַּאֲשֶׁר יָרִים מֹשֶׁה יָדוֹ וְגָבַר יִשְׂרָאֵל, *And it came to pass when Moshe raised his hand that Israel prevailed* (*Shemos* 17:11): "This teaches us that the world continues to exist in the merit of the 'raising of hands' (*nesias kapayim*)" — i.e., Bircas Kohanim.

A Shield Against Divine Anger

The *pasuk* (*Tehillim* 7:12) states: וְאֵל זֹעֵם בְּכָל יוֹם, *G-d is angered every day,* and *Chazal* (*Yerushalmi Sotah* 9:14) teach that R' Zeira said, "The initial curses are firmly established." *Chasdei David* (*Tosefta Sotah* 15:2) explains that each new daily curse does not supplant the curse that preceded it, but is added to, and compounds, all the previous curses. The *Yerushalmi* continues: "What annuls all these curses so that the world is able to continue its existence? R' Avin said in the name of R' Acha: Bircas Kohanim annuls all the curses."

Midrash Tehillim (7:12) cites a slightly different version of this statement of *Chazal*: "R' Acha said: If so (that G-d is angered), through what merit do we continue to exist? Through the merit of Bircas Kohanim."

Yet another version is found in *Midrash Shocher Tov* (7:9):

"R' Zeira said: Although G-d is angered every day, we are also sustained every day and protected from His anger. R' Acha said: In what merit are we sustained? In the merit of Bircas Kohanim."

Hashem promised Avraham Avinu (*Bereishis* 12:3), וַאֲבָרְכָה מְבָרְכֶיךָ וּמְקַלֶּלְךָ אָאֹר, *I will bless those who bless you, and he who curses you I will curse*. Rabbeinu Chaim Paltiel, one of the Tosafists, notes (*Bamidbar* 6:24) that it was not necessary to promise Avraham that the curses will be *annulled*, because through Bircas Kohanim, the curse of any wicked person loses all possible effect that it can have on the Jewish people.

Rabbeinu Bachaye writes (*Kad HaKemach, Erech Berachah*): "**It is well known that the entire universe is sustained through the merit of Bircas Kohanim**, as stated in *Midrash Tehillim*." Rabbeinu Bachaye cites the Mishnah's statement (*Sotah* 48a), "Rabban Shimon ben Gamliel said: From the day the Beis HaMikdash was destroyed, there is no day that is without its curse, and the dew does not descend in blessing, and the flavor has been removed from fruit." He then invokes R' Acha's statement: "Through what merit do we continue to exist? Through the merit of Bircas Kohanim."

Accordingly, *Sefer Koh Sevarechu* comments (Preface): "How appropriate and beneficial is the custom of those who live in Eretz Yisrael and those who have the custom to recite Bircas Kohanim daily, for 'there is no day that is without its curse,' and 'G-d is angered every day' — but the blessing of the Kohanim nullifies these curses."

The Strength to Prevail in Battle

Shir HaShirim states (3:7-8): הִנֵּה מִטָּתוֹ שֶׁלִּשְׁלֹמֹה שִׁשִּׁים גִּבֹּרִים סָבִיב לָהּ מִגִּבֹּרֵי יִשְׂרָאֵל. כֻּלָּם אֲחֻזֵי חֶרֶב מְלֻמְּדֵי מִלְחָמָה אִישׁ חַרְבּוֹ עַל יְרֵכוֹ מִפַּחַד בַּלֵּילוֹת, *Behold the resting place of Him to Whom peace belongs, with sixty of Israel's mighty encircling it. All of them gripping the sword, skilled in battle, each with his sword ready at his side, lest he succumb in the nights of exile*. The Midrash elaborates (*Bamidbar Rabbah* 11:3):

> R' Bivi said in the name of R' Elazar: These verses may be understood as an allusion to Bircas Kohanim. *Behold the resting place* — this refers to the Beis HaMikdash; *of Him to*

Whom peace belongs is the Holy One, Blessed is He. The *sixty of Israel's mighty* are the sixty letters that comprise the blessings of Bircas Kohanim; Bircas Kohanim is called *Israel's mighty* because it gives the Jewish people the strength to prevail over their enemies; alternatively, because the Name of Hashem, Who is mighty, appears in each of the three blessings. *All of them gripping the sword, skilled in battle* — the blessings of the Kohanim battle to protect us against all the misfortunes mentioned in the Torah. *Each with his sword ready at his side* — if someone sees a vision in a dream in which there is a sword cutting through his legs [a reference to one's descendants; *Maharzu*], what should he do? He should arise early and stand before the Kohanim to hear Bircas Kohanim. If he does so, no harm will befall him. Thus, the Kohanim are commanded, *So shall you bless Bnei Yisrael....*

Similarly, *Targum* renders the above verses as follows: "How beautiful are the Kohanim when they stand upon the *duchan* and spread out their hands to bless the Jewish people with the sixty letters that were given to Moshe Rabbeinu. **The Bircas Kohanim encircles them like a tall, strong, protective wall, and the success of all the mighty warriors of Israel comes through that blessing."**

Shlomo HaMelech's Throne and Temple

Otzar Midrashim (*Midrash Shlomo HaMelech*, p. 527) teaches that Shlomo HaMelech, with Divine inspiration, modeled his throne after Hashem's Throne of Glory. Images of certain celestial beings were engraved on the back, and sculptures of others stood in the front. Sixty mighty warriors were stationed there, with the sixty letters of Bircas Kohanim written upon their foreheads.

Targum (*Shir HaShirim* 3:7) teaches that when Shlomo HaMelech built the Beis HaMikdash in Yerushalayim, Hashem said: "How beautiful is this Beis HaMikdash that was built for Me through the hands of the king, Shlomo ben David! And how beautiful are the Kohanim when they spread their hands and stand on their *duchan* to bless the Jewish people with the sixty letters that were transmitted to Moshe Rabbeinu! And that *berachah* surrounds [the people] like a high and mighty wall, and through it all the mighty ones of Israel prevail and are victorious."

Kol Bo[1] teaches that it was Shlomo HaMelech who instituted that the daily Bircas Kohanim be performed during Shacharis, and he hinted at this in the above verse in *Shir HaShirim* (3:7): *Behold the resting place of Him to Whom peace belongs, with sixty of Israel's mighty encircling it.* The "sixty of Israel's mighty" is an allusion to the sixty letters of Bircas Kohanim.

Silencing the Satan

Rashi writes the following, in *Sefer HaPardes* (*Hilchos Rosh Hashanah*):

> The *sixty of Israel's mighty* (*Shir HaShirim* 3:7) are the sixty letters of Bircas Kohanim. The reason they are called "mighty" is that Hashem Himself gives His consent to these blessings when they are uttered by the Kohanim, as it says: *They shall place My Name upon Bnei Yisrael, and I will bless them.*
>
> The might of the blessings is manifested in their ability to silence the Satan and to prevail over him. We are taught in a Baraisa (*Bava Basra* 16a) that the Satan is the *yetzer hara,* and he is the Angel of Death as well. He first entices a person to sin and then ascends to the Heavenly Court to prosecute the sinner. When his victim is found guilty, the Satan descends once again and takes his life. The mighty Bircas Kohanim impedes the Satan from engaging in such actions, and expels him from our midst. The Kohanim are the "mighty of Israel," because only they have the ability to offer up sacrifices on our behalf. **Any non-Kohen, even someone as great as King David, is disqualified from doing so.**

---

1. *Hilchos Tefillah siman* 11, cited in *Eliyahu Rabbah* (*siman* 121). In the *Teshuvos* of *Maharil Diskin* (*Kuntres Acharon* #199), where he discusses the issue of mourners reciting Bircas Kohanim, he writes that one should take into consideration that the practice of *duchaning* daily during Shacharis was instituted by Shlomo HaMelech.

Foiling an Evil Eye

The passage of Bircas Kohanim is followed by the words וַיְהִי בְּיוֹם כַּלּוֹת מֹשֶׁה לְהָקִים אֶת הַמִּשְׁכָּן, *It was on the day that Moshe finished erecting the Mishkan* (*Bamidbar* 7:1). What is the connection between these two topics? The Midrash (*Bamidbar Rabbah* 12:4) explains this with a parable:

There was once a king whose daughter was engaged to be married. At the *kiddushin* ("betrothal")[2] ceremony, the king prepared a lavish banquet with much pomp and splendor. Unfortunately, this aroused the envy of many onlookers, and the *ayin hara* that resulted caused great harm to the princess. When it came time for the wedding, the king was not taking any more chances. He had an amulet written for his daughter, and instructed her to wear it at all times, to ward off any further *ayin hara*.

So it was when the Torah was given to the Jewish nation, continues the Midrash. Our standing at Mount Sinai was comparable to a *kiddushin* between us and Hashem, as Hashem told Moshe (*Shemos* 19:10), לֵךְ אֶל הָעָם וְקִדַּשְׁתָּם הַיּוֹם וּמָחָר וְכִבְּסוּ שִׂמְלֹתָם, *Go to the people and sanctify them today and tomorrow*. The Torah describes the spectacular nature of this event: *The entire people saw the thunder and the flames, the sound of the shofar and the smoking mountain* (*Shemos* 20:15). This public event engendered an *ayin hara* against the people, and ultimately led to the *Luchos* being broken. Therefore, when it came time to erect the Mishkan (symbolizing that the Shechinah would now dwell together with us, representing "*nisuin*"), Hashem first gave us the blessings of Bircas Kohanim to protect us from *ayin hara*.

When Mercy Prevails

Zohar (*Nasso* 147b) states: "Whoever is distressed by his dream shall come when the Kohanim are raising their hands and say the *Ribbono Shel Olam* prayer. What is the reason? **It is because Mercy**

2. A Jewish marriage is effected in two steps. The first step is *kiddushin*, which is performed by the groom giving a ring or something else of value to the bride. At this point she is a married woman, but they do not begin married life together until after the *nisuin* (wedding), which takes place when they stand together under the *chuppah*.

prevails in all the worlds at that time. Whoever prays due to his distress, Judgment will turn into Mercy for him."

Annulling Frightening Dreams

R' Yehoshua Ibn Schweib, one of the closest disciples of Rashba, advises (*Derashos Ri Ibn Schweib, Nasso*) that if someone experienced a frightening dream, such as if he saw a sword on his neck, he should arise early the next morning and go to shul to hear Bircas Kohanim; he should pay attention to the *berachos* and answer amen. At that point, he says, there is no need to fear the dream anymore, even if it shook him up and alarmed him, for this *berachah* will nullify it.

Grateful for Hashem's Blessing

The Gemara (*Berachos* 55b) teaches that if one had a dream but is uncertain whether the dream presaged good or evil, he should recite a prayer beginning *Ribbono Shel Olam* during Bircas Kohanim. The question is, how are we permitted to recite this prayer when we are supposed to be paying attention to the *berachah*?

Beis Yosef (130:1) addresses this and cites an answer found in the *teshuvos* of the Rishonim. Since we are taught that Bircas Kohanim has the power to ameliorate a bad dream, this prayer has a direct connection to Bircas Kohanim. Therefore, it is a fulfillment of *Chazal*'s teaching (*Sotah* 40a): "Is there any servant who receives his master's blessing and is not attentive to it and does not graciously demonstrate appreciation?" By praying for one's dreams during Bircas Kohanim, one demonstrates that he values and is grateful for Hashem's blessing.

Nullified by Sixty

Toras Chaim (*Bava Kamma* 55a) and *Noam Elimelech* (*Terumah* 27:1) give the following explanation for why Bircas Kohanim is effective in nullifying a bad dream: *Chazal* (*Berachos* 57b) teach that although dreams are mostly meaningless, one-sixtieth of a dream is prophetic. We are also familiar with the principle that undesirable substances (such as non-kosher food) become nullified when mixed with other substances in a ratio of one to sixty.

Now, Bircas Kohanim itself is considered a type of prophecy, because the purpose of every prophecy is to deliver a message from Hashem to the people, and that is exactly what the Kohanim are doing; Hashem specifically commanded them to convey these *berachos* to the Jewish people. That is why we are forbidden to gaze at the hands of the Kohanim during Bircas Kohanim — for just as the Shechinah rests upon a *navi* when he is delivering his prophecy, so too, the Shechinah is upon the hands of the Kohanim when they *duchan*.

When a person mentions his dream during Bircas Kohanim, the one-sixtieth of it that is prophetic blends with the sixty letters of the *berachos* of the Kohanim, which are *entirely* prophecy, and becomes nullified. Since the prophetic portion of the dream is mixed with sixty times as much other prophecy, it takes on the identity of the larger part of the mixture, and it is changed into *berachah*.

Channeling Blessing Directly From Hashem

R' Aharon Leib Shteinman would often illustrate the greatness of Bircas Kohanim with this simple but profound thought:

Imagine that one of the holy *Tannaim* were alive in our days — for example, R' Shimon bar Yochai, to whom all the deep secrets of Torah were revealed, and who was continuously involved in Torah study (*Shabbos* 11a); or R' Chanina ben Dosa, in whose merit the entire world received sustenance (*Berachos* 17b), and when he prayed for the ill he immediately knew if his prayers were accepted and if the person would live or die (*Berachos* 34b). We have no way to conceive of the greatness of such *Tannaim*. **Yet if they were alive, even in our generation, they would humbly stand every day before a Kohen for Bircas Kohanim, with great concentration.** Even if the Kohen is the simplest of men, not distinguished in his service of Hashem in any way, they would stand before him in awe in order to receive his *berachah*!

Although this Kohen does not personally amount to anything compared to a *Tanna*, he is nevertheless endowed with the power to channel *berachah* from Hashem Himself to all other Jews — an ability he has inherited directly from Aharon HaKohen, which no human being other than a Kohen possesses!

The Best Blessing of All

R' Dovid Cohen, Rosh Yeshivah of Yeshivas Chevron, writes in his approbation to this *sefer*:

> Many years ago, I went to speak to the rosh yeshivah, R' Aharon Leib Shteinman, and he said, "It is a great wonder to me when I see people who need salvation seeking to receive *berachos*, and many times even traveling great distances for this purpose, even though they have no guarantee that the *berachah* of the *gadol* will be fulfilled. Yet it does not enter their minds that right nearby, they have the opportunity to receive a *berachah* every single day, and Hashem Himself promises that this has the power to bring about an abundance of blessing. That is the *berachah* that the Kohanim recite every day — and these same people do not put in any effort to pursue the *berachos* of Bircas Kohanim!"
>
> Ever since, I have become aware that it is a worthwhile pursuit to find ways **to awaken the hearts of our fellow Jews, so that they come to appreciate the greatness that lies in the mitzvah of hearing Bircas Kohanim.**

Hashem Joins His Voice to That of the Kohanim

When the Jewish people entered Eretz Yisrael for the first time, they were instructed to go to Mount Gerizim and Mount Eval, where six tribes would ascend one mountain and the remaining tribes the other mountain. The elders of the Kohanim and Leviim were to stand in the middle and recite twelve blessings and twelve curses, and the entire nation would answer amen to each one. With regard to this event, the Torah states (*Devarim* 27:14): וְעָנוּ הַלְוִיִּם וְאָמְרוּ אֶל כָּל אִישׁ יִשְׂרָאֵל קוֹל רָם, *The Leviim shall speak up and say to every man of Israel in a raised voice. Yerushalmi* (*Sotah* 7:2) understands the term "*kol rom*" to mean "together with the voice of the Exalted (*rom*) One." That is, Hashem merged His voice with the voices of the Kohanim and Leviim, so that the people heard the voices combined.

The halachah is that Bircas Kohanim must also be recited *"b'kol rom"* (*Sotah* 38a and *Shulchan Aruch* 128:14), and *Yerushalmi* (ibid.) adds that Hashem, **so to speak, joins His voice with the voices of the Kohanim when they recite the blessings.** *Tur* (ibid.) and *Bach* (128:8) cite the *Yerushalmi* and explain that if the Kohanim do as they are commanded, and bless the people with concentration and with a warm heart, Hashem will join with Kohanim in blessing the people.

R' Aharon Leib Shteinman (*Ayeles HaShachar, Bamidbar* 6:23) quotes the *Yerushalmi* and *Tur* and adds that this is an enormous merit that every Jew, in every generation, possesses — **the opportunity to hear the voice of Hashem when he listens to Bircas Kohanim!**

Moreover, we are well aware of Hashem's intense love for the Jewish people. (If we would only love Him to the same extent, we would be a fortunate people indeed!) However, His love for us does not manifest itself equally at all times; there are moments when Hashem reveals a much greater love than He does at other times, and one of those moments is Bircas Kohanim. The Kohanim are commanded to channel Hashem's *berachah* to us "with love," which indicates that this is a time when Hashem is prepared to show us an extraordinary measure of love. That being the case, it is incumbent upon us, while listening to Bircas Kohanim, to strengthen our own love for Hashem, so that He will reflect that love back to us as well.

Hearing Hashem's Voice

In *K'Ayal Taarog* (*Hilchos Tefillah*, p. 202), R' Aharon Leib notes **that since the destruction of the Beis HaMikdash, the one opportunity we have to form a direct bond with Hashem is Bircas Kohanim**. The *pasuk* that says *You shall place My Name upon Bnei Yisrael* indicates that when the Kohen recites Bircas Kohanim, the Shechinah rests upon his hands, and he is enabled to transmit the *berachah* directly from Hashem to Klal Yisrael.

This helps us understand the words of *Rambam*, who writes (*Hilchos Tefillah U'Nesias Kapayim* 15:7): "The Kohanim [are chosen to] perform the mitzvah that the Holy One, Blessed is He, in His Mercy, commanded the Jewish people — for it is His desire that the Kohanim should transmit the *berachah* of Hashem to the Jewish people."

At *Mattan Torah,* Hashem spoke to Klal Yisrael. They actually heard Him speak, and even the nations of the world were allowed to hear His voice. This phenomenon was never repeated. At no other time did Hashem speak to a human; even the prophets did not hear from Him directly, only through a vision or a dream.

Nevertheless, if a person desires to hear the voice of Hashem speaking, it is possible to do so during Bircas Kohanim, as we see from the *Yerushalmi* and *Tur*, for, as *Rambam* explains, it is not the Kohen who has the power to bless; Hashem is the one Who blesses. Hashem says, *"Yevarechecha,"* and His word is channeled through the Kohanim. Hashem says, *"V'yishmerecha,"* and that utterance is channeled through the Kohanim as well, and so forth. The only difference is that at *Mattan Torah* we were able to sense that Hashem was speaking, and today we do not sense the voice of Hashem, which is sounded in unison with the Kohanim.

A Time of Heavenly Favor

R' Chaim Vital, in *Pri Eitz Chaim,* citing Arizal (*Shaar Chazaras HaAmidah,* ch. 4), says that one must have intense concentration during Bircas Kohanim. When the Kohanim raise their hands to bless the people, the Shechinah rests upon their hands and they become filled with a Heavenly flow of blessing. At that moment all are blessed from the Highest Source, and it is an *eis ratzon* — a time of Heavenly favor.

R' Yaakov Abuchatzeira writes (*Pituchei Chosam, Nasso*) that Bircas Kohanim contains infinite greatness. We know this from the words of *Zohar* and Arizal, who reveal to us that at the time of Bircas Kohanim all the Upper Worlds achieve perfection, from beginning to end, and blessing descends upon all of the worlds, Upper and Lower.

R' Shabse Horowitz, son of the *Shelah,* writes (*Shefa Tal,* p. 10):

> Be aware that when the Kohanim *duchan* it is an *eis ratzon* — a moment of Divine favor, love, and kindness, and a time when the trait of *rachamim* — Divine mercy — is dominant. This is hinted at in the wording of the *berachah* that the Kohanim recite before Bircas Kohanim: *Blessed are You, Hashem... and has commanded us to bless His people Yisrael*

with love. Thus, it is a time of love and endearment, and a time of *ratzon* and *rachamim*. Hashem commanded the Kohanim to bless the Jewish people with love at a *time* of Divine love and mercy."

R' Aharon Leib Shteinman writes (*Ayeles HaShachar, Bamidbar* 6:23) that just as the Kohanim are commanded to bless the Jewish people *b'ahavah*, with love, the Yisraelim should also work at this time to strengthen their unconditional love for Hashem, and then Hashem will reciprocate and increase the blessing.

Opening the Pipelines of Mercy

Malbim writes (*Bamidbar* 6:23):

> Hashem, in His goodness, is prepared and willing at all times to pour down kindness and blessing from its source in Heaven, which is always open, as David HaMelech has said (*Tehillim* 75:9): כִּי כוֹס בְּיַד ה׳ וְיַיִן חָמַר מָלֵא מֶסֶךְ וַיַּגֵּר מִזֶּה, *For there is a cup in Hashem's hand, with strong wine of full mixture which overflows from it*. All that is needed is people who are worthy of receiving the flow of blessing because of their righteous deeds. However, Hashem also made it possible **even for those who are not deserving to receive the blessings,** and that is through His chosen holy emissaries on earth — the Kohanim, who are empowered to open the pipelines of blessing through their prayers and *berachos*, and have that blessing pour down upon the Jewish people. **They raise up their ten fingers and thereby open the ten pipelines from Heaven.**

Similarly, Rabbeinu Yonah writes (*Shaarei HaAvodah*), "The Kohanim who blessed the Jewish people with raised hands and with their ten fingers would remember and keep in mind the ten *sefiros*, which include all of Hashem's creations." (The *sefiros* are a Kabbalistic concept referring to ten attributes through which Hashem is perceived and the aspects of how His blessing flows to the physical world.)

Acting Out the Blessing

Kedushas Levi shares a novel understanding of the phrase כֹּה תְבָרְכוּ אֶת בְּנֵי יִשְׂרָאֵל, *So shall you bless Bnei Yisrael.* He says that the word *koh* (so) implies that the Kohanim are to "act out" the blessing of Hashem. They spread their hands over the congregation as if to shower them with *berachah,* so that Hashem will be pleased that they wish to bless His people, and He will respond by blessing them Himself. Hashem's actions, as it were, mirror the actions of the Kohanim.

Direct Blessing

Alshich offers a deeper understanding of Bircas Kohanim (*Toras Moshe, Bamidbar* 6:24), which begins with the words *May Hashem bless you and safeguard you.* We ask to receive the *berachah* directly from Hashem and not through an angel. Not only with regard to wealth and other worldly blessings do we desire to be blessed directly from Hashem, but even with regard to *shemirah* (protection), which is often granted through an intermediary, as it is written (*Tehillim* 91:11): כִּי מַלְאָכָיו יְצַוֶּה לָּךְ לִשְׁמָרְךָ בְּכָל דְּרָכֶיךָ, *He will charge His angels for you, to protect you in all your ways,* and it is written (*Shemos* 23:20), הִנֵּה אָנֹכִי שֹׁלֵחַ מַלְאָךְ לְפָנֶיךָ לִשְׁמָרְךָ בַּדָּרֶךְ, *Behold! I send an angel before you to protect you on the way.*

Now, it is common for a king who has already done a number of favors for his close friend to lose some interest in the friendship. When he sees his friend, he no longer has the same loving expression on his face that he used to. Hashem does not treat us that way. Even after He has blessed us and safeguarded us Himself, and not through an angel, He gives this to us as a free gift (*matnas chinam*).

The Instrument and the Vessel

In his commentary on Chumash (*Bamidbar* 6:27), R' Shimshon Raphael Hirsch explains: It is not the Kohanim who bless the Jewish people, for the words that come from their mouths do not have the power of blessing in and of themselves. Rather, their mission is merely to *place My Name on Bnei Yisrael and I* — I alone — *shall bless them.* They are assigned to "place" the Name of Hashem upon the Jewish people so that they become, as it were, a *merkavah* ("chariot") for the Shechinah. The Kohanim convey the message that we look only to Hashem for every blessing, every protection, every revelation, every ability that He grants us, every gift, and every moment of peace in our lives. When we recognize that all these come only from Hashem, that recognition itself serves to honor His Name. Hashem is revealed through all the kindness He bestows upon us, and the Kohanim are the instrument through which the Name of Hashem is placed upon the Jewish nation. As for the congregation, they are to stand and prepare themselves to be a vessel to receive the *berachah* from Hashem, and then Hashem will surely bless them.

No Need for Any Other Berachos

R' Moshe Halberstam writes (*Haskamah* to *HaBerachah HaMeshuleshes*):

> I found in the writings of my father, the Tchakaver Rav, that his great-grandfather, the Divrei Chaim of Sanz, would refrain from giving *berachos* to anyone on Yom Tov, since Bircas Kohanim is recited then. He would say that on this day *berachos* are reserved for the Kohanim, adding that the *berachos* we receive from the Kohanim come from Hashem Himself, through the Kohanim, and are so great that there is no need for any other *berachos*.

R' Moshe Halberstam adds, based on his own understanding, that this is applicable in *chutz laAretz*, where Bircas Kohanim is recited only on Yom Tov. In Eretz Yisrael, where the custom is to *duchan* every day, it would seem that one need not take this approach. This author (who is a descendant of the Divrei Chaim) merited to show R' Chaim Kanievsky what was quoted in the name of the Divrei Chaim. I asked R' Chaim if he agrees with R' Moshe Halberstam's addition, and he said he did not. R' Chaim said that on a day a person merits to hear Bircas Kohanim there is no need to obtain a blessing from even a *gadol hador*, even if he resides in Eretz Yisrael, as he has been blessed by Hashem during Bircas Kohanim.

All-Encompassing Blessing

The third *berachah* of Bircas Kohanim begins: יִשָּׂא ה׳ פָּנָיו אֵלֶיךָ, *May Hashem lift His countenance to you. Sifrei* (*Nasso* 42) interprets this to mean "Hashem shall remove His anger from you." *Netziv* (*Emek HaNetziv, Sifrei* ibid.) explains, based on *Midrash Rabbah*, that the word יִשָּׂא, *lift,* can also be understood as "remove," and the word פָּנָיו, *His countenance,* can mean "His anger." He adds that although we may be deserving of Hashem's anger because of our sins, if we repent, this *berachah* has in it the power to cause our repentance to be accepted and to save us from the punishments that we might have otherwise suffered.

Sifrei adds many different meanings that are contained in the three verses of Bircas Kohanim, and *Netziv* explains that all these teachings are based on one principle: **Every *berachah* in the universe, up to Hashem's Throne of Glory, is included in these few words of Bircas Kohanim.** Therefore, it is forbidden to add to them. One who attempts to add only diminishes, for he makes it seem as though there is more blessing to be had than that which is included in these *berachos.*

Similarly, *Abarbanel* writes (*Bamidbar* 6:23): The *berachos* of Bircas Kohanim include long, successful life and peace in every sense of the word, in this World and even in the World to Come, as the *pasuk* says, יָבוֹא שָׁלוֹם יָנוּחוּ עַל מִשְׁכְּבוֹתָם, *He will come in peace; they will rest on their resting places* (*Yeshayah* 57:2; this *pasuk* indicates that the *berachah* of *shalom* is needed even after one leaves this world). These short *berachos* include every type of good that a person could possibly desire, and no person should forego the chance to receive them.

R' Yitzchak Aramah (*Akeidas Yitzchak, Shaar* 74) writes that these three *berachos* (which are actually six, since each one contains two *berachos*) include within them a blessing for every possible need that a human being might have. Whatever one seeks from Hashem throughout his life can be attained through Bircas Kohanim.

Ohr HaChaim (*Bamidbar* 6:24) explains that the blessing of יְבָרֶכְךָ ה׳, ***May Hashem bless you,*** **is so great that it requires** **וְיִשְׁמְרֶךָ**, **a special blessing from Hashem to help safeguard and maintain this infinite blessing.**

Ralbag (*Bamidbar* 6:23) observes that the purpose of the mitzvah of Bircas Kohanim is for us to receive continuous blessing from Hashem throughout our lives, so that we humans, who are born incomplete and lacking wisdom, will be able to grow and work toward perfection, through the influence of these *berachos*.

Burn Remedy

Pele Yoetz (*os kaf*) writes: I would like to convey to this generation that there is a tried-and-tested *segulah* (remedy) for a person who has suffered burns. Simply, the patient, or someone else on the patient's behalf, should recite Bircas Kohanim three times, concentrating on the words.

A Significant Passage

Mishnah Berurah (669:15) states that there are passages of the Torah whose *aliyos* we have the custom to sell separately. One of the five significant passages the *Mishnah Berurah* lists is that of Bircas Kohanim.

Chapter 4
The Privilege – and Responsibility – of the Kohanim

Not Just Messengers

S*fas Emes* (*Nasso* 5760) quotes a Midrash that states: "So says the Holy One, Blessed is He, to the Kohanim: Do not bless the Jewish people merely because I commanded you to do so, as though you are performing a chore that you would like to be done with as quickly as possible. Instead, focus on the blessings with your heart."

This teaches us that although the power of Bircas Kohanim is a gift from Hashem, and it is He Who blesses the Jewish people, the Kohanim should not think that they have no connection to the *berachah* and are only serving as messengers from Hashem. Rather, it is Hashem's will that they should personally desire to bless His people out of the goodness of their hearts, and when they do so, their blessing becomes a *berachah* from Hashem Himself. Thus, when the Torah instructs the Kohanim, אָמוֹר לָהֶם, *saying to them*, it means they should say words that come from the heart.

Warmth and Affection

The Torah introduces the mitzvah of Bircas Kohanim with the word אָמוֹר, *say*, rather than using the more common term דַּבֵּר, *speak*. *Maor VaShemesh* (*Bamidbar* 6:23) explains that the word

אֱמוֹר is an expression of warmth and affection. The *pasuk* is hinting to us that one who wishes to bless the Jewish people needs to have this quality — he must love his brethren fiercely, with all his heart and soul. He should love even the least worthy member of his people as he loves himself, and because of his love, he should praise them and extol their virtues before their Father in Heaven. This will awaken Hashem's great mercy and lovingkindness for His children, and this will draw down upon them all types of blessings.

With Love

Magen Avraham states (128:18), based on *Zohar,* that the blessing of the Kohen must be transmitted with love. *Zohar* (p. 147b) teaches that if a Kohen does not love the people he is blessing, or if they do not love him, he should not *duchan*. It seems that this is the basis of the wording of the *berachah* that the Kohanim recite before *duchaning*: *... and has commanded us to bless His people, Yisrael, with love*.

Mishnah Berurah rules (128:37) that if a Kohen cannot bless the congregation "with love," it is preferable that he exit the shul before the blessing of *Retzei* and not bless the congregation.

Why does Bircas Kohanim require love more so than other *berachos* or mitzvos?

R' Yaakov Emden writes (*Siddur Beis Yaakov, Hilchos Nesias Kapayim*):

> I have explained in *Mor U'Ketziah* (128) that the reason Bircas Kohanim must be recited "with love" is that otherwise, the *berachah* can be described, in the words of Shlomo HaMelech (*Mishlei* 27:6), as וְנַעְתָּרוֹת נְשִׁיקוֹת שׂוֹנֵא, *and superfluous are the kisses of a foe*. That is, a blessing from an enemy is no blessing at all. For this reason, the blessings of Bilaam ultimately devolved into curses for the Jewish people, as *Chazal* have taught (*Sanhedrin* 102b). Accordingly, for the *berachos* of the Kohanim to be effective, they must come from a source of love, as our Sages said (*Zohar, Nasso* 147b): "One who wishes to bless his friend must do so with a full heart."

The Most Difficult Mitzvah

What is the most difficult mitzvah to fulfill? The Vilna Gaon is quoted as saying that it is the mitzvah to be in a state of *simchah* for the entire seven days of Yom Tov, without the slightest feeling of sadness or distress. The Gerrer Rebbe, the Pnei Menachem, gave his own answer: He said it is the mitzvah for a Kohen to feel only pure love for all the people he is blessing during Bircas Kohanim, even when there is someone he dislikes among the congregation.

Kohanim Who Perform Acts of Kindness

R' Yisrael of Shklov writes (*Pe'as HaShulchan, Hilchos Eretz Yisrael* 2:16): "We have a tradition from the early *poskim*, based on Kabbalah, that one should endeavor to receive Hashem's *berachah* through Kohanim who are *baalei chesed* — that is, those who are regularly involved in performing acts of kindness for others."

Who Is "Them"?

Ibn Ezra (*Bamidbar* 6:27) explains an ambiguous phrase that appears in the Torah regarding Bircas Kohanim: The last *pasuk* in the passage states, וְשָׂמוּ אֶת שְׁמִי עַל בְּנֵי יִשְׂרָאֵל וַאֲנִי אֲבָרְכֵם, *Let them place My Name upon Bnei Yisrael, and I shall bless "them."* "Them" can refer to the Kohanim, in which case Hashem is saying, "I shall bless those who bless My people," or it can refer to the Jewish people themselves, meaning that when the Kohanim bless them, Hashem fulfills the blessing. In my opinion, says *Ibn Ezra*, both are included; Hashem blesses the Kohanim and the Jewish people together.

The Gemara (*Chullin* 49a) teaches that according to R' Yishmael, who was a Kohen, the *pasuk* means that when the Kohanim bless the people, Hashem blesses *the Kohanim*. R' Akiva, on the other hand, says that Hashem *affirms* the blessing of the Kohanim by blessing *Bnei Yisrael*. Nevertheless, the Kohanim do also receive a blessing from Hashem, as Hashem promised Avraham (*Bereishis* 12:3), *And I will bless those who bless you.*

Toras Chaim (ibid.) explains that R' Yishmael's position is more advantageous for the Kohanim, because it indicates that the Kohanim receive the exact same blessing as the rest of the people.

Thus R' Yishmael became known as "Yishmael the Kohen who always helps Kohanim."

Elsewhere, the Gemara (*Sotah* 38b) teaches that R' Yehoshua ben Levi said: Every Kohen who blesses the congregation is himself blessed, but one who does not is not blessed, for it is stated: *And I will bless those who bless you.* (This follows the opinion of R' Akiva.)

Sifrei (*Zuta, Nasso* 27) adds that lest one think that it is the Kohanim who bless the Jewish people, and if they do not wish to do so, the people are left with no blessing, the Torah states: ***And I shall bless them,* teaching us that the blessing comes from Hashem.** If the Kohanim bless the people, who blesses the Kohanim? The answer to this as well lies in the words *and I shall bless them.* When the Kohanim bless the Jewish people, Hashem blesses both — the people and the Kohanim themselves.

Toras Chaim (*Bava Metzia* 59a) notes that "*I shall bless them*" means that Hashem fills the Kohanim with immense *berachah,* so that they, in turn, are able to transmit the blessing of Hashem to the Jewish people in great abundance, and that is the concept behind the promise that Hashem made to Avraham, *I will bless those who bless you.*

Pray to Me That I Should Bless Them

Rashbam teaches (*Bamidbar* 6:23): The Kohanim are commanded, *So shall you bless Bnei Yisrael... Let them place My Name upon Bnei Yisrael, and I shall bless them.* Hashem is telling them, "Do not give your own blessing to the Jewish people, but pray to Me that *I* should bless them, and I will listen to your prayers and do as you request." This is reflected in the opening words of Bircas Kohanim: *May Hashem bless you....*

The Kohanim are Merely Saying the Words

The Kohanim are commanded: *So shall you bless Bnei Yisrael, "amor lahem"* — saying to them. What is meant by the phrase "saying to them"?

Abarbanel explains (*Bamidbar* 6:23): When Hashem blesses those whom He created — i.e., humans — He is directly conferring upon them the benefits of that blessing. When humans "bless" Hashem, on the other hand, it is an expression of praise and thanksgiving to Him. A third type of blessing is when humans bless one another. In this case, the one who offers the blessing is not directly bestowing any benefit upon his fellow man. **His *berachah* is only a prayer, appealing to Hashem to have mercy upon the recipient of the *berachah* and provide him with his needs.**

Thus, the *pasuk* uses the phrase "saying to them." Hashem is telling the Kohanim, "Do not think that you are actually giving any benefit to the Jewish people. You are merely 'saying' the words, and thereby entreating Hashem to bless the people; nothing more than that."

In a similar vein, *Chizkuni* states (ibid. 6:27): Lest the Kohanim think that they are the ones blessing the Jewish people, the Torah says: *and I shall bless them. Chizkuni* also observes that the words *let them place My Name* imply that the Kohanim are blessing the people with Hashem's Name, not with their own; indeed, each of the three verses of Bircas Kohanim includes the Name of Hashem.

The Torah says, with regard to the Kohanim, כִּי בָם בָּחַר ה׳ אֱלֹהֶיךָ לְשָׁרְתוֹ וּלְבָרֵךְ בְּשֵׁם ה׳, *For them has Hashem, your G-d, chosen to minister to Him and to bless with the Name of Hashem* (*Devarim* 21:5). R' Avraham ben HaRambam writes (*HaMaspik L'Ovdei Hashem,* ch. 28) that this *pasuk* establishes the Kohanim as the emissaries of Hashem to pray on behalf of the Jewish people. It is not their own *berachah*; rather, they are to say the words with their mouths and to pray in their hearts that the *berachah* be fulfilled. Hashem then accepts their prayer, and bestows good and lovingkindness upon His people.

Similarly, *Sefer HaEshkol* states (*Hilchos Bircas Kohanim*): Their *berachah* is no more than a prayer that Hakadosh Baruch Hu bless His nation, the Jewish people, as the Torah says, *Let them place My Name on Bnei Yisrael and I shall bless them.* When the Kohanim fulfill this mitzvah, I shall bless the Jewish people.

Bless With a Full Heart

The Midrash (*Bamidbar Rabbah* 11:12) notes that in the command to the Kohanim to bless the Jewish people — *So shall you bless Bnei Yisrael, saying to them* — the word אָמוֹר, *saying,* is written in its full form, with the letter *vav*. Hashem is telling the Kohanim, "I do not want you to hastily bless My people without putting your hearts into it, as though it is a chore you wish to be done with. Rather, have in your minds that the *berachah* should take hold upon them." The word is written in its full form to indicate that the Kohanim should give the *berachah* with their full hearts.

Yet there is a limit to how much time one should spend, as *Sefer HaBahir* states (138): "It is forbidden to prolong Bircas Kohanim for more than three hours (!) — one hour for each *berachah*, corresponding to the three *Avos* — so that the Kohanim should not appear as though they are 'bothering' Hashem with their persistence."

The Full Measure of Blessing

R' Eliezer Papo, author of *Pele Yoetz*, cautions (*Chesed L'Alafim* §10):

> The Kohen and the chazzan must take great care to pronounce each word slowly and precisely, with full concentration, and also to turn from side to side in the exact manner that is prescribed by halachah.[1] By doing so, they ensure that Hashem will approve of their *berachos*, and the congregation will receive the full measure of blessing.

Like Someone Counting Money

Yalkut Meam Loez (*Nasso*, ch. 6) teaches that the Kohen should feel awe and trembling when he stands to bless the Jewish people. He must know Who is standing above him, for it is no less than the Shechinah, and to where the sixty letters of Bircas Kohanim that he will utter are destined to go. With these thoughts in mind, he should make every effort to say each word with intense concentration, just as someone counts money, for every single letter of this *berachah* is like a precious pearl.

1. *Shulchan Aruch* (128:45) says that the Kohanim should face different directions during Bircas Kohanim, and *Mishnah Berurah* (128:168) explains that this is done so that Hashem should spread the blessing of the Kohanim to all the congregants that surround them.

Why a Stumbling Block?

The Gemara (*Sotah* 39a) states that when a Kohen begins going up to *duchan*, he should recite the following supplication:

> יְהִי רָצוֹן מִלְּפָנֶיךָ ה׳ אֱלֹקֵינוּ וֵאלֹקֵי אֲבוֹתֵינוּ, שֶׁתְּהֵא הַבְּרָכָה הַזֹּאת שֶׁצִּוִּיתָנוּ לְבָרֵךְ אֶת עַמְּךָ יִשְׂרָאֵל בְּרָכָה שְׁלֵמָה, וְלֹא יִהְיֶה בָּהּ שׁוּם מִכְשׁוֹל וְעָוֹן מֵעַתָּה וְעַד עוֹלָם.
>
> *May it be the will before You, Hashem, our G-d and the G-d of our forefathers, that this blessing with which You have commanded us to bless Your people Yisrael shall be a complete blessing and that there not be with it any stumbling block or sin, from this time until eternity.*

R' Moshe Mordechai Chodosh points out (*Kol HaTorah* journal, vol. 86, pp. 37-41) that **this is the only instance where a *yehi ratzon* recited before performing a mitzvah is sourced in a Gemara.** All other *tefillos* of this kind come from Kabbalistic sources. This seems perplexing — why would *Chazal* be concerned about "a stumbling block or sin" in the context of Bircas Kohanim more than any other mitzvah?

This is the explanation he gives:

> Bircas Kohanim is unique in that it must be done with love in order for it to be a complete mitzvah. Apart from the general requirement that one must have specific intention to fulfill whatever mitzvah he is performing, the Kohen must also engage his feelings and arouse in himself love and an *ayin tovah* ("good eye") toward the Jewish people. For this reason, there is great concern that a Kohen may fail to have the proper feelings, and the result would be a "stumbling block," Heaven forbid, instead of a blessing.
>
> That is why it has become an Ashkenazic custom overseas not to perform Bircas Kohanim during the week, for Shlomo HaMelech has said (*Mishlei* 22:9), טוֹב עַיִן הוּא יְבֹרָךְ, *One with a good eye shall be blessed,* and those who live outside of Eretz Yisrael are too preoccupied with their difficulties to have an *ayin tovah*. This is comparable to the halachah that a mourner does not *duchan*, which is for the same reason.
>
> From time to time I sense that there is a need to remind the Kohanim to think about the import and significance of

this mitzvah. They must be aware that without the proper *kavanah*, their *berachah* will be incomplete, and could end up as a "stumbling block" and a "sin." The *poskim* write that if a Kohen has resentment toward the congregation, he is not permitted to *duchan*, and that is the stumbling block we are worried about.

By the same token, if a Kohen does have the ability to *duchan* and he does not do so, he, too, has committed a "sin," for Hashem specifically appointed the tribe of Kohanim to bless His people, and He is prepared to allow His Shechinah to descend between their upraised fingers in order to shower the Jewish people with blessing. Therefore, a Kohen who does not appreciate his exalted status is certainly lacking in his love for the mitzvah, and that is considered a sin.

On the other hand, how exalted, indeed, can this mitzvah be for the Kohen who does have the proper esteem for it, and who does appreciate what it means to be a Kohen.

It is my belief that the Ponovezher Rav, who was a Kohen, acquired his remarkable and extreme love for every Jew through his daily recitation of Bircas Kohanim with love. It is said of the Chofetz Chaim as well that he became as great as he was through the mitzvah of Bircas Kohanim.

Historically, the Kohanim were the halachic teachers of the Jewish people and provided them with inspiration, as the Torah says about them (*Devarim* 33:10), יוֹרוּ מִשְׁפָּטֶיךָ לְיַעֲקֹב וְתוֹרָתְךָ לְיִשְׂרָאֵל, *They shall teach Your ordinances to Yaakov and Your Torah to Yisrael.* Whenever the prophets criticized the Jewish people for their failings, they always reproached the Kohanim first and foremost, for they bear responsibility for the entire people.

R' Avraham ben HaRambam writes (*HaMaspik L'Ovdei Hashem,* ch. 28) that while the Kohanim are reciting Bircas Kohanim, they should look toward the floor, like someone who is davening, in order to avoid looking at the people in the congregation and becoming distracted. Better still, there is a widespread custom among Kohanim to close their eyes altogether — and what a commendable custom it is! They must remain focused on the meaning of the *berachah* and think about nothing else.

Likewise, it is not appropriate for the congregation to gaze at the faces of the Kohanim, because that may divert their attention from the meaning of the *berachah*. The proper approach is to prepare oneself to receive the *berachah* and to concentrate on the words, in anticipation of receiving all the blessings they will bring.

With the Purest of Hearts and Intentions

R' Aharon Cohen, who was Rosh Yeshivah of Yeshivas Chevron, notes (*Beis Aharon, Bamidbar* 6:23) that in the command to the Kohanim to bless the Jewish people — *So shall you bless Bnei Yisrael, saying to them* — the word אָמוֹר, *saying,* is written in its full form, with the letter *vav*. Rashi there comments that the extra letter *vav* is similar to the extra *vav* in the word *zachor,* in the command to remember to keep Shabbos (*Shemos* 20:8). *Sifsei Chachamim* adds that this extra *vav* symbolizes that one must be careful to study the laws of Shabbos so that he will be able to keep Shabbos in the most befitting manner. R' Aharon explains that the reason Rashi is pointing this out here, regarding the word אָמוֹר, is to teach the Kohanim to bless Klal Yisrael with the purest of hearts and intentions. Just as one must study the laws of Shabbos beforehand, so that he will remember these laws and not desecrate Shabbos, so, too, the Kohanim should not be reciting idle words when they say Bircas Kohanim, but should prepare to fuse their words with love to Klal Yisrael from the depths of their hearts.[2]

Too Weak to Bless

R' Yitzchak Dovid Gutfarb once came to the home of the Chazon Ish to request a *berachah*. "I am feeling too weak right now," the Chazon Ish told him, "so I am not able to give you a *berachah*." R' Yitzchak Dovid suggested that perhaps he could say the words of the *berachah* himself, and the Chazon Ish would just say amen. The Chazon Ish thought about this for a few moments and then consented. R' Yitzchok Dovid said what it was he needed from Hashem, and the Chazon Ish responded, "Amen."

2. See above, where we cite the Midrash that says that we learn from the extra letter *vav* that a Kohen should recite Bircas Kohanim slowly, without rushing.

R' Leib Mintzberg of Yerushalayim's Masmidim *kehillah* noted a lesson to be learned from this incident: Couldn't the Chazon Ish have said a few words of *berachah,* using the same amount of effort that it took to excuse himself from doing so? Apparently not! The Chazon Ish understood that for a *berachah* to be meaningful, it must come from the depths of one's heart; one must truly beseech Hashem with the full intensity of his feelings. The Chazon Ish did not feel that he had the strength to give such a *berachah.* He even had to consider whether he had the ability to answer amen properly.

We see from the Chazon Ish, R' Mintzberg concluded, how much effort must go into a *berachah.* In particular, for a *berachah* like Bircas Kohanim that must be said "with love," a Kohen has to make sure to prepare himself beforehand.[3]

A Kohen's Blessing at Any Time

We find that Kohanim have the power to bless the Jewish people at all times, even not during Bircas Kohanim. While this type of blessing does not resemble the actual Bircas Kohanim, which is a direct blessing from Hashem, Hashem nevertheless grants a Kohen the special merit to bless at all times.[4]

In the winter of 5690/1930, the Belzer Rebbe sent his close follower, R' Dovid Schreiber, to intercede with the Polish government on behalf of the Jewish community, after harsh decrees had been enacted against them. The Rebbe told him that he must make a stop in Radin on the way, to receive a *berachah* from the Chofetz Chaim. He did so, and the Chofetz Chaim blessed him with the words of Bircas Kohanim.

R' Chaim Kanievsky would frequently ask R' Simchah HaKohen Kook, the chief rabbi of Rechovot, to bless him with the verses of Bircas Kohanim. At times, this happened at night, and someone asked Reb Chaim if a Kohen may recite Bircas Kohanim at night. R' Chaim replied that at night there is no mitzvah for the Kohen to bless, but he may still give this blessing by night or by day. Actually,

3. *Torah Vodaas* journal, 5765-7, p. 19.

4. For an example of this, see *She'eilos U'Teshuvos Binyan Shlomo* (vol. 2 #52), where R' Shlomo HaKohen of Vilna ends a letter to R' Chaim Berlin with the words of Bircas Kohanim.

he added, at night it is better, as there is no problem of *bal tosif*, since there is no mitzvah of Bircas Kohanim at night.[5]

Only in Your Dreams

R' Yitzchok Shaul Kanievsky, a son of R' Chaim, related the following anecdote:

> I was learning with Abba one afternoon when a person from a remote town in southern Israel came and told Abba he had an urgent matter to discuss with him. He explained that although he and his family were not known to be Kohanim, he had dreamed several times over the last few years that a distinguished-looking man with a long, flowing white beard came to him and told him that he was his paternal great-grandfather. He said he was given Divine permission to appear to him to inform him that he and his family were in fact Kohanim, and that he should *duchan* every day. Now the dream had recurred three nights in a row, so he made a special trip to ask Abba if he should begin to *duchan*.
>
> Abba told him that he was not permitted to *duchan* under any circumstances.
>
> "What should I tell my great-grandfather if he appears to me in a dream again?" he asked.
>
> Abba smiled and replied, "Tell him that from now on you will do daily Bircas Kohanim — but only in your dreams, and never when you are awake."

5. See Responsa of R' Chaim Kanievsky #507 regarding the advantage of a Kohen's blessing not during Bircas Kohanim.

Chapter 5
The Mitzvah of Bircas Kohanim in Contemporary Times

The mitzvah to perform Bircas Kohanim is a Torah obligation — *d'Oraysa* — even in our times, and many sources note that this is a daily obligation.

The Mishnah and Gemara (*Taanis* 26b) clearly state that the mitzvah of Bircas Kohanim is to be performed every single day during Shacharis and (when applicable) Mussaf. During Minchah, however, it is not performed, since drunkenness (i.e., a Kohen is prohibited from performing the *avodah* after drinking a *reviis* of wine) is prevalent at that time of the day. Thus, on a public fast day, when this is not a concern, the Kohanim do, in fact, *duchan* during Minchah.

Tanna D'Vei Eliyahu Rabbah (ch. 31) says about Aharon HaKohen: "He endeavored to make peace between the Jewish people and their Father in Heaven, between them and the Sages, between the Sages themselves, and between husband and wife. It is about him that the *navi* states: *Tell [each] righteous man that it is good; for they shall eat the fruit of their deeds* (*Yeshayah* 3:10), and *Thus said Hashem: Observe justice and perform righteousness…* (*Yeshayah* 56:1). Hashem, Who understands the hearts and intentions of men, was saying to Aharon, 'Your intention was for good — to make peace between Me and the Jewish people. Therefore, I will bring forth from you children who will atone for the Jewish people every year, and who will call down upon them the blessing of peace **every single day**, with the words, *May Hashem bless you... and establish peace for you.'"*

The Midrash (*Bereishis Rabbah* 66:2) describes the Jewish people as follows: "A nation whose Kohanim bestow (מְשִׂימִין) peace upon them **every day**, as it says in the Torah, *Let them place* (וְשָׂמוּ) *My Name,* and *May Hashem...establish* (וְיָשֵׂם) *peace for you.*"

In another Midrash (*Bereishis Rabbasi, Vayigash* 47:22), Hashem says to the Jewish people, "Your Kohanim are obligated to serve Me **every day**, by arising early in the morning and going to the synagogues to bless you."

Yerushalmi (*Nazir* 7:1) also states openly that the mitzvah of Bircas Kohanim applies every day.

Sefer HaChinuch teaches (Mitzvah 378): "The Kohanim are commanded to bless the Jewish people every day, as the Torah says, *So shall you bless Bnei Yisrael, saying to them....* One of the roots of this mitzvah is that Hashem, in His great kindness, desires to bless His people through His servants, who are continuously present in the Beis HaMikdash, and who are constantly thinking about serving Him. Their entire lives are bound up with fear of Hashem all day long; it is in their merit that the *berachah* takes effect, and the people are blessed in all their endeavors."

Likewise, *Meiri* (*Chullin* 49a) states that it is a positive Torah commandment for the Kohanim to bless the people every day.

Ralbag (*Parashas Nasso*) also says that the mitzvah is to bless the Jewish people every day.

Mabit writes (*Kiryas Sefer, Hilchos Tefillah* ch. 14 Mitzvah 19), based on the Gemara (*Sotah* 38a): "The Torah says, with regard to a Kohen, *for him has Hashem chosen from among all your tribes, to stand and serve in the name of Hashem, him and his sons, 'all the days'"* (*Devarim* 18:5). And since serving Hashem in the Beis HaMikdash is mentioned together with Bircas Kohanim in the *pasuk* that says *to serve Him and to bless in His Name,* we may compare one to the other. Thus, the mitzvah of Bircas Kohanim applies *all the days* — that is, every day of the year, in the Beis HaMikdash and in every other place."

The idea that Bircas Kohanim is a daily mitzvah can be found throughout the writings of the Rishonim and *poskim.*

Rambam writes (*Sefer HaMitzvos,* Positive Commandment 26): "Kohanim are commanded to bless the Jewish people **every day.** This is the mitzvah of *So shall you bless Bnei Yisrael, saying to them.*"

Rambam repeats this in his introduction to *Hilchos Tefillah*: "*Tefillah* includes two positive commandments ... and the second is for the Kohanim to bless the Jewish people **every day.**"

Similarly, when introducing his list of mitzvos in *Sefer Ahavah, Rambam* writes: "I will include in this list all the mitzvos that are performed on a continual basis, such as the mitzvah to love Hashem and to constantly remember Him, and the mitzvos of reading the *Shema,* praying, wearing tefillin, and Bircas Kohanim." He includes Bircas Kohanim among the six essential mitzvos that must be performed daily by every Jew, at all times and in every location.

This is also the explicit ruling of *Shulchan Aruch* (129:1).

Rashi (*Chullin* 133a, s.v. *Bein mibachutz*) states that Bircas Kohanim is a mitzvah that is performed both inside the Beis HaMikdash and outside, in the synagogue of every community. The same is found in *Tosafos* (*Menachos* 44a, s.v. *Kol Kohen*).

In the time of *Rashi,* Bircas Kohanim was performed daily in his locale, as we find in the *Machzor Vitri* and *Siddur Rashi,* authored by his close disciples. We also find in the writings of many other of the earlier Ashkenazic Rishonim that Bircas Kohanim was performed daily. (See chapter 15 for further discussion of this.)

Not a Rabbinic Mitzvah

R' Yaakov Emden, in *Mor U'Ketziah* (*Tur, Shulchan Aruch* 128), writes that performing Bircas Kohanim in our times, when we no longer have the Beis HaMikdash, is only a Rabbinic mitzvah. However, *Sdei Chemed* (vol. 9, *Kuntres Divrei Chachamim, siman* 64) points out that this contradicts what R' Yaakov Emden himself wrote in his *She'eilas Yaavetz,*[1] where he clearly maintains that it is a *d'Oraysa* obligation even today.

1. Vol. 1, *siman* 54. See also *Siddur R' Yaakov Emden* (*Hilchos Nesias Kapayim*), where he writes that even if Bircas Kohanim outside the Beis HaMikdash is *d'Rabbanan,* it is modeled after, and follows the same guidelines as, the *mitzvah d'Oraysa.* He also strongly praises the custom to *duchan* every day in Eretz Yisrael even today.

When the Chofetz Chaim wrote *Mishnah Berurah*, he was exceedingly careful to present the various opinions of the *poskim* in the most respectful terms, even when he disagreed with them. Yet with regard to the above view cited in *Mor U'Ketziah*, he writes in uncharacteristically strong terms (128:44):

> Be aware that Bircas Kohanim, even outside of Eretz Yisrael, is a Torah obligation; that is the consensus of all the *poskim*, based on the words of R' Yehoshua ben Levi, which we quoted above, in *se'if* 2 — not as *Mor U'Ketziah* concludes, that it is a Torah obligation only in the Beis HaMikdash. This was an error on his part, as he overlooked *Sifra* in *Parashas Shemini* (16) as well as *Sifrei* in *Parashas Shoftim* (51). He also seems to have disregarded *Yerushalmi Nazir*, which is quoted by *Tosafos Sotah* 38b (s.v. *Kol*). One of the scholars of our generation[2] pointed out to me that his words also conflict with *Bavli* (*Chullin* 133b). Aside from all these sources, the simple reading of the *pasuk*, *At that time, Hashem set apart the tribe of Levi... and to bless in His Name "until this day,"* (*Devarim* 10:8) clearly implies that the mitzvah remains in effect continuously.

Similarly, *Aruch HaShulchan* states (128:1): "There is a positive Torah commandment for the Kohanim to bless the Jewish people... and this mitzvah remains in effect continually, even in our times."

Kabbalistic Sources for Daily Bircas Kohanim

Many Kabbalistic sources stress the importance of performing Bircas Kohanim daily.

Zohar states (*Nasso*, p. 145): "The Kohanim are commanded to bless the people every day, by raising their fingers and reciting the blessing. This mitzvah causes a flow of blessing to all the worlds, Upper and Lower, for the deepest secrets of the universe are present within their raised fingers."

---

2. *Aderes* (*Zecher L'Mikdash*, vol. 2) writes that he was the one who pointed out to the Chofetz Chaim the proof from the Gemara in *Chullin* when they met in Warsaw in 1890. He then brings additional proof from other places in the Gemara that Bircas Kohanim is a *d'Oraysa* obligation even today.

R' Chaim Vital, the famed disciple of the Arizal, writes (*Shaarei Kedushah* vol. 1, *Shaar* 4): "One must exert all his energy to fulfill as many of the 613 mitzvos as can possibly be fulfilled in our times." He then goes on to list the mitzvos, and one of them is: "For the Kohanim to bless the Jewish people every day."

In *Shaar HaKavanos* (*Chazaras HaAmidah, Derush* #5), R' Chaim Vital reveals many deep, far-reaching kabbalistic secrets that lie within the mitzvah of Bircas Kohanim, and he places these teachings amid his discussion of the weekday davening. Clearly, he considered Bircas Kohanim to be a daily mitzvah.

Kaf HaChaim states (128:271): "We mentioned earlier (128:262), in the name of R' Chaim Vital in *Shaar HaKavanos*, that Bircas Kohanim is a necessary element of our prayer, and it **must be performed every day** during *Chazaras HaShatz*."

Later, he adds (128:262): "Likewise, during Shacharis of Tishah B'Av, here in Yerushalayim, in Congregation Khal Chassidim Beit El, where we follow the rulings of Arizal, our custom is to perform Bircas Kohanim [even during the weekday Shacharis]. The same is found in *Chesed L'Alafim*, [by R' Eliezer Papo, who cites the *Arizal*'s statement (128:18) that] the reason the practice of daily Bircas Kohanim was adopted is that Bircas Kohanim is an integral part of the prayers, which must be included in the chazzan's repetition of *Shemoneh Esrei*, as is written in *Shaar HaKavanos*. For this reason we are stringent, and do not allow this mitzvah to be omitted from the daily prayer."

Similarly, *Nagid U'Mitzvah*[3] states, in the order of the weekday prayers: "One must maintain great concentration during Bircas Kohanim. Additionally, the Kohen must raise his hands until they are actually at the same level as his head, and he should be very careful about this detail."

Siddur Chesed L'Avraham[4] says: "The Kohanim should prepare themselves to stand and serve in the Name of Hashem and bless the Jewish people in His Name. They must have in mind to fulfill the positive commandment of Bircas Kohanim, which is to be

---

3. A shorthand version of the writings of the Arizal, authored by R' Yaakov Tzemach, a close student and contemporary of R' Shmuel Vital, son of R' Chaim Vital.

4. Published by R' Avraham Toviano in Mantua, Italy, 1783. This *siddur* is based on the writings of Arizal and has been used by many chassidic Rebbes.

performed every day, as stated in *Tur* (128), *Rambam* (*Hilchos Nesias Kapayim* 14:1) and *Kisvei Arizal*."

Additionally, *Shulchan Aruch* of the *Arizal* (*Hilchos Tefillah, siman* 25) states that the Kohanim must concentrate when reciting Bircas Kohanim, "**and this should be done both on weekdays and on Shabbos.**"

Historic Sources for Daily Bircas Kohanim in Eretz Yisrael

Numerous sources indicate that Bircas Kohanim has been performed daily in Eretz Yisrael throughout the ages.

Darchei Tzion is a collection of letters that R' Ovadiah of Bartenura wrote to his family in Italy in 1488,[5] when he arrived in Eretz Yisrael, before settling in Yerushalayim. In one letter he writes (p. 14): "Every day, during every *tefillah* that includes Bircas Kohanim, the Kohanim here *duchan*, both on weekdays and on Shabbos."

The *mekubal* R' Moshe ben R' Mordechai Bassula (1480-1560) was a rav and rosh yeshivah in his hometown of Pesaro, Italy, and later moved to Tzfas, where he became a close disciple of R' Moshe Cordovero (the *Ramak*). In 1522 he published his *sefer, Masaos Eretz Yisrael,* in which he describes the customs of Yerushalayim. He writes: "Bircas Kohanim is performed here every day."

R' Shlomo Shlomil Minstrel of Tzfas, an Ashkenazi who lived in the generation after Arizal and authored *Shivchei HaAri* and other *sefarim*, writes (*Kovetz Al Yad,* vol. 3, p. 126): "Every day, the Kohanim go up to *duchan* before the chazzan reaches the *berachah* of *Sim Shalom,* and also during Minchah on fast days."

In the year 5382/1622, after R' Yeshayah HaLevi Horowitz, the *Shelah,* moved to Eretz Yisrael, he wrote to his family, who were still in Europe:[6] "Here, the Kohanim *duchan* every day, and I think of you during Bircas Kohanim, in order to bring their *berachah* upon your heads."

Likewise, R' Moshe ben R' Yisrael Naftali Hirsch (*Darchei Tzion,*

---

5. It is worth noting that this was sixty-two years before *Beis Yosef* was published. *Beis Yosef* cites the custom of daily Bircas Kohanim in Eretz Yisrael and commends the Kohanim who *duchan* there daily.

6. *Igros Eretz Yisrael* #35; *Toldos Chachmei Yerushalayim*, p. 154.

published in Frankfurt, Germany in the year 1650[7]) records that the custom of Ashkenazim in Yerushalayim is as follows: "After *Kedushah,* the Kohanim go out of the shul to wash their hands in the courtyard... When the chazzan finishes the *berachah* ending הַטּוֹב שִׁמְךָ וּלְךָ נָאֶה לְהוֹדוֹת, he calls out, 'Kohanim!' The Kohanim then begin to *duchan.* This takes place every morning during Shacharis, as well as during Mussaf on all days that Mussaf is recited."

R' Meir Poppirash and Mishnas Chassidim

In *Sefer Ohr Tzaddikim* (*Siman* 19, *Chazaras HaTefillah* #4), Maharam (R' Meir) Poppirash[8] — an Ashkenazi — writes explicitly that all communities worldwide should follow the custom of Eretz Yisrael to *duchan* every day, and twice on a day when there is Mussaf. The same ruling is found at length in *Mishnas Chassidim* (*Seder Kavanas Bircas Kohanim*), which was authored by R' Raphael Emmanuel Ricchi of Italy in the early eighteenth century. Both of these great men were known to be fluent in the teachings of the Arizal.

R' Yisrael of Shklov, a close student of the Vilna Gaon who moved to Eretz Yisrael at his rebbi's behest, writes (*Pe'as HaShulchan Hilchos Eretz Yisrael* 2:16): "It is a worthy custom in all of Eretz Yisrael that the Kohanim perform *nesias kapayim* every weekday, and on Yom Tov in Shacharis and Mussaf, and on Yom Kippur in Shacharis, Mussaf, and Neilah. That is also the custom in all Sephardic communities."

He adds: "The source of this custom is *Rambam* (*Hilchos Tefillah* 14:1) and *Beis Yosef* (129:1). It is only *Rema* (128:44) who excuses the Ashkenazic custom not to do so ... *Rama MiPano* (*She'eilos U'Teshuvos* 95), on the other hand, writes that this is a faulty custom (מִנְהָג גָּרוּעַ).[9] ... Thus, from the day we merited to establish our yeshivah in Eretz Yisrael and Yerushalayim, we have followed the custom that the Kohanim perform *nesias kapayim* every day, and

7. Not to be confused with the aforementioned work by the same name containing the letters of R' Ovadiah of Bartenura.

8. 1624-1662. Born in Krakow, Poland, he moved to Eretz Yisrael at the age of thirteen to study Kabbalah under the students of R' Chaim Vital. R' Meir authored thirty-nine *sefarim* before his untimely passing at age thirty-eight in Yerushalayim.

9. The opinion of *Rama MiPano* is discussed in greater depth in chapter 14.

on Shabbos and Yom Tov as required, which is also the correct thing to do according to the Vilna Gaon."[10]

In chapter 14, we will discuss why the practice of daily Bircas Kohanim was discontinued by Ashkenazic communities outside Eretz Yisrael.

10. The Vilna Gaon was of the opinion that even today, Bircas Kohanim should be performed daily in *chutz laAretz*. See chapter 15.

Part 2:

Vignettes From Our Torah Giants

Chapter 6
A Potent Blessing

One Who Wishes to Achieve Greatness in Torah Must Hear Bircas Kohanim

R' Avraham Yeshayah Bergman, a grandson of R' Elazar Menachem Shach, has been particular to hear Bircas Kohanim twice a day for the past thirty years. He recounts the incident that motivated him to take on this practice:

> One day, a *bachur* in the Ponovezh Yeshivah was not present at Shacharis. My grandfather, R' Shach, noticed and told the *bachur* to come to his office that evening. The student explained that he had overslept that morning, and had to daven in his room without a minyan. My grandfather told him that one who wishes to achieve greatness in Torah must hear Bircas Kohanim. Ever since, I make it a point to hear the *berachos* twice a day, to make sure that I have sufficient *kavanah* at least one of the times."

What Could Possibly Be Better for My Son?

R' Chizkiyahu Yosef Mishkovsky, *Mashgiach* of the Orchos Torah yeshivah in Bnei Brak, related that a certain *avreich* told him that the night before his son turned three, he took the child to the homes of several *tzaddikim*, hoping to receive a *berachah* for his son before his first haircut. Each time, he was told that the rav he was seeking was not available.

On his way home, the *avreich* had a thought: "Tomorrow, I will bring my son to shul to hear Bircas Kohanim, and in that way, he will receive a *berachah* directly from Hashem Himself. The Rambam writes (*Hilchos Tefillah* 15:7): 'The Kohanim perform their mitzvah as they are commanded, and Hakadosh Baruch Hu, in His mercy, blesses the Jewish people as He desires.'" When he came to this realization, he was filled with trust in Hashem, and said to himself, "What could possibly be better for my son than that?"

Iron Dome

R' Yitzchak Isaac Sher writes the following (*Leket Sichos Mussar*, vol. 3, p. 152), based on a *shmuess* he gave in Bnei Brak's Slabodka Yeshivah on 15 Iyar 5708 (May 24, 1948), in the midst of Israel's War of Independence:

> We heard the sirens and knew that we were in danger of an imminent attack from the Egyptian forces. I told the *talmidim* that our responsibility is to remain calm and not to be frightened or shaken. We are already in the best, most secure "bomb shelter" in the world — the *beis midrash* of our yeshivah. We, the *bnei hayeshivah*, are the true warriors. Any victory that occurs is our victory, for we are the ones who are praying, and it is through *tefillah* that we are able to ask Hashem to triumph over the enemies of the Jewish people. Have we not been taught that those who call out to Hashem sincerely and wholeheartedly are answered? If so, when we daven we must feel secure that our prayers will be accepted, and Hashem will send us salvation, and all those who are fighting this war will declare victory in the Name of Hashem.
>
> I then quoted *Targum Yonasan* (*Shir HaShirim* 3:7), which was shown to me by the Rosh Yeshivah of Yeshivas Chevron, R' Aharon Cohen. The *pasuk* says (*Shir HaShirim* 3:7), הִנֵּה מִטָּתוֹ שֶׁלִּשְׁלֹמֹה שִׁשִּׁים גִּבֹּרִים סָבִיב לָהּ מִגִּבֹּרֵי יִשְׂרָאֵל, *Behold the resting place of Him to Whom peace belongs, with sixty of Israel's mighty encircling it. Targum Yonasan* interprets the *pasuk* as follows: "How beautiful are the Kohanim at

the time that they spread their hands and stand upon the *duchan* to bless the nation of Yisrael with the sixty letters that were given over by Moshe Rabbeinu, and with that *berachah* they surround the Jewish people with a high and mighty wall of protection, through which the mighty ones of Yisrael are able to be strong and successful."

Chazal are teaching us who the true warriors are, and where their true strength lies — the strength that protects the Jewish people during wartime and allows them to be victorious. It is the power of Bircas Kohanim, the last remaining vestige of the *avodah* that took place in the Beis HaMikdash. We must believe in the power of this *berachah* more than we believe in the power of a *berachah* that we receive from a renowned *tzaddik*. We must enthusiastically pursue the opportunity to hear Bircas Kohanim, and pay attention to the *berachah* with all the reverence and trepidation that it deserves, in the same way that the Jewish people listened to the voices of the Kohanim in the Beis HaMikdash.

Certainly, at a time like this, when we are standing and davening to Hashem in hopes of His salvation, we must bear in mind what the true powers are that can bring us the merit to win the war. Firstly, the power of *bitachon* (trust in Hashem), with a full recognition of חֲזַק וְנִתְחַזַּק ... וַה׳ יַעֲשֶׂה הַטּוֹב בְּעֵינָיו, *Be strong and let us both be strong... and Hashem will do what is good in His eyes* (*II Shmuel* 10:12). Secondly, the power of *tefillah*, with a true expectation and trust in Hashem that He will bring salvation. Thirdly, the power of Bircas Kohanim, which carries a promise from the Torah itself — *Let them place My name upon Bnei Yisrael, and I shall bless them* (*Bamidbar* 6:27). And finally, the power of Torah, which is our guarantor to shield us and to save us, so that we may win the war.

The Blessing That Contains All Blessings

R' Yitzchak Weiss, a Belzer chassid who was killed during the Holocaust, writes (*Siach Yitzchak, Nasso*):

When someone asks for my *berachah* — the blessing of a simple Jew like me — I usually say, "May you be blessed with the *berachos* of Bircas Kohanim, with its sixty letters and with all the blessings that come forth from Bircas Kohanim, as revealed in the Gemara, *Midrashim*, and *Zohar*." Then, one Shabbos I had the merit to attend the *tish* of R' Yissachar Dov Rokeach, the Belzer Rebbe, for *seudah shlishis*. It was *Parashas Shemini* of the year 5669/1909, and he spoke about the *pesukim* of Bircas Kohanim. At the end of his talk, he said that his father, R' Yehoshua, the second Rebbe of Belz, used to bless people in just the way I described! I was extremely pleased to hear his words.

When R' Menachem Eliezer Moses was a young boy, his father once took him along with him as he accompanied the Chazon Ish on his daily morning walk. Menachem Eliezer had been taught to seek *berachos* from *tzaddikim* whenever he could, so he took this opportunity to ask the Chazon Ish for a *berachah*. The Chazon Ish said, "You should be blessed with the fulfillment of *Yevarechecha Hashem v'yishmerecha*, with every one of its many interpretations, as there is no greater blessing in the Torah than that blessing."[1]

Greater Than Any Tzaddik's Blessing

R' Shimshon Pincus taught (*Nefesh Shimshon* on *Tehillim*, p. 135):

The greatest *eis ratzon* (time of Heavenly Favor) that we have in our world is when the Kohanim are reciting Bircas Kohanim. At those moments the Gates of Heaven are literally wide open. What more do we need than that? יְבָרֶכְךָ ה׳ וְיִשְׁמְרֶךָ, *May Hashem bless you* — with prosperity! *And safeguard you* — from sin! יָאֵר ה׳ פָּנָיו אֵלֶיךָ וִיחֻנֶּךָּ — May Hashem shine His countenance upon you! וְיָשֵׂם לְךָ שָׁלוֹם — in the blessing of peace lies all the other blessings!

Once, a dear friend of mine was deathly ill, and it did not seem that he would survive. I had him in mind numerous times during Bircas Kohanim, and Hashem answered my prayers — my friend experienced a miraculous recovery!

1. As told to this author by R' Menachem Eliezer Moses.

The *Mashgiach* R' Eliezer Turk related (*Otzroseihem Amalei, Nasso*, p. 151):

> I know someone who went to the city of Ofakim early one morning to discuss with R' Shimshon Pincus a personal challenge he was facing. After R' Pincus heard the person's trouble he motioned to him to come with him into the adjacent room. R' Pincus told him that there is someone in this room who gives the most incredible blessings, which have an incredible impact in Heaven and don't go unanswered. The person was curious; who was the *tzaddik* who distributed such lofty blessings? In the room there was a minyan that was up to Shemoneh Esrei. R' Pincus told the person, "In a few short moments they will say Bircas Kohanim here. **The direct blessing of Hashem is greater than that of any human, even of the most righteous *tzaddikim*."**

Berachah Boomerang

When R' Aharon Leib Shteinman visited New York, after davening Shacharis at a *netz* minyan, he would join a Sephardic minyan for Bircas Kohanim. A traditional — but not fully observant — Kohen, whose children attended public school, davened in that shul, and after R' Aharon Leib heard Bircas Kohanim there for two consecutive days, the Kohen approached him. "It's the strangest thing," he began. "Lately, I feel a special connection to Hashem that I never felt before."

R' Aharon Leib encouraged him to seize the moment and make some changes in his life, particularly regarding the *chinuch* of his children. The man agreed to remove them from public school and register them in Jewish schools. "And what mitzvah should I work on?" he asked.

"Keeping Shabbos," R' Aharon Leib replied.

The Kohen maintained a connection with R' Aharon Leib over the next couple of years and visited him on his annual trips to Eretz Yisrael. Eventually, he and his family became Torah observant. This blessing in his life was brought about as a result of his serving as the conduit of the Bircas Kohanim heard by R' Aharon Leib.[2]

---

2. This story was told to the author by R' Moshe Shteinman, a son of R' Aharon

When the Kohen Couldn't Recall the Patient's Name

R' Gamliel HaKohen Rabinowitz[3] related: "My grandfather, R' Levi Rabinowitz, author of *Maadanei HaShulchan*, used to keep in mind the names of ill people and the like before he recited the daily Bircas Kohanim. Once, I gave him the name of a *choleh*, and a number of days later, the *choleh* passed away. I went to my grandfather that day to tell him that it was no longer necessary to daven for that individual, and then I asked him whether he had had the *choleh's* name in mind that morning. He told me that just that day, he was not able to recall the name, and he'd been anxious about it since. This brings to mind the Mishnah (*Berachos* 34b) that relates that R' Chanina ben Dosa would daven for *cholim*, and he said that when his *tefillah* did not go smoothly, he knew it was not accepted."

The Best Segulah for Parnassah

R' Yitzchak Zilberstein writes[4]:

> It causes me much heartache to see so many Jews mired in terrible financial difficulties, having accumulated so many debts that they cannot see any way out of their desperate situation. When these people come to me, I always advise them to seek the best possible means of achieving *parnassah* — and that is through Bircas Kohanim. I tell them they must make sure to hear Bircas Kohanim, and when the Kohanim raise their hands to bless the Jewish people, they should stand and listen in fear and awe, while picturing themselves as a vessel that is prepared to receive the *berachah*.

Leib, who accompanied his father on his trip to New York. See also the ArtScroll/ Mesorah biography of R' Aharon Leib, p. 227.

3. Author of *Gam Ani Odecha* and nephew of the well-known *mekubal* by the same name.

4. *Kol B'Ramah* Torah digest, 5768.

All-Inclusive Blessing

R' Yaakov Edelstein would advise those who approached him for a *berachah* due to difficulties they were facing to have in mind these difficulties while listening to Bircas Kohanim. R' Yaakov explained to his son, "When one hears Bircas Kohanim, it is the most opportune time to receive a *berachah* and salvation from one's troubles. I make sure to remind people about this, since Bircas Kohanim is done daily, and some people therefore don't realize what an incredible blessing it is." He also quoted the Brisker Rav's observation that Bircas Kohanim is greater than the blessing of the most righteous *tzaddik*, and added that the most appropriate place to have one's needs in mind is when the Kohanim say the word *shalom*, because the *berachah* of *shalom* includes everything.

Similarly, on many occasions R' Edelstein gave similar advice to those seeking to have children. Even if they lived in *chutz laAretz*, he would encourage them to hear Bircas Kohanim in a Sephardic minyan. He would tell the young couple to have their request in mind during Bircas Kohanim, and to answer amen to all three blessings with special concentration.

He told hundreds of Ashkenazim who resided overseas that they should try to attend a Sephardic minyan at least once a week to hear Bircas Kohanim, so that they could receive a Divine blessing and earn salvation in any area they needed, and many people were indeed helped by Hashem after going to hear Bircas Kohanim. R' Yaakov added that if the Kohen himself requires a *yeshuah*, he does not need to have anything specific in mind, as the blessing of the Kohanim themselves comes directly from Hashem.[5]

The Power of Even a Single Kohen's Blessing

This fascinating and eye-opening story was heard directly from the person involved.

The *netz* minyan of a certain shul in the Ramot neighborhood of Yerushalayim had only one Kohen to *duchan* each morning, and it happened that he was compelled to daven elsewhere for about three weeks. During this time, one of the members of the

5. Heard from his son R' Mordechai Shmuel Edelstein.

minyan was suddenly plagued by numerous misfortunes. Feeling overwhelmed by these hardships, he went to speak to R' Yaakov Edelstein, and poured out his heart to the venerable rav.

At first, R' Yaakov was stunned by the extent of this man's suffering and could not respond. Finally, after a few minutes he gently asked, "Tell me, have you been receiving the daily *berachah* of Bircas Kohanim?"

When the man explained that the regular Kohen in his minyan was absent, R' Yaakov told him to find another minyan, even if it would mean davening after *netz*. The man heeded R' Yaakov's advice, and a few weeks later, he returned to him and reported that most of his troubles had eased.

R' Yaakov replied, "This just demonstrates how the Bircas Kohanim of even a single Kohen has the capacity to protect us from adversity. We need no more proof than the fact that *Mishnah Berurah* (128:106) cites the opinion of those who permit a Kohen to interrupt his *Shemoneh Esrei* in order to *duchan* if he is the only Kohen available, but not if there is another Kohen in the shul who can do it."

R' Yaakov added that this also explains why Jews in Eretz Yisrael go to great lengths to ensure that there will be a Kohen present during Neilah on Yom Kippur. At that time the Gates of Heaven are open, and we can merit more blessing by rushing to ensure that we finish in time to *duchan* before sunset than by using these precious moments to concentrate more intently.

Like an Angel

R' Yisrael Zev Gustman recalled that when his rebbi, R' Shimon Yehudah HaKohen Shkop, would leave the front of the *beis midrash* after Bircas Kohanim, his face underwent a noticeable change. He no longer looked like an ordinary person; he had the appearance of an angel! R' Gustman told his student R' Eliezer Turk,[6] "We were all completely awestruck after he completed Bircas Kohanim, to the point that we were scared to look at his radiant face. He looked like a different person! I can never forget the glorious and formidable appearance of R' Shimon's face at that time."[7]

---

6. *Otzroseihem Amalei, Nasso,* p. 145.
7. See also *Torah Yevakesh MiPihu – Toldos R' Shimon Shkop,* author of *Shaarei Yosher*, p. 255.

More Divine Assistance

R' Yechezkel Abramsky said several times when he spoke publicly that on days when he concentrated during Bircas Kohanim, he saw more success and *siyata d'Shmaya* than he did on other days.[8]

8. As related by R' Gedaliah Eisenman, *Mashgiach* of Yeshivas Kol Torah in Yerushalayim.

Chapter 7
Cherishing Bircas Kohanim

A New Mitzvah

On 20 Elul 5684 (September 19, 1924), the *bachurim* of the Slabodka Yeshivah arrived in Eretz Yisrael to reestablish the yeshivah in Chevron. R' Menachem Mendel Sheinin, a *talmid* of the yeshivah, recalled that among them was the *tzaddik* R' Tzvi Kopshitz, who was a Kohen. R' Tzvi could not contain his excitement. He remained awake the entire night pacing eagerly back and forth, waiting for the morning to arrive. He told all those he met, "I will now have a new mitzvah to perform every day — the mitzvah of *v'ahavta l'rei'acha kamocha*, to love one's fellow Jew! Here in Eretz Yisrael the custom is to *duchan* every morning, and it must be done with love!"

Travel Insurance

R' Moshe Mordechai Chodosh, Rosh Yeshivah of Yeshivah Ohr Elchonon in Yerushalayim, recounted an incident that he heard from his father, R' Meir Chodosh, the *Mashgiach* of Yeshivas Chevron. After the yeshivah relocated from Slabodka to the city of Chevron, the Alter of Slabodka, R' Nosson Tzvi Finkel, wanted to move to Eretz Yisrael to reunite with his students. Due to his failing health, however, there was much concern that he would not be strong enough to adapt to a new climate. He traveled to Berlin to consult a doctor there about the matter, and the doctor gave his approval for the move.

Since he was already closer to his destination than before, he decided to continue on directly from Berlin to Eretz Yisrael, rather than first returning to Slabodka. He had one request, though. It was two weeks before Shavuos, and he wanted to remain in Berlin until after Yom Tov. Why? Because on Shavuos he would hear Bircas Kohanim, and he did not feel confident that he could travel safely to Eretz Yisrael without having the power of Bircas Kohanim to support him![1]

Immense Pleasure

The Minchas Elazar, R' Chaim Elazar Shapira of Munkacz, visited Eretz Yisrael in 1930 for thirteen days. The highlights of his trip are recorded by his disciple R' Moshe Goldstein in *Masa'os Yerushalayim*. Regarding their stop in Egypt, en route to Eretz Yisrael, he writes (p. 48): "Then we came to the great synagogue in the main town square of Alexandria, Egypt. It is an expansive, beautiful building, and the shul traces its history back to Eliyahu HaNavi. There our group davened Shacharis in our own separate minyan and we merited to include Bircas Kohanim, in accordance with the custom of Egypt and Eretz Yisrael."

Later, he writes (p. 106):

> In Eretz Yisrael the Kohanim perform Bircas Kohanim every day, both during Shacharis and Mussaf, as is the custom in Yerushalayim. This was an extremely enjoyable experience for the rav, to hear davening and Bircas Kohanim for the duration of his stay in Eretz Yisrael, day after day. He had immense pleasure each time, but the climax was on Shabbos, when he himself served as the chazzan for Shacharis, and he had the opportunity to call out the words of the *berachos* to the Kohanim, each word with trepidation and love. His intense joy was evident to all those in his presence.

1. *Kol Torah* journal, vol. 86, p. 37.

An Entire Glass of Vodka

R' Yitzchak Zilber related an incident that happened when he was still living in communist Russia. He was eating in the succah on the night of Shemini Atzeres, at the home of the Krogliak family, and among the guests was a Kohen. R' Yitzchak could not contain his excitement. In his minyan there was no Kohen that year, and he and his fellow congregants had not been able to hear Bircas Kohanim on Rosh Hashanah, Yom Kippur, or the first days of Succos. Finally, here was a Kohen — and in time for the last days of Yom Tov!

He immediately beseeched the guest to join their minyan the following morning, but the Kohen was not as enthusiastic as R' Yitzchak. "If you will drink down this entire glass of vodka," he said, "I'll come to your minyan!"

Without hesitating, R' Yitzchak poured the vodka down his throat, to the last drop. Now the Kohen had no choice but to come to shul. The next morning, the Kohen arrived at the minyan before the designated time, and R' Yitzchak was not yet there. As the minutes wore on, the Kohen began to get nervous, fearing that the vodka had made R' Yitzchak sick. But that was not the case. "In truth," R' Yitzchak said, "the vodka did not affect me in the slightest, as I was very excited to hear Bircas Kohanim, which I had not heard in a few months."[2]

Beyond His Limits

R' Aharon Cohen, one of the roshei yeshivah of Yeshivas Kness-es Yisrael–Chevron, had great love for the mitzvah of reciting Bircas Kohanim, and he made every effort to fulfill the mitzvah every day, with much enthusiasm. One of the reasons he rejoiced upon moving from Slabodka to Eretz Yisrael was that he now had the opportunity to *duchan* every day, rather than just on Yom Tov. His devotion to the mitzvah was especially manifest in the last years of his life, when he was suffering terribly from terminal cancer, yet he pushed himself beyond his limits to *duchan*.

The Vaad HaYeshivos had a hospitality apartment in

2. *L'Hisha'er Yehudi*, p. 306.

Yerushalayim's Beit HaKerem neighborhood, where people who were unwell could stay and rest. After R' Aharon underwent surgery, he stayed at this apartment for several weeks together with one of his *talmidim*, who tended to his needs. The *talmid* reported that R' Aharon exerted all his strength to be able to daven with a minyan, and even when he could not do so because of his poor health, he would nevertheless make an effort to come to *Chazaras HaShatz*, in order to *duchan*.

One Yom Tov, he was severely ill, and in the morning he could not come down the stairs to the shul. At some point, however, he began to feel slightly better, so he went down to the shul and asked people where he could find a minyan that had not davened yet. He was told that the nearest such place was at the other end of Beit HaKerem, a significant distance to walk even for a healthy person. Undeterred, R' Aharon gathered his strength and began the hike. When the day wore on and he failed to return, everyone was worried. It turned out that he actually did make it to the minyan, where he recited Bircas Kohanim and heard *Krias HaTorah* as well. But after all that, he was completely drained, and could not make his way back.

Someone close to him questioned, "Why was it necessary to go to such lengths? Does the mitzvah require a person to be *moser nefesh*?"

R' Aharon answered simply, "Should I give up a mitzvah as precious as this — *to bless His people, Yisrael, with love*? Are there any words to describe how valuable this mitzvah is?"

His impassioned answer left an everlasting impression on all who were present.

Similarly, on Purim 5721/1961, around three months before he passed away, R' Aharon was already critically ill, and he was in so much pain that he was barely able to sleep at night. The yeshivah was next door to his apartment, and on the night of Purim there was loud music and dancing in the yeshivah throughout the night. It became impossible for the rosh yeshivah to fall asleep at all. Nevertheless, when morning arrived, he somehow managed to make his way down to the yeshivah to *duchan*. He did not even seem to view his conduct as anything extraordinary![3]

---

3. *HaKohen HaGadol MeiEchav*, pp. 374-377.

Mysterious Cut

One summer, R' Aharon spent *bein hazmanim* in Bnei Brak, and would daven Shacharis every morning in the nearby Ponovezh Yeshivah. One morning, during *Chazaras HaShatz,* he went out of shul, as usual, to wash his hands for Bircas Kohanim. On the way back, he decided to return to the *beis midrash* through a different entrance, but failed to notice that there was a glass door there, and the result was a forceful collision between his head and the door. R' Aharon did not even notice, however, as his mind was totally immersed in his davening and in the anticipation of the mitzvah he was about to perform. He immediately went up to *duchan,* and only after he finished did the *Mashgiach,* R' Abba Grossbard, signal to him that there was blood streaming from his forehead. The wound was quickly bandaged, but when people asked him how he had gotten such a cut, he did not know what to answer!

In a *shmuess* in Ponovezh, R' Michel Yehudah Lefkowitz, who studied under R' Aharon in the Chevron Yeshivah, described R' Aharon's Bircas Kohanim and remarked, "Just by watching him, one could acquire infinite fear of Heaven. He was a genuinely G-dly person; something we no longer see today."[4]

Disturbing the Chazon Ish's Sleep

The Chazon Ish held a minyan on the roof of his house during the Yamim Noraim. One Yom Kippur, toward the end of his life, he began feeling faint in the middle of Mussaf. After *Kedushah,* he went downstairs to lie down, but before doing so, he left strict instructions with R' Avraham Greineman to wake him up in time for Bircas Kohanim. Shortly before Bircas Kohanim, R' Greineman went down to fulfill his assignment, but he was very hesitant about disturbing the Chazon Ish's sleep when he was in such frail condition, and he paced back and forth anxiously, trying to decide what to do. The problem was soon resolved, however, because the Chazon Ish suddenly sprang out of bed on his own and made his way back up to the roof.[5]

---

4. Ibid. p. 372.
5. *Maaseh Ish,* vol. 4, p. 117.

Accelerated Neilah

It was Yom Kippur 5684 (1924), the first year after the Alter of Slabodka moved to Eretz Yisrael and reestablished his yeshivah in the city of Chevron. When the yeshivah began Neilah, the Alter saw that the hour was late, and they would not be able to finish in time for Bircas Kohanim at their current pace.[6] Not wishing to miss out on Bircas Kohanim, he gathered a small group of *bachurim* and formed his own minyan, to daven Neilah faster. He explained that although this meant forfeiting the chance to daven Neilah slowly, it was worth it in order to perform the special mitzvah of Bircas Kohanim. When the remainder of the minyan saw this, they increased their own pace as well, and managed to finish in time to recite Bircas Kohanim.

R' Moshe Hillel Hirsch, Rosh Yeshivah of Yeshivas Slabodka in Bnei Brak, commented to this author that this practice continues until today in his yeshivah and in the Chevron–Yerushalayim yeshivah (an offshoot of Slabodka), due to the contagious devotion of the Alter, which had a lasting effect. This has become the practice in the vast majority of yeshivos in Eretz Yisrael as well. They make sure to perform Bircas Kohanim of Neilah before sunset, even though this requires that they daven Neilah at a faster pace, even rushing. Then, they recite *Avinu Malkeinu* and *kabbalas ol malchus Shamayim* slowly, so they can start Maariv at the designated time without having to take a break.

Similarly, since the establishment of Yeshivas Mir in Yerushalayim in 1944, the yeshivah has never missed Bircas Kohanim during Neilah, making sure to recite it before sunset. R' Tzvi Partzovitz, the Rosh Yeshivah of Yeshivas Mir's Modi'in Illit branch, shared this insight from his father, R' Nochum: "People think that the yeshivah makes sure to perform Bircas Kohanim before sunset on Yom Kippur so that Klal Yisrael should receive an extra blessing from Hashem, but the real reason is that since the Kohanim perform three positive mitzvos when they *duchan*, we are doing a *chesed* by hurrying our *tefillos* to enable them to do the mitzvah. That is the greatest source of merit for us at the conclusion of Neilah — doing a *chesed* for the Kohanim."

---

6. See chapter 41 for a discussion of whether Bircas Kohanim may be recited during Neilah after sunset.

Likewise, one Yom Kippur, the Brisker Rav asked the chazzan if he would finish Neilah in time for Bircas Kohanim, and he answered, "It depends how long it takes the Rav to daven." Hearing that, the Brisker Rav made sure to daven relatively quickly, in order to finish in time.

Until today, in the Brisker yeshivos, the descendants of the Brisker Rav always ensure that the Bircas Kohanim of Neilah takes place before sunset. His son R' Meir Soloveitchik commented that the most significant difference between his father's Yom Kippur davening in Europe and Eretz Yisrael was the Neilah service, as after they moved to Eretz Yisrael a big focus of their Neilah was ensuring that Bircas Kohanim would be performed before *shekiah*.

Worth Staying Up For

R' Yechiel Michel Stern related that every Shavuos morning, after he and his brothers had stayed up all night learning and had finished the morning prayers, their father, R' Moshe Aharon Stern, *Mashgiach* of Yeshivas Kamenitz, would insist on taking them on a detour. He said, "Today is the *yahrtzeit* of the Imrei Emes, and there will be hundreds of Kohanim davening in the Gerrer *beis midrash*. Let's go there and hear Bircas Kohanim!"

When his son attempted to explain that he was tired and had already heard Bircas Kohanim in his *netz* minyan from more than two Kohanim, R' Moshe Aharon would have none of it. He told his son, "If the Vilna Gaon were giving out *berachos*, would you say you're too tired? You would run for miles to get such a *berachah*! Hakadosh Baruch Hu Himself says וַאֲנִי אֲבָרְכֵם, *I will bless them*, and here you have an opportunity to get a *berachah* from Hashem through several hundred Kohanim. You can wait a bit longer before going to sleep!"[7]

Multiple Blessings

For many years, R' Meir Soloveitchik would circulate from one minyan to another in the Zichron Moshe shul, where numerous Shacharis minyanim take place every day, for the purpose of

7. *HaMashgiach* p. 311; *Otzroseihem Amalei Nasso* p. 145.

hearing Bircas Kohanim several times. Even if his minyan had two Kohanim, if he had extra time, he would go to another minyan to hear another Bircas Kohanim. He would frequently say, "Why don't people understand that it is worth running to hear Bircas Kohanim and receive a *berachah* from Hashem Himself?"[8]

For several years, R' Meir was accompanied by R' Yechezkel Sarna, the Rosh Yeshivah of Yeshivas Chevron. R' Meir's close friend R' Shlomo Zalman Zalaznik, Rosh Yeshivah of Yeshivas Eitz Chaim in Yerushalayim, would also try to hear multiple Bircas Kohanim blessings.[9]

Careful to Finish in Time

B'chol Nafshecha (p. 323), a Hebrew biography of the Rosh Yeshivah of Yeshivas Mir, R' Nosson Tzvi Finkel, describes how the Rosh Yeshivah would daven from a *siddur* word by precious word, as though he was counting money, pouring out his heart to Hashem. Even in the advanced stages of his illness, when he could barely function, he would continue his *Shemoneh Esrei* for an extended time. Yet he was always careful to finish before the chazzan reached Bircas Kohanim, so that he could move from the *mizrach* wall and stand before the Kohanim to receive the *berachah*.

8. *D'Chazitei L'Rabbi Meir*, by R' Shimon Yosef Meller.
9. *Sefer Yevarechecha*, p. 590.

Chapter 8
Dedication to the Mitzvah

Hearing Bircas Kohanim Daily, Everywhere in the World

Many *gedolim* living in Eretz Yisrael — including R' Yechezkel Sarna, R' Aharon Leib Shteinman, R' Simchah Zissel Broide, R' Chaim Pinchas Scheinberg, R' Moshe Shmuel Shapira, R' Shalom Schwadron, R' Moshe Mordechai Chodosh, R' Daniel Frisch (author of the *Masok MiDevash* commentary on *Zohar*), and many others — made an effort to continue hearing (or, in the case of R' Shalom, performing) Bircas Kohanim every day, as is the custom in Eretz Yisrael, when they traveled to *chutz laAretz*.

Almost every morning, they would visit a Sephardic shul, where Bircas Kohanim is recited daily, and that afforded them the opportunity to receive a *berachah* from Hashem, as the Torah promises to us. (R' Shteinman, R' Shapira, R' Sarna, and R' Broide davened in Ashkenazic shuls but went to a Sephardic shul to hear Bircas Kohanim after davening. R' Scheinberg, R' Chodosh, R' Frisch, and R' Schwadron usually davened the entire Shacharis in the Sephardic shul.)[1]

R' Gedaliah Honigsberg recounted that once, his grandfather R'

1. This was confirmed by the author with the children of all the above *gedolim*. For more on the topic of an Ashkenazi going to hear Bircas Kohanim in a Sephardic minyan in *chutz laAretz*, see chapter 17.

Aharon Leib Shteinman davened with a *netz* minyan on the plane as he returned from France, but there were no Kohanim on the flight. Immediately after landing in Eretz Yisrael, R' Aharon Leib and several people who accompanied him went directly to the Tiferes Tzvi-Itzkowitz shul in Bnei Brak, where they heard Bircas Kohanim.

Seeing Blessing in This World

R' Simcha Scheinberg, the current Rosh Yeshivah of Yeshivah Torah Ore and the only son of R' Chaim Pinchas, told this author that his father's love for the mitzvah of Bircas Kohanim was unquenchable. Before traveling overseas, he would inquire and make sure that he would be able to hear Bircas Kohanim in a Sephardic minyan during his journey.

I verified an incredible story that took place with a student of R' Chaim Pinchas who resided in New York. About forty years before R' Scheinberg's passing, he was in New York raising funds for his yeshivah. This student saw his rebbi's dedicated efforts to hear Bircas Kohanim daily, and asked him if he too should go to hear Bircas Kohanim every day, even as a permanent resident of *chutz laAretz*. R' Scheinberg replied that this is permitted and meritorious.[2] The person heeded R' Scheinberg's advice and has been going to hear Bircas Kohanim in a Sephardic shul almost daily. This person was blessed with incredible wealth and is today one of the leading philanthropists in the Torah world.

Standing at Attention

R' Bentzion Mutzafi relates that his father, the great *mekubal* R' Solomon Mutzafi, who was known to pray according to all the rulings of the Rashash's *Siddur HaKavanos*, was very particular to hear Bircas Kohanim every day. If it happened one day that there were no Kohanim in his own shul, he would go after davening to another shul to hear the *berachah*.

R' Bentzion also relates: It was my father's longstanding practice to pray with the sunrise every day of the week. After davening, we would go upstairs, or to the room adjoining the shul, where we

2. See chapter 17 for a discussion about residents of *chutz laAretz* going to a Sephardic minyan for Bircas Kohanim.

would spend some time studying Gemara together. When my father heard that the chazzan was almost up to Bircas Kohanim, he would interrupt our learning and instruct us to stand at attention to receive the *berachah* — even though we were not in the same room, or even on the same floor. We would remain standing until the completion of the *berachah*.[3]

Two Kohanim

R' Moshe Aharon Stern's children related that from the time he arrived in Eretz Yisrael as a young man, he insisted on hearing Bircas Kohanim from at least two Kohanim every single day. If the shul where he davened did not have two Kohanim, he would trek from neighborhood to neighborhood until he found a shul with two Kohanim, even if it meant forfeiting other important matters.

When the *Mashgiach* R' Yechezkel Levenstein was in Yerushalayim, he assembled a minyan of his students that he felt comfortable davening with, which would proceed at a slow pace, and R' Moshe Aharon was among them. As the Yamim Noraim approached, R' Chatzkel, as he was known, asked R' Moshe Aharon if their minyan would be able to daven together on Rosh Hashanah and Yom Kippur as well. When R' Moshe Aharon didn't immediately respond, R' Chatzkel said reproachfully, "I see that you are in doubt! Isn't it important to you to have a minyan like this, especially for the Yamim Noraim?"

R' Moshe Aharon explained, "If we won't have two Kohanim, I cannot daven here. Any other day, I can go to another shul afterward and hear Bircas Kohanim, but on Rosh Hashanah and Yom Kippur that is not possible."

R' Chatzkel answered, "Then do whatever it takes to get Kohanim. Just make sure we have our minyan and you are there!"

The final compromise was that R' Moshe Aharon would start off there, but if it turned out that their minyan did not have two Kohanim, he would daven elsewhere. He would not agree to forego Bircas Kohanim.[4] In fact, one year on Rosh Hashanah only one Kohen was present at the minyan, as the second designated Kohen

---

3. *Orchos Tzion*, vol. 2, pp. 251-252.
4. *HaMashgiach*, p. 309.

was unable to come, and R' Moshe Aharon politely excused himself and headed to another minyan to daven.[5]

Seeking a D'Oraysa Blessing

Similarly, R' Sroya Deblitzki of Bnei Brak was scrupulous to hear Bircas Kohanim from two Kohanim each day. For several decades he davened at *netz* every single day in Yeshivas Tiferes Tzion. If he didn't hear Bircas Kohanim from two Kohanim there, then despite his very busy learning schedule, he would go to another minyan to hear it there. R' Sroya did this in his later years as well, despite his weakness and illness. Even in the summer months, when sunrise was very early and the next minyan took place more than an hour later, he would not start his day without hearing Bircas Kohanim from two Kohanim.[6]

R' Sroya explained that although many Rishonim are of the opinion that one Kohen's recitation of Bircas Kohanim is also a fulfillment of the *mitzvah d'Oraysa*,[7] the halachah is that the chazzan may announce "Kohanim" only if there are two Kohanim present.[8] Since he wanted to be present for the fulfillment of this aspect of the mitzvah as well, he preferred to seek a minyan that had two Kohanim.[9]

On days when he went to another minyan to hear Bircas Kohanim from two Kohanim, if it was Shabbos or Rosh Chodesh, he made sure to hear both the Shacharis Bircas Kohanim as well as the Mussaf Bircas Kohanim, as he was of the opinion that according to both halachah and Kabbalah these are two separate obligations, and there are different Kabbalistic *kavanos* in the Bircas Kohanim of these two *tefillos*.[10]

To ensure that there would be two Kohanim at his regular minyan, R' Sroya would pay two Kohanim to attend.

---

5. As he related to R' Eliezer Turk, who worked alongside him in the Kamenitz Yeshivah. See *Otzroseihem Amalei, Nasso,* p. 147.
6. As related to this author by his only son, R' Dovid Deblitzki. See also *Derech Yesharah,* p. 216.
7. See chapter 30 for further discussion of this topic.
8. See *Shulchan Aruch* 128:10 and *Mishnah Berurah* §39.
9. Although the *Mishnah Berurah* (ibid.) does cite an opinion that Bircas Kohanim is a *d'Oraysa* even if "Kohanim" is not announced, R' Sroya took into account the other opinions as well.
10. *Derech Yesharah* ibid.

Blessing Everyone

One day, less than a year before R' Dovid Soloveitchik passed away, there were five Kohanim in his morning minyan. Although he was sitting near the chazzan, one of the Kohanim performed Bircas Kohanim close to R' Dovid, who had trouble hearing, to enable him to hear the words. The chazzan was behind this particular Kohen, however, and after Shacharis, R' Dovid told the Kohen that he should have been together with the other Kohanim at the *mizrach* wall, so that he would have included the chazzan in the *berachah*. The Kohen countered that there were four other Kohanim present and the chazzan received Bircas Kohanim from them, so he wanted to ensure that R' Dovid would be able to hear the *berachah*. R' Dovid responded that his father was scrupulous that all the Kohanim should face the rest of the congregants, so they should all include everyone in their *berachah*, including the chazzan.[11]

In this vein, R' Benzion HaKohen Kook writes (*Tziyunei Halachah*, p. 367):

> My rebbi, R' Yosef Shalom Elyashiv, was always careful to stand far enough from all the Kohanim so that he would not be in front of even one Kohen, which would disqualify him from receiving the blessing of that Kohen. One weekday morning, during the last years of R' Elyashiv's life, there were several Kohanim standing near the *aron kodesh* and the *mizrach* wall, and my son, who was *duchaning* (though he was not yet a bar mitzvah), was standing behind R' Elyashiv. When R' Elyashiv realized that my son was standing behind him, he quickly moved back a few feet, despite his weakness and fatigue, so that he would be standing in front of my son.[12]

Preparation

R' Dovid Soloveitchik, a son of the Brisker Rav, would stress that the need to ensure that a Kohen will be present for Shacharis and

---

11. *Acharon L'Dor Deah*, p. 443.

12. We also see the importance of the Kohen being in front of the entire congregation from R' Chaim Kanievsky's ruling (Responsa #83) that a Kohen is permitted to walk in front of someone davening *Shemoneh Esrei* in order to reach the *mizrach* wall so that he can be in front of the entire congregation.

Mussaf is akin to the need to prepare one's *dalet minim* before Succos. We all understand that if we are to have *dalet minim* on Succos, we cannot begin searching on Yom Tov, and the same is true of Bircas Kohanim; before the prayers, one must ensure that there will be a Kohen present.[13]

Similarly, during the eleven summers when R' Chaim Kanievsky went to Tzfas to rest, he agreed to go only if there would be two Kohanim present at a *netz* minyan in Tzfas, so that he could hear Bircas Kohanim daily.[14] While it is a custom in some chassidic synagogues in Tzfas that Bircas Kohanim is recited only during Mussaf of Shabbos, Rosh Chodesh, and Yom Tov,[15] R' Chaim was not ready to forgo this privilege.[16]

In the Most Suitable Fashion

For many years, R' Aharon Leib Shteinman would go to Yerushalayim for the first day of Pesach, to spend Yom Tov with his son R' Moshe. While he was there, he would daven Shacharis at the *netz* minyan of the Beis Yisrael shul in the Ezras Torah neighborhood. It happened a number of times that there was no Kohen at that minyan, so he would ask one of his grandsons to let him know when the next minyan was almost up to Bircas Kohanim, so he could go back to shul then. Even if the *netz* minyan had only one Kohen, he would return for the second minyan to hear Bircas Kohanim from two Kohanim, in order to be present for the optimal fulfillment of the mitzvah. When asked why he insisted on making such an effort, he would explain simply, "Bircas Kohanim is a *berachah* that is written in the Torah! I want to make sure I receive the *berachah* in the most suitable fashion."[17]

---

13. *Acharon L'Dor Deah*, biography of R' Dovid Soloveitchik by R' Shimon Yosef Meller, p. 441.
14. Heard from his son R' Yitzchak Shaul Kanievsky, who accompanied his parents to Tzfas each time for their brief five-day respite.
15. See chapter 18 for a discussion of Bircas Kohanim in Tzfas.
16. R' Shabse HaKohen Kubin, proprietor of the famed "Lulavei Kubin," was one of the Kohanim who *duchaned* nearly every day during R' Chaim's visits to Tzfas. For two summers, R' Chaim's nephew R' Dov HaKohen Kook (son-in-law of R' Yitzchak Zilberstein) joined R' Shabse and other Kohanim at the *minyan.*
17. *K'Ayal Taarog,* p. 201.

Chapter 9
Expressing Appreciation

Saying Thank You

R' Yechezkel Sarna, Rosh Yeshivah of Yeshivas Chevron, once did a certain favor for the Brisker Rav, and the Rav thanked him by saying, "*Yasher koach.*" R' Sarna objected, claiming that he did not deserve a *yasher koach*, because he was obligated to perform that particular mitzvah in any case. "Nevertheless," responded the Rav, "we find that the custom is to say *yasher koach* to the Kohanim after they *duchan*, even though they were obligated to do so. Apparently, it is appropriate to thank a person who fulfilled his obligation, since he provided you with a benefit." To this, R' Sarna countered, "That is indeed a fitting comparison — and that is why my custom is *not* to say *yasher koach* to the Kohanim!"[1]

The Custom to Say Yasher Koach

The source for our custom to say *yasher koach* to the Kohanim is *Mateh Ephraim* (592:11).[2] Additionally, the Mishnah (*Sheviis* 4:2) states that although any produce grown in Eretz Yisrael during the

1. *HaRav MiBrisk*, vol. 4, p. 459.
2. See *Aruch HaShulchan* 128:24, which states this is the accepted custom, and the Kohanim may reply *Beruchim tihyu. Mishnah Berurah* 128:60 cites this custom as well.

shemittah year is considered *hefker* (ownerless and free for the taking), someone who takes the produce is permitted to express his gratitude to the owner of the field. The *Rashash* there comments: "This is my explanation for the custom to say *yasher kochachem* to the Kohanim when they come down from the *duchan* — a custom that many people ridicule."

The *sefer Harerei Kedem*[3] relates that R' Moshe Feinstein would offer a *yasher koach* to the Kohanim as they returned to their seat after *duchaning,* even on Rosh Hashanah. This may seem surprising, in light of *Chayei Adam*'s ruling (141:9) that one is not permitted to speak from the beginning of shofar-blowing until he hears all one hundred shofar-blasts, including the ones that are sounded after *Aleinu.* Apparently, R' Moshe held that the *yasher koach* demonstrates that one is accepting the *berachah,* which is necessary, according to the opinion of *Sefer Chareidim*[4] that non-Kohanim have an obligation to receive the *berachah.* Therefore, thanking the Kohanim is an integral part of Bircas Kohanim and not an interruption.

R' Avrohom Biderman of ArtScroll/Mesorah, a *talmid* of R' Moshe Feinstein, added that on Rosh Hashanah at the Yeshivah of Staten Island, R' Moshe would tell each individual Kohen *yasher koach* immediately after Bircas Kohanim (without waiting until the conclusion of the shofar-blowing), and wish them that they should be *zocheh* to do the *avodah* in the Beis HaMikdash.

Not to Say Thank You

A dissenting view is that of R' Tzvi Hirsch, the Lisker Rav.[5] *Sefer Darkei HaYashar* (p. 48), authored by one of his disciples, gives this description of the Rosh Hashanah davening in Liska: The *tefillos,* including the shofar-blowing, took no more than three hours in all. After the Kohanim finished *duchaning,* the Rav would bang loudly on the *bimah* as a signal that no one should say anything to the Kohanim until after all the *tekios* had been sounded.

---

3. Vol. 1, p. 348, authored by R' Michel Shurkin of Yerushalayim.
4. See chapter 35.
5. Author of the *Ach Pri Tevuah,* he was a close disciple of the Divrei Chaim of Sanz and the rebbi of R' Yeshayah of Kerestir.

Yasher Koach From the Beis Yosef

In *chutz laAretz*, where the Kohanim *duchan* only on Yom Tov, the custom is that when they finish, everyone says, "*Yasher koach, Kohanim*," but in Eretz Yisrael, where Bircas Kohanim is performed on a daily basis, this is not the *minhag*. The Strikover Rebbe (*Dibros Kodesh, Emor* 5763) explains that since the *Beis Yosef* states (128:44), "*Yasher kocham* to those who reside in Eretz Yisrael and in Egypt, who perform Bircas Kohanim every day," the Kohanim no longer need a *yasher koach* from the congregation — they have already received that *berachah* from the great *Beis Yosef*!

Hugging and Kissing the Kohanim

Rav Simchah HaKohen Kaplan, who served as the Rav of Tzfas for many years, related publicly on numerous occasions that he merited to *duchan* in the minyan of R' Chaim Ozer Grodzinski in Vilna several times on Yom Tov, and the joy on R' Chaim Ozer's face at this time was palpable. After davening, the usually reserved R' Chaim Ozer could not contain his excitement. He would hug and kiss R' Simchah and the other Kohanim, telling them that they had a great merit to bestow Hashem's blessing on the people of Vilna.[6]

Earning Their Love

R' Yisrael Zev Gustman, Rosh Yeshivah of Yeshivas Netzach Yisrael in Yerushalayim, insisted on having two Kohanim *duchan* every morning.[7] (During the Yamim Noraim, he would try to have ten Kohanim present.[8]) If two Kohanim were not present, he would apologize to the congregants, but he would not allow *Chazaras HaShatz* to proceed until two Kohanim were found.[9]

---

6. *MiToras Simchah*, p. 78.
7. *Otzroseihem Amalei, Nasso*, p. 144.
8. See *Yadav Emunah* regarding the halachic practices of R' Gustman. This is based on the opinion of *Ohr Zarua* (411) regarding the advantage of ten Kohanim. See R' Chaim Kanievsky's responsa (#155), where he disagrees with the need to have ten Kohanim. We did extensive research and did not find that any *poskim* or *gedolim* besides R' Gustman went out of their way to have ten Kohanim.
9. Many other *gedolim* did the same; see above, chapter 12.

Those Kohanim who did agree to *duchan*, out of respect for R' Gustman, earned his endless gratitude. He would make a great effort to show them appreciation and to shower them with love and respect. He considered this an actual obligation, as he explained: "The Kohanim are commanded *to bless His people, Yisrael, with love*. That means it is up to us to see to it that the Kohanim love us. Why should any Kohen love Yisrael Zev Gustman, if I never showed *him* any warmth or love?"[10]

The Highlight of His Day

R' Nachman Biderman (brother of R' Meilich) related to this author that the joy that his grandfather, R' Moshe Mordechai of Lelov, had before and after Bircas Kohanim was palpable. R' Moshe Mordechai mentioned many times that hearing Bircas Kohanim was the highlight of his day. Every day after Bircas Kohanim, he waited for *Kaddish* after *Shemoneh Esrei* to be completed, and before *Ashrei* he walked over and wished each one of the Kohanim an individual and heartfelt *yasher koach*.

---

10. *Orchos Chassidecha*, p. 262.

Chapter 10
Respect for the Mitzvah

Standing Up for the Kohanim

Yerushalmi and *Bartenura* (*Bikkurim* 3:3) state that there is a mitzvah to stand up for those who are on their way to perform a mitzvah, and for this reason, people would stand when farmers in Eretz Yisrael came to Yerushalayim with their *bikkurim* fruit. Likewise, the custom is to stand when a baby is brought into the room for a *bris milah*.

On the basis of this *Yerushalmi*, R' Dov Berish Weidenfeld, the Tchebiner Rav, would stand up for the Kohanim as they passed by him on their way to *duchan*.[1]

Clearing a Path

The current Rosh Yeshivah of Yeshivas Ponovezh, R' Eliezer HaKohen Kahaneman, related that his grandfather, the Ponovezher Rav, R' Yosef Shlomo HaKohen Kahaneman, used to daven at the early minyan in Yeshivas Sfas Emes whenever he visited Yerushalayim. The Beis Yisrael of Ger would also daven there many mornings. In preparation for Bircas Kohanim, the Ponovezher Rav would wash his hands at the sink in the back of the shul and leave his shoes there. As the Ponovezher Rav headed toward the front of the shul in his socks, the Gerrer Rebbe would personally go ahead of him to clear a path, and he did the same on the way back!

---

1. *Mishmar HaLevi, Bechoros* §10.

Pushing Away the Shoes

When R' Moshe Shmuel Shapira, the Rosh Yeshivah of Yeshivas Be'er Yaakov, traveled from Eretz Yisrael to London to fundraise for his yeshivah, he would often go after davening to the Sephardic shul, Knesset Yechezkel, in Golders Green in order to hear Bircas Kohanim.[2]

R' Dov Schon, a close student of R' Moshe Shmuel who learned in Be'er Yaakov for several years, added that R' Moshe Shmuel was scrupulous about complying with the ruling of the *Mishnah Berurah* (128:15) that the Kohanim should not leave their shoes out in the open when they go up to *duchan*, as this is not respectful to the shul. When he noticed that some shoes were left in an open area, he would use his foot to gently push them under a bench or *shtender* so they would not be exposed during Bircas Kohanim.

Gentle Rebuke

R' Simchah Zissel Broide, the Rosh Yeshivah of Yeshivas Chevron, once saw two *bachurim* talking to each other during Bircas Kohanim. After davening, he approached them and said, "Imagine if you were in the presence of the greatest *tzaddik* of our generation, and you had come to him for a *berachah*. Would you be chatting with your friend? And here you are, receiving a *berachah* directly from Hashem."

Years later, one of those *bachurim* remarked, "The rosh yeshivah's gentle rebuke made such a deep impression on me that I am sure I will never speak during Bircas Kohanim again."[3]

It happened several times during *bein hazmanim* that the local minyan near the Chevron Yeshivah in Yerushalayim's Givat Mordechai neighborhood did not have a Kohen in attendance. Since there was another minyan starting after his minyan, R' Simchah Zissel would wait for the second minyan so that he could hear Bircas Kohanim. When a *bachur* questioned if it was worth the long wait for the second minyan to reach Bircas Kohanim, R' Simchah Zissel

---

2. Heard from his son R' Dovid Yitzchak Shapira, the current Rosh Yeshivah of Yeshivas Be'er Yaakov, and his host in London, R' Yitzchak Heitner.
3. Heard from the current rosh yeshivah, R' Dovid Cohen.

looked at the *bachur* in surprise and said, "Of course it's worth waiting to get a *berachah* from the Kohanim."[4]

When he had to travel for extended periods to the Johns Hopkins Medical Center in Baltimore for treatment of a severe eye condition, he would go to a local Sephardic shul several times a week before his medical appointments to merit hearing Bircas Kohanim.[5]

---

4. *Nesich Mamleches HaTorah,* on the life of R' Simchah Zissel, by R' Shimon Yosef Meller, p. 363.
5. Ibid.

Chapter 11
The Chofetz Chaim

A Fulfillment of "So Shall You Bless"

A remarkable story is told[1] of R' Akiva HaKohen (who passed away in 5256/1496) and his wife, who were blessed with twelve sons and thirteen daughters. R' Akiva was a great Torah scholar and extremely affluent as well. Unfortunately, he was envied by a number of people, who vented their jealousy by slandering him and forcing him to move from his native city of Ofan, Hungary, to Prague. In Prague, he continued to thrive and opened a yeshivah, which spread Torah wisdom throughout the city. Twelve of his daughters married Kohanim, and one of them, named Yocheved, married R' Shabse Sheftel HaLevi Horowitz, grandfather of the *Shelah*. (One of his twelve sons, R' Yitzchak Katz, married the daughter of the Maharal of Prague and headed the *beis din* of Nikolsburg.)

When R' Akiva went to *duchan* with his twelve sons and twelve sons-in-law, twenty-five Kohanim in all, he proudly said, "I am now fulfilling the mitzvah of כֹּה תְבָרְכוּ אֶת בְּנֵי יִשְׂרָאֵל, *So shall you bless Bnei Yisrael,* because the *gematria* (numerical value) of *koh* is twenty-five." R' Akiva's son-in-law R' Shabse, the Levi in the family, washed the hands of his father-in-law and all twenty-four brothers-in-law.

1. Introduction to the Maharal's *Megillas Yuchasin*, p. 30. R' Shlomo Kanievsky related that his father, R' Chaim, would repeat this story many times at the Shabbos meal.

In a related incident, someone once came to the Chofetz Chaim complaining about his financial stress and about how difficult it was for him to support his large family.

"How many children do you have?" the Chofetz Chaim asked.

"Seven, *bli ayin hara*."

The Chofetz Chaim was not impressed. "That's what you call a large family?" he exclaimed. "I knew a man with twenty-three children who didn't complain one-tenth of how much you are complaining!"

The man with twenty-three children was R' Chaim HaKohen Dvortsky, also known as R' Chaim Herliner, who lived near Radin. Once, when the Chofetz Chaim went to *duchan* together with R' Chaim, who was accompanied by his many children and grandchildren, R' Chaim made the same comment: "This is a fulfillment of the *pasuk* כֹּה תְבָרְכוּ."[2]

The Voice of a Young Boy

When R' Yehudah Zev Segal, the Manchester Rosh Yeshivah, was still a *bachur*, he had the privilege of spending two weeks in Radin, from Erev Yom Kippur until after Succos, basking in the exalted presence of the Chofetz Chaim. He reported[3] that when the Chofetz Chaim recited Bircas Kohanim on Yom Tov, his voice was like that of a young boy. R' Segal explained this based on an insight that the Chofetz Chaim himself wrote: The reason we enjoy hearing the sweet, pure voice of children is that they have not yet corrupted their gift of speech by speaking *lashon hara* and the like. That would describe the Chofetz Chaim as well, who retained the purity of his youth even in his old age.

No Change in Pronunciation

R' Aharon Leib Shteinman shared the following conversation that took place between a man named R' Eliyahu Tuvia and the Chofetz Chaim, which he heard directly from R' Eliyahu Tuvia himself.

R' Eliyahu Tuvia once had the opportunity to sit next to the Chofetz Chaim on a train ride to Warsaw. The Chofetz Chaim was

2. *Meir Einei Yisrael,* vol. 6, p. 331.
3. Ibid., vol. 4, p. 491.

traveling there to oversee the printing of his *Mishnah Berurah*, and he would need to be in Warsaw over Shavuos. This gave rise to a question:

"Should I *duchan* with my Lithuanian pronunciation," wondered the Chofetz Chaim, "or perhaps I should use the Polish pronunciation that the Warsaw community is more familiar with?"

R' Eliyahu Tuvia responded by quoting a certain *sefer*, which asserted that the Polish pronunciation is incorrect and should be disregarded. The Chofetz Chaim brushed off that comment with a dismissive wave of his hand. Later, R' Eliyahu learned why: It turned out that the *sefer* he had quoted was written by a *maskil* (a member of the anti-religious "enlightenment" movement).

In the end, the Chofetz Chaim chose to use the Lithuanian pronunciation.[4]

The Chofetz Chaim's Qualifications

When the Chofetz Chaim was asked to deliver the opening remarks for the first Knessiah Gedolah, he began by saying, "Among those gathered here are a number of great sages and *tzaddikim*. How do I have the right to speak in front of such *gedolim*, let alone to be the first! The Torah says, וְלֹא תַעֲלֶה בְמַעֲלֹת עַל מִזְבְּחִי אֲשֶׁר לֹא תִגָּלֶה עֶרְוָתְךָ עָלָיו, *You shall not ascend My altar on steps, so that your nakedness will not be uncovered upon it* (*Shemos* 20:23). This teaches us that one should not try to assume too high a position, as that will cause all his flaws to be exposed. However, I take solace in the fact that I do have two advantages over others. Firstly, I am a Kohen, and secondly, I have reached old age, *baruch Hashem*. Neither of these is my own personal achievement, but they entitle me to be honored. That is the type of honor I am able to accept." With that, the Chofetz Chaim proceeded to bless the assembled guests with the verses of Bircas Kohanim.[5]

Similarly, when the Chofetz Chaim delivered his historic address to a gathering of three thousand women in the main shul of Vilna, in the winter of 5691/1931, he ended by opening the *aron kodesh*, and, with tears streaming down his face, he recited the verses of

4. *Ayeles HaShachar, Nasso*. For further discussion of the practical halachah, which follows this practice, see chapter 45.
5. *Meir Einei Yisrael* vol. 4, p. 491.

Bircas Kohanim in a trembling voice, finishing with a blessing for *parnassah*, good health, and peace.[6]

A Glimpse of the Chofetz Chaim

R' Yitzchok Yedidyah Frankel, Chief Rabbi of Tel Aviv and father-in-law of R' Yisrael Meir Lau, would often recall the one opportunity he had to see the Chofetz Chaim. He was a *bachur* at the time, studying in yeshivah in Warsaw:

> One day, the electrifying news came to town that the Chofetz Chaim had organized a major convention for all the leading rabbanim of Europe, to discuss some harsh rulings of the Polish government, such as forcing the yeshivos to teach the local language — and the Chofetz Chaim himself would be coming to Warsaw! The entire city was abuzz with excitement, and I was filled with a burning desire to see the great *tzaddik* up close.
>
> When the auspicious day arrived, the streets of Warsaw turned black from the massive crowds. Tens of thousands of Jews turned out to greet the *gadol hador*. The people were crammed together to the point where it was almost impossible to move, but I kept davening that I would be in the right spot to catch a glimpse of the Chofetz Chaim. Hashem answered my prayer, and the path opened directly in front of me. Right there, in front of my eyes, the world-famous *gadol* was approaching! Just as the Chofetz Chaim was about to pass me, so close that I could have reached out and touched him, I blurted out in a voice I did not recognize, "Rebbi, please give me a *berachah*!"
>
> The Chofetz Chaim paused, and said humbly, "Why don't *you* give *me* a *berachah* instead?"
>
> I was speechless; I could not believe my ears. At last, I found my voice again, and pleaded, "But Rebbi is a Kohen and I am only a Yisrael!"
>
> At that, a hint of a smile flitted across the Chofetz Chaim's face, and he did give me a *berachah*. I will never forget this experience as long as I live.[7]

---

6. Ibid., vol 2, p. 511.
7. Ibid., vol. 3, p. 756.

A Blessing for Children

R' Yaakov Gellis of Yerushalayim recounted the story of a certain Yid he knew, R' Avraham Shimon Lipshitz, who was the *shamash* in "Nathan's shul." R' Avraham Shimon had been married for twenty years and had yet to be blessed with children. He asked R' Avraham Yisrael Gellis, R' Yaakov's father, to write a letter to the Chofetz Chaim on his behalf, and to request a *berachah*. R' Gellis did so, and included five liras with the letter, as a *"pidyon nefesh."*

A few weeks went by, and finally a reply came. The Chofetz Chaim wrote: "I have received your letter. I am not in the habit of giving *berachos*, nor am I worthy of doing so. I also don't accept money, and I was planning to send it back to you. However, I can tell from your writing that you are a *talmid chacham*, and I do not wish to be disrespectful toward *talmidei chachamim*. Therefore, I gave your money to the yeshivah; the receipt is attached. As far as the *berachah* is concerned, I give you the *berachah* of a Kohen, which Hashem has empowered me to do. May the couple merit to have healthy children."

One year later, R' Avraham Shimon was holding his first child in his arms. After that, they had a number of other children as well, all of whom built beautiful families.[8]

"I am Not a Rebbe!"

In 5671/1911, the Chofetz Chaim traveled to the city of Pietrekov, to arrange the printing of one of his *sefarim*. The print shop was located near the Gerrer *shtiebel*, and that is where he stopped in to daven Minchah and Maariv. In his characteristic humble manner, the Chofetz Chaim took a seat at the back of the shul, trying to avoid attention. This plan did not succeed, however, as by that time, he had already achieved worldwide renown, and it wasn't long before some people recognized him and began spreading the word that the short, ordinary-looking Yid in the back of the shul was none other than the venerable *gadol hador*. As soon as he finished davening, the entire congregation formed a line before him, hoping to get a *berachah*.

8. Ibid., vol. 3, p. 830.

The Chofetz Chaim looked on helplessly and said, "I'm not a Rebbe! What do you all want from me?"

One of the prominent members of the shul stepped forward and said, "The rav is a Kohen. Please — at least bless us with the blessing of a Kohen!"

When the Chofetz Chaim heard that, he acquiesced, giving each individual a blessing with the words of Bircas Kohanim.[9]

No Razor

R' Yekusiel Zalman HaLevi Levitas, the head of the Lonkova *beis din* in Poland, recounted that when he was learning in yeshivah in Vilna (in approximately the year 5660/1900), the Chofetz Chaim once spent a few days in the city to oversee the printing of his *sefarim,* and he davened in the same shul as R' Yekusiel Zalman.

R' Yekusiel Zalman writes, in an essay, that he noticed that the Chofetz Chaim was looking intently at a certain young man who was a regular in the shul. He asked who that young man was, and what he did for a living. Upon finding out that he was a barber, the Chofetz Chaim approached him and said, "I am sure that you close on Shabbos, but tell me — what do you do when a Jewish man comes into your shop and asks to be shaved with a razor?"

The embarrassed fellow began defending himself, "Rebbi," he said, "you must understand that I have young children at home who depend on me for their sustenance. If I refuse to serve the customers, I won't have even a dry crust of bread to feed my children!"

The Chofetz Chaim blessed the young barber with the words of Bircas Kohanim. The barber was humbled, and he made a firm commitment to never again shave a Jewish customer with a razor, but to use only a clipper. With that, the Chofetz Chaim gave him another *berachah* for success in business. It was not long afterward that the *berachah* was fulfilled, and the man became extremely successful and wealthy.[10]

---

9. Ibid., vol. 6, p. 494.
10. Ibid., vol. 3, p. 867.

I Cannot Stop!

R′ Dovid Teitz spent a great deal of time in the Chofetz Chaim's house during the last year of the *tzaddik*'s life. Shavuos marked the last time the Chofetz Chaim was able to perform Bircas Kohanim, as he passed away several months later, on 24 Elul 5693 (September 15, 1933). R′ Teitz related that he noticed that when the Chofetz Chaim went up to *duchan* that Shavuos, he did not lower his hands after finishing the *berachah*. Notwithstanding his advanced age, he kept his hands raised long after the other Kohanim, until he was explicitly told to put them down. When R′ Teitz asked the family about this unusual practice, they explained that the Chofetz Chaim, whose love for Klal Yisrael knew no bounds, had said many times, "**When I am blessing the Jewish people, I cannot stop!**"[11]

11. Ibid., vol. 6, p. 320.

Chapter 12
The Brisker Rav

A Blessing Worth Waiting For

R' Yitzchak Zev HaLevi Soloveitchik, the Brisker Rav, escaped during World War II to Eretz Yisrael, where he would daven with a minyan in his house. It happened several times during *Chazaras HaShatz* that the group suddenly realized that one of the two Kohanim who davened there regularly was not present. The Brisker Rav stopped the chazzan just before the *berachah* of *Retzei*, and sent someone to the Zichron Moshe shul to bring back an additional Kohen.[1] More than half an hour passed, with everyone waiting, and someone politely told the Brisker Rav that this didn't seem right. First of all, the halachah is that if one interrupts his *Shemoneh Esrei* for long enough to finish the entire *tefillah*, he must start over from the beginning. Besides, what of *tircha d'tzibbura* (inconveniencing the congregation unnecessarily)?

After davening, the Brisker Rav responded to both complaints. He said, "With regard to interrupting the *tefillah*, *Rema* (65:1) writes that the requirement to start over from the beginning applies only to someone who was forced to stop davening and was unable to continue. If someone decided on his own to pause for an extended time, he is permitted to continue from where he left off.

"As far as *tircha d'tzibbura* is concerned, think of it this way:

1. For a discussion of whether one Kohen suffices, see chapter 30.

There are many people who journey for days to receive a *berachah* from their Rebbe, even if they have to travel a great distance. These people are not even sure they will get a chance to meet with the Rebbe. Even if they do get an audience, they don't know if he will agree to give them the *berachah* that they seek. And even if they do get the *berachah*, they cannot be certain that it will come to fruition. Nevertheless, they make the trip on the chance that they will be blessed.

"Here, Hakadosh Baruch Hu Himself gives the Kohanim the power to bless the Jewish people, as the *pasuk* explicitly states, *Let them place My name upon Bnei Yisrael, and I shall bless them* (*Bamidbar* 6:27). You are *guaranteed* to receive Hashem's *berachah*!"

The Brisker Rav concluded, "That is why Bircas Kohanim is so important to me. It is worth waiting even longer than half an hour for this blessing."[2]

His son-in-law R' Yechiel Michel Feinstein later commented that when the Brisker Rav said that it was worth waiting to receive a *berachah* from a Kohen, he was merely attempting to appease the congregation. In reality, he delayed the *tefillah* for the simple reason that there is a mitzvah for the Kohanim to bless the people — not because of a personal desire to receive a *berachah*.[3]

Similar stories are told of other *gedolim* as well. R' Yisrael Zev Gustman would have the chazzan pause until two Kohanim were present (see chapter 9). Likewise, R' Hillel Kolodetsky related that when the Chevron Yeshivah in Yerushalayim did not have two Kohanim (which happened sometimes on Chol HaMoed or during *bein hazmanim*), R' Yechezkel Sarna, the rosh yeshivah, would stop the davening in the middle of *Chazaras HaShatz* until two Kohanim were present. Similarly, R' Simcha Scheinberg related that

2. R' Avraham Erlanger, as quoted in *Uvdos V'Hanhagos L'Beis Brisk* (vol. 3, p. 170). This author also heard from R' Chaim Kanievsky's close *talmid* R' Moshe Smotni that he was once present at the home of the Brisker Rav during *Chazaras HaShatz* when the Rav noticed that there was only one Kohen present, so he had the chazzan pause before *Retzei* for approximately twenty minutes until a second Kohen came. *Mishnah Berurah* (128:28) rules that it is permitted to pause before *Retzei* so that the Kohanim can come into shul. See R' Chaim Kanievsky's responsa (#115), where he writes that it is permitted for the chazzan to pause during *Chazaras HaShatz* and wait for a second Kohen to come.

3. *Uvdos V'Hanhagos L'Beis Brisk*, vol. 2, p. 45.

several times, during *bein hazmanim,* when there was only one Kohen present in Yeshivah Torah Ore, his father, R' Chaim Pinchas, stopped the chazzan during *Chazaras HaShatz* until a second Kohen arrived.

You Should Have Waited!

Several times, the Brisker Rav mentioned that he had learned how important Bircas Kohanim is from an incident that happened in his youth. His father, R' Chaim Brisker, once sent the young Yitzchak Zev to summon a particular individual, as he had a pressing matter to discuss with him. Understanding the urgency of the situation, the boy hurried to fulfill his father's instructions. When he returned home, and R' Chaim heard that he had called the person out of shul before Bircas Kohanim, R' Chaim scolded him, "How could you have deprived both him and yourself of such a lofty blessing, directly from Hashem? Although the matter was important, you should have waited!"[4]

Not Karaim

Someone who did not daven in the minyan of the Brisker Rav once told him that he felt bad that there had been only one Kohen at that morning's Shacharis, not two. After all, he said, according to the opinion of some Rishonim, *min haTorah* two Kohanim are required, and having one Kohen *duchan* is merely a *mitzvah d'Rabbanan.*[5]

Although the Brisker Rav himself paused *Chazaras HaShatz* several times so that two Kohanim would be present, he immediately retorted, "We are not *Karaim*!" (The *Karaim* were a sect that did not accept *mitzvos d'Rabbanan*). Even according to the opinion that one Kohen *duchaning* is a Rabbinic mitzvah, the magnitude of such a great *berachah* from Hashem should not be minimized.[6]

It is noteworthy that the Brisker Rav emphasizes, in his *chiddushim* (*Menachos* 44b), that according to *Rambam,* even with one Kohen, Bircas Kohanim is a mitzvah *min haTorah* and not a *d'Rabbanan.*

---

4. *HaRav MiBrisk,* vol. 4, p. 461, by R' Shimon Yosef Meller.
5. See chapter 30.
6. *HaRav MiBrisk,* vol. 2, p. 384.

Showing Appreciation

The mitzvah of Bircas Kohanim was very dear to the Brisker Rav. For that reason, he insisted, and made great efforts, to receive the *berachah* each day, and to ensure that there would be Kohanim present at the minyan in his house. At times, he would receive a large donation, and out of his love for the mitzvah he would use a generous portion of it to pay the Kohanim who came to daven in his house.[7]

The Mitzvah to Summon the Kohanim

R' Michel Feinstein related that the Brisker Rav was the one who called out "Kohanim" before Bircas Kohanim, since it is a special mitzvah to summon the Kohanim to *duchan*, as we derive from the *pasuk* אָמוֹר לָהֶם, *say to them* (*Bamidbar* 6:23).[8] His son R' Dovid continued this practice in his yeshivah. Currently, the Rav's grandson, R' Avraham Yehoshua Soloveitchik, calls out "Kohanim" before the daily Bircas Kohanim in his yeshivah.

Careful With Every Word

R' Shalom Schwadron, the "Maggid" of Yerushalayim, who was a Kohen, shared the following exchange that he personally had with the Brisker Rav:

One night, when the Brisker Rav was not feeling well, I was taking leave of him and I wished him *refuah sheleimah*. The Rav looked at me in surprise and asked, "Can one say Bircas Kohanim at night?" I answered that I was not offering a *berachah* as a Kohen, but merely in fulfillment of the *pasuk*, "*Tov ayin hu yevarech* (*one with a good eye will bless*)."

The Rav countered, "Where is there such a *pasuk*?"

Of course, he was correct. The *pasuk* (*Mishlei* 22:9) actually says, *Tov ayin hu* ***yevorach*** (*one with a good eye will* ***be blessed***), not *yevarech*. (My version of the *pasuk* is based on the Gemara, *Sotah* 38b.)[9]

---

7. Ibid., p. 459. Perhaps he gave this out of gratitude, rather than as payment for their Bircas Kohanim. (See R' Chaim Kanievsky's responsa #441.)
8. Ibid., vol. 4, p. 462. For a discussion of who should announce "Kohanim," see chapter 31.
9. *Uvdos V'Hanhagos L'Beis Brisk*, vol. 3, p. 237.

Chapter 13
The Story of Dr. Alvin Radkowsky

Dr. Avraham Yitzchak HaKohen (Alvin) Radkowsky was born in Elizabeth, New Jersey, in 1915, and lived for a number of years in Washington, D.C. Later, he moved to Silver Spring, Maryland, a suburb of Washington, where he was an active presence in the local shul and was involved in building the first *mikveh* in the area. Blessed with a brilliant mind and great power of concentration, he merited to study and complete the entire *Shas* in depth at least four times.

Dr. Alvin was a nuclear physicist and the chief scientist at the U.S. Navy Nuclear Propulsion Division for many years. His work in the 1950s led to major advances in nuclear-powered ship technology and civilian use of nuclear power. USS *Nautilus* (SSN-571) was the world's first operational nuclear-powered submarine, and the first submarine to complete a submerged transit of the North Pole, on August 3, 1958. Dr. Alvin worked on the "Nautilus Project" together with Admiral Hyman Rikover (also a Jew).

Dr. Alvin and his wife, Annette (Chanah), had one daughter, Gila,[1] and no sons. He always said that his biggest enjoyment in life was to go up to the *duchan* and bless the Jewish people. However, living outside Eretz Yisrael, he had the opportunity to fulfill this mitzvah only on Yom Tov. His dream was to move to the Holy Land, where he would be able to *duchan* every day. So it was that in 1972,

1. Mrs. Gila Chukat, who currently resides in Petach Tikvah, Israel. She graciously shared some information about her father with the author.

when he reached the earliest permitted retirement age (57), the family moved to Eretz Yisrael, settling in the Ramat Chen neighborhood of Ramat Gan.

A short time after settling there, he heard about the legendary Steipler Gaon, and went with a cousin of his to visit the great sage. Dr. Alvin was immediately captivated by the Steipler, and also by the integrity of the congregation in the local Lederman shul. He told the *gabbai* of the Lederman shul, R' Moshe Cohen, that since he had no sons, he felt that the privilege of being a Kohen would end with himself, and he therefore wanted to maximize his opportunity to recite Bircas Kohanim. Every Shabbos, he would walk an hour each way to and from the Lederman shul, just so he could experience the beautiful Shabbos davening there, and, of course, bless the congregants with Bircas Kohanim.

The Steipler took a liking to Dr. Alvin, and would refer to him as the *chacham olami*[2] (world-famous intellectual). Dr. Alvin later developed a warm relationship with R' Chaim Kanievsky and other illustrious Lederman shul members. He joined most of the *siyumim* in the shul, and would try to daven there as often as he could.

Dr. Alvin continued his career as a scientist after moving to Eretz Yisrael. He taught nuclear engineering at Tel Aviv University (1972-1994) and Ben Gurion University in Beer Sheva (1994-2002). In 1992, Dr. Alvin invented a new type of nuclear fuel called thorium, and started the Thorium Power Company. Thorium-fueled reactors allow nations the capability to generate energy while preventing them from using spent fuels to produce nuclear weapons.

It is speculated that Dr. Alvin was the nuclear scientist behind Israel's naval nuclear capability, and that he used his proximity to Ben Gurion University to assist Israel in its development of nuclear weapons, which was done with the consent of President Ronald Regan. It is impossible to confirm this, of course, as Israel, like most countries that have nuclear capabilities, keeps such information confidential. The fact that Ben Gurion University is not far from Israel's nuclear reactor in Dimona bolsters the postulation. Although Dr. Alvin "belonged" to the university and taught nuclear engineering there, some have conjectured that most of his time

---

2. See *Beis Imi*, authored by R' Chaim Kanievsky's daughter, Rebbetzin Ruti Tzivyon, ch. 18.

was dedicated to his research in Dimona, where he was heavily involved in assisting Israel to develop nuclear submarines.

Dr. Alvin's Innovation in the Lederman Shul

During the many times he *duchaned* at the Lederman shul, it disturbed him to see that some of the Kohanim left their shoes on the floor in a disorderly fashion and on public display.[3] After discussing this with the Steipler, Dr. Alvin came up with an innovation (perhaps not as ground-breaking as his nuclear patents, but an innovation nonetheless). He paid for a craftsman to build cubicles near the sinks outside the sanctuary, and also to install a carpet from the washing sinks until the *aron kodesh*, so that the Kohanim could keep their shoes in the cubicles and walk to the front of the shul on the carpet, without getting their socks dusty. The cubicles and carpet remained in the Lederman shul until after Dr. Alvin passed away in 5762/2002.[4]

Is a Kohen Obligated to Move to Eretz Yisrael to Duchan?

Rav Yitzchak Zilberstein discusses Dr. Alvin in his *teshuvos* (*Chashukei Chemed, Pesachim* 3b):

> **Q:** The brilliant scholar R' Avraham Yitzchak HaKohen Radkowsky moved from the United States to Eretz Yisrael to be able to recite Bircas Kohanim every day, and not just on Yom Tov. At the time he made this decision, there was a risk that he might lose his source of livelihood — his position as a nuclear scientist doing research for the U.S. government. Nevertheless, he chose to make the move, and Hashem blessed him with the *berachos* that are promised to Kohanim, and he was able to continue his successful career in his new home.
>
> Is a Kohen indeed obligated to move to Eretz Yisrael and endanger his *parnassah* for this purpose?

---

3. See *Mishnah Berurah* 128:15, which states that the shoes of the Kohanim should be placed in an inconspicuous place due to *kavod beis hamidrash*.
4. Heard from R' Chaim Kanievsky's son-in-law R' Yehoshua Tzivyon.

A: *Magen Avraham* (*O.C.* 13:8) rules that a person is not obligated to move to a different city in order to fulfill the mitzvah of *tzitzis*. Logic would seem to dictate that the same applies to moving to Eretz Yisrael in order to perform mitzvos, especially when there is a risk of losing one's livelihood. However, if one does move, he fulfills the mitzvah of וְיָרֵאתָ מֵאֱלֹהֶיךָ, *you shall fear your G-d* (*Vayikra* 25:17), as *Biur Halachah* implies.[5] Additionally, he fulfills the words of *Chayei Adam*, who writes (68:14): "One must run and pursue mitzvos, as Scripture states: וְנֵדְעָה נִרְדְּפָה לָדַעַת אֶת ה׳, *Let us know, let us strive to know Hashem* (*Hoshea* 6:3), and דֶּרֶךְ מִצְוֹתֶיךָ אָרוּץ, *I will run in the way of Your commandments"* (*Tehillim* 119:32).

One should make great efforts to fulfill mitzvos, and eagerly anticipate and aspire for such opportunities. This can be learned from the words וּשְׁמַרְתֶּם לַעֲשֹׂתָם, *you shall be careful to perform them* (*Devarim* 5:1). The word וּשְׁמַרְתֶּם can also connote anticipation (see *Bereishis* 37:11); thus, the Torah is instructing us to look forward to the moment that we will be able to perform a mitzvah, and this is also a fulfillment of the mitzvah to love Hashem.

5. Where he discusses Bircas Kohanim in 128:2, s.v. *Oh im amru.*

Part 3:

Bircas Kohanim Around the World

Chapter 14
Daily Bircas Kohanim in Eretz Yisrael and Chutz LaAretz

In chapter 5, we presented many halachic and Kabbalistic sources that emphasize that Bircas Kohanim is a daily mitzvah, even in our times. Indeed, Sephardic Jews throughout the world continue to perform Bircas Kohanim every day, but Ashkenazic Jews perform the mitzvah of daily Bircas Kohanim only in Eretz Yisrael.[1]

It is important to stress that although in Eretz Yisrael it has always been and remains the custom of Ashkenazim to perform Bircas Kohanim daily, for Ashkenazim in the Diaspora it is *prohibited* to perform Bircas Kohanim in an Ashkenazic shul at any time other than on Yom Tov. Most Ashkenazic communities in the Diaspora perform Bircas Kohanim on only thirteen days of the year — on the two days of Rosh Hashanah, on Yom Kippur, on the first two days of Succos, on Shemini Atzeres, on Simchas Torah,[2] on the first two and last two days of Pesach, and on the two days of Shavuos. Some chassidic communities in *chutz laAretz* have the custom to also perform Bircas Kohanim on Hoshana Rabbah and Shabbos Chol HaMoed as well, as we will discuss later (see chapter 40).

Many Rishonim and Acharonim offer possible reasons why Ashkenazim outside Eretz Yisrael do not perform this mitzvah daily,

---

1. With the exception of some chassidic communities in Tzfas, Teveriah, and Haifa who perform Bircas Kohanim only in Mussaf of Shabbos, Rosh Chodesh, and Yom Tov. See chapter 18 for a comprehensive discussion of this practice.
2. See chapter 40 regarding Simchas Torah.

but some Acharonim write that the reasons are not fully understood. Historically, there have been several unsuccessful attempts to reinstate daily Bircas Kohanim among Ashkenazic communities in *chutz laAretz,* notably by the Vilna Gaon, R' Chaim of Volozhin, and the *Baal HaTanya,* among others. *Aruch HaShulchan* writes that their lack of success seems to indicate that Hashem is preventing us from performing daily Bircas Kohanim outside of Eretz Yisrael, as we will see further.

Minhag Eretz Yisrael

In Eretz Yisrael, the custom of both Ashkenazim and Sephardim has always been to perform Bircas Kohanim every day during Shacharis, and during Mussaf on days when it is recited. In addition, Bircas Kohanim is performed during Minchah on fast days and during Neilah on Yom Kippur. This custom is mentioned by *Beis Yosef* (128:44) and *Taz* (128:37).[3] R' Yaakov Emden also writes, in his *Siddur* (*Hilchos Nesias Kapayim*), "How good and pleasant is the custom in Eretz Yisrael that the Kohanim *duchan* every day." *Mishnah Berurah* echoes this praise (128:164): "The practice in Eretz Yisrael and throughout Egypt is to perform Bircas Kohanim every day, and the *poskim* have lauded their custom." Likewise, *Aruch HaShulchan* (128:164) mentions that the custom in Eretz Yisrael and Egypt is to *duchan* daily, and adds that this is the custom of the entire continent of Asia.

Ashkenazim Outside Eretz Yisrael Who Wish to Duchan

Ashkenazi Jews outside Eretz Yisrael who wish to hear or perform Bircas Kohanim daily should be aware of the following halachos:

1. An Ashkenazi Jew who lives outside Eretz Yisrael may not perform Bircas Kohanim in an Ashkenazic congregation, except on Yom Tov, under any circumstances. This applies even to a new Ashkenazic community that is now being

3. The *Taz,* R' Dovid HaLevi Segal (1586-1667), passed away fifty-three years before the birth of the Vilna Gaon.

established in a previously uninhabited location; they may not deviate from the accepted custom. (See Responsa of R' Chaim Kanievsky #546.)

2. It is permitted for an Ashkenazi Levi or Yisrael who resides in *chutz laAretz* or is visiting from Eretz Yisrael to attend a Sephardic minyan for the express purpose of hearing Bircas Kohanim. According to some opinions, including that of R' Chaim Kanievsky, an Ashkenazi Kohen who resides outside Eretz Yisrael is permitted to attend a Sephardic shul every day for the purpose of *duchaning* in a Sephardic minyan. (See Responsa of R' Chaim Kanievsky #532-541; see also chapter 17.)
3. If a group of Ashkenazi Jews living in Eretz Yisrael form a temporary minyan outside Eretz Yisrael, and there are no other people in the minyan, they are permitted to perform Bircas Kohanim, since that is their custom when they are at home in Eretz Yisrael.[4]
4. According to some opinions, if an Ashkenazic minyan in *chutz laAretz* is composed primarily of permanent residents of Eretz Yisrael, *duchaning* is permitted. This is done in the city of Uman, Ukraine, all year round. (See below.)

Reasons for the Ashkenazic Custom

Considering the many authoritative sources we have quoted in the previous chapter describing Bircas Kohanim as a daily mitzvah even in our time, the Ashkenazic custom in the Diaspora to *duchan* only on Yom Tov requires explanation. A number of reasons are given, but, as we will see, they are all disputed by major halachic authorities.

Maharil, one of the later Rishonim, who passed away in 1427, gives this explanation[5]: "I heard from my esteemed father-in-law [R' Moshe Neumark], who was himself a Kohen, that it is because Kohanim have accepted upon themselves the custom to immerse in a mikveh before *duchaning,* a custom that is mentioned in *Hagahos*

4. See *Orchos Rabbeinu,* vol. 1, p. 67, which records that this was the view of the Steipler Gaon. His son, R' Chaim Kanievsky, rules similarly; see Responsa #546.
5. *She'eilos U'Teshuvos Maharil* (*Chadashos*) #21.

Maimoniyos. At times, it is difficult for a Kohen to immerse, especially in the cold weather in the winter, and the result is that he will be embarrassed by the fact that he is unable to *duchan.* And if he does go to immerse, that can cause him some embarrassment as well."

Maharil adds: "Another possible reason is that it takes a few minutes to perform the mitzvah, and many people cannot afford to take that time away from their work. Additionally, there is some concern about the reaction of non-Jews who see or hear about this ritual. In fact, I have seen places where they do not allow any non-Jew to be present when Bircas Kohanim is performed."

R' Yosef Karo (*Beis Yosef* (128:37) presents the opinion of *Maharil,* as quoted by *Sefer Agur* (*siman* 176), and objects: "*Maharil* has labored to justify the custom of his locale, but the reasons that he offers are inadequate. The explanation that it is due to a stringency that the Kohanim have taken upon themselves, to immerse, is illogical, for it is a stringency that results in a leniency; it dispenses with a mitzvah that is stated clearly in the Torah because of a stringency that is not stated anywhere! How can that be a justification to neglect three positive commandments every day? Granted, the Kohanim do not transgress any sin as long as they were not called up, but it is surely more desirable to fulfill three commandments each day than to immerse oneself, which is not a requirement at all! And so, ***yasher kocham* of those who live in Eretz Yisrael and in Egypt, who do *duchan* every day and do *not* immerse themselves!"**

Taz (ibid.) quotes *Beis Yosef* and adds: "If the Kohanim are concerned about *tumah,* they should have immersed themselves beforehand. And what about those who live in Eretz Yisrael and Egypt, who *duchan* every day — are they expected to be in a state of purity forever? Thus, it seems clear that they [the Kohanim who do not *duchan* daily] have no legitimate reason for their practice; one must surely not neglect this mitzvah for a stringency that has no basis in halachah."

Non-Jews at Bircas Kohanim

One of the reasons given for not performing daily Bircas Kohanim outside of Eretz Yisrael is that it was common for non-Jews to be present in the shul. *Maharil,* cited above, brings this as the third reason why Bircas Kohanim was not done in his locale (in addition to the issues of immersion and people losing time from work). The idea that a non-Jew should not be present during Bircas Kohanim is found in *Shulchan Aruch* (55:20), which states as follows: "If there is a minyan of men in one place, saying *Kaddish* or *Kedushah*, a person who is in a different location but is able to hear the *Kaddish* is permitted to respond. However, some say that this is allowed only if there is no foul matter, or a non-Jew, between him and the minyan."

In response to a question as to whether it is permissible to *duchan* when a non-Jew is present, *Chida* writes (*Shiurei Berachah*, beginning of *siman* 128): "Reciting Bircas Kohanim is an integral part of the prayers, and the Kohanim must not withhold their blessing from the Jewish people, even if a non-Jew is in the synagogue."

Elsewhere, he writes (*She'eilos U'Teshuvos Yosef Ometz, siman* 70): "If this is the reason for the custom not to perform Bircas Kohanim every day — that is, out of concern that there may be a non-Jew standing between the Kohanim and some members of the congregation, preventing them from responding amen — it is not an adequate reason, because *Beis Dovid*[6] states that the halachah of an intervening non-Jew applies only when the person responding to *Kaddish* is in a different room (or building) than the minyan he is responding with. In the case of Bircas Kohanim, where everyone is in the same room, the presence of a non-Jew has no effect, and it is not a reason to forego the mitzvah. If the argument is that non-Jews will see how Bircas Kohanim is performed and they will mock our practices, that is also not a consideration. We certainly must not abandon a Torah commandment, which is an essential part of our prayers, just to avoid the mockery of fools; this is self-evident."

Likewise, R' Chaim Kanievsky (Responsa #484-486) writes that even if a non-Jew is present in the shul, it is permitted to perform Bircas Kohanim.

Burdening the Congregation

Kol Bo (*siman* 125) and *Orchos Chaim* of R' Aharon of Lunil (*Hilchos Bircas Kohanim*) state that nowadays the custom is not to perform Bircas Kohanim daily; it is done only on Shabbos and Yom

6. *Siman* 32. Authored by R' Yosef Dovid of Salonica, Greece (1660-1736).

Tov. (Note that they include Shabbos.) They suggest that perhaps this is to avoid burdening the congregation (*tircha d'tzibbura*).

The Ashkenazic Practice, Codified in Halachah

Rema writes in his commentary to *Tur* (*Darkei Moshe* 128:21): "In my opinion, the reason offered for the custom not to *duchan* [namely, the requirement of immersion in a mikveh] is only secondary. The primary reason is so that people will not lose time from work, for in our countries, here in the Diaspora, the Kohanim and the rest of the congregation are stressed with the burden of making a living, and most people do not earn enough to provide their families with more than the bread that they need for their day-to-day survival. As a result, they are not in a state of joy on a day that they must go to work, and even on Shabbos,[7] their minds are distracted, thinking about all that transpired during the past week, and worrying about the week to come. The only time people have a true sense of *simchah* is on Yom Tov, for on Yom Tov the Torah commands us, *You shall rejoice on your festival*."

In his commentary on *Shulchan Aruch* (128:44), *Rema* writes, regarding *Shulchan Aruch*'s ruling that Bircas Kohanim is recited daily: "The custom in all these countries [where Ashkenazim live] is that Bircas Kohanim is performed only on Yom Tov, because at that time [the Kohanim] are enveloped by the joy of the Yom Tov, and are in a proper state of mind to bless the Jewish people. That is not the case on other days. Even on Shabbos, people are preoccupied, thinking about their livelihood and worrying about not being able to work that day. Even on Yom Tov, we *duchan* only during Mussaf, when people are about to leave shul and revel in the joy of Yom Tov."

Levush (ibid.) gives the same explanation as *Rema*. He writes: "When a person is not in a state of joy, he cannot *duchan*, and

7. *Maamar Mordechai*, by R' Mordechai Carmi (1749-1825) — a work that is frequently quoted in *Mishnah Berurah* — points out (128:45) that although *Orchos Chaim* of R' Aharon of Lunil and *Kol Bo* state that Bircas Kohanim was switched to only **Shabbos** and Yom Tov so as not to burden the congregation, *Rema* writes that Bircas Kohanim is not done on Shabbos, which is a more stringent position.

for that reason, it has become the widespread custom in all these countries not to perform Bircas Kohanim on a daily basis, even though, according to strict halachah, it should be done every day."

Lack of Immersion: Not a Reason to Refrain From Duchaning

It is worth noting that *Levush* does not mention *Maharil*'s concern regarding the requirement of the Kohanim to immerse in a mikveh before *duchaning*. Indeed, *Levush* (*Hilchos Krias Shema, siman* 88) clearly rules that immersion is not required today before Torah study, *tefillah*, or *Krias Shema*.

In fact, the *poskim* rule that a Kohen who did not immerse should nevertheless perform Bircas Kohanim. *Leket Yosher*, written by a disciple of *Terumas HaDeshen*, states (*Hilchos Bircas Kohanim*) that a Kohen who wishes to *duchan* is not required to refrain from marital relations the night before even if he will not be able to immerse in a mikveh before Bircas Kohanim. (This echoes the above ruling of *Beis Yosef*.)

R' Yaakov Emden addresses the issue of immersion before Bircas Kohanim, writing, in *Mor U'Ketziah*[8]: "It is very difficult to understand the reasoning behind this explanation. Granted, there is a widespread custom to immerse before a Yom Tov even nowadays, but there is no halachic source for doing so, for the custom was in effect only during the time of our Sages, when they still had the *parah adumah*, which allowed people to be purified from corpse-*tumah* and thereby be able to eat all their food in a state of *taharah* during the course of the Yom Tov. (Even those who did not eat all their food *b'taharah* all year were scrupulous about the matter during the Three Festivals.)

"Today, however, when we have no means of becoming *tahor*, immersing oneself does not accomplish that objective, and there is no more reason to do it on Yom Tov than at any other time. Therefore, it is obvious that the absence of immersion was certainly not the reason for canceling Bircas Kohanim."

8. *Siman* 128. Also printed in the *Siddur* of R' Yaakov Emden, *Hilchos Nesias Kapayim*.

Chayei Adam (32:11) also voices strong objection to the practice of choosing between Bircas Kohanim and immersion. He writes: "Although there are Kohanim who avoid performing Bircas Kohanim because they do not wish to neglect their marital obligations, and they believe that one may not *duchan* afterward until he immerses himself, it is not a sufficient reason to override a positive Torah commandment. It is better to *duchan* without immersing than not to *duchan* at all. Certainly, the notion that a Kohen who wishes to *duchan* is strictly forbidden to engage in marital relations causes one to transgress other sins, and it is a mistake, for there is no such prohibition at all; it is merely an erroneous stringency."

Similarly, *Mishnah Berurah* (128:165) states clearly that even if a Kohen didn't immerse (which he should do, *l'chatchilah*), he should still *duchan*.

R' Chaim Kanievsky also writes (see Responsa #169-171) that even if a Kohen did not immerse, it is permitted for him to ascend to the *duchan*.

Uncertain Lineage

R' Ephraim Zalman Margolis (1760-1828) writes, in *She'eilos U'Teshuvos Beis Ephraim* (O.C. 6): "The custom that we have today, which is to *duchan* only on Yom Tov — and, in some places, every Shabbos as well[9] — **dates back more than five hundred years**, as we find in *Tashbetz Kattan*, which was written by a student of *Maharam* of Rothenburg, the rebbi of the Rosh. The custom was established by scrupulous Torah authorities and was practiced in the presence of the greatest of the early *poskim*, such as *Maharam of Rothenburg* and his student, the *Tashbetz*; *Kol Bo*; *Maharil*; *Agur*; *Rema*; *Levush*; *Taz*; and *Magen Avraham*, as well as the leaders of every generation to this day." (*Beis Ephraim* also notes that the custom in Eretz Yisrael has always been to perform Bircas Kohanim daily.)

Beis Ephraim cites the aforementioned, widely accepted reasons for the Ashkenazic custom of reciting Bircas Kohanim in the Diaspora only during the festivals, and then adds an explanation of his own, which many do not agree with. He points out that Kohanim in our times can no longer trace their direct lineage back to Aharon

9. *Beis Ephraim* quotes the view of *Kol Bo* and R' Aharon of Lunil cited earlier.

HaKohen, and therefore there is a possibility that some, or many of them, are not Kohanim at all.

Opposition to Beis Ephraim

Maharit[10] rules, however, that "anyone who comes from a family that has a *chazakah* that they are Kohanim (and there is no reason to doubt their tradition), is, in my opinion, to be considered an authentic Kohen with regard to all halachos, even in our times, and even with regard to Torah laws."

Even *Rema*, who codified that Kohanim in *chutz laAretz* perform Bircas Kohanim only on Yom Tov, writes clearly (*Even HaEzer* 3:1) that Kohanim today have an unequivocal *chazakah* for Bircas Kohanim and for other matters; the only exception is that until the arrival of Mashiach we do not give the priestly gift of *terumah* to Kohanim.

Furthermore, *Pri Megadim* states (128:37, in *Mishbetzos Zahav*) that if a Kohen refuses to *duchan*, *beis din* has the right to force him to do so, even by physically beating him if necessary. If he continues refusing until it is already too late to *duchan*, he is to be punished with lashes. Clearly, then, *Pri Megadim*'s understanding is that those who have a tradition that they are Kohanim are assumed to be authentic Kohanim even in our times; if there were any doubt, we would not have a right to subject them to punishment.

Chasam Sofer held *Beis Ephraim* in the highest esteem, and considered him a leading halachic authority.[11] Yet he disagreed with *Beis Ephraim*'s explanation that Kohanim today no longer have a presumption of priestly lineage, as he writes to his father-in-law, R' Akiva Eiger (*She'eilos U'Teshuvos Chasam Sofer, Y.D.* 236), that the *chazakah* of Kohanim even in today's times is so strong that when Mashiach comes, all Kohanim will immediately be able to offer *korbanos* in the Beis HaMikdash.

My saintly ancestor, the Divrei Chaim of Sanz, writes unequivocally (*She'eilos U'Teshuvos Even HaEzer,* vol. 1. #10) that Kohanim even in today's times have a clear *chazakah*; he quotes the same from his father-in-law, R' Baruch Frankel.

---

10. R' Yosef of Trani (1568-1639), *She'eilos U'Teshuvos Maharit* 85 & 149. The same is found in the writings of his father, the *Mabit*, in *Kiryas Sefer* on *Rambam's Hilchos Issurei Biah*, ch. 20.
11. See, for instance, *She'eilos U'Teshuvos Chasam Sofer, O.C.* 41, *Y.D.* 209 & 235.

Sdei Chemed states (*Maareches* 20, *Klal* 92): "The majority of Torah authorities in recent generations were of the opinion that Kohanim in our times are to be considered definite Kohanim, with the full level of *kedushah,* in every aspect of halachah."

Aruch HaShulchan states (*Even HaEzer* 3:22): "Some mistakenly believe that Kohanim today are not full-fledged Kohanim, because they lack a family record that traces their lineage back to Aharon HaKohen. Heaven forbid to say such a thing! According to the strict halachah there is no such requirement at all, and the practice of researching and keeping such records in the past was done only to elevate and enhance the special status of Kohanim. Thus, any family that has a *chazakah* that they are Kohanim is to be treated as absolute Kohanim forever."

Elsewhere, *Aruch HaShulchan* adds (*Yoreh Deah* 305:55): "When Ezra ascended from Bavel to Eretz Yisrael to reestablish the Jewish community there, almost all Kohanim did have a document that traced their lineage, and that seemed to cast a shadow of doubt upon those Kohanim who did not. Nevertheless, Nechemiah ruled that they were all to be considered full-fledged Kohanim, and just as they were allowed to eat *terumah* in Bavel, they were allowed to eat it in Eretz Yisrael. It was about this ruling that *Chazal* state, 'Great is the power of *chazakah.*' All the more so today — when no Kohanim have documents of this sort, and therefore there is no reason to have suspicions about a Kohen who cannot trace his lineage — we must assume that they have a *chazakah*; far be it from us to cast doubts upon their status, even as an added, secondary argument to a halachic decision."

R' Shmuel Wosner (*She'eilos U'Teshuvos Shevet HaLevi,* vol. 4, *siman* 70) cites the opinion of *Maharit* and *Chasam Sofer,* who disagree with *Beis Ephraim,* and concludes that Kohanim in our times are to be considered full-fledged Kohanim, whose mitzvah of Bircas Kohanim is a Torah obligation.

The Impurity of the Lands of the Nations

Another reason given for the Ashkenazic practice of *duchaning* only on Yom Tov outside Eretz Yisrael relates to the concept that the lands of the nations are defiled by corpse-*tumah.* Non-Jews throughout the world often failed to mark their graves, and the

Sages therefore feared that a person walking outside Eretz Yisrael might unknowingly touch or move a small bone or other part of a corpse, rendering the person *tamei.* They therefore decreed that whoever walks in *chutz laAretz* must assume that he contracted *tumah* from parts of a dead body. This is known as *tumas eretz ha'amim* — *tumah* of the lands of the nations.

With regard to Kohanim, who are forbidden to expose themselves to corpse-*tumah, Halichos Shlomo* (*Hilchos Tefillah* 10:12) relates that R' Shlomo Zalman Auerbach was inclined to forbid Kohanim from leaving Eretz Yisrael, because besides the general prohibition against leaving Eretz Yisrael, which applies to everyone, *Shulchan Aruch* rules (*Y.D.* 369:1) that it is forbidden for a Kohen to enter any foreign land, even in our times. Similarly, *Pischei Teshuvah* quotes *Shevus Yaakov,*[12] which states: "If only all of my rulings would be as correct as this one [that *tumas eretz ha'amim* still applies today]!" *Shevus Yaakov* adds that we do not follow the leniency of *Maharshal,* who asserts that this *tumah* of overseas does not apply in our times.

Halichos Shlomo notes that R' Shlomo Zalman writes (*Chiddushei R' Shlomo Zalman, Shabbos* 15a): "It is questionable whether a Kohen who lives outside Eretz Yisrael is permitted to remain there, or if he is required to make every effort to relocate to Eretz Yisrael, if at all possible."

Based on this, R' Moshe Sternbuch suggests (*Teshuvos V'Hanhagos* vol. 4, #263) that one of the reasons Kohanim do not *duchan* daily in the Diaspora is that ideally, they should not be in lands other than Eretz Yisrael at all, and it is inappropriate for them to be blessing the Jewish people at the very moment that they are bringing the *tumah* of *eretz ha'amim* upon themselves. Even if it is not strictly forbidden for Kohanim to be outside Eretz Yisrael, that only explains why they are not transgressing a prohibition by being there, but the actual *tumah* is present nonetheless. Still, the custom is that they do *duchan* on Yom Tov, and the reason is that otherwise they may forget that they are Kohanim altogether; to avoid this, they perform the mitzvah a few times a year.

---

12. Vol. 2 #98. Written by R' Yaakov Reischer, 1661-1732.

Opposition to the Ashkenazic Custom

Rama MiPano[13] opposes the practice of *duchaning* only on Yom Tov, as he writes (*Teshuvos* 95): "The custom to refrain from daily Bircas Kohanim in most of the world is a *minhag garua* (faulty custom), out of concern for loss of time from work ... The Kohanim have become entangled in a grave error; however, they are not transgressing the positive commandment as long as they are not called up to *duchan*."

Magen Avraham (128:44) and many other Ashkenazic *poskim* cite this opinion of *Rama MiPano*.

R' Shmuel ben Yosef of Krakow,[14] who passed away in 1700, writes in *Olas Tamid* (128:100): "It is correct and proper in all places to avoid looking for strategies that negate a positive Torah commandment. Even though it is true that the Kohen does not transgress unless he is called [to *duchan*], nevertheless, [those who fail to *duchan* daily] are forfeiting the flow of blessing that comes down to this world through Bircas Kohanim."

Ba'er Heitev, a commentary on *Shulchan Aruch* written by R' Yehudah Ashkenazi of Tiktin, Poland, who passed away in 1743, quotes *Beis Yosef*'s statement that Bircas Kohanim is done daily and adds: "This is the appropriate and correct custom that should be practiced in all places."

R' Yaakov Pardo (1740-1819) writes (*Minchas Aharon, Klal* 16): "*Beis Yosef* and *Pri Chadash*[15] both write that we do not find in the Gemara or *poskim* the slightest reason to forbid daily Bircas Kohanim; and they surely would not neglect to mention it if there were any concern. The proof is from the custom of those who reside in Eretz Yisrael, who perform Bircas Kohanim every day. If people would listen to me, I would institute that custom in all

---

13. R' Menachem Azariah of Fano, Italy, 1548-1620. He was a close student of R' Moshe Cordovero and authored many works on halachah and Kabbalah. In 1574, R' Yosef Karo, the author of *Shulchan Aruch*, personally appointed R' Menachem Azariah to oversee the publication of his *sefer Kesef Mishneh* on *Rambam*.

14. R' Shmuel served as the lead *dayan* in Krakow for many years. *Olas Tamid*, a commentary on *Shulchan Aruch Orach Chaim*, is quoted dozens of times by *Magen Avraham* and *Mishnah Berurah*.

15. Written by R' Chizkiyahu da Silva of Yerushalayim (1659-1698).

Jewish communities throughout the world. The only reason they do not listen is because they are reluctant to lose any more time from work than they have to."

Efforts to Restore Daily Bircas Kohanim

Many halachic authorities over the generations have called for the restoration of the practice of daily Bircas Kohanim.

Netziv writes[16] that he heard (probably from R' Itzele of Volozhin) that the Vilna Gaon wanted to institute daily Bircas Kohanim even outside Eretz Yisrael, but Divine intervention stopped him from doing so. Just when he was about to launch this new practice, he was arrested and jailed in connection with a dispute regarding the rabbinate of Vilna. Undaunted, the Gaon's disciple R' Chaim of Volozhin attempted to continue the effort, and one day he announced that daily Bircas Kohanim would begin the following morning. That night, half the town burned down, including the *beis midrash*. At that point it became obvious that for some unknown reason, they were not meant to carry through with this plan.

This incident is also recorded in *Aliyos Eliyahu* (p. 32), which quotes R' Avraham Simchah of Amtzislav, a nephew and close disciple of R' Chaim of Volozhin, as saying, "It is possible that the reason they were prevented from changing the custom was so that there should not be any disparagement against earlier generations that did not reinstitute daily Bircas Kohanim."

Regarding this account of *Aliyos Eliyahu*, R' Yaakov Kamenetsky related that when R' Yisrael Salanter heard this story, he could not understand why R' Chaim of Volozhin had stopped his efforts, if he was convinced that this is what the Torah required. After all, the rule is *lo baShamayim hi* — halachah is not decided by signs from Heaven![17] R' Yisrael explained that since the *maskilim* were the ones who opposed the Vilna Gaon and burned down the *beis midrash* the first time, he was afraid they would burn down the *beis midrash* again.

Interestingly, R' Shlomo Lorincz writes (*BiMechitzasam*, vol. 2, p. 565) that the Steipler Gaon added that R' Chaim of Volozhin

16. *Meishiv Davar,* vol. 2, #104.

17. *BiMechitzas Rabbeinu*, collected sayings of Rav Yaakov Kamenetsky, p. 203. Heard directly from R' Shmuel Kamenetsky as well.

did in fact rebuild the *beis midrash* in Volozhin, and they did perform Bircas Kohanim there after it was rebuilt, as per the ruling of the Vilna Gaon. The Steipler said that human beings cannot comprehend "signs from Heaven," and the fact that the *beis midrash* burned down mysteriously was not a reason not to perform Bircas Kohanim.

Similarly, the *Alei Tamar* commentary on *Yerushalmi* (*Taanis* ch. 4) records this historical note: "In Lithuania, and even in the city of Vilna itself, most communities followed *minhag Ashkenaz*. Only in the *beis midrash* of the Vilna Gaon did people follow his customs, as recorded in *Maaseh Rav*. I also heard the same from a great Lithuanian scholar of advanced age, who remembered the practices he had seen in his youth — that Bircas Kohanim was performed on a daily basis only in the *beis midrash* of the Vilna Gaon and in one other minyan, in Kovno."

The Custom of R' Nosson Adler

It is known that the great rav and *mekubal* R' Nosson Adler (who was a Kohen) used to perform Bircas Kohanim in his own *beis midrash* in Frankfurt, Germany, during Shacharis every day, and during Shacharis and Mussaf on days when Mussaf was recited. He would comment that he is longing for the Beis HaMikdash to be rebuilt already so that he will be able to perform the actual *avodah*.[18]

However, his *talmid muvhak*, the Chasam Sofer, writes (*She'eilos U'Teshuvos, O.C.*, 23) that Kohanim outside of Eretz Yisrael should not *duchan* every day, because our *tefillos* are not said with proper concentration. *Tefillah* is comparable to a *korban*, which requires one's full mind and intent. Thus, the *berachah* of the Kohanim, which is part of *tefillah*, is surely not accepted if it is lacking *kavanah*. The exception is on Yom Tov, when our minds are free of distractions and concerns about our livelihood, and we are able to daven with *kavanah*; at such a time, it is possible for Bircas Kohanim to be accepted by Hashem.

18. This custom of R' Nosson Adler is recorded in many places, including *Chut HaMeshulash*, p. 20; *Derech HaNesher, siman* 31; *Toras Emes*, p. 47; and *Ateres Paz* 128:44.

The Vilna Gaon's Aspiration

Beis Yosef HeChadash contains an approbation written by R' Shmuel Heller, rav of the Ashkenazic community of nineteenth-century Tzfas, to the *sefer*'s author, R' Akiva Yosef Schlesinger. The letter is dated 14 Teves 5636/January 11, 1876, and it reads: "I can attest that I heard many times from R' Yisrael of Shklov, author of *Pe'as HaShulchan*, that the Vilna Gaon said he had two aspirations for which he would be willing to give up his Torah study and instead spend his precious time traveling from city to city in order to achieve them. **One of these was to institute daily Bircas Kohanim in all communities, even outside Eretz Yisrael."** R' Moshe Halberstam, who was married to R' Akiva Yosef's great-granddaughter, quotes the letter in an approbation to the *sefer HaBerachah HaMeshuleshes*, and writes that he has the original letter.

The Baal HaTanya's Efforts

The Baal HaTanya also attempted to restore the original custom of daily Bircas Kohanim outside Eretz Yisrael, but various obstacles and complications arose, and ultimately, he did not succeed in persuading the community to accept his proposition.[19]

In *Shulchan Aruch HaRav* (128:57), *Baal HaTanya* cites the "lack of joy" given as a reason for the custom not to *duchan* daily, and adds that this explanation is merely an attempt to justify our practice, but is not a sufficient reason to negate a positive Torah commandment. Echoing *Beis Yosef*, he adds, "*Yasher kocham* to those who live in Eretz Yisrael and the surrounding countries who do *duchan* every day, as *Chazal* have mandated, and thereby fulfill three positive commandments on a daily basis."

Similarly, *Aruch HaShulchan* (128:64) states that there is no adequate explanation for our practice of negating the positive Torah commandment of Bircas Kohanim all year long, and the *poskim* have already labeled it a "*minhag garua*" (faulty custom). "But what shall we do about it? **It is as though a Heavenly voice emanated to**

19. Recorded in *Likutei Sichos* (vol. 18, footnote 444) of the Lubavitcher Rebbe, R' Menachem Mendel Schneerson, and in his *Shaarei Halachah U'Minhag*, vol.1, *siman* 75.

prevent us from performing this mitzvah on a daily basis. I have a tradition that two *gedolei hador* from earlier generations, each one in his locale, attempted to reinstate daily Bircas Kohanim, and when the designated starting day arrived, their plans were thwarted and they did not succeed. This led them to conclude that it was a Heavenly decree to leave things as they are." (Presumably, the *gedolei hador* mentioned by *Aruch HaShulchan* are the Vilna Gaon, R' Chaim of Volozhin, or the *Baal HaTanya*.)

This is the definitive ruling for our times: An Ashkenazic minyan in *chutz laAretz* may not perform daily Bircas Kohanim.

Exception 1: Uman

In the early 1990s, when the communists lost their grip on the Ukraine and Jews were permitted to travel there, the question arose as to whether Ashkenazim from Eretz Yisrael should perform Bircas Kohanim daily when visiting the gravesite of R' Nachman of Breslov in Uman. Ever since this grave became accessible, tens of thousands of people, primarily Breslover chassidim, travel to Uman throughout the year, and especially for Rosh Hashanah.

R' Yisrael Yaakov Fisher, along with other rabbanim of the Eidah HaChareidis, ruled that these visitors are permitted to perform Bircas Kohanim every day in Uman. He explained that although the Ashkenazic custom outside Eretz Yisrael is to *duchan* only on Yom Tov, that applies to shuls whose congregants reside locally. The minyanim in Uman, on the other hand, were established not for local residents, but for visitors from abroad, and the vast majority of those are from Eretz Yisrael. That being the case, they are not bound by the custom of the city they are visiting, and are free to follow their own custom.

This situation is comparable to people from Eretz Yisrael forming their own minyan outside Eretz Yisrael, as discussed above. While the Steipler and his son R' Chaim Kanievsky permitted Israelis in *chutz laAretz* to perform daily Bircas Kohanim only on a temporary basis, R' Yisrael Yaakov Fisher was of the opinion that this may be done as long as the majority of the minyan of rotating visitors is from Eretz Yisrael, as is the case in Uman.

R' Yisrael Yaakov noted that although in earlier years, the Jewish community of Uman did not *duchan* every day, we may assume that once the communists came to power, there was no longer any observant Jewish presence remaining in that city. Thus, the group that began visiting Uman in recent times is considered to have founded a completely new community, unconnected to the original residents. Since this new "community" consists of visitors from abroad, the majority of whom live in Eretz Yisrael, they have the right to institute their own *minhagim*.

Based on this ruling of R' Yisrael Yaakov and the Eidah HaChareidis, the minyanim in Uman with a majority of Israeli congregants *duchan* during the weekday Shacharis all year round, and twice on days when Mussaf is recited.

Noted Breslov *mashpia* R' Yaakov Meir Schechter explained to this author that not only are visitors to Uman from Eretz Yisrael permitted to perform daily Bircas Kohanim, but they may very well be *obligated* to follow the custom of Eretz Yisrael, since *Pri Chadash* rules (*O.C.* 496) that when a new town is established, the people there must follow the customs of the place of origin of most of the residents. R' Yaakov Meir also pointed out that *Rema* rules similarly with regard to monetary matters (*Choshen Mishpat* 331:1), and that principle applies here as well. Therefore, Bircas Kohanim is performed in the city of Uman daily when the majority of congregants are from Eretz Yisrael.

Exception 2: The Hague

In *She'eilos U'Teshuvos V'Shav V'Rafa* (vol. 9, *siman* 12), R' Raphael Evers, the former chief rabbi of Holland, writes that the Ashkenazic community of The Hague, Holland, had the custom to perform Bircas Kohanim every Shabbos, during Mussaf. This practice traces back to the year 5626/1866, when a devastating cholera epidemic spread through the country. In response, R' Yissachar Berish Bernstein, rav of The Hague, called for Bircas Kohanim to be performed every Shabbos, because it is a known *segulah* to protect the community from plagues.[20] Even after the epidemic ended, it was decided to continue this practice of blessing the congregation, and so it remained for the next seventy-five years, until the outbreak of World War II.

---

20. See *Zera Kodesh* by R' Naftali of Ropshitz, *Lech Lecha; Birkei Yosef* 128:19; *Kaf HaChaim* 128:270.

Calling Up a Kohen to Duchan Against his Custom

The Gemara states (*Sotah* 38b), "R' Yehoshua ben Levi said: A Kohen who does not perform Bircas Kohanim transgresses three positive Torah commandments: (1) *So shall you bless Bnei Yisrael;* (2) *say to them*; and (3) *Let them place My Name upon Bnei Yisrael.*"

Shulchan Aruch rules (128:2) that a Kohen who is called up to *duchan* and fails to do so is in violation of these three mitzvos.

Therefore, in *chutz laAretz,* where the Ashkenazic custom is to *duchan* only on Yom Tov, one must be very careful not to tell an Ashkenazi Kohen to go up to the *duchan* on any other day. If the Kohen is called up to *duchan* during *Chazaras HaShatz* on a day when the custom is not to *duchan,* it is questionable if he is required to go up to *duchan,* even though that is in violation of the prevailing custom.

Pri Megadim states (*Eishel Avraham* 129:1): "During a weekday Shacharis one would be justified in saying, *'im alah lo yeireid'* — once he has gone up [to *duchan*], he should not come down [without *duchaning*]. During a weekday Minchah, however, if he went up in error, he *should* come down."

Maharsham writes (*Teshuvos,* vol. 8, *siman* 25): "In our times, even outside Eretz Yisrael, if a Kohen is called up to *duchan,* he has a Torah obligation to *duchan* even on weekdays."

Sefer Koh Sevarechu[21] states: "If a Kohen is called up on a day that, in his community, they do not *duchan,* it is a bona fide 'calling' for Bircas Kohanim, and the Kohanim are obligated to respond by going up to *duchan*; if they fail to do so, they fall into the trap of transgressing a Torah commandment. Although there may be room to disagree, it is, at the very least, a question of a Torah obligation (*d'Oraysa*), and as such, one must be stringent and go up to perform the mitzvah."

21. By R' Yehoshua Elazar HaKohen Chimtzi (1795-1881), *Maareches* 20, *siman* 2.

Questionable Obligation

The following ruling of R' Moshe HaLevi Mintz (*She'eilos U'Teshuvos Maharam Mintz* #12) underscores the problem of calling up a Kohen to *duchan* against his custom.[22] He writes that although a Kohen who did not do an *akirah* (move from his place) during the blessing of *Retzei* does not *duchan*,[23] he is not sure what the halachah would be if, after the blessing of *Retzei*, a Yisrael tells a Kohen who did not do an *akirah* to *duchan*. In such a case, it is unclear whether the Kohen is required to ascend to the *duchan*.

Thus, we see that even in a case where a Kohen is not halachically obligated to *duchan*, if he is told explicitly to ascend to the *duchan*, that might make Bircas Kohanim mandatory. Although *Mishnah Berurah* (128:9) cites *Magen Avraham*'s opinion that he is not permitted to ascend in this case, and he does not violate the positive commandment of Bircas Kohanim when he remains in his place, *Eliyahu Rabbah* (128:4) quotes *Maharam Mintz* and says it is possible that once the Yisrael tells the Kohen to *duchan* he is obligated to do so. Therefore, even though there is a strong, established custom among Ashkenazim in *chutz laAretz* not to *duchan* daily, if a Yisrael tells a Kohen to *duchan*, he is likely obligated to do so.

---

22. 1415-1480. He was the *rav* of Mainz, Germany, and several other German communities.

23. See 128:8 regarding the requirement of an *akirah*. See also chapter 26.

Chapter 15
History of the Ashkenazic Custom: Geonim and Rishonim

When did Ashkenazim in the Diaspora stop performing daily Bircas Kohanim? As we will see below, during the time of the Geonim and early Rishonim, daily Bircas Kohanim was still a universal practice, even among Ashkenazim outside Eretz Yisrael. We know that Bircas Kohanim was recited daily in the minyanim of *Rashi*, the *Baalei Tosafos, Rokeach,* and other Rishonim in Europe.

Apparently, the custom of *duchaning* only on Yom Tov first became prevalent at the end of the period of the Rishonim.

Maharil: The Turning Point

In a discussion regarding the *halachos* of a Kohen who is a mourner, *Binyan Shlomo*[1] states (vol. 1, *siman* 10):

> My heart tells me that *Mordechai* and *Hagahos Maimoniyos,* who rule that a Kohen should not *duchan* during *aveilus* (mourning), were not speaking about Bircas Kohanim on Yom Tov, for in their time it was still a universal custom to perform Bircas Kohanim every day, in accordance with Torah law, and as the custom still remains today in Eretz Yisrael and in Sephardic communities.

1. Authored by R' Shlomo HaKohen of Vilna, 1828-1905. He was one of the rabbanim who gave an approbation to *Mishnah Berurah*.

Our custom of limiting the mitzvah to Yom Tov is not found in any of the *sefarim* written by Sephardic *poskim*. It seems that [refraining from daily Bircas Kohanim] did not become a widespread custom at all until the time of Maharil, as the first one to record the custom was *Agur*, in the name of Maharil, as quoted by *Beis Yosef*. Thus, it became an accepted custom only in Ashkenazic communities, since Maharil himself lived in such a community, and set the foundation for many of the Ashkenazic customs that are practiced today. The Sephardim, on the other hand, never accepted any such custom, because none of the Sephardic *poskim* ever made mention of it.

We see, then, that it was around the time of Maharil (1365-1427) that Ashkenazic communities in the Diaspora stopped performing daily Bircas Kohanim.[2]

Geonic Sources for Daily Bircas Kohanim

A careful reading of rulings of the Geonim makes it clear that Bircas Kohanim was a universal daily practice in their times.[3]

Sheiltos D'R' Hai Gaon (*Bamidbar* 5, #123) questions why it is that Bircas Kohanim is performed all year round only during Shacharis and not Minchah, with the exception of Minchah on public fast days. (The answer given, based on the Gemara's statement in *Taanis* 26b, is that drunkenness is more prevalent in the afternoon, after eating a meal, but this is not a concern on a fast day.) The same is found in *Halachos Gedolos* (*Hilchos Kohanim*), a halachic work dating back to the time of the Geonim, and in *Teshuvos Geonei Mizrach U'Maarav* (*siman* 46, 48). Plainly, it was understood by the Geonim that the mitzvah of Bircas Kohanim is to be performed during Shacharis on a daily basis.

Likewise, in *Seder HaTefillah* of R' Amram Gaon and the *Siddur* of R' Saadiah Gaon, Bircas Kohanim is clearly a part of the weekday Shacharis prayer. In addition, R' Amram Gaon writes that on Tishah

2. Many Ashkenazic customs were recorded by *Maharil*, as he was one of the last Rishonim.
3. The Geonic period began in approximately the year 589, with the reopening of the yeshivah in Pumbedisa, and ended in approximately 1038 with the passing of R' Hai Gaon.

B'Av, Bircas Kohanim is to be performed during Minchah as well, indicating that Bircas Kohanim was not limited to Yom Tov.

R' Amram Gaon writes that on all fast days the Kohanim *duchan* during Minchah, with the exception of Yom Kippur, when Bircas Kohanim is done during Neilah instead. That, he says, is the custom in both yeshivos (Sura and Pumbedisa, the great academies of Bavel).

It is clear, then, that in the days of the Geonim, Bircas Kohanim was performed during Minchah on all fast days, except Yom Kippur, in addition to Shacharis of every day.

Summoning the Kohanim

Additionally, the *Siddur* of R' Saadiah Gaon states (p. 39), regarding weekday Shacharis, that if there is a Kohen in the congregation, he should bless the people after the chazzan says the words הַטּוֹב שִׁמְךָ וּלְךָ נָאֶה לְהוֹדוֹת. He goes on to explain that the *berachah* of *Retzei* was specifically added to *Shemoneh Esrei* in order to summon the Kohanim to perform Bircas Kohanim during Shacharis.

This idea is echoed by many other Geonim and Rishonim as well. *Sefer HaEshkol*[4] (*Hilchos Bircas Kohanim*) teaches that the first words of the *berachah* of *Retzei* were inserted into *Shemoneh Esrei* for the purpose of summoning the Kohanim to come forward for Bircas Kohanim. Therefore, he rules, during Minchah, when there is no Bircas Kohanim, one omits the opening phrase of the *berachah*, and begins with the words אִשֵּׁי יִשְׂרָאֵל.[5]

Likewise, R' Saadiah Gaon writes in a *teshuvah* that the opening phrase of *Retzei* should not be recited during Minchah, unless it is a fast day, and those who *are* accustomed to recite it every day during Minchah are in error — for it is meant as a signal to the Kohanim, who move in the direction of the *duchan* upon hearing those words. Rather, one should begin the *berachah* from אִשֵּׁי יִשְׂרָאֵל, for the Kohen is not required to come forward when he hears only that part of the *berachah*. One exception to the rule is Yom Kippur: Although Bircas Kohanim is not performed during Minchah of Yom Kippur, the custom is nevertheless to recite the entire *berachah* of *Retzei*.

---

4. By R' Avraham ben R' Yitzchak of Narbonne, France (1085-1158).
5. See *Nachal Eshkol* commentary #19.

A similar ruling regarding the *berachah* of *Retzei* is found in the *teshuvos* of R' Sherira Gaon as well.[6]

R' Avraham ben Nosson HaYarchi (1155-1215), who lived in France and Germany and then in Spain, records that this was the practice in some places (*Sefer HaManhig, Hilchos Tefillah*): "I saw that in Toledo [Spain] and its surrounding cities the custom is to skip the opening of the *berachah* of *Retzei* during Minchah and begin with the words אִשֵּׁי יִשְׂרָאֵל וּתְפִלָּתָם... The exception is Minchah of a fast day, when they do begin with *Retzei*. The reason for this custom is that the first words of *Retzei* are not said unless the Kohanim are preparing to perform the actual mitzvah of Bircas Kohanim."

Tur and *Beis Yosef*, however, state (*O.C.* 120) that our custom is to recite *Retzei* during Minchah every day; see there for the explanation.

In any event, we can deduce that Bircas Kohanim was recited during Shacharis every day during the period of the Geonim, most of whom resided in the Diaspora.

What Did Rashi Do?

Machzor Vitri[7] was authored in 1208 by Rabbeinu Simchah, one of Rashi's prime disciples, and cites many *halachos* and customs. It states (#130): "After *Modim*, the Kohanim perform Bircas Kohanim. On Yom Tov, Chol HaMoed, and Rosh Chodesh, this is done during Shacharis and Mussaf, and on weekdays, only **during Shacharis** — except on fast days, when it is done during Minchah as well."

In *Siddur Rashi*, which was compiled by several of Rashi's students and is quoted by many Rishonim, we find a similar paragraph, whose wording is almost identical to that of *Machzor Vitri*: "After *Modim*, when the chazzan finishes the *berachah*, the Kohanim perform Bircas Kohanim. On Yom Tov, Chol HaMoed, and Rosh Chodesh, this is done during Shacharis and Mussaf, and on weekdays, only **during Shacharis** — except on fast days, when it is done during Minchah as well."

Clearly, in the time of Rashi — an Ashkenazi living in France — Bircas Kohanim was still performed every day.

---

6. See also *Rashi, Berachos* 11b, s.v. *V'avodah*, and *Sefer HaManhig* (in *Hilchos Taanis*).

7. *Machzor Vitri* is cited by Rashi's grandson Rabbeinu Tam several times in *Tosafos*, and by dozens of other Rishonim.

The Custom of Marseilles

Sefer HaMinhagos,[8] which records the *minhagim* of Marseilles, France (an Ashkenazic region), states as follows: "After the chazzan finishes the *berachah* of *Modim*, if there are Kohanim present, they perform Bircas Kohanim. **This applies to Shacharis** and Mussaf, as well as Minchah of every fast day, with the exception of Yom Kippur, when it is done during Neilah instead. **If there are no Kohanim to *duchan*, then the *Elokeinu V'Elokei Avoseinu* prayer is recited**."

Sefer HaEshkol

Sefer HaEshkol, written in twelfth-century France, also implies that Bircas Kohanim was performed there daily, as he writes (*Hilchos Tefillin*): "Some Geonim have written that a Kohen is not obligated to wear tefillin on his arm. Certainly this was true when Kohanim performed the *avodah* in the Beis HaMikdash, because there may not be any separation between the priestly garments and the skin. When a Kohen is performing Bircas Kohanim he is exempt as well, due to the principle that a person who is occupied with one mitzvah is exempt from other mitzvos during that time; however, in that case he is exempt from wearing head-tefillin as well. **Our custom is to continue wearing tefillin, but to remove the straps from one's fingers while raising one's hands to *duchan*.**"

Obviously, *Sefer HaEshkol* took it for granted that Bircas Kohanim is performed *at a time when one wears tefillin* — i.e., on weekdays.[9]

Rokeach

An even clearer proof is found in the words of *Rokeach*[10] (*Hilchos Tefillah* #323), who lived in Germany: "Today, Bircas Kohanim is performed during Shacharis, and during Minchah (of fast days)."

---

8. Written by R' Moshe ben R' Shmuel of Marseilles, France, approximately one hundred years after Rashi's passing.
9. For more regarding a Kohen removing the straps of the tefillin from his fingers during Bircas Kohanim, see chapter 29.
10. R' Elazar of Worms (1160-1234), one of the *Baalei HaTosafos*.

Shibbolei HaLeket

Similarly, *Shibbolei HaLeket*[11] states, in his discussion of the order of the weekday prayers (*siman* 23):

> When the chazzan reaches the *berachah* of *Sim Shalom,* **the Kohanim go up to *duchan*.** If there is no Kohen present, and therefore the chazzan recites the passage beginning *Elokeinu V'Elokei Avoseinu,* the question arises: Does the congregation respond amen after each of the three *berachos* as they do during Bircas Kohanim, or should they make a distinction between the *berachah* of a Kohen and that of the chazzan?
>
> This question was posed to R' Hai Gaon, and he answered that our custom is not to respond amen to each *berachah*. Although Bircas Kohanim consists of three *berachos* when it is recited by a Kohen, it is treated as only one when the chazzan prays that Hashem should bless us with the verses used by the Kohanim, **as there is no Kohen present to bless the people.**

Obviously, *Shibbolei HaLeket* held that Bircas Kohanim is to be performed every day, since he placed this halachah in the order of the weekday prayers.

Sefer HaAgudah

Rabbeinu Alexander HaKohen,[12] a disciple of *Rosh,* served as Rav in the German cities of Cologne, Worms, and Frankfurt, and authored *Sefer HaAgudah*. He was killed during the Erfurt massacre of 1349, six years before Maharil was born. A clear indication that he did indeed *duchan* during Shacharis, and not just during Mussaf of Yom Tov, can be found in this ruling of his (*Megillah* #34): "After the Kohanim *duchan,* they put their shoes back on, and, in

11. Written by R' Tzidkiyah ben R' Avraham of Rome, Italy (1210-1275). During his youth he studied in Wurzberg, Germany, where he recorded customs and collected halachic rulings of French and German Torah scholars. *Shibbolei HaLeket* focuses primarily on *Orach Chaim* and includes halachic decisions, commentary on the prayers, and explanations of customs.

12. *Sefer HaAgudah,* a halachic work structured according to the order of the Gemara, is cited by many Rishonim, and is frequently quoted by *Rema*.

the process, they inevitably touch their feet and shoes. That being the case, unless they choose to remain barefoot, it is appropriate for them to wash their hands again **before davening or reciting *Hallel*, and that is what I have become accustomed to do.**"

Now, as we know, *Hallel* is recited only during Shacharis. Evidently, then, Rabbeinu Alexander HaKohen was "accustomed" to *duchaning* during Shacharis, even though he was an Ashkenazi living in Germany!

Sefer HaAgudah continues: "On Yom Kippur, Bircas Kohanim is performed during Neilah, but not during Minchah, because one may confuse it with Minchah of the rest of the year, when the Kohanim are not permitted to *duchan* because they might be intoxicated at that time of day. On a fast day, however, when Minchah is customarily recited at the end of the day, it is comparable to Neilah, and Bircas Kohanim should be performed."

Once again, we can infer that during his lifetime the common practice was to *duchan* every day, as the only reason it was not done during Minchah of a regular day was out of concern for intoxication.

R' Avraham ben Rabbeinu Azriel of Prague

Another indication that Bircas Kohanim was performed by Ashkenazim during Shacharis (and not only during Mussaf, as is the case in the Diaspora today) can be found in the words of R' Avraham ben Rabbeinu Azriel of Prague, a close disciple of Rokeach. He writes in *Arugas HaBosem*, which was published in 1234: "**We take the lulav in hand before the *berachah* of *Retzei* and Bircas Kohanim, just before beginning *Hallel*.** Just as Bircas Kohanim brings about goodwill between the Jewish people and their Father in Heaven, so too, the Four Species bring us goodwill with regard to the rainfall of the upcoming year, and that is why these two mitzvos are connected. Also, just as Bircas Kohanim contains sixty letters, so too, the lulav has sixty leaves — thirty on each side of the branch."

Evidently, the custom in his community was to perform Bircas Kohanim before *Hallel* is recited, which is during Shacharis.

Avudraham

In his discussion of the weekday Shacharis prayer, *Avudraham*[13] writes: "Some [non-Kohanim] have the custom during Bircas Kohanim to recite verses that correspond to each of the words of the *berachah*, and this is not an appropriate practice."

Avudraham places this law of Bircas Kohanim in the section dealing with weekday prayers, clearly indicating that it is to be performed every day.

Tosafos

Tosafos (*Taanis* 26b) state that the common practice today is for Bircas Kohanim to be performed during Minchah on fast days, close to sunset. *Tosafos* add that on Yom Kippur, when Minchah is recited earlier in the day, Bircas Kohanim is not performed during Minchah, but later, during Neilah, instead.

From this halachah we can infer that although Bircas Kohanim is performed during Minchah only on a fast day, it is certainly performed during Shacharis, which was traditionally the primary time of the mitzvah.

Similarly, *Sefer Mitzvos HaGadol* (*Mitzvas Asei* 20) states that Bircas Kohanim is performed on public fast days that are declared when there is a lack of rain, as well as on Yom Kippur, during Shacharis, Mussaf, and Neilah — but not during Minchah of Yom Kippur, out of a concern that one might confuse it with a weekday Minchah; on a weekday people may be intoxicated in the afternoon, and therefore *Chazal* forbade *duchaning*. On Tishah B'Av, Shivah Assar B'Tammuz, and the like, when there is no Neilah, and Minchah is recited close to sunset, Bircas Kohanim *is* performed, because it is comparable to Neilah of Yom Kippur.

Additionally, *Sefer HaMitzvos HaKattan* states (Mitzvah 113): "On Yom Kippur, the Kohanim perform Bircas Kohanim three times during the day — Shacharis, Mussaf, and Neilah — but not during Minchah, as it could be confused with a weekday Minchah.

13. R' Dovid ben R' Yosef Avudraham lived in Spain during the thirteenth century. His eponymous work, published in 1340, is a collection of halachos, *minhagim*, and commentaries on the prayers.

Minchah on Yom Kippur is recited while it is still early in the day, and for that reason the chazzan does not recite *Elokeinu V'Elokei Avoseinu*. During Minchah of other fast days, however, Bircas Kohanim is recited, because Minchah takes place near sunset, and it is comparable to Neilah, where there is no concern of intoxication. All the rest of the year, Bircas Kohanim is not performed during Minchah, since there is a concern that people may be intoxicated at that time of day."

Our Birthright

While it is clear from all these ancient sources that Bircas Kohanim was a daily practice even among Ashkenazim in the Diaspora up to the time of the early Rishonim, this custom may no longer be followed today by Ashkenazim outside Eretz Yisrael, as the later Ashkenazic Rishonim instituted that Bircas Kohanim should be recited there only on Yom Tov. This was codified by *Rema* as the authoritative halachah for all Ashkenazim in *chutz laAretz*.

Nevertheless, we do see that Bircas Kohanim is not merely an abstract footnote at the conclusion of the Yom Tov davening, but was an integral part of the daily davening for all of Klal Yisrael up to the period of the later Ashkenazic Rishonim.

One practical halachic ramification of this discussion is that if an Ashkenazi happens to daven in a Sephardic minyan in *chutz laAretz*, he should not leave the shul before *Retzei*, but should receive the *berachah* from his Sephardic brethren, as it is his birthright as well.

Chapter 16
Daily Bircas Kohanim: A Universal Sephardic Practice

Unlike Ashkenazic communities in the Diaspora, which perform Bircas Kohanim only on Yom Tov, Sephardic communities throughout the world *duchan* every day of the year.

Considering the power of Bircas Kohanim, which is a blessing directly from Hashem, it is a great merit and privilege for Sephardi Jews to be able to perform this mitzvah on a daily basis everywhere in the world.

Powerful Spiritual Secrets

Ben *Ish Chai* writes (First year, *Tetzaveh* §4): "Any Kohen who recites Bircas Kohanim is himself blessed from Hashem. With much praise to the Holy One, Blessed is He, we have merited to carefully fulfill this mitzvah here in the city of Baghdad on a daily basis, and that is the appropriate practice that should be instituted in all communities, for these blessings have the capacity to draw bountiful goodness from Heaven to all the worlds — Upper and Lower — and they contain within them the deepest and most powerful spiritual secrets. Fortunate is the eye that witnesses it!"

Not to Miss an Opportunity to Bless the Jewish People

R' Eliezer Papo, the author of *Pele Yoetz,* states, in *Chesed L'Alafim*[1]:

> A Kohen who blesses the Jewish people is himself blessed by Hashem, and thus, if he does not do so, he forfeits a great deal of goodness, and demonstrates that he has no desire for mitzvos, and no interest in Hashem's blessing ... Therefore, a Kohen who fears Hashem and loves His mitzvos will not miss an opportunity to *duchan* and to bring pleasure to his Creator, for indeed, it pleases Hashem to bless the Jewish people.
>
> **How good and pleasant is the custom that is practiced in many places, that the Kohanim *duchan* every day;** it is appropriate to do so in every community, and not to seek excuses to forego this positive Torah commandment. Although the Kohen does not transgress the commandment unless he is called up, nevertheless, he is depriving the congregation of an outpouring of blessing that comes to the Upper and Lower Worlds through the Bircas Kohanim.
>
> The mitzvah contains within it deep spiritual secrets and hidden meanings, but as a general rule, the Kohanim should simply have in mind that their actions should be accepted in Heaven, and should contain within them all the intentions of Aharon HaKohen and of the other Kohanim throughout the generations.[2]

In *Pele Yoetz* (*Erech Kohen*) he writes: "Kohanim must be extremely diligent about performing the few [*Kehunah*-related] mitzvos that remain for them in our times, such as the mitzvah to bless the Jewish people, which is a fulfillment of three Torah commandments. Moreover, the Kohen who blesses the people is himself blessed directly from Hashem, as the Torah says, *and I shall bless them*. How misguided are those Kohanim who step out of shul in order to avoid blessing the Jewish people, and thereby forfeit so

1. 128:1; this is also quoted in *Kaf HaChaim* (128:15).
2. See Responsa of R' Chaim Kanievsky #357, where he writes that the Kohanim should have in mind the meaning of the words.

much good for themselves! **If only I were a Kohen, I would surely *duchan* every single day!"**

No Opposition to the Sephardic Custom

The Sephardic custom to *duchan* every day is a practice that traces back to the days of Aharon HaKohen, continuing through the times of the Beis HaMikdash and all through the ages. It is the Ashkenazic custom in *chutz laAretz* of *duchaning* only on Yom Tov that is questionable, and indeed, many halachic authorities — including prominent Ashkenazic *poskim* of earlier generations — are perplexed by the practice.[3]

For instance, R' Yisrael of Shklov, a close student of the Vilna Gaon who moved to Eretz Yisrael, writes (*Pe'as HaShulchan, Hilchos Eretz Yisrael* 2:16) that the custom in Eretz Yisrael — to perform Bircas Kohanim every day — is highly commendable. He notes that this is also the custom of Sephardic communities around the world, based on *Rambam* and *Beis Yosef*; although *Rema* rules that the Ashkenazic custom is not to do so, *Rama MiPano* (*Teshuvos* #95) describes this as a "faulty custom."

R' Shlomo HaKohen of Vilna (1828-1905) writes, in a discussion regarding the halachos of a Kohen who is a mourner (*Binyan Shlomo,* vol. 1, *siman* 10):

> Our [Ashkenazic] custom of limiting the mitzvah [of Bircas Kohanim] to Yom Tov **is not found in any of the *sefarim* written by Sephardic *poskim.*** It seems that [refraining from daily Bircas Kohanim] did not become a widespread custom at all until the time of Maharil, as the first one to record the custom was *Agur,* in the name of Maharil, as quoted by *Beis Yosef.* Thus, it became an accepted custom only in Ashkenazic communities, since Maharil himself lived in such a community, and set the foundation for many of the Ashkenazic customs that are practiced today. **The Sephardim, on the other hand, never accepted any such custom, because none of the Sephardic *poskim* ever made mention of it.**

Aruch HaShulchan[4] states that in all Sephardic communities and Arab countries, the custom is to perform Bircas Kohanim every day

3. See chapter 14. Nevertheless, it is forbidden to change this custom.
4. 127:4.

during Shacharis. Elsewhere he writes[5] that in Eretz Yisrael, Egypt, and throughout Asia the Kohanim *duchan* every day.

Kaf HaChaim (128:271) quotes *Rama MiPano* and adds: "*Sheyarei Knesses HaGedolah*[6] (128:27) writes that we do not follow the custom of *Rema* in this case."

Likewise, *Maaseh Rokeach* (*Hilchos Tefillah* 14:1) quotes *Rama MiPano*, and maintains that Bircas Kohanim should be performed every day.

A Defect in Our Prayer

R' Ovadiah Hadayah (1889-1969), who served as rosh yeshivah of the famed Yeshivat HaMekubalim Beit El in Yerushalayim, writes (*She'eilos U'Teshuvos Yaskil Avdi*, vol. 7, *siman* 44):

> Even where there is a longstanding custom not to *duchan* every day, the *poskim* are of the opinion that it would be a great achievement if someone could abolish that custom and restore the ancient practice of performing the mitzvah daily. Although we always avoid casting aspersions on customs, for they are considered like part of the Torah, it does not apply in this case, for it is an improper custom (as noted by *Rama MiPano* and others), and anyone who can succeed in discontinuing it will be blessed in this world and the next.
>
> Indeed, he will be considered a "*mezakeh es harabbim*" — one who brings merit to the public — firstly, because he will enable the Kohanim to fulfill three positive Torah commandments every day, and secondly, because Bircas Kohanim will bring down great blessing upon the entire world. Moreover, it will correct a defect in the prayer, which is now missing this essential element.

All Sephardic Congregations Should Duchan

In some Sephardic shuls in Djerba and Amsterdam, Bircas Kohanim was performed only during Mussaf of Shabbos, Rosh

5. 128:64.

6. By R' Chaim Benveniste (1603-1673), Rav in Izmir, Turkey, and a close student of *Mabit*, R' Yosef Trani of Tzfas.

Chodesh, and Yom Tov. R' Ovadiah Yosef rules,[7] however, that *all* Sephardic congregations throughout the Diaspora should follow the custom to *duchan* every day, and adds that even those few Sephardic congregations who do not do so are permitted to change their custom and begin performing Bircas Kohanim daily. R' Ovadiah is following the opinion of *Rambam* and *Shulchan Aruch* (129:1) that Bircas Kohanim should be performed during Shacharis even on Shabbos and weekdays.

Similarly, *Kaf HaChaim* (128:274), citing *Sheyarei Knesses HaGedolah,* relates that a certain city had the custom to perform Bircas Kohanim only on Yom Tov, but at one point, for a particular reason, they decided to include Shabbos as well. Later, the reason for doing so became irrelevant, and the question arose as to whether they should revert to their original custom of not *duchaning* on Shabbos. *Sheyarei Knesses HaGedolah* responded that this would be inappropriate; on the contrary, it would be better if they would institute Bircas Kohanim every day!

7. See *Yalkut Yosef* 128:17.

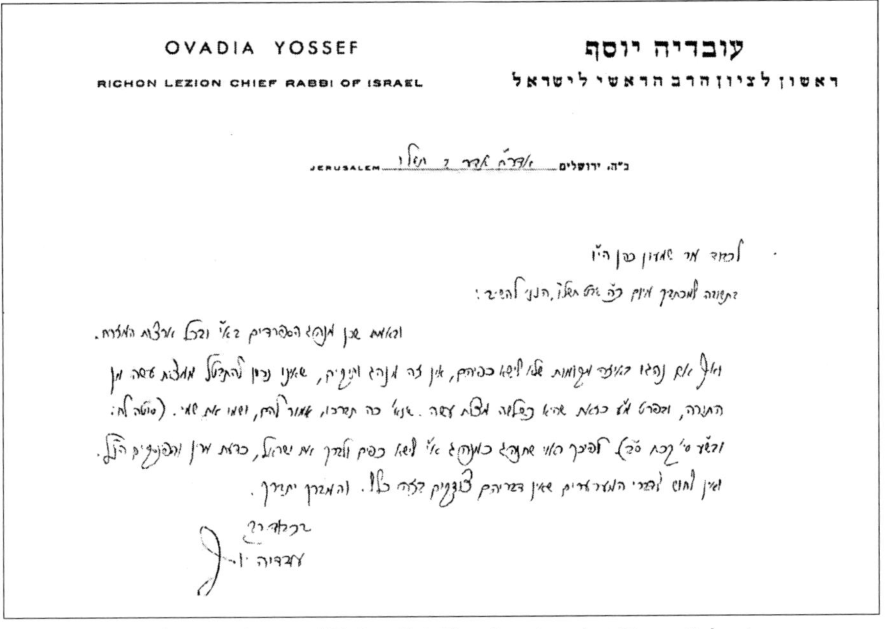

OVADIA YOSSEF	עובדיה יוסף
RICHON LEZION CHIEF RABBI OF ISRAEL	ראשון לציון והרב הראשי לישראל

ב"ה, ירושלים [illegible] JERUSALEM

לכבוד מר שמעון כהן הי"ו

[illegible]

הנה אמת שכן מנהג הספרדים בא"י ובכל ארצות המזרח.

[illegible]

Handwritten letter of R' Ovadiah Yosef stating that Bircas Kohanim should be performed daily in all Sephardic congregations

No Credit to Shabsai Tzvi

The most well-known and destructive false messiah in our history was the infamous Shabsai Tzvi, who arose in the seventeenth century and declared himself to be the savior of the Jewish people. For a number of years, he captured the hearts of a great number of Jews, who were willing to follow his every instruction and to adopt many practices that he instituted. In the Sephardic Spanish-Portuguese community of Amsterdam, followers of Shabsai Tzvi instituted that Sephardim should perform Bircas Kohanim every Shabbos. It is unknown why the Spanish-Portuguese community of Amsterdam did not perform Bircas Kohanim daily, like all other Sephardim worldwide.[8] In this regard, they conducted themselves like the Ashkenazim, and performed Bircas Kohanim only on Mussaf of the festivals.

When Shabsai Tzvi was finally exposed as a fraud and a heretic, and was compelled by the Turkish sultan to convert to Islam, the question arose as to whether those who had accepted the practice of *duchaning* every Shabbos should continue to do so, since it is, in fact, the custom of most Sephardic communities around the world.

This interesting query was presented to R' Yaakov Sasportas of Amsterdam (1610-1698), who was one of Shabsai Tzvi's earliest and most forceful opponents. He wrote a four-volume work against Shabsai Tzvi, which he called *Tzitzas Novel Tzvi*, and he responds to the above question as follows (*She'eilos U'Teshuvos Ohel Yaakov* #68-70):

> Who would take the mitzvah of Bircas Kohanim lightly, Heaven forbid? Even if the Kohen reciting the *berachah* is unworthy to be the conduit of blessing, it takes effect just the same, as *Chazal* have taught us in *Yerushalmi* (*Gittin* 5:9): Do not say, "This Kohen is guilty of engaging in forbidden relations and murder — *he* is going to bless me?" Says the Holy One, Blessed is He, "Is he, then, the one who blesses you? It is I Who shall bless you, as the Torah states, *and I shall bless them*!"

---

8. The *sefer Noheg Katzon Yosef*, written by R' Yosef HaLevi Kushman of Frankfurt, Germany, in 1718, states clearly that the Sephardim of Amsterdam did indeed perform daily Bircas Kohanim. Perhaps this was a result of the ruling of R' Yaakov Sasportas cited here.

> Moreover, *Yerushalmi* teaches (*Sotah* 9:14) that there is no day whose curses are not greater than the day before, and the only thing that protects us from the curses is Bircas Kohanim.
>
> Aside from all that, Bircas Kohanim is a positive commandment of the Torah, and the more we are able to perform it, the better.

Nevertheless, he concludes, in his opinion, the practice should be discontinued until three festivals have passed, as we do not want a mitzvah and a holy practice to be traced to Shabsai Tzvi; it would be a disgrace if that public sinner got any credit for this. After the three festivals have passed, he writes, and the congregation wants to revert to its previous custom, it is worthwhile for them to initiate even daily Bircas Kohanim. On the contrary, people will talk about the time when they abstained from doing Bircas Kohanim for a period of time because of the involvement of a *rasha,* and it will be a disgrace for Shabsai Tzvi.

R' Sasportas concludes, "The above applies only if the mitzvah will not be attributed to that wicked heretic. If that is not the intention, then I say, '*Yasher kocham* of those who follow the custom of *duchaning* every day,' as *Beis Yosef* writes with regard to those living in Eretz Yisrael."

Reinstituting the Bircas Kohanim Custom in Amsterdam

R' Eliezer Yehudah Waldenburg (*She'eilos U'Teshuvos Tzitz Eliezer,* vol. 7, #6) was asked whether a Sephardic community in Amsterdam that was still not performing daily Bircas Kohanim should begin to do so. He answered by referencing the above *teshuvah* of R' Yaakov Sasportas, adding: "Since much time has passed, and the custom is no longer attributed to that evil heretic, it is indeed appropriate to reinstitute it. Thus, it is permitted and it would be fitting for the communities that originate from Amsterdam and its environs to *duchan* every Shabbos and every day of the week, so as not to separate themselves from the Sephardic communities around the world."

The Custom in Djerba

Several shuls on the Tunisian island of Djerba had the custom to perform Bircas Kohanim only in Mussaf of Shabbos, Rosh Chodesh, and Yom Tov. (Shuls in other cities in Tunisia, such as Yeshivat Kisei Rachamim in the capital city of Tunis, founded by R' Tzemach Mazuz, did perform daily Bircas Kohanim.)

Responding to the query of a community that moved from Djerba to Eretz Yisrael, R' Binyamin Yehoshua Zilber ruled (*She'eilos U'Teshuvos Az Nidberu,* vol. 2, #62) that once they arrive in Eretz Yisrael, it is incumbent upon them to perform daily Bircas Kohanim, like all other Sephardim worldwide.

Even in a House of Mourners

R' Yihya Saleh (1713-1805), known as *Maharitz,* was a revered Yemenite *posek*. In his commentary on the *siddur* (*Hilchos Shemoneh Esrei*), he expounds in several places on the importance of daily Bircas Kohanim. He also writes that the Yemenite custom for many generations has been to *duchan* daily, even in a house of mourning, and if the mourners themselves are Kohanim, they should *duchan* as well, even during *shivah*.[9] He writes:

> There are those whose custom is that Kohanim do not *duchan* if they are in mourning, and some say it is not done at all in a house of mourning. However, I have a tradition that for many generations Bircas Kohanim was performed in a house of mourning, even by the mourner himself. Indeed, for what reason should a mourner refrain from fulfilling three positive commandments, when everyone agrees that he is obligated in all mitzvos of the Torah?
>
> If one wishes to argue that a mourner should not perform the mitzvah because he is not in a state of joy, that is not sufficient reason to negate three positive commandments, for where do we find that one who is not joyful is not permitted to *duchan*?
>
> The proof that this is not the case is the fact that so much ink has been spilled just to negate the opinion of those

9. See chapter 38 for a discussion of the various halachic opinions on this matter.

who say a bachelor should not *duchan*, because he is not in a state of joy. Later, I saw in *Pri Chadash* (*se'if* 43) that the opinion that a mourner does not *duchan* has no explanation and is totally unfounded.

Protection Against the Nazis

R' Eliezer Brezel[10] writes (glosses to *Sefer HaAgudah, Sotah* 38a): "During the difficult years of the Holocaust, it was revealed to me in a dream that Yerushalayim would not suffer from the Nazis, because Bircas Kohanim is recited there every day. I also heard from *gedolei Yisrael* that Yerushalayim was spared from the many earthquakes that struck Eretz Yisrael because of the daily Bircas Kohanim there."

The author of *VaAni Avaracheim* makes this observation in his introduction: When we contemplate all the tragic events of the Holocaust, we notice a pattern, although we cannot fathom Heaven's calculations. The amount of suffering and persecution that each community endured seems to be in direct proportion to the frequency that Bircas Kohanim was recited in that location. As a general rule, those places where the custom was to *duchan* every day, as is practiced in all Sephardic communities worldwide, or at least every Shabbos, suffered less than other places, where Bircas Kohanim is recited only on Yom Tov. The former category includes North Africa and Italy, despite the fact that those countries were allied with Germany. Moreover, the downfall of the Nazis began in Egypt, when they were heading toward Eretz Yisrael, and in both of those places, the custom throughout the generations was to *duchan* every day.[11]

10. 1910-2007. He was a prominent *talmid chacham* and Karlin-Stolin chassid in Yerushalayim who authored many *sefarim*, including a commentary on the *Sefer HaAgudah*.

11. Other sources mention that besides performing daily Bircas Kohanim, Sephardic congregations are more careful not to talk during davening. *Tosafos Yom Tov* and others wrote, after the Chmielnicki massacres of 1648, that Ashkenazic communities should be more careful not to talk during the prayers.

Chapter 17
Ashkenazim in Chutz LaAretz: Benefiting From the Berachah

Does the daily Bircas Kohanim performed in Eretz Yisrael extend to those in *chutz laAretz* who do not have the benefit of this *berachah* every day?

R' Moshe Chagiz[1] writes (*Eileh HaMitzvos*, Positive Commandment 148): "People living outside Eretz Yisrael who are supporting those who live in the Land, enabling them to fulfill the mitzvah of *yishuv Eretz Yisrael*, will be rewarded by being included in the Bircas Kohanim that is recited there. It is considered as though the Kohanim have in mind to bestow the *berachah* upon them, and as though they have in mind to receive the *berachah* (as we find with regard to all *berachos*, that the intention of both, the person reciting the *berachah* and the person who is receiving it, is necessary). It would also be ideal for the chazzan (outside Eretz Yisrael), when he says the words בָּרְכֵנוּ בַּבְּרָכָה הַמְשֻׁלֶּשֶׁת ... הָאֲמוּרָה מִפִּי אַהֲרֹן וּבָנָיו..., *Bless us with the three-verse blessing ... said by Aharon and his sons...*, to have in mind in that prayer the Kohanim in Eretz Yisrael who are reciting Bircas Kohanim. The *berachah* will surely take effect for all those who are included."

Most *poskim*, however, are of the opinion that Bircas Kohanim

1. 1671-1750. He was born in Yerushalayim and spent several decades in Amsterdam and Italy. In 1737 he left Europe and settled in Tzfas, where he passed away.

is not effective for those in another country, and definitely cannot "spread" overseas.[2]

R' Moshe Feinstein (*Igros Moshe, O.C.*, vol. 2, #31) states unequivocally that the *berachos* of a Kohen in one city do not extend to another city. He writes: "The Gemara (*Sotah* 38b) says that in a congregation that consists entirely of Kohanim, all of them should *duchan* together. The Gemara then asks: To whom is their blessing addressed, if no other congregants are present? And the Gemara answers: It is addressed to their brethren who are working in the fields and cannot be present. Now, why doesn't the Gemara simply answer that the blessing is addressed to the entire Jewish people? The obvious conclusion is that **the *berachah* is exclusively for those who live in the same city, as implied by the fact that the Gemara — as well as *Rambam* and *Shulchan Aruch* — mentions the fields, which refers to the surrounding local area."**

R' Shlomo Zalman Auerbach is quoted (*Halichos Shlomo, Hilchos Tefillah* 10:7) as saying that the "people in the fields" include only those who are presently in the same country. Thus, those who reside outside of Eretz Yisrael cannot receive the *berachah* through Kohanim in Eretz Yisrael. Even if a Kohen has in mind to bless someone who is in a different country, it would not be effective. (While this is similar to the opinion of R' Moshe Feinstein, R' Moshe specified that Bircas Kohanim extends only to the same city, but R' Shlomo Zalman said it extends to the same country — a remarkable *chiddush*.)

Having in Mind a Particular Individual

While performing Bircas Kohanim, may a Kohen have a particular individual in mind?

---

2. Several contemporary *sefarim* relate that one year, before Rosh Hashanah, R' Chaim Brisker sent a letter to the *Ohr Samei'ach*, R' Meir Simchah HaKohen of Dvinsk. In that letter, he reportedly asked R' Meir Simchah to have him in mind when reciting Bircas Kohanim during the upcoming *Yamim Noraim*. However, it is unclear what exactly was written in the letter, because no copy of the letter has ever been found, and the exact contents of the letter were never recorded. When R' Yosef Shalom Elyashiv was asked about this letter, he replied that if such a letter did exist, it was probably a request for a *bircas tzaddik*, as one should not have in mind a specific individual during Bircas Kohanim. See *Tziyunei Halachah*, p. 333.

When R' Yosef Shalom Elyashiv was asked this question, he responded (*Tziyunei Halachah,* p. 333): "It has no effect; the *berachah* must include everyone equally. Even when *Chazal* said that the workers in the fields are included, it does not mean that a Kohen can be in one place and direct his *berachah* toward someone who is in a different place. Moreover, even if he has in mind to include everyone who is present, but especially one specific person among them, that also has no effect; it contradicts the concept of blessing everyone together."

Similarly, R' Nissim Karelitz rules (*Chut Shani, Hilchos Bircas Kohanim* 128:7): "A Kohen must not have in mind that his *berachah* should be just for one particular person (for example, if that person asked him to do so). However, if he wishes, he may mention the person's name before he begins to *duchan.*"

R' Chaim Kanievsky also writes clearly (Responsa #366-368) that it does not help for a Kohen in Eretz Yisrael to have in mind someone in another city or overseas, as the *berachah* does not spread to another city or country, even if a Kohen in Eretz Yisrael has the person in mind. R' Chaim notes, however, that a Kohen may have in mind an individual in his city before Bircas Kohanim. (R' Chaim says it is permissible for a Kohen to have a Yisrael in mind during Bircas Kohanim, but it is preferable for the Kohen to have him in mind before Bircas Kohanim.)

Some Value

R' Moshe Sternbuch agrees that if a Kohen has in mind to bless someone who is not in the city, it would not be considered as though that person actually received Bircas Kohanim. Nevertheless, he suggests that it still does have some value, albeit not comparable to one who actually hears Bircas Kohanim.

For a number of years, R' Sternbuch served as a rav in Johannesburg, South Africa, and during that time he wrote (*Teshuvos V'Hanhagos,* vol. 1 #130):

> We who are outside of Eretz Yisrael yearn very much for Bircas Kohanim, which is a *berachah* directly from Hashem, and here we sorely miss it. Still, the truth is that the *"am sheb'sados"* (people working in the fields), who are not able to be present during Bircas Kohanim, are included in

the *berachah*. Perhaps we who live overseas, and also have no way to be present, can be included as well, and can receive the *berachah* through the Kohanim in Eretz Yisrael.

However, I am inclined to say that the main *berachah* is only for those who are standing before the Kohanim, or for members of that congregation who live in the city but are unable to attend, for some unavoidable reason. Nevertheless, if the Kohanim do have in mind only one specific individual from outside Eretz Yisrael, and mention his name before they begin to *duchan*, it is perhaps effective to bring Hashem's blessing upon that person, who, to some extent, can also be described as *am sheb'sados*.

When I am outside Eretz Yisrael, my practice is to ask two Kohanim to have me in mind every day before they *duchan*. In this way, I, too, am able to be included in a *berachah* from Hashem through the Kohanim, who have direct access to the Shechinah. I also make a point of paying them a specified amount for the service.

Elsewhere, however, R' Sternbuch writes (*Teshuvos V'Hanhagos*, vol. 4 #39) that this is not as effective as receiving the actual Bircas Kohanim:

"Some suggest that the entire Jewish people, even those who reside outside Eretz Yisrael, are considered *am sheb'sados*, and are thus included in Bircas Kohanim, since they, too, are *anusim* — that is, they are unable to be present due to circumstances beyond their control. However, it seems to me that the intention of *Chazal* was primarily to include only members of that particular congregation, who are unable to be there just that day because they are working in the fields. There is no indication that those who are not part of the same congregation as the Kohanim who are performing Bircas Kohanim, and are located elsewhere, can be included as well."

Later (ibid., vol. 6 #40), R' Sternbuch adds: "It seems that those who cannot be present receive the *berachah* only in a general, inclusive way, while those who are actually in the shul each receive their own individual *berachah*, as per the wording of the *berachos* themselves — e.g., יְבָרֶכְךָ ה', *May Hashem bless 'you'* (singular)."

In a conversation with this author, R' Sternbuch explained that it is a good idea for Ashkenazim who reside overseas to ask two Kohanim in Eretz Yisrael to have them in mind before Bircas Kohanim. He noted that, as he writes above, he himself did this when he was a rav in South Africa, but added emphatically that this is not remotely equivalent to an actual Bircas Kohanim; it is merely a semblance of Bircas Kohanim. Since he was unable to hear the *berachah* every day, however, it was his way of being connected with the general Bircas Kohanim.

Guidelines for Ashkenazim in a Sephardic Shul in Chutz LaAretz

R' Chaim Kanievsky was of the opinion that if a group of Ashkenazim who reside *outside* Eretz Yisrael travel to another part of the world (outside Eretz Yisrael), even to an uninhabited island, it is prohibited for them to *duchan* there in an Ashkenazic minyan.[3] This would be the case even if there was never a Jewish community in that location, as performing daily Bircas Kohanim would be a violation of the Ashkenazic custom.[4]

However, R' Chaim held that it *is* permitted for Ashkenazi Kohanim who reside outside Eretz Yisrael to *duchan* in a Sephardic minyan (following the Sephardic custom to *duchan* every day). This is not considered a violation of the Ashkenazic custom, since the Bircas Kohanim is taking place in a Sephardic minyan. Furthermore, R' Chaim actively encouraged Kohanim in *chutz laAretz* to *duchan* in an established Sephardic minyan, so that they could fulfill three positive Torah commandments.[5]

R' Chaim told his disciple R' Shimon Brecher, an Ashkenazi Kohen living in *chutz laAretz,* to go to *duchan* at a Sephardic minyan on a daily basis. R' Shimon accepted this advice, and performed the mitzvah daily for at least seven years, until he passed away, on 12 Cheshvan 5781/October 30, 2020. He would usually daven

3. If they reside in Eretz Yisrael, however, they are permitted to form their own, exclusive minyan and to *duchan* even outside of Eretz Yisrael; see chapter 14.
4. See Responsa #546.
5. See Responsa #532-541. This ruling also appears in a number of *sefarim* that quote R' Chaim; see, for example, *Simchas Avraham,* p. 417, and *Simchas Mordechai,* p. 258.

at sunrise in an Ashkenazic minyan, then take off his tefillin, but continue wearing his tallis, and drive to a local Sephardic minyan for Bircas Kohanim.

The following is a brief summary of the rulings R' Chaim gave R' Shimon with regard to Bircas Kohanim[6]:

1. It makes no difference whether one davens Shacharis with the Sephardim, or davens in an Ashkenazic minyan and then goes to the Sephardic shul for Bircas Kohanim.
2. It is permissible to leave one's own Ashkenazic minyan right after *Shemoneh Esrei* in order to get to the Sephardic minyan on time.
3. After parking one's car, going from the car to the Sephardic shul in order to *duchan* counts as the *akirah* (moving from one's place) that is required during the *berachah* of *Retzei.*
4. If the Kohen wants, he may use the Sephardic pronunciation of the words during Bircas Kohanim.
5. This author was once present when R' Shimon reported to R' Chaim that people had told him it is preferable for an Ashkenazi not to *duchan* in a Sephardic minyan every day overseas. R' Chaim responded that this is no different from Ashkenazim from *chutz laAretz duchaning* daily when they are in Eretz Yisrael.

A clear source for the ruling that an Ashkenazi Kohen is permitted to *duchan* at a Sephardic minyan outside Eretz Yisrael is found in *Reishis Bikkurim* (*siman* 4), authored by R' Betzalel HaKohen of Vilna (1820-1878). He writes, about his trip to Trieste, Italy in Elul 5624/1864: "The custom in this city is to *duchan* every Shabbos. On Shabbos Parashas Shoftim, I davened in a Sephardic minyan, and they honored me to be the only Kohen who said Bircas Kohanim aloud, while all the other Kohanim stood next to me and fulfilled their obligation by listening to my *berachos*. That is their custom — to perform Bircas Kohanim through *'shomei'a k'oneh'* (listening as the equivalent of speaking)."[7]

---

6. For more on these rulings, see *Shamanu Kein Ra'inu* ch. 7, pp. 213-221.
7. The isolated custom of *shomei'a k'oneh* practiced in Trieste, Italy, led to many halachic *teshuvos* on this topic; most *poskim* disagree with this practice.

Not to Miss a Single Day

Kol Chotzev, a biography of R' Shalom Schwadron authored by his grandson R' Yaakov Ariel, relates (p. 126) that R' Shalom, who was a Kohen, would make prodigious efforts to *duchan* every morning at a Sephardic minyan during his numerous trips to the United States. When he stayed in Brooklyn, the closest such minyan — the *netz* minyan of Beit Knesset Bnei Yosef, headed by R' Chaim Benoliel — was located quite a distance from the home where he stayed. Nevertheless, R' Shalom would not allow himself to miss a single day. Rain or snow, heat or cold — he was always there, always on time.[8]

Similarly, the current Toldos Aharon Rebbe, R' Dovid HaKohen Kahn of Yerushalayim, and the Pinsk-Karlin Rebbe, R' Aryeh HaKohen Rosenfeld of Yerushalayim, do their utmost whenever they travel abroad to be present during Bircas Kohanim in a Sephardic minyan, so they can bless the congregation and earn three daily mitzvos.

Two Separate Courts

The prohibition of *lo sisgodedu* (*Devarim* 14:1) — which can be interpreted as, *You shall not split into many agudos* (groups) — forbids a community to divide itself into different factions, with each group observing the Torah differently. Is it a halachic problem, then, if Ashkenazim in a certain city do not *duchan* daily, and Sephardim in the same city do?

R' Shmuel Wosner (*Shevet HaLevi,* vol. 4, *siman* 70) addresses this question and answers that this is not a case of *lo sisgodedu* at all, especially because the Ashkenazic and Sephardic communities are considered like two separate *batei dinim* (courts) in one city, each of which is entitled to follow its own rulings.[9]

---

8. R' Shlomo Wahba of Brooklyn, who drove R' Shalom to the minyan every morning, recalls that the joy R' Shalom exhibited when he arrived was intense. At R' Shlomo's request, R' Shalom would "pay" for the ride by sharing some *divrei Torah*. As they walked from the car to the shul, R' Shalom would caution R' Shlomo to be quiet. He said, "We do not wish to lose the mitzvah of davening at *netz* by waking those who are still sleeping." (This is also cited in the *Kol Torah* Journal, #79.)

9. *Eishel Avraham* states that *lo sisgodedu* does not apply to Bircas Kohanim; see chapter 40.

Following the Customs of a Sephardic Minyan

R' Moshe Feinstein writes (*Igros Moshe, O.C.,* vol. 3, #89) that when one is davening in a shul whose customs differ from his own, he must conform to the *minhagim* of that shul wherever deviating from their custom will be noticeable. For example, if they recite *Vidui* and *Yud-Gimmel Middos* before *Tachanun,* he should follow suit. If he does not, he may be in violation of the prohibition of *lo sisgodedu,* which forbids us to form separate groups, with each one following a different custom.

His *talmid* R' Ephraim Greenblatt writes (*Rivevos Ephraim,* vol. 6, *siman* 57): "I was asked by an Ashkenazi Kohen who was davening in a Sephardic minyan whether he should *duchan.* I responded that since it is the custom of that congregation, he should. I also heard from my friend R' Yerachmiel Adler, who is a Kohen, that he had posed the same question to R' Dovid Feinstein, and was told that if you daven with Sephardim you must follow their custom and *duchan* with them. Later, I came across the *sefer Mayim Chaim,* authored by R' Chaim Dovid HaLevi, who rules this way as well. He writes (vol. 1, #4) that even in those communities that continue their custom not to *duchan* every day, an Ashkenazi Kohen is not prohibited to *duchan* when he davens in a Sephardic minyan. On the contrary, it is an opportunity for him to fulfill a mitzvah together with his Sephardic brethren, and it should be done with a *berachah.* This is the clear and obvious halachah."

Other Opinions Regarding Kohanim Duchaning at a Sephardic Minyan

In contrast to the opinion of R' Chaim Kanievsky discussed above, R' Shlomo Zalman Auerbach is quoted (*Halichos Shlomo* ch. 10) as saying that an Ashkenazi Kohen who lives outside Eretz Yisrael should not deliberately go to a Sephardic shul in order to *duchan.* However, a Kohen who resides in Eretz Yisrael and presently finds himself in another country *is* permitted to do so. Similarly, R' Bentzion Kook reports that R' Yosef Shalom Elyashiv was uncomfortable with the practice of Kohanim who live in *chutz laAretz* attending a Sephardic minyan there for the purpose of *duchaning*.[10]

While these *poskim* question the appropriateness of a Kohen *duchaning* in a Sephardic minyan overseas, which is an *active* divergence from the Ashkenazic custom, they all agree that it is perfectly acceptable for a non-Kohen to go to hear Bircas Kohanim at a Sephardic minyan even on a daily basis.

Non-Kohanim Attending a Sephardic Minyan

Besides encouraging Ashkenazi Kohanim in *chutz laAretz* to attend a Sephardic minyan, R' Chaim encouraged thousands of Ashkenazi Leviim and Yisraelim living outside Eretz Yisrael to go to hear Bircas Kohanim in a Sephardic minyan (see introduction to this book).[11] On many occasions, visitors from other countries would approach R' Chaim to seek his *berachah* for various challenges and difficulties they were going through, and R' Chaim would advise them to go to a Sephardic minyan to hear Bircas Kohanim and to have in mind that they should merit a salvation.[12]

R' Chaim Kanievsky's Advice

R' Binyomin Carlebach, rosh yeshivah in Yerushalayim's Yeshivas Mir, related: "Approximately ten years before R' Chaim's *petirah*, the young son of a family I was acquainted with in the United States was diagnosed with a dire medical condition, and the doctors feared the worst. The family approached me and requested that I go to Bnei Brak and ask R' Chaim what the family could do as a merit for his recovery. When R' Chaim heard about the boy's severe medical issue, he told me that I should tell the father to attend daily Bircas Kohanim in a Sephardic minyan in the United States, as a *zechus* for a *yeshuah*. With Hashem's help, their son recovered and is today a vibrant and healthy *chashuveh bachur*."

10. See *Tziyunei Halachah*, p. 418.

11. Other *gedolim*, including R' Yaakov Edelstein and R' Chaim Pinchas Scheinberg, strongly encouraged Yisraelim from *chutz laAretz* who needed a *yeshuah* to go to hear Bircas Kohanim at a Sephardic minyan.

12. See *Rav Chaim Kanievsky on Shidduchim* (ArtScroll/Mesorah), p. 318.

Not to Make it a Daily Practice

R' Shmuel Kamenetsky told this author that if there would be a Sephardic shul near his home in Philadelphia, and it would not interfere with his daily schedule, he would make it his habit to try to hear Bircas Kohanim daily. R' Shmuel added that he often tells his students and family members that a *berachah* directly from Hashem is more powerful than a *berachah* from any intermediary, including a *tzaddik*.

R' Shmuel explained that since *Biur Halachah* (beginning of *Hilchos Nesias Kapayim*) quotes *Sefer Chareidim*'s view that it is a mitzvah for a Yisrael to hear Bircas Kohanim, he would certainly want to fulfill this mitzvah on a daily basis.[13] He also noted that although an Ashkenazi Kohen who resides outside Eretz Yisrael is not obligated to perform daily Bircas Kohanim — because the *minhag* is so strong that it completely overrides the commandment of the Torah — if an Ashkenazi Kohen wants to *duchan* in a Sephardic minyan, it is permissible for him to do so, but he would advise him not to do it daily, as the Ashkenazic custom in *chutz laAretz* is to *duchan* only on Yom Tov.

He added that if the Kohen goes to *duchan* in a Sephardic minyan one day a week, that is not considered uprooting any custom, and it is permissible *l'chatchilah*.

In the Footsteps of the Baal HaTanya

The Lubavitcher Rebbe, R' Menachem Mendel Schneerson, also strongly encouraged those who are able to hear Bircas Kohanim in a Sephardic minyan to do so, as he stated:[14]

> The custom in many communities, especially among our Sephardic brethren, is to perform Bircas Kohanim every

13. The Chazon Ish was of the opinion that the halachah is not in accordance with *Sefer Chareidim*, who holds that there is a specific mitzvah for a non-Kohen to hear Bircas Kohanim. Nevertheless, R' Chaim Kanievsky, who consistently followed the rulings of the Chazon Ish, still maintained that it is meritorious and highly recommended for a non-Kohen to hear Bircas Kohanim. See Responsa #163.

14. In a *sichah* delivered on *Motzaei Shabbos* 9 *Sivan* 5744/June 9, 1984 (*Sefer Toras Menachem, Hisvaaduyos* 5744, p. 446).

> day. That being the case, every individual (especially if he lives in one of the large cities that have numerous shuls catering to all types of Jewish communities) has the option of going to a shul that performs Bircas Kohanim and thereby receiving all the *berachos*, even if he is Ashkenazi and does not have the custom to *duchan* every day.

Sefer Hisvaaduyos of 1992 records that on 6 Cheshvan of that year, the Lubavitcher Rebbe told then-Sephardic Chief Rabbi of Israel R' Mordechai Eliyahu:

> The Sephardim are very fortunate that they have the merit of performing Bircas Kohanim every day, and not just on Yom Tov. The *Baal HaTanya* wanted to institute the custom of *duchaning* on a daily basis in his shul as well. He made an effort to do so but was not able to get the community to accept the practice.

Traveling for the Berachah

Some *gedolim* in *chutz laAretz* make it a point, despite their busy schedules, to hear Bircas Kohanim as frequently as they can. This author was present several times at a Sephardic minyan in the United States where R' Elya Ber Wachtfogel, Rosh Yeshivah of Yeshivas Zichron Moshe of South Fallsburg, was also present. Sometimes he davened the entire Shacharis with the Sephardim, and other times he came after he had already davened, just to hear Bircas Kohanim.

During the summer months, when many Jews vacation upstate near his yeshivah and form numerous minyanim, R' Elya Ber goes to hear Bircas Kohanim almost daily in a Sephardic minyan. In a conversation, he related that during the winter months, he goes to New York or New Jersey at least once a week to be blessed with Bircas Kohanim, despite having to travel more than two hours each way.[15] He tries to attend several Sephardic minyanim on the same trip, to compensate for the days that he is unable to travel the long distance.

---

15. R' Elya Ber explained that he usually goes on days when he does not give *shiur* in his yeshivah, so as not to cause *bittul Torah* for his *talmidim*. He also does his best to learn while traveling, as well as between the different Sephardic minyanim.

Chapter 18
Chassidic Communities in Tzfas, Teveriah, and Haifa

Although the custom throughout Eretz Yisrael, for both Sephardic and Ashkenazic Jews, has always been to recite Bircas Kohanim daily, certain chassidic communities in Tzfas, Teveriah, and Haifa do not follow this practice.

Chassidim everywhere else in Eretz Yisrael do perform daily Bircas Kohanim, but for at least the last century, it has been somewhat of a status quo for chassidic communities in these northern cities to recite Bircas Kohanim only during Mussaf, on all days that it is recited: Shabbos, Rosh Chodesh, Yom Tov, and Chol HaMoed. This is unlike the Ashkenazic practice in *chutz laAretz,* where Bircas Kohanim is performed only on Yom Tov.

Interestingly, the first known mention of this custom is by R' Chaim Siton, a Sephardic scholar who lived in Tzfas (1871-1916). In his *sefer Eretz Chaim* (*siman* 128), published in 5668/1908, he writes: "Although *Beis Yosef* praised those who perform Bircas Kohanim daily, we find mentioned in the Rishonim, the *Orchos Chaim*, and the *Kol Bo* that it is a burden upon the congregation to do Bircas Kohanim daily [as it adds too much time to the weekly prayers]. Seemingly, that is the reason that the Ashkenazim in Tzfas perform Bircas Kohanim only on Shabbos."

Compromise

R' Moshe Sternbuch writes (*Hilchos HaGra U'Minhagav* #109) that although there is no concrete halachic reason not to do daily Bircas Kohanim in Tzfas and Teveriah, it can be speculated that the custom originated when groups of chassidim arrived in those cities[16] from overseas, where they were accustomed to *duchan* only on Yom Tov. He adds that we do not know who initiated the custom, as there is no documented source for it, but we can guess that the chassidic communities of Tzfas and Teveriah settled on a compromise between their previous custom of performing Bircas Kohanim only on Yom Tov, which was the practice in Europe, and the custom of Eretz Yisrael, which was to *duchan* every day.[17]

R' Sternbuch adds that it is clear that in the time of the Arizal and the Kabbalists of Tzfas, prior to the arrival of the chassidim, Bircas Kohanim was performed daily. R' Yeshayahu HaLevi Horowitz (1555-1630), the *Shelah*, also writes that when he was in the Galilee,[18] Bircas Kohanim was done daily.

Since this unique custom in Tzfas and Teveriah traces back at least a century, many established chassidic communities in Tzfas and Teveriah continue to perform Bircas Kohanim only during Mussaf on all days when it is recited.

Opposition to the Custom

This custom has been disputed by many halachic authorities, however, including chassidic *poskim*.

R' Chaim Meir Greenbaum, *dayan* of the Vizhnitz community in Haifa, compiled a pamphlet entitled *Koh Sevarechu Haifa*, in

16. The first large group of chassidim, disciples of the Baal Shem Tov, arrived in Tzfas in 5537/1767, and remained there for three years. They then moved to the city of Pekiin and later to Teveriah. The first large group of disciples of the Vilna Gaon (called "Perushim") arrived in Tzfas in 5568/1808. A second group of students of the Vilna Gaon arrived in 5569/1809; R' Yisrael of Shklov was among this second group. In 1815, R' Menachem Mendel of Shklov moved to Yerushalayim and helped develop the Ashkenazic community of Yerushalayim.
17. R' Yitzchok Yaakov Weiss (*She'eilos U'Teshuvos Minchas Yitzchak*, vol. 8 #1-2) quotes R' Moshe Sternbuch's speculative explanation as the probable reason for the custom in Tzfas and Teveriah.
18. See chapter 5.

which he published a number of letters written by *poskim* of our times regarding Bircas Kohanim in northern Eretz Yisrael. There, he writes that it is doubtful that the practice of *duchaning* only during Mussaf was instituted in Tzfas by the great chassidic leaders R' Menachem Mendel of Vitebsk and R' Avraham HaKohen of Klassik, who arrived there in 1767 and stayed there for only three years.[19]

R' Binyamin Yehoshua Zilber[20] points out (*She'eilos U'Teshuvos Az Nidberu,* vol. 11, #43) that even if we assume that this custom was established when the first chassidim came to Tzfas, which was thirty years before the *talmidim* of the Vilna Gaon arrived, we see that R' Yisrael of Shklov did perform daily Bircas Kohanim in Tzfas nonetheless.[21] Evidently, he felt that the practice of the chassidic community for the preceding three decades (if indeed the practice was not to *duchan* daily) did not obligate the community of the Vilna Gaon's disciples to deviate from the established custom in Eretz Yisrael of daily Bircas Kohanim, which the Vilna Gaon tried unsuccessfully to introduce even in the Diaspora.

R' Menachem Mendel of Kamenitz (1800-1873), who spent some time with the Perushim community of R' Yisrael of Shklov in Tzfas, writes the following, in *Koros HaItim*: "I took up a dwelling in the neighborhood of the Perushim, in the same courtyard as R' Zalman Cohen. On that street there is a shul and a *beis midrash* that follow the customs of the Perushim, and every morning after davening, R' Yisrael of Shklov delivers a lecture on a *daf* of Gemara and on Chumash with the commentary of *Rashi.* **Their custom is that the Kohanim *duchan* every day."**

R' Shlomo Shlomil Minstrel of Tzfas, an Ashkenazi who lived in the generation after the Arizal and authored *Shivchei HaAri* and other *sefarim,* writes (*Kovetz Al Yad,* vol. 3, p. 126): "**Every day, the**

19. He quotes several letters from chassidim who were in Tzfas during those three years, which indicate that the chassidim at that time did not have their own shuls in Tzfas.

20. 1916-2008. He was one of the close disciples of the Chazon Ish and had a close personal relationship with several chassidic Rebbes. He authored many works on halachah and *mussar,* in addition to fourteen volumes of *teshuvos* called *Az Nidberu* in which he answered halachic queries from around the world.

21. In his *sefer Pe'as HaShulchan* (published in 1836), quoted above (see chapter 16), R' Yisrael of Shklov writes that it is the custom of the entire Eretz Yisrael to perform daily Bircas Kohanim.

Kohanim go up to *duchan* when the chazzan reaches the *berachah* of *Sim Shalom*, and also during Minchah on fast days."

Similarly, in Yeshivas Toras Eretz Yisrael in Tzfas, which was established in 1905 by R' Yaakov Dovid Wilovsky (known as the Ridbaz) and was one of the largest yeshivos in Israel at the time, Bircas Kohanim was performed on a daily basis.[22]

R' Binyamin Yehoshua Zilber[23] and R' Sroya Deblitzki[24] write that it would be a far-reaching merit if all the Ashkenazim in the Galilee would perform the great mitzvah of daily Bircas Kohanim.

Similarly, R' Chaim Kanievsky writes (Responsa #528) that those from other cities in Eretz Yisrael who visit Tzfas, or who open their own *beis midrash* in the Galilee, are surely permitted to form their own minyan and perform Bircas Kohanim.

On the few occasions when the Chazon Ish traveled to Tzfas in the summer, he davened in a minyan where Bircas Kohanim was performed every morning. Likewise, during the eleven summers when R' Chaim Kanievsky vacationed in Tzfas, he organized his own[25] *netz* minyan, in which daily Bircas Kohanim was performed as well (see Responsa #530).

Other Chassidic Communities in Tzfas

Although many chassidic communities in Tzfas have the custom to perform Bircas Kohanim only on Shabbos, Rosh Chodesh, Yom Tov, and Chol HaMoed, this definitely does not apply to *all* chassidic communities in the city. For instance, the chassidic community of Lelov in Tzfas does perform daily Bircas Kohanim, as per the directive of R' Moshe Mordechai of Lelov, and his son R' Shimon, who alternated between leading his chassidim in Bnei Brak and those in Tzfas. Additionally, the chassidic community of Breslov — which today is the single largest chassidic community in the city — as well as those of Biala and Sadigura perform Bircas Kohanim daily.

22. See *She'eilos U'Teshuvos Az Nidberu,* vol. 12, #24.
23. *Az Nidberu,* vol. 11, #43.
24. Noted *mekubal* of Bnei Brak, who conscientiously followed the customs of the Vilna Gaon. This is recorded in the *HaNe'eman* journal, year 17, issue 31.
25. Heard from the noted *mohel* R' Eliezer Lieberman of Tzfas, who hosted R' Chaim during ten out of those eleven years.

Meron

Interestingly, all communities in the town of Meron perform Bircas Kohanim daily, including chassidic congregations, despite the town's close proximity to Tzfas (approximately six miles, or ten kilometers). The reason is that the community of Meron was established, in 1949, primarily by inhabitants of other cities in Eretz Yisrael, whose custom was to perform daily Bircas Kohanim. Thus, for as long as the elders of Yerushalayim can remember, all chassidim who visit Meron, even for a short time, perform daily Bircas Kohanim there.[26]

Chassidic Communities in New Locations in Eretz Yisrael

As noted above (chapter 14), if a group of Ashkenazic Jews establishes a new community anywhere in the Diaspora, it is prohibited for them to institute daily Bircas Kohanim there, as the custom of all Ashkenazim outside of Eretz Yisrael is to *duchan* only on the festivals. Nevertheless, if a group of chassidim moves to Tzfas, Teveriah, or Haifa from a place in Eretz Yisrael where Bircas Kohanim is performed daily, R' Moshe Sternbuch, R' Moshe Shaul Klein, and R' Yaakov Meir Stern, and many other chassidic *poskim* (as well as R' Chaim Kanievsky) rule that the new community is *obligated* to continue performing Bircas Kohanim every day in those locations, in keeping with their original custom.[27] This was the reason R' Moshe Mordechai of Lelov and his son R' Shimon instituted daily Bircas Kohanim when their community opened their own shul in Tzfas, even though there were other established chassidic congregations there that did not do so.

R' Moshe Sternbuch rules[28] that it is not a violation of *lo sisgode-*

26. As heard by this author from R' Gamliel HaKohen Rabinowitz of Yerushalayim, who heard it from his father, R' Levi HaKohen Rabinowitz (1920-2015), author of *Maadanei HaShulchan*. Similar proof that the proximity of Meron to Tzfas does not obligate those in Meron to refrain from daily Bircas Kohanim is cited by R' Moshe Shaul Klein (*Koh Sevarechu Haifa*, p. 10), who explains that other cities in the Galilee do not have to follow the custom of Tzfas.
27. See *Koh Sevarechu Haifa*, and responsa of R' Chaim Kanievsky #530.
28. Ibid. p. 9.

du[29] if an Ashkenazic community initiates daily Bircas Kohanim anywhere in Eretz Yisrael, as that is the prevailing custom in Eretz Yisrael.

The Sanz Community in Teveriah

Several years ago, the Sanz-Klausenberg community of Netanya, seeking affordable housing, established a new satellite community in a previously uninhabited, mountainous area of Teveriah called Teveriah Illit (also known as Teveriah Shikun Dalet). Before the founding of this new community, the current Sanzer Rebbe, R' Tzvi Elimelech Halberstam, and other leaders of the Sanz community in Teveriah did extensive research to see if it was appropriate for the community to perform daily Bircas Kohanim, as its members had previously done before moving to Teveriah, or whether they were bound by the existing custom of other chassidic groups in Teveriah who did not perform the mitzvah daily.

After reviewing the topic in depth and discussing it with many other *poskim* in Eretz Yisrael, they made the decision to perform daily Bircas Kohanim in Teveriah Illit. The following summary of the relevant halachic considerations was articulated to the author by R' Zev Vaksberger, *Dayan* of the Sanz community of Teveriah, and R' Avraham Halberstam, son of the Sanz-Klausenberg Rebbe of Netanya:[30]

1. Although we assume that for approximately a century, most chassidim in Tzfas and Teveriah performed Bircas Kohanim only during Mussaf of Shabbos, Rosh Chodesh, and Yom Tov, there is no evidence that this custom originated with any of the disciples of the Baal Shem Tov, nor does anyone seem to know who actually instituted the custom.

2. If there is an independent community residing within another community, they are not obligated to take on the other community's stringencies. *Shulchan Aruch* (*O.C.* 468) and *Biur Halachah* of the Chofetz Chaim (s.v. *V'chumrei*) rule that a community that has the following three features qualifies as an independent

29. *Devarim* 14:1, which can be interpreted as, *You shall not split into many agudos* (groups). A community may not divide itself into different factions, with each group observing the Torah differently.

30. A similar summary appeared in the Sanz monthly newsletter, Av 5772/2022.

congregation: They have a separate shul with a daily minyan, their own rav who answers halachic queries, and their own mikveh. The Sanz community in Teveriah Illit meets these criteria.

3. Since the majority of those moving to Teveriah Illit were originally from Kiryat Sanz in Netanya, and others who joined the community originated in locations such as Yerushalayim and Bnei Brak, it would be considered abrogating their custom if they did *not* perform daily Bircas Kohanim in Teveriah Illit.

R' Vaksberger added that these considerations do not apply to the existing Sanz *beis midrash* in Tzfas, which was built many years earlier, and follows the custom of performing Bircas Kohanim only during Mussaf. Had Sanz established a community in the lower part of Teveriah, where many chassidic communities *duchan* only during Mussaf, he said, it is possible that they would have conformed with the custom of their immediate neighbors. However, their current location in Teveriah Illit is adjacent to a nearby large Ashkenazic-Litvish community called Nof Kinneret, where Bircas Kohanim is performed daily. It is also close to a large Sephardic neighborhood, where Bircas Kohanim is performed daily as well, and so it is unquestionably permitted for the new Sanz community to *duchan*, much to their delight.

Sephardic Opinions

R' Ovadiah Yosef writes, regarding those in the Galilee region who do not perform daily Bircas Kohanim:[31] "The default custom throughout Eretz Yisrael is for the Kohanim to *duchan* every day — weekdays, Shabbos, and Yom Tov — and Maran Beis Yosef praised this custom. It is true that there are Ashkenazim in some cities of the Galilee that do not *duchan* on weekdays, but it would be more correct for them, too, to adopt the custom of performing Bircas Kohanim every day, for it is pleasing in Hashem's eyes to bless the Jewish people."

R' Yehoshua Elazar HaKohen Chimtzi (1795-1881), who served as rav in Izmir, Turkey, for many years and subsequently moved to Haifa, writes (*Koh Sevarechu* 5:6) that the custom in Teveriah and Haifa

31. *Yalkut Yosef, Hilchos Tefillah* 128:17, p. 247. See also *Yechaveh Daas,* vol. 2 #13.

was to recite Bircas Kohanim even in a house of mourning, during *shivah*. It is clear that he is referring to the weekday Bircas Kohanim, as prayers are held in a house of mourning only on weekdays, not on Shabbos or Yom Tov.[32] In any case, we see that the Sephardic custom even in Haifa and Teveriah was to *duchan* daily, in keeping with the Sephardic custom everywhere else in the world.

R' Shach's View

R' Yitzchak Zilberstein (*Chashukei Chemed, Gittin* 2a) quotes the following letter from R' Elazar Menachem Mann Shach to R' Shalom Lopes, Chief Rabbi of the northern city of Acco: "There is no doubt that if it is possible to do so without *machlokes*, in a way that everyone will agree, it is proper to perform Bircas Kohanim every day, to fulfill a Torah commandment, as they are accustomed here [in Eretz Yisrael]. Even *Rema*'s statement (*siman* 128) that the custom was not to *duchan* daily applies only in the Diaspora, but in Eretz Yisrael the custom was to *duchan*, as *Mishnah Berurah* there explains."

Haifa

Although many chassidim in Haifa do not perform daily Bircas Kohanim, their status in this regard differs from those living in Tzfas and Teveriah. While Tzfas and Teveriah have long been home to established chassidic communities, the chassidim in Haifa have not been there for nearly as long. R' Binyamin Yehoshua Zilber speculates[33] that the chassidic community in Haifa was established by laymen from Tzfas and Teveriah who were accustomed to *duchaning* only during Mussaf, and they therefore continued this practice in Haifa. (Although Haifa is technically not part of the Galilee, and is not very close to Tzfas and Teveriah, it is closer to these cities than to Yerushalayim.) R' Chaim Meir Greenbaum, *Dayan* of the Vizhnitz community in Haifa, echoes this theory and says that this practice was never established as a *minhag*.

---

32. For an extensive discussion regarding Bircas Kohanim in a house of mourning, see chapter 38.
33. *She'eilos U'Teshuvos Az Nidberu*, vol. 11 #43. This is also cited by R' Moshe Sternbuch (*Koh Sevarechu Haifa*) as the reason for the custom in Haifa.

As in Tzfas and Teveriah, the Litvishe and Sephardic communities in Haifa do perform Bircas Kohanim every day. In nearby Rechasim (Kfar Chassidim), Bircas Kohanim is also performed daily by the Sephardic, Perushim, and Litvishe communities. In Yeshivas Knesses Chizkiyahu, founded by R' Elyah Lopian[34] and R' Noach Shimanovitz, Bircas Kohanim is performed daily, as is the case in Yeshivas Tiferes Yisrael (also known as Tiferes HaCarmel), whose rosh yeshivah, R' Raphael Shapira (a cousin and close student of the Brisker Rav), initiated daily Bircas Kohanim from the very first day the yeshivah opened. Similarly, Yeshivas Nachlas HaLeviim in Haifa, headed by R' Yisrael Meir Weiss (son-in-law of R' Chaim Shmulevitz), has performed daily Bircas Kohanim since its founding in 1986.

R' Wosner's Ruling

In 1979, several chassidic communities in Haifa seriously considered reinstituting daily Bircas Kohanim, but they were faced with a halachic quandary. Although no one knew who had established the custom to perform Bircas Kohanim only on days when Mussaf is recited, that had nevertheless been their practice for three decades.

The question was presented to the preeminent chassidic *posek*, R' Shmuel Wosner, who was inclined to permit daily Bircas Kohanim (*She'eilos U'Teshuvos Shevet HaLevi*, vol. 4 #70). He cites the *Sheyarei Knesses HaGedolah* and *Kaf HaChaim*, who emphasize the importance of daily Bircas Kohanim, and who both close by saying, "It would be even better if they would institute Bircas Kohanim every day." R' Wosner concludes his *teshuvah* somewhat equivocally, however, stating that those who have begun performing daily Bircas Kohanim cannot be compelled to revert to their former custom, but those who maintain the old custom also cannot be compelled to abandon it and begin performing daily Bircas Kohanim.

His close students, R' Moshe Shaul Klein and R' Yaakov Meir Stern, both explained[35] that although the end of the *teshuvah* was

34. R' Elyah Lopian insisted on daily Bircas Kohanim when the yeshivah moved to Kfar Chassidim; see *She'eilos U'Teshuvos Pe'as Sadecha*, vol. 2 #40.
35. Cited in *Koh Sevarechu Haifa*.

left purposely vague, R' Wosner was of the opinion that it would be preferable for the questioners to institute daily Bircas Kohanim in Haifa.

R' Moshe Halberstam, another chassidic *posek*, was of the opinion[36] that it was a good idea for the chassidim in Haifa to institute daily Bircas Kohanim, but he deferred to the *posek* R' Yitzchak Yaakov Weiss, head of Yerushalayim's Eidah HaChareidis, who wrote a detailed halachic response in *Minchas Yitzchak* (vol. 8 #1) explaining that although there is no documented reason for the chassidic custom in Haifa, it is preferable that no change should be made to the existing custom, which had been in place for many years.

R' Binyamin Yehoshua Zilber wrote several halachic rebuttals[37] to this ruling of *Minchas Yitzchak*, and explained that the principle that we maintain a status quo even when the reason for it is not known cannot override the three *mitzvos asei* of Bircas Kohanim. He explains that this is very different from the custom in the Diaspora to *duchan* only on Yom Tov, which was instituted by the later Rishonim, and cannot be overridden.[38] Similarly, R' Sroya Deblitski emphatically implored all residents of Haifa to perform Bircas Kohanim daily.[39]

New Chassidic Communities in Haifa

At the time the *Minchas Yitzchak* issued his ruling, there were two main chassidic groups in Haifa: Seret-Vizhnitz and Makava. Few other chassidic shuls existed there.

Approximately a decade before the publication of this book, however, many other groups of chassidim moved to Haifa, primarily young couples who could not afford the spiraling housing prices of Yerushalayim or Bnei Brak. These chassidim had always performed daily Bircas Kohanim, living as they did in cities where this was the practice, and in light of the above guidelines of *Biur Halachah*, several of these groups continued the practice of daily Bircas Kohanim when they moved to Haifa, since they constituted an independent community living within an existing community.

36. Cited in *Teshuvos HaPoskim* of R' Meir Katz, *Siman* 6 *Teshuvah* 12.
37. See *She'eilos U'Teshuvos Az Nidberu*, vol. 11 #43, 49; vol. 12 #24; vol. 13 #35.
38. See chapter 14.
39. See the *HaNe'eman* journal, year 17, issue 31.

Vizhnitz Communities in Haifa

One of the largest chassidic communities worldwide is Vizhnitz, whose headquarters are located in Bnei Brak, with many satellite *kehillos* throughout Eretz Yisrael. In 1936, after the passing of the Vizhnitzer Rebbe, R' Yisrael Hager, his son R' Chaim Meir assumed the mantle of leadership, while R' Chaim Meir's younger brother, R' Baruch, established a chassidic court and yeshivah in the town of Seret, Romania, becoming known as the first "Seret-Vizhnitz" Rebbe. After World War II, in 1951, R' Chaim Meir reestablished his chassidic court in Bnei Brak, while R' Boruch moved to Haifa in 1957 with a contingent of his chassidim and established a neighborhood called Ramat Vizhnitz.

Although both R' Chaim Meir and R' Baruch closely adhered to the customs of Vizhnitz, R' Baruch adopted the practice of other chassidim in Haifa to perform Bircas Kohanim only on days when Mussaf is recited, while the Vizhnitz chassidim in Bnei Brak and other cities throughout Eretz Yisrael performed daily Bircas Kohanim. (In the Seret-Vizhnitz *beis midrash* in Bnei Brak, and in all other Seret-Vizhnitz shuls in Eretz Yisrael, Bircas Kohanim *is* performed daily.)

Vizhnitz Bnei Brak in Haifa

R' Moshe Sternbuch ruled[40] that even though the established Seret-Vizhnitz community in Haifa performs Bircas Kohanim only during Mussaf, the Bnei Brak Vizhnitz community may — and are likely halachically obligated to — continue their practice of daily Bircas Kohanim when they open a new *kehillah* in Haifa, since they have their own shul and community, as per the guidelines outlined in *Biur Halachah*. R' Moshe Sternbuch emphasized that daily Bircas Kohanim is advisable because of all the mitzvos that the Kohanim fulfill, and the incredible blessing that all of Klal Yisrael receives from Hashem as a result.

R' Yaakov Meir Stern points out[41] that since the reason for the custom in Haifa is unknown, and we also do not know who

40. *Koh Sevarechu Haifa,* p. 9.
41. Ibid., p. 14.

instituted it, an assumption can be made that this practice was not established by *gedolim*, and communities in Haifa are therefore encouraged to perform Bircas Kohanim daily, especially since the Kohanim fulfill three *mitzvos asei* by doing so.

R' Moshe Shaul Klein, a close disciple of R' Wosner and a prominent Vizhnitzer chassid and rav, adds that today, the concept of an "established community" that can impose its customs on an entire city no longer exists, even in places like Tzfas and Teveriah, and it is permitted for the newcomers to continue their own custom of daily Bircas Kohanim.[42]

Impact of the Covid-19 Pandemic

When the Covid-19 pandemic struck, most shuls around the world, including those in Haifa, were shut down as a safety precaution. Medical authorities in Eretz Yisrael and elsewhere allowed limited outdoor minyanim, however, provided that the congregants kept a distance from one another and did not travel far from home.

Since these backyard and porch minyanim were composed of immediate neighbors, it turned out that in Haifa, some of the chassidim who were not accustomed to *duchaning* daily formed a minyan together with other Jews who did perform daily Bircas Kohanim, whether these were Sephardim, Litvaks, or chassidim originating from other cities. All the participants in these ad hoc minyanim were enthusiastic about performing daily Bircas Kohanim, because we are taught that if a plague strikes a city, the merit of Bircas Kohanim can protect against the plague.[43]

After several weeks or months, when the shuls finally reopened, a question was presented to the *poskim* as to whether these chassidim should revert to performing Bircas Kohanim during Mussaf only.

In response, the following words of R' Shmuel Wosner (*Shevet HaLevi,* vol. 4 #70) were heavily quoted: "*Sheyarei Knesses HaGedolah,* in his gloss to *Beis Yosef, siman* 128, quoted in *Kaf HaChaim* 128:274, states: 'If a city was accustomed to *duchan* only on Yom Tov, and a situation arose that compelled the rabbanim

---

42. Ibid., p. 11.

43. See *Zera Kodesh* by R' Naftali of Ropshitz, *Lech Lecha; Birkei Yosef* 128:19; *Kaf HaChaim* 128:270.

of the city to implement Bircas Kohanim on Shabbos as well, then even after the situation is resolved it is inappropriate to go back to their former custom and stop *duchaning* on Shabbos. On the contrary, **it would be even better if they would institute Bircas Kohanim every day**!' Clearly, then, it is not considered a deviation from the custom of the community if they continue daily Bircas Kohanim."

Chassidic *poskim* R' Shamai HaKohen Gross, R' Menachem Mendel Shafran, R' Betzalel Wekselstein, and R' Shaul Alter all concurred, based on the above ruling of R' Wosner, that once the chassidim in Haifa had started performing daily Bircas Kohanim in their backyard and porch minyanim, **they should continue doing so in the shuls of Haifa every day until Mashiach comes.**[44] They all point out that an important factor in their ruling is that there seems to be no credible source or reason for the original "custom" of not performing daily Bircas Kohanim in Haifa. They add that if a new community moves to Haifa that meets the halachic requirements cited above by *Biur Halachah*, they, too, are permitted to perform daily Bircas Kohanim.

Makava

The introduction of daily Bircas Kohanim in Haifa due to the Covid-19 pandemic prompted the *Gaavad* of Makava,[45] R' Shimon Lemberger, to institute daily Bircas Kohanim in his community in Haifa.

In a conversation with this author, R' Lemberger explained that when his father, the Ateres Moshe, who founded the Chassidus, decided in the late 1970s to maintain the status quo of performing Bircas Kohanim only on days when Mussaf is recited, he shared with R' Shimon that his decision was predicated on sensitive, time-specific circumstances,[46] and he made it very clear that he would be in

44. Their written letters appear in *Koh Sevarechu Haifa,* pp. 16-19, and in *Maasaf Simchas Torah,* vol. 1, pp. 709-716.

45. In Makava, the leader of the Chassidus is called "*Gaavad*" (an acronym for *gaon av beis din*) instead of Rebbe.

46. R' Shimon noted that the *Minchas Yitzchak*'s *teshuvah* was based on the same sensitive circumstances that his father was concerned about, and that the *Minchas Yitzchak* would also have allowed daily Bircas Kohanim once these circumstances were no longer relevant, as is the case today. R' Moshe Shaul Klein states *Koh Sevarechu Haifa* (p. 11) that the *Minchas Yitzchak* would very

favor of instituting daily Bircas Kohanim should those reasons no longer apply. In light of the recent changes made by other communities in Haifa, R' Shimon said, the basis of his father's ruling no longer applied, so the main Makava shul in Haifa started performing daily Bircas Kohanim on Erev Rosh Hashanah 5783. Smaller Makava shuls in the vicinity of Haifa had already started performing daily Bircas Kohanim when they reopened after the Covid-19 pandemic, as per the Gaavad's directive.[47]

Overseas: No Change

During the Covid-19 pandemic, this author merited to be in the presence of R' Chaim Kanievsky and presented him with the following question, which was asked by a prestigious scholar in *chutz laAretz*: Considering that the merit of Bircas Kohanim can save the inhabitants of a city, as noted by R' Naftali of Ropshitz, *Birkei Yosef,* and *Kaf HaChaim,* is it permitted to perform Bircas Kohanim daily in an Ashkenazic minyan overseas as a merit to halt the pandemic?

R' Chaim was very emphatic in his reply. He ruled that despite the danger associated with the pandemic, it is absolutely forbidden for an Ashkenazic minyan in the Diaspora to perform daily Bircas Kohanim, as we must comply with the long-standing custom instituted by Maharil and codified by *Rema,* which remains in full effect outside Eretz Yisrael.[48] R' Chaim added, however, that if it is a Sephardic minyan that davens *nusach Eidot HaMizrach,* Bircas Kohanim may be recited, and it would be meritorious for Ashkenazi Kohanim to join them in reciting Bircas Kohanim, and for Yisraelim to hear their Bircas Kohanim.

The Practice Today

Today, most chassidim who reside in Tzfas, Teveriah, and Haifa do perform daily Bircas Kohanim.

---

likely be in favor of daily Bircas Kohanim, due to the different circumstances now.

47. For a written summary of the opinion of the *Gaavad* of Makava, see *Koh Sevarechu Haifa,* p. 20.

48. See chapter 14.

Chapter 19
Bircas Kohanim at the Kosel

It was the summer of 5730/1970, and in Eretz Yisrael the air was filled with tension. The Arab world was still in shock over Israel's miraculous victory in the Six Day War, and they were not taking it well. Terror attacks in Israel persisted, and many Jews felt insecure.

During that time, R' Menachem Mendel Gefner, a devout Chassid of Vizhnitz, decided to arrange for a mass Bircas Kohanim. What better way could there be to bring a flow of *berachah* down to Klal Yisrael in their time of need? After all, *Chazal* teach us (*Midrash Tehillim* 7): "Rabban Shimon ben Gamliel said: From the day the Beis HaMikdash was destroyed, there was never a day without curse … R' Acha said, "If so, in what merit have we survived? In the merit of Bircas Kohanim."

The idea came to R' Menachem Mendel one day during a conversation he had with his friend R' Shmuel Hominer, a noted *tzaddik*. R' Shmuel raised an intriguing question: "Why is it," he asked, "that the only *yahrtzeit* date mentioned in the entire Torah is that of Aharon HaKohen, on Rosh Chodesh Av? As the *pasuk* says, וַיַּעַל אַהֲרֹן הַכֹּהֵן אֶל הֹר הָהָר עַל פִּי ה׳ וַיָּמָת שָׁם בִּשְׁנַת הָאַרְבָּעִים לְצֵאת בְּנֵי יִשְׂרָאֵל מֵאֶרֶץ מִצְרַיִם בַּחֹדֶשׁ הַחֲמִישִׁי בְּאֶחָד לַחֹדֶשׁ, *Then Aharon the Kohen went up to Mount Hor at the word of Hashem and died there, in the fortieth year after Bnei Yisrael went forth from the land of Egypt, in the fifth month on the first of the month* (*Bamidbar* 33:38). Surely there is a reason the Torah wanted us to know the exact day of Aharon's death. There must be a hidden power in this day to bring about salvations for the Jewish people in the merit of Aharon HaKohen, about whom the *Zohar* states (*Parashas Tzav*), "It was in the merit of the holy Aharon HaKohen that Klal Yisrael were redeemed from exile."

Upon hearing R' Shmuel's words, R' Menachem Mendel — always a man of vision and action — quoted a *pasuk* that discusses the spiritual revival of the Jewish nation after Chizkiyahu HaMelech restored the glory of Torah scholarship to Klal Yisrael. At that time, he arranged for them all to come together to bring the *Korban Pesach* in the Beis HaMikdash, and the *pasuk* says, וַיָּקֻמוּ הַכֹּהֲנִים הַלְוִיִּם וַיְבָרְכוּ אֶת הָעָם וַיִּשָּׁמַע בְּקוֹלָם וַתָּבוֹא תְפִלָּתָם לִמְעוֹן קָדְשׁוֹ לַשָּׁמָיִם, *The Kohanim and the Leviim got up and blessed the people, and He listened to their voice, and their prayers reached His holy abode in Heaven* (*II Divrei HaYamim* 30:27). "There you have it!" exclaimed R' Menachem Mendel. "Bircas Kohanim with a multitude of people is the secret to having our prayers answered!"

And that is how, in the midst of a Torah discussion, the novel idea of a mass Bircas Kohanim at the Kosel was born — and it seemed obvious to them that this event should take place on Aharon HaKohen's *yahrtzeit*.

ברכת כהנים המוני ליד הכותל המערבי

ביום הששי עש"ק פ' מטות מסעי ראש חדש אב יומא דהילולא דאהרן כהנא קדישא
כמבואר מפורש בתורה בפ' השבוע.

והנה מובא בספה"ק דביומא דהילולא באה נשמת הצדיק לעוה"ז ומשתחוה לד' בהר הקודש אשר בירושלים:

לכן יתאספו ביום הזה כל בני אהרן הכהנים על יד הכותל המערבי ושם ישא אהרן את ידיו יחד עם בניו הכהנים לברך את ישראל באהבה אשרי הזוכה לברך ולהתברך ביום הגדול הזה על יד המקום הקדוש הזה ע"י הכהנים הקדושים הרבים וכדכתיב בדה"י ב-ל ויתקדשו הכהנים לרוב ויברכו -העם וישמע לקולם ותבא תפילתם השמים **וע"י הברכה הרבה הזו יושפע שפע רב ברכות על כל ישראל והימים האלו יתהפכו מאבל ליום טוב ולששון ולשמחה בב"א.**

סדר היום תפילת שחרית בשעה 7 בדיוק ברכת כהנים דשחרית בשעה 8 בדיוק ברכת הכהנים ההמוני בתפילת מוסף בשעה 8.45

Poster announcing the first mass Bircas Kohanim

This discussion took place at the end of Tammuz, just a few days before Rosh Chodesh Av, so R' Menachem Mendel had no time to lose. He immediately began enlisting Kohanim and getting commitments from them to attend. His goal? To assemble seventy-one Kohanim, corresponding to the number of judges in the Great Sanhedrin, which used to convene in the Beis HaMikdash, not far from where the mass Bircas Kohanim would be recited. But then, on

Erev Rosh Chodesh, when almost everything had been arranged, R' Menachem Mendel suddenly fell ill. He was bedridden for days, and the event was canceled. It was a clear sign from Heaven that the time had not yet come.

The month of Av went by, and Elul as well. A new year began, and everyone was preoccupied with preparations for the Yamim Tovim. The Bircas Kohanim project was put aside and almost forgotten.

Then, one day, R' Menachem Mendel received a visit from R' Mechel Hominer, the son of R' Shmuel, who was an expert in deciphering ancient handwritten manuscripts from *gedolim* of the past. Excitedly, R' Mechel pulled out a bundle of such manuscripts, selected one, and handed it to R' Menachem Mendel. It was a commentary on the Torah authored by the *Rokeach*, R' Elazar of Worms, who was one of the *Baalei Tosafos*. The great men of his generation had said of the *Rokeach* that all his teachings were transmitted to him directly by Eliyahu HaNavi.

In his commentary on *Parashas Tetzaveh* he writes, "Aharon HaKohen's name is mentioned three hundred times in the three *Chumashim* of *Shemos, Vayikra*, and *Bamidbar* combined. If three hundred Kohanim would stand together on Har HaZeisim and recite Bircas Kohanim, it would hasten the coming of Mashiach."

When R' Menachem Mendel read these words, his determination to arrange a mass Bircas Kohanim was rekindled with even greater passion. He felt that Hashem had deliberately postponed it for his own benefit, so that the words of the *Rokeach* could inspire others.

"This being the case," R' Menachem Mendel said, "seventy-one Kohanim will not do at all. We must gather at least three hundred! Obviously, we cannot bring Kohanim to Har HaZeisim in our times, since it has become a cemetery, but on the other hand, we now have access to the Kosel, and there is plenty of space in front of it to accommodate thousands of Jews — a phenomenon that was impossible to imagine in the days of the Rishonim! And what place on earth could be more appropriate for this mitzvah than the last standing remnant of the Beis HaMikdash!"

To bolster his words, R' Menachem Mendel quoted the Midrash (*Bamidbar Rabbah* 11:2) that interprets the words הִנֵּה זֶה עוֹמֵד אַחַר כָּתְלֵנוּ, *He was standing behind our wall* (*Shir HaShirim* 2:9) as a reference to the Western Wall of the Beis HaMikdash, which will never be destroyed. The Midrash explains that this is because the Shechinah is on the west side. The Midrash adds that the next words of the *pasuk*, מַשְׁגִּיחַ מִן הַחַלֹּנוֹת, *observing through the windows*, mean between the shoulders of the Kohanim, and the phrase that follows, מֵצִיץ מִן הַחֲרַכִּים, *peering through the lattices*, means between the fingers of the Kohanim. And the next words (v. 10), עָנָה דוֹדִי וְאָמַר לִי, *My beloved called out to me and said*, are a reference to Hashem's promise of וַאֲנִי אֲבָרְכֵם, *and I will bless them*, through Bircas Kohanim.

R' Menachem Mendel's heart told him that he was on the threshold of restoring a practice reminiscent of the past glory of Bircas Kohanim in the Beis HaMikdash, a practice that had the potential to change the destiny of Klal Yisrael and perhaps to bring the final *Geulah*.

He did not rely upon his own sentiments, however, but went to consult with three *gedolei Yisrael*. His first stop was in Bnei Brak, to visit his Rebbe, the Imrei Chaim of Vizhnitz. The Rebbe listened carefully to all the details of the plan, added his own comments and insights, and then said, "Do not fear anyone or anything! Hashem will assist you, and you will surely succeed!"[1]

Next, he approached the Beis Yisrael of Ger, who was an expert in identifying old manuscripts. When R' Menachem Mendel showed him a copy of the document that had been unearthed by R' Mechel Hominer, the Rebbe examined it carefully, and confirmed that it was indeed the handwriting of the Rokeach. He approved of R' Menachem Mendel's idea in theory, but added, "Getting together three hundred Kohanim does not sound like such an easy undertaking."

R' Menachem Mendel laughed and said, "That's why I'm here — to receive the Rebbe's *berachah*!"

The Rebbe did give him a *berachah*, and went further than that — at the next major gathering of Gerrer chassidim, he encouraged all of them to attend the first-ever mass Bircas Kohanim at the Kosel.

1. Two years later, in Adar 5732/1972, the Vizhnitzer Rebbe asked R' Menachem Mendel when the next mass Bircas Kohanim was to take place, and when R' Menachem Mendel said, "On 19 Nissan, the fourth day of Chol HaMoed," a pained look crossed the Rebbe's face. "Who knows if I will merit to be there?" he said sadly. Indeed, his soul departed on the ninth of Nissan.

The third *gadol* that R' Menachem Mendel met with was the Steipler, R' Yaakov Yisrael Kanievsky. The Steipler gave his wholehearted blessing to the endeavor, and added this advice: "I am not qualified to discuss matters of Kabbalah, but I sense that you should forego all unnecessary fanfare. If not, I fear that the Satan will get involved and place obstacles in your path. Do what is needed, but skip the commotion, as we find in the Midrash (*Tanchuma, Ki Sisa* 31) that the first set of *Luchos* given to Klal Yisrael were broken because they were given in public, with much fanfare, so an evil eye affected them."

Fortified by the *berachos* of the *gedolei hador* and enlightened by their wise counsel, R' Menachem Mendel set out to turn concept into reality. This was no simple task. Countless impediments and naysayers arose, one after another. If not for the words of the Vizhnitzer Rebbe ringing in his ears — *Do not fear anyone or anything* — R' Menachem Mendel might have given up, but due to the support he had received, he was able to persevere.

One day, he met the Slonimer Rebbe, R' Avraham Weinberg, and told him of the difficulties he was facing. The Rebbe was deeply moved, and he said, "You have already received the *berachos* of the *gedolei hador*. Go with this power, and do not slack off! Heaven forbid that you should be discouraged by cynics and complications!"

R' Menachem Mendel was determined to hold the event at the earliest possible opportunity. He chose Tuesday, 3 Kislev 5732/1971, explaining that it was the third day of the week, on the third day of the third month, and Bircas Kohanim is called the *berachah hameshuleshes* — the three-*pasuk berachah*. Following the Steipler's advice, he avoided major advertising, and simply posted a number of small notices in various locations, as well as a modest ad in the *Hamodia* newspaper.

Yerushalayim can get quite stormy and windy at that time of year, and on the days leading up to 3 Kislev, the weather was not at all suitable for outdoor events. R' Menachem Mendel began to fear that all his efforts would be in vain. How could he gather three hundred Kohanim to recite Bircas Kohanim in the midst of a downpour? For that matter, how could he expect any Yisraelim to show up and *receive* the *berachah*? His resolve began to weaken. Perhaps this should be postponed until Pesach?

Then he took hold of himself and said, "No! I trust in the *berachos* of the *gedolim*!" And behold — on Tuesday the third of Kislev, as dawn broke, the heavy clouds covering the skies of Yerushalayim suddenly parted. Beautiful, clear sky appeared, and the rain stopped completely.

The neighboring streets and alleyways filled with streams of people from across the spectrum of Jewish society making their way to the Kosel. Tens of thousands of people — old and young, men, women, and children; what a breathtaking sight!

The Arabs living in the Old City were dumbfounded. They were familiar with Jewish holidays, but as far as they knew, none of them fall on 3 Kislev. "What is happening today?" they asked. "Isn't it an ordinary weekday?"

"Bircas Kohanim," came the answer.

"Is that a new holiday?"

"Yes. It's from R' Menachem Mendel Gefner."

The Gefner name was actually well known to the local Arabs. The Gefners had been living in the Old City for decades, and Rebbetzin Esther Mirel Gefner ran a small grocery. The news spread quickly among the local Arabs, and the words "Gefner's holiday" were passed from one to the next.

The Kosel plaza filled quickly, and was soon packed with people. The crowd parted slightly each time a Kohen arrived and made his way to the front. There was great anticipation in the air, as people sensed that they were about to recapture the spiritual elevation of the service in the Beis HaMikdash so long ago.

At exactly seven a.m., R' Menachem Mendel arose to open the ceremony. With great joy, he said, *"Beruchim haba'im b'sheim Hashem.* We are assembled here today, at the last remnant of the Beis HaMikdash, to daven together and receive a *berachah* from hundreds of Kohanim. How fortunate are we that Hashem has brought us to this place and time, to follow in the footsteps of our forefathers who prayed on this very mountain, where all the *tefillos* of the world gather and ascend to Heaven." He continued speaking for several minutes, describing the importance of the Kosel and of Bircas Kohanim. Then, they began davening Shacharis.

Finally, the anticipated moment arrived. Hundreds of Kohanim crowded together in rows, facing thousands of *mispallelim*. The

Kohanim represented every Jewish community — Sephardim and Ashkenazim, chassidim and Litvaks. They stood shoulder to shoulder by the ancient stones of the Kosel, covering their heads and hands with their talleisim, looking like waves cresting in the ocean. The chazzan finished the *berachah* of Modim as loudly as he could, and the words הַטּוֹב שִׁמְךָ וּלְךָ נָאֶה לְהוֹדוֹת were followed by a thunderous "AMEN." Suddenly, there was complete silence, as though the universe had come to a standstill. Then, echoing from the loudspeakers: "*KO-HA-NIM*!"

The Kohanim began chanting the *berachah* in unison, ending with a loud, "*B'-AH-HA-VAH*!" The electrified masses found their voices and responded once again, "AMEN!" In a beautiful sing-song, the Kohanim began, "*YEVARECHECHA HASHEM V'YISH-MERECHA*."

"AMEN!" came the response.

The words of the Kohanim pierced every heart and purified every soul. Undoubtedly, these *berachos* were ascending directly to Heaven and would bring an immediate response.

R' Menachem Mendel related that a short time after the event, a group of six young *baalei teshuvah* came to visit him, and, with tear-filled eyes, they expressed their gratitude to him, explaining that they had been so moved by the Bircas Kohanim that they had decided to change their entire way of life and come closer to Hashem. They had all since joined yeshivos that cater to beginners. R' Menachem Mendel also received countless letters and phone calls thanking him for all he had done, as many people felt certain that in the merit of their presence at that great gathering, they had experienced salvations in their lives.

R' Menachem Mendel succeeded in organizing over fifty of these mass Bircas Kohanim events at the Kosel in his lifetime, on Chol HaMoed and other special occasions. No matter what obstacles arose, he made sure that the Bircas Kohanim would take place. After practically every one of these, he saw miracles performed for those in attendance: hopelessly ill people who recovered, single people who found *shidduchim*, barren couples who were blessed with children, and homes where strife was replaced with harmony.[2]

---

2. This account was adapted from *Olamo shel Chassid*, a biography of R' Menachem Mendel Gefner.

An Exquisite Opportunity

The *tzaddik* R' Eliyahu Roth of Zvhil would walk to the Kosel each Chol HaMoed, along with thousands of other Jews, to participate in the mass Bircas Kohanim. Although his home was a significant distance from the Kosel, he was stringent to avoid traveling by car on Chol HaMoed, so he always made the trek by foot. He was never alone on his walk, though, for he was consistently accompanied by a sizable entourage of admirers, who were eager to hear his inspiring words.

All along the way he would say, "Do you know where we are headed? We are going to hear Bircas Kohanim!" With palpable excitement he would go on to describe what an exquisite opportunity this was: "The Torah says: *They shall place My Name upon Bnei Yisrael.* It is as though the Kohanim are taking the Name of Hashem, so to speak, and placing it upon the heads of those who are receiving the *berachah*! And what does Hashem say when the Kohanim bless the Jewish people? *And I shall bless them*! I, Myself, shall bless them! We are on our way right now to receive Hashem's great and holy Name upon our heads, channeled through hundreds of Kohanim! And all this to take place in the holiest location in the entire world!"

He would repeat these thoughts numerous times, with unwavering enthusiasm, which was so contagious that all those around him would get caught up in it. He would frequently speed up his pace with bursts of energy, brimming with anticipation to arrive at the Kosel and take part in the great mitzvah.[3]

Why R' Chaim Kanievsky Didn't Attend

In recent decades, every Chol HaMoed, thousands of Jews from all walks of life gather at the Kosel to hear Bircas Kohanim from hundreds of Kohanim at once. R' Chaim Kanievsky never attended this mass Bircas Kohanim, however. Most other *gedolei Yisrael* did not participate in this event, either.

For approximately the last thirty years of R' Chaim's life, he visited the Kosel every Chol HaMoed, Pesach and Succos, but he

3. *Ish Chassid Hayah*, p. 338.

would go in the evening to daven Maariv, and would not attend the morning Bircas Kohanim. This seems puzzling, considering his deep appreciation of this mitzvah. Furthermore, when people who were seeking salvation approached him, he would frequently advise them to have their needs in mind during Bircas Kohanim, which is the greatest source of blessing. Why, then, did he never participate in the mass Bircas Kohanim?

Someone also pointed out to R' Chaim that in such a large gathering of Kohanim — over two thousand — there would undoubtedly be a number of Kohanim with a definitive *chazakah* (proven priestly lineage). Yet when questioned by letter-writers about his reluctance to attend the mass Bircas Kohanim at the Kosel, he answered in writing (several times) that two Kohanim are enough to perform the *mitzvah d'Oraysa*.

His son R' Yitzchak Shaul Kanievsky and his close student R' Uri HaKohen Tieger explained that when asked this question verbally, R' Chaim would smile and reply that he relies on the Chazon Ish's ruling (*Hilchos Sheviis* 5:12) that Kohanim have a *chazakah* even in our times, and we allow Kohanim to perform the mitzvos of Bircas Kohanim and *pidyon haben* with a *berachah* even though they cannot trace their lineage.[4] Although we do not rely on this *chazakah* to give them *terumah*, that is only because we do not want to encourage people to falsely claim to be Kohanim in order to get *terumah* that they are not entitled to receive.

In the words of R' Yitzchak Shaul Kanievsky: "Abba frequently said there is no difference between two Kohanim, twenty, two hundred, or two thousand Kohanim. That's why he never went to hear the large Bircas Kohanim on Chol HaMoed at the Kosel. Abba did say that perhaps this gathering had the advantage of בְּרָב עָם הַדְרַת מֶלֶךְ, *A multitude of people is a king's glory* (*Mishlei* 14:28), but that was not enough of a reason for him to go. As long as he heard Bircas Kohanim daily from two Kohanim, he was satisfied."

The above ruling of the Chazon Ish is quoted several times in R' Chaim's *Derech Emunah*.[5]

---

4. See chapter 14 for a discussion regarding relying on the *chazakah* of Kohanim.
5. See, for example, *Hilchos Terumos* 6:20.

R' Chaim Shmulevitz's View

From June 1967, when the Kosel was liberated from the Jordanians, R' Chaim Shmulevitz, Rosh Yeshivah of Yeshivas Mir, would go to daven at the Kosel at least once a week on Friday afternoon, and often for Maariv during the week as well. Interestingly, he did not encourage people to attend Bircas Kohanim at the Kosel, nor did he attend himself. If he went to the Kosel on Chol HaMoed, it was for Maariv.

His grandson R' Tzvi Partzovitz, Rosh Yeshivah of Yeshivas Mir–Modi'in Illit, related: "My grandfather told me that since the vast majority of *poskim* write that Kohanim even in today's generation have a full *chazakah* of *Kehunah,* there is no difference between hearing Bircas Kohanim from two Kohanim or from many more. He added that he always enjoyed hearing the Bircas Kohanim of R' Chaim HaKohen Kamil. When asked about the concept that it is a glory to the King when a mitzvah is performed by many people at once (see *Zevachim* 14b), he answered that in the yeshivah he can receive the *berachah* through more than two Kohanim as well, and among them is R' Chaim Kamil, whose Bircas Kohanim was fiery and thunderous. To him, that was worth as much as the *berachos* of many Kohanim together at the Kosel."

R' Meir Shmulevitz, R' Chaim's son, added: "When people approached my father for a *berachah,* he would often advise them to be present when R' Chaim Kamil was *duchaning,* as the intensity of his Bircas Kohanim would be an additional merit for them."

Part 4:

Facets of the Mitzvah

Chapter 20
The Holiness of the Tribe of Levi and the Kohanim

Divinely Named

Rashi (*Bereishis* 29:34) notes that with regard to the naming of all of Yaakov's other sons, the Torah states, "She called," indicating that it was Yaakov's wife who gave the name, but regarding Levi the verse states, "He called." What does this wording convey? *Rashi* cites the Midrash that relates that when Levi was born, Hashem sent the angel Gavriel, who brought the baby before Him, and Hashem gave him this name, Levi, and bestowed upon him the twenty-four gifts granted to Kohanim, who are from the tribe of Levi. Because Hashem sent along gifts with the child, He called him Levi (a term that connotes accompaniment). The verse uses the masculine form "He called" to indicate that Hashem gave Levi his name.

An Impressive List of Scholars

In the introduction to his *She'eilos U'Teshuvos Shoel U'Meishiv*, R' Yosef Shaul HaLevi Nathansohn humbly explains why he deemed himself eligible to render halachic decisions:

> The Gemara states (*Yoma* 26a): You will not find Torah scholars who decide the law except for those who descend

> from the tribe of Levi, about whom it is written: *They shall teach your ordinances to [the Children of] Yaakov* (*Devarim* 33:10), or from the tribe of Yissachar, about whom it is written: *Of the tribe of Yissachar, men with understanding of the times, to know what Israel should do* (*I Divrei HaYamim* 12:33).
>
> Based on this, *Rambam* writes (*Hilchos Shemittah* 13:12) that the tribe of Levi was set aside to serve Hashem and to teach the Jewish people the laws of the Torah and the proper way to conduct their lives.
>
> Therefore, although I am not one of those exceptional individuals that *Rambam* is describing, who have devoted their entire lives to Torah study, I am nevertheless from the tribe of Levi, and so I thought that perhaps I, too, might merit to add my humble teachings to those great members of my tribe whose halachic rulings are accepted by our entire people. For example: *Sma* and *Shach*, who were Kohanim, *Taz, Magen Avraham*, and *Shelah*, who were Leviim, and, in more recent times, *Noda BiYehudah* and *Haflaah*, who were Leviim as well, and the *Ketzos*, who was a Kohen.

R' Nosson Gestetner (*L'Horos Nassan al haTorah, V'zos HaBerachah*) adds to this impressive list: the *Aruch HaShulchan*, R' Yechiel Michel HaLevi Epstein; the *Maharsham*, R' Shalom Mordechai HaKohen Schwadron; and the Chofetz Chaim, R' Yisrael Meir HaKohen Kagan, whose rulings in *Mishnah Berurah* are accepted throughout the Jewish world. He also adds his own rebbi, R' Shmuel HaLevi Wosner, author of *Shevet HaLevi*, who personally ordained hundreds of today's leading halachic authorities.

Seize the Opportunity!

When R' Shimon Schwab was studying in the Mir Yeshivah, he once went to visit the Chofetz Chaim, and he would often recall their memorable meeting. The great sage opened the conversation with a question:

"Are you a Kohen? Or a Levi?"

"No, I am a Yisrael," he responded.

"Do you understand what a difference there is between me, a Kohen, and you, who are only a Yisrael? When Mashiach comes, we will all go to Yerushalayim, and every Jew will want to perform the *avodah* of the *korbanos* in the Beis HaMikdash. Everyone will run up to the gates, but when they get there, the gatekeepers will inspect each person, and at that point, you and I will be separated. I will be allowed to enter the inner sanctuary, while you will be left standing outside. Those who are not able to enter will feel a burning jealousy as they watch all the Kohanim and Leviim pass through the gates."

The Chofetz Chaim then continued, "Do you know the reason for this separation between us? It is because three thousand years ago, after the sin of the Golden Calf, Moshe called out, '*Mi laShem eilai* — whoever is for Hashem, join me!' (*Shemos* 32:26) My great-grandfathers responded to Moshe's call, but yours did not. So it was that my ancestors merited the status of *Kehunah* for all their generations, while everyone else remained non-Kohanim.

"Why am I telling you this? Because every Jew will have moments in his life when a voice inside of him will call out, '*Mi laShem eilai*!' When that day comes, seize the opportunity! Do not hesitate, for you may lose your chance forever. Do not repeat the mistake of your ancestors. Step forward immediately, and do whatever needs to be done for the honor of Hashem!"[1]

Most Prophets were Kohanim

Rabbeinu David HaKochavi writes (*Sefer HaBattim*, Mitzvah 25):

> It is fitting that this *berachah* should come through the Kohanim, the teachers of Torah, for they are blessed with Hashem's Providence and are thus able to bring Providence upon others. When He gave the commandment of Bircas Kohanim, Hashem said, *Let them place My Name upon Bnei Yisrael.* Hashem's "Name" is His essence, and "placing His Name" upon the Jewish nation refers to an exalted level of *dveikus* — attachment to Hashem — which brings in its wake Hashem's Providence.

1. *Likutei Maamarei Chofetz Chaim*, p. 168.

The Tosafist Rabbeinu Chaim Paltiel observes (*Vayikra* 21:1) that the majority of prophets were Kohanim, who stayed in the Beis HaMikdash. Included in this category were Yirmiyah, Uriah, Yehoyada, Zechariah, and many others.

Chapter 21
Washing the Hands of the Kohanim

B*eis Yosef* (128:6) explains that a Levi should wash the hands of the Kohen because a Kohen should be purified by someone who also possesses sanctity, as *Zohar* states (*Nasso* p. 146) that the Kohen should sanctify his hands by a holy hand. "What is the holy hand?" asks the *Zohar*. "It is the Levi, from whose hands the Kohen needs to accept the holiness of the water, as it is written that you shall sanctify the Leviim ... From here we understand that **every Kohen who recites Bircas Kohanim needs to be sanctified through one who is already sanctified, in order to add holiness upon his holiness.**"

An additional reason why a Levi washes the Kohen's hands, says *Aruch HaShulchan* (128:15), is to replicate the service in the Beis HaMikdash, where the Leviim were subservient to the Kohanim.

Aderes (*Zecher L'Mikdash*, vol. 2, *Erech Leviim*) gives another reason why the Leviim wash the hands of the Kohanim. He cites *Zohar*'s statement (*Nasso*, p. 146) that through this action, blessing descends from Heaven, but notes that if this were the only reason, it would suffice for one Levi to wash the hands of all the Kohanim, and it would not be necessary for any other Leviim to go out and miss *Chazaras HaShatz*. Therefore, he continues, it seems that the primary reason this custom was instituted was so that there would be a remembrance of the Leviim's role in the Beis HaMikdash, where they were chosen to assist the Kohanim in their *avodah*. This explains why *all* the Leviim participate in the mitzvah of washing the Kohanim's hands, even at the expense of missing *Chazaras*

HaShatz — because if not for this service, there is no other active mitzvah the Leviim can do to demonstrate their special status with regard to the *avodah* in the Beis HaMikdash.

An Honor to the King

R' Eliyahu Guttmacher, a student of R' Akiva Eiger, writes in a *teshuvah* (*Michtav MeEliyahu,* p. 77):

> I was asked by members of the Neustadt community if their new practice, to have the Kohanim wash their hands in a separate room at the entrance to the shul rather than doing so in the shul itself, is appropriate.
>
> Let it be known that there is no room for such a practice! Heaven forbid to allow such a breach in our tradition! Consider this: There is nothing left for us from all the service that was performed in the Beis HaMikdash except Bircas Kohanim — who would dare to undermine this mitzvah in any way? It is as though he is poking his fingers into Hashem's eyes, so to speak!
>
> If you are concerned about the commotion that is caused by washing in the shul, you must know that this is actually an *honor* to Hashem! When the chazzan says, וְהָשֵׁב כֹּהֲנִים לַעֲבוֹדָתָם וּלְוִיִּם לְשִׁירָם וּלְזִמְרָם, *Restore the Kohanim to their service and the Leviim to their song and music,* and from all sides, Kohanim and Leviim stream hastily toward the washing area — that is a great *nachas* for Hashem, and a bit of a consolation for the loss of the Beis HaMikdash! How can you describe it as a "disturbance" in the shul? The Gemara (*Yoma* 24b) clearly says that the reason lotteries were conducted throughout the day in the Beis HaMikdash (to choose which Kohanim were to perform which *avodah*), rather than simply making one lottery in the morning, was specifically in order to create a hubbub in the *Azarah.* Rashi explains: "That is an honor to the King!"

Abundant Gratitude and Intense Joy

Yesod V'Shoresh HaAvodah (*Shaar* 8) teaches that at the time the Levi pours water over the hands of the Kohen, he should fill his heart and his thoughts with abundant gratitude and intense joy over the fact that Hashem chose him and created him as a member of the holiest segment of His nation.

Likewise, he says, the Kohen himself should fill his heart with immense gratitude that he was chosen to be among the holy descendants of Aharon — when he goes up to *duchan,* and even more so when he says the words *Who has sanctified us with the holiness of Aharon,* as well as on days that we don't *duchan* and he hears the chazzan say, *Bless us with the blessing … that was said from the mouth of Aharon and his sons, the Kohanim, Your holy people.*

"You are a Newcomer!"

The *Mashgiach* R' Yerucham Levovitz, who was a Levi, relates (*Daas Torah, Noach, Maamar* 1): "Once, when I was a student in Kelm, and the Kohanim had just finished washing their hands to *duchan,* I saw the Alter of Kelm pick up the basin of water to bring it outside. I immediately sprang forth and attempted to take the basin from his hands. He gave me a stern look and said, 'You are a newcomer! You have no idea what is going on around you!' And he would not allow me to help him with the task."

Depriving Me of My Obligation

The Brisker Rav, R' Yitzchak Zev HaLevi Soloveitchik, followed the practice of washing the hands of the Kohanim before they went to *duchan.* The Rav's custom was to wash the hands of only those Kohanim who were over bar mitzvah.[1]

When R' Raphael Kook, the Chief Rabbi of Teveriah, was still living in Yerushalayim, he used to daven almost every Shabbos at the Brisker Rav's home.

One Shabbos, after he started to daven there, the Brisker Rav stood by the sink to wash R' Raphael's hands. R' Raphael would not hear of this; how could he allow himself to be served by someone of such great stature? The Brisker Rav persisted in his request to wash R' Raphael's hands, but when he saw how adamant R' Raphael was, he relented and returned to his seat. After davening, when

1. *HaRav MiBrisk,* vol. 4, p. 462.

R' Raphael went over to the Brisker Rav to say *gut Shabbos*, the Rav was displeased with him, and said, "How can you deprive me of my obligation to wash the hands of the Kohen?"[2]

Mitzvah Object

When R' Chaim Brisker was asked what the Yisraelim should have in mind during Bircas Kohanim, he responded, "They should think that they are a *cheftza d'mitzvah* (mitzvah object), which the Kohanim are using to fulfill the mitzvah of Bircas Kohanim."[3]

His son, the Brisker Rav, applied this reasoning to a Kohen as well. Once, a certain *talmid chacham* who was a Kohen was davening at the home of the Brisker Rav. During *Chazaras HaShatz*, when this Kohen saw the Rav approaching the sink with a washing cup in hand, he recoiled in alarm, and said that he could not possibly allow the Brisker Rav to serve him by washing his hands. The Rav responded, "Do you think I am serving *you*? I am fulfilling my mitzvah to pour water on the hands of the Kohanim. You are nothing more than a *cheftza d'mitzvah*!"[4]

Rav Meir Soloveitchik, a son of the Brisker Rav, was scrupulous to wash the hands of the Kohanim daily. Only in his final years when he had great difficulty walking did he stop washing their hands.[5]

In Time to Wash

R' Shaul Kravitz, a disciple of R' Yerucham, related that although the *Mashgiach* usually davened a very long silent *Shemoneh Esrei*, on Yom Tov he would make sure to finish in time to wash the hands of the Kohanim for Bircas Kohanim.[6]

R' Shmuel Dovid Friedman, author of *Sdei Tzofim*, is a Kohen, and he describes the time he davened in the Bnei Brak *beis midrash* of the great *posek hador*, R' Shmuel HaLevi Wosner, on a regular weekday. R' Shmuel Dovid was accompanied by his sons

---

2. *Uvdos V'Hanhagos L'Beis Brisk*, vol. 1, p. 244.
3. As recorded by R' Aharon Leib Shteinman (*Ayeles HaShachar, Bamidbar* 6:23).
4. *HaRav MiBrisk* ibid.
5. *D'Chazitei L'Rabbi Meir*, by R' Shimon Yosef Meller, vol. 2, p. 61.
6. Heard from his son R' Aharon Meir Kravitz. See Responsa of R' Chaim Kanievsky #27, which states that this is the correct practice.

and grandsons, and when the time came to prepare for Bircas Kohanim, they all made their way to the sink area outside the *beis midrash*. R' Wosner was over a hundred years old at the time, but that did not deter him from fulfilling his role as a Levi, and he left his seat at the front of the *beis midrash* and went outside to wash the hands of the Kohanim. It was a remarkable sight; here was a venerable sage who carried the most difficult halachic questions on his shoulders, yet he insisted on personally washing the hands of every Kohen, young and old, including a number of R' Shmuel Dovid's grandsons who were no more than bar mitzvah age.

To get a better understanding of R' Wosner's perspective, it is worth studying what he himself had to say about the subject (*Shevet HaLevi,* vol. 8, 47:3):

> There is a question as to whether it is proper for the Leviim to go outside and wash the hands of the Kohanim at the expense of missing the opportunity to answer amen to the *berachos* of the chazzan. *Beis Yosef* himself writes that he did not have a source for allowing this until he found it in *Zohar* and in *Sifra D'Tzniusa*. Having the Leviim wash the hands is a valuable custom that is practiced in all Jewish communities throughout the world. The reason for it is that the holiness of the Kohanim is augmented by having the sanctity of the Leviim added to it through their participation in the mitzvah, and it is of such importance that one need not be concerned about the fact that they will not be able to answer amen.

Washing as a Team

Mekor Chaim (128:6), written by the author of *Chavos Yair*, describes how the handwashing was done in Germany: Before each Bircas Kohanim, during Shacharis and Mussaf,[7] the eldest Levi would honor three Leviim from the congregation to perform the handwashing service together, as a team. One carried a pitcher of water, another carried a bowl to pour the water into, and the third

---

7. The custom in Germany was to perform Bircas Kohanim twice on every day of Yom Tov (including Rosh Hashanah and Yom Kippur), during Shacharis and Mussaf. See chapter 40.

carried a towel. The three of them would circulate through the shul and stop by each Kohen to wash his hands.

No Shortcuts

In Eretz Yisrael, where Bircas Kohanim is performed every morning, there are some Kohanim who wash their own hands rather than having a Levi do it. R' Moshe Feinstein (*Igros Moshe, O.C.*, vol. 4, #127) notes that this is not appropriate. He points out that *Shulchan Aruch* states clearly that a Levi should wash the Kohen's hands — and R' Yosef Karo, the author of *Shulchan Aruch*, was a Sephardi, which means that even outside of Eretz Yisrael, Bircas Kohanim was performed every day in his community. Obviously, he did not consider that a reason to change the *minhag*. The reason some Kohanim choose to wash their own hands is that they don't want to be bothered with having a Levi do it every day; it is quicker for them to do it themselves. They take a lenient position, R' Moshe explains, because the *minhag* to have a Levi wash their hands is based not on halachah, but on Kabbalah, in accordance with the *Zohar*. Nevertheless, he concludes, they are incorrect; the correct practice is for the Leviim to wash the hands of the Kohanim daily.

(See chapter 24 for laws related to washing the hands of the Kohanim.)

Chapter 22
The Chazzan's Role

Calling Out Each Word

During Bircas Kohanim, the chazzan calls out each word of the blessing, one word at a time, and the Kohanim repeat each word after him (see *Shulchan Aruch* 128:13). *Rabbeinu Bachaye* (*Bamidbar* 6:23) offers a fascinating explanation for this procedure: The Gemara (*Sotah* 38b) states that a Kohen who blesses the people is himself blessed, as the Torah says, *And I will bless those who bless you*. What happens is that as the chazzan calls out each word, Hashem's blessing flows down from Heaven and rests upon the Kohanim. The Kohanim then in turn bestow the blessing upon the Jewish people.

Although *Shulchan Aruch* rules (128:13) that the Kohanim initiate by saying the word *yevarechecha*, the *Rema* (ibid.) disputes this, citing the Rishonim who say that the chazzan utters the word *yevarechecha* as well. He writes this is the custom of the Ashkenazic communities. (See chapter 33 for further discussion of this topic.)

Threefold Blessing

Sifsei Kohen al HaTorah offers a novel insight regarding the custom for the chazzan to call out each word of Bircas Kohanim, and then for the Kohanim to repeat it. This way, he explains, the blessing begins with a Yisrael (the chazzan), continues with the Kohanim, and ends with Hashem Himself. Thus, it becomes a threefold *berachah*. Furthermore, Bircas Kohanim consists of three *pesukim*, which also makes it a threefold blessing, and Shlomo HaMelech, in his wisdom, assures us, וְהַחוּט הַמְשֻׁלָּשׁ לֹא בִמְהֵרָה יִנָּתֵק, *A three-ply cord is not easily severed* (*Koheles* 4:12).

No More, No Less

Another reason for the custom for the chazzan to call out each word is cited by R' Shlomo HaKohen in his *teshuvos* (*Binyan Shlomo, siman* 1), quoting his brother R' Betzalel HaKohen. He explains that the mitzvah of Bircas Kohanim is subject to the negative commandments of לֹא תֹסֵף עָלָיו וְלֹא תִגְרַע מִמֶּנּוּ, *You shall not add to it and you shall not subtract from it* (*Devarim* 13:1), which forbid us from augmenting or subtracting from any mitzvah. Therefore, the chazzan calls out one word at a time, to make certain that no word is inadvertently repeated or omitted. This is comparable to the Kohen Gadol's counting the number of times he sprinkled the blood of the offerings on Yom Kippur ("*Achas* — one; *achas v'achas* — one and one; *achas u'shtayim* — one and two," etc.), to ensure that no more or less than the required number of sprinklings would take place.

Why the Amud Is Not at the Front of the Shul

At the end of R' Yechezkel Shraga Halberstam of Shinov's *Divrei Yechezkel*, his disciple recounts the following (p. 315):

> In the year 5648 (1888), I was in Shinov, and had the merit to be at the table of the Shinover Rebbe, who was known to reveal amazing Torah insights as he ate his meal. He told us that he had received an inquiry from another town: "Some of the members of the shul there wanted to place the *amud* (lectern) of the chazzan up against the front wall of the shul, rather than placing it a few feet back so that the chazzan faces the *aron kodesh*; others were strongly opposed to the idea. They asked me to send them a source for our custom that the chazzan does not stand all the way up front. In truth, the *poskim* do not speak about this question, and I did not know how to respond. I was feeling very distressed over the matter. Soon after that, however, the answer was

revealed to me in a dream. The reason we do not place the *amud* against the front wall is that then, the chazzan would be standing behind the Kohanim when they *duchan*, and those who stand behind the Kohanim are not included in their *berachah*!"

No Semblance of Bircas Kohanim

Mishmeres Shalom[8] presents a novel suggestion for Ashkenazim who reside outside of Eretz Yisrael:[9]

> The congregation should endeavor to choose a Kohen to be the chazzan for Shacharis, especially on Shabbos, and even more so for Mussaf on Shabbos, Rosh Chodesh, and Chol HaMoed. The reason I say so is so that the chazzan will recite the *tefillah* beginning *"Elokeinu V'Elokei avoseinu,"* asking that Hashem bless us with the *berachah* of Bircas Kohanim — and if he himself is a Kohen, it will be as though he performed Bircas Kohanim!

However, R' Moshe Sternbuch[10] forcefully rejects this supposition. He writes:

> The proposal of *Mishmeres Shalom* is inconceivable — Heaven forbid to say such a thing! First of all, the mitzvah of Bircas Kohanim cannot be fulfilled *at all* unless the Kohen raises his hands and faces the congregation; this is an essential requirement, as explained in *Mishnah Berurah* (128:52). Therefore, the chazzan, who does not raise his hands and face the congregation, is certainly not fulfilling the mitzvah. Moreover, it is *forbidden* for him to have the intention to perform the mitzvah, because one who attempts to perform a mitzvah in a way that is not in accordance with halachah transgresses the sin of *you shall not subtract* (from the mitzvos of the Torah).
>
> *Rambam* writes explicitly (*Hilchos Tefillah* 15:7) that the

---

8. 10:9. This *sefer*, authored by R' Shalom Perlow (1851-1925), rav of Brahin, Belarus, is an organized collection of *minhagim*.
9. We did an extensive search and did not find any earlier *sefarim* that suggested this.
10. *Teshuvos V'Hanhagos*, vol. 2 #105.

> *berachah* comes not from the Kohanim, but from the Holy One, Blessed is He. Hashem decreed, however, that the blessing should be *channeled* through the Kohanim, and that takes place when they raise their hands and recite the words of the *berachah*. If they do not raise their hands and face the congregation, it is not Bircas Kohanim. In conclusion, having a Kohen as the chazzan accomplishes nothing.

R' Chaim Kanievsky (Responsa #551) also strongly disagrees with *Mishmeres Shalom* and writes that even if the chazzan in *chutz laAretz* is a Kohen, there is no semblance of Bircas Kohanim.

Chapter 23
Women Hearing Bircas Kohanim

Should Women Attend?

Why do *Chazal* (*Sotah* 38b) mention only that the "people in the fields" (who are unable to come to shul) are included in Bircas Kohanim; what about women and young children, who also cannot be in shul?

Aruch HaShulchan explains (128:38): When a husband or father receives the *berachah* from the Kohanim, it automatically follows that his family and household are included — for if his wife and children are not blessed, what could be a greater curse for him than that? As David HaMelech puts it (*Tehillim* 128:3-4): אֶשְׁתְּךָ כְּגֶפֶן פֹּרִיָּה בְּיַרְכְּתֵי בֵיתֶךָ בָּנֶיךָ כִּשְׁתִלֵי זֵיתִים סָבִיב לְשֻׁלְחָנֶךָ. הִנֵּה כִי כֵן יְבֹרַךְ גָּבֶר יְרֵא ה׳, *Your wife will be like a fruitful vine in the inner chambers of your home; your children will be like shoots of olive trees surrounding your table. Indeed, for so is the man who fears Hashem blessed.* Thus, it goes without saying that one's family members are included in the *berachah*. Similarly, *Taz* (§22) states that a wife is blessed through her husband, and children through their father. *Magen Avraham* (§37) likewise states that a wife is blessed through her husband.

R' Moshe Feinstein writes (*Igros Moshe, O.C.*, vol. 5 #20):

> There is certainly an obligation upon every individual to come to shul, if there is one in the city, in order to hear Bircas Kohanim. Although *Chazal* made an allowance for those who are working in the fields of that city, and said they are

included in the *berachah* even if they do not come, *Tosafos* there cite the Gemara, which states that the workers in the field are considered *anusim* (unable to attend), but all those who are in the city are not *anusim* and are not excused from coming to hear the *berachos*. Of course, outside of Eretz Yisrael, where Bircas Kohanim is recited only on Yom Tov, when work is forbidden, the leniency for "workers in the field" is not applicable at all. However, mothers who must stay home to take care of their young children are certainly *anusim*, and are included in the *berachah*. The same applies to one who is tending to the needs of a sick person.[1]

The above seems to indicate that single girls and unmarried women should make the effort to attend Bircas Kohanim.

Some have the custom to bring very young children, even newborns, to shul on Yom Tov to hear Bircas Kohanim. R' Chaim Kanievsky writes (Responsa #504) that this practice has merit.

Not a Time-Related Mitzvah

Minchas Chinuch (Mitzvah 378) cites *Sefer Chareidim*'s view that there is a mitzvah obligation upon non-Kohanim to receive the *berachah*, adding that some argue that women are not included in this obligation, for the following reason: The Torah says with regard to Kohanim (*Devarim* 21:5), כִּי בָם בָּחַר ה׳ אֱלֹהֶיךָ לְשָׁרְתוֹ וּלְבָרֵךְ בְּשֵׁם ה׳, *For them has Hashem, your G-d, chosen to minister to Him and to bless with the Name of Hashem*, drawing a parallel between Bircas Kohanim and the *avodah* in the Beis HaMikdash. (Since both are mentioned in the same *pasuk*, we may learn the laws of one from the other. This method of deriving Torah laws is known as a *hekesh*.) Thus, it would seem that just as the *avodah* cannot be performed at night, so too Bircas Kohanim may not be performed at night. If so, it is a time-related mitzvah, and therefore women are exempt. However, the Gemara (*Taanis* 27a) clearly states that this *hekesh* is only an *asmachta* — a support for Rabbinic rulings. **Therefore, Bircas Kohanim may technically be performed at any time, and women are included in the mitzvah.**

---

1. Elsewhere, R' Moshe explains (ibid., vol. 2 #31) why Bircas Kohanim in one city cannot extend past that city, and surely not to overseas locations.

Behind the Kohanim

Rokeach (*Hilchos Tefillah* #323) points out that those who are standing behind the Kohanim cannot receive the *berachah*. If, however, they are facing the Kohanim, they do receive the *berachah*, even if they are behind a wall or partition, **such as women in the *ezras nashim*.**

Similarly, R' Eliyahu ben R' Yitzchak, a disciple of Rokeach, writes in *Sefer HaAsufos* (*Siman* 571; quoted in *Kovetz Shittos Kammai, Sotah* 38b): "When the Kohanim perform Bircas Kohanim, they must have in mind the entire Jewish people, and everyone, including those who are working in the fields, receives the blessing — **even the women who are on the other side of the wall, for the wall does not separate between them and the Kohanim."**

Ben Ish Chai (*Chukei Nashim*, ch. 43) writes that a woman who makes an effort to come to shul on Shabbos, sees the *sefer Torah*, responds amen at the appropriate times, and **listens to Bircas Kohanim is assured of receiving great reward in this world.**

Placement of the Ezras Nashim

On several occasions, when R' Chaim Kanievsky was asked whether an *ezras nashim* may be constructed in a room in front of the main shul, he answered that this should not be done, as the women will not be facing the Kohanim and will therefore not be included in Bircas Kohanim. (See Responsa #230.)[2]

He also writes (Responsa #229, 238) that as long as the *ezras nashim* is located in front of the Kohanim and the women face the Kohanim, they receive the *berachah*, even if they are on a higher floor or in an elevated area.

R' Chaim notes, as well (Responsa #242), that if the women are standing in front of where the Kohanim are standing (such as if the women's section is situated at the side of the men's section, rather than behind it), before Bircas Kohanim they should move back to face the Kohanim, so they can be included in the *berachah*.

---

2. Similarly, in *She'eilos U'Teshuvos Kinyan Torah* (vol. 5, #10), R' Avraham Dovid Horowitz of Yerushalayim's Eidah HaChareidis (who passed away in 2004) writes that a shul should be built with the women's section situated in such a way that the women can receive the blessing of Bircas Kohanim.

She Should Go to Hear Bircas Kohanim

R' Ezriel Barr related the following: My sister once had a frightening dream during a pregnancy. I approached the Chazon Ish and he said, "She has nothing to worry about. She should go to shul for Bircas Kohanim and recite the *Ribbono Shel Olam* prayer, as *Chazal* advise (*Berachos* 55b)."[3]

Similarly, a grandson of the Steipler Gaon recounted that once, his sister experienced a frightening dream during the Nine Days, and she went to her grandfather (the Steipler) to seek his advice. He told her to recite the *Ribbono Shel Olam* prayer in shul when the Kohanim *duchan*.[4]

A questioner wrote to R' Chaim Kanievsky that his wife, who was the director of a day camp, had dreamt that a horrific tragedy occurred in which she and several girls from the camp were injured in a trip that was scheduled for the next week. He asked R' Chaim if the trip should be canceled, and R' Chaim responded (Responsa #377) that if his wife goes to shul to hear Bircas Kohanim and recites the *Ribbono Shel Olam* prayer to negate bad dreams, she can participate in the trip as planned.

Elsewhere (Responsa #376), R' Chaim notes that if a woman has a bad dream and wishes to negate it, **she herself has to go to shul to hear Bircas Kohanim and say the *Ribbono Shel Olam* prayer; her husband cannot do this on her behalf.**

From the Terror in the Nights

A student of R' Moshe Shmuel Shapira in Yeshivas Be'er Yaakov, R' Dov Schon (who currently resides in the United States), recounted the following incident:

> When I was learning in Be'er Yaakov, I once got called to the office to take an emergency phone call. It was my father on the line, and for him it was very early in the morning, when most people are still sleeping. He explained that my grandmother had just experienced a frightening dream and was very shaken by it. He wanted me to get advice from

3. *Maaseh Ish,* vol. 3, p. 164.
4. *Orchos Rabbeinu,* vol. 2, p. 159.

the Rosh Yeshivah. I went to R' Moshe Shmuel and he said, "The Sephardim *duchan* every day even outside of Eretz Yisrael. It is worthwhile for your grandmother to go immediately to a Sephardic shul and stand in the women's section facing the Kohanim when they *duchan*. If she does so, no harm will befall her or her family."

He then opened a Gemara and read aloud: "One who sees a dream and does not understand what he has seen should arise early in the morning and stand before the Kohanim when they spread their hands [to perform Bircas Kohanim]" (*Berachos* 55b). He pointed to the commentary of R' Nissim Gaon, printed in the margin of the page, which states that the reason for doing so is explained in *Midrash Tanchuma* (*Nasso* 9), which gives the following interpretation of the words in *Shir HaShirim* (3:7-8) הִנֵּה מִטָּתוֹ שֶׁלִּשְׁלֹמֹה שִׁשִּׁים גִּבֹּרִים סָבִיב לָהּ מִגִּבֹּרֵי יִשְׂרָאֵל. כֻּלָּם אֲחֻזֵי חֶרֶב מְלֻמְּדֵי מִלְחָמָה אִישׁ חַרְבּוֹ עַל יְרֵכוֹ מִפַּחַד בַּלֵּילוֹת, *Behold the resting place of Him to Whom peace belongs, with sixty of Israel's mighty encircling it. All of them gripping the sword, skilled in battle, each with his sword ready at his side, lest he succumb in the nights of exile*:

"*Sixty mighty ones* alludes to the sixty letters of Bircas Kohanim. *All of them gripping the sword* — for the Name of Hashem is in each one of the *berachos*. *Each with his sword at his side* — this teaches us that even if a person dreamed that there was a drawn sword placed on his neck, or about to cut off his leg, he should arise early in the morning and go to the synagogue, to save himself from the terror of what he saw at night in his dream, and he should be present as the Kohanim raise their hands (to perform Bircas Kohanim). This will nullify his bad dream, and this is what the *pasuk* refers to with the words *from the terror in the nights*."

Incredible Salvations

R' Nissim Karelitz was a leading rav and *posek* in Bnei Brak, and many people facing challenges and troubles sought his counsel. In her later years, his wife, Rebbetzin Leah (the daughter of R' Tzvi

Kopshitz; see chapter 7) would ask the petitioners for their name and their mother's name. She would go to shul approximately twice a week, and during Bircas Kohanim she would have in mind all the misfortunes she had heard during the week. She told her children that she saw incredible salvations for those for whom she or others prayed during Bircas Kohanim.[5]

5. Heard from her son R' Shmuel Karelitz. This is also recorded by her nephew R' Eliezer Turk, *Otzroseihem Amalei, Nasso,* p. 151.

Part 5:

Laws and Customs

Chapter 24
Washing Hands Before Bircas Kohanim: A Halachic Perspective

Although Kohanim, like all Jews, are required to wash their hands in the morning before davening, they are also required to wash their hands (up to the wrist) again before performing Bircas Kohanim. This should be done before the chazzan begins the *berachah* of *Retzei.*[1] The Gemara (*Sotah* 39a) derives the obligation of handwashing from the verse שְׂאוּ יְדֵכֶם קֹדֶשׁ וּבָרְכוּ אֶת ה׳, *Lift your hands in the Sanctuary and bless Hashem* (*Tehillim* 134:2).[2] Based on this *pasuk*, the Gemara there states: "R' Yehoshua ben Levi said: Any Kohen who has not washed his hands may not lift them up to pronounce Bircas Kohanim."

1. If the Kohen's hands remained clean since he washed them earlier that morning, and there is no water available for him to wash again, he is permitted to rely on the morning handwashing and *duchan*.[3]

2. If the Kohen's hands are still clean, and in order for him to get to the sink to wash again he has to walk within four *amos* in front of someone who is davening *Shemoneh Esrei*, it is preferable for him to

1. *Shulchan Aruch* 128: 6; *Mishnah Berurah* §19.
2. See *Shulchan Aruch* ibid.
3. *Mishnah Berurah* (128:20) writes that as long as he is sure that his hands did not touch unclean areas of his body, one may rely on *Rambam* (*Hilchos Nesias Kapayim* 15:5), who is of the opinion that a special washing is not necessary if one's hands are still clean since washing that morning. See *Kesef Mishneh* on *Rambam* there, and *Beis Yosef* 128:6, quoting a letter from R' Avraham ben HaRambam in which he writes that his father and other Torah leaders were of the opinion that one may rely on his earlier *netilas yadayim* for Bircas Kohanim.

rely on the morning washing rather than walk to the sink.[4] If his hands are not clean, he is required to wash them, even if that entails passing within four *amos* in front of someone davening *Shemoneh Esrei*. Similarly, he may walk within four *amos* of someone davening *Shemoneh Esrei* in order to reach the *duchan* at the front of the shul.[5]

3. The Kohen does not recite a *berachah* when he washes his hands for Bircas Kohanim.[6]

4. The hands of the Kohen should be washed until the wrist[7] with a *reviis* of water,[8] poured from a utensil by a person (and not directly from the sink).[9]

5. Although for all other prayers, if one does not have access to water he may use other cleansing agents,[10] for Bircas Kohanim the only acceptable method of purifying one's hands is washing them with water.[11]

6. It is necessary to pour water over the hands of the Kohen only one time.[12]

7. Although the Kohen should make sure his hands are clean before washing them, if there is a *chatzitzah* (obstruction, such as a Band-aid) on the Kohen's hand that prevents the water from reaching that area, he is still permitted to perform Bircas Kohanim.[13]

8. When one washes *netilas yadayim* on the morning of Tishah B'Av or Yom Kippur, he is permitted to wash only his fingers. Nevertheless, a Kohen's entire hands may be washed for Bircas

---

4. Responsa of R' Chaim Kanievsky #82.
5. Responsa of R' Chaim Kanievsky #72.
6. *Shulchan Aruch* 128:7: If the Kohen already recited the *al netilas yadayim* blessing on the morning handwashing, he should not repeat the blessing when he washes his hands for Bircas Kohanim. See also *Mishnah Berurah* 128:21. This is unlike the opinion of *Tur* that one should make a *berachah* when washing for Bircas Kohanim. *Darkei Moshe* on *Tur* states that since *Rambam* is of the opinion that this additional handwashing is not necessary at all, we follow the rule of *safek berachah*; i.e., when there is a doubt, we do not recite a *berachah*.
7. *Rambam* (*Hilchos Nesias Kapayim* 15:5) writes that it is comparable to a Kohen who purifies his hands before the service in the Beis HaMikdash. See also *Shulchan Aruch* 128:6; *Mishnah Berurah* §21.
8. *Mishnah Berurah* 128:21; *Shaar HaTziyun* §25.
9. See *Mishnah Berurah* 128:21, citing the Acharonim.
10. As discussed in *Shulchan Aruch* 92:4.
11. See *Mishnah Berurah* 128:19.
12. See Responsa of R' Chaim Kanievsky #1.
13. See Responsa of R' Chaim Kanievsky #19.

Kohanim.[14] In Eretz Yisrael and in Sephardic congregations worldwide, where Bircas Kohanim is recited on Yom Kippur three times (Shacharis, Mussaf, and Neilah), it is permitted to wash the Kohen's entire hands before all three recitations of Bircas Kohanim.[15]

9. If the chazzan is a Kohen, and the shul follows the custom that a chazzan who is a Kohen performs Bircas Kohanim,[16] he may rely on the handwashing of the morning rather than exit the shul in the middle of *Chazaras HaShatz*.[17]

10. The Kohen should be careful not to converse with anyone after washing his hands for Bircas Kohanim, which would be an interruption (*hefsek*) between washing his hands and performing the mitzvah of Bircas Kohanim.[18]

The Role of the Levi

11. To add to the sanctity of the mitzvah, the hands of the Kohen should be washed by a Levi. *Beis Yosef* (128:6) explains, based on the *Zohar*, that the reason a Levi should wash the hands of the Kohen is so that the Kohen will be purified by someone who also possesses sanctity.[19] The *Mordechai*, a *Rishon*, actually refers to the Levi as the *"nosen mayim"* ("water pourer").[20]

12. *Aruch HaShulchan* (128:15) presents an additional reason for having a Levi wash the Kohen's hands: During the time of the Beis HaMikdash, the Leviim served and assisted the Kohanim in their performance of the *avodah* (Divine service), and the mitzvah of Bircas Kohanim is modeled after the *avodah* in the Beis HaMikdash.

13. *Shulchan Aruch* (128:6) states that a Levi must wash his own hands before washing the hands of the Kohen. *Rema* argues, however, noting that the custom in Ashkenazic communities is to be lenient and rely on the Levi's morning handwashing. All agree that if the Levi's hands are unclean before washing, or if his

---

14. See *Mishnah Berurah* 613:7.
15. See Responsa of R' Chaim Kanievsky #17.
16. For a discussion of this halachah see chapter 43. Also see *Shulchan Aruch* 128:20 and *Mishnah Berurah* §75.
17. See *Chayei Adam* 32:26; *Aruch HaShulchan* 128:33, and *Kaf HaChaim* 128:120.
18. *Biur Halachah* 128:6.
19. See chapter 21, where we elaborate on this idea and cite the *Zohar* that is the source of this idea.
20. See *Mordechai* (*Megillah* §817), also cited in *Beis Yosef* here.

attention to keeping his hands clean has lapsed, then he should wash his own hands before washing the hands of the Kohen.[21]

14. Even in Eretz Yisrael, where Bircas Kohanim is performed daily, the Levi should wash the hands of the Kohen every day, including the weekdays, even if he finds this inconvenient.[22]

15. Even if the only Levi present is below the age of bar mitzvah, it is preferable for him to wash the hands of the Kohen rather than the Kohen washing his own hands.[23] Even if there are adult Leviim there as well, the minor may wash the hands of the Kohanim together with the adults.[24]

16. Most *poskim* hold that if there are several Leviim, they should all wash the hands of the Kohen by holding the washing cup together.[25]

17. It is permitted for a Levi to leave the main room of the shul for the purpose of washing the hands of the Kohanim, even when this will cause him to miss part of *Chazaras HaShatz* and lose the opportunity to answer amen and *Modim d'Rabbanan*.[26]

Although a Levi is not obligated to walk out unless there are no

---

21. See *Mishnah Berurah* 128:23.

22. R' Moshe Feinstein points out (*Igros Moshe, O.C.,* vol. 4, #127) that R' Yosef Karo resided in Eretz Yisrael, where Bircas Kohanim is performed on a daily basis, and he clearly states in *Shulchan Aruch* that the Levi should wash the hands of the Kohen every day. See also Responsa of R' Chaim Kanievsky #36.

23. Responsa of R' Chaim Kanievsky #39.

24. Responsa of R' Chaim Kanievsky #40.

25. See *Leket HaKemach HeChadash* 128:45, which notes that in Ashkenazic communities, several Leviim wash the hands of the Kohanim together, while in Sephardic communities only one Levi washes the hands of the Kohanim. R' Yosef Shalom Elyashiv also ruled that several Leviim may wash the hands of the Kohen (*Tziyunei Halachah,* p. 348). See also Responsa of R' Chaim Kanievsky #21, where he writes as well that it is proper for several Leviim to wash the hands of the Kohen together.

26. *Aderes* (cited in chapter 21) explains why *all* the Leviim participate in the mitzvah of washing the Kohanim's hands, even at the expense of missing *Chazaras HaShatz* — because if not for this service, there would be no active mitzvah the Leviim could do today to demonstrate their special status with regard to the *avodah*.

This is also the opinion of R' Shmuel HaLevi Wosner (*Shevet HaLevi,* vol. 8 #47), R' Yosef Shalom Elyashiv (*Tziyunei Halachah,* p. 348), and R' Chaim Kanievsky (Responsa #22), who all agree that multiple Leviim should wash the hands of the Kohanim even at the cost of missing part of *Chazaras HaShatz,* as this is the mitzvah given to the Leviim.

other Leviim available to wash the Kohen's hands,[27] he is permitted to do so even when several other Leviim go out as well, even though they will all miss part of *Chazaras HaShatz*.[28]

18. It is prohibited for a Levi or a *bechor* to walk within four *amos* in front of someone davening *Shemoneh Esrei* in order to wash the hands of a Kohen.[29]

19. If the Kohen washed his own hands because there was no Levi (or *bechor*) available, and a Levi came in afterward, there is no need for the Levi to wash the Kohen's hands again.[30]

20. There is no obligation for the Kohen to dry his hands with a towel after washing them; if he prefers, he may allow them to air-dry.[31]

21. Even if the Levi is a greater Torah scholar or a more virtuous person than the Kohen, most *poskim* are of the opinion that he should still wash the hands of the Kohen.[32] The *sefer She'eilas Yaakov*[33] contains a letter that the author wrote to R' Yosef Shaul HaLevi Nathanson[34] inquiring whether or not R' Yosef Shaul followed the custom of washing the hands of the Kohanim. He replied: "I wash the hands of the Kohanim for Bircas Kohanim, and am careful to do so exactly in accordance with the halachah."

22. Even if the Levi is a rebbi or rosh yeshivah, he should still wash the hands of his students who are Kohanim, especially if there are no other Leviim present.[35]

23. Despite the significance of having a Levi wash the hands of the Kohen, if he fails to do so he is not penalized (such as by being

---

27. *Mishnah Berurah* (128:22) states that one should have a Levi perform the handwashing. For an explanation of *Mishnah Berurah*, see Responsa of R' Chaim Kanievsky #25.

28. *Shevet HaLevi* ibid. See also Responsa of R' Chaim Kanievsky #30.

29. Responsa of R' Chaim Kanievsky #75.

30. Responsa of R' Chaim Kanievsky #50.

31. Responsa of R' Chaim Kanievsky #8.

32. *Mishnah Berurah* (128:22) states that a Levi is required to wash the hands of a Kohen even if the Kohen is unlearned. This is the opinion of *Aruch HaShulchan* (128:15) as well; see chapter 21, where we record an incident with the Brisker Rav and R' Raphael HaKohen Kook.

33. Ch. 7; authored by R' Yaakov HaLevi Prager (1849-1918).

34. Author of *She'eilos U'Teshuvos Sho'el U'Meishiv*.

35. Responsa of R' Chaim Kanievsky #48. Also see chapter 21, in which we describe how R' Shmuel HaLevi Wosner washed the hands of his young students.

disqualified to receive the *aliyah* of Levi).[36]

Bechor in Place of a Levi

24. If there are no Leviim present, a *bechor* who is a *peter rechem* (i.e., firstborn of his mother; whether or not he is his father's firstborn is irrelevant) is given the honor of washing the hands of the Kohen, since he also has an elevated level of *kedushah* vis-à-vis the *avodah* in the Beis HaMikdash.[37]

25. If neither a Levi nor a Yisrael who is a *bechor* is available, a Kohen should not wash the hands of his fellow Kohanim, even if he is a *bechor*.[38]

26. A Yisrael who is not a *bechor* should not wash the hands of the Kohanim. In the absence of a Levi or a *bechor*, the Kohanim should wash their own hands.[39]

27. R' Chaim Kanievsky was a *bechor*, and when he was a child, he washed the hands of the Kohanim at the *netz* minyan of the Chazon Ish every morning.[40] Originally, there was no Levi present, but even when a Levi, R' Yosef Dinkels, joined the minyan, he continued washing the hands of the Kohanim together with R' Yosef.[41]

28. Even in the last years of R' Chaim's life, he would look around to see if a Levi was present. If there was no Levi, he would go out during *Chazaras HaShatz* to wash the hands of the Kohanim.[42]

---

36. *She'eilos Teshuvos Hillel Omer* (#87), quoting R' Reuven HaKohen Katz (rav and rosh yeshivah of Petach Tikvah when R' Chaim Kanievsky learned there); *Yalkut Yosef* 128:23.

37. *Bach* (128:3), citing *Maharil*; *Magen Avraham* (128:7); *Mishnah Berurah* 128:22.

38. See Responsa of R' Chaim Kanievsky #42.

39. This is clearly stated in the *Zohar* cited above. See also *Mishnah Berurah* 128:22; Responsa of R' Chaim Kanievsky #41.

40. Responsa of R' Chaim Kanievsky #54.

41. See *Minchas Todah*, authored by R' Chaim's grandson R' Gedaliah Honigsberg.

42. R' Chaim's son R' Yitzchak Shaul related that before Bircas Kohanim, R' Chaim would look toward the place where his *mechutan* R' Meir HaLevi Honigsberg sat. If he saw that R' Meir was not present, he would head out with a smile to wash the hands of the Kohanim. R' Yitzchak Shaul added that several times he was in shul with his father when there was no Levi present, and one of the Kohanim suggested that perhaps they should wash their own hands, in deference to R' Chaim's towering stature as a *talmid chacham*. R' Chaim waved dismissively at the idea, and said this is a special mitzvah that he eagerly awaits the opportunity to perform.

Chapter 25
Ascending to the Duchan

Throughout the Talmud, Bircas Kohanim is described as "ascending" to the *duchan*,[1] and the same expression is found in the *poskim*. Similarly, people commonly refer to Bircas Kohanim as *duchaning*.

The literal translation of ***duchan* is a raised platform or stage**. Is it, in fact, necessary (or preferable) for Bircas Kohanim to be performed on a raised platform, or is it described as "going up" only because it was commonly done that way?

When performing Bircas Kohanim in the Beis HaMikdash, the Kohanim stood on the stairs leading up to the *Ulam*. The Mishnah (*Tamid* 7:2) describes this in detail:

> All the Kohanim now came and stood on the twelve steps in front of the *Ulam*. When arranging themselves on the steps, the first five Kohanim who merited to work inside the *Heichal* stood to the south of their fellow Kohanim, and there were five vessels in their hands ... After the other Kohanim finished bringing the *tamid's* limbs to the *Mizbei'ach*, they joined the first five Kohanim on the steps to recite Bircas Kohanim. They blessed the nation with one blessing.
>
> They recited the same verses whether in the Beis HaMikdash or not, except that outside the Beis HaMikdash, the Kohanim say it as three separate blessings, pausing after

---

1. *Shabbos* 118b; *Rosh Hashanah* 28b and 31b; *Sotah* 38b and 40a; *Kiddushin* 71a; *Menachos* 44a.

each of the three verses for the people to answer amen, but in the Beis HaMikdash they said all the verses together as one long blessing, because the practice in the Beis HaMikdash was not to answer amen after blessings.

In his *sefer Derech Chochmah,*[2] R' Chaim Kanievsky writes that there were at least three platforms in the Beis HaMikdash for the express purpose of Bircas Kohanim.

The question now is whether standing on a raised platform (or stairs) is required outside the Beis HaMikdash as well.

Levush states:[3] "The term *'duchan'* that is widely used means a platform — that is, the platform upon which the Kohanim stand when performing Bircas Kohanim. That is why we frequently find the phrase 'ascending' to *duchan* — meaning going up onto the platform to bless the people."

Likewise, the Midrash teaches[4]: "Those who are standing behind the Kohanim are not included in the *berachah,* and for that reason, the Kohanim 'go up' to the *aron kodesh,* so that all the people will be facing them."

Similarly, *Pri Megadim* explains:[5] "'*Duchan'* refers to the place that the Kohanim ascend to for Bircas Kohanim; see *Levush* (quoted above). In our times, they stand on the platform in front of the *aron kodesh* or on the steps leading up to it."

Aruch HaShulchan[6] describes the *duchan* as follows:

> The Kohanim are meant to stand primarily in front of the *aron kodesh,* an area known as the "*duchan,*" just as they stood on a "*duchan*" in the Beis HaMikdash — that is, a designated place, such as a platform, as R' Ovadiah of Bartenura explains in his commentary to *Middos* (end of ch. 2). The word *duchan* is related to the word "*dachon,*" found in the Mishnah,[7] which is a shelf attached to the outside of a stove, where pots can be put down. Also, the *Targum* renders the *pasuk* (*Tehillim* 134:2) שְׂאוּ יְדֵכֶם קֹדֶשׁ וּבָרְכוּ אֶת ה׳, *Lift*

---

2. *Hilchos Beis HaBechirah* 6:6.
3. *Siman* 130.
4. *Bamidbar Rabbah* 11:3.
5. *Mishbetzos Zahav* 130:2.
6. 128:19.
7. *Keilim* 7:2.

> *your hands in the Sanctuary and bless Hashem,* to mean: "Raise your hands, Kohanim, on the holy *duchan*." Therefore, that is where the Kohanim must stand.
>
> If there are numerous Kohanim, those who cannot fit on the *duchan* should stand on the sides, against the front wall of the shul. This is the accepted practice in all countries. Accordingly, a Kohen may not remain standing by his own seat, for he is required to walk toward the *duchan*, as we have discussed in *se'if* 16. Many Kohanim stay in their place because they are unaware of this halachah, and we are obligated to instruct them not to do so.

Likewise, *Ben Ish Chai* writes:[8]

> The proper place for Kohanim to stand when blessing the people is upon a raised platform at the front of the shul, for the word "*duchan*" means a platform. Those who are lackadaisical about this, and just remain standing at ground level, are deviating from the words of our Sages. When *Chazal* say the Kohanim are to "ascend" to *duchan*, it is not a random expression; they meant it literally. Here in our city of Baghdad, the original practice of the Kohanim was to stand on the floor of the shul, but — thanks to Hashem — I succeeded in changing the custom and having them stand on the steps of the *aron kodesh*. It is appropriate to institute this practice in every community.

Kaf HaChaim[9] also emphasizes that the Kohanim must ascend the *duchan* and not stand on the floor, since this detail is mentioned in the Gemara (*Sotah* 40a). He adds that this is implied in the words of the *poskim* as well, and one should not deviate from the custom.

R' Ovadiah Yosef, however, writes:[10]

> It is clear that although standing on a raised platform is the optimal way to perform the mitzvah, there is absolutely no *obligation* to do so. In fact, *She'eilos U'Teshuvos Radbaz*[11] states that if the chazzan is the only Kohen in the shul, it

8. First year, *Tetzaveh* §5.
9. 128:13.
10. *Yechaveh Daas*, vol. 2 #13.
11. Vol. 1, *siman* 237.

is preferable for him to remain standing at the *amud* and have the congregation gather in front of him, so that he can face them without stepping out of his place when he recites the *berachos*. This is better than having him ascend to the *duchan*, because that is not a requisite part of the mitzvah. If such were not the case, what would happen if a group were davening in a place where there was no *duchan* and no *aron kodesh*? Would one say that the Kohanim are exempt from the mitzvah? Of course not! Obviously, then, the *duchan* is not a requirement.

Inspired to Ascend

After describing the inauguration of Aharon and his sons as Kohanim, the Torah says (*Vayikra* 9:22): וַיִּשָּׂא אַהֲרֹן אֶת יָדָיו אֶל הָעָם וַיְבָרְכֵם וַיֵּרֶד מֵעֲשֹׂת הַחַטָּאת וְהָעֹלָה וְהַשְּׁלָמִים, *Aharon raised his hands toward the people and blessed them; then he descended from having performed the sin-offering, the burnt-offering, and the peace-offering.* The *Netziv*, in *Haamek Davar*, offers the following insight: According to the simple understanding of the events described here, the mitzvah of Bircas Kohanim had not yet been given at that point, and that is why the Torah does not mention that Aharon's sons blessed the people as well. Rather, Aharon himself was inspired to ascend to a place that was elevated above the rest of the people and to bless them from that position; for this purpose, he chose to stand upon the *Mizbei'ach*. From that time on, it became customary for the Kohanim to stand in an elevated place when performing Bircas Kohanim.

R' Chaim Kanievsky's Rulings

Below is a summary of the rulings on this topic that appear in R' Chaim Kanievsky's responsa (#184-192):

1. It is preferable for the Kohanim to perform Bircas Kohanim on the platform in front of the *aron kodesh* and the steps leading up to it, if there is sufficient space there.
2. If there is not enough room on the steps for all the Kohanim, the ones who cannot stand on the steps should spread out along the front (*mizrach*) wall, and stand facing the congregation.

3. The Kohanim at the *mizrach* wall should not stand on a chair or bench to perform the mitzvah, but should remain standing on the floor.
4. There is no source for the common practice of putting down a carpet or floor-covering for the Kohanim to stand on during Bircas Kohanim. It is possible that the practice originally began when some Kohanim requested a carpet so that their feet would not become cold (since wearing shoes is not permitted when performing Bircas Kohanim).[12]

12. *K'Ayal Taarog* (Halachah, p. 192) notes that R' Aharon Leib Shteinman was of the same opinion as R' Chaim, that there is no requirement to spread out a carpet for the Kohanim to stand upon, and the only reason to do so is to protect their feet from the cold floor.

Chapter 26
Moving Toward the Duchan Before Bircas Kohanim

Shulchan Aruch rules (128:8), based on the Gemara (*Sotah* 38b), that the Kohanim must "uproot their feet" — that is, they must begin their ascent to the *duchan* — when the chazzan begins reciting the *berachah* of *Retzei*.[1]

Aruch HaShulchan[2] offers an important insight as to why the Kohanim prepare for Bircas Kohanim during the *berachah* of *Retzei*:

> There is a positive Torah commandment for the Kohanim to bless the Jewish people ... and this mitzvah remains in effect continually, even in our times. *Rambam*, in the beginning of *Hilchos Tefillah*, counts it as one of the 613 mitzvos ... Thus, even in our times, we have the mitzvah to perform Bircas Kohanim when we reach the conclusion of our prayer, which is a substitute for the *Korban Tamid*.[3] The "conclusion" of the prayer is when we come to the end of our requests — i.e., the *berachah* of *Shomei'a Tefillah*. This is followed by the *berachah* of *Retzei*, which begins with a prayer that Hashem accept our *tefillah*. That is why the

---

1. *Chayei Adam* (32:13) explains that we see from the Gemara that even a small step in the direction of the *duchan* is sufficient. See also Responsa of R' Chaim Kanievsky #60.
2. 128:1.
3. In the Beis HaMikdash, the *Tamid* was offered every morning and afternoon. Bircas Kohanim was performed after the morning offering.

Kohanim are obligated to start walking toward the front of the shul at this time in preparation for *duchaning*.[4]

1. Although the Kohanim do not have to actually reach the *duchan* until later, they must at least take a step in that direction during *Retzei*.[5]

2. The Kohanim should wash their hands before *Retzei*, so that they can begin walking toward the *duchan* as soon as the chazzan begins the *berachah*.[6]

3. Although ideally a Kohen should begin his ascent to the *duchan* as soon as the chazzan says the word *Retzei*,[7] he is permitted to *duchan* as long as he began his ascent before the congregation finished responding amen to the *berachah* of *Retzei*.[8]

4. If the Kohen did not begin his ascent until the end of the *Retzei* blessing, he may no longer *duchan* in that minyan. Furthermore, if he remains in the shul until the other Kohanim begin their *berachah*, he transgresses a positive commandment.[9] *Biur Halachah* (128:2) elaborates that this is true even if the Kohen regrets his failure to ascend to the *duchan* at the proper time and now wants to perform Bircas Kohanim, but cannot because halachah prohibits him from joining the other Kohanim on the *duchan*. Rather, this Kohen should leave the shul before the chazzan calls out "Kohanim," and should attempt to join another minyan so that he can begin the ascent to the *duchan* properly, at the beginning of *Retzei*.[10]

5. A Kohen who is eligible to *duchan* but for some reason does not want to do so must make sure to exit the shul before the chazzan calls out "Kohanim."[11] He should then remain outside for the

---

4. *Mishnah Berurah* (128:26) explains that we learn this from the verse וַיִּשָּׂא אַהֲרֹן אֶת יָדָיו אֶל הָעָם וַיְבָרְכֵם וַיֵּרֶד מֵעֲשֹׂת הַחַטָּאת וְהָעֹלָה וְהַשְּׁלָמִים, *Aharon raised his hands toward the people and blessed them; then he descended from having performed the sin-offering, the burnt-offering, and the peace-offering* (*Vayikra* 9:22). This indicates that Aharon recited the blessings before concluding the *avodah*. Likewise, the Kohanim must advance to the *duchan* before the chazzan finishes the *berachah* of *Avodah* (i.e., *Retzei*).

5. *Mishnah Berurah* 128:27.

6. Ibid.

7. *Mishnah Berurah* 128:25.

8. Ibid.

9. *Shulchan Aruch* 128:2

10. Responsa of R' Chaim Kanievsky #137.

11. *Shulchan Aruch* 128:4

duration of Bircas Kohanim. *Biur Halachah* adds that if the Kohen has no valid reason for leaving shul to avoid Bircas Kohanim, although he may not be transgressing the positive commandment to *duchan,* he has still committed a serious misdeed. This is comparable to someone who avoids the obligation of *tzitzis,* about whom our sources say that he will suffer punishment at a time of Divine anger (*idan rischa*).[12]

6. Even if the Kohen's reason for not stepping toward the *duchan* was that he was preoccupied with prayer, or some other circumstance beyond his control, he still may not *duchan.*[13] (Regarding a Kohen who is still in the middle of *Shemoneh Esrei,* see 15-17 below.)

7. If a Kohen has not yet washed his hands, and the chazzan has already begun *Retzei,* he should take a step toward the *duchan* and then quickly wash his hands before going up to perform the mitzvah. According to many authorities, walking out of the room to wash his hands is not sufficient as an *akirah,* even though he did "uproot his feet," because he did not move in the direction of the *duchan.*[14] Others maintain, however, that *b'dieved* (after the fact) the Kohen is permitted to *duchan* in this situation, since he did begin walking during *Retzei.*[15]

8. If a Kohen was near the end of *Shemoneh Esrei,* reciting the final paragraph of *Elokai Netzor,* when the chazzan reached *Retzei,* it is permitted for him to take a step toward the *duchan,* complete his *Shemoneh Esrei* if possible, and then perform Bircas Kohanim. If he is unable to complete *Elokai Netzor* during that time, he should perform Bircas Kohanim and recite *Elokai Netzor* afterward.[16]

---

12. *Biur Halachah* 128:4. The Gemara (*Menachos* 41a) states that generally, Hashem does not punish people for failing to perform a positive Torah commandment; people are punished only for violating negative prohibitions. However, in a period of Divine anger, punishment is meted out for negating positive mitzvos as well.

13. *Mishnah Berurah* and *Biur Halachah* 128:8. See below, where we note that a Kohen who will be performing Bircas Kohanim is permitted to take a small step toward the *duchan* during *Retzei* even if he is in the middle of *Shemoneh Esrei.*

14. *Mishnah Berurah* 128:28; *Shaar HaTziyun* ibid.

15. *Aruch HaShulchan* (128:16) is of the opinion that *b'dieved,* if one heads outside of the main room of the shul to wash his hands, he may *duchan,* as it is considered a partial ascent. This is also the opinion of R' Chaim Kanievsky; see Responsa #62.

16. Responsa of R' Chaim Kanievsky #90.

9. It is permitted for the chazzan to pray slowly or even to pause for a few minutes when he reaches *Retzei*, in order to allow the Kohanim sufficient time to reach the *duchan* or to reenter the room after washing their hands.[17]

10. If a Kohen went up to the *duchan* before *Retzei* for the purpose of performing Bircas Kohanim, he should also move forward slightly during *Retzei*, which will count as "uprooting his feet" to go toward the *duchan*;[18] however, if he did not do so, he may still perform Bircas Kohanim.[19]

11. Even a Kohen who davens at the *mizrach* wall (i.e., the front of the shul) and is already standing in the place where he will perform Bircas Kohanim should move his feet forward a bit during the *berachah* of *Retzei*, in order to fulfill the requirement of *akirah*.[20]

12. If the chazzan is a Kohen, and the shul follows the custom that a chazzan who is a Kohen performs Bircas Kohanim,[21] he should move slightly in the direction of the *duchan* when he reaches *Retzei*.[22]

13. If a Kohen was walking or traveling in a vehicle toward the shul as the chazzan was reciting *Retzei*, and he arrived after *Retzei* but in time for Bircas Kohanim, he is considered to have properly "uprooted his feet," as long as he was heading to shul for the purpose of performing Bircas Kohanim. If, however, he was going to shul without specific intent to *duchan*, and he arrived after the conclusion of *Retzei*, he is not considered to have begun his ascent on time, and he may not *duchan*.[23]

---

17. *Mishnah Berurah* 128:28; see also Responsa of R' Chaim Kanievsky #114. The Brisker Rav, R' Yitzchak Zev Soloveitchik, also followed this practice; see chapter 21.

18. Responsa of R' Chaim Kanievsky #61. This was also the opinion of R' Yosef Shalom Elyashiv (*Tziyunei Halachah* p. 349) and R' Shmuel Wosner (*Shevet HaLevi*, vol. 8 #23).

19. *Tziyunei Halachah* of R' Elyashiv, p. 351.

20. Responsa of R' Chaim Kanievsky #60. see also R' Yosef Shalom Elyashiv, *Tziyunei Halachah* p. 351.

21. See chapter 43 for an in-depth discussion. Also see *Shulchan Aruch* 128:20 and *Mishnah Berurah* §75.

22. *Mishnah Berurah* 128:106; *Ben Ish Chai, Tetzaveh* §18; *Kaf HaChaim* 128:50; Responsa of R' Chaim Kanievsky #394. See also R' Yosef Shalom Elyashiv, *Tziyunei Halachah*, p. 351.

23. *Mishnah Berurah* 128:28; Responsa of R' Chaim Kanievsky #58. *Mishnah*

14. If the Kohen was unable to begin his ascent during the *berachah* of *Retzei* due to circumstances beyond his control, it is preferable for him to leave the shul and not perform Bircas Kohanim in that minyan. He should perform Bircas Kohanim at a later minyan instead. If he already ascended the *duchan* in error, not realizing that he was not supposed to, he may remain there and perform Bircas Kohanim.[24]

15. **If there is only one Kohen present, and he is in the middle of *Shemoneh Esrei*, he is required to interrupt his *Shemoneh Esrei* in order to perform Bircas Kohanim, and then finish Shemoneh Esrei afterward.**[25] When the chazzan reaches *Retzei*, the Kohen (who is in the middle of davening) should pause and move slightly in the direction of the *duchan* so that he will be able to perform Bircas Kohanim and the congregation will not be deprived of this blessing. After completing Bircas Kohanim, he should return to his place and finish *Shemoneh Esrei*.[26]

16. *Aruch HaShulchan* rules[27] that if there is only one Kohen, and therefore he was not summoned to *duchan*, or a Kohen who was

---

Berurah (128:28) cites the opinion of *Chayei Adam* and *Shulchan Aruch HaRav* that if one left his home in order to perform Bircas Kohanim, he may recite Bircas Kohanim even if he was not in the shul during *Retzei*. *Mishnah Berurah* also cites other Acharonim who disagree, and does not clearly say which opinion one should follow. *Ben Ish Chai* (*Tetzaveh* §9) and *Kaf HaChaim* (128:54) both rule that if the Kohen had specific intent to go *duchan* at the time he was leaving his house, he may do so even if he arrived in the shul after *Retzei*. The *sefer Shamanu* (p. 229) records that my dear friend R' Shimon HaKohen Brecher would recite Bircas Kohanim at a Sephardic minyan when he was not in Eretz Yisrael. Usually, he would daven in an Ashkenazic minyan and then head to a nearby Sephardic shul to *duchan*. R' Shimon sometimes arrived after the *berachah* of *Retzei*, and he asked R' Chaim what to do in that situation. R' Chaim told him if he had in mind to go *duchan* at the time he left his car and began walking toward the shul, he is considered to have "uprooted his feet" and is permitted to *duchan*.

24. *Chayei Adam* 32:13; *Aruch HaShulchan* 128:16; *Shulchan Aruch HaRav* 128:13; *Biur Halachah* 128:8.

25. This requirement to interrupt *Shemoneh Esrei* to *duchan* underscores the importance of Bircas Kohanim, which is further underscored by the ruling of *Aruch HaShulchan* in 16 below.

26. As per the ruling of *Radbaz* (*She'eilos U'Teshuvos Radbaz*, vol. 1 # 293), which is quoted in *Magen Avraham* (128:40) and cited by *Shulchan Aruch HaRav* (128:43) and *Mishnah Berurah* (128:106) as the practical halachah.

27. 128:41.

summoned to *duchan*, is required to perform Bircas Kohanim even if doing so will cause him to miss *zman tefillah*. *Aruch HaShulchan* adds that a Kohen should not forgo Bircas Kohanim even to recite the complete *Krias Shema* on time, as Bircas Kohanim is a *d'Oraysa* obligation. Instead, if *zman Krias Shema* is approaching, a Kohen who has yet to recite *Krias Shema* should quickly recite the first verse of *Shema* (in fulfillment of the *mitzvah d'Oraysa* of *Krias Shema*) and then perform Bircas Kohanim.

17. If a Kohen is in the middle of *Shemoneh Esrei* and there are other Kohanim present, he does not need to interrupt his davening for Bircas Kohanim if he has not been summoned to *duchan*. There is a difference of opinion regarding whether he is required to interrupt his davening if he has been summoned. *Mishnah Berurah* (ibid.) cites *Magen Avraham*'s statement (based on *Radbaz* and other sources) that even when there are other Kohanim present, if a Kohen who is in the middle of *Shemoneh Esrei* is summoned to *duchan*, he becomes obligated to fulfill the mitzvah, and must interrupt his *tefillah*. However, *Mishnah Berurah* notes that *Eliyahu Rabbah* and R' Yaakov Emden (in his *Siddur*) disagree. They rule that if other Kohanim are present, the one who is in the middle of *Shemoneh Esrei* is not obligated to stop (even if he was called upon to *duchan*[28]).

One exception is if the Kohen has just ended the *berachah* of *Modim* and has not yet begun *Sim Shalom*. If Bircas Kohanim is inserted at that point of the *tefillah*, it is not considered an interruption, and the Kohen who is in the middle of *Shemoneh Esrei* should *duchan*. If he foresees that he will be up to *Sim Shalom* when the chazzan reaches Bircas Kohanim, he should move slightly toward the front of the shul when the chazzan begins *Retzei*.

28. Although interrupting *Shemoneh Esrei* is only a Rabbinic prohibition, and performing Bircas Kohanim when called upon to do so is a Torah commandment, in some instances, such as this one, the Rabbis insisted on compliance with their rulings even at the cost of performing a *mitzvah d'Oraysa* (*Eliyahu Rabbah*, cited in *Mishnah Berurah* ibid.).

Chapter 27
Prohibition to Wear Shoes

The *Tanna* Rabban Yochanan ben Zakkai instituted the prohibition against Kohanim wearing shoes when they ascend the *duchan*. The Gemara (*Sotah* 40a) presents two reasons for this prohibition, each of which has a different practical ramification:

1. It would be disrespectful toward the congregation for the Kohanim to wear shoes while blessing them, because shoes are typically unclean.
2. A strap of the Kohen's shoes may tear, prompting the Kohen to descend from the *duchan* to repair it. Meanwhile, those around him, noticing that he is not participating in Bircas Kohanim, will mistakenly assume that there is some flaw in his lineage that renders him unfit to perform the mitzvah.

Tosafos[1] offer a different reason (which is mentioned by others as well[2]):

3. The first time Hashem revealed Himself to Moshe Rabbeinu, He said, אַל תִּקְרַב הֲלֹם שַׁל נְעָלֶיךָ מֵעַל רַגְלֶיךָ, *Do not come closer to here, remove your shoes from your feet* (*Shemos* 3:5). This teaches us that when the Shechinah is revealed, one must remove his shoes. Bircas Kohanim is such an occasion.

---

1. *Tosafos al HaTorah, Shemos* 3:5.
2. *Sefer Chanukas HaTorah* (authored by R' Avraham Yehoshua Heschel of Krakow, rebbi of *Shach, Taz,* and many other Torah leaders; 1595-1663), *Likkutim* §204. *Imrei Emes* of Gur (*Imrei Emes al HaTorah, Nasso,* Year 1912) elaborates on this concept extensively.

1. Based on the first reason cited in the Gemara, all shoes that are worn outdoors, which may possibly be soiled, may not be worn, even if they have no laces. Since outdoor footwear is typically soiled, it is considered disrespectful to the congregation to wear such shoes during Bircas Kohanim.[3] *Rema*[4] writes that some are stringent only regarding shoes made of leather. Some rule that although ideally, one should wear only socks on his feet while *duchaning, b'dieved,* it is permitted to wear indoor slippers that do not have any laces, since those are not usually soiled.[5] However, this is not the preferred option, because other Kohanim may not know to differentiate between indoor slippers and outdoor footwear;[6] therefore, slippers should not be worn unless there is a pressing need.

2. If the Kohen's shoes have laces, he should untie them before washing his hands. He is permitted to wear his shoes until he goes up to the *duchan,* or even until the actual Bircas Kohanim, provided that he can remove his shoes without touching them with his hands. If removing the shoes in this fashion is impractical, he should remove them prior to washing his hands.[7]

3. When removing one's shoes at any other time, halachah mandates that the left shoe be removed before the right shoe.[8] When removing one's shoes for Bircas Kohanim, however, the right shoe is removed first.[9]

4. After the Kohanim remove their shoes, it is improper to leave them in plain sight; the shoes should be stowed beneath a chair, bench, or any other covering, in deference to the honor of the

---

3. *Shulchan Aruch* 128:5; *Mishnah Berurah* §15.
4. 128:5.
5. *Aruch HaShulchan* 128:12.
6. Rulings of R' Shlomo Zalman Auerbach in *Halichos Shlomo, Hilchos Tefillah* 10:11.
7. *Mishnah Berurah* 128:15.
8. *Shulchan Aruch* 2:5.
9. See Responsa of R' Chaim Kanievsky #172. See also *Daas Notah,* vol. 1, *Teshuvah* 149, for further analysis from R' Chaim. This halachah is also cited in the *luach* (calendar) of R' Yechiel Michel Tukachinsky, in the name of R' Avraham Yitzchak HaKohen Kook. This was also the opinion of R' Yosef Shalom Elyashiv (*Tziyunei Halachah,* p. 352) and R' Shlomo Zalman Auerbach, *Halichos Shlomo, Hilchos Tishah B'Av* 15:4.

shul.[10] It is also permitted to place them neatly in a covered corner adjacent to the *aron kodesh,*[11] since most of the congregants will not be able to see them there. One should make sure his shoes are neatly stowed away and covered regardless of whether one is davening in a *beis midrash* (such as in a yeshivah) or in a *beis knesses.*[12]

5. A Kohen may ascend the *duchan* wearing shoes if he places them neatly near or on the *duchan* after removing them.[13] He should try to cover the shoes completely, but as long as they are mostly covered, that is sufficient.[14]

6. When performing Bircas Kohanim, the Kohanim should wear socks.[15] While the Kohanim in the Beis HaMikdash did indeed serve barefoot, today this is considered improper, since one would not appear with bare feet in the presence of important people.[16] The *poskim* write that if a Kohen comes to shul without socks, he should be allowed to *duchan,* but should be told respectfully not to make this a regular occurrence.[17]

7. If the Kohen is wearing unusual, brightly colored socks, even if they are outlandish and unlike those worn by his fellow Kohanim, he is still permitted to ascend to the *duchan* with them.[18]

8. If a Kohen has a prosthetic leg,[19] or it is difficult for him to remove his shoes because of medical considerations, R' Moshe Feinstein writes that he is permitted to *duchan* even while wearing

---

10. *Mishnah Berurah* 128:15. See chapter 10, where we note that when R' Moshe Shmuel Shapira would see the Kohanim's shoes left out in the open, he himself would move them to a more discreet location.

11. See Responsa of R' Chaim Kanievsky #176.

12. See Responsa of R' Chaim Kanievsky #173.

13. See Responsa of R' Chaim Kanievsky #176. *Leket HaKemach HeChadash* (128:27) relates that in the minyan of the Chazon Ish, when the floor was cold, several Kohanim wore their shoes to the *duchan* and removed them right before Bircas Kohanim.

14. See Responsa of R' Chaim Kanievsky #175.

15. *Mishnah Berurah* 128:15.

16. See *Mishnah Berurah* (128:18), which states that in our times, going up to *duchan* barefoot is considered disgraceful.

17. See *Igros Moshe, O.C.,* vol. 2, #32. This is also the opinion of R' Chaim Kanievsky (Responsa #178).

18. *Igros Moshe* ibid.

19. See *Even Yisrael* by R' Yisrael Yaakov Fisher, vol. 7 #10, where he writes that it is permissible for a Kohen with a prosthetic leg to perform Bircas Kohanim if he is able to stand on one leg for the amount of time it takes to say the word *yevarechecha.* (He does not have to stand on one leg at that time; he just has to be able to.)

his shoes.[20] R' Ovadiah Yosef[21] permits shoes to be worn even in less pressing situations. He adds, however, that if a Kohen wears shoes, it is preferable that he remain on ground level at the front of the shul, rather than ascend the steps to the *aron kodesh* (in a shul where the *aron kodesh* is elevated), because if he does go up the stairs, it will be more noticeable that he is wearing shoes.

9. If the chazzan is a Kohen, and the shul has the custom that a chazzan who is a Kohen performs Bircas Kohanim,[22] he should remove his shoes prior to *Chazaras HaShatz*.[23]

10. R' Chaim Kanievsky would encourage Kohanim to wear slip-on shoes, without laces, all year round, so that they would not have to tie their shoes when they put them back on and then have to wash their hands again before continuing to daven.[24] He would say, "*Chaval* (what a pity) that every morning, after Bircas Kohanim, you need to wash your hands again after touching your shoes! Wearing slip-ons would save you time." R' Chaim himself wore only slip-on shoes, so that he wouldn't have to wash his hands each time he tied his shoes.

R' Chaim's son-in-law R' Yitzchak Kolodetsky, in his *sefer L'Shichno Sidreshu* (vol. 1, p. 24), makes a similar observation regarding the Chofetz Chaim: The Chofetz Chaim was particular to purchase only shoes that had no laces. This was a very worthwhile practice, for it saved him at least one minute a day — the time it takes to tie and untie one's shoes. In the course of a year, he gained over 360 minutes, which amounts to six hours, and in the course of seventy years (an average lifetime), he saved 420 hours!

11. Likewise, *Eliyahu Rabbah* states (§35): "Therefore, a Kohen should wear shoes that he can remove and put back on without touching them. If he does not have such shoes, it is preferable for him not to wear any shoes at all until after davening; that is also the opinion of *Sefer HaAgudah* (*siman* 34)."[25]

---

20. *Igros Moshe* ibid.
21. *Yechaveh Daas*, vol. 2 #13.
22. For a discussion of this subject, see chapter 43.
23. See *Kaf HaChaim* 128:120.
24. Heard from R' Shaya Epstein.
25. Cited in *Kaf HaChaim* (128:105), which also quotes the statement of *Sheyarei Knesses HaGedolah* (*Hagahos Beis Yosef* §9) that the Kohen must wash his hands after putting his shoes back on, unless he wears shoes that can be put on without touching them.

Chapter 28
Covering With a Tallis

During the time of the Beis HaMikdash, the Kohanim actually pronounced the *Shem HaMeforash*[1] (the Ineffable Name of Hashem) when performing Bircas Kohanim. Due to the intense holiness resting upon the hands of the Kohanim, one who looked at the hands of the Kohanim at this time could potentially suffer severe damage to his eyesight.[2] Therefore, during that period, it was forbidden for anyone — even the Kohanim themselves — to even glance at their hands during Bircas Kohanim.[3]

Now that, unfortunately, we no longer have a Beis HaMikdash, and the *Shem HaMeforash* is not uttered, it should be forbidden only to gaze at the hands of the Kohanim for an extended time, and an occasional glance should be permitted.[4] Nevertheless, although we do not need to be concerned about damaging our eyes, it is still preferable not to look at the hands of the Kohanim at all, as a remembrance of what took place in the Beis HaMikdash.[5]

In our times, it is a universal custom for both Kohanim and non-Kohanim to avoid looking at the hands of the Kohanim. Accordingly, during Bircas Kohanim the Kohanim use a tallis to cover

1. The *Shem HaMeforash* was pronounced during Bircas Kohanim until the passing of Shimon HaTzaddik, a disciple of Ezra HaSofer who served as the first Kohen Gadol in the second Beis HaMikdash; see *Yoma* 39b.
2. As discussed in *Chagigah* 16a.
3. As mentioned in chapter 29, practically speaking there was no concern that the Kohanim would see their own hands, because in the Beis HaMikdash the Kohanim raised their hands above their heads when reciting Bircas Kohanim.
4. *Mishnah Berurah* 128:89.
5. Ibid.

their hands and faces, while the other members of the congregation cover their faces with a tallis. Although most *poskim*[6] rule that the Kohanim should cover just their faces, while their hands should extend outside the tallis for the entire Bircas Kohanim, the custom of nearly all communities nowadays is for the Kohanim to cover their hands as well (see below for further elaboration).

There are two additional reasons for both Kohanim and non-Kohanim to cover their faces during Bircas Kohanim.

The first is so that they should not become distracted[7] and look around during Bircas Kohanim; rather, they should focus intently on the *berachah* that Hashem is bestowing upon them, without staring at the Kohanim or anything else.[8]

The second reason, which is given by *Zohar*[9] (as explained by *Kaf HaChaim*[10]), is that even in contemporary times the Shechinah still rests upon the hands of the Kohanim, and it is therefore forbidden to look at their hands.

Zohar states: "R' Yosi said: When the Kohen raises his hands, the people must not look at him, since the Shechinah rests upon his hands... Because the Holy Name rests on his hands, one must maintain a state of awe. Although one cannot see the Shechinah, one should not look at the hands of the Kohen, lest it appear that the congregation is acting disrespectfully toward the Shechinah."

This explanation for the prohibition to look at the hands of the Kohanim is mentioned by *Rashi*.[11] *Tosafos HaRosh*[12] elaborates on *Rashi*'s words, adding that although one's eyes were at risk of becoming damaged only in the Beis HaMikdash, it is forbidden to look at the hands of the Kohanim during Bircas Kohanim nowadays as well, since the Shechinah rests upon their hands at this time.

---

6. *Shulchan Aruch* 128:23; *Rema*; *Eliyahu Rabbah*; *Gra*; *Shulchan Aruch HaRav*; *Mishnah Berurah*.
7. *Yerushalmi Megillah* 4:8.
8. *Rambam, Hilchos Nesias Kapayim* 14:7; *Shulchan Aruch* 128:23.
9. *Nasso*, p. 147.
10. 128:143. The reason given by *Zohar* for why the prohibition remains in effect even in contemporary times is also cited in the commentary of *Rekanati* on the Torah, *Nasso*; *Sefer Chareidim*, ch. 45; *She'eilos U'Teshuvos Radbaz*, vol. 4 #80.
11. *Megillah* 24b. However, *Tosafos* (*Chagigah* 16a) disagree with *Rashi*'s explanation, and say the reason is to avoid distraction, as in *Yerushalmi* cited above.
12. *Megillah* 24b. See *Eliyahu Rabbah* 128:31 §55, which notes that according to *Rashi*'s explanation, one must be stringent even in our times.

Similarly, *Sefer HaEshkol*[13] rules that it is prohibited to gaze upon the hands of a Kohen during Bircas Kohanim because the Shechinah rests there. The *Nachal Eshkol* commentary on *Sefer HaEshkol* cites *Midrash Rabbah* on *Shir HaShirim*, which states, regarding the words דּוֹמֶה דוֹדִי לִצְבִי, *My beloved is like a gazelle* (2:9): "Hashem is compared to a gazelle. Just as a gazelle leaps through the forest from place to place, so does Hashem leap from one congregation to another, to bestow His blessing on the Jewish people at the time of Bircas Kohanim." Accordingly, Bircas Kohanim is a time of Divine Revelation, says *Nachal Eshkol*, so one must avoid glancing toward the Shechinah. *Sefer Daas Torah* of Maharsham on *Shulchan Aruch* (128:23) quotes this opinion of *Sefer HaEshkol*, echoing the prohibition to look at the hands of the Kohanim because the Shechinah rests there.[14]

One can attain extraordinary holiness by refraining from gazing at the Kohanim during Bircas Kohanim. Rabbeinu Chananel writes, in his *Sefer HaMiktzaos*, that the great *Tanna* R' Akiva was asked by his disciples how he achieved such an elevated level in Torah. One of the things that R' Akiva answered was that he never gazed at the Kohanim while they were on the *duchan*. The *Sefer HaMiktzaos* is quoted by several *poskim* as well.[15]

Halachos of Covering With a Tallis

1. According to the reason presented by *Zohar*, the Midrash, and some Rishonim and Acharonim, it is clear that one may not glance at the Kohen's hands at all during Bircas Kohanim.
2. The prohibition to gaze at the hands of the Kohanim begins when they say the word *yevarechecha*. It is permissible to look at their hands while they are reciting the *berachah* before Bircas Kohanim.[16]
3. Many have the custom that children come under their father's tallis during Bircas Kohanim, so that their eyes will be covered.

13. By Rabbeinu Avraham ben R' Yitzchak (1080-1158), father-in-law and rebbi of *Raavad*.
14. Other Rishonim and Acharonim discuss this as well. See chapter 1.
15. See *Pri Chadash* 128:30 and *Kaf HaChaim* 128:168.
16. Responsa of R' Chaim Kanievsky #273.

When R' Chaim Kanievsky was a child, his father followed this custom, and R' Chaim did so with his own children as well.[17]

4. Due to the great sanctity of Bircas Kohanim, the Kohanim should not be photographed or videoed during Bircas Kohanim.[18]

5. The Kohanim should not look around or become distracted while they recite Bircas Kohanim; rather, their eyes should face downward in the same way one stands in prayer,[19] for they are praying that Hashem should bless the Jewish people.[20]

6. The Kohanim should not look at their own hands during Bircas Kohanim. Therefore, it is customary for them to cover their faces with their talleisim.[21] However, it is permissible for them to glance at their hands to ensure that their fingers are spread out in the correct manner.[22]

7. *Beis Yosef*[23] praises those communities where the custom is that the Kohanim cover their hands and faces with a tallis so that they do not see the congregation and become distracted, and also so that the congregation will be prevented from seeing the hands of the Kohanim. *Rema*[24] states that in Europe the custom is for the Kohanim to cover their faces but keep their hands **outside** the tallis during the entire Bircas Kohanim. Interestingly, although many Acharonim concur with *Rema* on this matter,[25] *Kaf HaChaim* and *Aruch HaShulchan* state that it is the universal custom of both Sephardic and Ashkenazic congregations worldwide for the Kohanim to keep their hands (and faces) covered with a tallis during the entire Bircas Kohanim, so that non-Kohanim will not see their hands.[26]

---

17. Responsa of R' Chaim Kanievsky #288.
18. Responsa of R' Chaim Kanievsky #276, 277.
19. *Shulchan Aruch* 128:23.
20. *Mishnah Berurah* §88, citing *Levush*.
21. *Rema* 128:23.
22. Responsa of R' Chaim Kanievsky #284.
23. 128:23. *She'eilos U'Teshuvos Radbaz* (vol. 4 #6) explains that the reason the Kohanim cover their hands during Bircas Kohanim is that we are afraid that a member of the congregation will look at his hands; since the Shechinah rests on the hands of the Kohanim, they accepted this precaution upon themselves.
24. *Darkei Moshe* on *Beis Yosef* (ibid.) and in *Shulchan Aruch* 128:23.
25. *Mishnah Berurah* 128:91. This is also the opinion of *Levush, Eliyahu Rabbah, Gra, Shulchan Aruch HaRav*, and other Acharonim.
26. *Kaf HaChaim* (128:143) states that this is the custom of Yerushalayim and of Yeshivat Beit El of Kabbalah. See also *Aruch HaShulchan*'s statement (128:36) that keeping the hands covered is the custom that should be followed.

(This is indeed the practice in virtually all communities nowadays; see below for a notable exception.)

8. R' Moshe Feinstein[27] writes that although most early *poskim* rule that the Kohanim should keep their hands outside the tallis, the accepted custom is for them to cover their hands. He explains that although Ashkenazim generally follow *Rema*, in this situation we are concerned that some children will not go under their father's tallis and are at risk of being harmed as a result of seeing the hands of the Kohanim, so the hands of the Kohanim must be covered. Additionally, in many communities, unmarried men do not have a tallis to cover their eyes with, and they, as well as some women who can see the Kohanim, may not be aware that Bircas Kohanim is starting and might inadvertently glance at the Kohanim. For this reason, the Kohanim must be stringent and cover their hands as well as their faces.

9. Interestingly, the stringency of covering the Kohanim's hands results in a leniency. *Shulchan Aruch*[28] rules that a Kohen who has blemishes on his face or hands may not *duchan* unless he has been a resident of that city for thirty days, because his unusual appearance may cause people to gaze at him during Bircas Kohanim. However, since the custom nowadays is for a Kohen to cover his face and hands, there is no concern that anyone will become distracted by his physical blemishes, and he is therefore permitted to *duchan*.[29] *Rema*[30] and other Acharonim[31] point out that this applies only if *all* the Kohanim in the shul follow the custom to cover their faces and hands during Bircas Kohanim.[32]

10. A Kohen may use a non-kosher tallis for Bircas Kohanim if no kosher tallis is available. However, he should have in mind when

---

27. *Igros Moshe, O.C.*, vol. 5, #24.
28. 128:30 based on *Megillah* 24b.
29. 128:31; this is also explained in *Beis Yosef* 128:31.
30. 128:31.
31. *She'eilos U'Teshuvos Radbaz*, vol. 1 #39; *Magen Avraham* 128:31 §45; *Chayei Adam*, 32:4; *Shulchan Aruch HaRav* 128:46.
32. *Mishnah Berurah* (128:115), quoting the aforementioned Acharonim, clarifies that this is dependent only on the Kohanim. Even if it is the custom of the non-Kohanim to cover their faces during Bircas Kohanim, it does not suffice, because some may still gaze improperly, and there are also unmarried men who do not wear a tallis and are therefore at risk of gazing.

he dons the tallis that he is not intending to fulfill the mitzvah of wearing tzitzis.[33]

11. If there is no tallis available, the Kohen may use a coat or jacket (but not a towel)[34] to cover his hands, as the consensus today is that it is prohibited to *duchan* without a covering for his hands. If he does not have a jacket, he should leave the main room of the shul before *Retzei*, to avoid becoming obligated to *duchan* and being forced to do so with uncovered hands.[35]

12. If the only tallis in the shul is being used by the chazzan, it should be given to the Kohen during Bircas Kohanim.[36] (See Responsa of R' Chaim Kanievsky #305-307 for several other halachos pertaining to borrowing a tallis.)

13. In our times, the chassidic community of Munkacz is the only community in the world in which the custom is for the Kohanim to extend their hands outside their talleisim during Bircas Kohanim. This practice is based on the halachic opinion of the first Rebbe of Munkacz, the Shem MiShlomo,[37] whose grandson, the Minchas Elazar,[38] explains that since many halachic and Kabbalistic sources state that the hands of the Kohanim should be outside the tallis, this is the correct practice.[39] The Minchas Elazar recalls[40] that he was present when a Kohen was conversing with his grandfather (the Shem MiShlomo) and questioned this custom, noting that the custom of Kohanim in all other communities is to keep their hands covered while blessing the congregation. In response, the Shem MiShlomo announced before Mussaf of the following Yom Tov that the Kohanim should *not* cover their hands during Bircas Kohanim, but should keep them uncovered to conform with the opinion of several *poskim* and the Arizal.

---

33. Responsa of R' Chaim Kanievsky #302.
34. See Responsa of R' Chaim Kanievsky #294.
35. See Responsa of R' Chaim Kanievsky #290; R' Moshe Sternbuch, *Teshuvos V'Hanhagos*, vol. 2 #107; R' Ovadiah Yosef, *Yalkut Yosef* 128:100.
36. Responsa of R' Chaim Kanievsky #306.
37. R' Shlomo Spira, 1831-1893.
38. R' Chaim Elazar Spira, 1871-1937, Responsa Minchas Elazar, Vol. 3 #56.
39. The aforementioned *Kaf HaChaim* (128:143) is of the opinion that the statement in *Siddur Arizal* — that Kohanim should keep their hands outside the tallis during Bircas Kohanim — was written by a disciple of Arizal and not by Arizal himself.
40. In the aforementioned *teshuvah*.

14. R' Chaim Kanievsky writes (see Responsa #308) that even if a Kohen's ancestors had the custom to keep their hands uncovered during Bircas Kohanim, he is required to cover his hands if he is performing Bircas Kohanim in any shul in the world, except a Munkaczer shul.

15. R' Yehuda Fisher, son of R' Yisrael Yaakov Fisher,[41] related that although Yerushalayim's Zichron Moshe shul (which is a "minyan factory," with dozens of minyanim daily) has a longstanding policy to follow the *nusach* of the chazzan of each particular minyan, with regard to two practices his father was adamant that all minyanim follow the shul's custom regardless of the chazzan's own *minhag*. The first was that a Kohen must cover his hands during Bircas Kohanim, in keeping with the custom throughout the world. He advised Kohanim who wanted to keep their hands uncovered to perform Bircas Kohanim in a Munkaczer shul, but not in Zichron Moshe. (The second practice his father did not allow was for a *"chutz laAretz"* minyan to take place on Yom Tov Sheini in Zichron Moshe.)

41. 1928-2003. He authored the multi-volume *Even Yisrael* and was the rav of the famed Zichron Moshe shul in the Geulah neighborhood of Yerushalayim for several decades.

Chapter 29
Raising Hands

The Mishnah (*Sotah* 7:6) teaches that a Kohen must raise his hands when performing Bircas Kohanim, as derived from the *pasuk* וַיִּשָּׂא אַהֲרֹן אֶת יָדָיו אֶל הָעָם וַיְבָרְכֵם, *Aharon raised his hands toward the people and blessed them* (*Vayikra* 9:22). R' Ovadiah of Bartenura comments that although only Aharon is mentioned here, the same applies to all Kohanim, as we see from the words לַעֲמֹד לְשָׁרֵת בְּשֵׁם ה׳ הוּא וּבָנָיו כָּל הַיָּמִים, *to stand and to serve in the Name of Hashem, he [Aharon] and his sons all the days* (*Devarim* 18:5). This *pasuk* draws a parallel between Aharon and his sons, conveying that his sons, the Kohanim of all future generations, must also raise their hands when blessing the people. *Rambam* (*Hilchos Tefillah U'Nesias Kapayim* 14:11) and *Shulchan Aruch* (128:14) state as halachah that the Kohanim must bless the congregation with raised hands.

Rashi (*Sotah* ibid.) explains that the reason the Kohanim raise their hands when performing Bircas Kohanim is that in the Beis HaMikdash, the Kohanim pronounced the *Shem HaMeforash* during this blessing, so the Shechinah rested upon their hands, and it is not proper for a person's head to be more elevated than the resting place of the Shechinah. The exception was the Kohen Gadol; since he wore the *tzitz* on his forehead, which had the Name of Hashem engraved upon it, he was not permitted to raise his hands above his forehead.)[1] *Raavad* (*Tamid* 33b) offers an additional reason: He

1. See *Sotah* (ibid.).

explains that the Kohanim raised their hands above their heads so they should not inadvertently glance at their hands during Bircas Kohanim.

Shimon HaTzaddik was the first Kohen Gadol to serve in the second Beis HaMikdash. After he passed away, the Kohanim in the Beis HaMikdash discontinued the practice of pronouncing the *Shem HaMeforash*.[2] Nevertheless, the Kohanim continued to raise their hands while blessing the people, as the Mishnah states that the Kohanim outside the Beis HaMikdash (and in contemporary times) "lift their hands to the height of their shoulders."

There are differing opinions as to whether Kohanim are permitted to lift their hands above their heads when performing Bircas Kohanim.[3]

1. A Kohen who cannot raise his hands even briefly, because he is ill or his hands are paralyzed, should not perform Bircas Kohanim. Even if he is able to hold his hands up by tying them to a string connected to the ceiling or the like, it is not sufficient.[4]
2. If the Kohen is able to raise his hands for a few seconds at the beginning of Bircas Kohanim, he is permitted to *duchan*, even if he has to lower his hands to rest them between words, or while the other Kohanim are singing.[5] If the Kohen is able to lift only one of his hands, he is also permitted to *duchan*.[6] That said, every Kohen should make an attempt to keep both of his hands raised for the entire Bircas Kohanim, even if the Kohanim follow the custom to sing in order to give the congregation a chance to recite the prayer to nullify disturbing dreams.[7]

---

2. *Yoma* 39b; Rambam, *Hilchos Tefillah U'Nesias Kapayim* 14:10.
3. *Sefer Yerei'im* §269, *Ohr Zarua,* vol. 2 §411, and *Magen Gibborim* §12 prohibit this. However, *Raavad* (*Tamid* 33b) and R' Yaakov Emden (*Mor U'Ketziah* 128:11) rule that it is permitted. *Kaf HaChaim* (128:77) notes that the opinion of the *mekubalim* is that a Kohen may lift his hands above his head during Bircas Kohanim. However, *Tzitz Eliezer* (*She'eilos U'Teshuvos,* vol. 11 #6) brings from several *mekubalim,* including *Radbaz,* that according to Kabbalah a Kohen should not raise his hands above his head during Bircas Kohanim.
4. *She'eilos U'Teshuvos Noda BiYehudah, O.C.,* #5; cited in *Mishnah Berurah* 128:52.
5. *Mishnah Berurah* 128:52, based on the aforementioned *Noda BiYehudah* and *She'eilos U'Teshuvos Ksav Sofer, O.C.,* #13.
6. Responsa of R' Chaim Kanievsky #258.
7. See *Magen Avraham* 128:19, Responsa of R' Chaim Kanievsky #259.

3. *Tur* and *Shulchan Aruch*[8] state that the Kohanim should raise their hands to the height of their shoulders.

4. *Be'er Sheva*[9] is of the opinion that the Kohanim should raise their entire arms (from shoulder to fingertips) to the height of their shoulders. However, *Tosafos Yom Tov,* in his commentary to the Mishnah (*Sotah* ibid.), rules that the requirement for the Kohen to lift his hands is satisfied even if he elevates his hands only slightly. Similarly, *Chasam Sofer*[10] notes that the correct translation of "*nesias kapayim*" is lifting the *palms* of the hands, as opposed to *nesias yadayim,* which would mean lifting the entire arms. R' Chaim Kanievsky[11] writes that *b'dieved* we may follow the opinion of *Tosafos Yom Tov,* if the Kohen cannot raise his arm to the height of the shoulder.[12]

Hand height of the Kohanim
(Tallis is not shown over the hands for clarity)

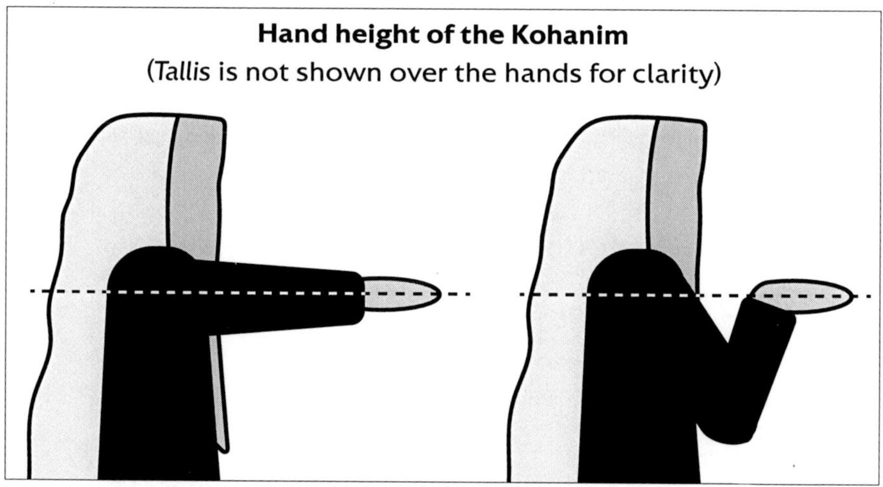

The Kohen on the left is positioning his arms correctly.
B'dieved, if the Kohen is ill or infirm, he may hold his hands as shown on the right.

8. 128:12.
9. *Sotah* 38b. This is also the opinion of *Mabit* (*Kiryas Sefer,* ch. 14).
10. *She'eilos U'Teshuvos, O.C.,* vol. 1, #194.
11. Responsa #247.
12. *Tziyunei Halachah* (p. 363) cites R' Yosef Shalom Elyashiv's ruling that *l'chatchilah* the entire arm should be raised to the height of the shoulder. However, if it is difficult for the Kohen, then *b'dieved,* as long as the palm of the hand is raised the Kohen is permitted to *duchan.*

5. Avnei Nezer[13] was asked about a Kohen whose hands had been amputated, leaving him with only the remainder of his arms, until the wrist. Was he permitted to *duchan*? He responded that the palms of the hands are the conduits to transmit the *berachah*, and therefore, in the absence of both palms, the Kohen may not *duchan*. He writes, however, that a Kohen is permitted to *duchan* if the palm of one hand is intact.

6. A Kohen should not wear gloves during Bircas Kohanim.[14]

7. Since many *poskim* say that the *berachah* is transmitted through the hands of the Kohanim, those that are receiving the *berachah* should ensure that they are standing in front of the *hands* of the Kohanim, rather than immediately in front of the Kohanim while their hands extend *past* the recipients (which might be comparable to standing *behind* the Kohanim).[15]

8. Just before performing Bircas Kohanim on a weekday (in a Sephardic minyan or in Eretz Yisrael), the Kohen should remove the tefillin strap from the palm of his hand.[16] *Sefer HaEshkol* states (*Hilchos Tefillin*): "Our custom is to continue wearing tefillin, but to remove the strap from one's fingers when raising one's hands to *duchan*."[17] R' Chaim Kanievsky concurs that the custom is to remove the strap before Bircas Kohanim.[18]

---

13. *She'eilos U'Teshuvos, O.C.*, #31; this opinion of *Avnei Nezer* is cited by many *poskim*, including R' Ovadiah Yosef (*Yabia Omer*, vol. 8 #13), who writes that even if all the Kohen's fingers have been amputated, he may still *duchan* if his palm is intact.
14. *Yabia Omer* ibid.
15. Responsa of R' Chaim Kanievsky #227.
16. See *Rif, Teshuvos, siman* 308; *Teshuvos HaGeonim* #11; *Mateh Yosef* (*O.C.* §2), authored by R' Yosef HaLevi of Egypt (1660-1713), offers several reasons why a Kohen should be careful to remove the tefillin strap from his fingers before Bircas Kohanim. R' Ovadiah Yosef (*Yalkut Yosef, Hilchos Tefillah* p. 224) rules that in light of the *teshuvos* of *Rif* and the Geonim, one should be stringent about this matter, and see to it that the strap is not on his hand.
17. *Sefer HaEshkol* took it for granted that Bircas Kohanim is performed at a time when one wears tefillin — i.e., on weekdays. As we explain in chapter 15, the custom of the earlier generations of Ashkenazim was to perform Bircas Kohanim on a daily basis all year round.
18. Responsa of R' Chaim Kanievsky #264.

Chapter 30
Summoning the Kohanim

When the Torah introduces the mitzvah of Bircas Kohanim, it says (*Bamidbar* 6:23), כֹּה תְבָרְכוּ אֶת בְּנֵי יִשְׂרָאֵל **אָמוֹר לָהֶם**, and *Onkelos* translates: כְּדֵין תְּבָרְכוּן יָת בְּנֵי יִשְׂרָאֵל **כַּד תֵּימְרוּן [יֵימְרוּן] לְהוֹן**, *So shall you bless Bnei Yisrael* ***when they [the people] say to [the Kohanim] that they should recite the blessing***. The Gemara (*Sotah* 38a) derives from this *pasuk* that a non-Kohen should summon the Kohanim to begin Bircas Kohanim,[1] and, since the *pasuk* says "to them" in the plural, there should ideally be at least two adult Kohanim performing the mitzvah.

1. In order for Bircas Kohanim to take place, it is necessary to have a minyan of ten men (which may include the Kohanim) from the time *Chazaras HaShatz* begins.[2] If *Chazaras HaShatz* began with exactly ten men, and then someone from the minyan stepped out, Bircas Kohanim cannot be performed, since there is no longer a minyan present. However, if the Kohanim already began to *duchan* with exactly ten men present, and then someone left, Bircas Kohanim should be completed, even though there is no longer a minyan.[3]

---

1. See *Shulchan Aruch* 128:10. *Onkelos*'s rendition is quoted by *Tur* and *Beis Yosef* (*siman* 128), and by many Acharonim. We learn from *Onkelos* that the Kohanim have to be called up; thus, in all likelihood, Kohanim who refuse to *duchan* are not in violation of the positive commandment to perform the mitzvah unless they were called up; see *Mishnah Berurah* 128:9.
2. See *Megillah* 23b; *Shulchan Aruch* 128:1.
3. *Biur Halachah* 128:1.

2. Although there is a minority opinion that Bircas Kohanim may be performed only in the presence of a *sefer Torah*, and also that it may not be performed outdoors, the accepted halachah and practice does not follow this opinion.[4]

3. According to some Rishonim, Bircas Kohanim is *d'Oraysa* (required by Torah law) only when there are at least two Kohanim blessing the congregation; if there is only one Kohen, his mitzvah is just a Rabbinic requirement. This is derived from the phrase אָמוֹר לָהֶם, *saying to "them,"* which is phrased in the plural. Therefore, to fulfill the *mitzvah d'Oraysa* according to this view, there must be a minimum of two Kohanim, who are called up by someone who is not a Kohen. Furthermore, according to these Rishonim, if only one Kohen is present, and he disregards the call to go up, he is not in violation of the mitzvah.[5] (Others disagree; see 8 below.)

4. Other Rishonim are of the opinion that *"amor lahem"* is written in the plural because the Torah is addressing Aharon HaKohen and his descendants, "saying to them" that they have been gifted with the mitzvah of Bircas Kohanim. According to this interpretation, there is no reason to say that two or more Kohanim are required in order to fulfill the *mitzvah d'Oraysa*.[6]

5. Some Rishonim say that even a single Kohen who ascends to *duchan* fulfills a *mitzvah d'Oraysa,* even if he was not called up by the congregation.[7]

---

4. *Mishnah Berurah* 128:1; *Chayei Adam* 32:15; *Shulchan Aruch HaRav* 128:18; *Ben Ish Chai, Tetzaveh* §13. R' Chaim Palagi, in his *sefer Chikekei Lev* (*siman* 4), cites seventeen different *poskim* who concur that the presence of a *sefer Torah* is not a requirement for Bircas Kohanim.

5. *Rabbeinu Peretz,* cited by *Tur* (*siman* 128), and *Rabbeinu Tam* (*Tosafos, Menachos* 44a) say that when there is only one Kohen present, and he does not respond to the call of "Kohanim," he is not in violation of the mitzvah.

6. This is the opinion of *Tur* himself — that even a single Kohen who does not *duchan* when called to do so is in violation of the commandment. He explains that אָמוֹר לָהֶם, *saying to them,* is written in the plural because it has a dual meaning — the Kohanim should say the words of the *berachos* to the Jewish people, and the Jewish people should call upon them to recite the *berachos*. At the same time, the simple understanding of the *pasuk* is that this commandment should be given to Aharon and his children, and that is why the plural form is used. The same idea is found in *Meiri* (*Sotah* 38b).

7. That is, even though he is not *obligated* to *duchan,* if he chooses to do so anyway, he fulfills a *mitzvah d'Oraysa. Maharam Mintz, siman* 12; *Minchas Chinuch,* Mitzvah 378:3.

6. All agree that if only one Kohen is present, he is required to recite the *berachah* of *asher kideshanu*, just as he would do if there were multiple Kohanim, and this is done even if the chazzan does not call him to ascend to the *duchan*.[8]

7. R' Chaim Kanievsky firmly maintained that Bircas Kohanim is required *min haTorah* only when performed by two or more Kohanim. It appears that this is the opinion of *Mishnah Berurah* as well.[9] However, as noted earlier (chapter 12), the Brisker Rav stated that even if the obligation for one Kohen to perform Bircas Kohanim is only *mid'Rabbanan*, it should be treated with the same gravity as if were *min haTorah*.[10]

8. According to some opinions, even when there is only one Kohen in the shul, if he disregards the summons (by the chazzan or a member of the congregation) to go *duchan*, he is in violation of the mitzvah.[11] Others are even more stringent, and maintain that he is obligated to *duchan* even without being called up, and if he does not do so, he is in violation of the mitzvah in this situation as well.[12]

9. If two concurrent minyanim[13] are taking place in the shul, and there are only two Kohanim available, it is best to have one

---

8. See *Mishnah Berurah* 128:39, that even those who say that one Kohen has only a *mitzvah d'Rabbanan* still agree that he is required to recite a *berachah* before performing Bircas Kohanim.

9. See *Biur Halachah* (128:25), *Mishnah Berurah* (§159) and *Shaar HaTziyun* (§38) there, and Responsa of R' Chaim Kanievsky #416, where he explains that this is the opinion of *Mishnah Berurah*.

10. As mentioned in chapter 12, someone once lamented to the Brisker Rav that there had been only one Kohen in his minyan, to which the Rav responded that it is only the Karaim who make light of a *mitzvah d'Rabbanan*. We also noted there that the Brisker Rav proves from the wording of *Rambam* that in his opinion even with one Kohen, it is a *mitzvah d'Oraysa*.

11. This is the opinion of *Shulchan Aruch* 128:2, as understood by *Olas Tamid* 128:8, *Maamar Mordechai* 128:5, and *Kaf HaChaim* 128:17. In the *sefer Ohr L'Tzion* by R' Benzion Abba Shaul (ch. 8), he brings proof from *Shulchan Aruch* 128:25 as well.

12. *Taz* 128:3. This is also the opinion of *Sefer Yerei'im* (§269). *Pri Megadim* expounds on the reason for his obligation. The *Taz* is also cited in *Mishnah Berurah* (§39).

13. R' Chaim Kanievsky received several inquiries regarding congregations that make separate minyanim for Mussaf when there is more than one person who has *yahrtzeit* that week and they both wish to daven at the *amud*. He also received the same question concerning a shul that had two concurrent minyanim on a regular basis.

minyan start a bit later than the other, and ask the Kohanim to *duchan* in both, so that both minyanim will be able to fulfill the mitzvah of Bircas Kohanim *mid'Oraysa.*[14] If this is not feasible, it is preferable to have both Kohanim in one of the minyanim, rather than one Kohen in each. This ensures that the Kohanim can fulfill the *mitzvah d'Oraysa* even according to the opinion that two Kohanim are required (even though this will leave one minyan with no Kohen at all).[15]

14. Responsa of R' Chaim Kanievsky #148.
15. See Responsa of R' Chaim Kanievsky #143-147. This was also the opinion of R' Aharon Leib Shteinman; see *K'Ayal Taarog, Hilchos Tefillah,* p. 196.

Chapter 31
Announcing "Kohanim!"

Mabit[1] writes that the one who announces "Kohanim" fulfills a *mitzvas asei.*

"Kohanim" is announced only when there are two Kohanim present and both are over the age of bar mitzvah.[2]

How Is "Kohanim" Announced?

Tur (128:10) cites three opinions:

1. ***Rabbeinu Tam*** (*Tosafos, Berachos* 34a) maintains that the chazzan may not be the one to announce "Kohanim," as it is considered an interruption of *Chazaras HaShatz*. Therefore, each shul should have a designated person who calls out "Kohanim" at the appropriate time.
2. ***Rambam*** (*Hilchos Tefillah* 14:8) and ***Shulchan Aruch*** (128:10) state that the chazzan should call out the word "Kohanim" as a signal for the Kohanim to begin the *berachah*. In their opinion, this is not considered an interruption, because

1. *She'eilos U'Teshuvos Mabit*, vol. 1 #64, and *Kiryas Sefer* on *Rambam* ch. 14.

2. *Mabit* (ibid.), cited in *Magen Avraham* (128:13) and *Mishnah Berurah* (§38). *Mishnah Berurah* points out that for those congregations where the chazzan recites *Elokeinu V'Elokei Avoseinu* before Bircas Kohanim (following the opinion of Rabbeinu Yehudah, which we discuss in the next section), it is preferable to announce the word "Kohanim" only when two adult Kohanim are present. However, if he did say the word "Kohanim" in a raised voice with only one adult Kohen present, one should not reprimand him, as it is not considered an interruption of the *tefillah*.

Bircas Kohanim is an essential part of the *tefillah*. Thus, just as the chazzan calls out each word of the *berachos* during Bircas Kohanim, and we do not consider that an interruption, so, too, he is permitted to announce "Kohanim" beforehand.[3]

3. ***Rabbeinu Yehudah*** (*Tosafos, Berachos* 34a) and **Maharam of Rothenburg** (cited in *Hagahos Maimoniyos, Hilchos Tefillah* 14:7) say that the chazzan should recite the prayer beginning *Elokeinu V'Elokei Avoseinu* in an undertone. Then, when he reaches the word "Kohanim," he should raise his voice, as a sign that the Kohanim should begin. *Hagahos Maimoniyos* states that this was originally the practice of his great teacher, the Maharam of Rothenburg, but later he concluded that the *Elokeinu V'Elokei Avoseinu* prayer should not be recited at all on a day that Bircas Kohanim is performed, and he retracted his opinion.[4] However, *Rema* writes that this is, in fact, the custom that should be followed, and he does not share the concern of Maharam of Rothenburg, since the prayer of *Elokeinu V'Elokei Avoseinu* is said quietly, and only the word "Kohanim" is pronounced aloud.

In Practice:

All of the three opinions outlined above are followed today, each by different communities.

1. ***Rabbeinu Tam***

Most yeshivos and Lithuanian communities in Eretz Yisrael follow the opinion of Rabbeinu Tam. That is, they appoint someone other than the chazzan to announce "Kohanim."[5]

---

3. As explained by *Mishnah Berurah* (128:34), who summarizes the opinion of *Rambam* based on the explanation of *Olas Tamid*.

4. For more on the retraction of Maharam of Rothenburg regarding reciting *Elokeinu V'Elokei Avoseinu* on a day that Bircas Kohanim is performed, see *Beis Yosef* 128:10 and *Biur HaGra* 128:21.

5. *Biur HaGra* 128:20; *Maaseh Rav* §168. *Chayei Adam* (32:15) states, as well, that this was the opinion of the *Gra*. This practice was also followed by the Chazon Ish; see *Kuntres Zichronos* of R' Chaim Kanievsky of the Chazon Ish (9:4), and Responsa of R' Chaim Kanievsky #199. In chapter 12, we noted that this was the practice of the Brisker Rav and his descendants as well. *Halichos Imrei Sofer* (§111) relates that the Rebbe of Erlau would call out "Kohanim" in his shul even

2. ***Rambam* and *Shulchan Aruch***

Sephardim, both in Eretz Yisrael and abroad, follow *Rambam,* and the chazzan calls out "Kohanim" in a loud voice. The *Elokeinu V'Elokei Avoseinu* prayer is not recited at all.[6]

3. ***Rabbeinu Yehudah***

In many Ashkenazic shuls outside Eretz Yisrael, and in some chassidic communities in Eretz Yisrael, the chazzan recites the *Elokeinu V'Elokei Avoseinu* prayer in an undertone, as per the opinion of Rabbeinu Yehudah. When he reaches the word "Kohanim," he pronounces it in a loud voice, to signal the Kohanim to begin Bircas Kohanim.[7]

---

when he was not the chazzan.

6. See *Kaf HaChaim* 128:71.

7. *Shulchan HaTahor* of the Komarna Rebbe (128:9) states that *Elokeinu V'Elokei Avoseinu* is not recited when the Kohanim perform Bircas Kohanim. *Piskei Teshuvos* (128:32) clarifies that in many chassidic communities in Eretz Yisrael, *Elokeinu V'Elokei Avoseinu* is not recited, and the chazzan is the one to call out "Kohanim," as is the custom of the Sephardim. R' Chaim Na'eh, in *Ketzos HaShulchan* (23:14), explains that *Shulchan Aruch HaRav* (127:2) seems to imply that *Elokeinu V'Elokei Avoseinu* is recited only outside Eretz Yisrael, where there is no daily Bircas Kohanim, and thus it became part of the prayer there. In Eretz Yisrael, however, where Bircas Kohanim is performed every day, there is no need to say it.

Chapter 32
The Elokeinu V'Elokei Avoseinu Prayer

1. *Shulchan Aruch* states (127:2) that if no Kohanim are present, the *Elokeinu V'Elokei Avoseinu* prayer is recited in place of Bircas Kohanim. *Rema* adds that this prayer is recited only during a *tefillah* when Bircas Kohanim could potentially be recited; namely, as *Mishnah Berurah* there notes, Shacharis and Mussaf, as well as Minchah on a public fast day. However, one does not answer amen after each blessing, because this is not an actual Bircas Kohanim.[1] Some congregations have the custom to say "*Kein yehi ratzon*" after each of the three blessings, in place of amen,[2] while others have the custom to say this phrase only after the last blessing (*v'yaseim lecha shalom*).[3]

2. As discussed in chapter 39, one who experiences a disturbing dream can nullify it by attending Bircas Kohanim and reciting the prayer that was composed for this purpose (printed in *siddurim*). However, one should not say this prayer when the chazzan recites

---

1. *Shulchan Aruch* 127:2. R' Moshe Sternbuch writes (*Teshuvos V'Hanhagos*, vol. 2 #101) that R' Chaim Brisker was of the opinion that if one does answer amen, he is in violation of *bal tosif*.
2. *Shulchan Aruch* ibid.; *Mishnah Berurah* (127:10) elaborates that although it is not Bircas Kohanim and for that reason we do not answer amen, nevertheless, we are beseeching Hashem to bless us with the same blessings He would have bestowed upon us had we received the *berachah* from the Kohanim, and therefore we respond, "*Kein yehi ratzon*" — may it be the will of Hashem.
3. *Magen Avraham* 127:5; cited in *Mishnah Berurah* (127:11).

Elokeinu V'Elokei Avoseinu in place of Bircas Kohanim. The *Rema* writes[4] that in a place where there is no Bircas Kohanim during Shacharis, the prayer for nullifying a bad dream may be recited during the prayer of *Sim Shalom*. R' Yaakov Emden, however, argues that this prayer is effective only in conjunction with the actual Bircas Kohanim.[5]

3. In an Ashkenazic minyan in the Diaspora, where Bircas Kohanim is not recited daily, **there is no advantage to having a Kohen serve as the chazzan in order for him to be the one to recite *Elokeinu V'Elokei Avoseinu*.** This prayer does not have the status of Bircas Kohanim in any way, and there is no difference whether it is recited by a Kohen or a non-Kohen.[6] For the same reason, it may not be recited while facing the congregation, and it is prohibited for a chazzan to raise up his hands or conform to any of the other requirements of Bircas Kohanim while saying it.[7]

4. *Mishnah Berurah*[8] states that if the chazzan forgot to say the *Elokeinu V'Elokei Avoseinu* prayer, it is not necessary to repeat *Chazaras HaShatz*. *Biur Halachah*[9] explains that this prayer was not recited in the time of the Gemara (see *Tosafos, Berachos* 34a), and we find opinions cited by *Tur* (ibid.) that one should not recite *Elokeinu V'Elokei Avoseinu* at all, so if it was omitted, there is certainly no need to repeat *Chazaras HaShatz*.

5. Whenever *Elokeinu V'Elokei Avoseinu* is recited (because there is no Kohen, or in an Ashkenazic minyan outside Eretz Yisrael), there is a protocol to be followed, as outlined in *Zohar*[10]: When the chazzan says the words "*Yevarechecha Hashem*," he faces the *aron kodesh*. When he says, "*v'yishmerecha*," he turns his face to the right. He then turns back to the *aron kodesh* and says, "*Ya'er Hashem*," and turns his face to the left when he says, "*panav eilecha*

4. 130:1.
5. *Siddur* of R' Yaakov Emden, in the name of his father, the Chacham Tzvi.
6. See chapter 22, where we present the ruling, issued by both R' Chaim Kanievsky and R' Moshe Sternbuch, that there is no advantage in choosing a Kohen to recite this prayer.
7. R' Moshe Sternbuch adds (ibid. #108) that if a chazzan mimics the requirements of Bircas Kohanim during the *Elokeinu V'Elokei Avoseinu* prayer, he is in violation of *bal tosif*.
8. 127:7.
9. Ibid., s.v. *Omer*.
10. *Zohar Chadash*, beginning of *Nasso*.

viychuneka." Finally, when he says, "*Yisa Hashem panav eilecha v'yaseim lecha shalom,*" he faces the *aron kodesh* once again. The Acharonim[11] explain that this is done in order to combine the less *chashuv* (distinguished) left side with the more *chashuv* right side; this has the effect of bringing more blessing upon the Jewish people.

Instructions for the *shaliach tzibbur*

At bold words he should face the direction of the arrow.
At non-bold words he should face the *aron kodesh*.

יְבָרֶכְךָ ד׳ **וְיִשְׁמְרֶךָ**

יָאֵר ד׳ **פָּנָיו** **אֵלֶיךָ** **וִיחֻנֶּךָּ**

יִשָּׂא ד׳ פָּנָיו אֵלֶיךָ וְיָשֵׂם לְךָ שָׁלוֹם

11. This *Zohar* is discussed by *Magen Avraham* (127:3), *Ba'er Heitev* (127:4), *Mishnah Berurah* (127:8), *Ben Ish Chai* (*Tetzaveh* §3), and *Kaf HaChaim* (121:7).

Chapter 33
Chazzan Calling Out the Words of Bircas Kohanim

Although the practice of the chazzan calling out the words of Bircas Kohanim to prompt the Kohanim is not found in the Talmud, it is mentioned in the Midrash,[1] and can be traced back to the times of the Geonim as well; R' Saadiah Gaon writes in his *Siddur*[2] that the chazzan reads the verses before the Kohanim. This practice is based on the phrase אָמוֹר לָהֶם, *saying to them,* which the Torah uses regarding the mitzvah of Bircas Kohanim.[3]

1. R' Shlomo HaKohen explains, in his *teshuvos, Binyan Shlomo* (*siman* 1), quoting his brother, R' Betzalel HaKohen, that the mitzvah of Bircas Kohanim is subject to the negative commandments of לֹא תֹסֵף עָלָיו וְלֹא תִגְרַע מִמֶּנּוּ, *You shall not add to it, and you shall not subtract from it* (*Devarim* 13:1), which forbid us to augment or subtract from any mitzvah. Therefore, the chazzan calls out one word at a time, to ascertain that no word is inadvertently repeated or omitted.

---

1. *Sifrei, Nasso* §39, and *Bamidbar Rabbah* 11:4. It is also cited by *Tosafos* (*Berachos* 34a) and many other Rishonim.
2. P. 39.
3. This is mentioned by several Rishonim, including *Machzor Vitri* (§130), authored by Rabbeinu Simchah, one of Rashi's closest disciples; *Orchos Chaim* (*Hilchos Nesias Kapayim* §6), authored by R' Aharon of Lunil; and *Sefer Yerei'im* §269. It is also cited by *Taz* (128:8).

Mishnah Berurah (128:49), citing *Pri Chadash*, adds that although this is the optimal procedure to follow, if the Kohanim decide to say the *berachos* on their own, without someone leading them, the mitzvah is still fulfilled.[4]

2. *Pri Chadash* (128:13) states that the chazzan is required to read the verses from a *siddur*; if he does not, the congregation should ask him to do so. *Ba'er Heitev* (128:23), *Mishnah Berurah* (128:49), and *Chayei Adam* (32:18) cite this as halachah.

3. The chazzan must raise his voice so that all the Kohanim hear each word[5] before they say it themselves. In response to a number of inquiries, R' Chaim Kanievsky wrote that the chazzan must say the words loudly enough for all the Kohanim to hear, but it is not necessary for the rest of the congregation to hear him (in contrast to the words of the Kohanim themselves, which should be loud enough for everyone to hear).

4. The Kohanim are required to wait for the chazzan to finish saying each word before they say it themselves,[6] and, likewise, the chazzan must wait for the Kohanim to finish reciting each word before he goes on to the next word.[7] The chazzan and the Kohanim should be careful not to recite the words at the same time, so that the Kohanim are heard distinctly and separately.[8]

5. *Meiri*[9] writes that an effort should be made to have the chazzan call out the words rather than another member of the congregation.

6. Although it is preferable for the chazzan to be the one who calls out the words before the Kohanim, we find in *Teshuvos HaGeonim*[10] that if the chazzan is fatigued and needs a short break during *Chazaras HaShatz*, it is perfectly acceptable for another

---

4. This is also noted by *Sefer Yerei'im* (§269) and *Shulchan Aruch HaRav* (128:21).
5. See Responsa of R' Chaim Kanievsky #206-213; see also *Tzitz Eliezer*, vol. 14 #17. The Gemara, *Rambam*, and *Shulchan Aruch* do not specify how loudly the chazzan should speak.
6. *Shulchan Aruch* 128:18.
7. *Mishnah Berurah* 128:68. *Shaar HaTziyun* (ibid.) explains that since *Rambam* and other *poskim* write that the chazzan should call out each word before the Kohanim, he must wait for them to finish saying each word before he calls out the next word.
8. *Mishnah Berurah* 128:67, based on *Shulchan Aruch HaRav*.
9. *Sotah* 38a.
10. Responsa #177.

person to call out the words in his stead, and, in fact, this was done occasionally in the yeshivah of the Geonim.

7. It is interesting to note that when the Chazon Ish served as chazzan, he would ask another person to call out the words of Bircas Kohanim, because he was concerned that he would become confused while calling out the words.[11] Nevertheless, in the minyan of the Chazon Ish, and in the Lederman shul of Bnei Brak, which stringently adheres to the rulings and customs of the Chazon Ish, the chazzan does recite the verses. (He does not, however, call out "Kohanim" before Bircas Kohanim, for the Chazon Ish, like most *poskim* of Lithuanian background, followed the opinion of Rabbeinu Tam that a designated member of the congregation who is not the chazzan calls out "Kohanim.")

8. R' Ovadiah Yosef[12] writes that it is permissible for someone other than the chazzan to call out the words of Bircas Kohanim, but this should not be done regularly.

Opinion That the Word Yevarechecha Is Not Recited by the Chazzan

Although all *poskim* agree that the chazzan (or another person) should call out the words of Bircas Kohanim, there are differing opinions among the Rishonim regarding the first word of the *berachah — yevarechecha*:

R' Saadiah Gaon[13] writes that the chazzan calls out all the words of Bircas Kohanim with the exception of *yevarechecha*.

Rambam (*Hilchos Tefillah U'Nesias Kapayim* 14:3) and *Shulchan Aruch* (128:13) concur with R' Saadiah Gaon, and state that the Kohanim say the word *yevarechecha* on their own, and the chazzan reads out all the words from that point on. R' Avraham ben HaRambam in his *sefer HaMaspik L'Ovdei Hashem* (ch. 28) rules in accordance with this opinion as well. It is also cited as halachah by *Pri Chadash* (128:13).

There are several reasons given for the opinion of R' Saadiah and *Rambam*:

---

11. See *Orchos Rabbeinu,* vol. 1, p. 66.
12. *Yabia Omer,* vol. 5 #22.
13. *Siddur Rav Saadiah Gaon,* p. 39.

1. *Beis Yosef* (128:13) writes that the reason the Geonim and Rishonim instituted that the chazzan should say the words before the Kohanim was so that the Kohanim should not become confused and forget which word they are up to. However, we are not concerned about the word *yevarechecha*, as that is the first word of Bircas Kohanim.[14] *Mishnah Berurah* (128:48) cites this explanation as well.[15]

2. *Mabit* (*Kiryas Sefer*, ch. 14) writes that the reason the Kohanim say *yevarechecha* without waiting for the chazzan is in order to avoid interrupting between the *berachah* of *asher kideshanu bikedushaso shel Aharon* and the performance of the mitzvah.[16]

3. *Shulchan Aruch HaRav* (128:21) offers a third explanation: When there are two or more Kohanim, and thus, the word "Kohanim" is called out (by either the chazzan or someone else), it is itself a request for the Kohanim to begin and say the word *yevarechecha*; therefore, there is no need for the chazzan to repeat the request by calling out *yevarechecha*. Once the Kohanim do say the word *yevarechecha*, the chazzan calls out the remaining words, so that the Kohanim do not become confused and forget what they are up to.[17] (Another reason for calling out the words is given by Rabbeinu Bachaye; see below.)

Opinion That the Word Yevarechecha Is Recited by the Chazzan

Tur (128:13) disagrees with *Rambam*, and states that the chazzan should call out *yevarechecha*. *Rema* (128:13) cites the opinion of

---

14. R' Yosef Karo, in *Kesef Mishnah* on *Rambam* (*Hilchos Tefillah U'Nesias Kapayim* 14:3), brings proof from the Gemara (*Sotah* 39b) that it is preferable for the Kohanim to initiate and say the word *yevarechecha*.

15. *Mishnah Berurah* (585:18 and in *Shaar HaTziyun* §31) states that although *Gra* implies that the halachah is in accordance with *Rambam*, we follow the opinion of *Tur*, as stated in *Rema* (cited below).

16. *Mabit* writes a similar idea (*Teshuvos Mabit*, vol. 1, #180).

17. This reason is cited by *Terumas HaDeshen* in the *sefer Leket Yosher* (p. 26), which we refer to later.

Tur and adds that *Hagahos Maimoniyos* and *Ran* are of this opinion as well, and that such is the practice of Ashkenazic communities.[18]

Ashkenazic and Sephardic Customs for Yevarechecha

1. If there is only one Kohen present, we do not call out "Kohanim" (because the phrase אָמוֹר לָהֶם, *saying to "them"* is written in the plural; see chapter 30). In this case, since the Kohen has not yet been called upon to begin the mitzvah, all agree that the chazzan should say *yevarechecha* before the Kohen.[19] In *Leket Yosher* (p. 26), *Terumas HaDeshen* explains that the word "Kohanim" is a call to the Kohanim to recite *yevarechecha*; therefore, there is no reason for the chazzan to repeat the request by calling out *yevarechecha*.[20] This does not apply, however, when only one Kohen is present and the word "Kohanim" is not called out.
2. If there is only one Kohen present, all *poskim*, both Sephardic and Ashkenazic, agree that the word *yevarechecha* is recited by the chazzan. Even when there is more than one Kohen, all Ashkenazim, who follow the opinion of *Rema*, have the custom that the chazzan says every word, including *yevarechecha*.
3. Interestingly, although Sephardim generally follow the rulings of *Rambam* and *Shulchan Aruch*, in this case, the vast majority of Sephardim throughout the world follow the opinion of *Tur* and *Ran*, that the chazzan does recite the word *yevarechecha*, even if there is more than one Kohen.

The Importance of the Chazzan Calling Out All Fifteen Words

As discussed in chapter 22, *Rabbeinu Bachaye* (*Bamidbar* 6:23) offers a fascinating explanation of why the chazzan calls out each

---

18. *Rema* also cites this in *Darkei Moshe* (on *Tur* 128:13).

19. *Maharam Mintz* (*siman* 12), cited in *Magen Avraham* 128:20 and *Mishnah Berurah* 128:47. This is mentioned in the writings of several Rishonim and *poskim*, including R' Avraham be HaRambam in his *sefer HaMaspik L'Ovdei Hashem*, ch. 28. *Kaf HaChaim* (128:83) writes that this is the halachah.

20. See above, that this is also the reason given by *Shulchan Aruch HaRav*.

word: The Gemara (*Sotah* 38b) states that a Kohen who blesses the people is himself blessed, as Hashem promised, וַאֲבָרְכָה מְבָרְכֶיךָ, *and I will bless those who bless you* (*Bereishis* 12:3). As the chazzan calls out each word, Hashem's blessing flows down from Heaven and rests upon the Kohanim. The Kohanim then bestow the blessing upon the Jewish people. The students of the Arizal, as well as *Ben Ish Chai,* cite Rabbeinu Bachaye's explanation in emphasizing the importance of reciting all fifteen words of Bircas Kohanim in this manner.

Many Sephardic *poskim* concur.

R' Eliezer Papo, author of *Pele Yoetz,* in his *sefer Chesed L'Alafim,*[21] writes that the chazzan *should* say the word *yevarechecha*. He points out that aside from the fact that the *mekubalim* of Yeshivat Beit El in Yerushalayim (who follow Arizal) conducted themselves this way, *Rambam* himself does not consider it mandatory for the Kohanim to initiate the first word, whereas *Tur* and other Rishonim hold that it *is* mandatory for the chazzan to call out the first word. Additionally, since all agree that the chazzan should call out *yevarechecha* when there is only one Kohen present, it is also permitted to do so when there is more than one.

Ben Ish Chai (*Halachos, Tetzaveh* §1) writes as follows:

> Here, in Baghdad, we followed the ruling of Maran [R' Yosef Karo] for many generations, and did not call out *yevarechecha*. However, several years ago, with much praise and gratitude to Hashem, I succeeded in changing the custom of all the synagogues in the city, and the chazzan now calls out the word *yevarechecha* as well. It is fitting to institute this ruling in all congregations throughout the world.

Ben Ish Chai then adds an important halachic insight that explains why he saw fit to diverge from the ruling of R' Yosef Karo:

> An added benefit has resulted from the introduction of this custom: Until now, the Kohanim would often finish reciting the *berachah* on the mitzvah, and begin the word *yevarechecha* immediately after the word *b'ahavah* at the end of their *berachah*. **This did not give the congregation a chance to respond amen.** Now, however, the Kohanim wait until the

21. 128:10.

word *yevarechecha* is called out, and there is ample time to respond amen to their *berachah*.

Ben Ish Chai discusses this in his responsa[22] as well, and concludes that this is the appropriate procedure.

Similarly, *Kaf HaChaim*[23] implies that the chazzan should always say the word *yevarechecha* just as he says all the other words of Bircas Kohanim.

The Change of Sephardic Custom in Eretz Yisrael

R' Ovadiah Yosef[24] writes extensively about his personal experience regarding the customs related to the word *yevarechecha*. When he was the chief rabbi of Cairo, around the year 1950, the Kohanim there said the word *yevarechecha* without being prompted, in accordance with the ruling of *Rambam* and *Shulchan Aruch*, and R' Ovadiah did not change the custom.

In 1968 he was appointed chief rabbi of Tel Aviv. There as well, Beit HaKnesset Ohel Moed followed the opinion of *Rambam*. That year, on Shabbos of *Parashas Nasso*, R' Ovadiah spoke about having the chazzan say the word *yevarechecha* before the Kohanim, pointing out the added benefit that the congregation would have time to respond amen to the *berachah* that the Kohanim recite before performing the mitzvah. After his speech, both the Kohanim and the congregants told R' Ovadiah that they would actually prefer to change their custom and have the chazzan recite the word *yevarechecha*. This has become the *minhag* of most Sephardic communities in Eretz Yisrael and around the world.

In contemporary times, most Sephardic communities throughout the world have the chazzan say *yevarechecha*, with the exception of Syrian communities outside Eretz Yisrael and many Yemenite communities in Eretz Yisrael and abroad. When there is only one Kohen present, the universal practice, even in Syrian and

22. *Rav Pe'alim*, vol. 3, *O.C. siman* 5.
23. 128:22. In his *sefer Lev Chaim* (vol. 3, *siman* 99) as well, *Kaf HaChaim* cites many sources that state that this is the preferred method.
24. See *Yechaveh Daas*, vol. 4 #10, and *Yalkut Yosef* 128:42 for a comprehensive discussion.

Yemenite communities, is that the chazzan does say the word *yevarechecha*.

Intense Concentration

Yesod V'Shoresh HaAvodah (5:6), when discussing the mitzvah of Bircas Kohanim, states the following:

> The chazzan must be very, very careful to recite the *berachah* with intense concentration, as the *Zohar* states: "It is fitting to arouse the hearts of those who serve as chazzan and to caution them to be exceedingly careful, when they reach Bircas Kohanim, to prepare their hearts in advance to say these three verses with the intention of bestowing blessing upon the Jewish people with a full heart, and not in the manner of one who is merely reading verses from the Torah."
>
> The chazzan must also be exacting in his pronunciation of the words, and pause between each one, so that the words do not run into one another.
>
> My brothers and dear friends! Please be aware and understand; ask yourself — if the chazzan recites the words without separating them properly, can it possibly find favor with the Creator?! ... Therefore, one must be very careful about this matter, and by doing so, he will bring blessing from Hashem upon His people.

Chapter 34
Turning to Face the Congregation

1. The Gemara (*Sotah* 39a) presents a *Yehi Ratzon* prayer that the Kohanim should recite upon ascending to the *duchan.*[1] This is cited as halachah in *Rambam,*[2] *Tur,* and *Shulchan Aruch.*[3]
2. The Kohanim are required to face the congregation during Bircas Kohanim.[4]
3. At what point should the Kohanim turn around to face the congregation? *Rambam*[5] writes that the *berachah* for the mitzvah of Bircas Kohanim is recited while facing the *aron kodesh,* and the Kohanim turn around only after reciting the *berachah.* However, *Tur* and *Shulchan Aruch*[6] state that the Kohanim recite the *berachah* facing the congregation.[7] The Chida writes, in *Birkei Yosef,*[8] that in order to accommodate both opinions, the Kohanim should compromise by facing the *aron kodesh* when they begin the *berachah,* and upon reaching the word וְצִוָּנוּ, they should turn around to

---

1. *Beis Yosef* 128:9 and *Rema* (ad loc.), in the name of several Rishonim, state that this prayer should be recited once the Kohanim are in the proximity of the *aron kodesh.* This prayer appears in chapter 51.
2. *Hilchos Tefillah U'Nesias Kapayim* 14:12.
3. 128:9.
4. As derived from the phrase אָמוֹר לָהֶם, *saying "to them"* (*Sotah* 38a); *Rambam* (*Hilchos Tefillah U'Nesias Kapayim* 14:11) and *Shulchan Aruch* (128:14) rule in accordance with this Gemara.
5. *Hilchos Tefillah U'Nesias Kapayim* 14:12.
6. 128:11.
7. This is the opinion of *Rashi* (*Sotah* 39b) as well.
8. 128:9; also cited in *Shaarei Teshuvah* 128:11.

face the congregation and complete the *berachah,* then recite Bircas Kohanim.[9] *Mishnah Berurah*[10] states that those Kohanim who are scrupulous in performing mitzvos should turn around to face the congregation while they say the word וְצִוָּנוּ, and then complete the *berachah*. Similarly, *Kaf HaChaim*[11] states that this is the custom that should be followed.

4. When the Kohanim turn around to face the congregation, they should turn to their right. Likewise, when they turn back to the *aron kodesh* at the conclusion of Bircas Kohanim, they should once again turn to their right. *Rambam*[12] adds that the source for this is the Gemara's statement (*Zevachim* 62b and elsewhere) that whenever one turns, he should turn to the right (when possible). This halachah is recorded in *Tur* and *Shulchan Aruch* as well.[13]

Swaying to Spread the Blessing

5. *Sefer Rokeach,*[14] cited in *Beis Yosef* and *Shulchan Aruch,*[15] describes in detail the manner in which the Kohanim should sway from side to side when reciting the *berachos*: As they say each of the following words, they are to sway from their right side to their left, with their hands outstretched: יְבָרֶכְךָ, וְיִשְׁמְרֶךָ, אֵלֶיךָ, וִיחֻנֶּךָּ, אֵלֶיךָ, לְךָ, and שָׁלוֹם.

Rambam does not mention this halachah, because it does not appear in the Gemara.[16]

6. *Levush*[17] explains that the purpose of swaying from side to side is in order to spread the *berachah* to all the congregants, including

9. *Leket Yosher* (*Hilchos Bircas Kohanim*), written by a student of the author of *Terumas HaDeshen,* concurs that the Kohanim should turn to face the congregation in the middle of the *berachah*. This is also cited as halachah by *Chayei Adam* (32:16).
10. §40.
11. 128:73.
12. *Hilchos Tefillah U'Nesias Kapayim* 14:13.
13. 128:17.
14. *Hilchos Bircas Kohanim* §323.
15. 128:45.
16. In the *Sefer HaMaspik L'Ovdei Hashem* (ch. 28), R' Avraham ben HaRambam presents a detailed overview of the laws of Bircas Kohanim, in a style similar to that of his father, and he, too, does not make any mention of this practice.
17. 128:45.

those who are not directly in front of the Kohanim. The *Levush* is cited by *Mishnah Berurah*[18] and *Kaf HaChaim*.[19]

7. There is no reason for the members of the congregation to stand directly in front of the Kohanim, as long as they are facing the Kohanim.[20]

In his later years, the Steipler Gaon (R' Chaim Kanievsky's father) would stand in front of the chazzan during Bircas Kohanim. R' Chaim was asked about this in writing several times, and he responded that his father had difficulty hearing and therefore moved close to the Kohanim to be able to hear them. R' Chaim also made it clear that there is no benefit to being in close proximity to the Kohanim or directly in front of them; all those who are in the shul and are facing the Kohanim are equally included in the *berachah*.[21]

8. When the chazzan begins the *berachah* of *Sim Shalom*, the Kohanim turn around to their right until they are facing the *aron kodesh*.[22] They may then lower their hands.[23]

9. The Kohanim are required to remain at the *duchan* until after the congregation responds amen to the *berachah* of *Sim Shalom*,[24] as *Sim Shalom* is the conclusion of Bircas Kohanim.[25]

10. *Mishnah Berurah*[26] states that in our times it is customary for the congregants to say *yasher koach* to the Kohanim,[27] and therefore, in order to prevent this from taking place in the middle of *Kaddish*, the Kohanim should remain at the *duchan* until the conclusion of *Kaddish*.

11. In most shuls throughout Eretz Yisrael, the congregants do not say *yasher koach* to the Kohanim. Nevertheless, R' Chaim Kanievsky writes that it is still preferable for the Kohanim to remain

---

18. §168.
19. 128:276.
20. *Shulchan Aruch* 128:24.
21. See Responsa of R' Chaim Kanievsky #222.
22. *Rambam* ibid. 14:13; *Shulchan Aruch* 128:17.
23. *Sotah* 39b; see also *Rambam, Hilchos Tefillah U'Nesias Kapayim* 14:6; *Shulchan Aruch* 128:15-16.
24. As stated in *Sotah* 39b, *Shulchan Aruch* 128:16, and *Rema* there.
25. See *Levush* 128:16.
26. §60.
27. For more on the *yasher koach* that the congregants say to express their thanks to the Kohanim, see chapter 9.

at the *duchan* until the conclusion of *Kaddish*.[28]

12. As the chazzan is saying *Sim Shalom*, the Kohanim recite the *Ribbono Shel Olam* prayer (cited in the Gemara),[29] asking Hashem to fulfill the *berachos* of Bircas Kohanim. At the same time, the Yisraelim recite the *Adir BaMarom* prayer.[30] The Kohanim and Yisraelim conclude their respective supplications at the same time as the chazzan concludes *Sim Shalom*, so that the congregation may respond amen to both the Kohanim and the chazzan at once.[31] (The *Ribbono Shel Olam* prayer for Kohanim and the *Adir BaMarom* prayer appear in chapter 51.)

13. The Kohanim are not allowed to converse with anyone until they have left the *duchan*.[32] This applies even if the Kohanim have already performed Bircas Kohanim in another congregation that morning.[33]

14. As they depart from the *duchan*, the Kohanim should remain facing the *aron kodesh* and take a step back before turning around, for they are taking leave of the Shechinah, which rests on upon them during Bircas Kohanim.[34]

---

28. Responsa of R' Chaim Kanievsky #430.

29. This prayer, which appears in chapter 51, is not to be confused with the *Ribbono Shel Olam* prayer recited by the congregation to nullify disturbing dreams.

30. See *Mishnah Berurah* 130:6. See also Responsa of R' Chaim Kanievsky #378-385 for a comprehensive discussion of the *Adir BaMarom* prayer.

31. See *Shulchan Aruch* 128:15 and *Rema* there.

32. *Mateh Moshe* §189 in the name of *Maharil*; quoted in *Mishnah Berurah* §58.

33. Responsa of R' Chaim Kanievsky #428.

34. *Magen Avraham* §25 (cited in *Mishnah Berurah* §61) references the Gemara's statement (*Yoma* 53a) that upon exiting the Holy of Holies after the Yom Kippur service, the Kohen Gadol would take a few steps back before turning around. Likewise, when the Kohanim would complete their service in the Beis HaMikdash, they would walk backwards a few steps before turning around.

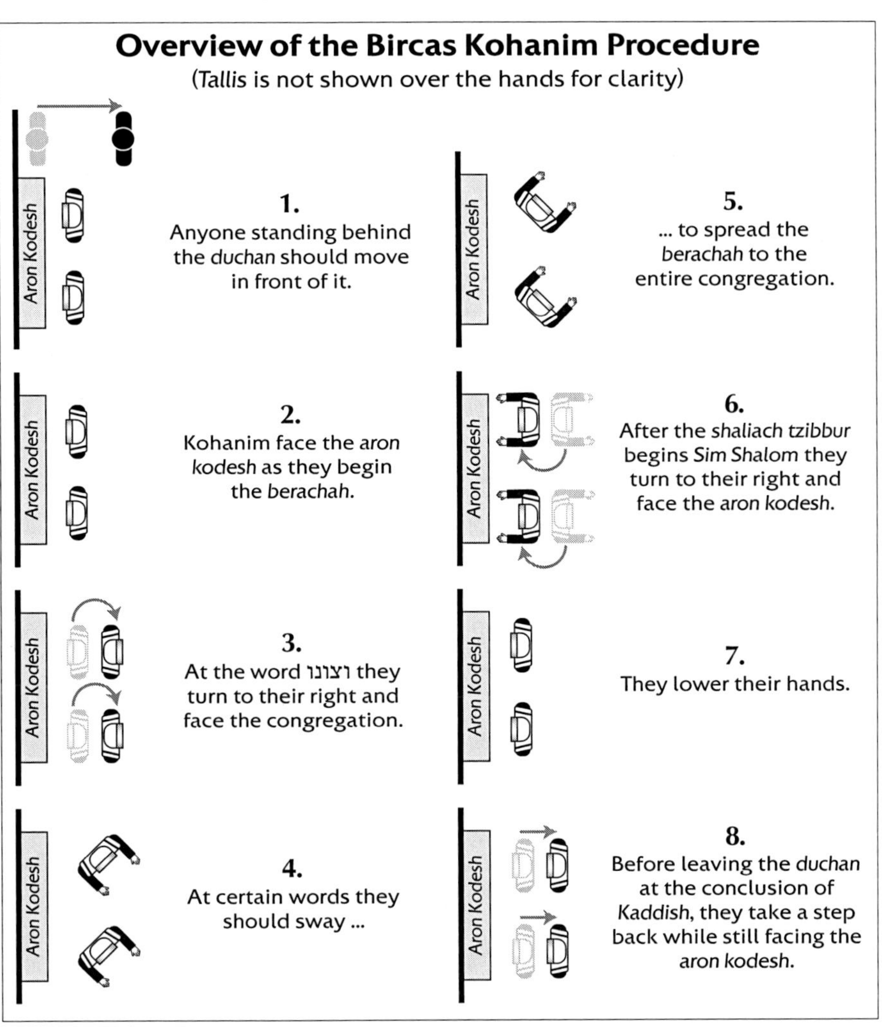
Overview of the Bircas Kohanim Procedure
(Tallis is not shown over the hands for clarity)
Aron Kodesh
1.
Anyone standing behind the duchan should move in front of it.
2.
Kohanim face the aron kodesh as they begin the berachah.
3.
At the word וצונו they turn to their right and face the congregation.
4.
At certain words they should sway ...
5.
... to spread the berachah to the entire congregation.
6.
After the shaliach tzibbur begins Sim Shalom they turn to their right and face the aron kodesh.
7.
They lower their hands.
8.
Before leaving the duchan at the conclusion of Kaddish, they take a step back while still facing the aron kodesh.

Chapter 35
The Obligation to Listen and Focus

1. *Sefer Chareidim*[1] holds that it is a *mitzvah d'Oraysa* (Torah-level commandment) for a non-Kohen to listen to Bircas Kohanim and receive the *berachos*. The Acharonim write that this is the opinion of other Rishonim as well.[2] *Biur Halachah*[3] cites the *Chareidim* at the beginning of *Hilchos Nesias Kapayim*,[4] and *Sefer Haflaah*[5] rules in accordance with the *Chareidim*. R' Moshe Feinstein also follows this opinion in several of his responsa.[6] However, *Ritva*[7] writes that there is no specific mitzvah for a non-Kohen to listen to

---

1. Ch. 4 §18. *Sefer Chareidim* was authored by R' Elazar Azikri of Tzfas (1533-1600), a contemporary of Beis Yosef, Arizal, and Radbaz. In the biography of the Chofetz Chaim by R' M. M. Yashar it is recorded that the Chofetz Chaim held the *Sefer Chareidim* in the highest esteem, to the extent that he delivered a *shiur* on the *sefer* to the students of his yeshivah in Radin. From the Chofetz Chaim's statement in *Mishnah Berurah* (156:4), one can see his great deference for the *Chareidim*.
2. See *Teshuvos Chasam Sofer, O.C.* #22; R' Yerucham Fishel Perlow on *Sefer HaMitzvos* of R' Saadiah Gaon (*Mitzvas Asei* 16).
3. 128:1.
4. R' Akiva Eiger in his commentary to *Shulchan Aruch* (128:1) cites *Sefer Chareidim* as well.
5. *Kesubos* 24b. *Sefer Haflaah* was authored by R' Pinchas HaLevi Horowitz of Frankfurt (1731-1805). This *Haflaah* is also cited in *Kaf HaChaim* (128:8) and *Shaarei Teshuvah* (128:1); this is also the opinion of the Mabit in *Igros Derech Hashem*, in a letter to the Chavos Yair (published in the back of *Teshuvos Chavos Yair*), R' Dovid Oppenheim writes that this is the opinion we follow; see *Shulchan HaTahor* of Komarna 128:3.
6. *Igros Moshe, O.C.*, vol. 3 #17, vol. 4 #21.
7. *Succah* 31b.

Bircas Kohanim. *Chazon Ish* also maintains that the halachah does not follow *Sefer Chareidim*.[8] Much has been written on this topic that is beyond the scope of this work.

2. Even according to those who disagree with *Sefer Chareidim*, it is still imperative for one to listen when Bircas Kohanim is recited in the shul where he is davening. If he is in the middle of *Shemoneh Esrei* he should pause to hear it.[9]

3. Although one who is already in the middle of *Shemoneh Esrei* may pause and listen, it is forbidden to begin *Shemoneh Esrei* if one knows that he will not finish in time for Bircas Kohanim. Instead, he should wait to hear Bircas Kohanim and then say the silent *Shemoneh Esrei*.[10]

4. *Igros Moshe*[11] rules that if one mistakenly started *Shemoneh Esrei* and is standing at the front wall of the shul, where he will not be facing the Kohanim,[12] he is permitted to change his location in the middle of *Shemoneh Esrei*, in order to stand in front of the Kohanim and be able to receive the *berachah*. This is not considered an interruption of *Shemoneh Esrei*, because Bircas Kohanim is an integral part of the *tefillah*.

5. *Tur* and *Shulchan Aruch*[13] state that it is forbidden for the members of the congregation to look around during Bircas Kohanim, because that causes one to become distracted and think about other matters.[14]

6. Similarly, *Ben Ish Chai*[15] writes that the congregants should keep their eyes closed and should not divert their minds to other matters; it should be as though they are in the middle of *Shemoneh Esrei*, and they should concentrate intently on the words of the *berachah*. *Ben Ish Chai* adds that even if someone is merely passing

---

8. See *Kuntres Zichronos* (9:1), in which R' Chaim Kanievsky compiled the rulings of the Chazon Ish; and Responsa of R' Chaim Kanievsky #116. Several other Acharonim quote the *Ritva* and follow his opinion.
9. See chapter 37 and Responsa of R' Chaim Kanievsky #118.
10. *Igros Moshe, O.C.*, vol. 4 #21, vol. 5 #20.
11. Ibid., vol. 5 #20.
12. See *Shulchan Aruch* 128:24.
13. 128:23. *Beis Yosef* explains that this is based on *Rambam, Hilchos Tefillah U'Nesias Kapayim* 14:7.
14. *Magen Avraham* ad loc. Cited in *Mishnah Berurah* §89.
15. First year, *Tetzaveh* §19.

through a shul to retrieve an item that he left behind, or the like, and he walks in while the Kohanim are *duchaning*, he must stand still and listen, and not leave until they finish.[16]

7. The Kohanim are required to stand during Bircas Kohanim, and the custom is that the rest of the congregation stands reverently as well. However, *Mishnah Berurah* notes[17] that while a Kohen who cannot stand without support may not *duchan*, a congregant is allowed to sit during Bircas Kohanim (if standing is difficult).

8. There seems to be a recent practice among some Yisraelim to open their hands, palms turned up, during Bircas Kohanim, to demonstrate that they are gratefully receiving the *berachah*. When R' Chaim Kanievsky was asked about this, however, he firmly maintained that there is no such *minhag*.[18]

R' Yisrael Yaakov Fisher also unequivocally stated that there is no known source for this practice. R' Yisrael Yaakov added that he never receives the question of whether non-Kohanim should fall to their knees during Bircas Kohanim, even though there *are* sources in the Rishonim for that *minhag* (although it should not be done today, since we do not have this custom).[19] Therefore, R' Yisrael Yaakov stated that people should not open their hands during Bircas Kohanim in order to "receive" the *berachah*.

9. Although some *siddurim* and *machzorim* print various *pesukim* next to the words of Bircas Kohanim, one should not say these *pesukim* during Bircas Kohanim; those who do say them are mistaken. Many Rishonim,[20] as well as *Tur, Shulchan Aruch*,[21] and *poskim* across the board (Ashkenazic and Sephardic), agree that this is an erroneous practice.[22] This is also the unequivocal ruling

16. See Responsa of R' Chaim Kanievsky #343, who writes the same.
17. 128:51.
18. See Responsa #353, 354.
19. The custom to fall to one's knees is recorded in *Machzor Vitri* (*siman* 130) and in *Siddur Rashi* (*siman* 508; cited in *Eliyahu Rabbah* §49): "When the Kohen begins to bless the congregation, [the non-Kohanim] fall on their knees."
20. Rabbeinu Chananel, cited in *Tosafos* (*Sotah* 40a); *Rif*; *Rosh*; and many others.
21. 128:26. This is also the opinion of *Rema* (ad loc.).
22. *Bach*; *Levush*; *Olas Tamid*; *Pri Chadash*; R' Eliezer Papo in *Chesed L'Alafim*; *Maamar Mordechai*; *Chayei Adam*; *Gra* in *Maaseh Rav* §166; *Shulchan Aruch HaRav*; Komarna Rebbe in *Shulchan HaTahor* (128:21); *Kaf HaChaim*; R' Ovadiah Yosef in *Yechaveh Daas*, vol. 5 #15, and others.

of *Mishnah Berurah*.[23] The Gemara[24] compares one who recites verses or is otherwise preoccupied during Bircas Kohanim to "a servant who is receiving a blessing from his master and is not attentive to the blessing" (which, of course, is a great affront to his master).[25]

10. The only prayers that one is permitted to recite during Bircas Kohanim are the *Ribbono Shel Olam* prayer to annul disturbing dreams and the *Yehi Ratzon* prayer at the end of the last *berachah* (printed in most *siddurim*; see chapter 51). These should preferably be recited only while the Kohanim are singing.[26]

11. It is forbidden to study Torah or be *maavir sidra* (review the weekly Torah portion) during Bircas Kohanim.[27] Even if a community has the custom to sing during Bircas Kohanim, one may not learn during the singing or at any other point during Bircas Kohanim.[28]

12. *Yosef Ometz*[29] states that if someone engages in idle talk during Bircas Kohanim, aside from not being included in the blessing, he is committing a serious sin. Similarly, R' Chaim Kanievsky[30] writes that if one learns Torah during Bircas Kohanim he does not receive the blessing.

13. R' Chaim Kanievsky[31] writes that if someone was present during Bircas Kohanim but inadvertently became distracted, he still receives the complete *berachah*. Even so, one should make a supreme effort to concentrate and not become distracted during the entire Bircas Kohanim.

---

23. §103.
24. *Sotah* 40a.
25. This Gemara is cited by several of the aforementioned Rishonim as the reason for the halachah.
26. *Tosafos* (*Sotah* 40a) explain that one is permitted to say the prayer in the middle of Bircas Kohanim because a bad dream can be a matter of *pikuach nefesh* (danger to life). See chapter 39.
27. *Sheyarei Knesses HaGedolah*; *Pri Chadash* §20; *Ba'er Heitev* §46.
28. Responsa of R' Chaim Kanievsky #341.
29. Written by Rabbeinu Yosef, *av beis din* of Frankfurt (1570-1637), §407 and 412.
30. Responsa #342.
31. Responsa #344.

14. *Yesod V'Shoresh HaAvodah*[32] states:

> We learned that when the Kohen raises his hands, the people must be in a state of awe and fear, and know that at that time goodwill prevails throughout the Worlds; the upper and lower Beings are blessed, and there is no Judgment among them all....
>
> One should fix his gaze on the floor as though he is actually standing in the middle of *Shemoneh Esrei*, as stated in *Shulchan Aruch* (128:23). One should concentrate on each and every word that comes from the mouths of the Kohanim and should not recite any of the *pesukim* that are printed in the siddurim, as is stated in *Shulchan Aruch* (ibid.).

32. *Shaar* 9, ch. 7.

Chapter 36
Positioning the Fingers

Although the Gemara and *Rambam* do not discuss how a Kohen should position his fingers during Bircas Kohanim,[1] we do find a source in the Midrash,[2] which mentions the special way the Kohen's fingers are to be arranged. The *poskim* cite a variety of customs in this regard, but each Kohen should follow the custom of his own family. Indeed, Rabbeinu Manoach, a disciple of Maharam of Rothenburg, writes[3] that since there is no Talmudic source for the positioning of the hands, each person should follow the tradition he has received.[4]

We will present some general halachos regarding the positioning of the hands, and then go on to describe the most common customs of how to position them.

1. It is important to note that if the Kohen cannot keep his fingers together as described by the *poskim*, he should still *duchan*, as the position of the fingers is not a requirement. Additionally, the Kohen should not place rubber bands or strings on his fingers to keep them together.[5]

---

1. This omission from the Gemara is noted by *Mordechai* (*Megillah* §816), cited in *Beis Yosef* (128:12). *Beis Yosef* adds that the way to position the fingers is not mentioned by *Rambam* at all, because it is not discussed in the Gemara.
2. *Tanchuma, Nasso* 15; *Bamidbar Rabbah* 11:2. *Midrash Tanchuma* is the source cited in *Biur HaGra* on *Shulchan Aruch* (128:12) and in *Mishnah Berurah* (§44).
3. In his commentary on *Rambam* (*Hilchos Tefillah U'Nesias Kapayim* 14:3).
4. In researching R' Chaim Kanievsky's customs, this author personally spoke to many of the Kohanim in the Lederman shul of Bnei Brak, where R' Chaim davened, yet none of them knew what was R' Chaim's opinion regarding how to position the fingers. Evidently, each one was following what his own father had taught him and saw no need to seek R' Chaim's ruling on this matter.
5. Responsa of R' Chaim Kanievsky #263; R' Ovadiah Yosef, *Yalkut Yosef* 128:50.

2. If it is tiring for the Kohen to keep his hands raised for the entire Bircas Kohanim, it is sufficient if he is able to raise his hands on his own when the verses are recited.[6] He should ensure that his fingers are positioned correctly while he recites the words, but he may relax them between the words or verses.[7]

3. *Hagahos Maimoniyos*[8] states that although the two hands should be connected during Bircas Kohanim, the right hand should be raised slightly higher than the left hand. This is derived from the *pasuk* וַיִּשָּׂא אַהֲרֹן אֶת ידו [יָדָיו] אֶל הָעָם וַיְבָרְכֵם, *Aharon raised his hands toward the people and blessed them* (*Vayikra* 9:22), where the word *yadav — his hands —* is spelled without the second *yud*, so it can be read as *yado — his hand* (singular), to teach us that one of the hands (the right one) should be elevated above the other one. This is the correct procedure according to Kabbalah as well.[9]

4. Even if a Kohen is left-handed, he should still make sure that his right hand is slightly higher than his left.[10]

Customs of How to Position the Fingers

The following is a partial overview, along with visual renderings, of the most common customs, which are observed by the vast majority of Kohanim. (There are a few other customs of how to position the fingers, which are observed by a small number of Kohanim.)

1. The Opinion of Tur and Shulchan Aruch

Tur and *Shulchan Aruch* state (128:12):

> They raise their hands to the height of their shoulders, elevating the right hand slightly above the left. They spread their hands and divide their fingers, to consciously create five *"avirim"* (lit., air spaces): one *avir* between the two fingers [on one side of each hand] and the two fingers [on the other side] (i.e., the space between the middle finger

6. See chapter 29.

7. See *Magen Avraham* 128:19, *Eliyahu Rabbah* 128:27, *Shulchan Aruch HaRav* 128:20, *Mishnah Berurah* §43.

8. *Hilchos Tefillah U'Nesias Kapayim* 14:3, cited in *Beis Yosef* 128:12 and *Mishnah Berurah* 128:42. This idea also appears in *Zohar, Nasso,* p. 146.

9. As cited in *Zohar* and *Beis Yosef* ibid.

10. Responsa of R' Chaim Kanievsky #254.

and the ring finger), one *avir* between each index finger and thumb, and another *avir* between the two thumbs. They spread their palms so that the inside faces the ground and the backs of their hands face heavenward.

This is the opinion of many *poskim*, including *Raviah, Mordechai, Rosh, Levush, Mateh Moshe, Magen Avraham, Shulchan Aruch HaRav, Aruch HaShulchan*, and *Mishnah Berurah*.

Tur explains that the concept of five *avirim* is hinted in the verse מֵצִיץ מִן הַחֲרַכִּים, *peering through the lattices* (*Shir HaShirim* 2:9). The letter *hei* has the numerical equivalent of five, which teaches us that the Kohanim should have five *avirim* when blessing Klal Yisrael.[11]

Shibbolei HaLeket (§23; cited in *Beis Yosef* 128:12) adds that the Kohanim position their fingers in a specific way to show that the Shechinah rests on their hands during Bircas Kohanim.

The *poskim* point out that although the right hand should be slightly elevated, the Kohen should do his utmost to keep his two thumbs connected to one another for the duration of Bircas Kohanim (with the right thumb higher than the left thumb), so that the five *avirim* remain intact.[12]

2. The Opinion of Zohar and the Vilna Gaon

Zohar (*Nasso,* p. 146) presents a differing opinion — that the five fingers of each hand should not touch each other at all, meaning that the hands should simply be spread out in a natural position. *Magen Avraham* states (128:19), however, that we do not follow this opinion. Interestingly, *Ben Ish Chai* notes[13] that in the writings of Arizal there is no mention that one should hold the fingers as described by *Zohar.* On the other hand, *Maaseh Rav* (§167) quotes the Vilna Gaon as saying that a Kohen should position his fingers in accordance with *Zohar,* with no *avirim,* and not as prescribed by *Tur, Shulchan Aruch,* and other *poskim.*

Ben Ish Chai[14] writes that he asked R' Eliyahu Mani of Yerushalayim/Chevron what was the custom of the Beit El yeshivah of *mekubalim,* and he was told that although the majority of Kohanim hold their

11. This is also cited in *Mishnah Berurah* (§45).

12. *Maharil, Hilchos Nesias Kapayim,* cited in *Beis Yosef* 128:12; *Magen Avraham* 128:19; *Mishnah Berurah* §43.

13. *Tetzaveh* §14. Also noted in *Nimukei Orach Chaim* 128:12.

14. Ibid.

fingers as prescribed by *Shulchan Aruch*, a minority of Kohanim do follow the opinion of *Zohar*.[15] In contrast to the Vilna Gaon's opinion, *Kaf HaChaim* (128:80) states that even according to the opinion of *Zohar* there are five *avirim* — in each hand (ten in total), whereas according to *Shulchan Aruch* there are five *avirim* in total.

3. Potential Compromise Opinion

Chavos Yair, in *Mekor Chaim* (*Orach Chaim* 128:12), offers a compromise approach, maintaining that there is no contradiction between *Zohar* and *Shulchan Aruch*. He writes that if the fingers are not held together, but are close to one another, it is not considered a disruption of the five *avirim*. This approach is also mentioned in *Nimukei Orach Chaim* of the Minchas Elazar (128:12) — that it is possible to simultaneously adhere to the opinions of both *Shulchan Aruch* and *Zohar*, as long as the fingers are close together, even if they are not touching each other. This position still has the five *avirim* described by *Tur* and *Shulchan Aruch*, but since the fingers are not attached completely, the opinion of *Zohar* is also satisfied.

Following One's Own Mesorah

Aruch HaShulchan (128:22) advises that one should try to position his fingers exactly as described by *Tur*, *Shulchan Aruch*, and the vast majority of Rishonim and *poskim*. Similarly, *Tzitz Eliezer* (vol. 11 #6) states that since *Tur*, *Shulchan Aruch*, and the vast majority of *poskim* rule in accordance with the first opinion, that is how the Kohanim should conduct themselves. However, a Kohen who has the custom to follow *Zohar* or the Vilna Gaon is permitted to do so, provided that it is not noticeable that he is positioning his fingers differently than the other Kohanim.

Tzitz Eliezer adds that one who changes his father's custom in order to follow the custom of *Zohar* should not feel that he is fulfilling the mitzvah in a more complete fashion than those who follow *Tur* and *Shulchan Aruch*.

The diagrams on the facing page show the above customs as well as other, less common opinions of how the fingers should be positioned.

---

15. R' Ovadiah Yosef rules (*Yalkut Yosef* #50) that the opinion of *Shulchan Aruch*, with the five *avirim*, should be followed, not the opinion of *Zohar*.

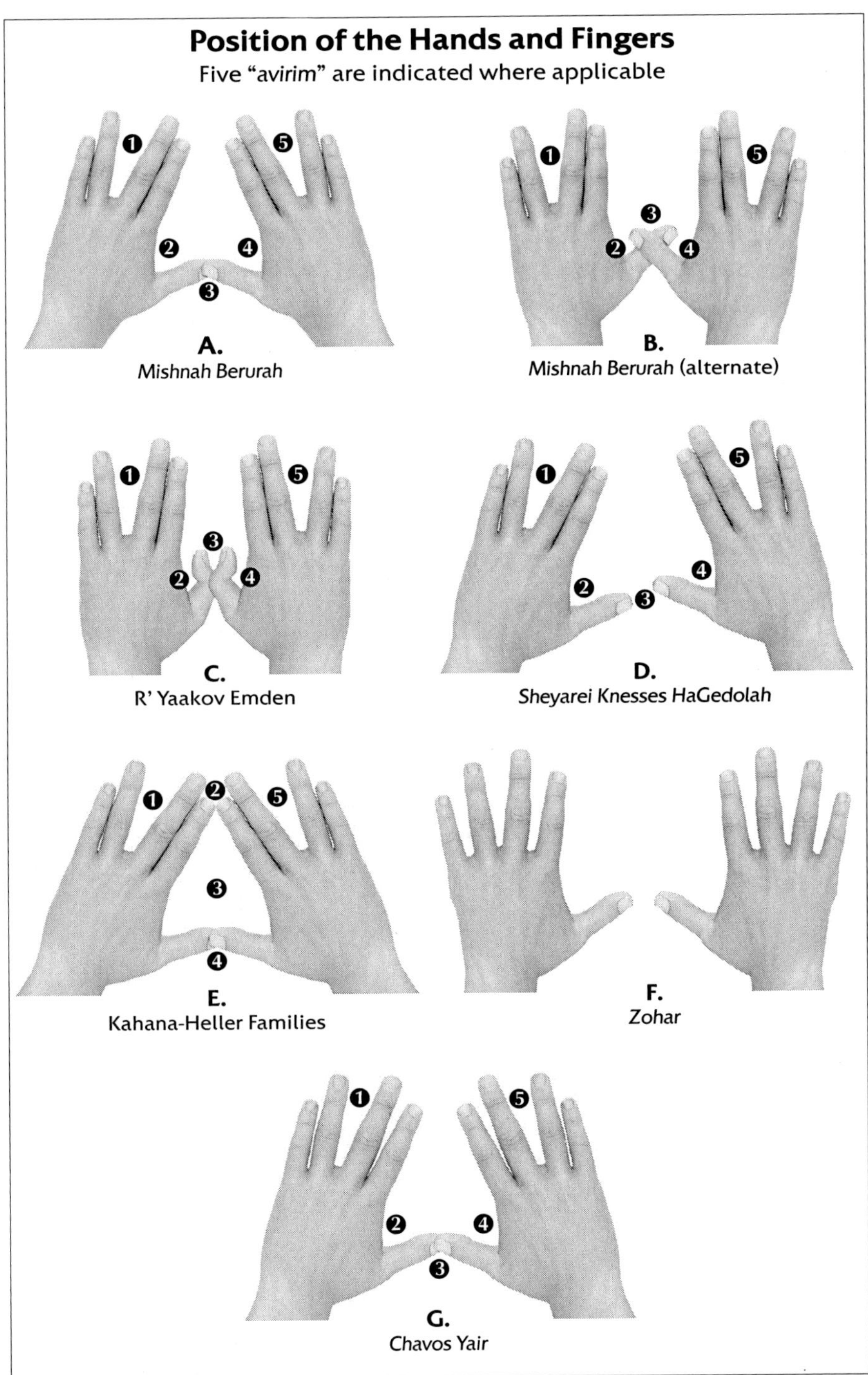
Position of the Hands and Fingers
Five "avirim" are indicated where applicable
A.
Mishnah Berurah
B.
Mishnah Berurah (alternate)
C.
R' Yaakov Emden
D.
Sheyarei Knesses HaGedolah
E.
Kahana-Heller Families
F.
Zohar
G.
Chavos Yair

Summary of Opinions

1. Opinions of the Poskim

Both Diagram A and Diagram B reflect the opinion of *Mishnah Berurah*. The difference is where the third *avir* should be.

Diagram A: The Most Common Custom

Here, the third *avir* is under the two thumbs. This custom, which is by far the most common among both Ashkenazim and Sephardim, reflects the opinion of *Maharil, Magen Avraham, Shulchan Aruch HaRav, Aruch HaShulchan,* and *Mishnah Berurah*.

Diagram B: Alternate

Some say that the aforementioned *poskim* have the third *avir* protruding outwards between the thumbs, rather than being blocked by the lack of an outward protruding *avir* between the thumbs.

Diagram C: Opinion of R' Yaakov Emden

R' Yaakov Emden[16] cites the opinion that if the tops of the thumbs are inverted and the thumbs are connected at the knuckles, there is an outward protruding *avir* between the thumbs. He points out that the two hands are still connected (conforming to *Maharil* and *Magen Avraham*, as mentioned above). This is also the opinion of R' Yaakov of Lissa, author of *Nesivos HaMishpat,* in his *sefer Derech Chaim* (*Hilchos Nesias Kapayim* 112:10) and in his *Siddur Derech Chaim* (Mussaf of *Shalosh Regalim* §10), and this view is also cited in *Kitzur Shulchan Aruch* (100:9). This opinion is followed by a number of Kohanim of German and Hungarian descent.

Diagram D: Opinion of Sheyarei Knesses HaGedolah

Sheyarei Knesses HaGedolah (on *Beis Yosef* 128:12) records that he saw that Rabbeinu Dovid HaKohen[17] did not connect his two hands (unlike the opinion of *Maharil* above). Rather, the fifth *avir* was in the space between the right and left hands, with the right

16. In his *Siddur* (*Hilchos Nesias Kapayim* #24) and in his *sefer Mor U'Ketziah* on *Tur*.

17. It is unclear who "Rabbeinu Dovid HaKohen" was. *Sheyarei Knesses HaGedolah* mentions him in one other place in *Hilchos Nesias Kapayim* as well.

hand slightly in front of the left hand. *Sheyarei Knesses HaGedolah* concludes that this is the custom one should follow.

Some Ashkenazim follow this custom and do not connect the two hands. R' Meir Aravah, a close disciple of R' Chaim Kanievsky and a Yisrael himself, writes in his *sefer Meir Oz* on *Mishnah Berurah* (128:12) that he asked R' Chaim what is the proper way for a Kohen to position his fingers during Bircas Kohanim, and R' Chaim responded that it should be done in accordance with the opinion of the *Sheyarei Knesses HaGedolah*; he also showed R' Meir how to hold that position. In a conversation with this author R' Meir added, "I noted that this is not the way that most *poskim* mention, and R' Chaim responded that this is the custom to be followed."

I also heard from the noted *posek* R' Simcha Bunim Cohen of Lakewood that before one Yom Tov, in the year 1979, he was in R' Moshe Feinstein's yeshivah, Mesivtha Tiferes Yerushalayim, and he asked R' Moshe how to perform Bircas Kohanim. R' Moshe responded by showing him to position his fingers in accordance with the opinion of the *Sheyarei Knesses HaGedolah*.

Diagram E: Opinion of the Kahana-Heller Family

Some of the descendants of the author of the *Ketzos HaChoshen* and his older brother, author of *Kuntres HaSefeikos*, have the custom to position their fingers as appears in Diagram E. They have five *avirim* as shown in the diagram, while keeping both hands connected at the thumbs and index fingers. This custom is followed by the Kahana branch of the Spinka Rebbes, who are direct descendants of the author of *Kuntres HaSefeikos* (there are several families of Spinka Rebbes; some are maternal cousins, and not all are Kohanim). Some Chabad Kohanim follow this custom as well. For more about this opinion see *She'eilos U'Teshuvos Beis Yisrael* (#18) written by R' Yisrael Landau, son-in-law of the famed R' Yeshayah of Kerestir.

2. Kabbalistic Opinion

Diagram F: Kabbalistic Opinion

In this position, which follows *Zohar* and the Vilna Gaon, the hands are simply spread out in a natural position, and the fingers of the two hands do not touch each other at all.

Diagram G: Compromise Opinion

This position, mentioned by *Chavos Yair* and others, follows the opinions of both *Shulchan Aruch* and *Zohar*: The fingers are held close together, creating the five *avirim* discussed by *Tur* and *Shulchan Aruch*, but do not touch each other, satisfying the opinion of *Zohar*.

Chapter 37
Answering Amen to Bircas Kohanim

1. The Mishnah[1] states that a chazzan should not answer amen after Bircas Kohanim because we are concerned that he may become confused. *Rashi*[2], *Rambam,*[3] and *Shulchan Aruch*[4] explain that he might forget what he was up to and call out the wrong *berachah* to the Kohanim.

2. *Midrash Rabbah*[5] states that if the chazzan is confident that he will not become confused he is permitted to answer amen to the *berachos* of the Kohanim.

3. Several Sephardic *poskim* rule that the chazzan should not answer amen even in our times, when he has a *siddur* and is less likely to become confused.[6] Many other *poskim,*[7] however, write that if the chazzan is davening from a *siddur,* we can assume that he will be able to maintain his concentration, and he is permitted to answer amen.

R' Moshe Feinstein[8] adds that answering amen to Bircas Kohanim,

1. *Berachos* 34a; cited in *Shulchan Aruch* 128:19.
2. *Berachos* ibid.
3. *Hilchos Tefillah U'Nesias Kapayim* 14:5.
4. 128:19.
5. Beginning of *Ki Savo*; cited in *Magen Avraham* (128:29) and *Pri Chadash* (128:20).
6. R' Eliezer Papo, *Chesed L'Alafim* 128:11; *Ben Ish Chai, Tetzaveh* §15; *Kaf HaChaim* 128:112.
7. *Sheyarei Knesses HaGedolah; Magen Avraham; Pri Chadash; Chayei Adam; Shulchan Aruch HaRav; Derech HaChaim* of the *Nesivos*.
8. *Igros Moshe, O.C.,* vol. 4 #21.

and thereby accepting the *berachos*, is an integral part of the mitzvah and is therefore more important than answering amen to any other *berachah*; for that reason, we are lenient in the case of a chazzan who has a *siddur. Mabit*[9] maintains that when a Yisrael answers amen to Bircas Kohanim he is fulfilling a positive commandment of the Torah; this opinion is cited by several Acharonim.[10] On the other hand, with regard to the *berachah* before Bircas Kohanim (*asher kideshanu bikedushaso shel Aharon…*), most *poskim* write that the chazzan should not answer amen. *Mishnah Berurah*[11] rules in accordance with that opinion.

4. One who is still in the middle of *Shemoneh Esrei* may not answer amen to Bircas Kohanim.[12] Even if one is davening the silent *Shemoneh Esrei* while following along with the chazzan's repetition, he should not answer amen, but should just pause and listen to Bircas Kohanim.[13] However, it is permissible to answer amen to Bircas Kohanim if one is in the middle of *Krias Shema*.[14]

---

9. *Kiryas Sefer, Hilchos Tefillah,* ch. 14.

10. *Igros Moshe* ibid. and vol. 2 #31; R' Moshe Sternbuch, *Teshuvos V'Hanhagos,* vol. 1 #117.

11. 128:71; also cited as halachah by *Kaf HaChaim* 128:112.

12. *Olas Tamid* §39; *Eliyahu Rabbah* §38; *Igros Moshe* (ibid.); *Shevet HaLevi*, vol. 3 #15; R' Chaim Kanievsky writes (Responsa #116) that this was the opinion of the Chazon Ish as well. R' Chaim also writes (#121) that if one does not pause to listen to Bircas Kohanim, he is not included in the *berachah*. See chapter 35, where we cite *Igros Moshe*'s ruling that one may not begin *Shemoneh Esrei* if he will not finish in time to hear Bircas Kohanim; he should wait until the completion of Bircas Kohanim and only then recite the silent *Shemoneh Esrei*, even if it means missing a large portion of *tefillah b'tzibbur*.

13. *Igros Moshe* 5:20; Responsa of R' Chaim Kanievsky #123.

14. Ibid., Responsa of R' Chaim Kanievsky #129.

Chapter 38
Mourners Reciting Bircas Kohanim

As we will see, there are varying customs with regard to an *avel* (mourner) performing Bircas Kohanim. The subject is not discussed at all in the Gemara, *Rambam*, or *Tur*. We will trace the halachah from its earliest sources down to the opinions of contemporary *poskim*.

1. *Shibbolei HaLeket* (*Hilchos Tefillah* §23) explains, citing Rabbeinu Yitzchak ben Yehudah (one of the *Baalei Tosafos*), that since mourners are lacking *simchah* (joy), it became customary for them not to perform Bircas Kohanim.[1] Similarly, *Mordechai* (*Megillah* §817) writes that a Kohen who is in the year of mourning for a parent should make sure to exit the shul before the Kohanim are called up to *duchan*, because if he is present at that time, he will become obligated to perform the mitzvah.

Beis Yosef (128:43) states that although Sephardic communities do not follow the custom cited by *Shibbolei HaLeket*, a mourning Kohen should nevertheless rely on this opinion during the week of *shivah* and refrain from performing Bircas Kohanim then. In that situation, he should walk out before the chazzan begins the

---

1. *Shibbolei HaLeket* (*Hilchos Tefillah* §23) also says in the name of Rabbeinu Yitzchak ben Yehudah that for the same reason, a Kohen who is not married should not perform Bircas Kohanim. However, *Shulchan Aruch* (128:44), *Rema* (ibid.), and other *poskim* write that we do not follow this custom, and any Kohen over the age of thirteen should perform Bircas Kohanim, even if he is the only Kohen present. (*Mishnah Berurah* 128:161; *Aruch HaShulchan* 128:62. See also R' Ovadiah Yosef in *Yabia Omer*, vol. 9 #108.)

berachah of *Retzei,* in order to avoid transgressing the three positive commandments for a Kohen to recite Bircas Kohanim. Similarly, *Shulchan Aruch* (128:43) rules that after *shivah* a Kohen should *duchan,* but during *shivah* he should leave the shul before the call of "Kohanim."

2. *Rema* writes (ad loc.) that a Kohen should not *duchan* for the entire period of mourning, including the twelve months of mourning that are required for the loss of a father or mother, and that is indeed the custom in Ashkenazic communities.[2]

Mishnah Berurah (§157) explains that the mourners may forego reciting Bircas Kohanim only if they were not called up to *duchan.* Thus, they must go out before the chazzan reaches the *berachah* of *Retzei,* to avoid becoming obligated to *duchan.* The reasoning for this is that refraining from *duchaning* during the mourning period is merely a custom, not an obligation, and Kohanim who are present when the call to *duchan* is issued are bound by the same obligation to *duchan* as non-mourners.[3]

Opinion That Kohanim Who Are Mourners Should Duchan Even During Shivah

3. *Radbaz*[4] maintains that a Kohen should *duchan* even during *shivah,* even if he is lacking *simchah.* He adds that the *Rashba*[5] was asked whether a Kohen who is unmarried or is otherwise not in a state of *simchah* is permitted to *duchan,* and he responded: "I have never heard of this concept from any of my teachers, nor have I seen it in the writings of any Torah sages. Perhaps there is some Midrash that says words to that effect, but I do not believe it appears anywhere in our Talmud."

R' Eliezer Papo (in his *sefer Chesed L'Alafim*[6]) and *Kaf HaChaim*[7]

---

2. As will be noted below, this is applicable in the Diaspora only. In Eretz Yisrael, the custom is for all mourners to begin to *duchan* right after *shivah.*
3. See *Shulchan Aruch* 128:43; *Taz* §26; *Biur HaGra* §79; *Biur Halachah* s.v. *Yeitzei;* and *Siddur R' Yaakov Emden, Hilchos Bircas Kohanim* §4.
4. *Teshuvos,* vol. 1 #1, and vol. 4 #128.
5. *Teshuvos,* vol. 1 #85.
6. 128:18.
7. 128:262. *Kaf HaChaim* quotes several Kabbalistic sources that indicate that Bircas Kohanim should be performed even by mourners.

are among those who rule that Kohanim should perform Bircas Kohanim even during *shivah*.

R' Yihya Saleh (1713-1805), known as *Maharitz*, was a revered Yemenite *posek*. In his commentary on the *siddur* (*Hilchos Shemoneh Esrei*), he expounds in several places about the importance of performing Bircas Kohanim every day. He also writes that this has been the Yemenite custom for many generations, even in a house of mourning. Moreover, he adds, if the mourners themselves are Kohanim, they should *duchan* as well, even during *shivah*. *Maharitz* concludes with the words of *Pri Chadash* (*se'if* 43) that the opinion that a mourner does not *duchan* has no explanation and is totally unfounded.

Maharil Diskin[8] writes that we should take into consideration that Shlomo HaMelech was the one who instituted that Bircas Kohanim be performed every day during davening, as *Kol Bo* informs us. Therefore, we should not take the matter lightly, and Kohanim should *duchan* even during *shivah*.

Members of the large, extended Kopshitz family of Kohanim follow the opinion that a Kohen who is a mourner is permitted to *duchan* even during *shivah*. This was confirmed to the author by R' Nosson Kopshitz, who is a noted rav in Beit Shemesh; he relates that he did so himself when he was sitting *shivah*. Furthermore, he reported that his father, R' Tzvi Kopshitz, also performed Bircas Kohanim when he was an *avel*, and his father said that in Eretz Yisrael we follow the ruling of *Maharil Diskin*. R' Nosson Kopshitz added that when his brother passed away, he *duchaned* together with his brother's sons in the *shivah* house. There were more than ten Kohanim sitting *shivah*, and they all performed Bircas Kohanim. *Gesher HaChaim*[9] quotes several additional sources for this custom and concludes that it is the *minhag* of several distinguished families in Yerushalayim. (This is not the general practice, however; see #7 below.)

4. Kohanim who perform Bircas Kohanim during *shivah* are permitted to do so even while wearing the clothing that was torn for *kriah*.[10]

---

8. *Teshuvos Maharil Diskin*, *Kuntres Acharon* #199.
9. Written by R' Yechiel Michel Tukachinsky; vol. 1, ch. 20.
10. R' Yisrael Yaakov Fisher, *Teshuvos Even Yisrael*, vol. 8 #10.

Difference Between Communities in Eretz Yisrael and Abroad

5. While the aforementioned *Rema* states that a Kohen should not *duchan* for the entire period of mourning (twelve months after the loss of a parent and thirty days after the loss of any other immediate relative), the *poskim* note that this is applicable only in Ashkenazic communities in the Diaspora, where Bircas Kohanim is performed only on Yom Tov. In Eretz Yisrael and in Sephardic communities worldwide, where Bircas Kohanim is performed every day, Kohanim resume *duchaning* immediately after *shivah*.[11]

Orchos Rabbeinu[12] offers this insight from the Chazon Ish: The *Rema* was discussing the Diaspora, where Bircas Kohanim is performed only on the Festivals. Since it is such a rare mitzvah, it generates great *simchah*, which is not appropriate for those in the year of mourning. However, in Eretz Yisrael, where Bircas Kohanim is an everyday occurrence, Kohanim may recite it immediately after *shivah*.

6. If a mourning Kohen from abroad travels to Eretz Yisrael after *shivah*, he should perform Bircas Kohanim while in Eretz Yisrael, even if he does not perform Bircas Kohanim during the Festivals at home.[13]

The Prevalent Opinion: Mourning Kohanim Do Not Duchan During Shivah

7. In most communities in Eretz Yisrael and in Sephardic communities throughout the world, who perform Bircas Kohanim on a daily basis, a Kohen does not *duchan* during *shivah* (following the opinion of *Shulchan Aruch*). However, as *Shaarei Teshuvah* states,[14]

---

11. *Gesher HaChaim* (ibid.); Klausenberger Rebbe, *Teshuvos Divrei Yatziv,* vol. 1 #71; R' Shmuel Wosner, *Teshuvos Shevet HaLevi*, vol. 1 #43. R' Moshe Sternbuch (*Teshuvos V'Hanhagos,* vol. 3 #49) also writes that the Ashkenazic custom in Eretz Yisrael is that a mourning Kohen performs Bircas Kohanim after *shivah*.
12. Vol. 3, p. 212.
13. Heard from R' Chaim Kanievsky.
14. *O.C.*, 121:2.

the custom in these communities is that other Kohanim, who are not *aveilim*, do perform Bircas Kohanim in the *shivah* house.

8. *Orchos Rabbeinu*[15] relates that the Chazon Ish held that Bircas Kohanim should be performed in a *shivah* house, but only by other Kohanim, not the mourners themselves.[16] He adds that when the mother of the Chazon Ish, Rebbetzin Leah Karelitz, passed away, the Ponovezher Rav, R' Yosef Shlomo HaKohen Kahaneman, attended the Shacharis minyan in the *shivah* house in Bnei Brak, and the Chazon Ish told him to *duchan*.

9. Similarly, *Ben Ish Chai* writes:[17]

> If a Kohen is in shul during his week of *shivah*, he should step out before the Kohanim are called to *duchan*. After *shivah*, however, he is permitted to *duchan*. Others are of the opinion that he may *duchan* even during *shivah*, and he will be blessed for doing so. The custom in Yerushalayim is for Bircas Kohanim to be performed even in a *shivah* house, and that is the custom I have instituted here, in Baghdad, as well. However, it should be performed only by other Kohanim, not the mourners themselves. Thus, the mourners should go to another room before the chazzan begins *Retzei*.

R' Ovadiah Yosef[18] also maintains that other Kohanim (but not the mourners) should perform Bircas Kohanim in a house of mourning.

10. Likewise, *Gesher HaChaim*[19] writes that the custom of Ashkenazim in Eretz Yisrael is for mourners to perform Bircas Kohanim, except during the week of *shivah*. Even then, other Kohanim who are not mourning do *duchan* in the *shivah* house, and the mourners walk out before *Retzei*.

---

15. Vol. 3, p. 212.
16. See also Responsa of R' Chaim Kanievsky #411.
17. *Tetzaveh* §22.
18. *Yabia Omer, Yoreh Deah,* vol. 4 #32.
19. Vol. 1, ch. 20. This is also cited in *Ketzos HaShulchan, siman* 23, authored by R' Avraham Chaim Na'eh.

Kohanim Duchaning on Shabbos During Shivah

11. With regard to a mourner performing Bircas Kohanim on Shabbos during *shivah, Pri Chadash* states (128:43): "In my opinion, a Kohen who is a mourner should *duchan,* so as to fulfill the three commandments, and he will be blessed for it, because there is no reason for this custom of not performing Bircas Kohanim when in mourning, and it has no basis in halachah."

Sephardic communities follow this ruling, that Kohanim during *shivah* should *duchan* on Shabbos, as R' Ovadiah Yosef writes[20] that to refrain from performing Bircas Kohanim on Shabbos is a public display of mourning (*"aveilus b'farhesia"*).[21] Therefore, a mourner during *shivah* is permitted to *duchan* on Shabbos even if there are other Kohanim present.

12. Similarly, *Netziv*[22] writes that in Eretz Yisrael, where Bircas Kohanim is performed every day, a mourner during the week of *shivah* should *duchan* on Shabbos and Yom Tov; otherwise, it would be a public display of mourning, which is not permitted on Shabbos.[23] Outside of Eretz Yisrael, on the other hand, where Bircas Kohanim is performed only on Yom Tov, it is not so noticeable if a Kohen skips Bircas Kohanim.

13. Although a mourner is obligated in all mitzvos, and that includes Bircas Kohanim, *Mishnah Berurah* (128:157) states that he should *not* perform Bircas Kohanim during *shivah,* even on Shabbos and even if there is no other Kohen available; accordingly, he should leave the shul before *Retzei.*[24]

---

20. *Yabia Omer, Yoreh Deah,* vol. 4 #32; R' Shlomo HaKohen of Vilna, in *Teshuvos Binyan Shlomo* (#10), writes that one may rely on *Pri Chadash* and ascend to the *duchan* on Shabbos.

21. The laws prohibiting a public display of mourning on Shabbos are found in *Yoreh Deah* 393:3.

22. *Teshuvos Meishiv Davar,* vol. 1 #47.

23. See the opinion of R' Ovadiah Yosef in *Yabia Omer,* below, regarding the issue of a public display of mourning as it pertains to Bircas Kohanim.

24. *Mishnah Berurah* adds that if the Kohen did *not* leave before *Retzei,* he is required to *duchan.*

14. On Shabbos in Eretz Yisrael, if a mourner is the only Kohen present, *Aruch HaShulchan*[25] rules that he is required to *duchan* even if he was not called upon to do so. As mentioned in the previous paragraph, *Mishnah Berurah* disagrees.

When a Mourner Is the Only Kohen Present

15. Although *Rema* rules that a mourner does not perform Bircas Kohanim during the entire mourning period, *Mishnah Berurah*[26] states that after the *shivah* he **should** *duchan* if he is the only Kohen available, or if there is only one other Kohen besides him. This applies even in the Diaspora.

Mishnah Berurah bases this on *She'eilos U'Teshuvos Knesses Yechezkel*[27] (#12),[28] which is cited by *Ba'er Heitev, Nesivos* (in his *sefer Derech HaChaim*), and R' Akiva Eiger.[29]

The Elokeinu V'Elokei Avoseinu Prayer

16. With regard to reciting the *Elokeinu V'Elokei Avoseinu* prayer in a house of mourning, there is a difference between those who live in Eretz Yisrael and those (Ashkenazim) who live abroad. Since Ashkenazim in the Diaspora do not perform Bircas Kohanim on a daily basis, the *Elokeinu V'Elokei Avoseinu* prayer is not recited in a house of mourning.[30] In Eretz Yisrael and in Sephardic communities, however, where Bircas Kohanim is performed every day, and, according to many opinions, even in a house of mourning (see above), the prayer is recited if Bircas Kohanim is omitted.[31]

---

25. 128:61.
26. 128:159.
27. Written by R' Yechezkel Katzenellenbogen (1670-1749), who was a rav in Altona, Germany.
28. R' Chaim Kanievsky notes, in his responsa (#416), that *Mishnah Berurah* diverges from *Knesses Yechezkel*, who says that a mourner may *duchan* if he is the *only* Kohen present. *Mishnah Berurah*, on the other hand, rules that he may *duchan* even if there is one other Kohen present, so that the mitzvah can be performed by two Kohanim.
29. See *Shaar HaTziyun* §127.
30. *Mishnah Berurah* 121:3.
31. See *Shaarei Teshuvah* 121:1; the aforementioned *Orchos Rabbeinu*, citing Chazon Ish; *Gesher HaChaim*; *Ketzos HaShulchan* (ibid.); Responsa of R' Chaim Kanievsky #542.

Bircas Kohanim on Rosh Hashanah and Yom Kippur

17. According to some authorities, even Kohanim in the Diaspora who follow the custom of not performing Bircas Kohanim while in the period of mourning should *duchan* on Rosh Hashanah and Yom Kippur.

R' Moshe Sternbuch[32] writes that mourners who reside outside Eretz Yisrael and follow the custom of not performing Bircas Kohanim on Yom Tov should make an exception for Rosh Hashanah and Yom Kippur. The reason is that these are days of judgment, and, unlike the Festivals, they are not days of complete joy. He adds that when he was the rav of Johannesburg, South Africa, he instituted that Kohanim who are mourners should perform Bircas Kohanim on Rosh Hashanah and Yom Kippur.

R' Yisrael Yaakov Fisher[33] agrees with the ruling of R' Moshe Sternbuch, but not with his reasoning, for it can be proven that Rosh Hashanah and Yom Kippur *are* days of joy. Rather, mourners should perform Bircas Kohanim on Rosh Hashanah and Yom Kippur specifically because these are exalted days, and the Jewish people are in great need of the blessing that comes through these *berachos*.

Custom for Mourners to Follow Shulchan Aruch

18. *Shulchan HaTahor*,[34] by the Komarna Rav, states that even outside Eretz Yisrael the mourner **should** *duchan* after *shivah*, as we do not follow the opinion of *Rema* with regard to this halachah. This was also the custom in the city of Munkacz.[35]

32. *Teshuvos V'Hanhagos*, vol. 3 #49.
33. *Halichos Even Yisrael*, vol. 2, ch. 6.
34. 128:25.
35. *Darchei Chaim V'Shalom*, p. 126.

Chapter 39
Nullifying Bad Dreams

1. The Gemara (*Berachos* 55b) states that if a person had an unsettling dream and is unsure of its meaning, he should say the *Ribbono Shel Olam* prayer during Bircas Kohanim. (This prayer appears in the *siddur* and can be found in chapter 51.) It is clear, however, from the words of the Midrash[1] in several places that Bircas Kohanim has the capacity to alter the effect of frightening dreams on its own, even if one does not recite the prayer.

2. *Tosafos*[2] explain that the reason this prayer may be said in the middle of Bircas Kohanim is that a person who experiences such a dream may potentially be in danger if the dream is not nullified. *Tosafos* add that for the same reason, one who has a frightening dream is permitted to fast a *taanis chalom* even on Shabbos if he wishes.

3. Chazon Ish held that in our times[3] one should not fast a *taanis chalom* on Shabbos but should instead recite the *Ribbono Shel Olam* prayer during Bircas Kohanim. He maintained that many of our dreams do not presage anything, but are merely the product of the emotional stresses that occupied one's mind throughout the day.[4]

---

1. *Bamidbar Rabbah* 11:3. See also *Tanchuma, Nasso* §9, and *Shir HaShirim Rabbah* §3. The full wording of the Midrash is quoted in chapter 3.
2. *Sotah* 40a.
3. See *Igros Chazon Ish,* vol. 2 #149; *Orchos Rabbeinu,* vol. 3, p. 213; *Maaseh Ish,* vol. 1, p. 160.
4. This is comparable to *Mishnah Berurah*'s statement (*Shaar HaTziyun* 220:1),

The relative of a woman who experienced an ominous dream asked the Chazon Ish if the woman should follow the advice given in *Siddur Yaavetz,* that one should fast even if it is Shabbos. The Chazon Ish responded, "I myself have had such dreams numerous times, and I pay no attention to them. The correct thing to do is to recite the *Ribbono Shel Olam* prayer during Bircas Kohanim." [5]

4. *Beis Yosef*[6] explains that since Bircas Kohanim has the power to ameliorate foreboding dreams, reciting the *Ribbono Shel Olam* prayer is not considered a prohibited distraction.[7] He adds, citing *Maharil,*[8] that to the contrary, when one recites the prayer he demonstrates an appreciation of the enormous blessing within Bircas Kohanim — that it even has the capacity to ward off potential danger.[9]

5. The chazzan is not permitted to recite the *Ribbono Shel Olam* prayer, as it is considered an unwarranted interruption.[10] Likewise, if a Kohen had a distressing dream, he may not say this prayer; however, his dream becomes nullified without the prayer, simply by his performing Bircas Kohanim.[11]

6. The reason we pray at this time to nullify dreams is explained in *Zohar*[12] as follows: "Whoever is distressed by his dream should come when the Kohanim are raising their hands and say the *Ribbono Shel Olam* prayer. What is the reason? It is because Mercy prevails in all the worlds at that time. Whoever prays due to his distress, Judgment will turn into Mercy for him."

---

citing several Rishonim, that if one is in distress and then experienced a disturbing dream, we can assume that the dream was caused by his distress.

5. *Igros Chazon Ish* ibid.; R' Yosef Shalom Elyashiv ruled that one should follow the opinion of Chazon Ish and say the *Ribbono Shel Olam* during Bircas Kohanim but not fast on Shabbos. See *Tziyunei Halachah,* p. 433.

6. 130:1.

7. The Gemara (*Sotah* 40a) states that it is offensive for someone to be distracted during Bircas Kohanim, as it shows a lack of appreciation for Hashem's blessing.

8. *Teshuvos* #148.

9. In chapter 3, we quoted *Toras Chaim*'s statement (which is also cited in *Noam Elimelech*) that since the Gemara (*Berachos* 57b) states that a dream contains a sixtieth of prophecy, the sixty powerful letters of Bircas Kohanim nullify the foreboding "prophecy" within the dream through the principle of *bittul b'shishim* (i.e., if one of the ingredients in a mixture is only one-sixtieth of the entire mixture, it is considered to be nullified).

10. *Rema* 128:45; *Mishnah Berurah* §173.

11. See Responsa of R' Chaim Kanievsky #372.

12. *Nasso,* p. 147b.

Similarly, *Tosafos* (*Sotah* 39b) state that the reason one says this prayer during Bircas Kohanim is that it is an *eis ratzon* — a time of Divine favor.

7. *Taz* and *Magen Avraham*[13] both write that the *Ribbono Shel Olam* prayer should not be said daily, but only on Yamim Tovim, or by an individual who experienced a disturbing dream the night before.

8. *Pri Chadash* and *Pri Megadim*[14] both explain that we see from *Tosafos* (cited above) that it is permissible to recite *Ribbono Shel Olam* during Bircas Kohanim only because of the danger associated with foreboding dreams. If one did not have such a dream, it is better to listen to Bircas Kohanim silently and not recite this prayer at all.

Mishnah Berurah notes,[15] however, that although some people may not recall having had any bad dreams since the last time they heard Bircas Kohanim, on Yom Tov everyone may nevertheless say this prayer (which begins, "I have dreamed a dream") because it is presumed that one did, in fact, have some disturbing dreams since the last Yom Tov, but he forgot them. *Mishnah Berurah*[16] adds that if one said the prayer on the first day of Yom Tov, he should not say the words "I have dreamed a dream" on the second day, unless he actually had a disturbing dream the night before.

9. In most Ashkenazic communities outside Eretz Yisrael, where Bircas Kohanim is performed only on Yom Tov, the custom is for the Kohanim to sing a wordless tune before saying the last word of each verse, so that the congregants will have time to recite the *Ribbono Shel Olam* prayer.[17]

10. Generally, the congregants recite *Ribbono Shel Olam* before the Kohanim say the words *v'yishmerecha* and *viychuneka* at the end of the first two verses. While the Kohanim are singing the end of the third verse, before the word *shalom*, many have the custom to recite the *Yehi Ratzon* prayer that appears in the *siddur*.[18]

---

13. 130:1.
14. Ibid.
15. 130:1.
16. *Biur Halachah* 130:1, following the opinion of *Machatzis HaShekel*.
17. *Rema* 128:45.
18. While the *Ribbono Shel Olam* prayer appears in the Gemara, the *Yehi Ratzon* does not. It is found in the *siddur Shaarei Tzion*, authored by R' Nosson ben R'

11. *Mishnah Berurah*[19] states that the custom of the Vilna Gaon was to recite *Ribbono Shel Olam* all three times, and not to recite the *Yehi Ratzon* prayer at all. *Mishnah Berurah*[20] maintains that it is preferable to do as the Vilna Gaon did, because the *Yehi Ratzon* prayer is lengthier than *Ribbono Shel Olam*, and it is better if the Kohanim do not take such a long break before completing their *berachah*.

12. When the Kohanim sing before the end of each verse, they should all sing the same tune; if they sing more than one tune, some Kohanim may become confused and forget which word they were up to.[21] *Mishnah Berurah*[22] explains that even though the chazzan calls out each word before the Kohanim, there is still a risk of confusion if the Kohanim sing multiple tunes.

13. When Yom Tov falls on Shabbos, *Ribbono Shel Olam* is not recited, unless one experienced a distressing dream, in which case that individual is permitted to recite the prayer.[23] The same applies when Yom Kippur falls on Shabbos.[24]

14. Unlike the Vilna Gaon, who recited *Ribbono Shel Olam* at the end of all three *berachos*, *Kaf HaChaim*[25] states that according to *Arizal*,[26] *Ribbono Shel Olam* should be recited only one time — and that one time should be before the last word of the final verse (*"shalom"*).

Moshe Hannover (1610-1683), a Polish-born disciple of *Maharsha*. *Shaarei Tzion* was published in Prague in the year 1662. Several years before the publication of his *siddur*, R' Nosson went to Italy to study Kabbalah from R' Chaim HaKohen of Syria, one of the closest disciples of R' Chaim Vital, who traveled to Italy at that time to publish his *sefarim*. (See the complete prayers with translation in chapter 51.)

19. 130:5.

20. 65:4.

21. *Shulchan Aruch* 128:21; based on *Terumas HaDeshen* §26.

22. §82.

23. *Eliyahu Rabbah* 130:10; cited in *Mishnah Berurah* (130:4) as the halachah. Interestingly, the custom in Volozhin was to recite the *Ribbono Shel Olam* prayer during Bircas Kohanim even when Yom Tov fell on Shabbos; see the *Netziv's Meishiv Davar*, vol. 1 #47. *Leket HaKemach HeChadash* (128:207) relates that this was the custom of the chassidim in Belz as well.

24. *Igros Moshe, O.C.*, vol. 3 #18.

25. 130:1.

26. *Shaar HaKavanos*, p. 51. See also *Pri Eitz Chaim, Shaar Chazaras Amidah,* ch. 10.

The custom of Chabad is to recite *Ribbono Shel Olam* one time, dividing it between the verses of Bircas Kohanim: Approximately one-third of the *Ribbono Shel Olam* prayer is said before the ending of each of the three verses, and the prayer is completed before the Kohanim end with the word *"shalom."*[27] This is also the custom cited in *Shulchan HaTahor* of Komarna.[28]

15. In Eretz Yisrael and in Sephardic communities worldwide, where Bircas Kohanim is performed every day, in most congregations the Kohanim do not sing to make time for people to recite *Ribbono Shel Olam,* even on Yom Tov. The prayer is not recited by the whole congregation, but only by an individual who experienced a disturbing dream the night before.[29] This was the custom of the Chazon Ish and remains the custom of the Lederman shul.[30]

Some have the custom that on Yom Tov, the Kohanim sing only at the end of the last verse (before the word *shalom*).[31]

16. If one is in Eretz Yisrael, where *Ribbono Shel Olam* is not recited by the congregation, and he has a disturbing dream, he may recite the prayer while listening to the Kohanim *duchan.*[32] If

---

27. See *sefer Hayom Yom* (section on Shavuos) written by the Lubavitcher Rebbe R' Menachem Mendel Schneerson, who compiled the customs of Chabad that he heard from his father-in-law, R' Yosef Yitzchak Schneerson.
28. 130:4.
29. See *Ihr HaKodesh V'HaMikdash* by R' Yechiel Michel Tukachinsky, vol. 3 #25.
30. See *Orchos Rabbeinu,* vol. 1, p. 67. This is also the custom of the Ponovezh and Chachmei Lublin yeshivos in Bnei Brak, and many chassidic communities in Eretz Yisrael, including Ger. Although most chassidim who reside outside of Eretz Yisrael do sing during Bircas Kohanim to allow time for *Ribbono Shel Olam,* Ger and Munkacz do not recite the *Ribbono Shel Olam* or *Yehi Ratzon* prayers; see *Darchei Chaim V'Shalom* §186.
31. This is the custom of the yeshivos of Mir, Slabodka, and Chevron, and several other chassidic communities in Eretz Yisrael. Interestingly, when R' Aharon of Belz moved to Eretz Yisrael, the Belz Chassidus adopted the custom of Eretz Yisrael of no singing at all during Bircas Kohanim. Several years before the publication of this book, a delegation of Kohanim from outside Eretz Yisrael approached the current Belzer Rebbe and told him that many of the chassidim who come to spend Yom Tov with the Rebbe in Yerushalayim feel they are missing out on the chance to recite the *Ribbono Shel Olam* prayer. After serious consideration, the Belzer Rebbe agreed to accommodate them, and since then, the Kohanim sing three times during Bircas Kohanim while some of the congregants recite *Ribbono Shel Olam* and *Yehi Ratzon,* as is done in other parts of the world.
32. *Beis Yosef* cited above.

he finds it difficult to say the prayer and listen at the same time, he can say an abridged version of *Ribbono Shel Olam* or simply have in mind that his dream should be nullified.[33] Others advise that he should recite *Ribbono Shel Olam* immediately after the conclusion of Bircas Kohanim.[34]

17. If a woman has a disturbing dream and wishes to nullify it, she should attend Bircas Kohanim herself to say *Ribbono Shel Olam*. It is not adequate for her husband to recite the prayer on her behalf.[35]

33. Responsa of R' Chaim Kanievsky #369, 370.

34. This was the practice of *Chasam Sofer*; see *sefer Chut HaMeshulash*, p. 143, *Shiurei R' Yosef Shalom Elyashiv, Berachos* 55b; *Tziyunei Halachah*, p. 432.

35. *Igros Chazon Ish*, vol. 2 #149; R' Yosef Shalom Elyashiv, *Tziyunei Halachah*, p. 434; Responsa of R' Chaim Kanievsky #376.

Chapter 40
Varying Customs on Yom Tov and Simchas Torah

Although in Eretz Yisrael it is, and always has been, the custom of Ashkenazim *and* Sephardim to perform Bircas Kohanim on a daily basis, Ashkenazic congregations in the Diaspora are forbidden to perform Bircas Kohanim at any time other than during Mussaf of the Yamim Tovim.[1] Certain communities, however, do perform Bircas Kohanim on some additional festive occasions, as we will explain.

Communities of German Descent ("Yekkes")

The practice of German communities differs from the custom specified by *Rema*, who writes (128:44) that Bircas Kohanim is performed on the Festivals only during Mussaf and not during Shacharis.

The German custom is to perform Bircas Kohanim during both Shacharis and Mussaf of every Yom Tov and three times on Yom Kippur (during Shacharis, Mussaf, and Neilah). As opposed to most Ashkenazic congregations in the Diaspora, which fulfill the mitzvah only thirteen times a year,[2] those who daven in a *Yekkishe*

1. On Simchas Torah, most Ashkenazic communities outside Eretz Yisrael perform Bircas Kohanim during Shacharis rather than Mussaf; see below.
2. On the two days of Rosh Hashanah, one day of Yom Kippur, the first two days of Succos, Shemini Atzeres and Simchas Torah, the first two and last two days

shul, such as Khal Adas Yeshurun (KAJ) in New York's Washington Heights neighborhood, merit hearing Bircas Kohanim twenty-seven times over the course of the year.

The following sources all indicate that the accepted custom throughout Germany, for many centuries, has been to *duchan* on Yom Tov not only during Mussaf, but during Shacharis as well:

- ❒ Maharam of Rothenburg (*Minhagei Maharam, Hilchos Bircas Kohanim*): "Our custom is to go up to *duchan* every Yom Tov during Shacharis and Mussaf, and, on Yom Kippur during Neilah as well."
- ❒ *Minhagei Maharil*[3] (*Hilchos Yom Tov*): "On all Yamim Tovim, the Kohanim go to *duchan* during Shacharis just as they do during Mussaf. I later saw that the custom in other countries is to *duchan* only during Mussaf, and I do not at all understand how such a custom came about."
- ❒ *Sefer HaMinhagim* of R' Yitzchak Isaac Tirna[4] states (*Hilchos Rosh Hashanah* and *Hilchos Pesach*) that Bircas Kohanim is performed on Yom Tov during Shacharis and Mussaf.[5]
- ❒ R' Yair Chaim Bachrach, known as the Chavos Yair (1639-1702), was the rav in several German communities. In *Mekor Chaim* (*Orach Chaim* 128:6) he describes how the handwashing procedure before Bircas Kohanim was done in Germany, and writes: "Before each Bircas Kohanim, during **Shacharis and Mussaf....**" Additionally, *Mekor Chaim* states (128:44): "The custom in many places is to *duchan* on Yom Tov only during Mussaf (with the exception of Simchas Torah), and that is what is done in Prague.

---

of Pesach, and on the two days of Shavuos. See below regarding the various customs that are followed on Simchas Torah.

3. See chapter 14. *Maharil* is the source cited in *Beis Yosef* for the Ashkenazic custom to perform Bircas Kohanim only on Yamim Tovim.

4. R' Yitzchak Isaac Tirna passed away in 1425. He was a contemporary of *Maharil*, and frequently corresponded with him, as both of them studied under R' Avraham Klausner, whose *Sefer HaMinhagim* is cited many times by *Rema*. This *Sefer HaMinhagim* states clearly that Bircas Kohanim is performed on Yom Kippur during Shacharis, Mussaf, and Neilah.

5. See citation below from *Sefer HaMinhagim*, that on Simchas Torah, Bircas Kohanim should be performed only during Shacharis, since an atmosphere of levity might reign during Mussaf of that day.

However, our practice is to *duchan* during Shacharis as well as Mussaf, and that is the custom of Germany."

- ❒ *Sefer Minhagim d'Kehillah Kedoshah Vermaiza* (Worms; *Hilchos* Shacharis of Yom Tov §48)[6]: "Bircas Kohanim is performed at the conclusion of Shacharis and during Mussaf, even when Yom Tov falls on Shabbos."
- ❒ *Sefer Minhagei Kehillah Kedoshah Magence* (Mainz; p. 7):[7] "The Kohanim go up to *duchan* during Shacharis and Mussaf of Rosh Hashanah, Yom Kippur, and all Festivals, even when Yom Tov falls on Shabbos. On Yom Kippur they *duchan* during Neilah as well, if there is sufficient time."
- ❒ *Noheg Katzon Yosef* (*Hilchos Yom Tov* §6):[8] "In the city of Frankfurt, Bircas Kohanim is performed even when Yom Tov falls on Shabbos, and the Kohanim go up to *duchan* during Shacharis and Mussaf."

Yom Kippur

1. As discussed in chapter 14, Bircas Kohanim is performed by Ashkenazim in Eretz Yisrael, and by Sephardim throughout the world, three times on Yom Kippur — in Shacharis, Mussaf, and Neilah (provided that the congregation reaches Bircas Kohanim before nightfall). In *Hilchos Nesias Kapayim* (128:44), *Rema* writes that the custom of some Ashkenazic communities (in the Diaspora) is to recite Bircas Kohanim on Yom Kippur during Shacharis and Neilah in addition to Mussaf. Later, however, in the halachos of Yom Kippur (623:5), *Rema* writes that the accepted custom is not to perform Bircas Kohanim during Neilah. *Mishnah Berurah* (623:9) explains that the custom evolved because Neilah frequently ends after nightfall, and Bircas Kohanim must take place during the day.[9]

2. In Lithuanian and yeshivah communities outside Eretz Yisrael, Bircas Kohanim is recited on Yom Kippur only during Mussaf,

---

6. Written by R' Yosef HaLevi Manzpach (also known as R' Yuspa Shamash), 1604-1678.

7. Published in 1862.

8. Authored by R' Yosef ben Moshe HaLevi Kushman; published in 1718.

9. In chapter 41, we note that some *poskim* allow Bircas Kohanim to be recited (*b'dieved*) until 13.5 minutes after sunset. Other *poskim* maintain that it must be done before sunset.

and in some chassidic communities, it is recited during Shacharis in addition to Mussaf.

3. The *Rosh* (*Yoma* 87a) writes that *minhag Ashkenaz* is to perform Bircas Kohanim during Neilah and not during Minchah. (The *Rosh* is stressing that Bircas Kohanim is performed during Neilah instead of Minchah; he therefore does not mention Bircas Kohanim at Shacharis.) In this vein, *Shulchan HaTahor* of Komarna states:[10] "On Yom Kippur, Bircas Kohanim is performed during Shacharis, Mussaf, and Neilah. One should not deviate from this custom, for it is the Ashkenazic custom of our ancestors, going back many generations."

4. Minchas Elazar of Munkacz writes:[11] "We follow the custom of my great-grandfather, R' Tzvi Elimelech Spira of Dinov, author of *Bnei Yissaschar.*[12] Even though he greatly cherished the mitzvah of Bircas Kohanim ... his congregation would perform it only during Shacharis and Mussaf of Yom Kippur, and not during Neilah. Instead, the chazzan would just recite the *Elokeinu V'Elokei Avoseinu* prayer, since it was already past nightfall by the time they reached the end of Neilah."[13]

We may infer from this that strictly speaking, it was the custom of the Bnei Yissaschar to *duchan* during Neilah; however, it was never feasible to do so in practice, since Neilah always extended until after sunset. Thus, they performed Bircas Kohanim only during Shacharis and Mussaf.

5. Although the Chasam Sofer did not follow the custom of his rebbi, R' Nosson Adler of Frankfurt, Germany, who performed Bircas Kohanim every day,[14] nor the general custom of his hometown of Frankfurt, where Bircas Kohanim was performed on Yom Tov during Shacharis as well as Mussaf, he did institute in his city, Pressburg (and its yeshivah), that Bircas Kohanim be performed on

---

10. 129:2. See also 128:26, where he writes that Bircas Kohanim should be performed three times on Yom Kippur even if Yom Kippur falls on Shabbos.
11. *Nimukei Orach Chaim* 623:5.
12. 1783-1841. He was a nephew of R' Elimelech of Lizhensk, and his *sefer* was called *Bnei Yissaschar* because he was told by his Rebbe, the Chozeh of Lublin, that he descended from the tribe of Yissachar.
13. See also *Darchei Chaim V'Shalom* of Munkacz §180. This custom is continued today in Munkacz congregations outside Eretz Yisrael.
14. See chapter 14.

Yom Kippur during both Shacharis and Mussaf.[15] (Until the Chasam Sofer made this change, the custom there was to perform Bircas Kohanim only during Mussaf.)

Hoshana Rabbah

To this day, Satmar,[16] Munkacz, and Komarna communities around the world (among other chassidic communities) perform Bircas Kohanim during Mussaf of Hoshana Rabbah. Minchas Elazar[17] states that this was the custom of his great-grandfather, the Bnei Yissaschar. *Ateres Paz* on Bircas Kohanim[18] lists several chassidic Rebbes who had Bircas Kohanim performed in their minyan on Hoshana Rabbah. He writes that since a Yom Tov atmosphere prevailed in those minyanim during Mussaf, Bircas Kohanim was performed as on other Yamim Tovim.

Simchas Torah

In Eretz Yisrael, the custom in all communities is to *duchan* on Shemini Atzeres/Simchas Torah during Shacharis and Mussaf, with no exceptions.[19]

For those who reside outside Eretz Yisrael, *Machzor Vitri*,[20] in specifying the order of davening on Simchas Torah, notes that Bircas Kohanim is performed during Mussaf of Simchas Torah (in addition to Shacharis, see footnote[21]). However, *Sefer HaMinhagim* of R' Yitzchok Isaac Tirna[22] states that the Kohanim *duchan* only during Shacharis. He explains that they refrain from performing Bircas Kohanim during Mussaf because the congregants are in a lightheaded state of mind, and in their levity they throw items

15. *Minhagei Chasam Sofer*, ch. 7.
16. This practice was instituted by Rabbeinu Yoel of Satmar on Hoshana Rabbah of the year 1932/5693. See *Yemei HaMelech*, ch. 8.
17. *Nimukei Orach Chaim* 623:5. See also *Darchei Chaim V' Shalom* of Munkacz §180.
18. §107; written by R' Pinchos HaKohen Schwartz in 1928.
19. See R' Yechiel Michel Tukachinsky, *Ir HaKodesh*, vol. 3, ch. 25. He adds that the Kohanim are cautioned not to become intoxicated.
20. *Seder Succos V'Shemini Atzeres* §423.
21. See chapter 15, where we note that at the time of the publication of *Machzor Vitri*, Bircas Kohanim was still performed daily even in the Diaspora.
22. *Hilchos Shemini Atzeres*.

across the shul. *Levush*[23] adds that Bircas Kohanim is not recited during Mussaf because the congregation is occupied with the celebration of Simchas Torah, which often leads to intoxication. *Eliyahu Rabbah*[24] relates that the general custom in Prague was to perform Bircas Kohanim during Mussaf,[25] but there was one shul in the city that did it during Shacharis.[26]

Mishnah Berurah[27] states that some communities have the custom to perform Bircas Kohanim on Simchas Torah during Shacharis, while others do so during Mussaf. *Mishnah Berurah* concludes that each community should follow its own custom, and the Kohanim, for their part, must be careful not to become intoxicated before performing the mitzvah.

German Custom on Simchas Torah

Chavos Yair (*Mekor Chaim* 128:44) cites *Eliyahu Rabbah*'s ruling that Bircas Kohanim on Simchas Torah is performed during Mussaf, and then writes: "Our practice is to *duchan* during Shacharis as well as Mussaf, and that is the custom of Germany."

Sefer Minhagim D'Kehillah Kedoshah Vermaiza (*Minhagim* of Simchas Torah §188, 190) also states clearly that Bircas Kohanim is performed on Simchas Torah during both Shacharis and Mussaf.

Likewise, *Noheg Katzon Yosef*[28] states that Bircas Kohanim should be performed during both Shacharis and Mussaf of Simchas Torah. He adds that the Kohanim should be careful not to become intoxicated.

Why Lo Sisgodedu Does Not Apply

As a general rule, when there are differing opinions in halachah, a community should follow one uniform practice. This principle is

---

23. *O.C.* 669; cited in *Mishnah Berurah* 669:17.
24. In his commentary to *Levush*, §6, and in his *sefer*, 669:20.
25. This was the custom of Komarna chassidim as well. See *Shulchan HaTahor*, 129:1.
26. See citation below of *Eishel Avraham*, who explains that there is no issue of *lo sisgodedu* if different congregations in the same town follow different customs for Bircas Kohanim.
27. 669:17.
28. *Hilchos Shemini Atzeres* §6; authored by R' Yosef ben Moshe HaLevi Kushman, and published in 1718.

derived from the commandment of *lo sisgodedu*,[29] which can be understood to mean, "Do not divide into different groups."[30] However, notes *Eishel Avraham* (Butchatch),[31] if some congregations perform Bircas Kohanim on Simchas Torah during Shacharis and others perform it during Mussaf, there is no issue of *lo sisgodedu*.

He explains that it does not appear as though they are following two different sets of halachos, because the only reason not to perform Bircas Kohanim on Simchas Torah is out of concern that the Kohanim might be intoxicated. Thus, people will assume that those who are not performing the mitzvah are intoxicated and those who are performing it are not intoxicated; all of them are following the same halachah.

R' Shmuel Wosner was also of the opinion that *lo sisgodedu* does not apply in such a case.[32]

Is it Appropriate to Become Intoxicated on Simchas Torah?

Since many *poskim* write that Bircas Kohanim on Simchas Torah should be performed during Shacharis rather than Mussaf, out of concern for intoxication, it appears that intoxication on Simchas Torah was a common occurrence. Some *gedolim* expressed their disapproval of this practice. R' Aryeh Leib HaKohen, son of the Chofetz Chaim, wrote:[33] "My father told me that the only mention of intoxication in Tanach is in connection to Purim, which is referred to as יְמֵי מִשְׁתֶּה וְשִׂמְחָה, *days of feasting and joy* (*Esther* 9:22). Thus, my father was opposed to people becoming intoxicated on Simchas Torah. The joy one should aspire to attain on Simchas Torah should be acquired through Torah and mitzvos, as the *pasuk* states (*Tehillim* 19:9), פִּקּוּדֵי ה׳ יְשָׁרִים מְשַׂמְּחֵי לֵב, *The orders of Hashem are upright, gladdening the heart*."

Similarly, *Menuchah U'Kedushah*[34] states that it is forbidden to become intoxicated on Simchas Torah.

---

29. *Devarim* 14:1; lit. *Do not cut yourselves*.
30. See *Yevamos* 13b.
31. 128:44.
32. See *She'eilos U'Teshuvos Shevet HaLevi*, vol. 4 #70
33. *Sichos Chofetz Chaim*, vol. 1 #29.
34. Vol. 2 §19; authored by R' Yisrael of Ponovezh, who was a close disciple of R' Chaim of Volozhin; published in 1864.

The Brisker Rav is quoted[35] as saying that there is no source for the practice of some people to become intoxicated on Simchas Torah. We find this opinion in the writings of some prominent chassidic Rebbes as well. Minchas Elazar states[36] that many chassidic leaders did not allow any intoxication during Simchas Torah. His great-grandfather, the Heichal Berachah of Komarna,[37] cites R' Elimelech of Lizhensk, who strongly prohibited all alcoholic beverages on Simchas Torah, so that alcohol would not have any part in the pure, holy *simchah* of the Yom Tov. This was also the practice of many other Rebbes, including the Rebbe of Toldos Aharon,[38] and is recorded in the *sefer Mishmeres Shalom*.[39]

Simchas Torah in Lakewood

In Beth Medrash Govoha of Lakewood, New Jersey, during the lifetimes of the yeshivah's distinguished founder, R' Aharon Kotler, and his son R' Shneur, the yeshivah would daven Shacharis (including the Torah reading) and Mussaf, make Kiddush, and then have *hakafos*. Since there was no Kiddush before Mussaf (and therefore no concern of intoxication), the Kohanim performed Bircas Kohanim only during Mussaf.

At some point, the yeshivah switched to holding the Kiddush and *hakafos* between Shacharis and Mussaf. When that change was implemented, opening the possibility of people becoming intoxicated before Mussaf, Bircas Kohanim was moved to Shacharis. However, there were those who preferred the original schedule, and several "side" minyanim were formed, in which Kiddush was not made before Mussaf. The question now arose: Should Bircas Kohanim in those minyanim be performed during Shacharis or Mussaf?

R' Yaakov Ephraim HaKohen Forchheimer, esteemed *posek* of Beth Medrash Govoha, attended one of those minyanim, and upon his suggestion the decision was made to perform Bircas Kohanim during both Shacharis and Mussaf. (R' Forchheimer is of Yekkish descent and davened for many years in Khal Adas Yeshurun of Washington Heights, where he *duchaned* on Simchas Torah during both

35. *Emek Berachah*, p. 127.
36. *Shaar Yissachar, Chodesh Tishrei* §20.
37. *Vayikra* 11:47.
38. *Zechor L'Avraham*, vol. 3 §57.
39. *Siman* 47.

Shacharis and Mussaf, in accordance with the German custom; see above.) This practice continues until today in various minyanim of Beth Medrash Govoha (most notably the minyan of R' Yehoshua Krupenia, a son-in-law of R' Shneur Kotler).[40]

Shabbos Chol HaMoed

The custom of Satmar shuls throughout the world is to perform Bircas Kohanim during Mussaf of Shabbos Chol HaMoed.[41] The Kohanim recite Bircas Kohanim without singing, as the *Ribbono Shel Olam* prayer is not recited by the congregation on Shabbos. *Machzor Satmar* for Pesach[42] states that this custom began after the Satmar Rebbe, R' Yoel Teitelbaum, visited Eretz Yisrael in the year 1932. Upon meriting to hear Bircas Kohanim on a daily basis there, he was overcome with longing for the mitzvah, and that year he instituted Bircas Kohanim on Shabbos Chol HaMoed in the city of Satmar. This practice has continued in Satmar communities worldwide until today.

---

40. This author spoke to R' Forchheimer, who clarified that his ruling was only for Simchas Torah, not other Yamim Tovim, and is meant only for minyanim that were newly established or that took place in private residences; it is for the purpose of satisfying all the differing customs among the congregants as to whether Bircas Kohanim should be performed during Shacharis or Mussaf. Also, it is applicable only if there is no Kiddush before Mussaf.

One Simchas Torah, I davened at a *netz* minyan in Lakewood that took place in a private residence, and there was no break for Kiddush between Shacharis and Mussaf. As might be expected, a lively dispute erupted as to when Bircas Kohanim should be performed. The organizer of the minyan asked me to clarify the position of R' Chaim Kanievsky on this matter, and when I later discussed the question with R' Chaim, I mentioned the ruling of R' Forchheimer. R' Chaim agreed with that ruling and added that in the case of a newly formed minyan that did not have an existing custom, it would be permissible to perform Bircas Kohanim on Simchas Torah (but not other Festivals) during both Shacharis and Mussaf, provided that there is no concern of intoxication. If the minyan already has an existing *minhag*, however, they should not change it.

41. In Eretz Yisrael, Satmar shuls perform Bircas Kohanim during Shacharis and Mussaf on Shabbos Chol HaMoed, as on every Shabbos.

42. P. 693. See also *Yemei HaMelech* ch. 8.

Chapter 41
Fast Days

The Gemara (*Taanis* 26b) states that Bircas Kohanim is performed only during Shacharis and not Minchah, because people are frequently intoxicated in the afternoon (as opposed to the morning, when they have not yet had their first meal of the day), and a Kohen who is intoxicated may not perform Bircas Kohanim.[1] *Rambam*[2] and *Shulchan Aruch*[3] rule in accordance with this Gemara.

The Gemara, *Rambam*, and *Shulchan Aruch* add that on public fast days, since there is no concern of intoxication, Bircas Kohanim is performed during Minchah as well. Additionally, the Gemara says that we are not afraid that a Kohen who performs Bircas Kohanim during Minchah on a fast day will become confused and do the same on a regular day, because Minchah on a fast day generally takes place toward the end of the day. *Rashi*[4] explains that on other days of the year most people davened Minchah earlier, but on fast days it was customary to daven just before nightfall so it should be noticeably different from the daily Minchah, and therefore, people realize that Minchah on a fast day is different.[5]

1. For more details about this prohibition see chapter 46.
2. *Hilchos Tefillah U'Nesias Kapayim* 14:1.
3. 129:1.
4. *Taanis* 26b s.v. *Kivan*.
5. See also *Magen Avraham* 129:2 and *Aruch HaShulchan* 129:2, who point out, based on this Gemara, that on non-fast days, the original custom was to daven Minchah several hours before nightfall.

The following halachos are applicable to congregations that *duchan* daily (meaning those in Eretz Yisrael, and Sephardic congregations worldwide):

1. Although Bircas Kohanim is performed during Minchah of a fast day, if a Kohen broke his fast before Minchah because he was ill or weak, *Pri Chadash*,[6] *Chida*,[7] and *Kaf HaChaim*[8] rule that it is prohibited for him to *duchan*; therefore, he must exit the shul before *Retzei*. However, *Ginas Veradim*[9] rules that it is permissible for him to *duchan*; since most people are fasting that day because of the communal *taanis*, it will not be confused with a regular day. All agree that he may perform Bircas Kohanim during Shacharis even if he was not fasting then.[10]

2. Some *poskim* maintain that if the only Kohen present at Minchah broke his fast,[11] or if there is only one other Kohen, and if they join together, Bircas Kohanim will be able to be performed with two Kohanim, it is permissible for him to *duchan*.[12] However, R' Chaim Kanievsky[13] held that even in this case the Kohen is prohibited to *duchan*, even if he broke his fast due to unavoidable circumstances (*oness*).

3. Many *poskim* write that Bircas Kohanim during Minchah of a fast day should be performed only after *Minchah Ketanah* — preferably within a half-hour before sunset — but not at *Minchah Gedolah* (which may be recited from one half-hour after halachic midday).[14]

---

6. 129:2.
7. *Machazik Berachah, Kuntres Acharon* §1.
8. 129:5.
9. *Klal* 1 §49. R' Yosef Shalom Elyashiv (*Tziyunei Halachah*, p. 406) and R' Sroya Deblitzki (*Zeh HaShulchan* 128:34) rule in accordance with *Ginas Veradim*.
10. See Responsa of R' Chaim Kanievsky #421.
11. R' Yechiel Michel Tukachinsky, *Luach Eretz Yisrael* on *Tzom Gedaliah*.
12. *Halichos Shlomo*, ch. 10, quoting R' Shlomo Zalman Auerbach. However, it has been pointed out in the name of R' Shlomo Zalman that if there are more than two Kohanim present, the Kohen who broke his fast should follow the ruling of *Pri Chadash* and not perform Bircas Kohanim during Minchah.
13. See Responsa of R' Chaim Kanievsky #422.
14. *Ben Ish Chai, Tetzaveh* §23, and in his responsa, *Rav Pe'alim*, vol. 4, *siman* 5; *Siddur Eitz Chaim* of R' Yihya Saleh; *Kaf HaChaim* 129:7; *Shevet HaLevi*, vol. 8 #23; *Yalkut Yosef* 129:2; R' Sroya Deblitzki, *Zeh HaShulchan*, *siman* 128.

4. *Chazon Ish,*[15] however, is of the opinion that since *Chazal* allowed Bircas Kohanim at Minchah of a fast day, it is permissible to *duchan* even when davening *Minchah Gedolah.*[16] This is the practice of the Lederman shul and some yeshivos in Eretz Yisrael.[17]

5. R' Moshe Sternbuch[18] and R' Binyamin Yehoshua Zilber[19] write that one should make an effort to daven Minchah close to sunset on fast days; however, if it is difficult to do so, one may rely on the Chazon Ish[20] and daven Minchah with Bircas Kohanim even as early as *Minchah Gedolah.*[21]

No Choice But to Duchan

On one fast day in Bnei Brak, the Ponovezher Rav came to daven Minchah in the main shul of the city. The people there realized that he must have had a good reason for not davening in the yeshivah, as he usually did, and they were correct. R' Kahaneman was not able to fast that day due to health concerns, and for that reason he did not wish to *duchan* during Minchah. To daven in the yeshivah and not *duchan* would be tantamount to a public announcement that he was not fasting, and he preferred to avoid the attention, so he came to this shul instead. As the chazzan was about to reach the *berachah* of *Retzei,* R' Kahaneman quietly made his way toward the

15. *O.C., siman* 20.

16. For an explanation of the Chazon Ish's position, see *Kehillos Yaakov, Berachos siman* 29; R' Chaim Kanievsky in *Shoneh Halachos* (129:2); and Responsa of R' Chaim Kanievsky #419.

17. Including Ponovezh and several others. R' Eliezer Kahaneman, one of the current roshei yeshivah of Ponovezh, told this author that the yeshivah has followed this ruling of the Chazon Ish since its inception.

18. *Moadim U'Zmanim,* vol. 7 §248.

19. *Pnei Baruch* on *Chayei Adam, Klal* 32, footnote.

20. In the yeshivos of Chevron and Mir in Yerushalayim, Minchah on fast days takes place late in the afternoon, so that Bircas Kohanim may be performed according to all opinions.

21. R' Sternbuch and R' Zilber add that the *sefer Chiddushei Dinim L'Rabbanei Yerushalayim HaKadmonim* (published in 1509/5269), which records the rulings of the ancient rabbanim of Yerushalayim, states clearly that it is permitted to perform Bircas Kohanim on a fast day even during *Minchah Gedolah.* (As noted in chapter 14, it has always been the custom in Eretz Yisrael to perform daily Bircas Kohanim.)

exit, so as not to be in shul for *Retzei*, which would obligate him to stay for Bircas Kohanim.

However, one fellow noticed that R' Kahaneman was about to leave, and decided to voice his objection. He jumped out of his seat and said to R' Kahneman, "Why are you going out? Aren't you a Kohen?"

Once he heard the man's words, R' Kahaneman had no choice. The halachah is that a Kohen who is called upon to *duchan* and does not do so is in violation of a positive Torah commandment, so he went up to *duchan*.[22]

Ashkenazic Congregations Outside Eretz Yisrael

Outside Eretz Yisrael, where Ashkenazic communities perform Bircas Kohanim only on Yom Tov, the *Elokeinu V'Elokei Avoseinu* prayer is recited during Minchah of fast days, just as it is recited every day during Shacharis.[23]

Bircas Kohanim During Neilah

1. On Yom Kippur, in Eretz Yisrael and in Sephardic communities worldwide, Bircas Kohanim is performed during Neilah instead of Minchah[24] (as well as during Shacharis and Mussaf). In most Ashkenazic communities outside Eretz Yisrael, it is performed on Yom Kippur only during Mussaf.
2. Although Bircas Kohanim is not performed during Minchah on Yom Kippur, *Rema*[25] writes that the *Elokeinu V'Elokei Avoseinu* prayer is recited by the chazzan, because if a Kohen *would* go up to *duchan* during Minchah (even though he was not supposed to), we would not tell him to go down.[26]

---

22. *Aleinu L'Shabei'ach, Nasso*, p. 115; *K'Ayal Taarog*, p. 195.
23. See *Rema* 566:8 and *Mishnah Berurah* §23.
24. *Taanis* 26b; *Rambam, Hilchos Tefillah U'Nesias Kapayim* 14:2; *Shulchan Aruch* 129:1.
25. 129:2. This is the Ashkenazic custom; Sephardim do not recite the *Elokeinu V'Elokei Avoseinu* prayer during Minchah of Yom Kippur.
26. As per *Rambam* and *Shulchan Aruch* (ibid.), who rule that if a Kohen went up to *duchan* we do not stop him, since there is no concern of intoxication on Yom

Outside Eretz Yisrael, in communities where Bircas Kohanim is performed only during Mussaf of Yom Kippur, *Elokeinu V'Elokei Avoseinu* is recited during Shacharis, Minchah, and Neilah.[27]

3. Even if the Kohanim will not be present during Neilah and they *are* present during Minchah, the Kohanim should still not perform Bircas Kohanim during Minchah.[28]

Neilah After Nightfall

Several Rishonim had a version of *Talmud Yerushalmi*[29] that states: "Just as the *avodah* in the Beis HaMikdash may be performed only during the daytime, so too, Bircas Kohanim may be performed only during the daytime."

1. *Maharil*[30] writes that it is permissible to perform Bircas Kohanim during Neilah of Yom Kippur even if it is already past nightfall. He explains that although the *avodah* in the Beis HaMikdash was performed primarily by day, the Gemara (*Berachos* 26b) points out that the *avodah* of burning the remnants of the afternoon *Tamid* offering on the *Mizbei'ach* did take place at night, and therefore, it is also permitted to perform the mitzvah of Bircas Kohanim after sunset. This is the opinion of several other Rishonim as well,[31] and R' Yaakov Emden[32] rules in accordance with this opinion. *Machatzis HaShekel*[33] explains that just as the *Tamid* offering was sacrificed during the day and completed at night, so too, since most of Neilah was recited during the day, it may be completed at night.

2. The vast majority of Rishonim, however, are of the opinion that Bircas Kohanim may be recited only by day. *Hagahos Maimoniyos*[34] records that the practice of his rebbi, Maharam of Rothenburg,

---

Kippur, and we do not want people to think he was sent down because of some doubt about his lineage.

27. *Mishnah Berurah* 129:8.
28. See Responsa of R' Chaim Kanievsky #427.
29. *Taanis* 4:1. This *Yerushalmi* is quoted by *Rosh*, *Sefer HaEshkol*, and *Hagahos Maimoniyos*, but does not appear in our version of *Yerushalmi*.
30. *Hilchos Yom Kippur, siman* 10; also cited by *Rema* (*Darkei Moshe* 623:2).
31. *Raviah* §877; *Ohr Zarua* §413.
32. *She'eilas Yaavetz* #51.
33. 623:3.
34. *Hilchos Yom Kippur.*

was to skip some of the *piyutim* during Neilah, to ensure that Bircas Kohanim would take place before sunset. After Bircas Kohanim, the congregation would recite whatever they had skipped, and conclude Neilah with the *Avinu Malkeinu* prayer. This is cited as the halachah by most Acharonim, who recommend that an effort should be made to perform Bircas Kohanim before sunset, even if it entails reciting the *piyutim* afterward.[35]

3. "*Bein hashemashos*" (twilight) is the time period that begins at sunset and ends when three medium-sized stars become visible in the night sky. "Day" ends and "night" begins sometime within this period, but we do not know exactly when that transition takes place.[36] Thus, *Mishnah Berurah* states that the issue of whether Bircas Kohanim may be performed during *bein hashemashos* is an unresolved question.[37] With regard to Eretz Yisrael, several *poskim* maintain that it is permitted to *duchan* until 13.5 minutes after sunset, since Bircas Kohanim is a Torah obligation (*d'Oraysa*) and we are stringent regarding *d'Oraysa* obligations (*safek d'Oraysa l'chumra*), so Bircas Kohanim may be performed even when there is doubt as to whether it still day.[38] Others, however, are of the opinion that Bircas Kohanim may not be performed after sunset under any circumstances.[39]

---

35. *Beis Yosef* 623; *Magen Avraham* 623:3; *Mishnah Berurah* 623:8.

36. See *Mishnah Berurah* 233:14. The view of the Geonim, which is followed by *Gra*, is that *bein hashemashos* begins immediately at sunset, and may end as soon as 13.5 minutes after sunset. *Shulchan Aruch, Yoreh Deah* 266:9, seems to follow this opinion.

37. *Shaar HaTziyun* (623:13) cites *Pri Megadim*, who is uncertain whether it is permissible to perform Bircas Kohanim during *bein hashemashos*. Likewise, *Mishnah Berurah* suggests that it may be permissible to do so until it is definitely night, but he remains inconclusive about the matter.

38. Opinion of R' Shlomo Zalman Auerbach and R' Yosef Shalom Elyashiv, recorded in their approbations to *HaMachzor L'Yom Kippur HaMeforash*. This is the opinion of R' Moshe Sternbuch (*Moadim U'Zmanim*, vol. 8 §62) as well. For an in-depth discussion of the subject, see R' Ovadiah Yosef's *Yechaveh Daas* (vol. 6 #40) and *Yabia Omer* (vol. 9 #58). R' Ovadiah also holds that *b'dieved*, it is permitted to perform Bircas Kohanim until 13.5 minutes after sunset. He stresses, however, that in his minyan they would announce before Neilah that the congregants should not sing, which would slow the pace of the chazzan; this was done to ensure that Bircas Kohanim could be recited before sunset (see footnote below regarding the personal practice of R' Ovadiah when he served as chazzan during Neilah).

39. *Orchos Rabbeinu* (vol. 2 p. 211) states in the name of R' Chaim Kanievsky

4. Even according to the opinions that Bircas Kohanim may be performed up to 13.5 minutes after sunset, this is only *b'dieved*; it is preferable to complete Bircas Kohanim before sunset.[40]

5. As noted in chapter 7, many yeshivos in Eretz Yisrael, including Mir, Chevron, and Brisk, are particular to complete Bircas Kohanim of Neilah before sunset.

that the Chazon Ish did not permit Bircas Kohanim after sunset. This is also the opinion of R' Yisrael Yaakov Fisher (*Halichos Even Yisrael* 20:4) and R' Shmuel Wosner (*MiBeis HaLevi, Hilchos Yom Kippur,* ch. 9); they emphasize that the mitzvah may not be performed even one minute after sunset.

40. See *Yabia Omer,* vol. 9 #58, where R' Ovadiah writes that when he served as chazzan for Neilah, he made sure that he kept a pace at which the Kohanim could recite Bircas Kohanim five minutes before sunset, and he announced before Neilah that no congregant should attempt to slow the pace of the prayer. See also *Mishnas HaGrish* (p. 416), which records that R' Yosef Shalom Elyashiv would ensure that his minyan could perform Bircas Kohanim before sunset. On occasions when it was getting late, he told them to omit the *Avinu Malkeinu* prayer at the conclusion of Minchah so they could start Neilah earlier, to ensure that they would perform Bircas Kohanim before sunset.

Chapter 42
Halachos of Yom Tov Sheini for Travelers

A Kohen From Eretz Yisrael Who Is Abroad on Yom Tov Sheini

1. Considering that Bircas Kohanim is part of davening, if a particular Kohen is not obligated in the *tefillah* that is being recited, should he nevertheless perform Bircas Kohanim? For example: In Eretz Yisrael, each Yom Tov is observed for just one day (with the exception of Rosh Hashanah), while outside Eretz Yisrael, most Yamim Tovim are for two days.[1] A person from Eretz Yisrael who is spending Yom Tov Sheini in another country is forbidden to do *melachah*, in deference to the local practice. However, he recites the weekday *tefillos* (as opposed to the *tefillos* for Yom Tov) and is required to put on tefillin[2] in private.[3] If he is a Kohen, should he perform Bircas Kohanim during Mussaf even though he is not required to daven Mussaf?[4]

1. See *Beitzah* 4b; *Rambam, Hilchos Yom Tov* 1:21; *Shulchan Aruch* 496:1.
2. This query relates to the second day of Shavuos, and the final day of Succos and of Pesach, when abroad it is Yom Tov Sheini and in Eretz Yisrael it is not Yom Tov. A Kohen is permitted to perform Bircas Kohanim during Mussaf according to all opinions if it is Chol HaMoed for him, since he, too, is obligated to recite Mussaf.
3. See *Shulchan Aruch* 496:3 and *Mishnah Berurah* §13 for other relevant *halachos*.
4. During Shacharis, even though he recites a different *Shemoneh Esrei*, he is

This question is the subject of intense debate among the *poskim*. *Shaarei Teshuvah*[5] quotes a number of Acharonim who discuss the matter, and concludes that it is preferable for the Kohen from Eretz Yisrael not to *duchan* during Mussaf, since he is not obligated to recite that *tefillah*.[6] *Shaarei Teshuvah* adds, however, that if the visitor from Eretz Yisrael is the only Kohen in that shul, he is permitted to perform Bircas Kohanim with a *berachah*. If he chooses to *duchan* together with other Kohanim, it is preferable for him not to recite the *berachah* before Bircas Kohanim.[7]

Igros Moshe[8] is more lenient and allows a Kohen from Eretz Yisrael to participate in Bircas Kohanim during Mussaf of Yom Tov Sheini. R' Yosef Shalom Elyashiv[9] permits this as well, even when there are other Kohanim present. He explains that according to the strict halachah, Bircas Kohanim should be performed every day even outside Eretz Yisrael, and it is only because of a custom that it is not performed daily. That being the case, if the custom on that particular day *is* to perform Bircas Kohanim outside Eretz Yisrael, it is permissible for a Kohen from Eretz Yisrael to do so even if he is not obligated in that specific *tefillah*.

Visitors to Eretz Yisrael on Yom Tov Sheini

2. If a group of people who reside abroad are in Eretz Yisrael for Yom Tov and they join together for a Yom Tov Sheini minyan,[10] but they have no Kohen from outside Eretz Yisrael to *duchan* for them, *Shaarei Teshuvah*[11] says that according to most opinions, a

---

permitted to perform Bircas Kohanim (if he is davening in a Sephardic minyan).

5. 496:4.

6. *Shaarei Teshuvah* also cites the opinion of R' Moshe ben Chaviv and *Zera Avraham* that it is permissible for him to *duchan*. However, *Teshuvos Ginas Veradim, Klal* 1 *siman* 13 (written R' Avraham ben R' Mordechai HaLevi) raises some doubt with regard to reciting a *berachah*.

7. This is the opinion of *Ginas Veradim*, which is cited by R' Akiva Eiger in his commentary to *Shulchan Aruch* (128:44), and by *Kaf HaChaim* (128:21).

8. Vol. 4 #106.

9. *Tziyunei Halachah*, p. 420.

10. It is a common practice for visitors to Eretz Yisrael to form their own minyanim for Yom Tov Sheini. However, *Mishnah Berurah* (496:13) is of the opinion that this should not be done; instead, one should daven at home in private without a minyan.

11. Ibid.

Kohen who resides in Eretz Yisrael may perform Bircas Kohanim for that minyan during Mussaf. R' Shmuel Wosner[12] writes that although *Shaarei Teshuvah* does permit it, there is some doubt as to whether that is the accepted halachah.

3. If visitors to Eretz Yisrael from abroad form their own minyan on Yom Tov (or Shabbos), they should *duchan* during Shacharis and Mussaf, even though at home they *duchan* only during Mussaf.[13]

---

12. *Teshuvos Shevet HaLevi*, vol. 3 #96.
13. See Responsa of R' Chaim Kanievsky #544.

Chapter 43
A Chazzan Who Is a Kohen

Chazal and the *poskim* discuss a situation where the chazzan is himself a Kohen. The question is how to deal with the potential conflict between his responsibilities as the chazzan and his obligation to perform Bircas Kohanim. The Mishnah (*Berachos* 34a) states that if a Kohen is the chazzan, even if he is the only Kohen in the shul, he should not perform Bircas Kohanim. *Rashi* (ibid.) explains that if the chazzan were to perform Bircas Kohanim in public, there is a concern that his "fear of the congregation" will cause him to lose his focus on the *tefillah*. The Mishnah concludes, however, that if the chazzan is confident that he will be able to maintain proper concentration, he is permitted to *duchan*. Interestingly, the Gemara there does not have any comment or discussion about the latter part of the Mishnah.

1. *Shulchan Aruch* (128:20) explains that if the chazzan is the only Kohen in the shul, we allow him to *duchan* (if he can maintain his concentration), because we do not want the congregation to miss even one opportunity to receive the blessing of Bircas Kohanim.[1]

---

1. This ruling is affirmed by many *poskim*. We see from here the critical importance of the congregation hearing Bircas Kohanim, to the extent that this can at times can override a halachah. Similarly, we noted in chapter 26 that if there is only one Kohen in a minyan, he is required to take a step in the direction of the *aron kodesh* during *Retzei* and interrupt his *Shemoneh Esrei* to perform Bircas Kohanim; afterward, he can complete *Shemoneh Esrei* from the place he was up to.

2. *Mishnah Berurah* (128:72-76) states that this is permitted only when we are certain that the chazzan will not become confused and will be able to continue the *tefillah* from where he left off. This is the situation in contemporary times, since every chazzan has a *siddur* in front of him. *Mishnah Berurah* adds, however, that if there is another Kohen in the shul who can *duchan* instead, the chazzan should not *duchan* even if he has a *siddur*.[2]

Pri Chadash,[3] however, states firmly that a chazzan who is confident that he will be able to return to the *berachah* of *Sim Shalom* without confusion is permitted to *duchan* even if there are other Kohanim *duchaning* in that minyan. *Pri Chadash* proves from *Midrash Rabbah, Rosh*, and *Rabbeinu Manoach* that this is the halachah to be followed. Similarly, R' Yaakov Emden writes, in several places,[4] that a Kohen who is a chazzan should perform Bircas Kohanim together with the other Kohanim.

3. *Mishnah Berurah*[5] concludes that since the opinion of *Pri Chadash* is that a chazzan may *duchan* even when there are other Kohanim, and since the only concern of *Shulchan Aruch* is that the chazzan might become confused (for example, if he does not have a *siddur* to daven from), one should not protest if a chazzan who is a Kohen chooses to *duchan*. Additionally, although *Magen Avraham* (128:31) disagrees with *Pri Chadash*, he concedes that some Kohanim do have the custom to *duchan* when serving as the chazzan, even when there are multiple Kohanim present. (The fact that *Magen Avraham* mentions this seems to indicate that he would agree that one need not protest if a Kohen chooses to follow the opinion of *Pri Chadash*.)

4. All agree that if someone in the congregation summoned the chazzan (who is a Kohen), either before or during the *berachah* of *Retzei*,[6] to ascend to the *duchan* or to wash his hands,[7] the chazzan becomes obligated to *duchan*, lest he be in violation of

---

2. *Mishnah Berurah* 128:76.
3. 128:20.
4. *Lechem Shamayim* (*Berachos* 5:4), *She'eilas Yaavetz*, vol. 1 §54, *Mor U'Ketziah, siman* 128, *Siddur R' Yaakov Emden, Hilchos Nesias Kapayim* §6, 7.
5. *Shaar HaTziyun* 128:64.
6. *Mishnah Berurah* (128:74).
7. *Mordechai* (*Megillah* §817) writes that if the Kohen is reminded to wash his hands for Bircas Kohanim and he does not *duchan*, he violates three positive commandments.

a positive Torah commandment.[8] Even if he is concerned that he may become confused, and be unable to finish the *tefillah* properly, that possibility does not override the *mitzvas asei*, and he must *duchan*.[9]

5. In *Kuntres Zichronos* (9:5),[10] R' Chaim Kanievsky writes that although the Chazon Ish initially ruled that a Kohen who is serving as the chazzan should *duchan*, he later changed his opinion, and ruled that the chazzan should not *duchan* in *any* situation, even if he is the only Kohen present.

6. In the Lederman shul of Bnei Brak, where the congregation strictly adheres to the rulings and customs of the Chazon Ish, they do not allow a Kohen to serve as the chazzan for *Chazaras HaShatz*. R' Chaim Kanievsky relates (Responsa #400) that the Chazon Ish insisted upon this stringency even if the Kohen was observing a *yahrtzeit* for a parent, or was in the year of mourning for a parent, when it is customary to serve as the chazzan. R' Chaim added that it is more beneficial for the soul of the deceased parent if the son *duchans* than if he serves as the chazzan. In his responsa, R' Chaim explains that Bircas Kohanim is a fulfillment of three *mitzvos d'Oraysa*, and that certainly takes precedence over serving as a chazzan.

7. *Maaseh Ish*[11] records an episode that highlights and underscores this opinion of the Chazon Ish. A Kohen by the name of R' Yitzchak Halberstadt was davening in the *netz* minyan of the Chazon Ish on the day of his father's *yahrtzeit*. He wanted to serve as chazzan for the entire *tefillah* as a merit for his father's soul, but the Chazon Ish told him that he should not daven the *Chazaras HaShatz* portion. "You are well-intentioned," the Chazon Ish said. "But although it is a merit for your father's soul to recite *Chazaras HaShatz* and have the congregation respond amen to your *berachos*, it will be a greater merit for him if you perform Bircas Kohanim."

8. Despite the opposition of the Chazon Ish, most Ashkenazic communities in Eretz Yisrael, including Lithuanian yeshivah

8. *Rema* 128:20, based on *Mordechai* (ibid.) and *Hagahos Maimoniyos*.

9. *Mishnah Berurah* 128:75. *Shaar HaTziyun* (ibid.) lists the Acharonim who are of this opinion.

10. See also *Orchos Rabbeinu*, vol. 1, p. 66.

11. Vol. 2, p. 95.

communities, follow the ruling of *Pri Chadash* and R' Yaakov Emden, and allow a Kohen who is the chazzan to *duchan*.[12] Similarly, in the vast majority of chassidic communities in Eretz Yisrael and abroad, Kohanim do perform Bircas Kohanim while serving as chazzan, even when there are other Kohanim present.[13] However, in Sephardic communities throughout the world, Kohanim do not serve as the chazzan for *Chazaras HaShatz*, even when they are in mourning, so that they should be able to perform Bircas Kohanim.[14]

9. Others are of the opinion that if there are *two* other Kohanim present, a chazzan who is a Kohen should not *duchan*, but if there is only one, the chazzan who is a Kohen should *duchan* together with him, to satisfy the opinion that a minimum of two Kohanim is required to fulfill the *mitzvah d'Oraysa*.[15]

10. If the chazzan is performing Bircas Kohanim, a non-Kohen should be designated to announce "Kohanim" and to be the

---

12. This practice follows the ruling of Rabbeinu Moshe of Evreux, France, one of the closest disciples of Rabbeinu Shimshon of Shantz and one of the most prominent authors of *Tosafos*. The *sefer Al HaKol* (ch. 7), written by a disciple of Rabbeinu Moshe, states: "Rabbeinu Shimshon (of Shantz) ruled that even if there are other Kohanim performing Bircas Kohanim in a congregation, if the chazzan is a Kohen, he should perform Bircas Kohanim together with the other Kohanim." Regarding the practical application of this halachah, see R' Yechiel Michel Tukachinsky's *Ir HaKodesh* (vol. 3, p. 242) and *Sefer Eretz Yisrael* (2:2). R' Avraham Chaim Na'eh writes, in *Ketzos HaShulchan* (23:42), that the custom of Eretz Yisrael is that a chazzan who is a Kohen performs Bircas Kohanim even if there are other Kohanim in the minyan. R' Yosef Shalom Elyashiv is also quoted as saying that one should follow the custom of Eretz Yisrael; see *Tziyunei Halachah*, pp. 381-382. *K'Ayal Taarog* (*Hilchos Tefillah*, p. 190) relates that in the daily Shacharis minyan that took place for many years in the home of R' Aharon Leib Shteinman, there were times that a Kohen was the chazzan, and he did *duchan*. When they asked R' Aharon Leib about this practice, he replied that since there are different customs, he will not voice an objection.

13. *See Shulchan HaTahor* of the Komarna Rebbe (128:19). *Ateres Paz* on Bircas Kohanim (§59) states that the custom of his grandfather, R' Avraham Yehudah HaKohen Schwartz (1824-1883; author of *Kol Aryeh*), was to perform Bircas Kohanim while serving as chazzan even when other Kohanim were present. This was also the custom of the Munkacz Chassidus; see *She'eilos U'Teshuvos Minchas Elazar* (vol. 1 #48), which adds that we have seen many *gedolim* who were Kohanim perform Bircas Kohanim while serving as chazzan. See also *Darchei Chaim V'Shalom* of Munkacz, p. 126.

14. See *Kaf HaChaim* (128:117) and R' Ovadiah Yosef (*Yalkut Yosef* 128:56).

15. R' Binyamin Yehoshua Zilber, *She'eilos U'Teshuvos Az Nidberu*, vol. 13 #34; R' Shlomo Zalman Auerbach, as quoted in *Halichos Shlomo* (*Hilchos Tefillah* 10:7).

"makri" who calls out the words of the *berachah* one at a time for the Kohanim to repeat.[16]

11. Most *poskim* hold that when a Kohen serves as the chazzan and performs Bircas Kohanim, after *duchaning* he should continue *Chazaras HaShatz* and recite the final *berachah* of *Shemoneh Esrei* — as opposed to having the *makri* take over for him.[17]

12. If the chazzan is *duchaning,* he should remove his shoes and wash his hands before beginning *Chazaras HaShatz* — even though, technically, he can skip the handwashing and rely on the morning handwashing he performed before davening.[18] He is also required to make an *"akirah"* (to take a step toward the *duchan*) right before, or during, *Retzei.*[19] If the chazzan forgot to remove his shoes before *Chazaras HaShatz,* he is permitted to remove them before Bircas Kohanim.[20]

13. If the chazzan is *duchaning,* he should not ascend the steps to the *aron kodesh.* Rather, he should stand in place and turn around to face the congregation while reciting the *berachah.* The congregants should do their utmost to position themselves in front of him, so that they may be included in his blessing.[21] The chazzan should turn around in the same exact fashion as the other Kohanim, even though he is in the middle of reciting *Chazaras HaShatz.*[22]

16. *Shulchan Aruch* 128:22.
17. *Mishnah Berurah* 128:87.
18. *Chayei Adam* 32:26; *Aruch HaShulchan* 128:33.
19. *Shulchan Aruch* 128:20.
20. Responsa of R' Chaim Kanievsky #180.
21. *She'eilos U'Teshuvos Radbaz,* vol. 1 #237; also cited in *Kaf HaChaim* (128:120), who adds that he saw Kohanim who were great scholars rely on their morning handwashing when they served as a chazzan. Also, they remained at the *amud* and did not ascend the steps to the *aron kodesh;* they did, however, turn around to face the congregation. See also Responsa of R' Chaim Kanievsky #396.
22. Responsa of R' Chaim Kanievsky #397.

Chapter 44
Reciting Bircas Kohanim — and Its Blessing — Multiple Times

The Gemara relates (*Sotah* 39a):

> The disciples of R' Elazar ben Shamua asked: On account of which meritorious practice have you attained longevity? R' Elazar ben Shamua (who was a Kohen) replied: "I never raised my hands to perform Bircas Kohanim without first reciting a blessing."

The Gemara continues:

> What blessing does a Kohen recite before performing Bircas Kohanim?
>
> R' Zeira said in the name of R' Chisda: בָּרוּךְ אַתָּה ה׳ אֱלֹהֵינוּ מֶלֶךְ הָעוֹלָם אֲשֶׁר קִדְּשָׁנוּ בִּקְדֻשָּׁתוֹ שֶׁל אַהֲרֹן וְצִוָּנוּ לְבָרֵךְ אֶת עַמּוֹ יִשְׂרָאֵל בְּאַהֲבָה, *Blessed are You, Hashem, our God, King of the universe, Who has sanctified us with the holiness of Aharon and has commanded us to bless His people, Yisrael, with love.*

1. The Gemara (*Rosh Hashanah* 28b) teaches that it is permitted for a Kohen to perform Bircas Kohanim multiple times in one day (each time at another minyan).
2. Based on this Gemara, *Rambam,*[1] *Tur*, and *Shulchan Aruch*[2] rule that a Kohen may *duchan* many times a day, each time at a sepa-

1. *Hilchos Tefillah U'Nesias Kapayim* 15:11.
2. 128:28.

rate minyan, but they do not mention if he must recite a new blessing before each Bircas Kohanim.

3. *Maharam Mintz* writes[3] that each time a Kohen performs Bircas Kohanim, he recites a *berachah,* just as he recites this *berachah* repeatedly on Yom Kippur, when performing Bircas Kohanim during Shacharis, Mussaf, and Neilah. *Maharam Mintz* adds that each time a Kohen performs Bircas Kohanim, even many times in one day, he fulfills another mitzvah. This is stated clearly by *Meiri*[4] and many Acharonim.[5] *Mishnah Berurah*[6] adds that the Kohen recites another *berachah* even if all the minyanim take place in the same shul.[7]

4. *Tosafos*[8] explain that there is no issue of *bal tosif* (the prohibition against adding to a mitzvah of the Torah) if a Kohen performs Bircas Kohanim multiple times, just as one is permitted to blow the shofar for a number of different congregations on the same day.

5. If a Kohen already performed Bircas Kohanim during Shacharis, then even if he was told to *duchan* again during Mussaf and did not do so, most *poskim* agree that he is not in violation of the three relevant commandments, since he did perform the mitzvah once that day.[9] However, he *is* forfeiting an additional mitzvah.

Chasam Sofer,[10] however, holds that on a day that Bircas Kohanim is recited twice, such as during Shacharis and Mussaf, each one is a separate *mitzvah d'Oraysa*. Therefore, a Kohen who was told to *duchan* during Mussaf and did not do so is in violation of the mitzvah, even if he already *duchaned* during Shacharis. However,

---

3. In his *teshuvos* (#12, addressed to R' Yisrael Isserlein, the *Terumas HaDeshen*); this is cited by many Acharonim, including *Magen Avraham* (128:3) and *Mishnah Berurah* (§11 and §106).

4. *Rosh Hashanah* 28b. *Maharam Mintz* cites additional Rishonim who concur with this opinion.

5. R' Akiva Eiger in *Derush V'Chiddush* on *Rosh Hashanah* 16b; *Chida* in *Birkei Yosef, Shiurei Berachah* 128:3; *Minchas Chinuch* (Mitzvah 378); *Shulchan Aruch HaRav* 128:41; and many others.

6. 128:11, 106.

7. See Responsa of R' Chaim Kanievsky #437, that even if the minyanim are located adjacent to one other and are all taking place within a short timeframe, the Kohanim should recite a new blessing each time.

8. *Rosh Hashanah* 16b, 28b. Cited as halachah in *Mishnah Berurah* (§106).

9. *Shulchan Aruch* 128:3; see also *Mishnah Berurah* §11. See also *She'eilos U'Teshuvos Maharam Mintz* §12 and *Mabit* in *Kiryas Sefer,* ch. 14.

10. Responsa #22, and in his commentary to *Shulchan Aruch* 128:3.

Shulchan Aruch HaRav[11] and *Mishnah Berurah*[12] write that performing Bircas Kohanim again during Mussaf is only a Rabbinic mitzvah and not a Torah obligation — but, of course, a second *berachah* is recited, as with any Rabbinic mitzvah. The Acharonim point out that even according to the opinion that the Kohen does not violate a prohibition by refusing to *duchan* a second time, he is not permitted to remain in the shul to hear Bircas Kohanim from his fellow Kohanim while he himself does not *duchan*, unless he is in the middle of *Shemoneh Esrei* and cannot leave.[13]

6. If the chazzan mistakenly omitted *Yaaleh V'Yavo* during *Chazaras HaShatz* of Shacharis on Rosh Chodesh, and only realized this at the end of *Chazaras HaShatz*, such as during *Sim Shalom*, he is required to return to the *berachah* of *Retzei*. In this situation, if Bircas Kohanim was already performed during the first recitation, it should not be performed again.[14]

7. There are a number of mitzvos that are done by speaking but may be fulfilled by listening, in accordance with the principle of *shomei'a k'oneh* (i.e., listening is equivalent to speaking). Bircas Kohanim is an exception to the rule. Each individual Kohen is required to recite the blessing before *duchaning*, and the actual *pesukim* of Bircas Kohanim; it is not sufficient to just listen to another Kohen reciting the *berachos*.[15]

---

11. 128:4.
12. 128:106 and *Shaar HaTziyun* §81.
13. *Pri Megadim* 128:3; *Mishnah Berurah* §11.
14. See R' Tzvi Pesach Frank, *Teshuvos Har Tzvi*, vol. 1 #61; Responsa of R' Chaim Kanievsky #446. In the aforementioned *teshuvah* of the *Chasam Sofer*, he writes that Bircas Kohanim may not be performed twice during the same *tefillah*, but he does not offer a specific example of when this might be relevant. It has been noted that this ruling of the Chasam Sofer is applicable in the case of a chazzan who forgot *Yaaleh V'Yavo*.
15. See *Teshuvos Mabit*, vol. 1 #180; *Mishnah Berurah* §41; *Kaf HaChaim* 128:74. See also Responsa of R' Chaim Kanievsky #386.

Chapter 45
Ashkenazic and Sephardic Pronunciation

1. Ashkenazim and Sephardim use different pronunciations for Hebrew words, but since most congregations are accustomed to hearing a variety of dictions, it is permitted for an Ashkenazi Kohen to recite Bircas Kohanim with his customary pronunciation even when performing the mitzvah in a Sephardic shul. Likewise, a Kohen who is a Sephardi may recite Bircas Kohanim with his usual pronunciation in an Ashkenazic shul.[1]

2. Ideally, a Kohen should pronounce the words of Bircas Kohanim in accordance with his own dialect. However, if a Kohen is davening in a minyan that uses different pronunciation (e.g., an Ashkenazi in a Sephardic minyan), and he finds it difficult to say the words differently than the other Kohanim, he is permitted, *b'dieved,* to recite the blessings with the same pronunciation as the other Kohanim.[2]

---

1. R' Yosef Shalom Elyashiv, *Tziyunei Halachah,* p. 338; R' Ovadiah Yosef, *Yalkut Yosef* 128:67; Responsa of R' Chaim Kanievsky #330. See also chapter 11, where we cited a similar idea in the name of the Chofetz Chaim.

2. R' Chaim Kanievsky (Responsa #331). In this vein, R' Elyashiv points out (*Tziyunei Halachah* ibid.) that had the *Rambam* been a Kohen, he would have used the Sephardic pronunciation for Bircas Kohanim, as would have been done by all the other great Sephardic Rishonim who were the leaders of Klal Yisrael.

Chapter 46
Performing Bircas Kohanim While Intoxicated

The Gemara (*Taanis* 26b) states that a Kohen who is intoxicated may not perform Bircas Kohanim. The Gemara explains that the mitzvah of Bircas Kohanim appears in the Torah immediately after the laws of the *nazir*,[1] to teach us that just as a *nazir* may not drink wine, a Kohen may not drink wine before performing Bircas Kohanim. The Gemara adds, however, that Bircas Kohanim is comparable to the service in the Beis HaMikdash, and therefore, a Kohen who wishes to *duchan* is permitted to drink up to one *reviis* of wine, just as the Kohanim in the Beis HaMikdash were forbidden only to drink a *reviis*. *Mishnah Berurah* (128:137) explains that the restriction on drinking wine before performing Bircas Kohanim is subject to the same guidelines as drinking wine before offering a sacrifice in the Beis HaMikdash.

1. *Shulchan Aruch* (128:38) states that if a Kohen drank a *reviis* of wine, he may not perform Bircas Kohanim until the effect of the wine dissipates.[2]
2. Although the Gemara and *Shulchan Aruch* forbid only wine, the *poskim* write that other alcoholic beverages, such as whiskey,

---

1. A *nazir* is a person who accepts upon himself the vow of *nezirus*, upon which it becomes forbidden for him to consume wine or grape products, cut his hair, or come into contact with corpse-*tumah*.
2. See *Shulchan Aruch* 99:2 for the halachic guidelines for removing the effects of wine.

bourbon, and the like, are also included in the prohibition. However, a Kohen who consumes one of these beverages is not disqualified until he reaches a certain level of intoxication (regardless of the amount imbibed), whereas one who drinks wine is allowed only up to one *reviis*, as discussed above.[3]

3. *Chayei Adam*[4] rules that if a Kohen is weak and has a medical need to make Kiddush and eat before Mussaf, he should drink less than a *reviis* of wine, so as not to forfeit the mitzvah of Bircas Kohanim. *Mishnah Berurah*[5] notes that since wine in our times is diluted, the Kohen may drink an exact *reviis* for Kiddush and still perform Bircas Kohanim during Mussaf. Elsewhere, *Mishnah Berurah*[6] mentions that taking a short nap counteracts the effect of wine. *Pri Megadim*[7] states that if the Kohen who is weak eats a *k'zayis* of bread after making Kiddush, he is still permitted to *duchan* afterward, as the food mitigates the possible intoxicating effect of the Kiddush wine.

4. A Kohen is permitted to make Kiddush on grape juice before Bircas Kohanim.[8] However, it is preferable for him to hear a non-Kohen make Kiddush.[9]

5. *Mishnah Berurah*[10] cites *Levush*'s observation that since many people become intoxicated on Simchas Torah, some have the custom to refrain from performing Bircas Kohanim on that day. *Mishnah Berurah* also quotes *Eliyahu Rabbah*, who writes that one shul in Prague had the custom to perform Bircas Kohanim on Simchas Torah during Shacharis, while others did so during Mussaf.

---

3. *Mishnah Berurah* (§141) cites the opinion of *Magen Avraham* that after imbibing other alcoholic beverages (besides wine) the Kohanim are not disqualified until they are as completely intoxicated as Lot was during the incident involving his daughters (see *Bereishis* 19:30-38). *Mishnah Berurah* and *Biur Halachah* conclude, however, that we follow the opinion of most other Acharonim, that once they reach the point where they are not fit to "speak before the King" (a lower level of intoxication), they may no longer *duchan*.
4. 32:7.
5. See *Biur Halachah* 286:3.
6. 99:13.
7. 286:2.
8. See Responsa of R' Chaim Kanievsky #475 and *Teshuvos Az Nidberu* of R' Binyamin Yehoshua Zilber, vol. 6 #6; *Shiurei R' Yosef Shalom Elyashiv, Berachos* 35b, *Tziyunei Halachah* of R' Elyashiv, p. 428.
9. *Shulchan Aruch HaRav* 128:5; *Kitzur Shulchan Aruch* 100:3.
10. 669:17.

Kohanim must be careful not to become intoxicated before they have done the mitzvah, concludes *Mishnah Berurah*. (See chapter 40, where we discuss the common custom today to perform Bircas Kohanim on Simchas Torah during Shacharis.)

In *Kuntres Zichronos* (see chapter 48), R' Chaim Kanievsky writes that on Simchas Torah the Chazon Ish would make a kiddush for the congregation in his house before *hakafos* (it seems that he did so because he received the honor of *Chassan Torah* every year; see *Rema* 669:1), and he would instruct the Kohanim not to drink wine, so that they would be able to *duchan* during Mussaf (see 128:38 and *Mishnah Berurah* 669:16).[11]

11. Although the Chazon Ish sponsored the kiddush, he did not eat anything himself (see chapter 48).

Chapter 47
A Kohen Who Is a Sinner

The *Yerushalmi* states (*Gittin* 5:9):

> In order that you should not say, "So-and-so (who is a Kohen) commits adultery and murder — and *he* is the one who blesses us? Of what value is his blessing?" The Holy One, Blessed is He, therefore declares, "He is not the one who actually blesses you; it is I, as the Torah states: *Let them place My Name on Bnei Yisrael, and I shall bless them.*"

Rambam elaborates (*Hilchos Tefillah U'Nesias Kapayim* 15:6-7, cited in *Tur, siman* 128):

> As long as a Kohen does not have any of the specific defects that disqualify him from Bircas Kohanim, he is permitted to *duchan* and should not be prevented from doing so. This includes someone who is not a scholar, is not careful in his mitzvah observance, has a bad reputation among people, or is known to be dishonest in his business transactions. The mitzvah of Bircas Kohanim applies to *every* Kohen, and the fact that he is a sinner is no reason for him to add another sin — that is, the sin of failing to fulfill this positive commandment. Lest you ask, "How can the blessing of such a commoner be of any value?" you must know that the blessing does not depend on the Kohen; rather, it comes from Hashem Himself, as the Torah states: *Let them place My Name on Bnei Yisrael, and I shall bless them.*

Better to Let Them Duchan

R' Yitzchok Kosovsky, author of *She'eilas Yitzchak,* sent a letter to his brother-in-law, R' Chaim Ozer Grodzinski, asking whether he should allow Kohanim who desecrate Shabbos to *duchan,* as *Shulchan Aruch* seems to indicate that it is not permitted (128:37). R' Chaim Ozer responded (*She'eilos U'Teshuvos Achiezer,* vol. 3, 25), "You are correct in your fear that by not allowing them to *duchan* they may come to forget that they are Kohanim altogether. This can lead them to serious transgressions, such as marrying women who are forbidden to Kohanim, or entering a cemetery and the like. It is preferable to let them *duchan,* and treat them as *tinokos shenishbu* (infants who were taken captive by non-Jews and raised without Torah values), as the Aruch LaNer, R' Yaakov Ettlinger, is inclined to rule (*Binyan Tzion, Teshuvah* 23), with regard to wine that is touched by such people."

A similar opinion is expressed by Chazon Ish (*Hilchos Shechitah,* ch. 1), R' Yitzchak Elchonon Spektor (*Igros,* vol. 1, 61), and R' Moshe Feinstein (*Igros Moshe,* vol. 1 #33).

A Kohen Who Murdered

1. The Gemara[12] and *Shulchan Aruch*[13] rule that if a Kohen killed someone, he should not perform Bircas Kohanim. According to some *poskim,* this restriction does not apply to a Kohen who killed accidentally, or even to one who killed deliberately, but then sincerely repented.[14]

12. *Berachos* 32b.
13. 128:35. *Rema,* as explained by *Mishnah Berurah* §130, rules leniently even for a Kohen who killed intentionally, provided that he repented completely.
14. See *Mishnah Berurah* 128:130 and *Biur Halachah* there (s.v. *Asah Teshuvah*) quoting *Gra,* that according to *Shulchan Aruch* the Kohen is permitted to perform Bircas Kohanim if he repented. This is also the opinion of *Shulchan Aruch HaRav* 128:50. Other *poskim* disagree, stating that if a Kohen killed someone intentionally he is banned from performing Bircas Kohanim even if he repented. If the Kohen was involved in a fatal car accident that was not his fault, it is permissible for him to perform Bircas Kohanim. See R' Ovadiah Yosef, *Yechaveh Daas,* vol. 5 #16; *Teshuvos Shevet HaLevi,* vol. 1 #43; and Responsa of R' Chaim Kanievsky #463.

2. If a Kohen killed someone, even intentionally, while serving in the military, he is still permitted to perform Bircas Kohanim.[15]

3. A Kohen who publicly embarrassed someone is permitted to perform Bircas Kohanim,[16] even though the sin of embarrassing another Jew in public is tantamount to murder.[17]

15. *Igros Moshe, Y.D.,* vol. 2 #158; R' Ovadiah Yosef, *Yechaveh Daas,* vol. 2 #14; Responsa of R' Chaim Kanievsky #461.
16. *Teshuvos Shevet HaLevi,* vol. 8 #172; *Teshuvos L'Horos Nassan,* vol. 8 #2; Responsa of R' Chaim Kanievsky #464.
17. *Bava Metzia* 58b. See also *Rambam, Hilchos Deios* 6:8.

Chapter 48
Kuntres Zichronos

R' Chaim Kanievsky kept a notebook that he called *Kuntres Zichronos* in which he recorded all the practices of his great teacher, the Chazon Ish. Shortly after R' Chaim passed away, his family published the notebook, to share it with Klal Yisrael. Here is what he wrote about Bircas Kohanim (an English translation follows the Hebrew):

סימן ח׳

א) כשהיה ש״ץ לא הקריא לכהנים יברכך רק אחר (עיין ברכות ל״ד א׳ תוספות ד״ה לא ובאורח חיים סימן קכ״ח סי״ג).

סימן ט׳

א) שמעתי שלא הסכים לדעת החרדים שיש מצות עשה על ישראל לשמע ברכת כהנים (מובא בבאור הלכה ריש סימן קכ״ח).

ב) שאלתי אם עדין שוכב במטתו ושומע ברכת כהנים אם צריך לירד לעמד לפני הכהנים והשיב דהוי כעם שבשדות דהברכה גם עליהם (עיין ארח חיים סימן קכ״ח והכא עדיף).

ג) בשמחת תורה לפני הקפות היה נותן קדוש בביתו עבור הצבור (כנראה משום שהיה חתן תורה עין רמ״א סימן תרס״ט), וצוה לכהן שלא ישתה יין כדי שיוכל לישא כפיו במוסף (עיין אורח חיים סימן קכ״ח סעיף ל״ח ובמשנה ברורה סימן תרס״ט ס״ק ט״ז) והוא בעצמו לא טעם עמהם כלום.

ד) תבת כהנים היה רגיל להקרות בעצמו ולא הש״ץ (ועין במעשה רב סימן קס״ח ועין לעיל סימן ח׳ אות נ״ט איך נהג כשהיה ש״ץ).

ה) בתחלה היה דעתו שכהן ש״ץ ישא כפיו ואחר כך חזר בו ואמר

שלא ישא כפיו ואפלו אין כהנים אחרים (כן העידו כמה עדים ועין סימן קכ״ח סעיף כ׳).

ו) כמדמה לי שהכהן משכונת בורובוב אמר לי שמרן אמר לו כשהיה יארצייט שמוטב שישא כפיו ולא יעבר לפני התבה (שזה דאוריתא וזה דרבנן).

ז) צוה לר״ש כהן ז״ל שבנו ישא כפיו חצי שנה לפני הבר מצוה (עין סימן קכ״ח סעיף ל״ד ומשנה ברורה ס״ק קכ״ג).

ח) יש אומרים משמו שכהנים נושׂאים כפיהם בבית האבל (רמ״ג וכן שמעתי גם כן, וזה בארץ ישׂראל שנושׂאים כפים כל יום).

ט) אבל תוך ל׳ על אביו ואמו נושׂא כפיו (בן ר״ש כהן בשם אביו ז״ל ועין ארח חיים סימן קכ״ח סעיף מ״ג אך יש לומר דבארץ ישׂראל שאני).

י) שמענו שהקפיד שלא לבקש לכהן לצאת קדם קריאת התורה כדי לקרא לאחר במקומו שאין זה וקדשתו (רמ״ג), ומכל מקום לפעמים במקום צרך גדול כגון שהיו חיובים לעליות התיר לבקש מהכהן שיצא (כן שמעתי).

Siman 8

1. When he (the Chazon Ish) served as the chazzan, he did not call out the words of Bircas Kohanim (*"Yevarechecha,"* etc.) himself, but assigned someone else to do it. (See *Berachos* 34a, *Tosafos* s.v. *Lo*, and *O.C.* 128:13.)

Siman 9

1. I heard that he did not agree with the opinion of *Sefer Chareidim* that there is a positive commandment for non-Kohanim to hear Bircas Kohanim (see *Biur Halachah*, beginning of *siman* 128).
2. I asked him this question: If one is still lying in bed and he hears Bircas Kohanim from a nearby shul, is he is obligated to immediately get out of bed and stand up before the Kohanim? He answered that such a person is comparable to the *am sheb'sados* (people working out in the fields), who are included in the *berachah* without hearing it (see *Shulchan Aruch* 128, and the case of one who is lying in bed is even better than the situation discussed there).

3. On Simchas Torah he would make a kiddush for the congregation in his house before *hakafos* (it seems that he did so because he received the honor of *Chassan Torah* every year; see *Rema* 669:1), and he would instruct the Kohanim not to drink wine, so that they would be able to *duchan* during Mussaf (see *Shulchan Aruch* 128:38 and *Mishnah Berurah* 669:16). Although he sponsored the kiddush, he did not eat anything himself.

4. He would call out the word "Kohanim!" himself, rather than having the chazzan do it (see also *Maaseh Rav, siman* 168, and see above, *siman* 8, as to how he conducted himself when he served as the chazzan).

5. Initially, he ruled that a Kohen who is serving as the chazzan should *duchan*, but he later changed his opinion on the matter, and ruled that the chazzan should not *duchan* (heard from numerous witnesses; see *Shulchan Aruch* 128:20).

6. A Kohen from the Ramat Gan neighborhood told me that the Chazon Ish told him it is better to *duchan* on the day you have *yahrtzeit* than to serve as the chazzan, as most non-Kohanim do (because Bircas Kohanim is a *mitzvah d'Oraysa* and davening is only *d'Rabbanan*).

7. He instructed R' Shlomo Cohen to have his son begin *duchaning* a half-year before his bar mitzvah (see 128:34 and *Mishnah Berurah* #123).

8. Some say in his name that Kohanim should *duchan* even in a mourner's home; heard from R' Meir Greineman. I heard this myself as well. (Of course, this applies only in Eretz Yisrael, where Bircas Kohanim is performed every day.)

9. A mourner, even within the first thirty days after losing one of his parents, should *duchan* (heard from the son of R' Shlomo Cohen in the name of his father; see 128:43; however, it is probable that the halachah differs for those who reside in Eretz Yisrael.)

10. I heard that he was insistent that one should not tell a Kohen to step out of the shul before the Torah reading so that the first *aliyah* could be offered to a non-Kohen, as this negates the mitzvah of *V'kidashto* (*Vayikra* 21:8; heard from R' Meir Greineman). Nevertheless, in times of great necessity, when there were many people who had to receive *aliyos*, he did allow for the Kohen to be asked to leave (that is what I heard).

Chapter 49
Shoneh Halachos: Laws of Nesias Kapayim

The following halachic rulings are taken from R' Chaim Kanievsky's *Shoneh Halachos*, which is a summary of the halachos presented in *Mishnah Berurah*. (We received R' Chaim's permission and encouragement to publish these in this book.)

Siman 128

Torah Commandment

1. The mitzvah for a Kohen to recite Bircas Kohanim is *d'Oraysa* (required by Torah law), even outside Eretz Yisrael. *Sefer Chareidim* states that the non-Kohanim, who stand silently, facing the Kohanim and having in mind to receive the *berachah*, are also included in the mitzvah.[1]

Minyan

2. A minyan of at least ten men is required for Bircas Kohanim. The Kohanim themselves are included in the ten, even if they are the majority. (If the minyan consists of only Kohanim, see #51 below.) This requirement to have ten men is *d'Rabbanan* (a Rabbinic requirement). *Pri Megadim* questions whether a sleeping person may be counted as one of the ten.[2]

---

1. *Biur Halachah* s.v. *Kasav; Shaar HaTziyun* §137.
2. *Se'if* 1,2; *Mishnah Berurah* §1,2; *Biur Halachah* s.v. *Ein.*

3. If the chazzan began *Chazaras HaShatz* with ten people and then some walked out, although he does finish the remainder of *Chazaras HaShatz*, Bircas Kohanim is not recited. However, if the Kohanim already began to *duchan* before the minyan dispersed, they may finish.[3]

If Someone Claims to Be a Kohen

4. According to some *poskim*, anyone who claims to be a Kohen is believed with regard to Bircas Kohanim, and we allow him to *duchan*. The *minhag* is in accordance with this opinion.[4]

Is a Sefer Torah Required?

5. According to a minority opinion, Bircas Kohanim may be recited only in a place where there is a *sefer Torah*; however, almost all Acharonim disagree.[5]

A Non-Kohen

6. A non-Kohen is forbidden to *duchan* even if he does so together with Kohanim. If he does *duchan* (with his hands raised like a Kohen), he transgresses a positive commandment, because the Torah specifically instructs Kohanim to recite the blessing: כֹּה תְבָרְכוּ, *so shall you bless* (*Bamidbar* 6:23) — *"you,"* the Kohanim, and no one else.

This raises the question of how it is that even non-Kohanim commonly use the words of Bircas Kohanim to bless each other when they are parting ways (and some fathers have the custom to bless their children with the words of Bircas Kohanim on Friday night). Perhaps the explanation is that since everyone knows that Bircas Kohanim is recited only during davening, it is self-understood that one's intention is not to fulfill the mitzvah of Bircas Kohanim at this time, but merely to borrow the words of the *pesukim* to use as a personal blessing.[6]

---

3. *Mishnah Berurah* §1; *Biur Halachah* s.v. *B'pachos*.
4. *Mishnah Berurah* §1.
5. Ibid.
6. *Se'if* 1; *Mishnah Berurah* §3,6; *Biur Halachah* s.v. *D'zar*. See also *Chazon Ish*, *Kesubos* 89:16.

7. A *chalal* (disqualified Kohen[7]) has the same status as a non-Kohen, and he may not *duchan*.[8]

Removing Shoes

8. The Kohanim may not go up to *duchan* while wearing shoes, whether or not the shoes have laces.[9] Boots that come up to one's knees are permissible; however, according to some opinions, if the boots are made from leather they may not be worn.

It is also improper to *duchan* barefooted; one should be wearing socks.[10]

9. Out of respect for the shul, the Kohen should not leave his shoes out in the open, but rather in a discreet location. They should preferably be removed before he washes his hands, but if it is possible to remove the shoes without touching them, he may do so after washing as well.[11]

Washing Hands

10. Even though the Kohanim, like everyone else, wash their hands in the morning before davening, they must wash them again, until the wrist,[12] before *duchaning* (see #11 below).

The Kohen should use only water to clean his hands at this time, not other cleansing agents.

According to some, this washing is comparable to a Kohen washing his hands before performing the *avodah* in the Beis HaMikdash. Thus, the water should be poured from a vessel, by a person; it should not be discolored, and the vessel should contain at least one *reviis* of water.[13]

---

7. For example, if one's father is a Kohen and his mother was divorced before marrying him; since such a marriage is forbidden for a Kohen, the child is a *chalal*.
8. *Biur Halachah* s.v. *V'ein*.
9. The reason the Kohen must remove his shoes is that the shoes may be soiled, and that is not considered respectful to the congregation. There is also a concern that he may be compelled to tie them while the other Kohanim are *duchaning*, and this may lead some to conjecture that he is not *duchaning* with the others because he is not qualified to be a Kohen. Nevertheless, the rule applies to all shoes, even if they have no laces.
10. *Se'if* 5; *Mishnah Berurah* §15-18.
11. *Mishnah Berurah* §15.
12. Even on Tishah B'Av and Yom Kippur; *Mishnah Berurah*, 613:7.
13. *Se'if* 6; *Mishnah Berurah* §19,21.

11. If there is no water available, the Kohen may rely upon his morning handwashing, provided that he did not get distracted from guarding the cleanliness of his hands the entire time, and he knows that he did not touch any part of his body that is normally kept covered.[14]

12. It is preferable not to pause between washing and reciting Bircas Kohanim for longer than it takes to walk twenty-two *amos* (about twenty-two average paces). Therefore, the Kohanim should wash only when the chazzan is up to the *berachah* of *Retzei,* and the chazzan himself should not say the *berachah* too slowly. The Kohanim should also refrain from speaking from the time they wash until they *duchan.*[15]

13. A Levi should pour the water onto the hands of the Kohen. Even if the Levi is a *talmid chacham* (Torah scholar) and the Kohen is an *am haaretz* (unlearned), the Levi is still required to serve the Kohen; that is certainly the case if at least one of the Kohanim is also a *talmid chacham.*

If no Levi is available, the water should be poured by a *bechor* — someone who is a firstborn to his mother. If there is no *bechor* either, then the Kohen should wash his own hands, rather than be served by a Yisrael.[16]

14. The common practice is to allow a Levi to wash the Kohen's hands even if the Levi did not wash his own hands first. However, if the Levi has not been attentive to what his hands are touching, it is preferable that he wash his hands first; all the more so if he knows that he touched an unclean part of his body.[17]

15. Even if the Kohen touched an unclean part of his body, the custom is that he does not recite the *berachah* of *al netilas yadayim* when he washes. Nevertheless, since there is some question about this, a G-d-fearing Kohen will make every effort to keep his hands clean from the time he washes them in the morning, in order to avoid the uncertainty regarding the *berachah.*[18]

---

14. *Mishnah Berurah* §20; *Shaar HaTziyun* ad loc.
15. *Biur Halachah* s.v. *Chozrin.*
16. *Se'if* 6; *Mishnah Berurah* §22.
17. *Se'if* 6; *Mishnah Berurah* §23.
18. *Se'if* 7; *Mishnah Berurah* §24.

A Kohen Who Doesn't Duchan

16. A qualified Kohen who does not go up to *duchan* violates the positive commandment of כֹּה תְבָרְכוּ, *so shall you bless* (*Bamidbar* 6:23), and it is considered as though he transgressed two other mitzvos as well: אָמוֹר לָהֶם, *say to them* (ibid.) and וְשָׂמוּ אֶת שְׁמִי, *Let them place My Name* (ibid. v. 27). However, this applies only if he was in the shul when the chazzan called out, "Kohanim!" or he was told to go up or to wash his hands.[19]

17. A Kohen is not obligated to *duchan* more than once a day, but if he does choose to *duchan* a second time, he must repeat the *berachah* (*Asher Kideshanu*...).[20]

18. The mitzvah of Bircas Kohanim does not override the Kohen's prohibition to expose himself to the *tumah* of a corpse. Therefore, if he learns that there is a corpse in the shul, he must walk out immediately, even if he has already gone up to *duchan*. However, if the corpse is not in the same room, but in an adjoining room, in which case the prohibition to expose himself to it is only *d'Rabbanan*, the Kohen is not obligated to leave once he has washed his hands. Even in such a case, if he finds out about the corpse before washing, it is preferable that he leave the building.[21]

19. If a Kohen is feeling weak and he prefers not to *duchan*, he should leave the shul before the chazzan begins *Retzei*. Technically, he is permitted to come back in after the chazzan has already called out, "Kohanim," but the custom is that he should stay out until after Bircas Kohanim so that no one should question his status as a Kohen.[22]

If he is not feeling weak, and he is able to *duchan*, he is forbidden to walk out and thereby disregard the mitzvah of Bircas Kohanim.[23]

Moving From One's Place

20. When the chazzan begins the *berachah* of *Retzei*, every Kohen must move from his place toward the *duchan*. *B'dieved* (after the fact), if a Kohen did not begin moving immediately, he may still

---

19. *Se'if* 2; *Mishnah Berurah* §7,10; *Biur Halachah* s.v. *Im* and s.v. *Oh*.
20. *Se'if* 3; *Mishnah Berurah* §11; *Shaar HaTziyun* §81.
21. *Mishnah Berurah* §8.
22. *Se'if* 4; *Mishnah Berurah* §12,13.
23. *Biur Halachah* ibid., s.v. *Einam*.

go up toward the *duchan* as long as the chazzan did not yet finish *Retzei.*

Akiras makom — moving from one's place — is done *after* washing one's hands; therefore, the Kohanim should wash their hands before *Retzei,* to allow themselves time to move from their places during *Retzei.*[24]

21. A Kohen who did not move from his place until after *Retzei* may not go up to *duchan*. If he goes up in any case, may he *duchan*? It depends: If the cause of his not moving on time was something beyond his control (an *oness*), he may remain where he is and *duchan*; otherwise, he must exit the shul.[25]

22. If he did not move from his place until after *Retzei,* but now someone tells him to go *duchan,* he is still not permitted to do so. However, some *poskim* question this ruling, and therefore the Kohen should leave the shul before anyone has a chance to tell him to go up.[26]

23. If the Kohen did move during *Retzei,* but in the wrong direction — that is, further away from the *duchan* — it is not considered *akiras makom*. Therefore, to avoid that scenario, if the Kohanim who went out to wash have not yet come back into the room when the chazzan is ready to say *Retzei,* and we don't know whether they have started moving toward the *duchan,* we tell the chazzan not to begin *Retzei* until they come in.[27]

24. If a Kohen left his house to go to shul, and he walked in after *Retzei,* that is not considered *akirah,* and he may not go up to *duchan,*[28] unless he left his house with the specific intent of going to shul in order to *duchan*. However, according to some opinions, even in the latter case it is not considered *akirah* unless his house is close enough to the shul that he heard the chazzan begin *Retzei.*[29]

---

24. *Se'if* 8; *Mishnah Berurah* §25,27.
25. *Se'if* 8; *Mishnah Berurah* §29; *Biur Halachah* s.v. *Aval.*
26. *Se'if* 9; *Biur Halachah* s.v. *Shuv.*
27. *Mishnah Berurah* §28.
28. If he did go up, however, he is not required to step down.
29. *Mishnah Berurah* §28; *Shaar HaTziyun* ad loc.

Modim

25. The Kohanim stand at the *duchan*, facing the *aron kodesh*, until the chazzan finishes the *berachah* of *Modim*. The Kohanim say *Modim d'Rabbanan* along with everyone else, and then they say the following *tefillah*:

> יְהִי רָצוֹן מִלְּפָנֶיךָ ה׳ אֱלֹהֵינוּ וֵאלֹהֵי אֲבוֹתֵינוּ, שֶׁתְּהֵא הַבְּרָכָה הַזֹּאת שֶׁצִּוִּיתָנוּ לְבָרֵךְ אֶת עַמְּךָ יִשְׂרָאֵל בְּרָכָה שְׁלֵמָה, וְלֹא יִהְיֶה בָהּ שׁוּם מִכְשׁוֹל וְעָוֹן מֵעַתָּה וְעַד עוֹלָם.
>
> *May it be Your will, Hashem, our G-d and the G-d of our forefathers, that this blessing with which You have commanded us to bless Your people Yisrael shall be a complete blessing, and that it not have any impediment or sin, from this time until eternity.*

They should finish this *tefillah* at the same time that the chazzan finishes the *berachah* of *Modim*, so that the congregation can respond amen to both simultaneously. The Kohanim themselves must also answer amen to the chazzan's *berachah*.[30]

"Kohanim!"

26. If two or more Kohanim are present, the chazzan summons them by saying the word "Kohanim." This is not considered an interruption, since it is necessary for the *tefillah*. The common practice is for the chazzan to quietly say the *tefillah* beginning אֱלֹהֵינוּ וֵאלֹהֵי אֲבוֹתֵינוּ בָּרְכֵנוּ בַּבְּרָכָה..., *Our G-d and the G-d of our forefathers, bless us with the blessing...* until the word "Kohanim," which he says aloud, and then he concludes in an undertone, with the words[31] עַם קְדוֹשֶׁךָ כָּאָמוּר, *Your holy nation, as it says*.[32]

27. If only one Kohen over bar mitzvah is present, the chazzan does not summon him. However, where the custom is to say the *tefillah* of אֱלֹהֵינוּ וֵאלֹהֵי אֲבוֹתֵינוּ בָּרְכֵנוּ בַּבְּרָכָה..., there is no harm in saying the word "Kohanim" aloud, because it is not an interruption in the *tefillah* in any case.[33]

---

30. *Se'if* 9, 10; *Mishnah Berurah* §30-32.
31. In some communities the congregation says these three words aloud, but not the Kohanim.
32. *Se'if* 10; *Mishnah Berurah* §34-36.
33. *Se'if* 10; *Mishnah Berurah* §38,39; *Shaar HaTziyun* ad loc.

28. The *berachah* that the Kohanim recite before Bircas Kohanim includes the phrase וְצִוָּנוּ לְבָרֵךְ אֶת עַמּוֹ יִשְׂרָאֵל בְּאַהֲבָה, *and has commanded us to bless His people Yisrael with love*. If a Kohen hates the congregation, or if they hate him, it is actually dangerous for him to *duchan*, and therefore he should walk out before *Retzei* unless he can overcome this inclination and remove the hatred from his heart. However, if two of the Kohanim hate each other, they are still permitted to *duchan* together, and one does not have the right to tell the other, "You *duchan* during Shacharis and I will *duchan* during Mussaf."[34]

Turning to Face the Congregation

29. After the Kohanim are summoned, they turn around to face the congregation. In most shuls, the *aron kodesh* is on the east wall, and thus the Kohanim are now facing toward the west. If the *aron kodesh* is located on the north wall (and the chazzan is facing east), some *poskim* say they should stand facing south, with their backs to the *aron kodesh*, while others say they should stand with their backs to the east wall of the shul, facing west, while the congregation stands face to face with them.[35]

30. The Kohanim begin the *berachah* אֲשֶׁר קִדְּשָׁנוּ בִּקְדֻשָּׁתוֹ שֶׁל אַהֲרֹן וְצִוָּנוּ לְבָרֵךְ אֶת עַמּוֹ יִשְׂרָאֵל בְּאַהֲבָה while they are still facing the *aron kodesh*, and they turn as they are reciting the *berachah* so that they finish the last words facing the congregation.

Every Kohen should recite the *berachah* himself, as opposed to one Kohen reciting it for all the rest.[36]

Nesias Kapayim — Raising One's Hands

31. The Kohanim raise their hands, palms down, to shoulder height, and spread their fingers to create five air spaces: each hand's index finger and middle finger should be separated from the other two fingers of that hand, forming a "V"; the index fingers, in turn, are separated from the thumbs, forming two more air spaces. The fifth space is created by placing the right thumb over the left (the

34. *Mishnah Berurah* §37.
35. *Se'if* 10; *Mishnah Berurah* §37.
36. *Se'if* 11; *Mishnah Berurah* §40,41.

right hand is held slightly higher than the left hand). (See diagrams in chapter 36.)

Some *poskim* say that if holding the hands in this position causes the Kohen fatigue, he may relax his hands between one word of the *berachah* and the next, and certainly between the verses.[37]

32. The chazzan says each word of Bircas Kohanim out loud, reading it from a *siddur*, and the Kohanim repeat after him, one word at a time. At the end of each *pasuk*, the congregation responds amen. *Pri Chadash* states that although *l'chatchilah* (ideally), it is a mitzvah for the chazzan to call out the words for the Kohanim, if he did not do so, the mitzvah of Bircas Kohanim is nevertheless fulfilled.[38]

Essential Requirements

33. Raising one's hands while reciting Bircas Kohanim is required by Torah law,[39] and the mitzvah cannot be fulfilled without it. Therefore, a Kohen who is not able to hold his hands up may not *duchan*. Even if he devises a way of keeping them raised, such as with strings or the like, that is not considered "raising" one's hands. As we mentioned earlier, if he can hold them up as he says each word that is sufficient, and he is permitted to lower them between words.[40]

34. Bircas Kohanim must be recited in *Lashon HaKodesh* (the original Hebrew),[41] and the Kohanim must stand while reciting the words.[42] (Those receiving the *berachah*, on the other hand, are permitted to sit, as long as they face the Kohanim. Nevertheless, it is proper for them to stand out of reverence for the mitzvah.)

Hereagain, if a Kohen is too weak to stand without being supported, he may not *duchan*.[43]

---

37. *Se'if* 12; *Mishnah Berurah* §43.
38. *Se'if* 13; *Mishnah Berurah* §49.
39. This is derived from the *pasuk* וַיִּשָּׂא אַהֲרֹן אֶת יָדָיו אֶל הָעָם וַיְבָרְכֵם, *Aharon raised his hands toward the people and blessed them* (*Vayikra* 9:22).
40. *Se'if* 14; *Mishnah Berurah* §50,52.
41. We learn this from the words כֹּה תְבָרְכוּ, *so shall you bless* (*Bamidbar* 6:23).
42. We learn that Bircas Kohanim is considered "*avodah*" (Divine Service) from the phrase לְשָׁרְתוֹ וּלְבָרֵךְ בִּשְׁמוֹ, *to serve Him and to bless in His Name* (*Devarim* 10:8), and all *avodah* must be performed while standing, as the Torah says, לַעֲמֹד לְשָׁרֵת, *to stand and serve* (*Devarim* 18:5).
43. *Se'if* 14; *Mishnah Berurah* §51.

35. The Kohanim must pronounce the words loudly enough for the entire congregation to hear.[44] Thus, a Kohen who is not able to speak loudly may not *duchan*, and should preferably walk out before *Retzei*.[45]

36. The requirements for the Kohanim to stand, face the congregation, and recite the *berachos* in *Lashon HaKodesh* are all *d'Oraysa*, and the mitzvah cannot be fulfilled any other way. Any Kohen who cannot meet these conditions should preferably step out before *Retzei*.[46]

After the Berachah

37. After they have finished reciting the three *pesukim* of Bircas Kohanim and the chazzan has begun *Sim Shalom*, the Kohanim turn around to face the *aron kodesh* once more, and recite the following *tefillah*:

> רִבּוֹנוֹ שֶׁל עוֹלָם עָשִׂינוּ מַה שֶּׁגָּזַרְתָּ עָלֵינוּ, אַף אַתָּה עֲשֵׂה עִמָּנוּ כְּמָה שֶׁהִבְטַחְתָּנוּ: הַשְׁקִיפָה מִמְּעוֹן קָדְשְׁךָ, מִן הַשָּׁמַיִם, וּבָרֵךְ אֶת עַמְּךָ אֶת יִשְׂרָאֵל, וְאֵת הָאֲדָמָה אֲשֶׁר נָתַתָּה לָנוּ — כַּאֲשֶׁר נִשְׁבַּעְתָּ לַאֲבֹתֵינוּ — אֶרֶץ זָבַת חָלָב וּדְבָשׁ.
>
> *Master of the universe, we have done what You have decreed upon us; may You also do for us as You have promised us: Gaze down from Your holy abode, from the heavens, and bless Your people, Yisrael, and the ground that You have given us, as You swore to our fathers, a land flowing with milk and honey.*

They should finish this *tefillah* at the same time the chazzan finishes the *berachah* of *Sim Shalom*, so that the congregation can respond amen to both simultaneously. On Rosh Hashanah and Yom Kippur, when the chazzan sings *Hayom Te'amtzeinu* before *Sim Shalom*, the Kohanim should wait before reciting the *tefillah*, in order to finish along with the chazzan. If they finish too soon, they should add the *tefillah* of *Adir BaMarom* (see below, *siman* 130).

The Kohanim themselves also must answer amen to the chazzan's *berachah*.[47]

---

44. As the *pasuk* states, אָמוֹר לָהֶם, *saying to them* (*Bamidbar* 6:23).
45. *Se'if* 14; *Mishnah Berurah* §53.
46. *Mishnah Berurah* §50.
47. *Se'if* 15; *Mishnah Berurah* §54,56.

38. The Kohanim are not permitted to turn around until the chazzan begins *Sim Shalom,* and they are not permitted to lower their hands until after they turn around.

They are not permitted to speak until they step down from the *duchan,* and they may not step down until the majority of the congregation has answered amen to the *berachah* of *Sim Shalom*. Now that it has become customary to express gratitude to the Kohanim by saying "*yasher koach,*" it is preferable for the Kohanim to remain in place until after *Kaddish* so that they and the congregation will not get distracted and neglect to respond to *Kaddish*.[48]

39. Whenever a Kohen turns around, either to face the congregation or toward the *aron kodesh,* he should turn to his right (clockwise), even if he is left-handed.[49]

40. When coming down from the *duchan,* a Kohen should not walk with his back to the *aron kodesh* but should turn sideways, so that he is facing slightly in the direction of the *aron kodesh,* in the manner of a student who is taking leave of his teacher.[50]

41. Upon returning to their seats, the Kohanim should avoid touching their shoes. If a Kohen did touch his shoes, he must wash his hands before continuing to daven.[51]

Wait Your Turn

42. Throughout the Bircas Kohanim procedure, the chazzan, Kohanim, and congregation must wait for one another to finish what they are saying before moving on to the next step. Thus:

- ❒ The chazzan may not call out "Kohanim" until most of the congregation has finished saying amen to the *berachah* of *Modim.*
- ❒ The Kohanim may not begin the *berachah* of *Asher Kideshanu* until the chazzan finishes saying the word "Kohanim."
- ❒ The chazzan may not call out the first word, *yevarechecha,* until the Kohanim finish reciting the *berachah.*

---

48. *Se'if* 16; *Mishnah Berurah* §57-60.
49. *Se'if* 17; *Mishnah Berurah* §61; *Shaar HaTziyun* ad loc.
50. *Mishnah Berurah* §61.
51. *Se'if* 17; *Mishnah Berurah* §62.

- The Kohanim may not say *"yevarechecha"* until the chazzan finishes calling it out to them. The same applies to each word of Bircas Kohanim.
- Likewise, the congregation may not answer amen until the Kohanim finish saying the last word of each *berachah,* and the chazzan may not proceed with the next *berachah* until the congregation finishes saying amen.[52]

When Not to Say Amen

43. If the chazzan is davening by heart, he should not answer amen to Bircas Kohanim, as he may get confused and forget what he is up to. If he is davening from a *siddur,* however, and is thus not concerned about losing his place, he should answer amen.

According to some *poskim,* the chazzan should not answer amen to the *berachah* that the Kohanim say prior to Bircas Kohanim (*Asher Kideshanu*), as that would be considered an interruption in *Chazaras HaShatz.* It is proper to follow this opinion.[53]

If the Chazzan Is a Kohen

44. It is preferable that the one who calls out the words of Bircas Kohanim should not be a Kohen. Therefore, since our custom is that the chazzan is the one to call out the words, an effort should be made to find a non-Kohen to be the chazzan. In the event that the chazzan *is* a Kohen, a non-Kohen should stand near him and call out to the Kohanim, while the chazzan stands silently in his place. If this is also not feasible, then the chazzan himself should call out to the other Kohanim.[54]

45. If the chazzan is a Kohen, but there are other Kohanim in the shul besides him, he should not *duchan,* and no one should tell him to *duchan.* If someone does tell him (before or during the *berachah* of *Retzei*) to go up and *duchan,* then he is faced with a *mitzvas asei* to do so, and he has no choice; he must go up.

In those places where the custom is for the chazzan to *duchan* even if there are other Kohanim, it is possible that we are not

---

52. *Se'if* 18; *Mishnah Berurah* §8, 9, 63-69.
53. *Se'if* 19; *Mishnah Berurah* §71; *Shaar HaTziyun* ad loc.
54. *Se'if* 22; *Mishnah Berurah* §85-87; *Biur Halachah* s.v. *V'yikra; Shaar HaTziyun* ad loc.

required to object to the practice.[55]

46. If the chazzan is the only Kohen in the shul, and he is davening from a *siddur*, so he is confident that he won't get confused, he should *duchan*, in order to avoid forfeiting Bircas Kohanim altogether. When he reaches the *berachah* of *Retzei* he takes a step toward the *duchan*, and when he finishes the *berachah* of *Modim* he leaves his place completely to go up to the *aron kodesh* and faces the congregation. Another person takes his place by the *amud* and calls out the words of Bircas Kohanim. When he is finished reciting the *berachos*, the Kohen returns to the *amud* and concludes with *Sim Shalom*.[56]

Avoiding Distractions

47. The Kohanim are not permitted to switch tunes in the middle of Bircas Kohanim, as this tends to cause confusion, and they may forget which word they are up to. Likewise, they should all be singing the same tune, not several different tunes simultaneously.

Taz writes that the same applies to the chazzan. *Eliyahu Rabbah*, however, defends the practice of the chazzan switching tunes.[57]

48. When *duchaning*, the Kohanim should not look around or allow their thoughts to wander. Rather, they should lower their gaze in the manner of someone who is davening. The congregation, for their part, should also concentrate on the *berachah* while facing the Kohanim. They should not look at the faces of the Kohanim or at their hands, and certainly not anywhere else, so as not to get distracted.

Strictly speaking, nowadays, when the Kohanim do not utilize the Ineffable Name of Hashem, and the Shechinah does not rest upon their hands, a quick glance is not forbidden; only staring intensely in a way that causes distraction is forbidden. Nevertheless, the custom is to not look at all, as a remembrance of Bircas Kohanim in the Beis HaMikdash. Thus, it is common practice for the congregation to cover their faces with their talleisim during Bircas Kohanim.[58]

---

55. *Se'if* 20; *Mishnah Berurah* §72,74,75; *Shaar HaTziyun* §64.
56. *Se'if* 20; *Mishnah Berurah* §76-79,81.
57. *Se'if* 21; *Mishnah Berurah* §83,84.
58. *Se'if* 23; *Mishnah Berurah* §89,92.

49. The Kohanim should also not gaze at their own hands, and therefore the custom is for them to lower their talleisim over their faces and spread their arms outward so that their hands extend beyond the tallis.[59]

Who Receives the Berachah?

50. Those who are at home and have the ability to come to shul to hear Bircas Kohanim, but don't bother to do so, are not included in the *berachah*. On the other hand, the "people in the fields," meaning those who are out working in the fields, or whose circumstances do not allow them to come to shul, are included in the *berachah*.

Even those who are in shul must be standing in the right place to receive the *berachah*. If they are behind the Kohanim, either directly behind them or at an angle, they are not included. Thus, those who sit at the front wall of the shul must move to another place where they can face the Kohanim. *Bach* defends such people by asserting that since everyone pays for his own seat and does not have the right to take someone else's place, the people at the front are comparable to the people in the fields who are unable to be in front of the Kohanim. This is a weak argument, however, because it is not so difficult to find a different spot to stand in for the duration of Bircas Kohanim.

Those directly to the right or to the left of the Kohanim, and certainly those who are facing them, but at an angle, are included in the *berachah*; however, they should turn toward the Kohanim. If someone is directly to the right or left of the Kohanim, and he faces toward the back of the shul (the same direction that the Kohanim are facing), that may suffice for him to be included, but it is better if he faces the Kohanim.[60]

A Minyan of Only Kohanim

51. The basic mitzvah of Bircas Kohanim is for the Kohanim to bless the congregation. Therefore, as long as there is at least one non-Kohen in the shul, then even if all the other men are Kohanim, the Kohanim should all go up to bless that one non-Kohen. If there

---

59. *Se'if* 23; *Mishnah Berurah* §91.
60. *Se'if* 24; *Mishnah Berurah* §93,95,96; *Biur Halachah* s.v. *Afilu, Im, Aval*; *Shaar HaTziyun* ad loc.

are no non-Kohanim at all, then it depends: If the minyan consists of only ten Kohanim, they should all go up to *duchan*, except the chazzan, who serves as the *makri* (the one who calls out the words of the *berachos*). If there are more than ten in the minyan, then ten of the Kohanim (i.e., the chazzan and nine others) should remain in their places to receive the *berachah* and answer amen, and only those in excess of ten should *duchan*. This applies even when there are only eleven Kohanim in shul, and only one Kohen will be able to *duchan*. However, there is some uncertainty about that particular situation.[61]

Do Not Say Pesukim

52. During Bircas Kohanim, we are receiving a *berachah* directly from the King, and therefore it is appropriate to remain silent while listening to the words, and not to recite *pesukim* at this time. Some have the practice to say *pesukim* while the Kohanim are singing (between words), but this custom is not mentioned in any halachic source.[62]

No More and No Less

53. The Torah states: לֹא תֹסִפוּ עַל הַדָּבָר אֲשֶׁר אָנֹכִי מְצַוֶּה אֶתְכֶם וְלֹא תִגְרְעוּ מִמֶּנּוּ, *You shall not add to the word that I command you, nor shall you subtract from it* (*Devarim* 4:2). Thus, a Kohen who adds an extra *berachah* to Bircas Kohanim, or leaves out one of the three *berachos*, transgresses a Torah prohibition, if he does so while his hands are spread out, in the manner of Bircas Kohanim. If he adds a *berachah* after his hands are lowered, there is some doubt as to whether he transgresses this prohibition.

On the other hand, it is perfectly fine to fulfill the mitzvah numerous times in one day, as long as the Kohen says only the three *berachos* that the Torah prescribes. Although he is permitted to *duchan* as many times as he wishes, he is not *obligated* to do so more than once a day.[63]

---

61. *Se'if* 25; *Mishnah Berurah* §97,99,101; *Biur Halachah* s.v. *Yoser.*
62. *Se'if* 26; *Mishnah Berurah* §103.
63. *Se'if* 27; *Mishnah Berurah* §104,105,106; *Biur Halachah* s.v. *V'im.*

In the Middle of Shemoneh Esrei

54. If a Kohen is in the middle of *Shemoneh Esrei* and there are no other Kohanim in shul, and he was called to go *duchan,* some *poskim* say that he should interrupt his *tefillah* and *duchan,* and then finish *Shemoneh Esrei* after he returns to his place. Others say this is permitted only if he gets up to Bircas Kohanim in his own *Shemoneh Esrei* at the same time as the chazzan does. All agree that if he will become confused and be unable to continue *Shemoneh Esrei* afterward, he should not interrupt his *tefillah.*

In a situation where he is permitted to *duchan* in the middle of *Shemoneh Esrei,* he should take a step toward the front of the shul when the chazzan begins *Retzei,* and go up to the *duchan* when the chazzan reaches Bircas Kohanim.[64]

Didn't Daven Yet

55. A Kohen may *duchan* even if he has not yet davened. If this will cause him to miss *zman tefillah* (the latest time for *Shemoneh Esrei* of Shacharis), he should stay outside the shul and daven there. However, if people tell him to go up and *duchan,* he must do so, because at that point Bircas Kohanim is a *d'Oraysa* obligation, whereas *tefillah* at the correct *zman* is only a Rabbinic obligation. If he was told to go up and he is in danger of missing *zman Krias Shema,* he should say the first *pasuk of Shema* and then go up to *duchan.*[65]

Disfigured Face or Hands

56. A Kohen who has blemishes on his face or hands, which may cause people to gaze at them during Bircas Kohanim, may not *duchan.* This includes hands that are bent in an unusual way, white spots on his face or hands, etc. He is not obligated to leave the shul, but it is preferable for him to do so. If he did go up to *duchan,* however, he is not required to step down.[66]

57. Once the people in the city have become accustomed to the blemishes that a particular Kohen has, it is no longer forbidden

64. *Mishnah Berurah* §106; *Shaar HaTziyun* ad loc.

65. *Se'if* 29; *Mishnah Berurah* §107.

66. *Se'if* 30; *Mishnah Berurah* §108,110; *Biur Halachah* s.v. *Mi* and s.v. *L'chein.*

for him to *duchan*, as his unusual appearance will no longer attract undue attention. This includes any Kohen who has been living in the city for thirty days or more. Likewise, any facial discoloration or the like that is relatively common (e.g., freckles) does not disqualify him from *duchaning*.[67]

58. Where the custom is for the Kohanim to cover their faces and hands during Bircas Kohanim, we need not be concerned about blemishes that are thus concealed. However, if that is not the custom, a disfigured Kohen may not *duchan* even if he does cover his face and hands, and even if all the other Kohanim follow suit, so that the blemished Kohen does not stand out. Since this is not their usual custom, people will still look at them. If only the congregation covers their faces, but not the Kohanim, that does not suffice.[68]

59. A Kohen whose hands are stained with dye may not *duchan* unless the custom of that city is for the Kohanim to cover their hands, or if his hands are consistently stained and he has been living in the city for thirty days or more, or if the majority of people in that city do similar work that causes their hands to become stained.[69]

Other Disqualifications

60. A Kohen may not *duchan* with torn clothing that exposes his shoulders and arms, as this is disrespectful to the congregation.[70]

61. A Kohen who suffers from digestive issues and cannot control his bowels may not *duchan*; it is preferable that he step out of the shul before *Retzei*.[71]

Unable to Enunciate Certain Letters

62. A Kohen who is unable to enunciate certain letters — for example, the letter *shin* (ש) or the letter *ches* (ח) — may not *duchan*. However, if most of the people in that city mispronounce the letters

67. *Se'if* 30; *Mishnah Berurah* §108,113; *Biur Halachah* s.v. *Holech*.
68. *Se'if* 31; *Mishnah Berurah* §114-116.
69. *Se'if* 32; *Mishnah Berurah* §117,118.
70. *Mishnah Berurah* §111.
71. Ibid.

the same way, it is permitted. Thus, in our time, when most people do not know how to differentiate between the pronunciation of the letter *aleph* (א) and the letter *ayin* (ע), a Kohen who also does not know the difference may nevertheless *duchan*.[72]

Minimum Age

63. A minor may not *duchan* alone, but if he knows how to *duchan* properly he may do so (with the preceding *berachah*) together with adult Kohanim, in order to receive training in the performance of the mitzvah.

Once he has developed indications of physical maturity (i.e., two pubic hairs), or he has turned thirteen years old, in which case we presume that he has developed such indications, he is permitted to *duchan* by himself occasionally, but he may not do so on a constant basis until he has fully matured (i.e., when there is a full growth of hair). Where the custom is to *duchan* only on Yom Tov, that is considered "occasional," with the possible exception of Yom Kippur, which is the subject of disagreement among the *poskim*. According to other opinions, if this thirteen-year-old is the only Kohen in the congregation, he may even *duchan* by himself on a constant basis.

Once he has reached the age of eighteen, he is considered a mature adult regardless of the amount of hair he has developed.[73]

64. An adult who is so short that he could be mistaken for a child may not *duchan* alone unless he has a beard.[74]

After Drinking Wine

65. Bircas Kohanim is comparable to *avodah* (Divine service) in the Beis HaMikdash; therefore, if a Kohen drinks a whole *reviis* of undiluted wine at once, he may not *duchan* until he shakes off the effect of the wine (by walking, riding, or taking a nap, as prescribed in *O.C.* 99:2). If he drinks more than a *reviis*, then he may not *duchan* even if the wine is diluted and even if he drinks it in several sips (until he shakes off the effect of the wine).

---

72. *Se'if* 33; *Mishnah Berurah* §119,120; *Shaar HaTziyun* ad loc.
73. *Se'if* 34; *Mishnah Berurah* §121-123,125,126; *Biur Halachah* s.v. *Aval, U'mihu,* and *V'lo.*
74. *Biur Halachah* s.v. *U'mihu.*

If he drinks other intoxicating beverages, however, he is not forbidden to *duchan* unless he becomes so inebriated that it would be unfitting for him to speak to a king in his condition.

There is a disagreement among the *poskim* as to whether non-alcoholic wine has the status of wine with regard to this halachah.[75]

A Mumar

66. A Kohen who accepts any other religion, or who publicly desecrates Shabbos (which is comparable to idolatry[76]), is not allowed to *duchan* unless he does *teshuvah*.[77] In the opinion of *Rambam*, *teshuvah* is effective (to allow him to *duchan*) only if he merely *accepted* another religion, but if he actually performed an act of worship, he is never permitted to *duchan* again, even after he does *teshuvah*.

Someone who only *committed* himself to convert to another religion, but never carried out his intention, is not disqualified from Bircas Kohanim.[78]

Uncircumcised

67. An uncircumcised Kohen who refuses to undergo a *bris milah* is not permitted to *duchan*. However, if he is unable to undergo the procedure due to a life-threatening medical condition (for example, if his brothers died because of circumcision, and he is concerned that he may have the same condition they did), then he is not disqualified from Bircas Kohanim.[79]

Committed Murder

68. A Kohen who killed another person, even accidentally, is forbidden to *duchan* unless he does *teshuvah*.[80] However, if the victim did not die immediately, but only after some time passed, the Kohen is not disqualified, since it is possible that the actual

75. *Se'if* 38; *Mishnah Berurah* §138,141.
76. *Rashi Chullin* 5a.
77. Just as he is forbidden to perform *avodah* in the Beis HaMikdash.
78. *Se'if* 37; *Mishnah Berurah* §134-136.
79. *Biur Halachah* s.v. *V'im*.
80. We derive this from the *pasuk* וּבְפָרִשְׂכֶם כַּפֵּיכֶם אַעְלִים עֵינַי מִכֶּם ... אֵינֶנִּי שֹׁמֵעַ יְדֵיכֶם דָּמִים מָלֵאוּ, *When you "spread your hands," I will hide My eyes from you ... I will not listen; your hands are filled with blood* (*Yeshayah* 1:15).

death was caused by some other contributing factor. Some say that if the murder was deliberate, *teshuvah* does not help to allow him to *duchan*. It is unclear which opinion is to be followed in this case, but if he does go up to *duchan*, we do not send him away.

If a Kohen was forced to commit murder in order to save his own life, then even though one is not permitted to do so, he is nevertheless permitted to *duchan*. (He is certainly permitted to *duchan* if he killed someone in self-defense.)

If he accidentally killed a baby while trying to perform a *bris milah*, he is not disqualified from Bircas Kohanim, since his intention was to do a mitzvah.

If he struck a pregnant woman and caused her to miscarry, he is not disqualified, because one who kills a fetus is not liable for capital punishment.

Even if there is a widespread rumor that he committed murder, he is not disqualified until the rumor is substantiated. However, if he knows that the rumor is true, he should not *duchan*.[81]

Forbidden Marriage

69. If a Kohen is married to one of the women who is forbidden specifically to a Kohen (e.g., a woman who was divorced), he is not permitted to *duchan*, and he is not accorded any of the honors due to a Kohen (such as receiving the first *aliyah*), until he takes two steps: (a) He must commit himself to divorce his wife that very day, and (b) he must make a *neder al daas rabbim* (a type of vow that cannot be nullified by a *beis din* or a rav) that he will never again marry someone who is forbidden to Kohanim.[82]

Exposes Himself to Corpse-Tumah

70. A Kohen is forbidden to come into contact with, or to be under the same roof as, or to step over, a corpse (unless he is attending the funeral and being involved in the burial of his seven closest relatives). If he does so intentionally, he is disqualified from *duchaning* and from all the honors due to a Kohen until he does *teshuvah* and pledges in the presence of *beis din* to never repeat

81. *Se'if* 35,36; *Mishnah Berurah* §128-133; *Biur Halachah* s.v. *Afilu b'shogeg* and *Afilu assur*; *Shaar HaTziyun* §99,101.

82. *Se'if* 40; *Mishnah Berurah* §147,149; *Shaar HaTziyun* ad loc.

his sin. If he committed this sin only on rare occasions, and not regularly, it is questionable if the latter step is required.

For a Kohen who profits financially from exposing himself to corpses, a verbal pledge is insufficient; he must also make a *neder al daas rabbim* (see previous halachah) to reinforce the commitment.[83]

Chalal

71. A *chalal* is someone who was born from a marriage that is forbidden to a Kohen; for example, if his mother was divorced before marrying his father, who is a Kohen. A *chalal* has the status of a non-Kohen in all respects, and therefore may not *duchan*.[84]

Other Deficiencies

72. If a Kohen commits any other sin aside from those listed above, regardless of its severity, he is still allowed to *duchan*. This is true even if his immoral behavior is widely known and even if he clearly has not done *teshuvah*. As *Rambam* explains, just because he is a sinner, that is not a reason for him to commit an additional sin by failing to fulfill the mitzvah of Bircas Kohanim. And although one might think that the *berachah* of a wicked person has no value, that is an error, as the *berachah* does not come from the Kohen himself; he is merely a conduit to transmit a *berachah* from Hashem.[85]

Mourner

73. Bircas Kohanim should be recited in a state of *simchah*; therefore, one who is in mourning does not *duchan*. This includes a Kohen whose father or mother passed away within the past twelve months, or who lost another close relative[86] within the past thirty days. However, this applies only if there are two other Kohanim aside from him. If not, he is permitted to *duchan* unless he is in the middle of *shivah* (the first seven days of mourning).

---

83. *Se'if* 41; *Mishnah Berurah* §150,151; *Biur Halachah* s.v. *Nitma*.
84. *Se'if* 42; *Mishnah Berurah* §155,156.
85. *Se'if* 39; *Mishnah Berurah* §142-146.
86. I.e., brother, sister, son, daughter or wife.

A mourner who is not permitted to *duchan* should step out before *Retzei.* If he didn't, and the chazzan called out "Kohanim," he is required to go up to *duchan.* However, in the case of an *onen* (that is, before his deceased relative has been buried), some *poskim* say that even if he was called up, he does not *duchan.*[87]

Unmarried

74. There is an opinion that an unmarried Kohen does not *duchan,* since he is lacking *simchah* to some extent; however, the prevalent custom does not follow that opinion. On the other hand, if an unmarried Kohen *prefers* not to *duchan,* we do not oppose his preference. He should step out before *Retzei* so as not to be in shul when the chazzan calls out "Kohanim."[88]

On What Days Is Bircas Kohanim Recited?

75. The custom in many countries is to *duchan* only on Yom Tov, during Mussaf, when we are in a state of *simchah.* In Eretz Yisrael, the *minhag* is to *duchan* every morning, a practice that is highly praised by the *poskim.*[89]

Spreading the Blessing

76. When the Kohanim say the words יְבָרֶכְךָ, וְיִשְׁמְרֶךָ, אֵלֶיךָ, וִיחֻנֶּךָּ, אֵלֶיךָ, לְךָ, and שָׁלוֹם, they stretch out the last word in a sing-song, while turning left and then right, to "spread" the *berachah* to all those present. The Kohanim should stretch out only the last letter of each of these words, because until the last letter is pronounced, it is not a word at all. The same applies to any chazzan who is singing the words of davening — he should never extend the first half of a word, because half a word is meaningless.[90]

When to Say the Ribbono Shel Olam Prayer

77. The custom is that the congregation recites the prayer beginning *"Ribbono Shel Olam"* after the *makri* calls out the last word of each *pasuk* of Bircas Kohanim. While they are saying this *tefillah,*

---

87. *Se'if* 43; *Mishnah Berurah* §157-159; *Biur Halachah* s.v. *Yeitzei.*
88. *Se'if* 44; *Mishnah Berurah* §160,161,163; *Biur Halachah* s.v. *Yeitzei.*
89. *Se'if* 44; *Mishnah Berurah* §164,165.
90. *Se'if* 45; *Mishnah Berurah* §169.

the Kohanim remain silent or sing a tune until the congregation is finished, and then the Kohanim say the last word of the *pasuk*. The congregation should not take too much time saying this *tefillah*, as it creates an interruption between the call of the *makri* and the response of the Kohanim, especially if the Kohanim are remaining silent during that time.

The chazzan himself should not say *Ribbono Shel Olam*, as it would be an interruption in his *Chazaras HaShatz*. If someone other than the chazzan is the *makri*, he should also not say it, as he may forget which word he was up to. However, once he says the last word (*shalom*), he may say the *tefillah*.[91]

No Kohen, No V'sei'areiv

78. When there are no Kohanim in shul for *Chazaras HaShatz* of Mussaf, the custom is not to say the paragraph beginning *V'sei'areiv*.[92]

Not to Use the Services of a Kohen

79. With regard to a Kohen the Torah commands us, וְקִדַּשְׁתּוֹ, *You shall sanctify him* (*Vayikra* 21:8). This obligates us to treat a Kohen with great respect, and therefore, one is not permitted to have a Kohen serve him; it is akin to using a sanctified item for one's own needs (a sin known as *me'ilah*).

According to one opinion, however, a Kohen may forego his honor and choose to provide a service for a non-Kohen. According to other opinions, the Kohen may do so only if he has some personal benefit or financial gain from serving the non-Kohen. It is preferable to follow the first, more stringent opinion, especially in the case of a menial, degrading type of work.

It may be permissible for one Kohen to serve another Kohen, or for a Kohen who is an *am ha'aretz* (lacking in Torah knowledge) to serve another person, but it should still be avoided in the case of a degrading type of work.[93]

91. *Se'if* 45; *Mishnah Berurah* §173; *Biur Halachah* s.v. *Ub'shaah*.
92. *Mishnah Berurah* §173.
93. *Se'if* 45; *Mishnah Berurah* §175; *Biur Halachah* s.v. *Assur*.

Siman 129

During Which Tefillos Is Bircas Kohanim Recited?

1. In places where Bircas Kohanim is recited every day, it is recited only during the *tefillos* of Shacharis, Mussaf, and Neilah (on Yom Kippur — provided that it is still daytime), but not during Minchah, because some Kohanim may be intoxicated at that time of day. In places where Bircas Kohanim is recited only on Yom Tov, on all other days the chazzan says the paragraph of אֱלֹקֵינוּ וֵאלֹקֵי אֲבוֹתֵינוּ בָּרְכֵנוּ בַּבְּרָכָה... in place of Bircas Kohanim during those *tefillos*.[94]

2. On mandatory fast days, Bircas Kohanim is recited during Minchah as well (in places where it is recited every day), since the Kohanim are fasting and are not intoxicated. The exception to this rule is Yom Kippur, when Bircas Kohanim is recited during Neilah and not Minchah; the paragraph of אֱלֹקֵינוּ וֵאלֹקֵי אֲבוֹתֵינוּ בָּרְכֵנוּ בַּבְּרָכָה... is recited during Minchah.[95]

Siman 130

The Ribbono Shel Olam Prayer

1. If someone had a dream that is causing him distress, he should recite the *Ribbono Shel Olam* prayer three times during Bircas Kohanim the following morning (if he lives in a place where Bircas Kohanim is recited every day; if not, see next halachah). He should say this prayer one time before the end of each of the three *berachos*.

The first time he says it he should end with the word וְתִשְׁמְרֵנִי — corresponding to the word וְיִשְׁמְרֶךָ at the end of the first *berachah*; the second time he should end with וּתְחָנֵּנִי — corresponding to וִיחֻנֶּךָּ; the third time with וְתָבוֹא עָלַי בִּרְכַּת כֹּהֲנֶיךָ וְתִרְצֵנִי.

He should time his recital of the *tefillah* to finish at the same time that the Kohanim finish saying the last word of each *berachah*, so that when the congregation responds amen to the *berachah* of the Kohanim it will be a response to his *tefillah* as well. If he finishes

94. *Se'if* 1; *Mishnah Berurah* §2,8,9.
95. *Se'if* 1; *Mishnah Berurah* §10; *Shaar HaTziyun* ad loc.

before the Kohanim, he should add the *tefillah* of *Adir BaMarom*, and finish with the word *shalom* at the same time that the Kohanim say the word *shalom*, which will be followed by the amen of the congregation.

If there are no Kohanim present, or if one is in a place where Bircas Kohanim is not performed daily, one should say the *Ribbono Shel Olam* prayer while the chazzan is saying the *berachah* of *Sim Shalom*, and in this case as well, he should finish together with the chazzan in order to take advantage of the amen of the congregation. If he does not have enough time, he may begin the *tefillah* a bit sooner — when the chazzan begins saying the words of Bircas Kohanim (*yevarechecha*). If he finishes before the chazzan, he should add the *tefillah* of *Adir BaMarom*, as above. Some have the custom to say *Adir BaMarom* every day, when the chazzan gets up to the words *v'tov b'einecha* in the *berachah* of *Sim Shalom*.[96]

2. As noted, the *Ribbono Shel Olam* prayer is recited the morning after having a troubling dream. However, in places where Bircas Kohanim takes place only on Yom Tov, the custom is for the entire congregation to say it, on the presumption that everyone has such dreams from time to time, and it is highly likely that every person has experienced at least one disturbing dream since the last time Bircas Kohanim was recited.

This *tefillah*, like all personal supplications, is not recited on Shabbos, unless someone had a disturbing dream the night before.

According to some opinions, the *tefillah* is also not recited on Yom Tov Sheini (the second day of Yom Tov for those who live outside Eretz Yisrael), unless one had a troubling dream the night before, because the Bircas Kohanim that was recited on the first day of Yom Tov already covered all the earlier dreams. The custom, however, is to say it anyway. Perhaps the reason is that we are also concerned about dreams that *someone else* may have had about us. Even according to this *minhag*, one should not begin from the words חֲלוֹם חָלַמְתִּי, but from יְהִי רָצוֹן ... שֶׁיִּהְיוּ כָּל חֲלוֹמוֹתַי.[97]

96. *Se'if* 1; *Mishnah Berurah* §3-7,9,10.
97. *Se'if* 1; *Mishnah Berurah* §1,4,9; *Biur Halachah* s.v. *Man.*

Part 6:

Collected Responsa of Maran Harav Chaim Kanievsky

Chapter 50
R' Chaim's Responsa About Bircas Kohanim

For over five decades, R' Chaim responded in writing to requests for rulings and guidance regarding every area of Torah life. Graciously, he permitted the author to go through his huge archive and select the responses pertaining to Bircas Kohanim, the subject of this book. For the benefit of the reader, we have grouped the questions according to topics.

We urge the reader to study the underlying sources, not just the questions and answers, for a fuller understanding of the Rav's rulings.

R' Chaim insisted that we caution the reader not to decide halachic questions based on these letters. For halachic decisions, a rav must be consulted for a definitive ruling.

Please note: The English summaries do not reflect many of the nuances and details addressed in the *teshuvos*.

HANDWASHING BEFORE BIRCAS KOHANIM

Kohanim are to have their hands washed before each Bircas Kohanim, even if they washed their hands before davening or a previous Bircas Kohanim and even if they must rush their personal *Shemoneh Esrei.* It is preferable that the water be poured from a utensil and that it reach until the wrist, even on Yom Kippur and Tishah B'Av (when other handwashing is performed only until the knuckles). The water needs to be poured only one time. They may leave the actual shul for the short time needed to wash their hands, but they should return before *Retzei* in order to begin walking toward the front.

1

שאלה: כמה פעמים צריך ליטול כל יד לנשיאת כפים?

תשובה: פעם אחת.

2

שאלה: האם ראוי להתקין ברז בהיכל בית הכנסת עצמו כדי שלא יפסידו הכהנים והלויים עניית אמן בזמן שהולכים ליטול ידי הכהנים?

תשובה: כרצונכם.

3

שאלה: מהו המקור שכהנים צריכים לקדש ידיהם בבית המקדש בכלי, כדמשמע במשנה ברורה (סי' קכ"ח ס"ק כ"א), והעתיקו רבנו בשונה הלכות דין י'.

תשובה: זבחים כ"א ב'.

4

שאלה: אם יש מנין מצומצם בבית הכנסת, איך ינהגו הכהנים בנטילת ידים לברכת כהנים, האם להקדים לפני חזרת הש"ץ?

תשובה: מותר לצאת בשביל לחזור תיכף ואין מקלקל המנין.

5

שאלה: בבאור הלכה (סי' קכ"ח, ד"ה חוזרים ונוטלים), הביא מהמגן אברהם בשם תוספות (סוטה ל"ט, א' ד"ה כל) שצריך ליטול ידים סמוך לרצה, דאסור לשהות כדי הילוך כ"ב אמה בין נטילה לברכה. האם כהן שמתפלל במנין מצומצם יקפיד על זה, או שמא עדיף ליטול קודם חזרת הש"ץ כדי שלא יצטרך לצאת באמצע?

תשובה: אין קפידא שיצא.

6

שאלה: כהנים שיוצאים לנטילת ידים ומפסידים לשמוע חלק גדול של חזרת הש"ץ, למה אין עושים כמו שפסק הרמב"ם שאפשר לסמוך על הנטילה הראשונה בבוקר?

תשובה: כך מצותן.

7

שאלה: מה עדיף, האם ליטול ידים קודם ברכת כהנים ומשום הכי אינו יכול לעקור רגלים ברצה, או שמא עדיף לעשות נטילת ידים בתחילת חזרת הש"ץ ולעקור רגלים "ברצה"?

תשובה: תקדים קצת הנטילה שתוכל לעקור רגלים ברצה.

8

שאלה: האם הכהנים חייבים לנגב הידים אחר נטילת ידים לפני שעולים לדוכן?

תשובה: לא נזכר.

9

שאלה: כהן שנטל ידיו לברכת כהנים, ואחרי זה לחץ חבירו ידו בדרכו לדוכן, האם צריך לחזור וליטול?

תשובה: לא.

10

שאלה: בשלחן ערוך (סי' קכ"ח ס"ו): "אף על פי שנטלו הכהנים ידיהם שחרית חוזרים ונוטלים ידיהם וכו'", ובמשנה ברורה (סק"כ): "ואם אין לו מים כתבו האחרונים דנוכל לסמוך על שיטת הרמב"ם דסבירא ליה שיוצא בנטילת ידים שנטל בשחרית". ולפי זה מה הדין בכהן שעומד בסוף שמונה עשרה באמצע אלוקי נצור, שמשער שאם יאמר התחנונים האישיים שלו לא יהא לו מספיק זמן ליטול ידיו לנשיאת כפים, האם עדיף שלא יאמר הבקשות שלו ויטול ידיו, או שמא בכהאי גוונא יכול לומר בקשותיו ויסמוך על שיטת הרמב"ם?

תשובה: לא יאמר הבקשות.

11

שאלה: מה הדין בכהן שעמד בתפלה וגמר תפלתו כשהשליח ציבור היה כבר באמצע ברכת רצה, ואם ילך ליטול ידיו לא יגיע לברכת כהנים כלל, האם אפשר לסמוך על דעת הרמב"ם דמהני נטילת ידים של שחרית, או במה שנטל לקריאת שמע ותפלה, או שמא יצא לחוץ ולא ישא כפיו?

תשובה: אפשר להקל.

12

שאלה: האם צריך ליטול עד הפרק, והאם צריך ליטול בכלי, ואי לא, האם על כל פנים יש מעלה בכך?

תשובה: לכתחילה יש להשתדל כנטילת ידים לסעודה, עיין משנה ברורה ס"ק כ"א.

13

שאלה: מה הדין בנטילת ידים לכהנים, כשהמים לא הגיעו ממש עד הפרק [שזה דבר מאד מצוי] או שלא הגיעו ממש לכל המקומות בכף היד?

תשובה: יטול עוד קצת.

14

שאלה: כהן שנוטל ידיו לדוכן, האם יש ענין שיטול ידיו בשפע, כמו בנטילת ידים לסעודה (או"ח סימן קנ"ח סעיף י')?

תשובה: לא נזכר.

15

שאלה: נטילת ידים לדוכן האם דינה כנטילת ידים של שחרית לענין שלכתחילה צריך להקפיד בכל דיני נטילת ידים ובדיעבד אין מעכב?

תשובה: נכון.

16

שאלה: נטילת ידים לפני נשיאת כפים ביום הכיפורים ותשעה באב, אם הכהנים נוטלים כל היד או רק עד סוף קשרי אצבעותיו?

תשובה: נוטלין כל היד, עי' במשנה ברורה סי' תרי"ג ס"ק ז.

17

שאלה: נטילת ידים לפני נשיאת כפים ביום הכיפורים, האם נוטלין כל היד כל פעם שמברך בשחרית, מוסף, ונעילה?

תשובה: כן.

18

שאלה: הבאור הלכה (סי' קכ"ח סעיף ו) מביא מהמגן אברהם שצריך להסמיך נטילת ידי הכהנים לברכת כהנים כדי הילוך כ"ב אמה בין נטילה לברכה, מה עושה כהן שאינו יכול ליטול ידיו כ"כ סמוך לברכה?

תשובה: כיון שעושה מה שיכול הו"ל מסמיך.

19

שאלה: האם ברחיצת הכהן לעלות לדוכן חציצה מעכבת, ולא מצאתי מי שדיבר בזה.

תשובה: מסתבר דאין מעכב.

20

שאלה: האם הרגיל להאריך בתפילתו צריך לקצר כדי ליטול ידיו לנשיאת כפים אף ששמר ידיו מהנטילה שלפני התפילה, או לא?

תשובה: נכון ליטול.

HANDWASHING BY A LEVI OR A BECHOR

Before *Bircas Kohanim,* the hands of the Kohanim are washed by Leviim, and several Leviim may hold the cup together. If no Leviim are present or available (e.g., the Levi is still in the middle of his own *Shemoneh Esrei*), those who are *bechorim* (firstborn) take their place. Minor Leviim or *bechorim* may wash the hands of the Kohanim, and it is appropriate for Leviim who are Torah scholars to wash the hands of even unlearned Kohanim. However, although it is a mitzvah, there is no obligation for each individual Levi to wash the Kohen's hands, and if other Leviim are present, a Levi may choose to remain in shul to hear *Chazaras HaShatz*.

21

שאלה: האם נכון להקפיד שרק לוי אחד יטול ידיו של כהן העולה לדוכן?
תשובה: המנהג שהרבה לויים נוטלים.

22

שאלה: בשלחן ערוך (סי' קכ"ח סעיף ו') בדין שהלוי יוצק מים לכהנים, נסתפקתי כשכבר יש לוי שיוצק האם יש ענין שגם לויים נוספים ייצקו או שאין ענין ואין צורך?
תשובה: יש נוהגין כמה לויים יחד.

23

שאלה: כשיש יותר כהנים מלויים האם עדיף שלוי אחד יטול לבדו לכהן אחד וכן כולם, או אין שום חיסרון במה שכמה נוטלים ביחד?
תשובה: אין נ"מ.

24

שאלה: איתא בשלחן ערוך (סעיף ו') "והלוי יוצק מים על ידיהם". יש לעיין מה הדין כשיש שני לויים ושניהם נוטלים לכהן האם יוצאים ידי מצותן, שהרי קיימא לן במסכת שבת (צ"ג, א) דאם זה יכול וזה יכול שניהם פטורים, כי אם אחד יכול לעשות את המלאכה לבד והשני עזר לו אין זה נקרא עשיית מלאכה ופטור, ואם כן הוא הדין כאן כלפי הלוי שיכול לצקת מים לבד וחברו עוזר לו אין זה נקרא מלאכה של יציקת מים ואין יוצא ידי חובתו, או דלמא דרק בשבת בעינן כל מלאכה ולא חצי מלאכה, ואם יכל לעשות לבד וחברו עזר לו זה חצי מלאכה ופטור כמו שלא עשה כלל מלאכה, מה שאין כן כאן בדין יציקת מים על ידי הכהנים אין צריך מלאכה שלמה ואפילו בחלק מן המלאכה הלוי יוצא ידי חובתו?
תשובה: יוצאין.

25

שאלה: זכיתי לבקר את כת"ר ומששמע שאני לוי זכיתי לברכתו: "שתזכה ליטול ידים לכהנים". ולא זכיתי להבין בעוניי עומק מעלת דברי כת"ר, שהרי בבית המקדש, מקדשים הכהנים ידיהם ורגליהם מהכיור כמו בכל עבודה כמו שמשמע מהרמב"ם (הלכות נשיאת כפים פרק ט"ו הלכה ה') שכתב "כדרך שמקדשין לעבודה", ואף שכתב הרמב"ם (הלכות ביאת המקדש פרק ה' הלכה י') שאם קידש באחד מכלי השרת הרי זה כשר, אך כתב שם שאם קידש בכלי שרת בחוץ ועבד עבודתו פסולה, ואם כן כיצד יכנס הלוי לתוך העזרה לנטילת ידים. ועוד שאלה מהו המקור שהלוי יטול ידי הכהן?

תשובה: נטילת ידים לנשיאת כפים מקורו בגמ', ועל ידי לוי מקורו בזהר, ויתכן שהיה גם בבית המקדש.

26

שאלה: מה הטעם שהלויים שופכים מים על ידי הכהנים לברכת כהנים, הא בזמן בית המקדש הכהנים נטלו ידיהם בעצמם בלא לויים, ואם כן אמאי צריכים לויים האידנא?

תשובה: ע"ז נתמנו הלויים.

27

שאלה: אם יש לוי אחד בבית הכנסת, האם עדיף שיתפלל באריכות או בקצרה כדי להספיק ליטול ידים להכהן לפני ברכת כהנים?

תשובה: יזדרז.

28

שאלה: האם יש דין חינוך לאב לוי לחנך את בנו הקטן ליטול ידי כהן?

תשובה: כן.

29

שאלה: המשנה ברורה (סי' קכ"ח ס"ק כ"ב) דן בלוי תלמיד חכם אם צריך ליטול לכהנים וכתב דיש להחמיר, וכל שכן אם יש כהן אחד תלמיד חכם דמציל את כולם "ומחוייב" ליצוק אף על עם הארץ, וצריך ביאור מה מקור לחיוב זה דמשמע דזה חיוב גמור?

תשובה: כיון שהמנהג כך ע"פ קבלה.

30

שאלה: הסתפקתי כשהכיור נמצא מחוץ לבית המדרש, האם עדיף ללוי ליטול ידי הכהנים ולהפסיד חלק מחזרת הש"ץ או עדיף לשמוע חזרת הש"ץ?

תשובה: מצותו בכך.

31

שאלה: האם עדיף ללוי להשאר בבית הכנסת בחזרת הש"ץ ולענות אמן, או ללכת ליטול ידיהם של הכהנים?

תשובה: אם אין אחר ילך.

32

שאלה: בשלחן ערוך מבואר (סי' קכ"ח סעיף ו') שהלוי יוצק מים על ידיהם של כהנים, ובמשנה ברורה (ס"ק כ"ב) כתב שאם אין לוי אז בכור פטר רחם נוטל ידים לכהנים, ולכאורה משמע שהעיקר שהידים של הכהנים יהיו נטולות אם זה על ידי לוי או פטר רחם, ולא שהעיקר שהלוי יטול את הידים, ולכן ברצוני לשאול האם כשיש לוי שנוטל ידים לכהן ואני גם כן לוי, האם גם אני צריך לצאת ליטול ידים ולהפסיד על ידי זה את חזרת הש"ץ או לא?

תשובה: אם יש לוי אחר שיוצא אין אתה חייב.

33

שאלה: כתב לי כת"ר שעדיף ללוי ליטול ידי כל הכהנים, האם לוי מחויב ליצוק ידי כל הכהנים או סגי באחד או בשנים היכא דאינו רוצה להפסיד חזרת הש"ץ?

תשובה: יכול לרחוץ לאחד ולחזור אם הוא רוצה.

34

שאלה: האם לוי מחויב ליצוק ידי כל הכהנים או סגי באחד או בשנים?

תשובה: אם אין אחר מצוה שהוא ירחץ לכולם.

35

שאלה: האם מצוה על לוי ליטול ידי כהן גם כשיש כבר לויים אחרים שנוטלים להם?

תשובה: יש בזה ענין אבל לא חיוב.

36

שאלה: ראיתי נוהגים שאין מקפידים הלויים לרחוץ ידי הכהנים בימות החול, רק בשבת ויום טוב רוחצים ידיהם. מהו המקור לזה?

תשובה: אצלנו מקפידים.

37

שאלה: בנטילת ידים לברכת כהנים והלוי יוצק, האם זה ענין ללוי ליצוק, או לכהן שיצוק לו לוי שיש בו קדושה וצריך לחזר אחריו?

תשובה: ענין שלוי יצוק.

38

שאלה: האם זה שנוטלים הלויים את הידים לכהנים לפני ברכת כהנים הוא חובה או רשות?

תשובה: מצוה.

39

שאלה: האם לוי קטן מותר ליטול ידי כהנים לדוכן או לא משום שאין זה כבוד?

תשובה: מותר.

40

שאלה: כשיש בכור גדול ולוי קטן האם הבכור יוכל ליצוק מים לכהנים?

תשובה: גם לוי קטן יכול ליצוק.

41

שאלה: כשאין לוי או בכור האם יש ענין שכהן יצוק לכהן שגם בו יש קדושה?
תשובה: לא.

42

שאלה: אם אין לוי או בכור לרחוץ ידי הכהנים, האם כהן בכור יכול לרחוץ לכהנים אחרים מחמת הבכורה שבו?
תשובה: לא ירחוץ.

43

שאלה: אני כהן, ומצוי מאד כשהלוי נוטל ידי, אינו נוטל ידי בצורה טובה, ובגלל זה המים לא מגיעים לכל כף היד ממש, ואם אני אטול לבד מסתמא אני אטול יותר טוב על כל כף ידי, האם במקרה כזה הלוי צריך לימנע מליטול ידי?
תשובה: לא, רק תשתדל שיטול כראוי.

44

שאלה: במשנה ברורה כתב (ס"ק כ"ג) דכשהלוי הסיח דעתו מנטילת ידים של שחרית, צריך ליטול ידיו לפני שיטול לכהן, האם נוהגים כן למעשה?
תשובה: כן.

45

שאלה: לוי שיצא מבית הכסא ומצא כהן שרוצה ליטול ידיו לנשיאת כפים, האם הלוי נוטל ידי עצמו קודם ואחר כן נוטל לכהן או שמא יטול ידי הכהן מיד?
תשובה: כך הדין שנוטל לעצמו קודם.

46

שאלה: אני כהן והולך להתפלל בבית המדרש של מורי ורבי בעל "שבט הלוי" משום שנוטל ידי הכהנים, האם איכא בזה משום השתמשות בתלמיד חכם או לא?
תשובה: לא.

47

שאלה: ראיתי בקהילה א' שהאדמו"ר שלהם לוי, שמביאים קערה עם מים למקום שלו במזרח והכהנים מגיעים אליו שיטול את ידיהם. האם לדעת כת"ר יש בזה משום חסרון ב"וקדשתו" שהם הולכים אליו ולא הפוך?
תשובה: זה כבודם.

48

שאלה: ראש ישיבה או ר"מ בישיבה שהם משבט לוי, האם צריכים ליטול ידי בחורים כהנים בישיבתם לפני ברכת כהנים?
תשובה: כן.

49

שאלה: לוי שלומד בבית הכנסת, ורואה כהנים שבאים ליטול ידיהם לנשיאת כפים ואין להם לוי, האם מחויב ליטול להם, ואם לא האם על כל פנים ראוי שיטול להם?
תשובה: נכון שיטול.

50

שאלה: בשלחן ערוך (סי' קכ"ח סעיף ו') כתב שלוי נוטל לכהן, וכתב במשנה ברורה שם שאם אין לוי יטול בכור, והסתפקתי בכהאי גוונא שנטל בכור והגיע לוי, או נטל הכהן עצמו והגיע בכור או לוי, האם יש ענין או דין ליטול שוב כיון שכעת יש בכור או לוי, או שמא כיון שכבר נטל אין צריך לשוב וליטול?
תשובה: אין צריך ליטול שנית.

51

שאלה: במשנה ברורה (ס"ק כ"ב) כתב, שאם אין לוי, יוצק בכור פטר רחם מים על ידי הכהנים, כשנוטלים ידיהם לעלות לדוכן. ורציתי לשאול אם אין לוי, האם מוטל החיוב על הכהן לחפש אחרי בכור שיטול ידיו לדוכן, או שאין חיוב זה כלל על הכהן לחפש אחרי הבכור, אלא אם הבכור מרגיש שאין לוי, יש לו מצוה ללכת ליטול ידי הכהן?
תשובה: אין עליו חיוב.

52

שאלה: כשאין לוי בבית הכנסת ובכור רוצה ליטול לכהנים ידיהם, האם ראוי לו להפסיד לענות אמן ולשמוע חלק מחזרת הש"ץ בעבור זה?
תשובה: כן.

53

שאלה: בית הכנסת שיש בו לוי, ואינו נוטל ידי הכהנים לברכת כהנים (כגון שמאריך בתפילתו), האם חל חיוב על הבכורים, או לא כיון שיש שם לוי?
תשובה: אם אין לוי נוטל, מצוה על הבכורים.

54

שאלה: האם זה נכון כשהיה כת"ר ילד לפני הבר מצוה במנין של מרן החזון איש, שנטל ידים של הכהנים לפני שעלו לדוכן?
תשובה: נכון.

55

שאלה: מהי קדושתו של בכור שנוטל ידי הכהנים אם אין לוי?
תשובה: לעתיד לבא ישמש בעבודה ג"כ.

56

שאלה: האם גם בכור שהוא יוצא דופן נוטל ידים לכהנים במקום לוי?
תשובה: כן המנהג.

57

שאלה: בכף החיים (סי׳ קכ״ח ס״ק מ׳) כתב לגבי נטילת ידים לכהנים שאם אין שם לוי נוטלים בעצמם ואין הבכור נוטל להם, ע״כ, האם לפי זה אסור לבכור אשכנזי ליטול לכהן ספרדי?

תשובה: מותר אם מסכים.

MOVING TOWARD THE DUCHAN

The Kohanim must begin moving toward the *duchan* during *Retzei* (not afterward), even if they are in a different room, and even if they are in the middle of *Shemoneh Esrei*. They should move slightly even if they are standing near the *duchan* or are already standing on the *duchan*. A chazzan who is performing Bircas Kohanim should move forward slightly during *Retzei*.

58

שאלה: על מה סומכים הכהנים שעוקרין רגליהם לדוכן בברכת מודים נגד מה שמבואר בשלחן ערוך (סי׳ קכ״ח סעיף ח׳) ובמשנה ברורה?

תשובה: שלא כדין.

59

שאלה: נפסק (סי׳ קכ״ח סעיף ח׳) שצריך לעקור לנשיאת כפים ברצה, ויש להסתפק אם עקר באמן שענו הקהל על ברכת רצה אם יוכל לעלות, דהמשנה ברורה (ס״ק ס׳) כתב (לגבי שים שלום) ״דקודם אמן עדיין לא נסתיים הברכה״, ואם כן לפי זה עדיין זה נחשב שעקר בעבודה ויוכל לעלות האם למעשה יש לעלות?

תשובה: יתכן דמהני.

60

שאלה: כהן שכבר עומד במקום הדוכן האם יש לו דין לעקור רגליו ברצה, כגון כהן חזן, שרוצה לישא כפיו, האם הוא צריך לעקור רגליו ברצה, או שמספיק מה שהוא עומד במקום הדוכן?

תשובה: יעקור קצת.

61

שאלה: כהן שעקר רגליו קודם רצה, וכבר עומד על הדוכן לפני שהתחיל השליח ציבור רצה, האם שמיה עקירה?

תשובה: יזוז קצת.

62

שאלה: בשלחן ערוך (סי' קכ"ח סעיף ח') "כשמתחיל שליח ציבור רצה כל כהן שבבית הכנסת נעקר ממקומו לעלות לדוכן". והנה כהן שגמר שמונה עשרה סמוך לרצה ואם ילך ליטול ידיו לא יגיע לתוך בית הכנסת כדי לעקור רגליו למקום הדוכן עד שכבר התחיל השליח ציבור ברכת רצה, מה עדיף לו לעשות, שילך ליטול ידיו או שיעקור רגליו ברצה ולא יטול ידיו?

תשובה: אם מתחיל לילך בחוץ גם כן הוי כעקר.

63

שאלה: כהן המאריך בתפילתו, האם הא דבזמן עמידתו לשמונה עשרה, יהא דעתו לישא כפיו, חשיב כעקר רגליו, או שחייב לעקור שוב בעבודה, כשהוא עדיין עומד בשמונה עשרה?

תשובה: צריך לעקור.

64

שאלה: כהן שעקר רגליו אל הדוכן, ולאחר רצה גילה שדרך זו סגורה וחזר לאחוריו ללכת מדרך אחרת, האם עקירתו הראשונה שהתבטלה נחשבת עקירה?

תשובה: חשוב עקירה.

65

שאלה: כהן שעקר רגליו ב"רצה" לכיוון הדוכן אך החליט בינתיים לקחת ספר מהארון הנמצא בכיוון הנגדי של הדוכן ולא חזר ללכת לכיוון הדוכן רק בברכת מודים, האם בזה שהלך לכיוון מערב ביטל עקירה הראשונה ולא יוכל לעלות לדוכן?

תשובה: לא.

66

שאלה: האם אחרי שכהן נטל ידיו צריך לשוב למקומו ולעקור לדוכן רק ברצה?

תשובה: יכול לעקור קצת ברצה.

67

שאלה: השלחן ערוך (סי' קכ"ח סעיף ח') כתב כשמתחיל שליח ציבור רצה כל כהן שבבית הכנסת נעקר ממקומו לעלות לדוכן, וראיתי שיש כהנים שעולים לדוכן כשאמר השליח ציבור במוסף של יום טוב והשב כהנים לעבודתם, האם נכון לעשות זה?

תשובה: זה לפני רצה, ויזוז קצת ברצה.

68

שאלה: כהן שהיה במנין ועקר רגליו בכדי ללכת לשאת כפיו במנין בחדר צדדי, וכשהגיע שם אחזו במודים, האם מהני העקירה שלו מהמנין הראשון אם כוונתו היתה להגיע להמנין השני לברך?

תשובה: לכאורה מהני.

69

שאלה: כתבתי לכת"ר כהן שאוחז באמצע אלקי נצור והגיע השליח ציבור לברכת כהנים, האם יכול לעלות לדוכן. והשיב "יאמר יהיו לרצון ויפסע ויעלה". האם זה אפילו אם לא עשה שום עקירה ברצה?
תשובה: יעקור קצת ברצה.

WALKING IN FRONT OF SOMEONE DAVENING SHEMONEH ESREI

If necessary, the Kohen may walk in front of someone who is davening *Shemoneh Esrei* in order to ascend to the *duchan*, even if he has recited Bircas Kohanim that day already, but he should try to move beside the person, not directly in front of him. He may pass alongside someone davening *Shemoneh Esrei* even to wash his hands. He may not walk in front of someone davening *Shemoneh Esrei* on his way back after Bircas Kohanim.

70.

שאלה: האם מותר לעבור לפני המתפלל בשביל לעלות לדוכן לישא כפים, ומה הדין לעבור מן הצדדין בכדי ליטול ידיו?
תשובה: החזו"א התיר לעבור אבל בשביל ליטול ידיו לא שמעתי, ומן הצדדין בודאי יש להקל.

71

שאלה: האם מותר לכהן לעבור לפני המתפלל בשביל ליטול ידיו לברכת כהנים?
תשובה: שמעתי בשם החזון איש שמותר לכהן לעבור לישא כפיו שהיא דאורייתא, אבל לנטילת ידים צ"ע דיכול לסמוך על נטילת ידים שחרית, ומן הצד יש להקל.

72

שאלה: האם כהן יכול לעבור כנגד המתפלל ללכת ליטול ידיו, או כדי לישא כפיו על הדוכן, או שישא כפיו שלא על הדוכן?
תשובה: לישא כפיו התיר מרן החזו"א שזה דאורייתא, אבל ליטול ידיו איני יודע.

73

שאלה: בענין כהן שרוצה ליטול ידים לברכת כהנים, שמעתי בשם כת"ר שאם נטל שחרית וידיו נשארו נקיות אינו רשאי לעבור לפני המתפלל לצורך נטילה, ורק לצורך נשיאות כפים רשאי לעבור, האם זה נכון?

תשובה: נכון.

74

שאלה: כשהתירו לעבור לפני המתפלל לנשיאת כפים, האם זה גם לכהן שכבר נשא כפיו ורוצה ללכת למנין אחר כדי לישא כפיו שם?

תשובה: כן.

75

שאלה: האם מותר ללוי לעבור לפני המתפלל בשביל ללכת ליטול מים על ידיו של הכהן?

תשובה: לא שמענו.

76

שאלה: כשהכהן חייב ליטול ידיו מאחר שנטמאו, האם גם הלוי מותר לו לעבור לפני המתפלל ליטול לכהן?

תשובה: מסתבר שלא.

77

שאלה: כהן שגמר תפלתו שבלחש ועומד אדם תחתיו שאוחז באמצע שמונה עשרה, האם מותר לכהן לעקור כדי שיוכל ליטול ידיו קודם ברכת כהנים, או שמא דוקא לעלות לדוכן בלבד מותר לו לעקור דהיינו שיצטרך לחכות עד זמן שיוכל לעלות לדוכן?

תשובה: יפסע מן הצד אם אפשר.

78

שאלה: אם הכהן חייב בנטילה כגון שנגעו ידיו בדבר שחייב נטילה, ובהליכת הכהן ליטול ידיו צריך לעבור תוך ד' אמות של מתפלל האם עליו לצאת מבית הכנסת ולא ליטול כפיו?

תשובה: אם יכול לעבור מן הצד יותר טוב.

79

שאלה: האם חייב הכהן להמתין קצת עד אמצע חזרת הש"ץ אולי יגמור המתפלל שמונה עשרה ואז יפסע וילך לשאת כפיו, או כיון שהותר לו לפסוע אין צריך כלל לחכות ויכול מיד כשגמר שמונה עשרה לפסוע בתוך ד' אמות של חבירו?

תשובה: טוב שימתין.

80

שאלה: האם כשהולך לדוכן צריך להשתדל ללכת בדרך שלא יעבור כנגד המתפלל או מאחר והולך למצוה לא צריך לדקדק?

תשובה: בודאי טוב שלא יעבור אם אפשר.

81

שאלה: האם מותר לעבור לפני מתפלל בדרך לברכת כהנים כשיש דרך ארוכה יותר שלא לפני מתפלל?
תשובה: ילך בארוכה.

82

שאלה: אני כהן ורגיל להתפלל בקביעות בכותל המערבי תפילת שחרית, ויש ציבור גדול שמתפלל שם וכמעט אי אפשר ללכת לברז ליטול ידי ולא לעבור על אדם תוך ד׳ אמות של מתפלל שמונה עשרה, כיצד אעשה לענין נטילת ידים לברכת הכהנים, האם אפשר לעבור ליטול ידי, או עדיף לסמוך על שיטת הרמב״ם שאפשר לסמוך על נטילת ידים בבוקר אם לא נגע במקומות המכוסים עדיין?
תשובה: תסמוך על הרמב״ם.

83

שאלה: לא הבנתי מה ההיתר לכהנים לעבור לפני המתפלל כדי לישא כפים, הרי יכולים לקיים המצוה של נשיאת כפים גם בלי לעבור דהיינו שישא כפים במקומו (ורק יסתובב לאחוריו) ויברך לאלו שיהיו כנגדו כשמברך, וכי בגלל שיש מנהג ללכת ליד הארון קודש, מנהג זה ידחה איסור דרבנן ויוכל לעבור לפני המתפלל.
תשובה: צריך לעמוד לפני כל הצבור.

84

שאלה: האם יש היתר לכהנים אחרי שיורדים מהדוכן לעבור לפני המתפלל?
תשובה: בדרך חזרה צריך ליזהר, זה לא מצוה.

INTERRUPTING OR RUSHING DAVENING TO DUCHAN

A Kohen may *duchan* even if he is in the middle of *Pesukei D'Zimrah* or *Birchos Krias Shema*. If he does not go up to *duchan* during this time he must find another minyan to *duchan* in afterward. He may skip the prayer of *Elokai Netzor* in order to ascend to the *duchan*, and just say the verse beginning *Yiheyu l'ratzon*. Since Bircas Kohanim is a *d'Oraysa* obligation while *tefillah* is a *d'Rabbanan*, Bircas Kohanim takes precedence. Therefore, a Kohen should daven *Shemoneh Esrei* more quickly in order to be able to *duchan*, even if he is a visitor to Eretz Yisrael who is not accustomed to reciting Bircas Kohanim every day. If he came late to shul and does not have time to finish davening before reciting Bircas Kohanim he should wait to *duchan* and only then daven. If he begins *Shemoneh Esrei* after Bircas Kohanim, before the end of *Chazaras HaShatz*, that is still considered *tefillah b'tzibbur*. If no Kohen is present, the chazzan may pause *Chazaras HaShatz* so that people can go out and look for a Kohen.

85

שאלה: מהו כשיש מנין אחר בחדר שלצידו שאוחזים בברכת כהנים בשעה שכהן זה אוחז באמצע פסוקי דזמרה, האם מותר לו ללכת לשם ולעלות לדוכן באמצע פסוקי דזמרה?

תשובה: כן.

86

שאלה: כהן שהוא באמצע ברכת קריאת שמע והגיע השליח ציבור לנשיאת כפים, איך צריך לנהוג?

תשובה: צריך לעלות.

87

שאלה: כהן העומד בתפילתו בין הפרקים של קריאת שמע, או באמצע וקודם שמונה עשרה, והשליח ציבור הגיע כבר לברכת כהנים, האם רשאי הכהן לעלות אז לדוכן, ודומה לברכת הרעם והברק דרשאי בכהאי גוונא לברך, או דלמא כיון שמלבד הברכה מזכיר הפסוקים של יברכך וגו׳, אסור לו לעלות לדוכן, ויצטרך לצאת מבית הכנסת קודם שיגיע השליח ציבור לרצה?

תשובה: יעלה.

88

שאלה: האם רשאי הכהן לעלות לדוכן לברכת כהנים באמצע פסוקי דזמרה ובאמצע קריאת שמע וברכותיה, או דילמא אמרינן בזה ״עוסק במצוה פטור מן המצוה״, דכיון שעוסק בתפילתו, פטור מלעלות לדוכן?

תשובה: רשאי, ואם לא יעלה יצטרך לחפש אח״כ מנין אחר.

89

שאלה: נסתפקתי מה הדין בכהן שעומד אחר ישתבח לפני יוצר והגיע השליח ציבור לברכת כהנים, האם ישא כפיו או לא?

תשובה: ישא.

90

שאלה: כהן העומד בתפילת שמונה עשרה לאחר שים שלום קודם אלוקי נצור, האם מותר לדלג על אלוקי נצור, ויאמר יהיו לרצון בשביל שיספיק לעלות לדוכן ולישא כפיו?

תשובה: מותר, כי אלוקי נצור אינו חיוב.

91

שאלה: שאלתי את כת"ר האם מותר לכהן לעלות לדוכן כשאוחז בתפלת אלוקי נצור וכו', וענה לי שמותר רק יאמר יהיו לרצון קודם לכן, ונסתפקתי האם מותר לו להפסיק גם בכדי שהות שיספיק גם ליטול ידיו קודם נשיאת כפים (הגם שנטל ידיו בבוקר), או דוקא להפסיק בכדי שהות שיוכל לעלות לדוכן בלבד?

תשובה: אלוקי נצור אינו חיוב לומר.

92

שאלה: בענין הנ"ל האם כשגמר ברכת כהנים מותר לו לחזור למקומו להמשיך תפלת "אלוקי נצור" וכו', או שצריך להישאר על ידי הדוכן ושם להמשיך תפלתו?

תשובה: מותר.

93

שאלה: האם עדיף לכהן לפסוע מיד אחרי שמונה עשרה בלי לומר אלוקי נצור, בשביל לברך ברכת כהנים?

תשובה: כן, ויאמר יהיו לרצון אחר ברכת כהנים.

94

שאלה: האם רצוי להתפלל שמונה עשרה מהר בשביל להספיק לעלות לדוכן בברכת כהנים?

תשובה: כן.

95

שאלה: האם כהן חייב מדינא לקצר בתפילת שמונה עשרה בשביל שיספיק לברך ברכת כהנים?

תשובה: ראוי לעשות כן.

96

שאלה: אני כהן ובאתי מחוץ לארץ לביקור זמן קצר, והמנהג שלי בחוץ לארץ לישא כפים רק בחגים, והנה זה כמה שנים שאני מתפלל שמונה עשרה ארוך, ושאלתי היא האם אני מחויב להתפלל במרוצה כדי להגיע לישא כפי או לא, והאם יש חיוב גמור מדינא לבני חוץ לארץ, שלא באו לארץ ישראל להשתקע, ובדעתם לחזור לישא כפים?

תשובה: טוב שתזדרז כי נשיאת כפים דאורייתא ותפילה דרבנן.

97

שאלה: כהן שמאריך בתפלתו ולא מספיק ברכת כהנים, האם חל עליו חיוב ללכת למנין אחר ולברך ברכת כהנים?

תשובה: מצוה.

98

שאלה: כהן שהזדרז בשחרית לגמור שמונה עשרה על מנת שיוכל לברך ברכת כהנים, האם צריך להזדרז במוסף גם כן להספיק לברך ברכת כהנים?

תשובה: צריך.

99

שאלה: כהן שלא הספיק תפילתו עם החזן, האם יחכה עד החזרה ויתחיל עמידה עם החזן כדי שיענה קדושה, אף שיפסיד לעשות ברכת כהנים, או שמא עדיף שיתחיל מיד העמידה, אף שלא יספיק לענות קדושה, אך יספיק לברכת כהנים?

תשובה: יתחיל עם השליח ציבור ויאמר עמו קדושה, ולברכת כהנים יעקור קצת וישא כפיו.

100

שאלה: כהן שבא מאוחר לבית הכנסת והגיע לתפילת לחש שלו בסוף תפילת הלחש של הציבור, ואם יתחיל מיד לא יגמור לפני שיגיע השליח ציבור לקדושה אך יספיק לו הזמן כדי לעלות לדוכן, ואם יתפלל עם הש"ץ מילה במילה כדי לענות קדושה עם הציבור לא יעלה לדוכן כיון שיש שם כהנים אחרים, האם עדיף לענות קדושה עם הציבור ולא יעלה לדוכן, או לא לענות קדושה ויצא בשומע כעונה ויעלה לדוכן?

תשובה: לא יתפלל ויענה קדושה ויעלה לדוכן ואח"כ יתפלל.

101

שאלה: כהן שבא מאוחר לבית הכנסת והגיע לתפילת לחש שלו בסוף תפילת הלחש של הציבור, ואם יתחיל מיד לא יגמור לפני שיגיע השליח ציבור לקדושה אך יספיק לו הזמן כדי לעלות לדוכן, ואם יתפלל עם הש"ץ מילה במילה כדי לענות קדושה עם הציבור לא יעלה לדוכן כיון שיש שם כהנים אחרים, האם עדיף לענות קדושה עם הציבור ולא יעלה לדוכן, או לא לענות קדושה ויצא בשומע כעונה ויעלה לדוכן. וענה לי כת"ר שלא יתפלל אלא יענה קדושה ואחר כך יעלה לדוכן ואחר כך יתפלל. ורציתי לשאול עוד, מה יעשה אם בין כך ובין כך יעבור זמן תפילה וצריך הוא לעשות אחד מהדרכים הנ"ל מה יעשה?

תשובה: יצא חוץ לבהכ"נ ויתפלל בלי קדושה, ואחר כך יעלה לדוכן בבהכ"נ.

102

שאלה: כהן שאיחר לתפילה ויש לו שתי אפשרויות, או לחכות לחזרת הש"ץ כדי להרויח קדושה ועל ידי זה יפסיד ברכת כהנים, או להתחיל עכשיו שמונה עשרה ועל ידי זה יפסיד קדושה וירויח ברכת כהנים, מה עדיף?

תשובה: יברך ברכת כהנים ויתחיל אחר כך שמונה עשרה לפני שהש"צ יגמור, וחשיב תפלה בצבור.

103

שאלה: פעם שאלתי את כת"ר, כהן שבא לבית הכנסת והציבור באמצע שמונה עשרה, ויש לו אפשרות להתפלל מיד שמונה עשרה ויספיק נשיאת כפים אך יפסיד קדושה, ואם ימתין להתחיל עם השליח ציבור יספיק קדושה, אך יפסיד נשיאת כפים מה יעשה? וענה לי כת"ר "ימתין לשניהם", האם כוונת כת"ר שלא יתפלל שמונה עשרה מיד אלא ימתין לנשיאת כפים, ואחר כך יתפלל שמונה עשרה ביחידות?

תשובה: יכול להתחיל שמונה עשרה אחר נשיאת כפים. כל זמן שהש"צ מתפלל נחשב גם כן תפלה בצבור.

104

שאלה: כהן שיודע שעל ידי שישא כפיו [שהמבטלו, ביטל מצות עשה שהוא כשלש מצוות כמבואר בשו"ע], יפסיד תפילה בצבור, האם יעשה כן?

תשובה: מסתבר דברכת כהנים עדיפא.

105

שאלה: כהן שקם מאוחר ויש לו זמן מצומצם לתפילה, האם עדיף שיתפלל בצבור וילך באמצע חזרת הש"ץ (כי אין לו שהות להמתין לנשיאת כפים), או שיכנס למנין אחר שעומדים בחזרת הש"ץ ויוכל לישא את כפיו ויתפלל ביחידות?

תשובה: נשיאת כפים דאורייתא.

106

שאלה: אם הציבור התחיל להתפלל תפילת שמונה עשרה, האם כדאי להמתין לסוף חזרת הש"ץ כדי שאפשר יהיה לברך ברכת כהנים, ולהתפלל שמונה עשרה אחרי ברכת כהנים, או שמא עדיף להתחיל להתפלל שמונה עשרה מיד משום מצוה הבא לידך אל תחמיצנה, אך יש סיכוי שלא אגמור שמונה עשרה עד אחרי ברכת כהנים?

תשובה: תתחיל ש"ע אחר בר"כ.

107

שאלה: כהן ששכח יעלה ויבוא של שחרית ולא יספיק לחזור תפילת שחרית עד ברכת כהנים למתי ידחה את החזרה, האם כיון שנתחייב בחזרה צריך לעשותה מיד, ואף שיפסיד על ידי זה ברכת כהנים?

תשובה: לא ידחה את הברכת כהנים שהיא דאורייתא.

108

שאלה: כהן העומד בתפילת שמונה עשרה בשעה שהשליח ציבור אומר רצה ורואה שיוכל לגמור עד הטוב שמך וכו', האם יוכל בשעת רצה לעקור רגליו לצורך ברכת כהנים בכדי שיוכל לכשיגמור תפילתו לעלות לדוכן?

תשובה: יתכן שכן.

109

שאלה: האם לכהן, עדיף שיתפלל יותר בכוונה, ולא לעשות ברכת כהנים, או לא?

תשובה: ברכת כהנים עדיפא שהיא דאורייתא.

110

שאלה: כהן שמאריך בשמונה עשרה, ויש כהנים אחרים בהמנין שמברכים ברכת כהנים, האם כהן זה מתברך גם ככל שאר העם הישראלים?

תשובה: לא.

111

שאלה: כהן שכשאוחז בתפילה בלחש במחיה המתים סיים עמו השליח ציבור ביחד והקהל מתחיל קדושה ובאפשרותו כעת לומר קדושה עם הציבור אך הוא מעוניין להמשיך בתפילתו בזמן הקדושה ובפרט בשבת שזה ארוך, ולהספיק נשיאת כפים, האם רשאי להמשיך להתפלל או שמא מחוייב כעת לומר קדושה?

תשובה: יאמר רק קדוש וברוך וימשיך.

112

שאלה: בהא דמבואר במשנה ברורה (סי' קכ"ח ס"ק ק"ו) שכהן המתפלל שמונה עשרה ואין שם כהן אחר והגיע בתפילתו למקום ברכת כהנים, שמותר לו לעלות לדוכן ואחר שיגמור הנשיאת כפים ירד מהדוכן ויגמור תפלתו, האם מותר לו רק לרדת מהדוכן או גם לחזור למקומו שהתפלל שם שמונה עשרה?

תשובה: יתכן שיכול לחזור למקומו.

113

שאלה: במשנה ברורה (שם) הביא בשם הגאון יעב"ץ בסידורו "שלא להפסיק באמצע התפלה לנשיאת כפים כשעומד בברכה אחרת, אם לא שהגיע בתפלתו למקום ברכת כהנים שאז דעתו שמותר לו לעקור רגליו ולעלות לדוכן, שבמקום זה לא מקרי הפסק שהוא מעין שים שלום", האם היתר זה הוא דוקא בכהן יחיד או לא?

תשובה: אם אמרו לו עלה לדוכן הוי כמי שאין רק כהן א', עי' בשונה הלכות שם.

114

שאלה: אם התחילו חזרת הש"ץ כבר ואין כהן או כהנים בהמנין, האם יכול השליח ציבור להפסיק בחזרת הש"ץ לפני רצה אפילו שזה יקח כמה רגעים, בכדי להביא כהן או כהנים לנשיאת כפים?

תשובה: מותר.

115

שאלה: כת"ר כתב שמותר להפסיק בברכת רצה לקרוא לכהן מבית כנסת סמוך. האם זה רק באופן שיביאו שני כהנים ויקיימו מצוה דאורייתא, או שמותר גם באופן שיקראו רק לכהן אחד, שלכמה שיטות זהו רק דרבנן?

תשובה: גם א'.

INTERRUPTING DAVENING TO HEAR BIRCAS KOHANIM

A non-Kohen who is in the middle of *Shemoneh Esrei* when Bircas Kohanim is recited should stop and listen, without answering amen, even if he has heard Bircas Kohanim already. If he is davening *Shemoneh Esrei* along with *Chazaras HaShatz,* he may not answer amen even though the chazzan may. If he is in the middle of *Birchos Krias Shema,* he may answer amen only to the verses of Bircas Kohanim and not to the preceding blessing. One who has already davened and is learning in the shul while another minyan is in progress must stop to listen to Bircas Kohanim.

116

שאלה: דעת החרדים (הובא בבאור הלכה ריש הלכות נשיאת כפים) שיש מצוה על הישראל להתברך, אבל לכאורה דעת הריטב"א (סוכה לא, ב) דליכא מצוה על הישראל להתברך. האם יש נ"מ במחלוקת זו אי מותר להפסיק באמצע שמונה עשרה לשמוע ברכת כהנים, דלספר החרדים מותר, ולריטב"א אסור, או שאף להריטב"א מותר?

תשובה: גם החזו"א סבר דלא כהחרדים ומ"מ אמר שמצוה להפסיק ולשמוע.

117

שאלה: דעת מרן החזו"א שלא כהחרדים שאין מצוה להתברך בברכת כהנים, וראיתי שדעתו שאם אוחז בשמונה עשרה אחרי ברכת ההודאה מותר להפסיק לשמוע, ולשיטתו שאין מצוה להתברך, איך התיר להפסיק ולשמוע, ולמה לא הוי הפסק?

תשובה: לשמוע אינו הפסק.

118

שאלה: כשמתפלל עם השליח ציבור והגיעו לנשיאת כפים, האם ימתין או שימשיך שים שלום כשאומרים נשיאת כפים?

תשובה: טוב להמתין, וכן נהג מרן החזו"א זצ"ל.

119

שאלה: אדם שעומד בשמונה עשרה בסיום ברכת "הטוב שמך ולך נאה להודות", ושומע שהכהנים מתחילים לברך ברכת כהנים, האם יפסיק תפלתו וישמע ברכת כהנים, או שימשיך בתפלתו?
תשובה: יפסיק לשמוע ולא יענה אמן.

120

שאלה: להפוסקים שיש מצוה לישראל להתברך מפי הכהנים, האם כשהישראל עומד באמצע שמונה עשרה בעת ברכת כהנים, מקיים מצותו הגם שהוא ממשיך בשמונה עשרה, כי למעשה בירכו אותו, או שלא קיים מצותו, כי אינו שומע את הברכת כהנים שהרי ממשיך בתפלתו?
תשובה: יש לו לשתוק ולשמוע ואז קיים.

121

שאלה: כתב לי כת"ר דרצוי לישראל האוחז בשמונה עשרה דלחש שישמע לברכת הכהנים. וצריך בירור דנימא עוסק במצוה פטור מן המצוה?
תשובה: אינו חייב אבל אם עושה כן יש מצוה.

122

שאלה: יחיד העומד באמצע תפילת שמונה עשרה והגיע השליח ציבור לברכת כהנים, האם רשאי להמשיך בתפילתו לבל תופרע כוונתו, או שמא צריך להמתין לכוון לשמוע את ברכת כהנים?
תשובה: ימתין.

123

שאלה: המתפלל שמונה עשרה ושמע ברכת כהנים האם צריך להפסיק?
תשובה: אין חייב אבל יכול להפסיק ולשמוע, ונכון לעשות כן.

124

שאלה: מי ששמע ברכת כהנים קודם התפילה האם צריך להפסיק באמצע שמונה עשרה להאזין לברכת כהנים?
תשובה: טוב שיפסיק וישמע.

125

שאלה: האם כשחבירו מפסיק באמצע שמונה עשרה לברכת כהנים מותר לעבור לפניו ולא נחשב עובר לפני המתפלל?
תשובה: אסור.

126

שאלה: מי שעומד באמצע שמונה עשרה האם צריך להפסיק ולהאזין לברכת השליח ציבור כשאין כהנים ואומר אלוקינו ואלוקי אבותינו ברכנו בברכה המשולשת בתורה וכו'?
תשובה: לא.

127

שאלה: מבואר בשלחן ערוך (סי' קכ"ח סעיף י"ט) ששליח צבור לא יענה אמן על ברכת כהנים כיון שיכול להתבלבל, וכתב המשנה ברורה (ס"ק ע"א) שאם יש לו סידור מותר לשליח צבור לענות. האם הוא הדין נמי אם ישראל שמתפלל עם השליח צבור יכול להפסיק לענות אמן בשעת ברכת כהנים?

תשובה: לא.

128

שאלה: מה החילוק בין החזן שיכול לענות אמן על ברכת כהנים, לבין מי שהגיע בשמונה עשרה להטוב שמך שאינו יכול?

תשובה: החזן מצותו בכך אבל לא המתפלל איתו וכמו שאין אומר איתו עננו.

129

שאלה: אמן של ברכת כהנים מה דינו של ישראל להפסיק קריאת שמע וברכותיה?

תשובה: על הברכת כהנים אפשר לענות ולא על הברכה לפני ברכת כהנים.

130

שאלה: מי שהתפלל וכבר שמע ברכת כהנים ועכשיו לומד תורה בבית הכנסת בזמן שמנין אחר מתפלל, והגיעו לברכת כהנים האם חייב להפסיק?

תשובה: חייב.

WHEN THE KOHEN IS IN VIOLATION OF THE MITZVAH TO DUCHAN

A Kohen who is inside the shul and does not go up to *duchan* despite being called up violates three positive commandments, even if he is planning to *duchan* elsewhere. If he is not inside the shul, he does not violate these mitzvos but should try to find an opportunity to perform the mitzvah. According to some, a Kohen who consistently fails to *duchan* loses the privilege of being called to the Torah for an *aliyah*.

131

שאלה: בשלחן ערוך (סי' קכ"ח סעיף ב') כתב: "כל כהן שאין בו אחד מהדברים המעכבים, אם אינו עולה לדוכן אף על פי שביטל מצות עשה אחת, הרי זה כעובר בשלש עשה, אם היה בבית הכנסת כשקורא כהנים, או אם אמרו לו לעלות או ליטול ידיו", וכתב בבאור הלכה ד"ה אם היה: "לאפוקי אם היה אז חוץ לבית הכנסת כתב הר"ן דאינו עובר אפילו אם קראו לו לעלות". ונסתפקתי

מה נקרא "אם היה בבית הכנסת", האם דוקא בתוך בית הכנסת ממש, או גם בפרוזדור, מפני שהוא בתוך אותו בנין?
תשובה: דוקא בבהכ"נ.

132

שאלה: כהן שלא נמצא בבית הכנסת ברצה ואינו נושא את כפיו באותו היום, האם עובר על איסור?
תשובה: אין עובר, אבל נכון שילך לישא כפיו.

133

שאלה: כהן שקראו לו לעלות ועקר רגליו בעבודה ולא עלה לנשיאת כפים במנין הזה והלך למנין אחר ושם אמרו לו ועקר רגליו בעבודה ועלה, האם עובר על העשה כיון שמיד לא עלה, או שמא כיון שבסוף עלה לא ביטל העשה?
תשובה: יתכן שעבר.

134

שאלה: בקראו לכהן לעלות לדוכן ולא עלה כי רוצה לעלות במנין אחר האם עובר בעשה, ואם יעלה במנין אחר האם מתקן האיסור?
תשובה: עובר.

135

שאלה: כהן שרוצה לעשות ברכת כהנים במנין הרגיל שלו ובדרך לתפילה קוראים לו שיעשה ברכת כהנים במנין אחר, האם עובר על לאו כשאינו מגיע, או כיון שמתכנן לעשות ברכת כהנים בהמשך היום, אינו עובר על לאו?
תשובה: אין עובר אם לא נמצא בבהכ"נ ומ"מ טוב שיכנס.

136

שאלה: כהן שהתפלל במנין, ולא הספיק לעלות לברכת כהנים, מפני שהאריך בתפלה, האם מן הראוי שילך למנין אחר, והאם יש חיוב לעשות כן?
תשובה: יתכן שצריך לילך.

137

שאלה: כהן שלא הספיק לישא כפיו במנין שהתפלל בו, האם ראוי ללכת למנין אחר לישא כפיו?
תשובה: ראוי.

138

שאלה: אם רמזו לכהן בידים לעלות לדוכן ולא אמרו לו כלום, האם חייב מן התורה לעלות לדוכן?
תשובה: יתכן דחייב.

139

שאלה: האם כהן שלא עולה לדוכן בקביעות אינו יכול לעלות לתורה?
תשובה: יש אומרים כן.

THE ADVANTAGE OF HAVING TWO OR MORE KOHANIM

One who heard Bircas Kohanim from only one Kohen is not obligated to hear it from two or more Kohanim, but doing so is a worthy practice. There is no advantage to hearing Bircas Kohanim from a large group of Kohanim, as opposed to just two. It is preferable for a Kohen to perform Bircas Kohanim in a minyan where there is another Kohen, to fulfill the *d'Oraysa* obligation, rather than in a minyan where he is the only Kohen, even if that means the minyan will be left without a Kohen (unless he has already been called up to *duchan* in that minyan). If he did *duchan* as a lone Kohen, he should try to attend a second minyan in order to perform Bircas Kohanim with another Kohen, even at the expense of his Torah learning. It is better for a Kohen to *duchan* than to serve as the chazzan even if he has a compelling reason to lead the davening.

140

שאלה: מה הדין לישראל ששמע ברכת כהנים והיה רק כהן אחד וכעת יש לו אפשרות לשמוע משני כהנים האם יש ענין ללכת?

תשובה: אם רוצה לחזור לשמוע תבא עליו ברכה.

141

שאלה: אם נתברך מפי כהן אחד האם עליו לחזר אחר מנין בו מברכים ב' כהנים?

תשובה: אין חייב.

142

שאלה: ישראל שיכול להתפלל בשני בתי מדרש, באחד ישנם הרבה כהנים שיעלו על הדוכן, ובשני יש רק שני כהנים, האם עדיף ללכת לבית המדרש שיש הרבה כהנים?

תשובה: לא שמענו.

143

שאלה: איזהו דרך שיברור האדם, אם הוא כהן, האם יש מעלה להתפלל במנין שיש עוד כהן, ומצד שני בבית המדרש שהוא מתפלל מזמן לזמן אין עוד כהן, ויפסידו הצבור לשמוע ברכת כהנים. האם יתפלל במנין עם כהן אחר, או עם ציבור שהוא כהן יחידי?

תשובה: כשיש כהן א' הוא רק דרבנן, ילך למקום שיש עוד כהן.

144

שאלה: כהן שיש באפשרותו להתפלל בבית הכנסת שיש שם עוד כהנים או בבית הכנסת שאין שם כהנים כלל, האם יש להעדיף בית הכנסת שיש שם עוד כהנים משום מה שהובא בבאור הלכה (סי' קכ"ח סעיף כ"ה) שאז מקיים מצוה דאורייתא ומשום הכי כשעולה רק אחד לדעת איזה פוסקים הוא רק מצות עשה דרבנן, או שמא ילך להתפלל במקום שאין כהנים כלל בכדי לזכות הציבור שם בברכת כהנים?

תשובה: יותר טוב שיהי' במקום של דאורייתא.

145

שאלה: כשיש כמה כהנים בבית הכנסת ומבקשים מאחד הכהנים שיבוא לבית הכנסת שאין בו כהנים האם ילך, דמצד אחד עושה עמהם חסד שיהיה להם ברכת כהנים, אך מצד שני לסוברים שכהן יחיד חיובו רק מדרבנן מפסיד את המצוה מדאורייתא?

תשובה: מסתבר שאין לו להפקיע המצוה דאורייתא.

146

שאלה: לשיטת הראשונים שנשיאת כפים עם שני כהנים הוא מצוה מן התורה ואחד שנושא כפיו הוא דרבנן, האם לכהן מותר ללכת מבית הכנסת שהוא נמצא יחד עם חבירו לבית הכנסת שאין להם כהן שהוא יהיה יחידי, דהרי מבטל מצוה דאורייתא?

תשובה: אין ראוי.

147

שאלה: כשיש שני מנינים באותה שעה, כגון תפילת ותיקין שיש מנין נוסף בבית כנסת שני, ויש רק שני כהנים, האם ראוי לחלק, שכהן אחד יהיה במנין זה, והאחר בשני, או שמא עדיף שיברכו ב' במנין אחד, ובשני לא ישאו כפים כלל?

תשובה: לכאורה עדיף שנים במקום אחד.

148

שאלה: כהן שיש לו אפשרות להתפלל בא' משני מנינים, במנין אחד אין להם כהן אחר ומבקשים ממנו שיתפלל עמהם כדי שיזכו בנשיאת כפים, והוא יקיים בזה חסד, ובמנין השני יש עוד כהן ואז יהא הברכת כהנים מדאורייתא לכל הדעות, באיזה מנין יתפלל?

תשובה: יבקש מהם שא' יאחר קצת דיוכל להיות בב' המנינים.

149

שאלה: נכנס לבית הכנסת וראה שהוא כהן יחידי האם יכול לצאת למקום אחר שיש עוד כהנים, או דיש ריעותא משום אין מעבירין על המצוות?

תשובה: אם לא קראוהו עדיין רשאי לצאת.

150

שאלה: מי שהיה הכהן היחיד שנשא כפיו שזה רק ״דרבנן״ לכמה שיטות, האם צריך לילך לבית הכנסת אחר שיש שם עוד כהנים כדי לקיים ה״דאורייתא״?

תשובה: אין חייב.

151

שאלה: כהן שנשא כפיו כשהיה כהן היחיד בהמנין, האם ילך למנין אחר לברך ברכת כהנים אם יש שם עוד כהן שיברך איתו, כשיצטרך להפסיק באמצע הלימוד?

תשובה: כן.

152

שאלה: הנני רוצה לשאול אודות עובדא שנהגתי בעצמי שכאשר היו שני כהנים בבית הכנסת והציבור נחלק בתפילת מוסף לשני מנינים, עליתי לדוכן במנין אחד והכהן השני במנין השני, ושאל ממני אחד אם לא היה עדיף טפי לחוש לשיטת התוספות (מנחות מ״ד, א), שכהן אחד אינו מחויב בנשיאת כפים מדאורייתא, ולעשות יחד עם הכהן השני באותו מנין, אף שעל ידי כך ישאר אחד משני המנינים בלא כהן?

תשובה: זה שהעיר לך צודק.

153

שאלה: כהן שיש לו אפשרות לברך ברכת כהנים בשני מקומות: באחד יש מיעוט כהנים ורוב קהל ישראל, ובשני יש ריבוי כהנים ומיעוט קהל, היכן עדיף שיברך.

תשובה: רוב עם ובלבד שיהיו לפחות ב׳ כהנים.

154

שאלה: בית הכנסת שמתפללים בו שני כהנים כאשר אחד מהם הוא שליח ציבור ואינו נושא כפיו, האם יש לחשוש לשיטת רבנו פרץ (המובא בטור) וכן הוא בתוד״ה כל ״כהן״ (מנחות, מ״ד, א) בשם ר״ת והעתיקו החיי אדם בשם י״א, שגורם בזה לביטול מצות עשה דאורייתא של נשיאת כפים?

תשובה: נכון שהש״ץ לא יהיה כהן אפי׳ הוא חיוב וישא כפיו, וכן הורה החזו״א.

155

שאלה: האם יש מעלה מיוחדת כשיש עשרה כהנים שנושאים את כפיהם ואומרים ברכת כהנים ביחד (כמו שמשמע מדברי האור זרוע סי׳ תי״א), או שמא אין שום מעלה מיוחדת בזה שהם מספר עשר, חוץ ממה שיש רבוי כהנים?

תשובה: לא שמענו.

156

שאלה: האם יש ענין לישראל לשמוע ברכת כהנים מכמה שיותר כהנים או לא?

תשובה: לא שמענו.

157

שאלה: האם יש יותר ברכה בברכת כהנים אם יש הרבה יותר משני כהנים?
תשובה: אין נ"מ.

158

שאלה: האם יש יותר ענין בברכת כהנים כשיש אלף כהנים מאשר שני כהנים?
תשובה: אין נ"מ.

159

שאלה: האם יש חשיבות לנשיאת כפים של כהן צדיק אחד (כמו החפץ חיים), או של הרבה כהנים פשוטים?
תשובה: כהן א' דרבנן וב' כהנים דאורייתא.

THE MITZVAH TO HEAR BIRCAS KOHANIM (ACCORDING TO SEFER CHAREIDIM)

Even according to the *Sefer Chareidim*'s view, that a non-Kohen has a mitzvah to hear Bircas Kohanim, a woman is not obligated in this mitzvah. A non-Kohen does not make a *berachah* over this mitzvah since it is covered by the *berachah* of the Kohanim. If a non-Kohen did not hear Bircas Kohanim, he is not obligated to go to another minyan to hear it, but doing so is recommended.

160.

שאלה: לשיטת ספר החרדים (פרק ד' אות י"ח) שהובא בבאור הלכה (בתחילת סימן קכ"ח) שיש מצות עשה בשמיעת ברכת כהנים לישראל, אם גם אשה צריכה לשמוע, או שמא הוי מצות עשה שהזמן גרמא משום שאין ברכת כהנים בלילה?
תשובה: לכאורה פטורה.

161

שאלה: שיטת ספר חרדים שלישראל יש מצוה להתברך גם כן כמו שלכהן יש מצוה לברכו, אם כן מדוע לא תקנו לישראל ברכה גם כן?
תשובה: זה בכלל הברכה של הכהן.

162

שאלה: למה אין ברכה לישראל השומעים ברכת כהנים להחרדים דהוי מצוה?
תשובה: אינה מצוה בפני עצמה אלא נטפלים למצות הכהנים.

163

שאלה: אם לא קיים מצותו, כי עמד בשמונה עשרה ולא האזין לברכת כהנים, האם צריך ללכת לשמוע ברכת כהנים במקום אחר?
תשובה: החזו"א לא סבר כהחרדים ואין חיוב על הישראל.

164

שאלה: ידועה פלוגתת הראשונים, אי מצות ברכת כהנים נאמרה גם על הישראל, שמצוה הוא להתברך, מלבד מצות הכהן לברך, או שהמצוה נאמרה רק על הכהן, שהוא מצווה לברך, אך הישראל המתברך אינו מקיים מצוה בכך, מלבד מה שזוכה לברכת הכהן. [דעת החרדים (פרק ד' אות יח) דהישראל נמי מקיים מצוה, עי' הפלאה (כתובות דף כ"ד, ב), ואילו דעת הריטב"א (סוכה דף לא, ב) דהישראל אינו מצווה. והחתם סופר (שו"ת או"ח סי' קס"ז) הביא דכן שיטת רוב הפוסקים]. והנה בירושלמי (מגילה פ"ד ה"ח) איתא, דהטעם שאסור להסתכל על הכהנים בשעה שמברכים, שלא יסיח המסתכל דעתו מן הברכה [עי' תוס' (חגיגה דף טז ע"א ד"ה בכהנים), ובשו"ע (סי' קכ"ח סעיף כ"ג ובמ"ב ס"ק פ"ט)]. ויל"ע, להנך שיטות דאין הישראל מצווה להתברך, מאי חששא יש בזה שיסיח דעתו מן הברכה, הא אין מבטל בכך שום מצוה או חיוב המוטל עליו.
תשובה: מבזה המצוה.

165

שאלה: מנין שלא היו בו כהנים והשליח ציבור אמר או"א ברכנו בברכה המשולשת וכו', האם יש ענין ללכת למקום אחר לשמוע ברכת כהנים אפילו להשיטות שחולקים על ספר החרדים.
תשובה: יש ענין אבל לא חייבו.

166

שאלה: לפי הפוסקים שיש מצוה על הישראל להתברך מפי הכהנים, האם אסור לאדם לנסוע למקום שלא ימצא שם ברכת כהנים ונחשב שמבטל מצות עשה, שהרי מחויב להתברך מפי הכהנים, כמו שהכהן שלא בירך ביטל עשה?
תשובה: החזו"א לא חשש לדעה זו.

167

שאלה: לפי דברי החרדים דאף הישראל המתברך מהכהן בכלל המצווה ד"כה תברכו את בני ישראל", האם כשיש כמה כהנים שמברכים ביחד, מקיים כמה מצוות כמספר המברכים, או דילמא מקיים רק מצוה אחת דהוה כולא חדא ברכתא, ובפרט לדברי הרמב"ם בהלכות נשיאת כפים (פרק ט"ו הלכה ז) דאין קיבול הברכה תלוי בכהנים אלא בהקב"ה?
תשובה: מצוה א'.

168

שאלה: כת"ר כתב לי שהחזון איש לא סבר כשיטת החרדים שישראל מקיים מצוה כשמתברך מפי הכהנים. ולכאורה לדעת הר"ן רפ"ב דקידושין שכתב שהאשה גם כן מקיימת מצוה בנישואין כי היא מסייעת לבעלה לקיים המצוה, דבלעדיה לא יוכל הבעל לקיים המצוה, ונמצא נמי דישראל מקיים מצוה שמסייע לכהן לקיים מצוותו?
תשובה: אין שייך.

IMMERSION IN A MIKVEH BEFORE DUCHANING

It is praiseworthy, but not obligatory, for a Kohen who is in a state of impurity to immerse in a mikveh before Bircas Kohanim.

169

שאלה: בבית יוסף (סי' קכ"ח) כתב בשם האגור שמנהג הכהנים לטבול קודם נשיאת כפים אלא שלא הובא להלכה מפני שזו חומרא דאתי לידי קולא, אך במשנה ברורה (ס"ק קס"ה) הביא שלכתחילה יש לטבול בערב יום טוב משום נשיאת כפים שביום טוב. ילמדנו רבינו האיך נכון לנהוג למעשה כשבקל אפשר לטבול בכל יום לנשיאת כפים?
תשובה: הנזהר תבא עליו ברכה אך אינו חיוב.

170

שאלה: האם חייב או דבר נכון לכהן לילך למקוה כל יום לנשיאת כפים משום סלסול שנהגו הכהנים (הובא בבית יוסף סי' קכ"ח)?
תשובה: היום אינו חיוב.

171

שאלה: מכיון שאני ממשפחת הכהנים ברצוני לדעת ביום שאני צריך ללכת למקוה (טומאת קרי) ומשום איזו סיבה לא הלכתי למקוה, האם מותר לי לברך ברכת כהנים עד שאלך למקוה?
תשובה: המנהג להקל.

REMOVING SHOES BEFORE DUCHANING

The Kohen should remove his right shoe first when preparing to *duchan*. The shoes should be moved out of sight in deference to the shul or *beis midrash*, but they need not be completely hidden. A Kohen should wear socks to *duchan*, but may *duchan* without socks if he is not wearing them. A Kohen serving as chazzan who forgot to remove his shoes before *Chazaras HaShatz* should remove them before Bircas Kohanim.

172

שאלה: אני כהן, וראיתי בשם כת״ר שכאשר חולצים נעלים לעלות לדוכן יש לחלוץ קודם נעל ימין כי זה חליצה לצורך מצוה, ויש חולקים שלא מצאנו בגמ׳ ושו״ע חילוק בזה, ולכן יש לחלוץ נעל שמאל קודם כמו תמיד, כיצד נכון לנהוג?

תשובה: ימין תחילה.

173

שאלה: המשנה ברורה (ס״ק ט״ו) הביא וז״ל: ״ויש להצניע המנעלים שלא יעמדו בגלוי בבית הכנסת מפני הכבוד״, עכ״ל. ושאלתי היא האם גם בבית המדרש שלומדים בו בקביעות יש להחמיר בכך, או שהסיבה להצניע היא מפני שבתפילה עומדים לפני המלך ואם כן בבית המדרש אין להחמיר?

תשובה: טוב ליזהר.

174

שאלה: במשנה ברורה הנ״ל, האם חוששים משום כבוד הצבור או כבוד בית הכנסת, ונפקא מינה כשמצניע המנעלים בין העמוד להיכל שמפני כבוד הצבור זה מוצנע, אבל כלפי ההיכל זה גלוי?

תשובה: טוב ליזהר.

175

שאלה: לפי המשנה ברורה הנ״ל, אם הכהן מכניס הנעלים מתחת לספסל האם סגי שמקצת הנעל יהיה תחת הספסל אפילו שמקצתו בולט חוץ לספסל?

תשובה: מסתבר שיש להקל.

176

שאלה: האם מותר לכהן לעלות עם מנעלים לדוכן ולהוריד אותם שם בפינה המכוסה של הדוכן?

תשובה: כן.

177

שאלה: כהן שבא לבית הכנסת בסנדלים בלי גרבים האם יעלה לדוכן, דלכאורה מהמשנה ברורה (סי' קכ"ח ס"ק י"ח) משמע שרק לכתחילה לא יעלה אבל בדיעבד אפשר, אבל לכאורה יש לדון מצד זה שהעם יסתכלו בכהן אם יעלה לדוכן בלי גרבים וכמו ששנינו בשו"ע (סי' קכ"ח סעיף ל') שאם הכהן בעל מום בידיו או ברגליו לא ישא כפיו מפני שהעם יסתכלו בו ויסיחו דעתם מלכוון לשמוע הברכה, האם הוא הדין בענינינו יש לדון שאם הכהן יעלה לדוכן בצורה מתמיהה בלי גרבים יסתכלו בו ויסיחו דעתם?

תשובה: יעלה.

178

שאלה: המשנה ברורה כתב שאין לישא כפים יחף, שאינו כבוד. מה יעשה כהן שבא לבית הכנסת בלי גרביים, ומה יעשה אם כבר קראו כהנים?

תשובה: באין ברירה מסתמא יכול.

179

שאלה: כהן יחף ללא גרביים, האם יכול לישא כפיו כך, או יצא מחוץ לבית הכנסת?

תשובה: אם אין לו ברירה יתכן דיברך כך.

180

שאלה: ש"ץ שהוא כהן ושכח להוריד מנעליו קודם התפילה, מה עדיף שיעשה - יוריד מנעליו באמצע חזרת הש"ץ לפני "רצה" או לפני "ברכת כהנים", או שמא ישא כפיו עם מנעליו לרגליו, או שמא לא ישא כפיו?

תשובה: לכאורה יוריד מנעליו לפני ברכת כהנים.

181

שאלה: האם ההולך בתשעה באב ברחוב (וגם על החול) בגרביים לרגליו, יכול לעלות בהם לדוכן, האם עדיין לא דנים בזה דין מנעלים?

תשובה: מותר.

182

שאלה: עלה לדוכן ומריח ריח רע מאוד מהגרביים של העומד סמוך אליו, האם יכול לשאת כפיו?

תשובה: אינו ריח שאוסר.

183

שאלה: האם מותר לכהנים לא לעלות לדוכן כשהרצפה רטובה, ולא רוצים שירטבו להם הגרביים?

תשובה: ינגבו.

ASCENDING TO THE DUCHAN

It is preferable that the Kohen stand on the platform before the *aron kodesh*. If there is no platform, there is no need to stand on something else to raise himself off the floor. There is no halachic reason to place a rug or other covering on the floor where the Kohanim stand. The Kohanim recite a prayer after they *duchan* that the blessing be fulfilled, and they are allowed to do so even though the chazzan is reciting *Chazaras HaShatz*. This prayer is recited even on Shabbos, and even on Mussaf of Rosh Hashanah; it is not considered an interruption between the shofar sounds.

184

שאלה: האם יש ענין לעלות לדוכן או שמא אין נפק"מ ויכול לעמוד במזרח לא על הדוכן?

תשובה: משמע שיש ענין אם אפשר.

185

שאלה: כהן העומד בדוכן, האם יותר טוב לעמוד לפני ארון הקודש או דבכל מקום שעומד במזרח שוה?

תשובה: כרצונו.

186

שאלה: בית כנסת שאין בו דוכן לכהנים, והרצפה אינה גבוהה, האם יש לעלות על גבי כסא נמוך לשאת את כפיהם?

תשובה: לא.

187

שאלה: אם אין מקום על מדריגת ארון הקודש שהוא יותר גבוה, האם ראוי לכתחילה לעשות ברכת כהנים על גבי מקום גבוה?

תשובה: אינו צריך.

188

שאלה: האם יש ענין לעמוד על הדוכן לא ממול ארון הקודש או לא?

תשובה: אין נ"מ.

189

שאלה: כשעולה הכהן לפני ארון הקודש, האם יש ענין שיעמוד הכהן לצד ארון קודש שלא יהיה גביו נגד ההיכל?

תשובה: אחרי שחכמים התירו אין להחמיר.

190

שאלה: למה כהנים מקפידים לא לישא כפים כשרגליהם על הרצפה, רק שמים איזה סמרטוט וכו׳ האם יש ליזהר?

תשובה: אולי שלא יצטננו.

191

שאלה: האם יש שום ענין שהכהן יעמוד על שטיח בשעת ברכת כהנים. דהנה באשל אברהם בס״ח כתוב שאין שיעור לגובה הדוכן ומסיים כשיש ב׳ או אולי אפילו א׳ על הדוכן די, ואולי לכן נהגו לעמוד על גבי שטיח. אך צ״ע דאם הכהן עומד על גבי הדוכן אצל ארון הקודש למה בכלל יצטרך לעמוד על גבי השטיח, ולמה שמים שטיחים על גבי הדוכן?

תשובה: שלא יצטנן.

192

שאלה: בבית המדרש שכהנים נושאים כפים בקרקע שוה לציבור, האם יש להקפיד שיהיה שטיח שהכהנים יעמדו עליו כשנושאים כפים משום שלכתחילה הדוכן צריך להיות במקום גבוה קצת, האם כת״ר יודע קפידא על פי דין שכהן ישא כפיו דוקא על שטיח ולא על הרצפה?

תשובה: כמדומה שהמנהג משום קור.

193

שאלה: בשלחן ערוך (סי׳ קכ״ח סעיף ט׳) כתב, כשעוקרים כהנים רגליהם לעלות לדוכן אומרים יהי רצון מלפניך וכו׳ שתהא ברכה זו שצויתנו לברך את עמך ישראל וכו׳. וכן בסעיף ט״ו: ואומרים רבון העולמים עשינו מה שגזרת עלינו עשה אתה וכו׳. ומקור תפילות הללו מגמרא סוטה (ל״ט, א). אולם צריך ביאור תקנה זו, דהרי מפריע לכהנים להקשיב לחזרת הש״ץ?

תשובה: כבר יצאו ידי שמונה עשרה.

194

שאלה: בשלחן ערוך כתוב שהכהנים יגידו ברכה בלחש לפני ואחרי נשיאת כפים. ויש להקשות אם יש רק עשרה בבית הכנסת שאז צריכים כולם לענות לחזרת הש״ץ שלא יהיו ברכות לבטלה, מה עדיף לכהנים לעשות, שיגידו או שישתקו?

תשובה: שיגידו.

195

שאלה: בשלחן ערוך (סי׳ קכ״ח סעיף ט): כשעוקרים כהנים רגליהם לעלות לדוכן אומרים יהי רצון מלפניך ה׳ אלוקינו שתהא ברכה זו שצויתנו לברך את עמך ישראל ברכה שלמה ולא יהא מכשול ועון מעתה ועד עולם. ולא זכיתי להבין, מה החרדה הגדולה שלא מצינו אותה כמדומני בשום מצות עשה אחרת?

תשובה: לא יעכב עון ומכשול שתתקבל הברכה.

196

שאלה: האם בשבת הכהנים אומרים את היהי רצון שלפני ברכת כהנים, וכן הרבונו של עולם אחריו?

תשובה: אומרים.

197

שאלה: האם מותר לכהנים לומר היהי רצון שלפני נשיאת כפים ותפילת רבונו של עולם אחרי נשיאת כפים במוסף של ראש השנה, או שמא אסור להם משום הפסק בתקיעות?

תשובה: מותר.

ANNOUNCING "KOHANIM"

According to the *Shulchan Aruch*, the chazzan should be the one to call out "Kohanim." Others disagree, however, maintaining that another congregant should be the one to do this. If only one Kohen is present, even if there is a minor Kohen *duchaning* with him, "Kohanim" should not be announced.

198

שאלה: איתא במחבר (סי' קכ"ח סעיף י'): "קורא להם השליח ציבור כהנים", מה טעם אין נוהגין כן כמו שמבואר בחיי אדם, החזון איש ועוד אחרונים, אלא אחד מן הקהל קורא כהנים?

תשובה: שלא להפסיק בשמו"ע.

199

שאלה: מה מקור מנהגנו שהשליח ציבור אינו קורא כהנים אלא אחר, ודלא כהמשנה ברורה (סי' קכ"ח ס"ק ל"ד), והאם נכון הדבר שבמנין של החזו"א, היה החזו"א מקריא הפסוקים לכהנים ולא השליח ציבור?

תשובה: נכון, ושמעתי שהוא רצה את המצוה.

200

שאלה: כשהציבור לא אמר לכהנים קודם נשיאת כפים "כהנים" ואחד הכהנים התחיל לברך האם יצטרפו אליו שאר הכהנים?

תשובה: נכון להמתין.

201

שאלה: האם עדיף לכבד לאחד מהמתפללים לקרוא "כהנים" לפני ברכת כהנים?

תשובה: טוב לעשות כן.

202

שאלה: לנוהגים שהגבאי מכריז כהנים בעת חזרת הש"ץ, כיצד ינהג הגבאי בעת שיש רק כהן אחד גדול בר חיובא ויש עמו קטן שהגיע לחינוך שנושא גם כן כפיו, האם צריך להכריז כהנים, או עד כמה שאין שני כהנים בני חיובא לא יכריז?

תשובה: לא יכריז. עיין משנה ברורה ס"ק ל"ח.

THE BERACHAH BEFORE BIRCAS KOHANIM

Like other *berachos* recited over the mitzvos of Kohanim, the *berachah* recited before Bircas Kohanim does not contain the words *"asher kideshanu b'mitzvosav."* The text of this *berachah* was instituted by the Anshei Knesses HaGedolah, like all other *berachos*. One should not think in learning or read a *sefer* while the *berachah* is recited.

203

שאלה: מדוע בנוסח ברכת הכהנים, מברכים אשר קדשנו בקדושתו של אהרן, ואין מברכים כשאר ברכות המצוות אשר קדשנו במצוותיו?

תשובה: בכל מצות כהונה מברכין כן, עי' רמב"ם סוף הלכות תרומות.

204

שאלה: הכהנים מברכים לפני נשיאת כפים, "אשר קדשנו בקדושתו של אהרן" וכו'. ומה בירך אהרן הכהן בעצמו?

תשובה: ברכות תיקנו אנשי כנה"ג.

205

שאלה: האם בעת הברכה של "אשר קדשנו בקדושתו" מותר לישראלים לעיין בספר או להרהר בלימוד?

תשובה: טוב שלא.

CALLING OUT THE WORDS OF BIRCAS KOHANIM

The chazzan does not have to announce the words of Bircas Kohanim loudly, as the congregation is required to hear only the words of the Kohanim and not his words. Only the Kohanim are required to hear the chazzan announcing the words. The chazzan does not have to announce the words using the same pronunciation (e.g., Ashkenazi or Sephardi) as the Kohanim. The chazzan should wait until all of the Kohanim have finished saying each word before continuing to the next.

206

שאלה: כיצד צריך השליח ציבור להגיד לכהנים את פסוקי הברכה (יברכך וכו'), בקול נמוך או בקול רגיל?

תשובה: כרצונו.

207

שאלה: האם יש ענין שהחזן יאמר ברכת כהנים בשקט (כמו שמצוי בכמה וכמה חזנים)?

תשובה: אין חייבין להשמיע רק להכהנים.

208

שאלה: שליח ציבור המקריא לכהנים בברכת כהנים יברכך וכו', יש חזנים שמקריאים לכהנים בלחש, ויש חזנים שמקריאים בקול רם, כיצד צריך להקריא?

תשובה: שהכהנים ישמעו.

209

שאלה: ראיתי נוהגים בברכת כהנים שהמקריא קורא בלחש ביחס לשאר התפילה, האם כן נכון לעשות?

תשובה: כיון שאין מוציא רבים אין צריך קול רם.

210

שאלה: האם יש מקור שהחזן אומר ברכת כהנים בשקט?

תשובה: אין צריך, רק שהכהנים ישמעו.

211

שאלה: האם יש מקור למה שיש נוהגים שהשליח ציבור מקריא ברכת כהנים בקול רם?

תשובה: אין צריך להשמיע לכל הצבור אבל צריך להשמיע לכל הכהנים ששם.

212

שאלה: היכן המקור להלכה דבשעה שהשליח ציבור אומר יברכך וכו׳ לכהנים, צריך לומר בקול נמוך יותר מהכהנים?

תשובה: אין זה הלכה רק נוהגין כן בשביל שא״צ להשמיע לציבור רק לכהנים.

213

שאלה: האם רק הכהנים צריכים לשמוע החזן או גם הציבור, האם הוא חלק מחזרת הש״ץ?

תשובה: רק הכהנים.

214

שאלה: שליח ציבור שקורא יברכך בשביל הכהנים, והכהן לא שמע את השליח ציבור, אם יאמר עוד פעם יברכך?

תשובה: לא.

215

שאלה: בדברי הרמב״ם (פט״ו ה״א מנשיאת כפים) דאדם שהוא עלג לא ישא כפיו, האם גם כאן במקריא יש פסול זה?

תשובה: לא.

216

שאלה: כהן מעדות ספרד העולה לדוכן והשליח ציבור מעדת אשכנז, האם יקריא לכהן יברכך וגו׳ בהברה ספרדית כמו שהכהן עונה אחריו?

תשובה: לא.

217

שאלה: במשנה ברורה (ס״ק ס״ח) כתב שהמקריא לא יתחיל להקרות תיבה אחרת עד שיסיימו הכהנים התיבה שלפניה, והנה לפעמים יש כהן שמושך התיבה יותר משאר הכהנים, האם צריך המקריא להמתין אף עליו או די שימתין על רובם?

תשובה: טוב שימתין.

FACING THE CONGREGATION

The non-Kohanim, including the chazzan, must face the Kohanim while they *duchan*, but they may stand to the side facing the Kohanim, and do not have to face them directly. They must hear the Kohanim but do not have to be in close proximity to them. If one needs to move back in order to face the Kohanim, and someone is davening *Shemoneh Esrei* behind him, he should pass beside him. One should stand no further toward the front of the shul than where the Kohanim's hands are. If the *ezras nashim* is elevated, the women are still included in Bircas Kohanim provided they face the Kohanim and are not standing past where the Kohanim are. For that reason, one should not build an *ezras nashim* that is situated past where the Kohanim stand. Men or women who are standing past where the Kohanim stand should move back to be included in the *berachah*.

218

שאלה: במה שכתוב במשנה ברורה (ס"ק נ') שצריך פנים כנגד פנים, האם זה לעיכובא לגבי ישראל יחיד שאינו פנים כנגד פנים?

תשובה: יתכן שהוא לעיכובא דמקרא נפקא.

219

שאלה: האם יש ענין לעמוד ממש פנים כנגד פנים של הכהנים בשעת ברכת כהנים?

תשובה: אפשר לעמוד גם בצד ובלבד שיהיו הפנים לצד שהכהנים.

220

שאלה: במה שכתב בשלחן ערוך (סי' קכ"ח סעיף כ"ג) שיהיו פניהם כנגד פני הכהנים, האם מוזכר באיזה מקום שיש ענין להיות ממש פנים כנגד פנים לכהנים דהיינו מולם, או שאין בזה ענין כלל רק העיקר לא להיות מאחריהם, כי ראיתי אנשים שהקפידו להיות מול הכהנים ממש, וברצוני לדעת אם יש סמך לדבר?

תשובה: צדדין ולפניו כלפניו.

221

שאלה: העומד בצדדים שלפני הכהנים, דמבואר במשנה ברורה (ס"ק צ"ה) שהוא בכלל הברכה, ושאלתי את כת"ר אם מכל מקום לכתחילה צריך להפנות ראשו למול הכהנים, והשיבני שטוב שיפנה פניו ולא מעכב, והנני שואל אם כשאוחז בשמונה עשרה גם כן יעשה כן?

תשובה: יכול לעשות.

222

שאלה: ראיתי מובא בספר ארחות רבנו (חלק א' עמוד ס"ו), שבעל הקהלות יעקב היה נוהג בשעת ברכת כהנים לעמוד כנגד הכהנים ממש, האם היה הנהגה זו מצד הלכה או מצד סיבה אחרת, והאם יש להקפיד בזה?

תשובה: הוא שמע קשה, ועמד כן כדי שישמע היטב.

223

שאלה: ראיתי כמה בני אדם שבשעת ברכת כהנים הם הולכים למקום שהם לפני הכהנים ממש, וקשה הלא זהו הלכה מפורשת (סי' קכ"ח סעיף כ"ד) שמלפניהם ובצדיהם הם בכלל ברכה, ואם כן האם יש טעם להנהגה הזאת?
תשובה: כנראה שישמעו טוב.

224

שאלה: האם יש הידור להתקרב ככל האפשר לכהנים כדי שיהיה במצב כמו שאדם מדבר לחבירו?
תשובה: אין מקום כלל להדר והעיקר שישמעו.

225

שאלה: אדם שעומד אחורי הכהנים וממילא אינו בכלל ברכה וכמו שכתב השלחן ערוך (סי' קכ"ח סעיף כ"ד), האם מותר לו לעבור לפני המתפלל כדי להיות בכלל ברכה?
תשובה: יעבור מן הצד.

226

שאלה: האם החזן חייב להיות כנגד או שוה לכהנים, ואם הוא מאחורי הכהנים נחשב כעם שבשדות ויכול להקריא להם הפסוקים?
תשובה: צריך שיהא לפניהם.

227

שאלה: כתב הבאור הלכה (סי' קכ"ח סעיף כ"ד בסוף ד"ה אבל) בזה"ל: "ואפשר דאפילו עומד בשוה עם פני הכהנים דהיינו פניו לצד מערב גם כן בכלל ברכה הוא, דזה הוא גם כן בכלל מאמרם כדרך שאומר אדם לחבירו דמצוי כמה פעמים שבני אדם יושבים בשוה ומדברים", עכ"ל. יש להסתפק האם עומד בשוה היינו פניהם של הכהנים, או ידיהם של הכהנים?
תשובה: נכון לעמוד לפני ידיהם.

228

שאלה: האם יש להקפיד שהשליח ציבור יתפלל לפני הכהנים ולא מאחוריהם?
תשובה: כן.

229

שאלה: בענין ברכת כהנים יש להסתפק באותם האנשים העומדים על גבי הבימה שבבית הכנסת והוא גבוה יותר ממקום עמידת הכהן, וכן מי שעומד בעזרת נשים שהוא בקומה שניה האם הם בכלל הברכה, או האם צריך לעמוד על רצפת בית הכנסת ולא יעמוד גבוה מהכהנים כדי להיות נכלל בברכת כהנים?
תשובה: כולם בכלל הברכה.

230

שאלה: בונים בית כנסת בשכונתינו ורוצים שהעזרת נשים תהיה במזרחו של בית הכנסת, שאם בונים בצורה הזאת, יש אפשרות שהבית הכנסת יהיה יותר גדול. אך יש אומרים שאם עושים כן, כל שבת שבאות הנשים להתפלל שם, יהיו מאחורי הכהנים, ומבואר בשלחן ערוך (סי' קכ"ח סעיף כ"ד) שמי שמאחורי הכהנים אינם בכלל הברכה, האם מותר לבנות הבית כנסת באופן זה?

תשובה: אין לעשות כן.

231

שאלה: מי שהתפלל כבר, ולומד בעזרת נשים וחלון פתוח בינו לבין הכהנים המברכים ברכת כהנים, אי סגי בזה, או שיש להחמיר להיות דוקא בבית הכנסת ממש?

תשובה: סגי, אבל יותר טוב ליכנס.

232

שאלה: בבית הכנסת בעירי בנו ארון קודש ועמוד חזן לידו, ונמצא שהחזן אחורי הכהנים, האם זה בסדר?

תשובה: כדאי להזיז את העמוד מיד.

233

שאלה: האם הדין של "עם שאחורי הכהנים אינו בכלל ברכה" חל גם על השליח ציבור, שמקום עמידתו מאחורי הכהנים ולא דקדק לעמוד לפניהם?

תשובה: כן.

234

שאלה: חזן שמקום העמוד שלו הוא מאחורי הכהנים, ונמצא שבברכת כהנים, הוא עומד מאחורי הכהנים, האם רצוי לזוז ממקומו, לצורך ברכת כהנים לקבל ברכתם, או שמא לא יזוז ממקומו?

תשובה: לכתחלה לא יתפלל שם.

235

שאלה: במקום שיש כמה כהנים, והישראל עומד לפני כמה כהנים, אמנם הוא מאחורי כמה כהנים, האם יצא ברכת כהנים?

תשובה: מסתבר שאם הוא לפני קצת כהנים הוא בכלל ברכה, אך לכתחילה בודאי יש לעמוד לפני כולם.

236

שאלה: בברכת כהנים שעומדים יותר מעשרה כהנים ליד קיר המזרח וכהן אחד נעמד שורה לפניהם, האם חייבים הקהל לצאת ממקומם ולעמוד לפני כל הכהנים כולל כהן יחיד זה?

תשובה: ראוי לעשות כן.

237

שאלה: העומד נגד רוב הכהנים, אבל יש מקצת כהנים שהוא מאחריהם, האם יש לו ללכת לאחוריו כדי שיהיה נגד פני כל הכהנים ויתברך מכולם?
תשובה: יותר טוב נגד כולם.

238

שאלה: האם בברכת כהנים, בעזרת נשים כלול בברכה זו?
תשובה: כן.

239

שאלה: האם אפשר לכתחילה לעמוד בברכת כהנים מאחורי עמוד שבינו לבין הכהנים, שכתוב בשו"ע (סי' קכ"ח סעיף כ"ד) שמי שעומד לפני הכהנים אפילו מחיצה של ברזל אינה מפסקת בינו לבין הכהנים?
תשובה: כן.

240

שאלה: האם חייבים או שאסור להפסיק באמצע הלימוד כדי לשמוע ברכת כהנים, כשצריך בשביל זה לעבור לחדר אחר בשביל שיעמוד לפני הכהנים ולא מאחוריהם?
תשובה: נכון לעשות כן.

241

שאלה: בבתי הכנסת בציריך שוויץ, יש מנהג, שחלק מהנשים שמתפללות בעזרת הנשים, בשעת ברכת כהנים הופכות את עצמן בכיוון הפוך מהכהנים, האם זה מנהג שטות וראוי להעיר לנשים שזה גם בזיון לכהנים ולברכה?
תשובה: כמדומה שזה שלא כהלכה ואין לעשות כן.

242

שאלה: בהלכות נשיאת כפים מפורש (סי' קכ"ח סעיף כ"ד): "עם שאחורי הכהנים אינם בכלל ברכה", ואם כן צריך עיון למה אין הנשים העומדות בעזרת נשים והן אחורי כהנים הולכות איזה פסיעות להיות לפני הכהנים כמו אנשים, ואף על פי שמבואר בפוסקים (ערוך השלחן סי' קכ"ח סעיף ל"ח) דנשים יש להם ברכה מצד בעליהם מכל מקום מה נעשה עם אלמנות וגרושות ופנויות.
תשובה: באמת יש ללכת.

243

שאלה: אם התפלל במנין שלא היה להם כהנים ויש לו את האפשרות להמתין למנין אחר כדי לשמוע ברכת כהנים ולא המתין, האם הוא בכלל עם שבשדות?
תשובה: לא.

244

שאלה: המתפללים במזרח ומאריכים בתפילה עד אחר נשיאת כפים, האם זה הוי אנוס והוא בכלל הברכה?

תשובה: אין לנהוג כן.

245

שאלה: הא דאמרינן (סוטה דף ל"ח, ב) דעם שאחורי כהנים אינן בכלל ברכה, ונפסק גם בשלחן ערוך (סי' קכ"ח סעיף כ"ד), האם הוא אינו בכלל הברכה גם באופן שנמצא אחורי הכהנים מחמת שמאריך בתפילתו?

תשובה: יתכן.

RAISING THE HANDS AND POSITIONING THE FINGERS

Bircas Kohanim is unique in that the hands of the Kohanim must be raised while this blessing is given. Ideally, the Kohen's hands should be raised until shoulder level, but if he is ill or infirm he may lower his elbows and arms. The Kohen's right hand should be slightly higher than his left hand, even if he is left-handed. The Kohanim should keep their hands raised even while they are singing between the verses. If a Kohen cannot hold his fingers in the recommended position (to create the five *"avirim"*), he may nevertheless *duchan*. The tefillin straps should be removed from the fingers before *duchaning*. A Kohen may move his feet during Bircas Kohanim and does not have to keep them together, as in *Shemoneh Esrei*. There is no prohibition for a non-Kohen to position his fingers the way the Kohanim do during Bircas Kohanim, but he should not raise his hands the way the Kohanim do, as if performing Bircas Kohanim.

246

שאלה: הטור ושלחן ערוך קוראים את הלכות ברכת כהנים בשם "הלכות נשיאת כפים", (וכן מצינו בברכת יעקב "יתר שאת" בראשית מ"ט ג, וברש"י שם: לשון נשיאות כפים), והלא נשיאת כפים הוא רק אופן של הברכה, והוא רק דין אחד מדיני ברכת כהנים כדאיתא בגמרא (סוטה ל"ח, א) תניא כה תברכו בנשיאת כפים וכו', ולמה זה כל כך חשוב ועיקר שכל הברכת כהנים יקרא על שם נשיאת כפים?

תשובה: שכל הברכות שבעולם א"צ נשיאת כפים.

247

שאלה: במשנה ברורה (ס"ק נ') כתב דנשיאת כפים היא לעיכובא. ובשלחן ערוך (קכ"ח, י"ב) כתב שנשיאת כפים היינו כנגד כתפיהם. האם גם השיעור של נשיאת כפים הוא לעיכובא, ואם כן כשחזינן לכהן דלא עביד הכי, האם לענות אמן או לא?

תשובה: עי' תוי"ט פ"ז דסוטה מ"ו דכתב הגבהה בעלמא משמע, ולפ"ז כנגד כתפותיהם לכתחילה מדרבנן אבל אינו מעכב.

248

שאלה: בברכת כהנים שצריך להיות כפיהן כנגד כתפיהן, האם הכוונה לפני הידים לבד, או שצריך שהזרוע גם כן יהיה מוגבה כנגד הכתפיים.

תשובה: כמדומה שרק הכפות.

249

שאלה: בנשיאת כפים האם צריך שכל היד תהיה בגובה הכתף או רק כף היד?

תשובה: כף היד.

250

שאלה: האם מעכב בנשיאת כפים שגם המרפק יהיה בגובה כתפיו, או שסגי שיגביהנו קצת ורק כפיו כנגד כתפיו?

תשובה: כמדומה שאין מקפידין.

251

שאלה: כשכהנים נושאים כפיהם, האם צריכים רק להגביה היד שיהא בגובה הכתפיים, או שגם צריכים לפשוט כל הזרוע, או האם יכולים לכפוף הזרוע ולקרב הידים אצלם?

תשובה: לכאו' היד.

252

שאלה: אם רואה כהן שנושא רק כפות ידיו כנגד כתפיו כדעת האבני נזר (או"ח סי' ל"א), האם לגעור בו כיון שיש הסוברים שבעי נשיאת כל היד כולל הזרוע והאמה?

תשובה: אין למחות.

253

שאלה: בשלחן ערוך (סי' קכ"ח סעיף י"ב) כתב: ומגביהים ידיהם כנגד כתפותיהם ופושטים ידיהם, וכתב הרמב"ם (פרק י"ד, ט), הלשון ופושטין אצבעותיהם, וכן הוא ברש"י (סוטה לט, ב ד"ה לכוף). ויש להקשות כשהמקום דחוק אם מספיק בפישוט אצבעותיהם כנגד כתפותיהם, או שמא צריך דוקא פשיטת ידיהם?

תשובה: יתכן דמהני.

254

שאלה: בשלחן ערוך (סי' קכ"ח, סעיף י"ב) כתב: ומגביהים יד ימנית קצת למעלה מהשמאלית. האם גם כהן איטר יד יש להגביה יד ימנית קצת?
תשובה: כן.

255

שאלה: באיזה זמן צריכים הכהנים להגביה כפיהם לפשוט אצבעותיהם לנשיאת כפים, קודם הברכה של ברוך אתה ה' או אחר הברכה?
תשובה: כמנהגו.

256

שאלה: כשכהן עולה לברכת כהנים ומרים את הידים בהתחלת הברכה ולא כשמתחיל לברך יברכך, האם הוא עובר על בל תוסיף?
תשובה: אין בזה בל תוסיף.

257

שאלה: כתב המשנה ברורה (ס"ק נ"ב) כהן שלא יכול להגביה ידיו בלי סמוכין ועזרה, לא יכול לישא כפיו. מה הדין בכהן שיש לו גבס ביד אחת, ואינו יכול להגביהו בעצמו בלי עזרה של ידו השניה שלו, האם גם בכה"ג פסול לישא כפיו, או שמא מכיון שהוא עושה כן בעצמו בלי עזרה חיצונית, זהו נחשב כעושה בעצמו, ויכול לישא כפיו?
תשובה: מסתבר דיכול.

258

שאלה: כתב בשו"ת אבני נזר (או"ח סי' ל"א) שאם ל"ע נקטע כף יד אחת של כהן, וכף יד השני נשאר, שיכול לעשות ברכת כהנים. ויש להקשות שהרי מבואר במשנה ברורה (ס"ק נ"ב) בשם הנודע ביהודה, שכהן שאינו יכול להגביה שני ידיו לזמן מועט אינו נושא כפיו. מה הדין אם יכול רק להגביה ידו אחת בעזרת היד השניה לזמן מועט?
תשובה: מסתבר דמועיל.

259

שאלה: במקום שנוהגים לנגן בברכת כהנים ביום טוב, האם ידי הכהן צריכים להיות מורמות למעלה אז, או שמא יכול להניחם?
תשובה: ודאי יגביה, כיון שהטעם שמנגנים כדי שיוכלו לומר רבונו של עולם.

260

שאלה: בשלחן ערוך (סי' קכ"ח סעיף ט"ז) כתוב שהכהנים אינם רשאים להוריד ידיהם הפרושות עד שמחזירים את פניהם מהקהל. ביום טוב כשהציבור אומרים רבונו של עולם של הטבת חלום, והכהנים שרים, האם אז רשאים להוריד ידיהם?
תשובה: לכאו' יש ליזהר.

261

שאלה: האם שרי לכהן להניח ידיו בין מילה למילה מחמת עייפות וכדו'?
תשובה: לכתחילה אין לעשות.

262

שאלה: הנה מצינו בשו"ע שכתב גבי ברכת כהנים (סי' קכ"ח סעיף י"ב): "מגביהים ידיהם כנגד כתפותיהם וכו' וחולקים אצבעותיהם ומכוונים לעשות חמשה אוירים בין שתי אצבעות לשתי אצבעות", ובמשנה ברורה כתב הטעם לכך (ס"ק מ"ד): "וחולקים אצבעותיהם דאיתא בתנחומא פרשת נשא משגיח מן החלונות מציץ מן החרכים, משגיח מן החלונות מבין אצבעותיהם של כהנים, מציץ מן החרכים בשעה שפושטים כפיהם". האם דבר זה הוא לעיכובא בנוגע לאחד שאינו יכול לחבר שתי אצבעותיו ביחד ולעשות אויר אחד, והאם יש עצה לזה, ומנלן דין זה?
תשובה: אינו מעכב.

263

שאלה: כהן שאינו יכול לחבר בידו האחת הקמיצה עם הזרת, האם הוי ככהן שיש בידיו תחבושת וכדומה שעולה לדוכן כך אפילו בלא להפסיק הידים בה' אוירים, או שמא עדיף שיחבר אצבעותיו בחוט וכדומה?
תשובה: יעלה.

264

שאלה: האם בנשיאת כפים שבעינן ה' אוירין רצועות התפילין חוצצים להם?
תשובה: המנהג להוציא הרצועות.

265

שאלה: האם הכהנים חייבים להסיר רצועות התפילין לפני שעולים לדוכן?
תשובה: כך נוהגין.

266

שאלה: האם יכול כהן לישא כפיו עם תפילין קשורה לאצבעו, כאשר אין זה מפריע לה' אוירין שצריכים להיות בין אצבעותיו?
תשובה: אין ראוי.

267

שאלה: כהן בברכת כהנים שהפיל ספר קודש על הרצפה באמצע ברכת כהנים ואין אף אחד מן הקהל יכול להרימו, האם יכול הכהן להרים הספר אם לא יתבלבל בהמשך הברכה?
תשובה: כן.

268

שאלה: באמצע ברכת כהנים אם מותר לכהן להזיז את הרגלים?
תשובה: מותר.

269

שאלה: האם כהנים צריכים להשוות רגליהם בנשיאת כפים כמו בתפילת שמונה עשרה, דחשיב כהנים בשעת עבודה?

תשובה: לא שמענו.

270

שאלה: האם יש איסור לישראל לפרוש אצבעותיו ככהן?

תשובה: לא שמעתי כזה איסור.

271

שאלה: נשאלתי אם ישראל יכול לפשוט אצבעותיו ככהן, והראוני לעטרת זקנים (סי' קכ"ח אות ה') בשם הזוהר שאסור, ומה דעתו בזה, ואולי בישראל שאין חלות של ברכה יכול?

תשובה: לזקוף האצבעות הוא דבר אחר והיינו להרים ידיו למעלה מראשו.

NOT LOOKING AT THE KOHANIM

The congregation must face, but not gaze at, the Kohanim while they recite the actual words of Bircas Kohanim, even though they are covered in a tallis. It is not proper to photograph Bircas Kohanim. A Kohen may look at his own hands to see that they are positioned correctly. The custom is that young boys in shul go under their father's tallis during Bircas Kohanim so they should not see the Kohanim.

272

שאלה: בשלחן ערוך מובא (סי' קכ"ח סעיף כ"ג) שיש לעמוד בעינים למטה בברכת כהנים, ומובא בהמשך שם: "ויהיו פניהם כנגד פני הכהנים". קשה לי האיך צריכים לעמוד בשעת ברכת כהנים?

תשובה: צריך לעמוד נגד פניו ולא להסתכל עליו.

273

שאלה: בשלחן ערוך (סי' קכ"ח סעיף כ"ג) כתב דבשעה שמברכים הכהנים את העם לא יביטו ולא יסיחו דעתם וכו' ולא יסתכלו בהם. האם דין זה שאין להסתכל בכהנים הוא גם בעת שמברכים אשר קדשנו בקדושתו של אהרן, או רק בעת שאומרים פסוקי הברכה?

תשובה: רק בפסוקי הברכה.

274

שאלה: האם מותר להסתכל על הכהנים אחר שגמרו "שלום" אבל עדיין לא הפכו פניהם מהקהל ועודן בטלית?

תשובה: מותר.

275

שאלה: בהא דאמרו אל יסתכל בכהנים בשעת נשיאת כפים, והמסתכל עיניו כהות, האם בכלל זה גם כן היכא שכבר סיימו ברכתם (כבר אמרו "שלום") אבל עדיין ידיהם פרוסות?

תשובה: לא.

276

שאלה: האם יש מקום לאסור לצלם את הכהנים כשהם מברכים ברכת כהנים?

תשובה: אינו דרך ארץ.

277

שאלה: האם מותר לצלם ברכת כהנים או שמא אסור כשם שאסור להסתכל?

תשובה: אין ראוי.

278

שאלה: למה בזמנינו מקפידים לא להסתכל על ידי הכהנים בנשיאת כהנים, כיון שמכסין ידיהם בטלית ומשמע במשנה ברורה דמהני?

תשובה: שמא יוציא הכהן ידו.

279

שאלה: האם יש היום ענין לא להביט בכהנים, דהא מבואר ברמ"א (סי' קכ"ח, סעיף כ"ג) שלכן שמים טלית, ואם כן אחרי שיש טלית לכאורה יכול להביט בהם?

תשובה: יש ליזהר.

280

שאלה: במה שכתב הרמ"א (סימן קכ"ח, סעיף כ"ג) שיש מקומות שנהגו שהכהנים מכסים גם ידיהם בטלית כדי שלא יסתכלו העם בהם, האם האידנא שהכהנים מכסים גם ידיהם מותר לעם להסתכל עליהם, שהרי אין בעיה של היסח הדעת כי פניהם וידיהם מכוסות או שמא אסור גם האידנא?

תשובה: אין להסתכל.

281

שאלה: בחוץ לארץ שהכהנים שרים בעת ברכת כהנים ביום טוב, האם מותר להסתכל על הכהנים בשעה ששרים?

תשובה: ראוי לעצום עינים בברכת כהנים תמיד.

282

שאלה: כת"ר כתב לי שראוי לעצום עינים תמיד בברכת כהנים. ולא זכיתי להבין אמאי לעצום עינים, דהא די שלא יסתכל בכהנים, ובפרט שמכסים עצמם בטלית?

תשובה: כוונתי שראוי לעשות כן שלא יבוא להסתכל.

283

שאלה: במקום שבין כך אינו רואה הכהנים, אם צריך לעצום עיניו בשעת ברכת כהנים?

תשובה: אין צריך.

284

שאלה: כתב הרמ"א (סי' קכ"ח, סעיף כ"ג) דגם הכהנים לא יסתכלו בידיהם, ובמשנה ברורה (ס"ק פ"ט) כתב: "אבל ראיה קצת שרי דדוקא בזמן המקדש שהיו מברכין בשם המפורש וכו', ומכל מקום נוהגין גם עכשיו זכר למקדש שלא להביט בהם כלל". ויש לעיין אם מותר לכהן להסתכל בידיו כדי לראות אם הם פרושים כדין?

תשובה: מסתמא מותר.

285

שאלה: בענין התנהגות הציבור בעת ברכת כהנים, בחלק מהקהילות שהבנים נכנסים תחת טלית אביהם בעת הברכה, האם יש מקור וטעם למנהג? וויש לדון, שקורה הרבה שפני הבנים אינם נוטים אל מול הכהנים, וגם הבנים ואף האבות נוטים לטעות ולחשוב שהברכה עוברת מהאב לבן, לכן האם ראוי לבטל ולעורר אחרים לחדול ממנהג זה.

תשובה: זה מנהג יפה כדי שלא יסתכל, וכל הטענות אין בהן ממש.

286

שאלה: האם יש מקור לאלו הנוהגים לכסות את בניהם בטלית בשעת ברכת כהנים, והאם הוא מנהג נכון כי שמעתי מפקפקים בזה דנראה כאילו האבא גם פועל בברכה?

תשובה: מנהג נכון.

287

שאלה: למה נוהגים לכסות הבנים בטליתותיהם בשעת ברכת כהנים?

תשובה: שלא יסתכלו.

288

שאלה: כשהיה כת"ר ילד, האם אביו זצ"ל הכניס אותו תחת טליתו בשעת ברכת כהנים?

תשובה: כן.

289

שאלה: האם יש מקור למנהג שנהגו האבות להניח ידיהם בראש בניהם בשעת ברכת כהנים בבית הכנסת, האם משפיע משהו לקבלת הברכה?

תשובה: לא שמעתי מנהג זה.

COVERING WITH A TALLIS

A Kohen who does not have a tallis with which to cover himself should cover himself with his coat or jacket. If there is no alternative, two Kohanim may cover themselves with the same tallis. A hat may be worn under the tallis. A Kohen who wears a tallis only for Bircas Kohanim must recite a *berachah* over the tallis, even during *Chazaras HaShatz*. If he *duchans* a second time, during Mussaf, and dons the tallis again, he must recite the *berachah* on the tallis again. On a non-kosher tallis one does not say a *berachah*, but it may be worn for Bircas Kohanim if he does not have in mind to perform the mitzvah of tzitzis with it. If there is no spare tallis in the shul, the Kohen may borrow a tallis for Bircas Kohanim from the chazzan or another congregant, even if that person is in the middle of *Shemoneh Esrei*. If the Kohen's tallis falls off during Bircas Kohanim he should put it back on without a *berachah*.

290

שאלה: כהן שהיה אצל מנין בחורים בלי טלית ולא היה שם טלית בשבילו, אם חייב לישא את כפיו, או שמא פטור מחמת חסרון הטלית?

תשובה: ישים את מעילו במקום טלית.

291

שאלה: האם מותר לשני כהנים לישא כפים בטלית אחת?

תשובה: אם אין ברירה.

292

שאלה: אם יש טלית אחד, ויש שני כהנים מוכנים לישא כפיהם, מה עליהם לעשות?

תשובה: עי' סנהדרין כ' א.

293

שאלה: שאלתי את כת"ר מה יעשו שני כהנים שרוצים לישא כפיהם ויש רק טלית אחד. וענה לי עיין סנהדרין כ' עמוד א, ושם איתא שהיו מתכסין ששה תלמידים בטלית אחת, אולם לא הבנתי מה הכרעת כת"ר בזה האם מותר או אסור?

תשובה: כשאי אפשר באופן אחר מותר.

294

שאלה: האם מותר לכהן לישא כפיו במגבת כשאין לו טלית?

תשובה: ישים את מעילו.

295

שאלה: האם מותר לבחור לשאת כפים עם כובע תחת הטלית?

תשובה: מותר.

296

שאלה: האם יש הידור וחיבוב מצוה שיהיה לבחור כהן טלית משלו לנשיאת כפים, או אין הידור בזה?

תשובה: לא שמענו.

297

שאלה: ישראל שמעוטף בטלית גדול ומקיים מצוה בכל רגע ורגע ושכח באותו יום להניח טלית קטן, האם מחוייב ליתנו לכהן בחור קודם נשיאת כפים למרות שמפסיד מצוות ציצית באותם רגעים?

תשובה: אינו חייב אבל ראוי.

298

שאלה: כהן שלובש טליתו רק לברכת כהנים האם צריך לברך?

תשובה: כן.

299

שאלה: האם מותר לבחור לברך על טלית עבור ברכת כהנים באמצע חזרת הש"ץ?

תשובה: כן.

300

שאלה: כהן העולה לדוכן ונוטל טלית הקהל האם צריך לברך עליו?

תשובה: אם יודע שהוא כשר ולובשו למצוה.

301

שאלה: אני בחור ומלביש טלית רק לפני ברכת כהנים עם ברכה, ואחר כך אני מוריד הטלית. האם בברכת כהנים של מוסף אני צריך לברך שוב?

תשובה: כן.

302

שאלה: כהן בחור שאינו נוהג להתעטף בטלית (לפני נישואיו), ויש בבית הכנסת טלית פסולה, האם יכול להתעטף בה לברכת כהנים?

תשובה: אם מכוון לא לצאת מצות ציצית יש מקום להקל.

303

שאלה: האם הא דכתוב בפוסקים דמותר ללבוש טלית פסולה לברכת כהנים היכא דליכא אחר אם מכוון שלא לצאת, וצ"ע האם הלכה זו הוא דוקא אם לא נשא עדיין כפיו או מותר אפילו נשא כפיו?

תשובה: אפי' נשא.

304

שאלה: כהן שאין לו טלית לישא את כפיו ואמרו לו לעלות לדוכן, האם ישא את כפיו בלא טלית או שמא ילך לבית המדרש אחר מיד וישא שם את כפיו אם שם יש לו טלית?

תשובה: יכסה עם מעילו.

305

שאלה: כהן שצריך טלית לברכת כהנים, האם עדיף שיקח מאדם שמתפלל אף על פי שזה מפריע בתפילה או מהשליח ציבור שלכאורה זה פחות מפריע לו, אף על פי שזה אותו שמונה עשרה, וגם בשליח ציבור יש כבוד הציבור?

תשובה: כרצונו.

306

שאלה: אם יש רק טלית אחת בבית הכנסת, האם כהן יכול להוריד הטלית מהש"ץ באמצע שמונה עשרה כדי שיוכל לשאת כפיו עם טלית?

תשובה: כן.

307

שאלה: רציתי לשאול את כת"ר, אני בחור כהן שלומד בישיבה קטנה, ולפעמים בחזרת הש"ץ לפני ברכת כהנים צריך אני לקחת טלית ממי שיש לו טלית והוא עדיין מתפלל ואין מתפלל אחר שאפשר לקחת ממנו, האם מותר לי לקחת ממנו בעודנו מתפלל שמונה עשרה, ואת"ל שלא, האם מוטב שאצא החוצה ולא אקח טלית ממי שמתפלל. והנה מצד בין אדם לחבירו אינני שואל דהבחור שיש לו הטלית מרשה לקחת, אבל שאלתי מצד הלכות תפילה האם מן הראוי לקחת טלית בשביל לקיים המצוה?

תשובה: יתכן שמותר.

308

שאלה: כהן שיש לו מנהג מאבותיו לשאת כפיו כשידיו מגולות מחוץ לטלית (כמבואר ברמ"א סי' קכ"ח סעיף כ"ג), וכל בתי הכנסת בעירו נוהגים כמנהג העולם שידי הכהנים מכוסות בטלית בשעת נשיאת כפים, היכול לעשות כמנהג אבותיו לברך עם ידים שאינם מכוסות, אפילו ששאר הכהנים מכסים ידיהם?

תשובה: לא.

309

שאלה: האם מותר לכהן לישא כפים בטלית שפסיה כחולים במקום שחורים (שיש לחוש שזה יגרום שיסתכלו בו)?

תשובה: מותר.

310

שאלה: כהן שנפלה טליתו באמצע שמברך הקהל מה יעשה?

תשובה: ילבש בלי ברכה.

SAYING BIRCAS KOHANIM LOUDLY

The *berachah* before Bircas Kohanim should be recited loudly, so that everyone in the shul can answer amen. Each Kohen should say the words of Bircas Kohanim loudly enough to be heard throughout the shul. Even if the minyan consists only of Kohanim, they should *duchan* loudly.

311

שאלה: האם גם ברכת נשיאת כפים אשר קדשנו וכו׳ צריכה להיות בקול רם?
תשובה: ראוי כדי שיוכלו לענות אמן.

312

שאלה: מה השיעור של בקול רם שצריך שיהא בברכת כהנים, האם הכוונה שהיא בקול רם יחד עם שאר הכהנים (שהתוצאה תהיה שכולם ישמעו), או שכל כהן בפני עצמו צריך שיאמר אצלו בקול רם, והנפק״מ כשאחד מן הכהנים קולו לבד לא נשמע אלא עם שאר הכהנים, האם מתקיים ה׳בקול רם׳?
תשובה: לכאורה כל אחד צריך קול רם.

313

שאלה: כתב בשולחן ערוך (סי׳ קכ״ח סעיף י״ד) שצריך להגיד בקול רם, האם זה דין על כל הכהנים ביחד שיצא מהם קול רם שכולם ישמעו, או שזה דין על הכהן בפני עצמו, ונפקא מינא אם יש כהן שמדבר בלחש, האם יוכל להיות ביחד עם עוד כהנים או לא?
תשובה: כל כהן צריך לומר בקול רם.

314

שאלה: במשנה ברורה (ס״ק נ״ג) כתב דצריך שיאמר ברכת כהנים באופן שכל הקהל ישמע, ולפי זה כהן יחיד בבית הכנסת גדול שידוע לו שכל הקהל אינו שומעו, האם עדיף לא לעלות?
תשובה: בודאי יעלה ויגביה קולו.

315

שאלה: בהא דכתב המשנה ברורה (ס״ק נ״ג) שברכת כהנים צריך בקול רם דהיינו בקול בינוני לאפוקי בלחש, האם כשאומר בקול בינוני נשמע לציבור, אבל יש עמו עוד כהנים אחרים שמגביהים קולם יותר לכן קולו לא נשמע, האם צריך לומר בקול גדול כמותם?
תשובה: אם שומעים כל הקולות יחד סגי.

316

שאלה: מדוע ברכת כהנים נאמרת על ידי רבים, הרי יש כלל שתרי קלי לא משתמעי?

תשובה: אם כולם אותו הקול משתמע.

317

שאלה: מדוע בברכת כהנים אין בעיה של תרי קלי לא משתמעי?

תשובה: מצותן בכך.

318

שאלה: האם יש שיעור בדין קול רם בברכת כהנים דהיינו כל כחו, או די שמשמיע להציבור, וכן האם לומר בקול רם ממש כעין צעקה?

תשובה: אין לעשות דברים משונים.

319

שאלה: השלחן ערוך (סי' קכ"ח סעיף י"ד) כתב, אין מברכין (ברכת כהנים) אלא בלשון הקודש, ובעמידה, ובנשיאת כפים, ובקול רם. ובמשנה ברורה (ס"ק נ"ג) כתב שאם המתפללים רבים בעינן שיהא כל הקהל שומע ולא סגי בעשרה שומעים. והסתפקתי אם ישנם כהנים רבים וקולו אינו מורגש מחמת קולות שאר הכהנים, האם חשיב שאמר בקול רם, או שיש דין שישמעו הקהל את קולו דוקא?

תשובה: זה טוב.

320

שאלה: כהן ששמעו אותו מקצת המתפללים האם קיים המצוה, ואם כן, אם לא שמעו כל המתפללים האם קיים מצוה?

תשובה: אם השתדל שישמעו קיים.

321

שאלה: איתא בשלחן ערוך (סי' קכ"ח סעיף כ"ה), שבית הכנסת שכולה כהנים מברכים לעם שבשדות. האם בכהאי גוונא יכולים לברך בקול נמוך, דהרי בלאו הכי העם שבשדות אינו שומע?

תשובה: צריך בקול רם.

322

שאלה: כת"ר כתב לי שבמקרה של בית הכנסת שכולה כהנים, שמברכים לעם שבשדות, צריכים לברך בקול רם, מה הטעם בזה?

תשובה: אחר שאמרה תורה אמור להם כאדם האומר לחברו, זו צורת הבר"כ וגם כשאין ישראלים צריך לומר כאדם האומר לחברו.

323

שאלה: מה המקור שהכהן כשנושא כפיו יאמר יותר בקול מהחזן יברכך?

תשובה: כדי שכל הצבור ישמע.

324

שאלה: בברכת כהנים שצריך קול רם, כשיש בית הכנסת גדול האם מספיק שעד סוף הבית הכנסת ישמעו את כולם, או צריך שכל כהן וכהן ישמעוהו עד סוף הבית הכנסת?

תשובה: ישתדל מה שיותר בקול.

325

שאלה: בבית כנסת גדול מאוד, שאין כולם שומעים את הכהנים, גם כשאומרים בקול רם, האם לא ישא הכהן כפיו?

תשובה: יתקרבו הציבור.

SEPHARDIC AND ASHKENAZIC PRONUNCIATION

An Ashkenazi Kohen is permitted to *duchan* in a Sephardi shul (and vice versa) even though he pronounces the words differently. He should use his own pronunciation, but he may use the pronunciation of the congregation if he prefers.

326

שאלה: כהנים אשכנזים האם מותר להם לעלות לדוכן יחד עם הכהנים הספרדים בבית הכנסת של ספרדים, כיון שמבטאם שונה לגמרי בין במבטא האותיות ובין במבטא הנקודות?

תשובה: מותר.

327

שאלה: כהן אשכנזי המתפלל במנין ספרדי, האם מותר לו לומר פסוקי ברכת כהנים בהברה ספרדית?

תשובה: מותר.

328

שאלה: אשכנזי הנושא כפיו אצל הספרדים בהברה אשכנזית, האם נקרא דש בעירו, או שגם בזה יש חשש שמסתכלים בו מחמת השינוי?

תשובה: אם מתפלל שם הרבה פעמים הוי זה דש בעירו.

329

שאלה: כשכהן ספרדי מברך ברכת כהנים, והחזן מקריא במבטא אשכנזי, האם צריך הכהן גם כן לברך במבטא אשכנזי?

תשובה: אין צריך.

330

שאלה: כשיש כהן אשכנזי שמתפלל בבית כנסת ספרדי, האם עליו לברך ברכת כהנים בהברה ספרדית, או בהברה אשכנזית כמנהגו?

תשובה: כמנהגו.

331

שאלה: כהן אשכנזי שמברך ברכת כהנים בבית הכנסת של ספרדים, האם הוא צריך לומר אותה בהברה ספרדית?

תשובה: אם אין ברירה אחרת או שקשה לו.

STANDING DURING BIRCAS KOHANIM

One must stand reverently while reciting or listening to Bircas Kohanim. One does not have to stand and face the Kohanim during the preceding *berachah,* or if there is no Kohen and the chazzan substitutes the *"Elokeinu V'Elokei Avoseinu"* prayer. One who is too weak to stand may sit while hearing Bircas Kohanim.

332

שאלה: האם מותר לשבת בברכת כהנים?

תשובה: לא, עיין במשנה ברורה ס"ק נ"א.

333

שאלה: בברכת כהנים הציבור צריכים לעמוד, אם אין שם כהן והחזן אומר יברכך ד' וישמרך האם הציבור צריכים לעמוד אז, או דוקא אם יש ברכת כהנים?

תשובה: רק בברכת כהנים.

334

שאלה: האם צריך לעמוד לפני ברכת כהנים כשהכהנים מברכים אקב"ו לברך את עמו ישראל וכו' לפני ברכת כהנים?

תשובה: צריך לעמוד רק בברכת כהנים.

335

שאלה: האם הברכה אשר קדשנו בקדושתו של אהרן חשיב כחלק מנשיאת כפים לענין זה שצריך לעמוד פנים כנגד פנים באימה ובכובד ראש?

תשובה: לא.

336

שאלה: כתב המגן אברהם (סעיף קטן כ"ד) שמדינא אין חייב ישראל לעמוד בשעת ברכת כהנים, אמנם המשנה ברורה (ס"ק נ"א) מביא מהראשונים שהמנהג הוא שהכל עומדים, ובשם האשכול הביא שצריכים לעמוד לפני

הכהנים באימה ובכובד ראש. ישראל שאינו יכול לעמוד מחמת חולשה או חולי, האם עליו לצאת מהבית הכנסת לפני ברכת כהנים?
תשובה: יש מקום להקל.

ANSWERING AMEN

The congregation should say amen after all the Kohanim have finished reciting each verse of Bircas Kohanim. If one Kohen takes longer, amen should be recited after he finishes. A Kohen who finished before the other Kohanim should not answer amen. A non-Kohen who already heard Bircas Kohanim and hears it again must nevertheless answer amen.

337

שאלה: כשהכהנים מברכים את העם ורוב הכהנים מסיימים ביחד, אבל כהן אחד או שנים מאריכים יותר מן השאר ומסיימים לאחר כדי דיבור או בספק לאחר כדי דיבור מן הרוב, האם יש לענות אמן אחר שגמרו כל הכהנים, או אחר הרוב?
תשובה: אולי ימתין לכולם.

338

שאלה: נסתפק לן בברכת כהנים כשכהן אחד מאריך יותר מחבריו לאחר כדי דבור, אי בעינן עניית אמן גם אחר הכהנים שכבר גמרו?
תשובה: יש לענות אחר האחרון.

339

שאלה: כהן שסיים לפני אחיו הכהנים אחת מהברכות יותר מכדי דיבור, האם יכול לענות אמן אחר ברכותיהם, או שזה הפסק בין הברכות?
תשובה: לא יענה.

340

שאלה: ישראל שכבר שמע ברכת כהנים, וכעת הוא באמצע לימודו, ושומע ברכת כהנים, האם צריך לענות אמן על ברכת כהנים?
תשובה: צריך.

PROPER CONDUCT DURING BIRCAS KOHANIM

One may not learn Torah during Bircas Kohanim, even while the Kohanim are singing. If he does, he is not included in the *berachah*. If someone in the shul already heard Bircas Kohanim, he should stay and listen, as it is worth hearing it multiple times. One should concentrate on the *berachah*, but is included in it even if he was distracted. A Kohen who is davening *Shemoneh Esrei* and did not move toward the *duchan* during *Retzei* should remain silent during Bircas Kohanim. If someone came late to shul, after Bircas Kohanim began, it is worthwhile for him to hear even part of Bircas Kohanim. There is no reason for the listeners to open their hands during Bircas Kohanim to "receive" the *berachah*. One should not walk between the Kohanim during Bircas Kohanim, such as to remove a *sefer Torah* for another minyan, but should wait until they have finished.

341

שאלה: האם מותר לעיין בספר בשעת נשיאת כפים ביום טוב אם הכהנים שרים?

תשובה: אסור ללמוד בשעת נשיאת כפים.

342

שאלה: מי שלומד בשעת ברכת כהנים האם חלה עליו הברכה?

תשובה: לא.

343

שאלה: אדם ששמע כבר ברכת כהנים, ונכנס לבית הכנסת לאיזה ענין, ואחזו שם בברכת כהנים, האם צריך להשאר או שמא רשאי לצאת?

תשובה: נכון להשאר.

344

שאלה: מי שנמצא בבית הכנסת בשעת ברכת כהנים ולא הקשיב למה שמברכים הכהנים אלא הסיח דעתו, האם גם הוא נכלל בברכה, או שצריך להתרכז בברכת הכהנים כדי שיחול הברכה על המתברך?

תשובה: נכלל בברכה אבל טוב שיכוון.

345

שאלה: האם יש ענין לשמוע ברכת כהנים יותר מפעם אחת, כשלומד אחרי התפילה בבית הכנסת, ויכול לעבור בין חדרי התפילה?

תשובה: כדאי.

346

שאלה: כהן המתפלל שמונה עשרה ולא עקר רגליו ברצה ושומע ברכת כהנים האם ישתוק, דדמי לעבד שמברכין אותו ואינו מאזין?

תשובה: טוב שישתוק.

347

שאלה: בברכת כהנים שצריך להקשיב לברכת כהנים האם היינו שצריך להקשיב לכל מילה ומילה ולדעת שעכשיו הכהנים אומרים יברכך ועכשיו יאר ואחר כך ישא וכו', או שסגי "בכוונה כללית", שיודע שעכשיו "הכהנים מברכים" ורוצה "להתברך בכל ברכותיהם"?

תשובה: טוב לכוין הכל.

348

שאלה: האם שייך חצי ברכת כהנים, כגון שמגיע באיחור קצת והכהנים כבר אומרים יאר־ישא?

תשובה: שייך.

349

שאלה: לשיטת ספר החרדים (פרק ד' אות י"ח) שגם ישראל מקיים מצוה כששומע ברכת כהנים מהכהנים (הובא בבאור הלכה ריש סימן קכ"ח), יש לעיין אם נכנס הישראל באמצע ברכת כהנים, האם יעמוד שם לקבל לפחות חצי מהברכת כהנים, או לא, כיון דאיכא "בל תגרע" ששומע רק חצי מהברכת כהנים?

תשובה: לא שייך בזה לא תגרע.

350

שאלה: האם צריך לענות "ברוך הוא וברוך שמו" כשמזכירים שם ה' שלא באמצע ברכה, כגון בברכת כהנים?

תשובה: אין ראוי להפסיק.

351

שאלה: האם יש לומר ברוך הוא וברוך שמו אחר שאומרים הכהנים שם ה'?

תשובה: לא נהוג אצלנו.

352

שאלה: אלו שאומרים ברוך הוא וברוך שמו בברכת כהנים בכל שם, אם נכון עושין?

תשובה: יותר טוב שלא לומר כדעת הגר"א.

353

שאלה: האם יש ענין לישראל לפתוח הידים בברכת כהנים לקבל הברכה?
תשובה: לא שמענו.

354

שאלה: מה המקור למנהג מקצת אנשים שבשעת ברכת כהנים פותחים כפות ידיהם?
תשובה: לא שמענו מנהג כזה.

355

שאלה: מנין שמתפללים והגיעו לקריאת התורה ואין באותו חדר ספר תורה, ושלחו אדם להביא ספר תורה מהחדר הסמוך, והנה בדיוק כשמביא את הספר תורה הכהנים עומדים ליד ארון הקודש ומתחילים ברכת כהנים, האם יפלס דרך בין הכהנים ויוציא את הספר תורה, או ימתין עד שיסיימו ברכת כהנים?
תשובה: ימתין עד שיסיימו.

THE KAVANAH OF THE KOHANIM

During Bircas Kohanim, the Kohanim should have in mind to fulfill a *mitzvas asei d'Oraysa*. While reciting the words they should think about the simple meaning of the words, and have in mind in general that all the various deeper meanings should be fulfilled. One may ask a Kohen to have him and his specific needs in mind while reciting Bircas Kohanim. The Kohen may then have him in mind before reciting Bircas Kohanim, along with the rest of Klal Yisrael; he does not need to have him in mind during all of Bircas Kohanim. A Kohen does not have to think about his own needs during Bircas Kohanim, as he is automatically included in the blessing, but he may if he wishes. It does not help for a Kohen in Eretz Yisrael to think of blessing someone outside Eretz Yisrael during his Bircas Kohanim, even if the person pays him to have him in mind.

356

שאלה: אני כהן ובמה יש לכוין בנשיאת כפים?
תשובה: לקיים מצות עשה דאורייתא.

357

שאלה: האם בנשיאת כפים צריך לכוין הפירוש שפירש רש"י, או שמא סגי לכוין את פירוש המילים לבד?
תשובה: פירוש המילות.

358

שאלה: יש הרבה פירושים בברכת כהנים ולרוב אינו יכול לכוין כל הפירושים, האם כדאי שכל פעם יכוין על פירוש אחר, או שמא כדאי שיאמר הברכה בלא לכוין הפירוש ויתכוין שהברכה תחול עם כל הפירושים?

תשובה: יכוין פירוש המילות ושיחול ככל הפירושים.

359

שאלה: כהן המתבקש על ידי מישהו, לכוון עליו ביחוד בשעת נשיאת כפים, הרשאי לעשות כן?

תשובה: אם מכוין גם עליו רשאי.

360

שאלה: האם כהן צריך לכוין גם על עצמו בברכת כהנים, או שאין צורך כיון שכבר מתברך מהקב"ה, וכדאיתא בחולין (מ"ט, א)?

תשובה: אין צריך.

361

שאלה: כהן שיש לו צרה בתוך ביתו או שחלם חלום לא טוב, האם מותר לחשוב באמצע ברכת כהנים שהקב"ה ישפיע עליו ועל משפחתו דברים טובים?

תשובה: במחשבה מותר.

362

שאלה: מי שיש לו צרה האם יש איזה ענין או מעלה ללוי או לישראל לבקש מהכהן לפני נשיאת כפים שיכוין דעתו עליו בברכת כהנים?

תשובה: כן.

363

שאלה: הכהן שמברך ברכת כהנים ומכוין בברכה על פלוני, האם צריך לכוין על פלוני בעת כל מילה שהיא לנוכח כגון "יברכך" "וישמרך", או די שמכוין קודם הברכה דהיינו קודם שמברך אשר קדשנו במצוותיו ואז יכול לעיין בפתקא עם שמות ומועיל שפיר?

תשובה: די קודם הברכה.

364

שאלה: האם יכול לכוין בברכת כהנים על מישהו מסוים כגון חולה וכדומה, והאם יכול לכוון על בני משפחתו או על עצמו בכלל עם ישראל?

תשובה: יכול לכוון גם על אדם מסוים בכלל עם ישראל.

365

שאלה: כשרוצה הכהן לכוין בברכתו לפלוני האם יאמר בפיו קודם ברכת כהנים פלוני בן פלונית, או די שיחשוב קודם ברכת כהנים בלבו פלוני בן פלונית?

תשובה: לא יאמר כלום בפיו.

366

שאלה: אם מהני כשכהן בארץ ישראל מכוין לברך חבירו בחוץ לארץ בברכת כהנים, דיש לומר דאנן בחוץ לארץ הוו בגדר עם שבשדות דאניסי ושפיר מהני, או דילמא לא אמרינן כן ולא מהני אפילו אם מכוין בשבילו בהדיא?
תשובה: לא שייך.

367

שאלה: האם בן חוץ לארץ ראוי לבקש מכהן בן ארץ ישראל לכוין לכוללו בתוך ברכתו של ברכת כהנים בכל יום ויום, ואיך יעשה? שיכוין לשמו עם שם האב או שם האם, ומתי יכוין לכך?
תשובה: לכאורה אינו מועיל.

368

שאלה: ישראל הנמצא בחוץ לארץ, האם יכול לבקש או לשלם לכהנים בארץ ישראל או כהנים ספרדים בעירו שנושאים כפים בכל יום, שיכוונו גם עליו בשעת ברכת כהנים?
תשובה: אין לזה טעם.

NEGATING BAD DREAMS

If a person cannot concentrate on Bircas Kohanim while saying the *Ribbono Shel Olam* prayer to negate bad dreams, he should just think the prayer in his mind. The same applies to the Kohanim themselves. A listener can also recite a shortened prayer (see #370-371) and have in mind that the amen of the congregation should apply to that as well. The *Ribbono Shel Olam* prayer may be recited even on Shabbos. It must be said by the person who had the dream and not on behalf of someone else. One should not say other words of supplication during Bircas Kohanim. A woman who had a frightening dream should go to shul to hear Bircas Kohanim and recite the *Ribbono Shel Olam* prayer.

369

שאלה: מי שאומר הרבונו של עולם על חלומות רעים בשעת ברכת כהנים, ואינו יכול לשמוע ולכוין לברכת הכהנים האם כדאי לומר, או שאדם כזה עדיף שיוותר על אמירת הרבונו של עולם?
תשובה: יאמר בהרהור.

370

שאלה: אני חושש מעין הרע וכבר כמה שנים אני סובל מחלומות רעים, ברצוני לומר הנוסח המודפס בהסידור לבטל חלומות רעים, אך זה יקח כמעט כל הזמן של ברכת כהנים ויפריע לי לענות אמן על ברכת כהנים, האם יש עצה עבורי?

תשובה: אמור בברכת כהנים יהי רצון שיהא לי לברכה ולא ישלוט בי עין הרע, ויכוון כשהקהל עונים אמן שיכוונו גם על זה. ואם אתה כהן תחשוב על זה.

371

שאלה: מי שסובל מהרבה חלומות רעים, האם יש עצה עבורו?

תשובה: בברכת כהנים ב"ויחנך" יאמר שיהיו כל חלומותי עלי לטובה.

372

שאלה: מה יעשה כהן שחלם חלום רע, כיצד יאמר רבונו של עולם כנגד חלומות רעים?

תשובה: כהן יהרהר החלום בשעת בר"כ, כ"כ האחרונים.

373

שאלה: בשעת ברכת כהנים האם יכול הישראל לבקש עוד בקשות פרטיות בפה ולא במחשבה אחר שאומר בימים נוראים את התפילות שמודפס בהסידור?

תשובה: אין ראוי.

374

שאלה: האם מותר לומר "רבונו של עולם אני שלך וכו'" בברכת כהנים בזמן שהכהנים אומרים את המילים גם אם לא ראה החלום באותו לילה?

תשובה: מותר, אולי ראה ושכח.

375

שאלה: אחד שחלם חלום בשבת האם מותר לומר תפילת רבונו של עולם שאומרים בברכת כהנים בשבת?

תשובה: כן. עיין במשנה ברורה סי' ק"ל ס"ק ד.

376

שאלה: האם מועיל שליחות, שאדם יאמר תפילת "רבונו של עולם" לבטל חלומות רעים, בעת שהכהנים נושאים כפיהם, עבור אשתו או חבירו?

תשובה: לא.

377

שאלה: אשתי מנהלת קייטנה של בית יעקב, והנה לפני כמה ימים לפנות בוקר, חלמה אשתי חלום שקרה אסון משונה והיא ל"ע נפגעה ביחד עם כמה בנות מהקייטנה על טיול שאירגנו לשבוע הבא. רצינו לדעת האם צריכה לחשוש לזה, ולהימנע לנסוע על הטיול?

תשובה: אם תלך לבהכ"נ ותשמע ברכת כהנים ותגיד הרבונו של עולם יכולה לנסוע.

ADIR BAMAROM

The listeners recite *Adir BaMarom* after hearing Bircas Kohanim, while the chazzan is finishing *Sim Shalom,* even if they have not experienced bad dreams. This prayer is recited even on Shabbos. It may be recited even after the chazzan finishes *Sim Shalom.* It is not recited when Bircas Kohanim is not performed.

378

שאלה: מי אומר "אדיר במרום", האם כל הציבור או רק מי שחלם חלום, דבגמרא (ברכות נ"ה, ב') משמע שרק מי שחלם חלום?

תשובה: כל הצבור.

379

שאלה: האם אומרים "אדיר במרום" אחר נשיאת כפים גם אם לא חלם שום חלום?

תשובה: כן.

380

שאלה: כשיש נשיאת כפים בשבת שאין אומרים רבונו של עולם אני שלך וחלומותי שלך וכו', האם יש לומר "אדיר במרום"?

תשובה: המנהג לומר אחר בר"כ.

381

שאלה: מתי יש לומר "אדיר במרום", שהרי המשנה ברורה (סי' ק"ל ס"ק ו) כתב בשם הט"ז (ס"ק ב) שיגיד בשעה שהש"ץ מסיים וטוב בעיניך וכו', אמנם בערוך השלחן (סי' ק"ל ס"ק ג) כתב דהמנהג שלנו שאומרים אותו בשעה שהש"ץ אומר שים שלום, ומדייק כן מלשון הרי"ף שכתב "וכד מהדרי כהני אפייהו", ורצוני לדעת איך יש לנהוג למעשה?

תשובה: כהמ"ב.

382

שאלה: מדוע יש אומרים "אדיר במרום" מיד בסיום ברכת כהנים, הרי מבואר במשנה ברורה (סי' ק"ל ס"ק ו) דצריך לומר ב"וטוב בעיניך"?

תשובה: יש לנהוג כהמ"ב ולסיים עם הש"ץ.

383

שאלה: האם צריך לסיים "אדיר במרום" עם החזן בסוף שים שלום בכל יום במקום שאין אומרים ה"רבונו של עולם", כגון שלא חלם באותו לילה, האם צריך הישראל לגמור עם החזן?

תשובה: כן.

384

שאלה: אם שכחתי לומר "אדיר במרום" שאחר ברכת כהנים, ונזכרתי רק לאחר שהש"ץ סיים את ברכת "שים שלום", האם גם אז אפשר לומר "אדיר במרום"?
תשובה: יכול לומר.

385

שאלה: כשאין כהנים, והש"ץ אומר אלוקינו ואלוקי אבותינו וכו', האם הקהל אומרים אדיר במרום?
תשובה: א"צ.

A KOHEN WHOSE VOICE IS WEAK

A Kohen cannot fulfill the mitzvah of Bircas Kohanim by listening to other Kohanim (through the mechanism of *shomei'a k'oneh*), such as if he is hoarse or otherwise unable to speak loudly.

386

שאלה: כהן שאינו יכול לברך מחמת חולשתו האם יכול לברך בלי לומר כלום על ידי שומע כעונה?
תשובה: בברכת כהנים לא מהני שומע כעונה.

387

שאלה: בשונה הלכות (סי' קכ"ח דין ל"ז) הביא דברי המשנה ברורה שמי שקולו צרוד ואינו יכול לדבר כי אם בלחש אינו יכול לישא כפיו וטוב שיצא קודם רצה, וצ"ע דלפי מה שכתב החזו"א בסימן כ"ט דאמרינן שומע כעונה בברכת כהנים למה אינו יכול לישא כפיו הרי יכול לצאת על ידי שומע כעונה?
תשובה: לא נהגו.

388

שאלה: בקהלות יעקב (ברכות סי' י"ג) דן אי מהני שומע כעונה בברכת כהנים, ויש להסתפק בכהן צרוד שאינו יכול לברך רק בלחש, אם ראוי לבקש מחברו שיוציאו מדין שומע כעונה, דהמשנה ברורה (ס' קכ"ח ס"ק י"ד) כתב דכהן שקולו צרוד אינו יכול לישא כפיו, משום דבעינן שישמע הציבור. וכ"כ בבאור הלכה (סעיף כ"ז) דקול רם הוא לעיכובא. אמנם צריך להבין לפי זה, דהא בית הכנסת שכולה כהנים כולם עולים לדוכן ומברכין לאחיהם שבשדות, אף שאין איש שומע להם, ומשמע שאינו מעכב בדיעבד, (וכן נקט בעמק הנצי"ב, שקול רם אינו מעכב בדיעבד)?
תשובה: לא שייך להוציא.

A CHAZZAN WHO IS A KOHEN

If a chazzan who is a Kohen *duchans*, he should go out to wash his hands before *Chazaras HaShatz* even if the congregation is impatient. If he forgot to remove his shoes before *Chazaras HaShatz* he should remove them before Bircas Kohanim. He must move slightly from his place during *Retzei*, toward the *duchan*. He should recite Bircas Kohanim from there, and not ascend the platform before the *aron kodesh*. He may turn around normally to face the congregation, and does not need to keep his feet together, as during *Shemoneh Esrei*. The Chazon Ish ruled that a chazzan who is a Kohen should not *duchan* even if there are no other Kohanim, and a Kohen who has *yahrtzeit* should *duchan* rather than serve as chazzan. If a chazzan who is a Kohen does *duchan*, he should wait until the congregation finishes answering amen before continuing *Chazaras HaShatz*.

389

שאלה: כהן העומד באמצע שמונה עשרה, והגיע הש"ץ לברכת כהנים מביא המשנה ברורה (ס"ק ק"ו) דעת הפוסקים שאם הוא הכהן היחידי חייב להפסיק כדי לישא כפיו, אפילו לא קראו לעלות לדוכן (והיינו אחר שיעקור רגליו קצת ברצה). ויש להעיר בזה, דכיון שעוסק במצות תפילה למה לא אמרינן העוסק במצוה פטור מן המצוה?

תשובה: תפלה דרבנן ונ"כ דאורייתא.

390

שאלה: ש"ץ שהוא כהן ובאמצע חזרת הש"ץ הוא מסתובב לנשיאת כפים, האם עכשיו נאסר ד' אמות לעבור לפניו כלפי הציבור, או שרק לכיוון היכן שהוא מתפלל התפילה?

תשובה: עתה אין מתפלל אלא נושא כפיו.

391

שאלה: שליח ציבור כהן שגמר שמונה עשרה בלחש ורוצה ללכת ליטול ידים כדי לישא כפיו, אך הציבור מזרזים אותו להתחיל חזרת הש"ץ, האם עדיף להסתמך על הנטילה שלפני התפלה ולהתחיל מיד כמו שכתוב על כהן שלא הספיק ליטול והגיע זמן שצריך לגשת לברכת כהנים שיכול להסתמך על נטילה של קודם התפלה, או שמא עדיף ללכת ליטול?

תשובה: הצבור ימתין משהו.

392

שאלה: מי שהיה שליח ציבור והוא כהן, ושכח להוריד מנעליו, מה עדיף שיעשה, יוריד מנעליו באמצע שמונה עשרה לפני רצה (או לפני ברכת כהנים), או ישא כפיו עם מנעליו, או לא ישא את כפיו?
תשובה: יוריד מנעליו לפני ברכת כהנים.

393

שאלה: כהן שליח ציבור ששכח להוריד מנעליו קודם התחלת חזרת הש"ץ והתחיל החזרה, האם יוריד באמצע או שלא יברך ברכת כהנים?
תשובה: יוריד באמצע.

394

שאלה: באופן המבואר בשו"ע (סעיף כ) שהשליח ציבור כהן עולה לדוכן, ומבואר שצריך שיעקור מעט רגליו בעבודה, לא נתברר לי, מהו שיעור העקירה, האם צריך שתצא רגלו לגמרי ממקומה או שמא סגי בעקירה כזו שעדיין נשארת עקיבו במקום שהיו אצבעותיו תחילה.
תשובה: צריך לזוז ממקומו.

395

שאלה: שליח ציבור כהן העולה לדוכן האם צריך לעקור רגליו ברצה או שדי לו בעקירתו לפני חזרת הש"ץ?
תשובה: בשו"ע משמע שיעקור רגליו מעט.

396

שאלה: בשו"ת הרדב"ז (ח"א סי' רל"ז) ביאר שצריך שתהיה כל התפילה במקום אחד ולא בב' מקומות. כהן שליח ציבור שמברך, אם יכול לזוז קצת ברצה, ולהשאר בעמוד של השליח ציבור ולברך הציבור משם, ולא יעלה על מדריגת ארון הקודש?
תשובה: כן.

397

שאלה: כהן שהוא שליח ציבור בשחרית, ומנהג המקום שש"ץ כהן נושא כפיו, האם צריך כשמסובב עצמו אל מול פני הקהל באמצע הברכה לקפוץ כשרגליו ישרות דלא גרע מאמצע שמונה עשרה, או שיש להסתובב ככל כהן העולה לדוכן?
תשובה: ככל כהן.

398

שאלה: ברצוני לשאול את כת"ר האם נכונה השמועה כי מרן החזון איש זצ"ל נהג בבית מדרשו כשהשליח ציבור כהן, שאינו נושא כפיו כדברי מרן השולחן ערוך (קכ"ח, כ')?
תשובה: נכון.

399

שאלה: כהן שליח ציבור, האם יברך ברכת כהנים, והאם יש הבדל בין כהן יחיד או שיש עוד כהנים?

תשובה: החזו"א פסק שלא יעלה לדוכן אפי' אין כהנים אחרים.

400

שאלה: מה היה דעת מרן החזון איש לכהן שיש לו יארצייט על אביו האם יתפלל בעמוד?

תשובה: שמעתי שהחזו"א אמר ששליח ציבור כהן לא ישא כפיו אפי' אין כהנים אחרים. גם אמר לכהן שהי' לו יאר"צ שמוטב שלא יתפלל חזרת הש"ץ וישא כפיו.

401

שאלה: כהן שהוא בן יחיד האם הוא יכול להתפלל ביום היארצייט להוריו?

תשובה: כהן ראוי שלא יהא שליח ציבור אפי' הוא חיוב.

402

שאלה: כאשר הכהן הוא שליח ציבור ויש עוד אחד בלבד, האם כדאי שהשליח ציבור גם ישא כפיו כדי שיהיו שני כהנים ותהיה ברכת כהנים דאורייתא, אף למנהג הספרדים שכשיש כהן אחר, כהן שליח ציבור לא ישא כפיו?

תשובה: כמדומה שלא ישא.

403

שאלה: האם ראוי לכהן שהוא בתוך השנה שנפטר אביו או אמו שלא יגש לעמוד?

תשובה: יותר טוב שלא יעבור לפני התיבה.

404

שאלה: השער הציון (סי' קכ"ח ס"ק ס"ד) מביא מחלוקת הפוסקים לגבי ש"ץ שהוא כהן ויש עוד כהנים אחרים בלעדיו האם הש"ץ שהוא כהן ישא כפיו, דעת השלחן ערוך והמגן אברהם ורוב הפוסקים שלא ישא כפיו אף שמובטח שלא יטעה, אמנם דעת הפרי חדש להקל בזה, ומסיים השער הציון שבמקום שנהגו כוותיה אפשר שאין למחות. לדינא, מה ראוי לעשות?

תשובה: כפי המנהג.

405

שאלה: נשאלתי באופן שיש כמה חזנים ישראלים, ויש כהן שהוא בעל רגש גדול, והציבור מתרומם ומתפללים יותר טוב כשהכהן הוא הש"ץ, האם כדאי שיעלה כהן לשמש כש"ץ בתפילת שחרית או מוסף של שבת, שהרי בכך הוא מפסיד מצות עשה של נשיאת כפים?

תשובה: לא כדאי.

406

שאלה: האם מה שכתב המשנה ברורה (סי' קכ"ח סעיף כ'), דבאיכא כהנים אחרים לא יעלה השליח ציבור שהוא כהן לדוכן, הוא גם כשאינו עולה לדוכן ממש, אלא באופן שהסיר את נעליו לפני חזרת הש"ץ, ובעת שמגיע לברכת כהנים, נושא את כפיו במקומו בסמוך לעמוד?

תשובה: כן.

407

שאלה: בשלחן ערוך (סי' קכ"ח סעיף כ') אם שליח ציבור כהן וכו', ובשער הציון (אות ס"ד) מביא את האחרונים שסוברים שאפילו אם יש עוד כהנים נושא את כפיו, וקשה לי האם מותר לכהן להיות לכתחילה שליח ציבור?

תשובה: אם אין אחר ודאי מותר.

408

שאלה: בשלחן ערוך (סי' קכ"ח סעיף כ') כותב בנוגע לש"ץ כהן, אם יש כהנים אחרים, אינו עולה לדוכן, והרמ"א שם מביא שאם אמרו לש"ץ עלה לדוכן, או ליטול ידיו, מחויב מדאורייתא לעלות לדוכן אפילו אם יש כהנים אחרים. ויש להקשות, שהטעם שאינו צריך הש"ץ לעלות הוא בגלל שרבנן פטרוהו כדי שלא יתבלבל, אם כן למה עובר אם אינו עולה?

תשובה: כיון שהוא חשש רחוק עובר.

409

שאלה: ש"ץ שנשא כפיו האם צריך להמתין מלהחזיר פניו עד שיכלה אמן מפי הציבור, דבין כך אינו ממתין לשים שלום, שהוא האומרו?

תשובה: ימתין.

BIRCAS KOHANIM DURING THE MOURNING PERIOD

A Kohen who is an *avel* does not *duchan* during shivah even if no other Kohanim are present. In Sephardic communities and in Eretz Yisrael, other Kohanim in the shivah house who are not *aveilim* may *duchan*, as it is a *mitzvah d'Oraysa*, and after shivah a Kohen may *duchan*, even during *shloshim* or the year of mourning for a parent.

410

שאלה: בבית האבל כשהאבל כהן, ואין שם כהן אלא הוא האם יכול לישא כפיו?

תשובה: כמדומה שהאבל עצמו אין נושא כפיו בתוך ז'.

411

שאלה: האם בבית האבל מותר לכהנים שאינם אבלים לישא כפיהם או לא?
תשובה: החזו"א ציום לישא כפיהם.

412

שאלה: מה טעם שנוהגים כהנים אחרים (לא האבלים) לשאת כפים בבית האבל, הרי חסר לו בשמחה?
תשובה: מ"ע דאורייתא.

413

שאלה: לדעת מרן החזו"א וכן מנהג ירושלים (המובא בשערי תשובה סי' קכ"א סעיף ב') שכהנים אחרים עולים לדוכן, אבל הכהנים האבלים אינם עולים, מה הדין בבית האבל שהם כהנים ולא עולים, האם כהנים אחרים יכולים לעלות?
תשובה: יכולים.

414

שאלה: הענין שמובא בהלכה שכהן אבל אינו נושא כפים אלא יצא החוצה עד אחר אמירת כהנים, קשה לי היכי שרי לעבור על איסור שנאמר עליו בגמ' (ברכות ח', א') ועוזבי ד' יכלו?
תשובה: מי שעושה כהלכה ד' עושה ברכה ולא קללה.

415

שאלה: בספר ארחות רבנו (חלק ג' עמוד רי"ב) מובא בשם כת"ר שאבל בארץ ישראל נושא כפיו לאחר שבעה ימי האבילות כל י"ב חודש. האם נקטינן כן למעשה?
תשובה: כן.

416

שאלה: איתא במשנה ברורה (ס"ק קנ"ט) בנוגע לאבל: "ואם אין שם בבית הכנסת שני כהנים אחרים חוץ מהאבל, מותר להאבל לישא כפיו", עכ"ל. וכתב שם בשער הציון (אות קכ"ז): "תשובת כנסת יחזקאל [סימן י"ב] המובא בבאר היטב, והעתיקו גם בעל דרך החיים לדינא, ודלא כהמגן אברהם, וכן משמע גם כן בחידושי ר' עקיבא איגר, ויש להקל כמותם, דהרי בלאו הכי הוא רק מנהגא בעלמא", עכ"ל. ויש להקשות שבספר כנסת יחזקאל הוא כותב "נשאלתי בית הכנסת שאין כהנים כי אם אבלים אם רשאין לעלות לדוכן", והאריך שם להוכיח פסקו שפסק דמותר לאבלים לישא כפיהם, וסיים וכתב והסכימו עמי כל בעלי תריסין עכ"ל, ושם המדובר שאין כהנים בבית הכנסת בכלל, ולמה שינה המשנה ברורה ממה שכתוב בתשובת כנסת יחזקאל?
תשובה: משום דמדאורייתא רק ב' כהנים.

MINCHAH OF A FAST DAY

On a fast day (except Yom Kippur), Bircas Kohanim is recited at Minchah, even Minchah Gedolah. (Once Chazal instituted that Bircas Kohanim is recited at Minchah of a fast day, they did not differentiate based on when Minchah is said.) If a Kohen is not fasting, although he may perform Bircas Kohanim during Shacharis, he should not recite Bircas Kohanim during Minchah even if no other Kohen is present.

417

שאלה: בתענית ציבור, האם נושאים כפים כשמתפללים מנחה גדולה?

תשובה: כן.

418

שאלה: כהן הנוהג שאינו נושא כפיו בתענית ציבור במנחה גדולה, והזדמן לבית הכנסת שלנו שמתפלל מנחה גדולה גם בתענית ציבור, האם עדיף שיצא לחוץ קודם רצה?

תשובה: ישא כפיו.

419

שאלה: בהלכות נשיאת כפים (סי' קכ"ט, א) מובא שבתענית שאין בו נעילה, נושאים כפים בתפלת מנחה, ואף על פי שבמנחה של שאר ימים גזרו משום שכרות, מ"מ במנחה של תענית לא גזרו הואיל ותפלת מנחה סמוך לשקיעת החמה ולפיכך היא דומה לתפלת נעילה ואינה מתחלפת במנחה של שאר ימים, ומה שאין כן בתענית שיש בה נעילה אין נושאין כפים במנחה לפי שביום שיש בו נעילה מתפללים מנחה בעוד היום גדול כדי להתחיל נעילה קודם שקיעת החמה, לכן מתחלפת היא במנחה של שאר הימים שהיו נוהגים גם כן להתפלל בעוד היום גדול מפני שהיו רוצים לאכול אחר כך. וריהטת הדברים משמע דמה שנושאין כפים במנחה של תענית היינו רק כשמתפללים מנחה קטנה סמוך לשקיעה, ולא כשמתפללים מנחה גדולה דאז ליכא היכרא. אמנם בחזון איש (או"ח סי' כ') מסתפק לומר דצריך נשיאת כפים גם במנחה גדולה, ופירש שם בטעם הדבר לפי שגם בזמננו אנו מקדימים תפילת מנחה של תענית יותר מכל יום, וגם זה הוי היכר. ורציתי לשאול דאם כן אם מתפללים כל השנה מנחה גדולה כגון ב־12:30 בחורף ובתענית הלא גם לא מתפללים קודם, אם כן לפי זה לא נושאים כפים במנחה דתעניתא, שידוע שתלמידי החזו"א זצ"ל נושאים כפים בתענית מנחה גדולה אף על פי שכל השנה גם כן מתפללים מנחה גדולה, ורציתי לברר המקור?

תשובה: כן היתה תקנת חז"ל ולא חילקו בזה.

420

שאלה: אחר שלא מצינו בגמרא תענית (דף כ"ו, ב) שהתפללו מנחה גדולה בתענית ציבור, אם כן מעולם לא היה תקנה של נשיאת כפים בזמן מנחה גדולה, וכל התקנה היתה על מנחה בזמן נעילה שדומה לתפילת נעילה, ויש להקשות למה מותר לברך ברכת כהנים בזמן מנחה גדולה?
תשובה: לא פלוג רבנן.

421

שאלה: כהן שאינו מתענה בתענית ציבור מחמת חולי ל"ע, האם יעלה לדוכן לברכת כהנים בשחרית ובמנחה?
תשובה: יכול בשחרית אבל לא במנחה.

422

שאלה: כהן שאינו מתענה בתענית ציבור והוא הכהן היחידי בבית הכנסת האם יש לו לישא כפיו בתפלת מנחה?
תשובה: לא.

423

שאלה: האם כהן שחולה ואינו צם יכול לישא כפיו במנחה של תענית ציבור?
תשובה: עי' שונה הלכות סי' קכ"ט דין ב' שהמתענין עד חצי היום אין נושאין כפיהם.

424

שאלה: כהן שישב ללמוד בבית הכנסת בערב שבת צום עשרה בטבת, וקיבל עליו שבת מבעוד יום, ולפתע התארגנו להתפלל לשם מנחה לפני השקיעה, והסתפק הכהן אם מותר לו לעלות לדוכן כיון שכבר קיבל שבת ואולי עשאו על ידי זה ללילה?
תשובה: אין ראוי.

425

שאלה: בשער הציון (סי' קכ"ט ס"ק ה') שאומרים ברכת כהנים "דוקא בתענית ציבור גמור", ויש לדון בערב ראש חודש או בתענית בה"ב כשיש עשרה המתענים וקורין "ויחל" האם יאמרו ברכת כהנים בתפלת מנחה או לא, כיון שאינו תענית ציבור גמור?
תשובה: לכאורה אין לומר.

426

שאלה: כיון שהדין שבתשעת הימים קודם תשעה באב אסורים בשתיית יין, מדוע אין הכהנים נושאים כפיהם במנחה?
תשובה: זה רק מנהג.

427

שאלה: בשלחן ערוך (סי' קכ"ט סעיף א) מבואר שבמנחה של תענית יש נשיאת כפים. וביום כיפור עושים נשיאת כפים בתפילת נעילה בתנאי שיהיה

ביום. והסתפקתי באופן שיודעים שבודאי לא יהיה נשיאת כפים בנעילה משום שיהיה אחר השקיעה, האם יכולים לעשות נשיאת כפים במנחה כדין שאר תענית ציבור?
תשובה: לא.

DESCENDING FROM THE DUCHAN

A Kohen may not speak after Bircas Kohanim until he descends from the *duchan*, even if he has heard *Chazaras HaShatz* already. The Kohanim should descend only after the chazzan finishes *Kaddish* after *Sim Shalom*. If the congregants say *yasher koach* to the Kohanim, the Kohanim may respond by blessing them in return. A Kohen may bless someone with the words of Bircas Kohanim even not during davening.

428

שאלה: כתב במשנה ברורה (ס״ק נ״ח) וז״ל: ״ואינם רשאים לעקור, ויזהרו שלא ידברו עד שירדו מדוכנן אף שכבר הורידו כפיהם״ עכ״ל, ויש להקשות דהא בלאו הכי אסור לדבר בחזרת הש״ץ?
תשובה: אפילו כבר שמעו חזרת הש״צ במנין אחר.

429

שאלה: יש כהנים שיורדים מהדוכן לפני שהשליח ציבור סיים את הברכה המברך את עמו ישראל בשלום, האם יכולים לעשות כך, או מאחר ואומרים הרבונו של עולם עד שהשליח ציבור גומר את המברך את עמו ישראל בשלום אז נחשב שעדיין צריכים לעמוד בדוכן?
תשובה: אין ראוי.

430

שאלה: במשנה ברורה (ס״ק ס׳) כתב שהכהנים צריכים להישאר בדוכן עד אחר קדיש כדי שלא יגידו לכהנים ״ישר כח״ בקדיש ויכשלו האנשים בדיבור באמצע קדיש. האם כל דין זה שייך בחוץ לארץ אבל בארץ ישראל שנושאים כפים בכל יום אין צריך להישאר לקדיש?
תשובה: ראוי להשאר.

431

שאלה: מה הטעם שאין הכהנים רשאין לעקור רגליהם עד שיגמור שליח ציבור שים שלום (סוטה ל״ט ב, שלחן ערוך סי׳ קכ״ח סעיף ט״ז)?
תשובה: שלא יבלבלו ויתבלבלו.

432

שאלה: כהן לאחר נשיאת כפים האם הוא חייב לומר תחנון מיד אפילו קודם שישים הנעלים?

תשובה: כרצונו.

433

שאלה: האם יש ענין שהכהנים צריכים להקפיד לא להגיד "ברוכים תהיו" אחרי נשיאת כפים משום איסור בל תוסיף?

תשובה: אין מכוין להוספה.

434

שאלה: לשיטת הרמב"ם דאסור לכהן להוסיף ברכה על ברכת כהנים אפילו בלחש ובלא החזרת פנים ובלא נשיאת כפים כמבואר בבאור הלכה (סי' קכ"ח), יש לדון כשהעם אומרים אחר הדוכן ישר כח אי מותר לכהן לענות ברוך תהיה, אי איכא משום בל תוסיף?

תשובה: מותר.

435

שאלה: האם מותר לכהן לברך את חבירו שלא בשעת התפילה בנוסח של ברכת כהנים?

תשובה: מותר.

DUCHANING MORE THAN ONCE

A Kohen may *duchan* in multiple minyanim in a day, and should say a new *berachah* each time. On Shabbos, Yom Tov, and Rosh Chodesh, the Kohanim recite the *berachah* a second time before Bircas Kohanim of Mussaf, since much time has elapsed since they said it in Shacharis. It is a mitzvah for a Kohen to *duchan* a second time during Mussaf. A Kohen who already *duchaned* should not listen to Bircas Kohanim elsewhere in order to receive the blessing. A Kohen should not charge money for *duchaning*. If he already *duchaned* and is now learning in the shul and another minyan reaches Bircas Kohanim, he should *duchan* again. If a person heard Bircas Kohanim only during Shacharis and not Mussaf, it is worthwhile for him to go elsewhere to hear Bircas Kohanim again.

436.

שאלה: האם יכול לכוין בברכת אשר קדשנו כשמברך על ברכת כהנים פעם ראשונה על מנין אחר שיודע שהולך כעת לברך.

תשובה: אין לעשות כן, עיין משנה ברורה סי' קכ"ח ס"ק י"א.

437

שאלה: כהן שנושא כפיו בשני מנינים, בזה אחר זה, האם יכול לברך במנין הראשון הברכה "אשר קדשנו" וכו', ויפטור לו גם הברכת כהנים שהולך תיכף ומיד למקום אחר לברך ברכת כהנים, ויוכל להתחיל שם מיד ביברכך?

תשובה: לא, כי זה שתי מצות נפרדות.

438

שאלה: במקום שאני מברך ברכת כהנים לכמה מנינים, האם רצוי לברך על כל מנין, או אפשר לכוין במנין הראשון עבור כל המנינים? ואם אני מברך בכל מנין בנפרד, למה אין שאלה של ברכה לבטלה?

תשובה: מברכין על כל מנין.

439

שאלה: כהן שמברך ברכת כהנים בשחרית בשבת למה צריך לברך שוב "אשר קדשנו בקדושתו של אהרן וצונו לברך את עמו ישראל באהבה", כשנושא כפיו שוב במוסף, לכאורה יועיל הברכה שבירך בשחרית גם לברכת כהנים של מוסף, ויוכל להתחיל במוסף מיד ביברכך וכו'?

תשובה: הוי הפסק גדול והיסח הדעת.

440

שאלה: כהן שנשא כפיו כבר באותו יום ורוצה כעת להתברך מכהנים אחרים, האם טוב עושה או עדיף לשאת שוב כפיו?

תשובה: לא טוב.

441

שאלה: כהן שנשא כפיו פעם אחת באותו יום, האם יכול לדרוש כסף מציבור שמבקש שישא כפים בשנית?

תשובה: אין לעשות כן.

442

שאלה: ביום שעולים לדוכן שני פעמים כראש חודש, שבת, ויום טוב, האם יש חיוב לעלות בשניהם, או החיוב הוא ככל יום לעלות פעם אחת אלא שמקיים מצות עשה כשעולה פעם שניה?

תשובה: יש מצוה.

443

שאלה: שני כהנים בירכו בחול המועד בתפילת שחרית את הציבור, ואילו במוסף רק כהן אחד הספיק לגמור שמונה עשרה ובירך את הציבור, והכהן השני האריך בשמונה עשרה ולא בירך הציבור במוסף, האם עשה טוב, או שצריך היה להזדרז להספיק לברך ברכת כהנים גם במוסף?

תשובה: יש לו להזדרז ולברך.

444

שאלה: כהן שכבר התפלל ונשא כפיו ואחר כך יושב ולומד בבית הכנסת, ועתה בשעה שהמנין השני הגיע לברכת כהנים, האם יש מצוה או מעלה לעלות שוב, או שמא עדיף לצאת ולהמשיך לימודו בחוץ?
תשובה: יש ענין לעלות.

445

שאלה: מנין בשבת שהיו כהנים בתפילת שחרית אך לא היו כהנים בתפילת מוסף, האם יש לישראל להדר ללכת למקום אחר להתברך בברכת כהנים?
תשובה: יש ענין.

446

שאלה: הוי עובדא כאן באחד מבתי כנסיות שבירושלים בש"ק פר' נח ר"ח חשון, שהש"צ בתפלת שחרית שכח לומר יעלה ויבא, והמשיך בברכת הודאה, והכהנים עלו לדוכן, ובאמצע ברכת שים שלום, נזכרו, והעירו לש"צ שלא אמר יעלה ויבא, ולכן חזר והתחיל כדין מרצה. וכעת נשאלה השאלה לענין ברכת כהנים, האם יעלו הכהנים לדוכן שנית באותו תפילה?
תשובה: מסתבר דכבר יצאו ידי בר"כ, עי' באו"ח קפ"ח ט.

THE ADVANTAGE OF DAVENING IN A PLACE WHERE BIRCAS KOHANIM IS PERFORMED

It is preferable to daven in a smaller minyan where Bircas Kohanim is recited than in a larger minyan where it is not. It is also preferable to daven in a minyan where Bircas Kohanim is recited than in a *vasikin* minyan where it is not. One is not obligated to go to another minyan to hear Bircas Kohanim if there is no Kohen in his minyan, but it is worthwhile, if possible, even at the expense of his Torah learning. If a person can make it to shul on Yom Kippur for just a short time, such as if he is tending to an ill person, he should go for Bircas Kohanim.

447

שאלה: אם מתפלל שחרית במערת המכפלה ובתוך המערה יש מנין אך ללא ברכת כהנים, וברחבה בחוץ יש מנין עם ברכת כהנים, היכן עדיף להתפלל?
תשובה: במקום שיש ברכת כהנים.

448

שאלה: אדם שיש לו אפשרות או להתפלל בבית הכנסת שיש שם רוב עם, או בבית הכנסת שישמע שם ברכת כהנים, אבל אין שם ברוב עם, היכן עדיף שיתפלל?

תשובה: ברכת כהנים דאורייתא.

449

שאלה: יש לי אפשרות או להתפלל במנין של נץ אך אין כהנים בהמנין, או במנין במקום אחר שיש ברכת כהנים אך תפילת שמונה עשרה הוא אחרי זמן הנץ, לאיזה מנין עלי ללכת אם אי אפשר ללכת לשני המנינים?

תשובה: תלך לשמוע ברכת כהנים.

450

שאלה: נסתפקתי, כשיש שני בתי כנסת אם אלך לאחד אקבל עלייה לתורה, אבל הרבה פעמים אין שם כהן לברך את העם, ובשני יש כהן אבל לא אקבל עלייה, מה עדיף?

תשובה: ברכת כהנים עדיף.

451

שאלה: מה הדין כשעוד לא התחיל להתפלל ויודע שבמנין שבו יתפלל לא יהיה כהן, האם מחויב ללכת למנין אחר?

תשובה: אין חייב.

452

שאלה: היכא שלא היו כהנים במנין האם יש לישראל לטרוח לשמוע ברכת כהנים אפילו שימעט קצת על ידי זה מזמן הלימוד?

תשובה: ראוי.

453

שאלה: ישראל שלא שמע ברכת כהנים בשחרית, האם ילך לשמוע במנין אחר גם כאשר יגרם לו בטול תורה?

תשובה: יש ענין.

454

שאלה: כהן שכבר התפלל וכבר קיים מצות נשיאת כפים, ועתה יושב בסוכה סמוך לבית הכנסת, ושומע שכעת המנין בבית הכנסת באמצע חזרת הש"ץ, האם יעזוב את הסוכה כדי לקיים שוב פעם מצות נשיאת כפים, או עדיף שישאר בסוכה ויקיים מצוה של ישיבת סוכה.

תשובה: יעזוב.

455

שאלה: מי שמטפל באביו החולה ביום כיפור ויש לו חצי שעה שיכול לצאת מבית הכנסת להתפלל (שחרית, מוסף, מנחה או נעילה), לאיזה תפילה כדאי ללכת?

תשובה: לברכת כהנים.

456

שאלה: בחול המועד סוכות ובחול המועד פסח יש מי שדואג לערוך בכותל המערבי מעמד של ברכת כהנים בשחרית ובמוסף, ובאים שם יותר מאלף כהנים לברך את ישראל, האם מי שהתפלל ושמע כבר ברכת כהנים משני כהנים במקום אחר, יש לו ענין לנסוע לכותל המערבי ולהתברך מכל אותם כהנים?

תשובה: אם אין ביטול תורה.

A KOHEN WHO MURDERED

If a Kohen killed someone in self-defense, or by order of *beis din*, or inadvertently (such as a doctor who erred during surgery or a driver who ran over someone who dashed into the street), he may still *duchan*. A Kohen who shamed someone publicly may still *duchan*, even though shaming is tantamount to murder, since he did not kill with his hands, which he uses for *duchaning*. If a Kohen committed immoral acts with his hands, he may *duchan* once he has done *teshuvah*.

457

שאלה: כתוב בשלחן ערוך (סי' קכ"ח סעיף ל"ה) כהן אסור לו לעלות לדוכן אם הרג את הנפש. מה הדין כשהרג נפש על פי הדין של "הבא להרגך השכם להורגו" (ברכות נ"ח, א)?

תשובה: מותר.

458

שאלה: שליח בית דין שהוא כהן שביצע אחת מד' מיתות בית דין, אם הוא בכלל אין קטיגור נעשה סניגור?

תשובה: אם הרג כדין מותר לו לישא כפיו.

459

שאלה: כהן שהוא רופא מנתח ומת החולה מחמת טעות הרופא ולא מחמת רשלנות?

תשובה: בשוגג מקילין, עיין שונה הלכות סי' קכ"ח דין ע"ב.

460

שאלה: כהן שהרג בן נח אם רשאי לישא כפים?

תשובה: רשאי.

461

שאלה: חייל כהן שהרג נכרי במלחמה, האם רשאי לישא כפיו, והאם יש חילוק בין חייל המגן על ישראל, לחייל בצבא של גוים?

תשובה: מותר.

462

שאלה: כהן שהרג הנפש לא ישא כפיו, אם דוקא כשהרג בעודו כהן, או אף אם הרג מקודם, וכגון פנחס שהרג את זימרי קודם שנעשה כהן, האם אחר כך כשנתכהן נשא כפיו?

תשובה: אם הרג כדין בודאי נושא כפיו.

463

שאלה: בשלחן ערוך (סי׳ קכ״ח, סעיף ל״ה) מביא את ההלכה של כהן שהרג את הנפש, לא ישא את כפיו, והמשנה ברורה מביא הטעם משום שהרג בידיו אין קטגור נעשה סנגור. ולפי זה יש לשאול באופן שהיה אונס, כגון שנסע במהירות המותרת על פי החוק, ופתאום קפץ ילד לכביש, ולא הספיק לעצור והילד נהרג, האם מותר לישא כפיו?

תשובה: אונס רחמנא פטריה.

464

שאלה: כהן שהלבין פני חבירו ברבים, האם מותר לישא כפיו?

תשובה: מותר.

465

שאלה: איתא בברכות (ל״ב, ב) אמר רבי יוחנן כל כהן שהרג את הנפש לא ישא את כפיו שנאמר ידיכם דמים מלאו. לפי זה, כהן שפגע בחברו והלבין פניו, האם ישא את כפיו משום שנחשב כרוצח, דאיתא בבא מציעא (נ״ח, ב) תני תנא קמיה דרב נחמן בר יצחק, כל המלבין פני חבירו ברבים כאילו שופך דמים?

תשובה: לא הרג בידיו.

466

שאלה: לשון התוספות (יבמות ז׳, א׳ ד״ה שנאמר) ״לפי שהרג בידיו ואין קטיגור נעשה סניגור״. האם דוקא בהרג בידיו וכלשון הפסוק ״ידיכם״ דמים מלאו, או שמא גם בהרג ברגליו נפסל?

תשובה: רגל בכלל יד, עיין סוף פ״ד דזבים.

467

שאלה: נסתפקתי בכהן שעבר רח״ל על מה שאמרו בנדה (י״ג, ב): ידיכם דמים מלאו, אלו המנאפים ביד, אם מותר לשאת כפיו?

תשובה: אם עשה תשובה ישא כפיו.

AN ENEMY

If a Kohen is entangled in a financial dispute with another member of the congregation and the two are not on speaking terms, the Kohen may nevertheless perform Bircas Kohanim, having in mind to bless the entire congregation. A non-Kohen who vowed not to derive benefit from a Kohen may hear Bircas Kohanim from him. A Kohen who is a sinner may perform Bircas Kohanim, and is not considered an "enemy" of the congregation.

468

שאלה: כהן שהסתכסך עם אחד מהקהל בעניני ממונות ואינם מדברים זה עם זה, האם מותר לכהן זה לישא כפיו כשבעל ריבו בבית הכנסת, ואם מותר לו לישא כפיו האם על הישראל לצאת מבית הכנסת?

תשובה: שיכוין לברך את כולם.

469

שאלה: ישראל שמודר הנאה מכהן, האם יכול לשמוע ממנו ברכת כהנים?

תשובה: יכול, מצות לאו ליהנות ניתנו.

470

שאלה: מי שהדיר הנאה מכהן, האם מותר לשמוע ממנו ברכת כהנים?

תשובה: אין לכהן לכוין לשום אדם אלא עושין מצותו והקב"ה מברך כרצונו.

471

שאלה: כתב כת"ר בשונה הלכות (סי' קכ"ח דין ע"ז) וז"ל: "לא היו בו מהדברים המונעים נשיאת כפים הנזכרים בסימן זה אף על פי שאינו מדקדק במצות אפילו מצות חמורות כעריות וכדומה, והוא מפורסם לכל ברשעתו נושא את כפיו, ואפילו לא עשה תשובה שאין שאר עבירות חוץ מהנזכרים לעיל מונעים נשיאת כפים". ויש לשאול דבפשוטו אדם כזה הוא שונא לציבור, ואם כן איך נושא כפיו והרי אינו יכול לברך "באהבה" וכמו שהביא המשנה ברורה לדינא לעיל (ס"ק ל"ז)?

תשובה: אינו שונא.

A MINOR PERFORMING BIRCAS KOHANIM

It is not considered honorable to the congregation for a minor to perform Bircas Kohanim alone, as Hashem commanded that it be performed by adult Kohanim who are worthy of honor. Unmarried *bachurim* whose beard is not yet fully grown may *duchan* nonetheless, as the congregation forgoes its honor to allow them to perform Bircas Kohanim.

472

שאלה: כתב השלחן ערוך (סי' קכ"ח סעיף ל"ט): "כהן שאינו מדקדק במצות והעם מרננים אחריו, נושא את כפיו", וביאר המשנה ברורה (ס"ק קמ"ו): "אפילו לא עשה תשובה על חטאיו, והטעם כתב הרמב"ם (פט"ו ה"ז) ואל תתמה ותאמר ומה תועיל ברכת הדיוט זה שאין קבול הברכה תלוי בכהנים אלא בהקב"ה שנאמר ושמו את שמי על בני ישראל ואני אברכם, הכהנים עושין מצות שנצטוו בה והקב"ה ברחמיו מברך את ישראל כחפצו," עכ"ל. וצריכים להבין לפי זה, שבשלחן ערוך (סעיף ל"ד) כותב: "קטן שלא הביא שתי שערות אינו נושא את כפיו בפני עצמו כלל", וכתב המשנה ברורה (ס"ק קכ"ב): "אפילו באקראי שאין כבוד צבור להיות כפופין לברכת קטן". וצריך עיון, מה איכפת לן מי הוא הכהן למעט קטן, הרי הקב"ה מברך את ישראל, ואדרבה כבוד הוא להצבור כשהמברך הוא קטן, שנקי מחטא יותר מאשר בעל העבירה המפורסם הנ"ל?

תשובה: הרי צוה דוקא ע"י כהנים גדולים לפי שראוין לכבוד.

473

שאלה: מהו ההיתר לכהנים בחורים שלא נתמלא זקנם, לישא כפיהם בקביעות?

תשובה: הצבור מוחלים על כבודם.

INTOXICATION

A Kohen may drink milk before *duchaning*. He may *duchan* after drinking grape juice if he does not feel intoxicated. If a Kohen makes Kiddush before *duchaning,* such as on Rosh Hashanah between Shacharis and Mussaf, he should be very careful not to become intoxicated.

474

שאלה: ברמב"ם בהלכות ביאת מקדש (פרק א, הלכה ב) מבואר דחלב משכר, ויש לעיין לפי זה האם הכהנים צריכים להקפיד שלא לשתות חלב קודם נשיאת כפים?

תשובה: אין איסור בחלב.

475

שאלה: כהן ששתה רביעית מיץ ענבים האם אחר כך מותר לו לישא כפיו?

תשובה: אם אין מרגיש שכרות.

476

שאלה: האם יש ענין שכהן לא יעשה הקידוש ושלא יאכל לפני הדוכן כגון בראש השנה בין שחרית למוסף?

תשובה: יזהר מאד שלא ישתכר.

A KOHEN WITH A BLEMISH

A Kohen whose leg is in a cast and who is walking on crutches, but can stand independently, may *duchan*. If his hand is in a cast or bandage, or if he has a tattoo, he may also *duchan*, as it is covered by the tallis.

477

שאלה: מה הדין בכהן שרגלו מגובסת בגבס, וצריך לקביים כדי לעלות לדוכן, אכן בשעת הברכה הוא יכול לעמוד במקומו בלי סמיכה, האם יכול לשאת את כפיו, דמכיון שהצבור מסיח את דעתם לראות האם יסתדר לעמוד בלי סמיכה, אם כן אפשר שמהאי טעמא לא ישא את כפיו, או שמא אין זה נידון לפטרו משום היסח הדעת?

תשובה: לכאורה יכול.

478

שאלה: כהן שיש לו על ידו גבס או תחבושת, האם יש לו להמנע מלישא את כפיו?

תשובה: הרי מכסה בהטלית.

479

שאלה: מבואר בשו"ע (סי' קכ"ח סעיף ל') דכהן שיש לו מום לא ישא כפיו דכיון שהוא דבר מתמיה יבואו להסיח דעת מלשמוע הברכה. והנה מעשה בכהן ששבר רגלו ויש לו גבס על רגלו כולל כף הרגל והוא רוצה לשאת כפים, אמרתי שלכאורה אסור לו כיון דאין רגלו נראית כתיקונה ועוד דאינו יכול לעמוד בצורה יציבה וניכר שיש לו מום ברגלו, מה דעת כת"ר בזה?

תשובה: בזמנינו שמכסין הידים יש מקום להקל.

480

שאלה: כהן שעשה ל"ע כתובת קעקע על ידיו ועכשיו חזר בתשובה, האם מותר לישא כפיו אם מכסה ידיו על ידי טלית?

תשובה: מותר.

A NON-KOHEN RECITING BIRCAS KOHANIM

A non-Kohen may bless his friend with the words of Bircas Kohanim; the prohibition for a non-Kohen to recite Bircas Kohanim applies only in a minyan, with raised hands. Kohanim today are assumed to be kosher Kohanim.

481

שאלה: יש לעיין אם יש איסור לזר לברך חבירו בברכת כהנים יברכך וגו׳ יאר וגו׳ ישא וגו׳, ומבואר בש״ס דאסור משום דכתיב אתם ולא זרים, ולאו הבא מכלל עשה עשה, ולכאורה הא מעשים שבכל יום שאחד מברך חבירו בברכה זו, ואיך מברכים, ואולי כל האיסור רק עם הברכה שלפניה (אשר קדשנו וכו׳ לברך את עמו ישראל באהבה)?

תשובה: דוקא בצבור ובנשיאת כפים אסור, עיין באור הלכה ריש סי׳ קכ״ח.

482

שאלה: כהנים בזמן הזה איך נושאים כפיהם, והלא אם הם פסולים הוו כזרים, וזר העולה לדוכן עובר בעשה דאתם ולא זרים, למה התירו לישא כפיהם דיש בזה חשש איסור עשה, ואולי היה להם להתנות תנאי שאם אינם כהנים אין מתכוונים לברכה?

תשובה: אין איסור רק על מוחזק כזר.

483

שאלה: קשה לי, הרי היום הכהנים הם ספיקות, ואם כן כיצד יכולים לברך אקב״ו לברך את עמו ישראל באהבה, דלכאורה יהיו פטורים מברכה זו, מדין ספק ברכות להקל?

תשובה: מוחזקים כהנים.

BIRCAS KOHANIM IN THE PRESENCE OF A NON-JEW

Bircas Kohanim may be performed even if a non-Jew is present in the shul, such a worker or aide of an elderly individual.

484

שאלה: כתב בשו״ת מהרי״ל (חדשות סי׳ כ״א) שנמנעים בחוץ לארץ לישא כפים כיון שנמצאים גוים במקום שמתפללים. לפי זה האם יש לימנע גם

בזמנינו כשמתפללים בחלק הקדמי של הבית הכנסת ובזמן שנושאים כפים הגוי מנקה החלק האחורי או מתקן שם החשמל?
תשובה: יש להקל.

485

שאלה: האם מותר לשאת כפים כשיש נכרי בבית הכנסת?
תשובה: מותר.

486

שאלה: הנה, בשו"ת מהרי"ל (חדשות סי' כ"א), כתב: באגור נשאל גדול הדור מהרר"י מולין למה אין הכהנים נושאין כפיהן בכל יום מאחר שהוא מצות עשה, ובתוך התשובה כתב וז"ל: "וכן יש לומר מפני הגוים, וביש מקומות ראיתי שאין מניחין שום גוי בבית הכנסת בשעת נשיאות כפים וכיון שאין מזהירין, הכהן לא עבר", עכ"ל. מה לעשות במנין שמתפללים בבית אבות ושם עובדים גוים, והם מתהלכים הנה והנה לצורך הטיפול בזקנים, האם להשתדל למונעם מליכנס לחדר שמתפללים? והאם זה פוגם בסגולה של ברכת כהנים?
תשובה: כיון שהוא לצורך ישראל אין קפידא ואינו פוגם.

THE CHAZZAN'S SUBSTITUTE PRAYER

When responding *"Kein yehi ratzon"* to the *Elokeinu V'Elokei Avoseinu* prayer, our custom is not to mention anything else. One need not stand while the chazzan recites this prayer.

487

שאלה: כשאין כהנים, אומר הש"ץ אלוקינו ואלוקי אבותנו ברכנו בברכה המשולשת בתורה הכתובה וכו'. וראיתי חילוקי דעות במפרשי הסידור, האם אומר "המשולשת בתורה" ביחד, ושוב יאמר הכתובה וכו', או שיאמר "המשולשת", ואחר כך יאמר "בתורה הכתובה" ביחד, איזה דרך נכון לומר?
תשובה: הכל כוונה א'.

488

שאלה: מהו המקור שנוהגים קצת אנשים שבמקומות שאין נושאים כפים שכשהשליח ציבור אומר הנוסח יברכך ד' וישמרך אומרים כן יהי רצון בזכות אברהם אבינו וכן בשאר הפסוקים בזכות יצחק ויעקב?
תשובה: אצלנו לא נוהגים כן.

489

שאלה: כשהש"ץ אומר או"א ברכנו בברכה המשולשת כשאין כהנים, האם צריך לעמוד כשאומר יברכך וכו'?
תשובה: אין צריך.

490

שאלה: המשנה ברורה ועוד אחרונים (סי' קכ"ז ס"ק ח) מביאים מהזוהר הק', שאם אין בבית הכנסת כהנים, והש"ץ אומר: אלוקינו ואלוקי אבותינו ברכנו בברכה המשולשת וכו', "כשאומר יברכך ד' יראה לצד ההיכל, וישמרך יראה לצד ימין שלו, יאר ד' כלפי ההיכל, פניו אליך ויחונך יראה צד שמאל שלו, ליחדו בימין". ולכאורה כל זה לפי מה שהיה נהוג שהש"ץ היה עומד על הבימה מול ההיכל (וכמנהג הספרדים בזמנינו), אבל לפי מה שנהוג אצל רוב האשכנזים היום, שהש"ץ עומד מימין להיכל, לכאורה אין לש"ץ לכוון פניו ביברכך ה' לכיוון ההיכל, דצריך להתחיל ולהטות לימין ולא לשמאל, לכן האם יש לאשכנזים להטות באופן אחרת?

תשובה: אין נ"מ ולא פלוג.

ACCORDING HONOR TO THE KOHEN

The obligation to honor a Kohen extends to all matters, not just mitzvah matters. This obligation is incumbent upon both a Yisrael and a Levi. However, one may hire a Kohen to perform menial labor, for pay. The wife of a Kohen may ask her husband or son to perform menial tasks for her. A Kohen may help others if he wishes, and they may accept his help. Giving a Kohen a tallis for Bircas Kohanim is considered a form of honor. A Kohen should not be asked to leave the shul so that a non-Kohen can receive the first *aliyah* to the Torah, nor should the Kohen waive his right to have the first *aliyah* in favor of a non-Kohen. A Kohen or Levi should include that title when writing his name, so that his status should not be forgotten.

491

שאלה: החיוב כיבוד לכהן, האם הוא דוקא בדברים שבקדושה או בכל דבר?

תשובה: בכל דבר.

492

שאלה: האם מותר ליתן לכהן עבודה בזויה כגון שטיפת בית הכנסת וכיוצא בו תמורת תשלום?

תשובה: תמורת תשלום מותר.

493

שאלה: האם מותר לאשת כהן לבקש מבעלה לעשות מלאכה בשבילה, אפילו באופן שהוא אינו מוחל? וכן יש לעיין אם מותר לאם לבקש מבנה כהן לעשות מלאכה בשבילה, אולי נאמר דמצות כיבוד אב ואם דוחה מצות וקדשתו?

תשובה: כהן בכהן מותר (עי' בה"ל ס"ס קכ"ח) וי"ל דכהנת ככהן.

494

שאלה: החפץ חיים כתב (ספר המצות הקצר מצות עשה, מצוה נ) על מצות "וקדשתו" בזה"ל: ומחוייבים אנו לקדשו אפילו בעל כרחו אם אינו רוצה, שנאמר: וקדשתו, אפילו בעל כרחו. ויש להקשות ממה שכתב המשנה ברורה (סי' קכ"ח, ס"ק קע"ה) שכהן יכול למחול על כבודו?

תשובה: על בזיון לא.

495

שאלה: האם יש דין שללוי אסור להשתמש בכהן כמו בישראל?

תשובה: כמו בישראל.

496

שאלה: איתא ברמ"א (סימן קכ"ח סעיף מ"ה) שאסור להשתמש בכהן, והמשנה ברורה (ס"ק קע"ה) כותב שטוב להחמיר לכתחילה, ובשרויות בזויות בודאי יש ליזהר. האם מותר לכהן לעשות דבר ביזוי מרצונו ובפרט במקום מצוה כגון לעשות חסד (כמו לזרוק האשפה) או ביקור חולים?

תשובה: לכהן מותר.

497

שאלה: הנה היות והנני כהן, הרבה פעמים כאשר אני חפץ לעזור לאנשים ולסייע להם, מיד הם מסרבים וטענתם בפיהם שאסור להשתמש עמי מחמת מצות וקדשתו, אך מאידך אני טוען שאם כן בטלת מצות חסד משבט הכהנים, ובודאי שמה שאסור להשתמש בכהן אינו אלא כאשר מבקשים עזרה מהכהנים וכדו', אבל באופן שהכהן מציע עזרה מעצמו הרי יש לו בזה מצוה ולא מיקרי שמשתמשין עמו, ורציתי לדעת עם מי הצדק?

תשובה: מסתבר כדבריך.

498

שאלה: מובא במשנה ברורה (סעיף קטן קע"ה) שיש ליזהר להשתמש בכהן מנהג בזיון אבל האם להכהן להמנע לעשות הבקשה של הישראל מדין לפני עיור?

תשובה: אין כאן לפני עיור כיון שרוצה.

499

שאלה: האם נתינת הטלית לכהן לצורך עליתו לדוכן יש בו משום מצות וקדשתו?

תשובה: כן.

500

שאלה: אם יש כמה אנשים חיובים לעלות לתורה (בר מצוה, חתן, יארצייט), האם מותר לבקש מכהן לצאת מבית הכנסת בתחילת קריאת התורה ולתת את העליה לתורה לישראל?

תשובה: אין לעשות כן.

501

שאלה: אם יש כהן אחד בבית הכנסת והוא רוצה לתת העליה לתורה שלו לישראל, היכול ישראל לעלות לתורה "ברשות כהן"?

תשובה: אין לעשות כן, עיין במ"ב סי' קל"ה ס"ק ט.

502

שאלה: נוהגין שמי שהוא כהן או לוי כשכותב שמו כותב הכהן או הלוי, מהו המקור לכך?

תשובה: אהרן אחיך הלוי, שמות ד' י"ד.

503

שאלה: האם יש ענין לכהן או ללוי כשכותבים שמם להזכיר הכהן או הלוי?

תשובה: יש ענין שלא ישתכח הכהונה ושיוכלו להעיד עליו.

MISCELLANEOUS QUESTIONS

There are grounds for bringing babies and young children to shul to hear Bircas Kohanim, even though technically they are included in this blessing even when they are not in shul. A Kohen's blessing has value even when given outside the actual Bircas Kohanim in shul, and is akin to the *berachah* of a *tzaddik*. There is no basis for gathering a minyan in the house of an ill patient and blessing him with Bircas Kohanim not as part of davening.

Hashem gives His *berachah* via the Kohanim to grant them the merit of bringing this blessing to the Jewish people. Bircas Kohanim is recited in the singular because it refers to the entire congregation as a unit.

A Kohen who didn't have time to remove his tefillin yet may *duchan* during Mussaf in his tefillin even though the other Kohanim are no longer wearing theirs.

A Kohen should not *duchan* in a minyan that is davening Shacharis after *zman tefillah*.

A Kohen may recite Bircas Kohanim even before saying *Birchos HaTorah*. If he mispronounces the words, but all other people where he lives do the same, he may still *duchan*. A Kohen who is too weak to *duchan* must leave the shul before Bircas Kohanim even if people do not know that he is a Kohen.

504

שאלה: איתא במסכת סוטה (ל"ח, ב) דעם שבשדות הוי בכלל ברכה כיון דאניסי ואינם יכולים לבא, אם כן מה שנוהגים קצת בני אדם להביא קטנים בני יומן לבית הכנסת בשלש רגלים, הלא הקטנים אינם יכולים לבוא מעצמן, אם כן דינם לכאורה כעם שבשדות שהם בכלל ברכה, אם כן האם יש ממש במעשיהם?

תשובה: יש ענין.

505

שאלה: האם יסוד דברי המשך חכמה (סוף פרשת וירא) לגבי "ברכת צדיק" שהוא בזכות האמונה בו, קיים גם כן "בברכת כהנים" שלפי האמונה בהקדוש ברוך הוא, כך יתקיים הברכה?

תשובה: יתכן.

506

שאלה: האם החשיבות של ברכת כהנים הוא רק בנשיאת כפים בתפילה, או יש גם חשיבות של ברכה מכהן לישראל ואפילו שלא בשעת תפילה?

תשובה: בודאי יש ענין.

507

שאלה: העולם נוהגין לבקש מכהן עבור ברכתם, האם יש בברכת כהן בלי נשיאת כפים יתרון על פני ברכת מי שאינו כהן?

תשובה: כמו של צדיק.

508

שאלה: ראיתי נוהגין כשיש חולה מסוכן לאסוף עשרה כהנים בביתו, ומברכים אותו בברכת כהנים שלא בתוך התפילה. האם שפיר דמי לעשות הכי?

תשובה: לא שמענו.

509

שאלה: האם הברכה של ברכת כהנים בשבת יותר חשובה מהברכה בימות החול, כי בשבת נוסף גם הברכה של השבת כי היא מקור הברכה, כעין שמצינו בספרים הק' שלימוד בשבת שוה יותר מלימוד ביום חול, או שמצד הברכת כהנים אין הבדל בין שבת ליום חול?

תשובה: לא מצינו.

510

שאלה: מה הענין שהוצרך הקב"ה להעביר את הברכות דוקא דרך הכהנים ולא הוא בעצמו?

תשובה: כדי שיזכו בברכה.

511

שאלה: מה הענין שהוצרך הקב"ה להעביר את הברכות דווקא דרך הכהנים ולא הוא בעצמו, כמו לגבי עמל התורה ושמירת השבת שהקב"ה בעצמו מביא את הברכה על האדם, ולמה כאן בחר דרך הכהנים?

תשובה: כדי שיזכו הכהנים.

512

שאלה: למה ברכת כהנים נתקנה בלשון יחיד?

תשובה: כל הצבור כיחיד.

513

שאלה: כהן שעדיין לא חלץ תפילין ואוחזים בתפילת מוסף, האם יכול לעלות לדוכן עם תפילין למרות שהציבור אוחזים במוסף ולכולם אין תפילין?

תשובה: אם אין מספיק יכול.

514

שאלה: ציבור שמתפללים שחרית אחר זמן תפילה וקוראים לכהן שישא כפים עבורם, האם יעשה זאת?

תשובה: לא ילך.

515

שאלה: מנין שמתקיים לאחר זמן תפלה, האם רשאים הכהנים לברך שם ברכת כהנים?

תשובה: לא.

516

שאלה: אדם שהתפלל במנין שלא היו שם כהנים, וכעת נמצא במנין שמתפללים לאחר זמן תפילה והתחילו הכהנים שם לברך ברכת כהנים, האם ישמע עתה ברכת כהנים?

תשובה: ברכה לבטלה.

517

שאלה: כהן שאינו רשאי לישא כפיו, כגון שנשא גרושה וכיו"ב, ועלה לישא כפיו, ואי אפשר להורידו משם, כגון שהוא אלים, האם ימנעו מחמת זה שאר הכהנים מלברך?

תשובה: לא ימנעו.

518

שאלה: האם מותר לכהן לברך "ברכת כהנים" כשעדיין לא בירך "ברכות התורה"?

תשובה: מותר.

519

שאלה: אם אין עשרה ששמעו כל חזרת הש"ץ, האם מותר לכהן לברך נשיאת כפים?

תשובה: כן.

520

שאלה: בשלחן ערוך (סי' קכ"ח סעיף ל"ג) כתב: מי שאינו יודע לחתוך האותיות לא ישא את כפיו, וכתב שם המשנה ברורה ואם כל בני עירו קוראין כך מותר לישא כפים שם באותו מקום. וצריך ביאור דהרי ברכת כהנים חייב

בלשון הקודש דוקא, ואם כן מה מועיל שבני עירו קוראין כך, הרי הוא מחליף האותיות, ואין כאן לשון הקודש, ואף שהענין והמשמעות מובן לאנשי עירו, אבל לשון הקודש ליכא?
תשובה: זה נקרא לשון הקודש.

521

שאלה: בשלחן ערוך (סי' קכ"ח סעיף ד) איתא שכהן שאינו עולה לדוכן (מחמת שהוא חלש וכיו"ב) צריך לצאת מבית הכנסת עד שיגמרו ברכת כהנים, כדי שלא יאמרו שהוא פגום. מה הדין במי שנוסע למדינה אחרת שאין מכירים אותו, ואינם יודעים שהוא כהן, האם מותר לו להישאר שם?
תשובה: לא פלוג רבנן.

522

שאלה: ש"ץ בתפלת שחרית התחיל לומר שים שלום ושכח לקרוא כהנים לישא כפים, ומיד הפסיקוהו הציבור שלא ימשיך דיש כהנים, האם מותר להש"ץ להקריא אותם יברכך וכו', או שמא משום שהתחיל בדבר אחר ישתוק וימשיך התפלה אחרי סיום הברכה מכהנים, והמקריא יהא אחד מהציבור.
תשובה: מותר לו.

523

שאלה: הובא בשם ספר המקצועות שיש ליזהר לשאת כפיו אחר שנכנס לבית נדה, האם נכון לכתחילה לחשוש לזה?
תשובה: לא שמענו להקפיד.

524

שאלה: המשנה ברורה (סק"ב) מביא שכהנים ממנין העשרה וז"ל: "שהכהנים גם כן בכלל ברכה מדכתיב ואני אברכם כלומר לכהנים", עכ"ל. וקשה שהמשנה ברורה להלן (ס"ק נ"ה, וכן בס"ק קמ"ו) הביא דואני אברכם הוי על ישראל, והוא פלוגתת רבי עקיבא ורבי ישמעאל (חולין מ"ט, א). ואם כן, איך סתם המשנה ברורה פעם כדעת תנא אחד, ופעם כדעת תנא אחר?
תשובה: דרך המ"ב כך בהרבה מקומות משום שב' הדרשות נכונות.

525

שאלה: איתא בחולין (מ"ט, א) שרבי ישמעאל מסייע לכהני דס"ל שהם מתברכים מהקב"ה מהפסוק "ואני אברכם", ומסבירה הגמרא: דמוקי לה לברכת כהנים במקום ברכה דישראל. ופרש"י: דהכי עדיפא דמשמע שמתברכין הן עם השאר. ולכאורה משמע שלפי רבי עקיבא שהכהן מתברך מפסוק אחר "מואברכה מברכיך" אינו מתברך באותו ברכה כמו לישראל. להלכה מביא הרמב"ם הלכות תפילה ונשיאת כפים (פרק ט"ו הלכה י"ב) כרבי עקיבא. למה פוסקים בזה כמו רבי עקיבא?
תשובה: הלכה כר"ע מחברו.

526

שאלה: האם יש נפקא מינה להלכה בין רבי עקיבא לרבי ישמעאל?
תשובה: הנודר מהמתברכים מהכהנים.

527

שאלה: ביהי רצון שאומרים בסיום ברכת כהנים ביום טוב אומרים: ותתננו לאהבה לחן ולחסד ולרחמים בעיניך ובעיני כל רואנו וכו׳ כשם שנתת את יוסף צדיקך בשעה שהלבישו אביו כתונת פסים, לחן ולחסד ולרחמים בעיניך ובעיני כל רואיו. ולכאורה קשה הלא אדרבה בשעה שהלביש עליו כתונת פסים זה גרם קנאה להאחים כדאיתא בגמרא (שבת י, ב) לעולם אל ישנה אדם בניו בין הבנים שבשביל שני סלעים וכו׳?
תשובה: לא קאי על האחים שקינאוהו אלא על שאר העולם.

BIRCAS KOHANIM IN THE NORTH OF ERETZ YISRAEL

A minyan in a hotel in Tzfas may perform Bircas Kohanim on a regular day even if the hotel owner's custom is not to *duchan* daily. It is worthwhile for a person living in Tzfas whose shul does not perform Bircas Kohanim daily to go hear Bircas Kohanim in a minyan that does perform it. The same is true for a visitor.

528

שאלה: בית מלון בצפת שבאים לשם אורחים מירושלים ומבני ברק ומיתר הערים בהם מברכים ברכת כהנים בכל יום, האם הם יכולים לברך ברכת כהנים במלון, או שינהגו כמנהג בעל הבית של המלון שהוא שייך למקצת חסידים של צפת שאינם מברכים ברכת כהנים אלא רק בתפילת מוסף?
תשובה: יכולים כיון שהם ממקומות שמברכין.

529

שאלה: לגבי לא תתגודדו בברכת כהנים, בני ישיבה שלומדים בירושלים, שרוב ככל הבחורים שבה מתגוררים באיזור ירושלים ומרכז הארץ שנושאים כפים בכל יום, אבל יש בחור אחד שמתגורר בצפת, וכשהוא בצפת, מנהגו לשאת כפיו רק בתפילת מוסף, וכל הישיבה נוסעת למחנה קיץ בצפת, ושם מתפללים שחרית כל הישיבה ביחד, האם מותר להבחור לישא כפיו ביחד עם שאר תלמידי הישיבה?
תשובה: מותר.

530

שאלה: האם כשאנשי בני ברק באים לצפת, ומתפללים בבית הכנסת במנין של אנשי בני ברק גם כן אין לכהן לישא כפיו, ומה עושה כת"ר כשנוסע לצפת?

תשובה: יש שעושים שם כמו שנוהגים בני חוץ לארץ. אנו כשנוסעים לצפת נושאין כפים שם.

531

שאלה: בעיר שיש חלוקי מנהגים בין הקהילות, כגון צפת שבחלק מקהילות החסידים אין נושאין כפיהם בכל יום, ורק נושאים כפיהם בכל שבת וראש חודש במוסף, ואילו בקהילות ליטא, הספרדים, וחלק מקהילות החסידים נוהגין לישא כפיהם בכל יום, אם יש ענין לישראל ללכת לשמוע ברכת כהנים כשיטת ספר החרדים שעל הישראל המתברך מקיים מצות עשה וכל שכן על הכהן לברך לכולי עלמא, או שמא מכיון שבקהילתו אין נוהגין כך אין בכך ענין?

תשובה: טוב לעשות כן, אף דלא קי"ל כהחרדים.

BIRCAS KOHANIM OUTSIDE ERETZ YISRAEL

Bircas Kohanim is more potent than the blessing of a *gadol*.

If an Ashkenazi Kohen living outside Eretz Yisrael davens in a Sephardi minyan, he may *duchan* there. He may go to a Sephardi minyan specifically for this purpose, even on a daily basis, and this is a worthwhile practice. Similarly, Ashkenazi non-Kohanim may attend a Sephardi minyan in order to hear Bircas Kohanim. Visitors to Eretz Yisrael should follow the local practice of *duchaning* every day, and should do so during Shacharis of Yom Tov Sheini as well. They may *duchan* even on the plane to and from Eretz Yisrael. An Ashkenazi minyan in a new settlement outside Eretz Yisrael may not perform Bircas Kohanim. If a minyan is composed exclusively of residents of Eretz Yisrael who are visiting a place outside Eretz Yisrael, they may follow their custom of *duchaning* every day even there.

There is no point in having a Kohen serve as the chazzan in order to recite the *Elokeinu V'Elokei Avoseinu* prayer.

532

שאלה: כהן בן אשכנז שגר בחוץ לארץ שנזדמן לו להתפלל במנין של ספרדים הנוהגים לישא כפים בכל יום, האם יכול לעלות לדוכן, או שמא עדיף שיצא מבית הכנסת לפני ברכת "רצה" מאחר ואין מנהגו לישא כפים?

תשובה: מצוה לעלות.

533

שאלה: כהן אשכנזי שגר בחוץ לארץ ומתפלל במנין של ספרדים בחוץ לארץ בקביעות, שנוהגים לישא כפים בכל יום, והוא הכהן היחידי שם, האם רשאי גם הוא לישא כפים באותו מקום בשבילם, או שמא יותר טוב שיתחמק וימנע מלישא כפים שם, מאחר ומנהגו שלא לישא כפים בכל יום, וברצוני לדעת כיצד ינהג אותו הכהן?

תשובה: רשאי.

534

שאלה: האם כהן שהוא דר בחוץ לארץ רשאי ללכת לבית הכנסת של ספרדים לישא את כפיו, לאחר שגמר תפילתו בבית הכנסת שמתפלל נוסח אשכנז, או לא?

תשובה: מותר.

535

שאלה: כהן אשכנזי שגר כל חייו בחוץ לארץ שמנהגו לברך ברכת כהנים רק בהחגים, האם מותר ללכת ולהתפלל במנין של ספרדים בקביעות כל יום בימות החול ובשבת, אם המנהג שלו להתפלל נוסח אשכנז?

תשובה: מותר.

536

שאלה: כהן אשכנזי בחוץ לארץ שעולה לדוכן בקביעות במנין של הספרדים בימי החול או בשבת, האם יש לחוש לברכה לבטלה?

תשובה: פשיטא שאין זה ברכה לבטלה.

537

שאלה: כהן אשכנזי שנמצא במקום שאין נוהגים האשכנזים לברך ברכת כהנים, האם יש לו להשתדל להתפלל במנין של ספרדים או ללכת שם אחרי תפילתו כדי לברך?

תשובה: אין חייב אבל טוב שיעשה.

538

שאלה: אני כהן אשכנזי, ולצערי הנני גר בחוץ לארץ שנוהגים לשאת כפים רק ביום טוב לפי המבואר בהרמ"א (סי' קכ"ח סעיף מ"ד). אמנם, נכספה וגם כלתה נפשי לברך ברכת כהנים בכל יום או מידי שבת בשבתו, ושאלתי האם מותר לכתחילה ללכת לבית מדרש של אחינו בני יוצאי ספרד שאצלם מברכין ברכת כהנים בכל יום כדי לקיים מצות עשה?

תשובה: כן.

539

שאלה: האם לויים וישראלים אשכנזים תושבי חוץ לארץ יכולים ללכת לשמוע, או להתפלל כל יום במנין של ספרדים בחוץ לארץ, וכוונתם ללכת למנין של הספרדים הוא רק בכדי לשמוע ברכת כהנים?

תשובה: מותר.

540

שאלה: מובא בשו"ת בית אפרים סימן ו': "מנהג אשכנזים שלא לישא כפים בחו"ל הוא מנהג קדום ואסור לשנותו". האם מותר לכהן אשכנזי ללכת להתפלל אצל הספרדים?

תשובה: במקום דיש ספרדים והולך להתפלל אצלם מותר.

541

שאלה: כהן אשכנזי בחוץ לארץ שאין נושאים כפים בכל יום, האם כדאי לו ליכנס לבית הכנסת של ספרדים כדי לקיים מצות נשיאת כפים?

תשובה: כדאי.

542

שאלה: בארץ ישראל, המנהג בבית אבל שהכהנים (לא האבלים עצמם) נושאים כפיהם, אמנם המשנה ברורה (סי' קכ"א ס"ק ו') כתב שאין אומרים הזכרת ברכת כהנים של אלקינו ואלוקי אבותינו וכו' בבית האבל, האם יש לנהוג כן בחוץ לארץ?

תשובה: כן.

543

שאלה: בענין ברכת כהנים נהוג כאן בארץ ישראל כמעט בכל המקומות, שהכהנים נושאים כפיהם בכל יום, ויש שערערו בכהן שגר בחוץ לארץ שמגיע לביקור בארץ ישראל, איך יכול לישא כפיו, שהרי כתב הרמ"א שבמדינות אשכנז נהגו שלא לשאת כפים רק במוסף של יום טוב שאז שרויים בשמחה, ואם כן טוענים וכי בארץ ישראל יותר שמחים מאשר בחוץ לארץ, ולכן טוענים שהנוהגים כהרמ"א צריכים לשאת כפים רק במוסף של יום טוב, מה דעת כת"ר בזה?

תשובה: בארץ ישראל עלו תלמידי הגר"א והנהיגו כדעת הגר"א לישא כפים כל יום.

544

שאלה: בני חוץ לארץ הנמצאים בארץ ישראל ביום טוב שני ועושים מנין לעצמם, האם נושאים כפים בשחרית או לא?

תשובה: יעשו.

545

שאלה: כשנוסע במטוס מארץ ישראל או לארץ ישראל, האם ישא כפיו כהן אשכנזי שגר בחוץ לארץ שמתפלל שחרית במטוס?

תשובה: יכול לישא.

546

שאלה: ראיתי בספר ארחות רבנו (חלק א' עמוד ס"ז) כי מרן בעל הקהלות יעקב זצ"ל פסק שאם ציבור בני ארץ ישראל יש להם מנין נפרד בחוץ לארץ

יכולים לישא כפים כל יום כמנהג ארץ ישראל ולא כמנהג חוץ לארץ. אם הקימו ישוב יהודי חדש בחוץ לארץ שלא היה בו מנהג אחר קודם, לכאורה מותר לישא כפים כל יום, שכידוע אדיר היה חפצם של הגר"א והגר"ח מוולאז'ין לשנות המנהג בחוץ לארץ, לכן במקום חדש האם ראוי לעשות כן?
תשובה: אין לעשות כן, ושאני התם שהיה עראי.

547

שאלה: מנין של נופשים ומבריאים המתפללים במנין מיוחד בחוץ לארץ ואין עמם מתושבי חוץ לארץ, האם עליהם לישא כפים שם?
תשובה: לכאורה ינהגו כבני ארץ ישראל כיון דאין שם בני חוץ לארץ.

548

שאלה: לענין ברכת כהנים, האם אילת נחשב כחוץ לארץ?
תשובה: אילת חוץ לארץ.

549

שאלה: אם אני מגיע לאילת עם קבוצה ממקום אחר בארץ ומארגנים בבית הכנסת מנין נפרד, האם אני יכול לישא כפים כמו הדין של קבוצה של עשרה אנשים שבאים מארץ ישראל לחוץ לארץ ויכולים לישא כפים, אפילו שבבית כנסת שהם מתפללים אין עושים נשיאת כפים, או שמא אין לשנות ממנהג הבית כנסת?
תשובה: יכולים.

550

שאלה: בן אשכנז הגר בחוץ לארץ וצריך ישועה, מה עדיף לעשות, ללכת לגדול הדור להתפלל עבורו, או שילך בעצמו למנין של אחינו בני ספרד לשמוע ברכת כהנים?
תשובה: ברכת כהנים עדיף.

551

שאלה: בחוץ לארץ שאין נשיאת כפים אלא ביום טוב, האם יש איזה הידור או ענין שכהן יהיה השליח ציבור ובאמירת אלוקינו ואלוקי אבותינו ברכנו בברכה המשולשת בתורה וכו' יהיה נחשב קצת כברכת כהנים או שאין בזה כלום?
תשובה: לא מועיל.

Part 7:

The Text of Bircas Kohanim and Its Associated Tefillos

At this point, the Kohanim must begin their ascent to the *duchan*.

רְצֵה Be favorable, HASHEM, our God, toward Your people Yisrael and their prayer, and restore the service to the Holy of Holies of Your Temple. The fire-offerings of Yisrael and their prayer accept with love and favor, and may the service of Your people Yisrael always be favorable to You.

On Mussaf of Yom Tov, most congregations recite וְתֶעָרֵב.
When וְתֶעָרֵב is not recited, the chazzan continues וְתֶחֱזֶינָה עֵינֵינוּ (below).

Congregation, followed by chazzan:

וְתֶעָרֵב May our entreaty become pleasing before You as an elevation-offering and as a sacrifice. Please, O Merciful One, in Your abounding mercy return Your Presence to Zion, Your city, and the order of the Temple service to Yerushalayim. And may our eyes behold when You return to Zion in mercy, that we may there serve You with awe as in days of old and as in earlier years.

Chazzan concludes:

Blessed are You, HASHEM, for You alone do we serve, with awe.

וְתֶחֱזֶינָה May our eyes behold Your return to Zion in compassion. Blessed are You, HASHEM, Who restores His Presence to Zion.

(Cong. and Kohanim—Amen.)

Chazzan recites the entire מוֹדִים aloud, while the congregation recites מוֹדִים דְּרַבָּנָן softly. All bow at מוֹדִים and straighten up at 'ה.

מוֹדִים We gratefully thank You, for it is You Who are HASHEM, our God and the God of our forefathers for all eternity; Rock of our lives, Shield of our salvation are You from generation to generation. We shall thank You and relate Your praise[1] — for our lives, which are committed to Your power and for our souls that are entrusted to You; for Your miracles that are with us every day;

MODIM OF THE RABBIS

מוֹדִים We gratefully thank You, for it is You Who are HASHEM, our God and the God of our forefathers, the God of all flesh, our Molder, the Molder of the universe. Blessings and thanks are due Your great and holy Name, for You have given us life and sustained us. So may You continue

(1) Cf. *Tehillim* 79:13.

At this point, the Kohanim must begin their ascent to the *duchan*.

רְצֵה יהוה אֱלֹהֵינוּ בְּעַמְּךָ יִשְׂרָאֵל וּבִתְפִלָּתָם, וְהָשֵׁב אֶת הָעֲבוֹדָה לִדְבִיר בֵּיתֶךָ. וְאִשֵּׁי יִשְׂרָאֵל וּתְפִלָּתָם בְּאַהֲבָה תְקַבֵּל בְּרָצוֹן, וּתְהִי לְרָצוֹן תָּמִיד עֲבוֹדַת יִשְׂרָאֵל עַמֶּךָ.

On Mussaf of Yom Tov, most congregations recite וְתֶעֱרַב. When וְתֶעֱרַב is not recited, the chazzan continues וְתֶחֱזֶינָה עֵינֵינוּ (below).

Congregation, followed by chazzan:

וְתֶעֱרַב לְפָנֶיךָ עֲתִירָתֵנוּ כְּעוֹלָה וּכְקָרְבָּן. אָנָּא, רַחוּם, בְּרַחֲמֶיךָ הָרַבִּים הָשֵׁב שְׁכִינָתְךָ לְצִיּוֹן עִירֶךָ, וְסֵדֶר הָעֲבוֹדָה לִירוּשָׁלָיִם. וְתֶחֱזֶינָה עֵינֵינוּ בְּשׁוּבְךָ לְצִיּוֹן בְּרַחֲמִים, וְשָׁם נַעֲבָדְךָ בְּיִרְאָה כִּימֵי עוֹלָם וּכְשָׁנִים קַדְמוֹנִיּוֹת.

Chazzan concludes:

בָּרוּךְ אַתָּה יהוה, שֶׁאוֹתְךָ לְבַדְּךָ בְּיִרְאָה נַעֲבוֹד.

וְתֶחֱזֶינָה עֵינֵינוּ בְּשׁוּבְךָ לְצִיּוֹן בְּרַחֲמִים. בָּרוּךְ אַתָּה יהוה, הַמַּחֲזִיר שְׁכִינָתוֹ לְצִיּוֹן.

(.אָמֵן — Cong. and Kohanim)

Chazzan recites the entire מוֹדִים aloud, while the congregation recites מוֹדִים דְּרַבָּנָן softly. All bow at מוֹדִים and straighten up at 'ה.

מוֹדִים אֲנַחְנוּ לָךְ שָׁאַתָּה הוּא יהוה אֱלֹהֵינוּ וֵאלֹהֵי אֲבוֹתֵינוּ לְעוֹלָם וָעֶד. צוּר חַיֵּינוּ, מָגֵן יִשְׁעֵנוּ אַתָּה הוּא לְדוֹר וָדוֹר. נוֹדֶה לְּךָ וּנְסַפֵּר תְּהִלָּתֶךָ[1] עַל חַיֵּינוּ הַמְּסוּרִים בְּיָדֶךָ, וְעַל נִשְׁמוֹתֵינוּ הַפְּקוּדוֹת לָךְ, וְעַל נִסֶּיךָ שֶׁבְּכָל יוֹם עִמָּנוּ,

מודים דרבנן

מוֹדִים אֲנַחְנוּ לָךְ, שָׁאַתָּה הוּא יהוה אֱלֹהֵינוּ וֵאלֹהֵי אֲבוֹתֵינוּ, אֱלֹהֵי כָל בָּשָׂר, יוֹצְרֵנוּ, יוֹצֵר בְּרֵאשִׁית. בְּרָכוֹת וְהוֹדָאוֹת לְשִׁמְךָ הַגָּדוֹל וְהַקָּדוֹשׁ, עַל שֶׁהֶחֱיִיתָנוּ וְקִיַּמְתָּנוּ. כֵּן

and for Your wonders and favors in every season — evening, morning, and afternoon. The Beneficent One, for Your compassions were never exhausted, and the Compassionate One, for Your kindnesses never ended[1] — always have we put our hope in You.

to give us life and sustain us and gather our exiles to the Courtyards of Your Sanctuary, to observe Your decrees, to do Your will, and to serve You wholeheartedly. [We thank You] for inspiring us to thank You. Blessed is the God of thanksgivings.

For all these, may Your Name be blessed and exalted, our King, continually forever and ever.

While the chazzan recites וְכֹל הַחַיִּים, the Kohanim recite יְהִי רָצוֹן silently:
The chazzan bends his knees at בָּרוּךְ; bows at אַתָּה; straightens up at 'ה.

וְכֹל Everything alive will gratefully acknowledge You, Selah! and praise Your Name sincerely, O God of our salvation and help, Selah! Blessed are You, HASHEM, Your Name is "The Beneficent One" and to You it is fitting to give thanks.

יְהִי רָצוֹן May it be Your will, HASHEM, our God and the God of our forefathers, that this blessing which You have commanded us to bestow upon Your nation Israel be a full blessing, that there be in it neither stumbling block nor sin from now and forever.

(Cong. and Kohanim—Amen.)

In some communities, the chazzan recites the following in an undertone.
In all communities, when there is more than one Kohen, the word כֹּהֲנִים is recited aloud by the chazzan or a designated congregant, as a formal summons to the Kohanim to bless the people. In some communities the congregation, but not the Kohanim, responds, עַם קְדוֹשֶׁךָ כָּאָמוּר, aloud:

אֱלֹהֵינוּ Our God and the God of our forefathers, bless us with the three-verse blessing in the Torah that was written by the hand of Moshe, Your servant, that was said by Aharon and his sons, the

Kohanim,

Your holy people — as it is said:

The Kohanim recite the following blessing aloud, in unison:

בָּרוּךְ Blessed are You, HASHEM, our God, King of the universe, Who has sanctified us with the holiness of Aharon, and has commanded us to bless His people Yisrael with love.

(Cong. but not chazzan—Amen.)

(1) Cf. *Eichah* 3:22.

וְעַל נִפְלְאוֹתֶיךָ וְטוֹבוֹתֶיךָ שֶׁבְּכָל עֵת, עֶרֶב וָבֹקֶר וְצָהֳרָיִם. הַטּוֹב כִּי לֹא כָלוּ רַחֲמֶיךָ, וְהַמְּרַחֵם כִּי לֹא תַמּוּ חֲסָדֶיךָ,[1] מֵעוֹלָם קִוִּינוּ לָךְ.

תְּחַיֵּנוּ וּתְקַיְּמֵנוּ, וְתֶאֱסוֹף גָּלֻיּוֹתֵינוּ לְחַצְרוֹת קָדְשֶׁךָ, לִשְׁמוֹר חֻקֶּיךָ וְלַעֲשׂוֹת רְצוֹנֶךָ, וּלְעָבְדְּךָ בְּלֵבָב שָׁלֵם, עַל שֶׁאֲנַחְנוּ מוֹדִים לָךְ. בָּרוּךְ אֵל הַהוֹדָאוֹת.

וְעַל כֻּלָּם יִתְבָּרַךְ וְיִתְרוֹמַם שִׁמְךָ מַלְכֵּנוּ תָּמִיד לְעוֹלָם וָעֶד.

While the chazzan recites וְכֹל הַחַיִּים, the Kohanim recite יְהִי רָצוֹן silently:
The chazzan bends his knees at בָּרוּךְ; bows at אַתָּה; straightens up at ה׳.

וְכֹל הַחַיִּים יוֹדוּךָ סֶּלָה, וִיהַלְלוּ אֶת שִׁמְךָ בֶּאֱמֶת, הָאֵל יְשׁוּעָתֵנוּ וְעֶזְרָתֵנוּ סֶלָה. בָּרוּךְ אַתָּה יהוה, הַטּוֹב שִׁמְךָ וּלְךָ נָאֶה לְהוֹדוֹת.

יְהִי רָצוֹן מִלְּפָנֶיךָ, יהוה אֱלֹהֵינוּ וֵאלֹהֵי אֲבוֹתֵינוּ, שֶׁתְּהֵא הַבְּרָכָה הַזֹּאת שֶׁצִּוִּיתָנוּ לְבָרֵךְ אֶת עַמְּךָ יִשְׂרָאֵל בְּרָכָה שְׁלֵמָה, וְלֹא יִהְיֶה בָּהּ שׁוּם מִכְשׁוֹל וְעָוֹן מֵעַתָּה וְעַד עוֹלָם.

(Cong. and Kohanim — אָמֵן.)

In some communities, the chazzan recites the following in an undertone. In all communities, when there is more than one Kohen, the word כֹּהֲנִים is recited aloud by the chazzan or a designated congregant, as a formal summons to the Kohanim to bless the people. In some communities the congregation, but not the Kohanim, responds, עַם קְדוֹשֶׁךָ כָּאָמוּר, aloud:

אֱלֹהֵינוּ וֵאלֹהֵי אֲבוֹתֵינוּ, בָּרְכֵנוּ בַבְּרָכָה הַמְּשֻׁלֶּשֶׁת, בַּתּוֹרָה הַכְּתוּבָה עַל יְדֵי מֹשֶׁה עַבְדֶּךָ, הָאֲמוּרָה מִפִּי אַהֲרֹן וּבָנָיו

כֹּהֲנִים

עַם קְדוֹשֶׁךָ — כָּאָמוּר:

The Kohanim recite the following blessing aloud, in unison:

בָּרוּךְ אַתָּה יהוה אֱלֹהֵינוּ מֶלֶךְ הָעוֹלָם, אֲשֶׁר קִדְּשָׁנוּ בִּקְדֻשָּׁתוֹ שֶׁל אַהֲרֹן, וְצִוָּנוּ לְבָרֵךְ אֶת עַמּוֹ יִשְׂרָאֵל בְּאַהֲבָה.

(Cong. but not chazzan — אָמֵן.)

The related verses in small print that appear beneath the words of the Kohanim's blessing are not recited.

May [He] bless you

May HASHEM bless you from Zion, Maker of heaven and earth.[1]

— HASHEM —

HASHEM, our Master, how mighty is Your Name throughout the earth![2]

and safeguard you.

Safeguard me, O God, for in You have I taken refuge.[3]

Outside Eretz Yisrael (and in some congregations in Eretz Yisrael), when Yom Tov is on a weekday, the Kohanim sing an extended chant before saying וְיִשְׁמְרֶךָ, and the congregation recites the following supplication in an undertone. When the Kohanim conclude וְיִשְׁמְרֶךָ, the congregation and chazzan respond אָמֵן.

רִבּוֹנוֹ Master of the world, I am Yours and my dreams are Yours. I have dreamed a dream but I do not know what it indicates. May it be Your will, HASHEM, my God and the God of my forefathers, that all my dreams regarding myself and regarding all of Yisrael be good ones — those I have dreamed about myself, those I have dreamed about others, and those that others dreamed about me. If they are good, strengthen them, fortify them, make them endure in me and in them like the dreams of the righteous Yosef. But if they require healing, heal them like Chizkiyah king of Yehudah from his sickness; like Miriam the prophetess from her *tzaraas*; like Naaman from his *tzaraas*; like the waters of Marah through the hand of Moshe our teacher; and like the waters of Yericho through the hand of Elisha. And just as You transformed the curse of the wicked Bilaam from a curse to a blessing, so may You transform all of my dreams regarding myself and regarding all of Yisrael for goodness. May You protect me, may You be gracious to me, may You accept me. Amen.

May [He] illuminate

May God favor us and bless us, may He illuminate His countenance with us, Selah.[4]

— HASHEM —

HASHEM, HASHEM, God, Compassionate and Gracious, Slow to anger, and Abundant in Kindness and Truth.[5]

The related verses in small print that appear beneath the words of the Kohanim's blessing are not recited.

יְבָרֶכְךָ

יְבָרֶכְךָ יהוה מִצִּיּוֹן, עֹשֵׂה שָׁמַיִם וָאָרֶץ.[1]

יהוה

יהוה אֲדוֹנֵינוּ, מָה אַדִּיר שִׁמְךָ בְּכָל הָאָרֶץ.[2]

וְיִשְׁמְרֶךָ.

שָׁמְרֵנִי, אֵל, כִּי חָסִיתִי בָךְ.[3]

Outside Eretz Yisrael (and in some congregations in Eretz Yisrael), when Yom Tov is on a weekday, the Kohanim sing an extended chant before saying וְיִשְׁמְרֶךָ, and the congregation recites the following supplication in an undertone. When the Kohanim conclude וְיִשְׁמְרֶךָ, the congregation and chazzan respond אָמֵן.

רִבּוֹנוֹ שֶׁל עוֹלָם, אֲנִי שֶׁלָּךְ וַחֲלוֹמוֹתַי שֶׁלָּךְ. חֲלוֹם חָלַמְתִּי וְאֵינִי יוֹדֵעַ מַה הוּא. יְהִי רָצוֹן מִלְּפָנֶיךָ, יהוה אֱלֹהַי וֵאלֹהֵי אֲבוֹתַי, שֶׁיִּהְיוּ כָּל חֲלוֹמוֹתַי עָלַי וְעַל כָּל יִשְׂרָאֵל לְטוֹבָה — בֵּין שֶׁחָלַמְתִּי עַל עַצְמִי, וּבֵין שֶׁחָלַמְתִּי עַל אֲחֵרִים, וּבֵין שֶׁחָלְמוּ אֲחֵרִים עָלָי. אִם טוֹבִים הֵם, חַזְּקֵם וְאַמְּצֵם, וְיִתְקַיְּמוּ בִי וּבָהֶם כַּחֲלוֹמוֹתָיו שֶׁל יוֹסֵף הַצַּדִּיק. וְאִם צְרִיכִים רְפוּאָה, רְפָאֵם כְּחִזְקִיָּהוּ מֶלֶךְ יְהוּדָה מֵחָלְיוֹ, וּכְמִרְיָם הַנְּבִיאָה מִצָּרַעְתָּהּ, וּכְנַעֲמָן מִצָּרַעְתּוֹ, וּכְמֵי מָרָה עַל יְדֵי מֹשֶׁה רַבֵּנוּ, וּכְמֵי יְרִיחוֹ עַל יְדֵי אֱלִישָׁע. וּכְשֵׁם שֶׁהָפַכְתָּ אֶת קִלְלַת בִּלְעָם הָרָשָׁע מִקְּלָלָה לִבְרָכָה, כֵּן תַּהֲפוֹךְ כָּל חֲלוֹמוֹתַי עָלַי וְעַל כָּל יִשְׂרָאֵל לְטוֹבָה, וְתִשְׁמְרֵנִי וּתְחָנֵּנִי וְתִרְצֵנִי. אָמֵן.

יָאֵר

אֱלֹהִים יְחָנֵּנוּ וִיבָרְכֵנוּ, יָאֵר פָּנָיו אִתָּנוּ, סֶלָה.[4]

יהוה

יהוה יהוה, אֵל רַחוּם וְחַנּוּן, אֶרֶךְ אַפַּיִם וְרַב חֶסֶד וֶאֱמֶת.[5]

---

(1) *Tehillim* 134:3. (2) 8:10. (3) 16:1.(4) 67:2. (5) *Shemos* 34:6.

His countenance

Turn Your face to me and be gracious to me, for alone and afflicted am I.[1]

for you

To You, HASHEM, I raise my soul.[2]

and be gracious to you.

Behold! Like the eyes of servants unto their master's hand, like the eyes of a maid unto her mistress's hand, so are our eyes unto HASHEM, our God, until He will favor us.[3]

Outside Eretz Yisrael (and in some congregations in Eretz Yisrael), when Yom Tov is on a weekday, the Kohanim sing an extended chant before saying וִיחֻנֶּךָּ, and the congregation recites the following supplication in an undertone. When the Kohanim conclude וִיחֻנֶּךָּ, the congregation and chazzan respond אָמֵן.

רִבּוֹנוֹ Master of the world, I am Yours and my dreams are Yours. I have dreamed a dream but I do not know what it indicates. May it be Your will, HASHEM, my God and the God of my forefathers, that all my dreams regarding myself and regarding all of Yisrael be good ones — those I have dreamed about myself, those I have dreamed about others, and those that others dreamed about me. If they are good, strengthen them, fortify them, make them endure in me and in them like the dreams of the righteous Yosef. But if they require healing, heal them like Chizkiyah king of Yehudah from his sickness; like Miriam the prophetess from her *tzaraas*; like Naaman from his *tzaraas*; like the waters of Marah through the hand of Moshe our teacher; and like the waters of Yericho through the hand of Elisha. And just as You transformed the curse of the wicked Bilaam from a curse to a blessing, so may You transform all of my dreams regarding myself and regarding all of Yisrael for goodness. May You protect me, may You be gracious to me, may You accept me. Amen.

May [He] turn

May he receive a blessing from HASHEM, and just kindness from the God of his salvation.[4] And he will find favor and good understanding in the eyes of God and man.[5]

— HASHEM —

HASHEM, find favor with us, for You have we hoped! Be their power in the mornings, and our salvation in times of distress.[6]

פָּנָיו

פְּנֵה אֵלַי וְחָנֵּנִי, כִּי יָחִיד וְעָנִי אָנִי.[1]

אֵלֶיךָ

אֵלֶיךָ יהוה נַפְשִׁי אֶשָּׂא.[2]

וִיחֻנֶּךָּ.

הִנֵּה כְעֵינֵי עֲבָדִים אֶל יַד אֲדוֹנֵיהֶם, כְּעֵינֵי שִׁפְחָה אֶל יַד גְּבִרְתָּהּ,
כֵּן עֵינֵינוּ אֶל יהוה אֱלֹהֵינוּ עַד שֶׁיְּחָנֵּנוּ.[3]

Outside Eretz Yisrael (and in some congregations in Eretz Yisrael), when Yom Tov is on a weekday, the Kohanim sing an extended chant before saying וִיחֻנֶּךָּ, and the congregation recites the following supplication in an undertone. When the Kohanim conclude וִיחֻנֶּךָּ, the congregation and chazzan respond אָמֵן.

רִבּוֹנוֹ שֶׁל עוֹלָם, אֲנִי שֶׁלָּךְ וַחֲלוֹמוֹתַי שֶׁלָּךְ. חֲלוֹם חָלַמְתִּי וְאֵינִי יוֹדֵעַ מַה הוּא. יְהִי רָצוֹן מִלְּפָנֶיךָ, יהוה אֱלֹהַי וֵאלֹהֵי אֲבוֹתַי, שֶׁיִּהְיוּ כָּל חֲלוֹמוֹתַי עָלַי וְעַל כָּל יִשְׂרָאֵל לְטוֹבָה — בֵּין שֶׁחָלַמְתִּי עַל עַצְמִי, וּבֵין שֶׁחָלַמְתִּי עַל אֲחֵרִים, וּבֵין שֶׁחָלְמוּ אֲחֵרִים עָלָי. אִם טוֹבִים הֵם, חַזְּקֵם וְאַמְּצֵם, וְיִתְקַיְּמוּ בִי וּבָהֶם כַּחֲלוֹמוֹתָיו שֶׁל יוֹסֵף הַצַּדִּיק. וְאִם צְרִיכִים רְפוּאָה, רְפָאֵם כְּחִזְקִיָּהוּ מֶלֶךְ יְהוּדָה מֵחָלְיוֹ, וּכְמִרְיָם הַנְּבִיאָה מִצָּרַעְתָּהּ, וּכְנַעֲמָן מִצָּרַעְתּוֹ, וּכְמֵי מָרָה עַל יְדֵי מֹשֶׁה רַבֵּנוּ, וּכְמֵי יְרִיחוֹ עַל יְדֵי אֱלִישָׁע. וּכְשֵׁם שֶׁהָפַכְתָּ אֶת קִלְלַת בִּלְעָם הָרָשָׁע מִקְּלָלָה לִבְרָכָה, כֵּן תַּהֲפוֹךְ כָּל חֲלוֹמוֹתַי עָלַי וְעַל כָּל יִשְׂרָאֵל לְטוֹבָה, וְתִשְׁמְרֵנִי וּתְחָנֵּנִי וְתִרְצֵנִי. אָמֵן.

יִשָּׂא

יִשָּׂא בְרָכָה מֵאֵת יהוה, וּצְדָקָה מֵאֱלֹהֵי יִשְׁעוֹ.[4]
וּמְצָא חֵן וְשֵׂכֶל טוֹב בְּעֵינֵי אֱלֹהִים וְאָדָם.[5]

יהוה

יהוה, חָנֵּנוּ, לְךָ קִוִּינוּ, הֱיֵה זְרֹעָם לַבְּקָרִים, אַף יְשׁוּעָתֵנוּ בְּעֵת צָרָה.[6]

---

(1) *Tehillim* 25:16. (2) 25:1. (3) 123:2. (4) 24:5. (5) *Mishlei* 3:4. (6) *Yeshayah* 33:2.

His countenance

Do not hide Your countenance from me in a day that is distressing to me; lean Your ear toward me; in the day that I call, speedily answer me.[1]

to you

To You I raised my eyes, O You Who dwells in the Heavens.[2]

and establish

And they shall place My Name upon the Children of Yisrael, and I shall bless them.[3]

for you

Yours, HASHEM, is the greatness, the strength, the splendor, the triumph, and the glory, even all that is in heaven and earth; Yours, HASHEM, is the kingdom and the sovereignty over every leader.[4]

peace.

"Peace, peace, for far and near," says HASHEM, "and I shall heal him."[5]

Outside Eretz Yisrael (and in some congregations in Eretz Yisrael), when Yom Tov is on a weekday, the Kohanim sing an extended chant and the congregation recites the following supplication in an undertone. [The Divine Name that appears here in brackets and bold type should be scanned with the eyes but not spoken.] When the Kohanim conclude שָׁלוֹם, the congregation and chazzan respond אָמֵן.

יְהִי רָצוֹן May it be Your will, HASHEM, my God and the God of my forefathers, that You act for the sake of the holiness of Your kindness and the greatness of Your mercies which reach out, and for the sake of the sanctity of Your Name — the great, the mighty, and the awesome; composed of twenty-two letters which derive from the verses of Bircas Kohanim [**אנקת״ם פסת״ם פספסי״ם דיונסי״ם**]; spoken by Aharon and his sons, Your holy people — that You be near to me when I call to You; that You listen to my prayer, my plea, and my cry at all times, just as You listened to the cry [**אֶנְקַת**] of Yaakov, Your perfect one, who is called "a wholesome man" [**תָּם**]. And may You bestow upon me and upon all the souls of my household, our food and our sustenance — generously and not sparsely, honestly and not in forbidden fashion, pleasurably and not in pain — from beneath Your generous hand, just as You gave a portion [**פַּסַּת**] of bread to eat and clothing to wear to our father Yaakov who is called "a wholesome man" [**תָּם**]. And may You grant that we find love, favor, kindness, and mercy in Your eyes and in the eyes of all who behold us; and that my words in Your service be heard;

---

(1) *Tehillim* 102:3. (2) 123:1. (3) *Bamidbar* 6:27. (4) *I Divrei HaYamim* 29:11.
(5) *Yeshayah* 57:19.

פָּנָיו

אַל תַּסְתֵּר פָּנֶיךָ מִמֶּנִּי בְּיוֹם צַר לִי, הַטֵּה אֵלַי אָזְנֶךָ, בְּיוֹם אֶקְרָא מַהֵר עֲנֵנִי.[1]

אֵלֶיךָ

אֵלֶיךָ נָשָׂאתִי אֶת עֵינַי, הַיֹּשְׁבִי בַּשָּׁמָיִם.[2]

וְיָשֵׂם

וְשָׂמוּ אֶת שְׁמִי עַל בְּנֵי יִשְׂרָאֵל, וַאֲנִי אֲבָרְכֵם.[3]

לְךָ

לְךָ יהוה, הַגְּדֻלָּה וְהַגְּבוּרָה וְהַתִּפְאֶרֶת וְהַנֵּצַח וְהַהוֹד, כִּי כֹל בַּשָּׁמַיִם וּבָאָרֶץ,
לְךָ יהוה, הַמַּמְלָכָה וְהַמִּתְנַשֵּׂא לְכֹל לְרֹאשׁ.[4]

שָׁלוֹם.

שָׁלוֹם שָׁלוֹם לָרָחוֹק וְלַקָּרוֹב, אָמַר יהוה, וּרְפָאתִיו.[5]

Outside Eretz Yisrael (and in some congregations in Eretz Yisrael), when Yom Tov is on a weekday, the Kohanim sing an extended chant and the congregation recites the following supplication in an undertone. [The Divine Name that appears here in brackets and bold type should be scanned with the eyes but not spoken.] When the Kohanim conclude שָׁלוֹם, the congregation and chazzan respond אָמֵן.

יְהִי רָצוֹן מִלְּפָנֶיךָ, יהוה אֱלֹהַי וֵאלֹהֵי אֲבוֹתַי, שֶׁתַּעֲשֶׂה לְמַעַן קְדֻשַּׁת חֲסָדֶיךָ וְגֹדֶל רַחֲמֶיךָ הַפְּשׁוּטִים, וּלְמַעַן טָהֳרַת שִׁמְךָ הַגָּדוֹל הַגִּבּוֹר וְהַנּוֹרָא, בֶּן עֶשְׂרִים וּשְׁתַּיִם אוֹתִיּוֹת הַיּוֹצְאִים מִן הַפְּסוּקִים שֶׁל בִּרְכַּת כֹּהֲנִים **[אנקת״ם פסת״ם פספסי״ם דיונסי״ם]** הָאֲמוּרָה מִפִּי אַהֲרֹן וּבָנָיו עַם קְדוֹשֶׁךָ, שֶׁתִּהְיֶה קָרוֹב לִי בְּקָרְאִי לָךְ, וְתִשְׁמַע תְּפִלָּתִי נַאֲקָתִי וְאֶנְקָתִי תָּמִיד, כְּשֵׁם שֶׁשָּׁמַעְתָּ אֶנְקַת יַעֲקֹב תְּמִימֶךָ הַנִּקְרָא אִישׁ תָּם. וְתִתֶּן לִי וּלְכָל נַפְשׁוֹת בֵּיתִי מְזוֹנוֹתֵינוּ וּפַרְנָסָתֵנוּ — בְּרֶוַח וְלֹא בְצִמְצוּם, בְּהֶתֵּר וְלֹא בְאִסּוּר, בְּנַחַת וְלֹא בְצַעַר — מִתַּחַת יָדְךָ הָרְחָבָה, כְּשֵׁם שֶׁנָּתַתָּ פִּסַּת לֶחֶם לֶאֱכוֹל וּבֶגֶד לִלְבּוֹשׁ לְיַעֲקֹב אָבִינוּ הַנִּקְרָא אִישׁ תָּם. וְתִתְּנֵנוּ לְאַהֲבָה, לְחֵן וּלְחֶסֶד וּלְרַחֲמִים בְּעֵינֶיךָ וּבְעֵינֵי כָל רוֹאֵינוּ, וְיִהְיוּ דְבָרַי נִשְׁמָעִים לַעֲבוֹדָתֶךָ,

just as You granted Yosef, Your righteous one — at the time that his father garbed him in a fine woolen tunic [פַּסִּים] — that he find favor, kindness, and mercy in Your eyes and in the eyes of all who beheld him. May You perform wonders and miracles [וְנִסִּים] with me, and a goodly sign; grant me success in my ways; place in my heart the power of understanding, to understand, to be wise, to fulfill all the words of Your Torah's teaching and its mysteries; save me from errors; and purify my thinking and my heart for Your service and Your awe. May You prolong my days [insert the appropriate words— and the days of my father, my mother, my wife, my husband, my son(s), my daughter(s)] with goodness, with sweetness, with an abundance of strength and peace. Amen: Selah.

The chazzan immediately begins שִׂים שָׁלוֹם; the Kohanim turn back to the Ark, lower their hands, and recite their concluding prayer רִבּוֹנוֹ שֶׁל עוֹלָם; and the congregation recites אַדִּיר בַּמָּרוֹם. Many are careful to conclude their prayers simultaneously with the chazzan's conclusion of הַמְבָרֵךְ אֶת עַמּוֹ יִשְׂרָאֵל בַּשָּׁלוֹם.

Kohanim:

רִבּוֹנוֹ Master of the world, we have done what You have decreed upon us, now may You also do as You have promised us: Look down from Your sacred dwelling, from the heavens, and bless Your people, Yisrael, and the earth which You have given us — just as You have sworn to our fathers — a land that flows with milk and honey.[1]

Congregation:

אַדִּיר Mighty One on high, He Who dwells in power! You are Peace and Your Name is Peace! May it be acceptable that You grant us and all of Your people, the House of Yisrael, life and blessing for a safeguard of peace.

Chazzan continues:

שִׂים שָׁלוֹם Establish peace, goodness, blessing, graciousness, kindness, and compassion upon us and upon all of Your people Yisrael. Bless us, our Father, all of us as one, with the light of Your countenance, for with the light of Your countenance You gave us, HASHEM, our God, the Torah of life and a love of kindness, righteousness, blessing, compassion, life, and peace. And may it be good in Your eyes to bless Your people Yisrael, in every season and in every hour with Your peace. Blessed are You, HASHEM, Who blesses His people Yisrael with peace. (Cong. and Kohanim—Amen.)

(1) *Devarim* 26:15.

כְּשֵׁם שֶׁנָּתַתָּ אֶת יוֹסֵף צַדִּיקֶךָ — בְּשָׁעָה שֶׁהִלְבִּישׁוֹ אָבִיו כְּתֹנֶת **פַּסִּים** — לְחֵן וּלְחֶסֶד וּלְרַחֲמִים בְּעֵינֶיךָ וּבְעֵינֵי כָל רוֹאָיו. וְתַעֲשֶׂה עִמִּי נִפְלָאוֹת **וְנִסִּים**, וּלְטוֹבָה אוֹת, וְתַצְלִיחֵנִי בִּדְרָכַי, וְתֵן בְּלִבִּי בִּינָה לְהָבִין וּלְהַשְׂכִּיל וּלְקַיֵּם אֶת כָּל דִּבְרֵי תַלְמוּד תּוֹרָתֶךָ וְסוֹדוֹתֶיהָ, וְתַצִּילֵנִי מִשְּׁגִיאוֹת, וּתְטַהֵר רַעְיוֹנַי וְלִבִּי לַעֲבוֹדָתֶךָ וּלְיִרְאָתֶךָ. וְתַאֲרִיךְ יָמַי [insert the appropriate words — וִימֵי אָבִי / וְאִמִּי / וְאִשְׁתִּי / וּבַעְלִי / וּבְנִי / וּבָנַי / וּבִתִּי / וּבְנוֹתַי] בְּטוֹב וּבִנְעִימוֹת, בְּרֹב עֹז וְשָׁלוֹם, אָמֵן סֶלָה.

The chazzan immediately begins שִׂים שָׁלוֹם; the Kohanim turn back to the Ark, lower their hands, and recite their concluding prayer רִבּוֹנוֹ שֶׁל עוֹלָם; and the congregation recites אַדִּיר בַּמָּרוֹם. Many are careful to conclude their prayers simultaneously with the chazzan's conclusion of הַמְבָרֵךְ אֶת עַמּוֹ יִשְׂרָאֵל בַּשָּׁלוֹם.

Kohanim:

רִבּוֹנוֹ שֶׁל עוֹלָם, עָשִׂינוּ מַה שֶּׁגָּזַרְתָּ עָלֵינוּ, אַף אַתָּה עֲשֵׂה עִמָּנוּ כְּמָה שֶּׁהִבְטַחְתָּנוּ: הַשְׁקִיפָה מִמְּעוֹן קָדְשְׁךָ, מִן הַשָּׁמַיִם, וּבָרֵךְ אֶת עַמְּךָ אֶת יִשְׂרָאֵל, וְאֵת הָאֲדָמָה אֲשֶׁר נָתַתָּה לָנוּ — כַּאֲשֶׁר נִשְׁבַּעְתָּ לַאֲבֹתֵינוּ — אֶרֶץ זָבַת חָלָב וּדְבָשׁ.[1]

Congregation:

אַדִּיר בַּמָּרוֹם, שׁוֹכֵן בִּגְבוּרָה, אַתָּה שָׁלוֹם וְשִׁמְךָ שָׁלוֹם. יְהִי רָצוֹן שֶׁתָּשִׂים עָלֵינוּ וְעַל כָּל עַמְּךָ בֵּית יִשְׂרָאֵל חַיִּים וּבְרָכָה לְמִשְׁמֶרֶת שָׁלוֹם.

Chazzan continues:

שִׂים שָׁלוֹם, טוֹבָה וּבְרָכָה, חֵן וָחֶסֶד וְרַחֲמִים, עָלֵינוּ וְעַל כָּל יִשְׂרָאֵל עַמֶּךָ. בָּרְכֵנוּ אָבִינוּ, כֻּלָּנוּ כְּאֶחָד, בְּאוֹר פָּנֶיךָ, כִּי בְאוֹר פָּנֶיךָ נָתַתָּ לָּנוּ, יהוה אֱלֹהֵינוּ, תּוֹרַת חַיִּים וְאַהֲבַת חֶסֶד, וּצְדָקָה, וּבְרָכָה, וְרַחֲמִים, וְחַיִּים, וְשָׁלוֹם. וְטוֹב בְּעֵינֶיךָ לְבָרֵךְ אֶת עַמְּךָ יִשְׂרָאֵל, בְּכָל עֵת וּבְכָל שָׁעָה בִּשְׁלוֹמֶךָ. בָּרוּךְ אַתָּה יהוה, הַמְּבָרֵךְ אֶת עַמּוֹ יִשְׂרָאֵל בַּשָּׁלוֹם. (Cong. and Kohanim — אָמֵן.)